BTEC NATIONAL
Book 2
Public Services

Nick Cullingworth
with Steve Benson

Nelson Thornes

Published in 2008 by:
Nelson Thornes Ltd
Delta Place
27 Bath Road
CHELTENHAM
GL53 7TH
United Kingdom

08 09 10 11 12 / 10 9 8 7 6 5 4 3 2 1

A catalogue record for this book is available from the British Library

ISBN 978 0 7487 8191 1

Cover photograph by Thinkstock/Alamy
Illustrations by Pantek Arts Ltd
Page make-up by Pantek Arts Ltd, Maidstone, Kent

Printed and bound in Slovenia by Korotan

Contents

Introduction

Millions of people work in Britain's public services. They include firefighters, police officers, soldiers, sailors, air crew, prison officers, civil servants, teachers and nurses. Their work is varied, exciting, demanding, responsible – and vitally important. In Britain the importance of the public services is widely recognised and billions of pounds are spent on them. They provide secure, relatively well-paid jobs and excellent careers for the right people. Because of these advantages many people want to work in the public services – and this is where BTEC National Public Services courses come in. These courses tell you what the public services are all about, and prepare you for public service work. They won't ensure that you get into a public service – but they will get you off to a flying start by giving you the knowledge and skills you need, both for public service work and for further studies.

How do you use this book?

Covering nine of the most popular specialist units from the new 2007 specification, this book, together with Book 1, has everything you need if you are studying BTEC National Certificate or Diploma in Public Services. Simple to use and understand, it is designed to provide you with the skills and knowledge you need to gain your qualification. We guide you step-by-step towards your qualification, through a range of features that are fully explained over the page.

Which units do you need to complete?

BTEC National Public Services Book 2 provides coverage of nine specialist units for the BTEC National Certificate or Diploma in Public Services. To achieve the Certificate, you are required to complete five core units plus seven specialist units that provide for a combined total of 720 guided learning hours (GLH). To achieve the Diploma, you are required to complete six core units plus twelve specialist units that provide for a combined total of 1080 guided learning hours (GLH). Each unit in Book 1 and Book 2 requires 60 guided learning hours. Together *BTEC National Public Services Book 1* and *BTEC National Public Services Book 2* provide you with coverage of the following:

BTEC National Public Services Book 1 Core and Specialist Units	BTEC National Public Services Book 2 Specialist Units
Unit 1 **Government, Policies and the Public Services***	Unit 8 **International Perspectives for the Uniformed Public Services**
Unit 2 **Team Leadership in the Uniformed Public Services***	Unit 10 **Skills for Land-based Outdoor and Adventurous Activities**
Unit 3 **Citizenship, Contemporary Society and the Public Services***	Unit 12 **Crime and its Effects on Society**
Unit 4 **Team Development in Public Services***	Unit 13 **Command and Control in the Uniformed Public Services**
Unit 5 **Understanding Discipline within the Uniformed Public Services***	Unit 14 **The Planning for and Management of Major Incidents**
Unit 6 **Diversity and the Public Services***	Unit 15 **Responding to Emergency Service Incidents**
Unit 7 **Physical Preparation and Fitness for the Uniformed Services**	Unit 16 **Uniformed Public Services Employment**
Unit 9 **Outdoor and Adventurous Expeditions**	Unit 17 **Understanding the Criminal Justice System and Police Powers**
Unit 22 **Understanding Aspects of the Legal System and Law Making Process**	Unit 18 **Understanding Behaviour in Public Sector Employment**

*Denotes a Core unit

Is there anything else you need to do?

1 Do all the work the tutors set you.

2 Never be afraid to ask for help if you need it.

3 Develop your fitness, 'people skills' and sense of responsibility.

4 Get wise to the internet - and use the internet wisely.

5 Visit the public services and meet the people who work in them.

Turn over now for your guide to the features of this book.

We hope you enjoy your BTEC course – Good Luck!

Features of this book

UNIT 8

International Perspectives for the Uniformed Public Services

This unit covers:
- International organisations that exist and how they impact on UK public services
- Causes of war and conflict and the effects of conflict on UK uniformed public services
- How the public services deal with the problem of international and domestic terrorism
- Understanding human rights and human rights violations, showing how UK uniformed public services are used in a humanitarian role.

Thanks to **globalisation** Britain is increasingly affected by what goes on in the rest of the world. This is keenly felt by the uniformed public services, which are having to adapt to new pressures at an ever-increasing rate.

This unit covers the international influences that affect the work of the British uniformed public services. It begins by examining international organisations such as the EU and the changes they have brought about in our uniformed public service work.

Then it looks at war and the part played by our uniformed services.

The next section of the unit covers terrorism, its origins and types and the challenges it poses to the uniformed services.

The final section of the unit deals with human rights, human rights violations, and the overseas humanitarian work of the British uniformed public services.[/

Learning objectives

At the beginning of each Unit there will be a bulleted list letting you know what material is going to be covered. They specifically relate to the learning objectives within the specification.

Grading criteria

The table of grading criteria at the beginning of each unit identifies achievement levels of pass, merit and distinction, as stated in the specification.

To achieve a **pass**, you must be able to match each of the 'P' criteria in turn.

To achieve **merit** or **distinction**, you must increase the level of evidence that you use in your work, using the 'M' and 'D' columns as reference. For example, to achieve a distinction you must fulfil all the criteria in the pass, merit and distinction columns. Each of the criteria provides a specific page number for easy reference.

grading criteria	To achieve a **Pass** grade the evidence must show that the learner is able to:	To achieve a **Merit** grade the evidence must show that the learner is able to:	To achieve a **Distinction** grade the evidence must show that the learner is able to:
	P1 describe the key international organisations, showing how their decisions impact on the UK public services	**M1** analyse how decisions made at international level affect the operations of UK public services	**D1** analyse the causes of two recent conflicts, and their impact on UK uniformed public services
	P2 outline the structure and decision-making processes of the European Union, identifying five key decisions that have affected UK uniformed public services	**M2** explain how the European Union has influenced the operation of one uniformed public service	
	P3 summarise the common causes of war and conflict, illustrating the spectrum of conflict and its effects on the uniformed public services	**M3** compare in detail the causes of a low intensity and high intensity conflict and its effects on the uniformed public services	
	P4 describe the methods used by terrorists, identifying the types of counter-terrorist measures used to combat it	**M4** explain the types of counter-terrorist measures used to combat terrorism	

activity
GROUP WORK

P2

Give a presentation suitable for a Britain–Europe friendship society outlining the organisation and decision-making systems of the EU, and describing five key EU decisions that have affected UK public services. (Back up your presentation with notes, handouts and visual aids showing that all group members have fulfilled the grading criteria.

case study 8.5 — **Article 5**

The key article in the Treaty states:

The Parties agree that an armed attack against one or more of them in Europe or North America shall be considered an attack against them all and consequently they agree that, if such an armed attack occurs, each of them, in exercise of the right of individual or collective self-defence recognised by Article 51 of the Charter of the United Nations, will assist the Party or Parties so attacked by taking forthwith, individually and in concert with the other Parties, such action as it deems necessary, including the use of armed force, to restore and maintain the security of the North Atlantic area.

Any such armed attack and all measures taken as a result thereof shall immediately be reported to the Security Council. Such measures shall be terminated when the Security Council has taken the measures necessary to restore and maintain international peace and security.

Source: NATO

activity
GROUP WORK

In what ways do treaties like this make the world a safer place, and in what ways do they make the world more dangerous?

remember

The total amount of money spent by the UN in military activities is only 2% of world military spending

The UN is funded by the member states, on a roughly pro-rata basis, which means that the amount of money they give each year is linked to their own GDP (wealth). Twenty per cent of the world's wealth is American, and they pay 22% of the annual UN budget (i.e. slightly more than they should). The UK pays 2.2% of the UN budget whereas China, whose GDP is only slightly less than Britain's, pays 0.4%. Many countries fail to pay as much as they should to the UN for a variety of reasons. The overall regular budget is $3 billion, roughly £2 billion. This sounds like a lot of money, but the UK police alone cost around £15 billion a year.

 Annual Report and Accounts 2005–06, Ministry of Defence (www.mod.uk)

 Link More detail can be found in Book 1, Unit 5, page 194

Progress Check

1. Outline the role of the House of Commons in deciding government policies
2. Why is the House of Commons more powerful than the House of Lords?
3. Give four roles of the Prime Minister
4. Name four government departments which have responsibility for at least one uniformed public service
5. What are the three main kinds of election that take place in England? What extra kind of election do they have in the rest of Britain?
6. Give five campaigning methods used by major political parties before a general election
7. Where do the police get their money from?
8. What are the main roles of (a) ministers and junior ministers and (b) civil servants in a government department?
9. What does accountability mean, and why does it matter?
10. Which uniformed public services have an ombudsman and what is the ombudsman's role?
11. Name four duties of a police authority
12. Outline the main stages that a Bill goes through in Parliament
13. Name three international influences on British government policy

Activities

are designed to help you understand the topics through answering questions or undertaking research, and are either *Group* or *Individual* work. They are linked to the grading criteria by application of the D, P, and M categories.

Case studies

provide real life examples that relate to what is being discussed within the text. It provides an opportunity to demonstrate theory in practice.

An **activity** that is linked to a Case study helps you to apply your knowledge of the subject to real life situations.

Keywords

of specific importance are highlighted within the text, and then defined in a glossary at the end of the book .

Remember boxes

contain helpful hints, tips or advice.

Information bars

point you towards resources for further reading and research (e.g. websites).

Links

direct you to Book 1 and to other parts of Book 2 that relate to the subject currently being covered.

Progress checks

provide a list of quick questions at the end of each Unit, designed to ensure that you have understood the most important aspects of each subject area.

Acknowledgements

The authors and publishers would like to thank the following for permission to reproduce material.

Acas, American Society for International Law, Armed Forces Assembly of WEU, Association of Chief Police Officers, *Black's Law Dictionary*, Centrex, Criminal Cases Review Commission, Europol, I-land Internet Service, the *Guardian* Unlimited, Gwent Police, the *Independent*, The Kepplewray Project, Lancashire County Council, Liverpool City Council, Merseyside Fire and Rescue Service, the Metropolitan Police Authority, MidEast Web for Coexistence RA, Ministry of Defence, National Occupational Standards, NATO, NCALT, Oxford University Cave Club, Rizer, Robinwood Activity Centres, Shropshire and Wrekin Fire Authority, Surrey Police Association, Sussex Police Authority, *The Times*, United Nations, West Midlands Police, West Yorkshire Police Authority, The World Bank, Youth Justice Board,

Crown copyright material is reproduced with the permission of the Controller of Her Majesty's Stationary Office © Crown Copyright.

Every effort has been made to contact copyright holders, and we apologise if any have been overlooked. The publishers will be happy to rectify any errors or omissions in this respect at the earliest opportunity.

Picture credits

Alamy: Figs 8.6, 10.3, 12.1, 12.3, 12.9, 13.14, 14.2, 14.5, 15.4, 15.6, 15.9, 16.2, 16.6, 16.7, 17.2, 17.5, 17.8, 18.4, 18.5.

Getty: Figs 8.3, 8.5, 13.7, 13.16.

iStock: Figs 10.5, 10.9.

UNIT 8

International Perspectives for the Uniformed Public Services

This unit covers:

- International organisations that exist and how they impact on UK public services
- Causes of war and conflict and the effects of conflict on UK uniformed public services
- How the public services deal with the problem of international and domestic terrorism
- Understanding human rights and human rights **violations**, showing how UK uniformed public services are used in a humanitarian role

Thanks to **globalisation** Britain is increasingly affected by what goes on in the rest of the world. This is keenly felt by the uniformed public services, which are having to adapt to new pressures at an ever-increasing rate.

This unit covers the international influences that affect the work of the British uniformed public services. It begins by examining international organisations such as the EU and the changes they have brought about in our uniformed public service work.

Then it looks at war and the part played by our uniformed services.

The next section of the unit covers terrorism, its origins and types and the challenges it poses to the uniformed services.

The final section of the unit deals with human rights, human rights violations, and the overseas humanitarian work of the British uniformed public services.

To achieve a **pass** grade the evidence must show that the learner is able to:	To achieve a **merit** grade the evidence must show that, in addition to the pass criteria, the learner is able to:	To achieve a **distinction** grade the evidence must show that, in addition to the pass and merit criteria, the learner is able to:
P3 summarise the common causes of war and conflict, illustrating the spectrum of conflict and its effects on the uniformed public services Pg 26	**M3** compare in detail the causes of a low intensity and high intensity conflict and its effects on the uniformed public services Pg 26	
P4 describe the methods used by terrorists, identifying the types of counter-terrorist measures used to combat it Pg 40	**M4** explain the types of counter-terrorist measures used to combat terrorism Pg 40	
P5 describe the key features of the United Nations Universal Declaration of Human Rights, explaining how human rights have been violated in one international country Pg 41		
P6 describe the humanitarian role played by the UK uniformed public services in an international situation Pg 44		

International organisations that exist and how they impact on UK public services

International organisations fall into a number of categories:

■ Organisations with official government backing from the countries involved:

- The United Nations (UN). This is a unique organisation with 192 member countries (as at 2007). Each country sends official representatives (ambassadors) to observe and participate in the organisation's work.

- Regional groupings of states on a continental basis, with both political and **economic** aims, e.g. the EU, the African Union, the League of Arab States.

- Countries bound together by military or security treaties, e.g. the North Atlantic **Treaty** Organisation (NATO), the Organization for Security and Cooperation in Europe (OSCE).

- Organisations with shared economic aims which are not regionally based, e.g. G8 – the group of the eight richest nations in the world, of which Britain is a member, OPEC – the Organisation of Petroleum Exporting Countries.

- Organisations formed to deal with a specific issue, e.g. the US-led **coalition** which invaded Iraq in 2003.
- Organisations with **cultural** links based on colonial history, e.g. the Commonwealth, *L'Organisation Internationale de la Francophonie*.
- Regional organisations with environmentally linked aims (some of which relate to protection, some relate to **sustainable** management), e.g. Indian Ocean Tuna Commission.
- **Regulatory** organisations, e.g. International Atomic Energy Agency, International Civil Aviation Organisation.

■ International organisations which are independent of governments:

- These are mainly **pressure groups** such as Greenpeace and Amnesty International, cultural and religious organisations, industrial bodies – and then a host of other organisations of varying degrees of importance and legality ranging from the Red Cross to Al-Qaida.

United Nations

The UN is the main body working for world peace, human rights and for cultural and educational development. It was set up in 1945 at the end of World War II and originally had only 50 members. Its aims are set out in the United Nations **Charter**.

---

case study 8.1

Preamble to the United Nations Charter

WE THE PEOPLES OF THE UNITED NATIONS DETERMINED

to save succeeding generations from the scourge of war, which twice in our lifetime has brought untold sorrow to mankind, and

to reaffirm faith in fundamental human rights, in the dignity and worth of the human person, in the equal rights of men and women and of nations large and small, and

to establish conditions under which justice and respect for the obligations arising from treaties and other sources of international law can be maintained, and

to promote social progress and better standards of life in larger freedom,

AND FOR THESE ENDS

to practice tolerance and live together in peace with one another as good neighbours, and

to unite our strength to maintain international peace and security, and

to ensure, by the acceptance of principles and the institution of methods, that armed force shall not be used, save in the common interest, and

to employ international machinery for the promotion of the economic and social advancement of all peoples

Source: United Nations

---

activity
INDIVIDUAL WORK

Search the UN website (www.un.org/) to find examples where each of these aims has recently been carried out by the United Nations.

Structure and institutions

The structure of the United Nations is extremely complex. Figure 8.1 shows some of the main **institutions** within the organisation.

UN institutions

Note that specialised agencies such as the World Bank are not UN agencies, but they work very closely with the UN.

The UN is funded by the member states, on a roughly pro-rata basis, which means that the amount of money they give each year is linked to their own **GDP** (wealth). Twenty per cent of the world's wealth is American, and they pay 22% of the annual UN budget (i.e. slightly more than they should). The UK pays 2.2% of the UN budget whereas China, whose GDP is only slightly less than Britain's, pays 0.4%. Many countries fail to pay as much as they should to the UN for a variety of reasons. The overall regular budget is $3 billion, roughly £2 billion. This sounds like a lot of money, but the UK police alone cost around £15 billion a year.

Extra funding is given by some member countries (such as Britain) to the UN for peacekeeping duties – and British military personnel are actively involved in a range of UN peacekeeping duties.

> **remember**
>
> The total amount of money spent by the UN in military activities is only 2% of world military spending

The Security Council

The UN Security Council was set up in 1946 with the aim of ensuring that the world would remain at peace. It has five permanent members: Britain, the US, France, Russia and China. There are 10 non-permanent members who serve for two years only. The UN Security Council is the most powerful institution in the UN because it has the power, under the UN Charter, to require governments to take certain actions in certain situations.

Figure 8.1 UN institutions

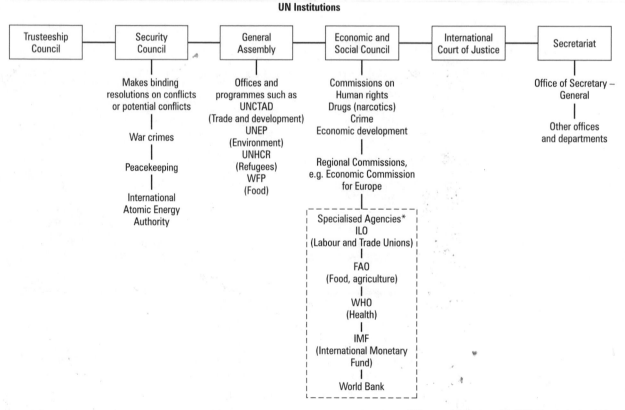

* These are independent of the UN but work closely with it.

Brief history

A *very* brief history is given on the previous page. Further details can be found on the UN website.

www.un.org

Roles

- To try to resolve disputes by peaceful means.
- To pass UN **resolutions** requiring countries and organisations which are at war to stop fighting, or agree to certain international measures.
- To send peacekeeping forces to unstable areas.
- To decide on **sanctions** or other 'punishments'.
- To decide on military action.
- To suspend countries from the rights and privileges of UN membership.

Peacekeeping and peacemaking

Peacekeeping is a complex and difficult role which can involve anything from attacking **insurgents** to ensuring that local children get to school safely. It includes creating peaceful conditions so that a war-torn **infrastructure** of bombed roads, poor water supplies and damaged electricity networks can be rebuilt. In Iraq it has meant setting up local and even a national government, and supporting other institutions. It also includes reorganising and retraining the police and army of the war-affected countries so that, when peacekeepers eventually leave, law and order will remain.

> **remember**
> Peacekeeping can include fighting, e.g. against insurgents.

Peacemaking

This is an ambiguous term. It can mean fighting (as in Afghanistan in 2006) to subdue forces (the Taliban) which were prepared to take on the British and other NATO-backed armies. It can also mean negotiation and **diplomatic** activity to arrange cease-fires, as has happened from time to time in Palestine.

UK service involvement (e.g. peacekeeping missions, disaster relief)

The UN Security Council and its decisions are important for Britain's armed forces and any other uniformed public services (such as the police) who might undertake training or advisory work in areas which have recently been at war. This is because British uniformed services participate actively in several of the UN's peacekeeping operations. According to the MOD Annual report for 2005/06, British forces were involved in UN peacekeeping missions in Cyprus, the Democratic Republic of Congo, Georgia, Liberia, Sierra Leone and Sudan.

Annual Report and Accounts 2005–06, Ministry of Defence (www.mod.uk)

The armed forces carry out relief work in some major disasters – mainly those that affect Britain in some way. An example of this was the help they gave in the Pakistan Earthquake in the winter of 2005/06.

European Union

The European Union (EU) started in 1957 with the Treaty of Rome. This created the European Economic Community. The founding members were France, West Germany, the Netherlands, Belgium, Italy and Luxembourg. In its early years it was successful in raising the standard of living in these countries which were still recovering from the ravages of World War II. In 1973 the UK, Ireland and Denmark joined. From 1979 onwards citizens of member countries were able to elect Members of the **European**

case study
8.2

Pakistan earthquake

We also provided four C-130 Hercules to the NATO airbridge to transport aid into Pakistan (one of these C-130s was not in the event required), and one RAF C-17 aircraft transported two civilian helicopters from Seville to Pakistan. An 86-man party of Royal Engineers (supported by Royal Marines) constructed emergency shelters for villagers in remote areas above 5,500 ft. Further assistance included a two-person Mobile Air Operations Team, a four-person Mobile Medical Team, an Operational Reconnaissance Team, four **logistics** planners deployed to the UN Joint Logistics Centre and various personnel to the Joint Force Air Component Command, and 23,000 vegetarian and Halal ration packs.

Source: Annual Report and Accounts 2005–2006, Ministry of Defence

activity

GROUP WORK

Think of as many reasons as you can why the armed forces help in relief work of this kind.

---

remember

A constitution is a list of laws, rules, rights and responsibilities.

Parliament (MEPs). In the 1980s Greece, Spain and Portugal joined and in 1987 the Single European Act set out a programme designed to create a 'single market' with a minimum of **trade barriers** and restrictions between member countries.

In 1993 the Maastricht Treaty and in 1999 the Treaty of Amsterdam strengthened the ties between member countries and put forward the idea of a single currency – the euro. In 1995 Austria, Finland and Sweden joined the EU. The Schengen agreements allowed for the free flow of European citizens between countries without passport checks (though the UK opted out of this). The euro was introduced in 2002 and became the common currency in 12 EU countries which wanted to join the system and which fulfilled certain economic standards. In 2003 the EU started its own peacekeeping force, coordinating its work with NATO. In 2004 a **Constitution** for Europe including all of the main laws of previous treaties, plus some extra ones, was written. However, it was rejected in **referendums** in France and the Netherlands. The constitution was mothballed until 2007 when a new version was put forward.

Membership

Membership of the EU has continued to grow and the member countries at the beginning of 2007 were as follows.

- Member States: Germany, France, Italy, the Netherlands, Belgium, Luxembourg, Denmark, Ireland, the UK, Greece, Spain, Portugal, Austria, Finland, Sweden, Czech Republic, Cyprus, Estonia, Latvia, Lithuania, Hungary, Malta, Poland, Slovenia and Slovakia.

- New Member States: Bulgaria and Romania.

- Candidate countries: Croatia, the Former Yugoslav Republic of Macedonia and Turkey.

Other countries, such as Serbia and Montenegro (now independent from Serbia), are also beginning the application processes.

Structure and institutions

remember

The aim of separation of powers is to prevent a government becoming dictatorial.

The EU is a highly complex **bureaucratic** organisation which is partly but not wholly democratic. In other words, not all of the powerful people in the EU have been elected by the public (of any country) for the posts they now hold. The EU is made up of 'institutions' which roughly follow the western democratic system of 'separation of powers'. This means the EU has a **legislature** (the **European Commission** and the European Parliament), which makes laws, a **judiciary** (The European Court of Justice)

Figure 8.2 Structure of the
European Union

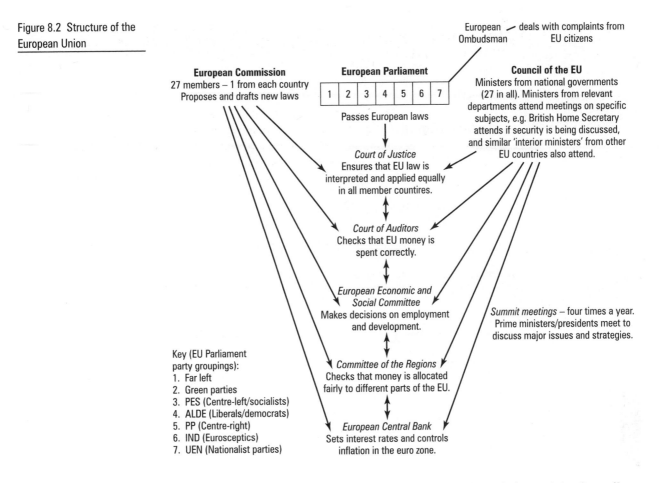

European Ombudsman — deals with complaints from EU citizens

European Commission
27 members – 1 from each country
Proposes and drafts new laws

European Parliament

| 1 | 2 | 3 | 4 | 5 | 6 | 7 |

Passes European laws

Council of the EU
Ministers from national governments (27 in all). Ministers from relevant departments attend meetings on specific subjects, e.g. British Home Secretary attends if security is being discussed, and similar 'interior ministers' from other EU countries also attend.

Court of Justice
Ensures that EU law is interpreted and applied equally in all member countires.

Court of Auditors
Checks that EU money is spent correctly.

European Economic and Social Committee
Makes decisions on employment and development.

Summit meetings – four times a year. Prime ministers/presidents meet to discuss major issues and strategies.

Key (EU Parliament party groupings):
1. Far left
2. Green parties
3. PES (Centre-left/socialists)
4. ALDE (Liberals/democrats)
5. PP (Centre-right)
6. IND (Eurosceptics)
7. UEN (Nationalist parties)

Committee of the Regions
Checks that money is allocated fairly to different parts of the EU.

European Central Bank
Sets interest rates and controls inflation in the euro zone.

which interprets laws, and an **executive** (the European Commission and the **Council of the European Union**) which sees that the laws are put into effect. These three branches of the EU government are all largely independent from each other so that they can check and question each others' work.

Structure of the EU

The three top institutions are the Parliament, the European Commission and the Council of the European Union.

Council of Ministers (now called the Council of the European Union)

This institution holds major meetings on important European issues. The people attending the meetings are the ministers in charge of government departments in each of the Member States. Only ministers who in their own country are responsible for the subject under discussion attend any particular meeting, so if the meeting was about defence, 27 defence ministers, one from each EU country, would attend.

European Commission

In 2007 this important but unelected body had 27 members who had been appointed by the national governments of Member States. Their job is to propose new laws and – with the help of EU civil servants – draft them (write them) for debate by the European Parliament.

European Parliament

This consists of 785 Members of the European Parliament (MEPs) all of whom are elected in European elections. Less than one-third are women. They come from all EU countries, in numbers which are roughly proportional to the population of each member country. The EU Parliament itself is not set out like the House of Commons, with a government and an opposition. Instead it sits in a kind of semicircle with the left wing at one side, the right wing at the other, and the centre parties in the middle.

The parties are grouped into blocks. Labour MEPs sit with **socialists**, while Conservative MEPs sit with the European People's Party, a right-of-centre grouping including German Christian Democrats and the centre-right parties of other EU countries. The role of the EU Parliament is to debate and pass (or not pass) laws proposed to it by the EU Commission, and to plan the spending of the €100 billion EU budget (around £65 billion).

Issues that affect the public opinion of the EU

Public opinion of the EU differs widely from one EU country to the next. British people are on average much less enthusiastic about the EU than people in other EU countries. For example, in the autumn of 2006 39% of British people polled by Eurobarometer thought that Britain had benefited by its membership of the EU, while 87% of Irish people thought Ireland had benefited from EU membership! In the EU as a whole 54% of the general public believe their own country has benefited from EU membership.

Negative British views about the EU could be influenced by the following factors:

- The anti-European stance of the press.

- Traditional scepticism (doubtfulness) towards the EU in the Conservative party.

- **Nationalism** – the belief that 'British is best'.

- The feeling that EU membership is eroding the UK's independence; dislike of EU laws which seem to interfere with the British way of life.

- Language and cultural links with the US, Australia, etc. which may seem stronger than with mainland Europe.

Positive British views towards the EU may be influenced by:

- A love of Europe, European culture, sport and the way of life, and the association of Europe with holidays.

- High levels of education which, according to opinion polls, make people more supportive of the EU.

- Profitable trade links between the UK and Europe.

- The idea that the EU is a force for peace, stability and improved human rights.

> **remember**
>
> The public's views of the EU can change quickly, and present negative views may reflect negative views expressed by the press and politicians.

Eurobarometer surveys

(http://ec.europa.eu/public_opinion/index_en.htm)

Enlargement of the EU

This is a complex political issue. It has led to large numbers of workers from the **accession countries** such as Poland, Hungary, etc. coming to the UK, Spain and other western European countries to work. Though, at least in the short term, this movement benefits the British economy, it is unpopular among many British people who feel either that their own jobs are under threat or that 'foreigners' will end up 'scrounging' off the state. People also have concerns about the cultural effects of society becoming ever more diverse. There are particularly mixed feelings about the long-term possibility of Turkey joining the EU. If Turkey did join it would be the biggest and most populous EU Member State. The British government is (at present) in favour of Turkey's application, but many people feel that Turkey is not really a European country, it has a poor human rights record, and that if it joins the EU it will mainly benefit the countries in the east of Europe rather than Britain.

Constitution

The EU Constitution which was drawn up in the form of a treaty in 2004 was a legal document rather like the US or French constitutions, putting in writing the rights, responsibilities and main laws governing the citizens of EU countries. It had to be agreed by all Member States in order to be brought into effect. Governments in mainland

Europe were mostly in favour of the constitution, feeling that it would lead to more freedom and prosperity. Workers and **left-wing** socialists were strongly against it because it did not give enough protection to working people. Right-wing parties did not like it because it undermined the national independence of Member States. Some countries decided to hold referendums (in 2005) to see whether their people approved the constitution. This was done in France, the Netherlands and Luxembourg.

Luxembourg (a country with a population smaller than Nottingham) voted in favour of the EU Constitution, but both France and the Netherlands voted against. This shock result caused a political earthquake in the EU. The referendum was not held in Britain, but opinion polls suggested the British would have rejected the EU Constitution if a referendum had been held. In 2007 a new version of the constitution came out, but it is not yet clear if it will be accepted by all member states.

case study 8.3

Public opinion

Table 8.1 UK public opinion on Europe

Opinion	UK public (%)	EU average (%)
A positive image of the EU	28	46
EU membership is good for our country	34	53
Trust in own country's government	24	30
Trust in the EU	26	45
The EU's priority should be fighting terrorism	46	27
The EU's priority should be fighting poverty and social exclusion	33	43

Source: Eurobarometer 66, Public Opinion in the European Union, autumn 2006

Table 8.2 UK public opinion about responsibilities of the EU

Issue	UK government should be responsible (%)	Jointly – UK and EU (%)
Fighting crime	69	28
Immigration	63	33
Protecting the environment	No info	55
Terrorism	35	61
Scientific and technological research	38	56

Source: Eurobarometer 66, Public Opinion in the European Union, autumn 2006

activity
INDIVIDUAL WORK

Do you personally agree or disagree with the majority in each of these categories? What are your reasons?

remember

Countries want
the advantages of
EU membership
but they are afraid
of losing their
independence.

Superpower or super-state

It is hard to define the exact nature of the EU, or what its long-term future will be. Some politicians have seen it as a kind of 'United States of Europe', aiming to challenge US supremacy in the world or at least to become a **superpower** in its own right. Others have seen it as a kind of gigantic 'nanny state' interfering in everybody else's business while being corrupt and inefficient with a lot of old European politicians feathering their own nests. Still others see the EU as a force for good, upholding human rights and **democracy**, looking after its people, and laying the foundations of a peaceful and prosperous Europe for the future. People in Britain tend not to like it much, but few serious politicians ever suggest that Britain should leave the EU – even though the idea might be popular. Britain wants to benefit economically from the EU, but is reluctant to get rid of the pound and use euros instead.

Decision-making process within the EU

The key players in EU decision making are the European Commission, the European Parliament and the Council of the European Union. But the ideas they decide on may come from **summit** meetings of EU leaders, or from treaties such as the Treaty of Nice where major policy decisions are made about things like enlargement.

In **legislative** decision making (drawing up new laws) the ideas usually come from the European Commission. The stages are as follows:

1. The Commission puts a proposal for a new law to the Council.

2. The Council discusses the proposal and reaches a 'common position' on it.

3. This is passed to the Parliament which debates the common position, examines it and, usually, makes amendments.

4. The amended text is sent back to the Council and to the Commission.

5. The Commission gives its opinion on Parliament's amendments.

6. (a) If the Commission is not in favour of the amended text, it can only become law if the Council are in unanimous agreement that it should become law.

   (b) If the Commission is in favour of the amended text it will become law provided that the Council also supports the amended text by a majority.

As in the British Parliament, proposed new laws are examined by committees set up by the main legislative bodies as well as by the bodies themselves.

There are differences in detail in the way that the EU Parliament, Commission and Council deal with new laws. There are three main variations on the decision-making process, each with its own name:

- Consultation: Parliament can change the proposed new law.

- Assent: Parliament must either accept or reject the new law – it cannot change it.

- Co-decision: If Parliament and the Council disagree, the proposed law is put before a conciliation committee made up of Council and Parliament representatives. If the committee agrees the proposed law can go ahead, the law goes back to Parliament and the Council, and it is passed.

Qualified majority voting

There are 27 countries in the EU so when there is a meeting of the Council of the EU there are 27 government ministers, one from each country. When the Council or the Commission (which also has 27 members) vote, they use a system called qualified majority voting, so that the vote of a member from a big country such as Germany has more weight than the vote from a member from a small country such as Malta.

EU laws have different names according to how wide their scope is and how they are applied. The main ones are explained below:

- Decision: an Act which applies to particular, named people and must be obeyed in its entirety.

- Regulation: a rule which applies generally in the EU. It must be obeyed in its entirety but does not need to be passed (like a directive) by national governments.

- Directive: an instruction given to the governments of Member States to change their laws (using their national Parliaments) so that their national laws harmonise (i.e. are in agreement) with EU laws.

The EU also issues Opinions and Recommendations. These put an obligation on Member States but they are not legally binding (i.e. compulsory) like Decisions, Regulations and Directives. They can be compared to a Code of Practice in English law.

UK service involvement

UK uniformed services **liaise** closely with their EU counterparts, and this liaison is getting closer all the time. This applies both to the armed forces and to uniformed services such as the police and customs officers. The main reasons for this closer liaison are:

- The increasing number of international threats to both British and European security.

- EU Directive 2004/38/EC which gave EU citizens the right to move freely and live in different Member States.

The EU has security and defence arrangements to which the UK contributes. These are the Common Foreign and Security Policy (CFSP) and the European Security and Defence Policy (ESDP). These follow a plan called the European Security Strategy (ESS).

Services from different EU countries can work together through the CFSP or through bilateral agreements (i.e. between two member countries). Such agreements are useful in major civil emergencies, for example forest fires in the Mediterranean countries where teams of fire-fighters can be quickly drafted in from other countries including Britain.

The armed forces of EU countries are involved with the EU (or European) Rapid Reaction Force (ERRF). This is an arrangement set up since 1999 as a result of which up to 60,000 military personnel, mainly soldiers, can be made available to deal with international crises. These are normally crises which:

- have not yet developed into full-scale wars

- are not being dealt with by the US Military or NATO.

Originally there were fears of a **conflict of interest** between the ERRF and NATO but, perhaps because most EU countries are NATO members, the two have been able to work together, most notably in the Balkans since 2003.

European police cooperation and their organisations

Police **coordination** among EU countries, including Britain, is rapidly developing. The main organisation is Europol, which shares information among EU member country police forces. There is also a European Police Chiefs Task Force, to ensure coordination at the top level. And there is police involvement in the European Rapid Reaction Force, since the ERRF is concerned mainly with peacekeeping. There is a good deal of cooperation on crime prevention through the EU Crime Prevention Forum. A recent visible example of EU police cooperation was in the 2006 World Cup, held in Germany, where British and German police worked closely and successfully together.

Current issues

The main current issues are:

- Illicit drug trafficking.

- Illicit immigration networks.

- Terrorism.

- Forgery of money and other means of payment.

- Trafficking in human beings.

- Child pornography.

remember

Organisations such as the OSCE (an independent NATO-like organisation) and Interpol have similar aims to the EU organisations, and liaise with them and the British authorities.

- Illicit vehicle trafficking.
- Money-laundering.

Europol (www.europol.europa.eu/index.asp?page=facts&language=en)
(plenty of information on European police cooperation)

Illegal immigrants and border control

Illegal immigration takes two main forms:

1. People coming to Britain on temporary visas and then disappearing without trace into the community.

2. People trafficking.

People trafficking is a serious and increasing form of international crime which demands international solutions in the form of greater intergovernment and police cooperation.

People trafficking has a 'complex organisation, and is linked to facilitating crimes such as document **counterfeiting**. The same is true for illegal immigration'
(EU Organised Crime Threat Assessment 2006, Europol www.europol.europa.eu/index.asp?page=home&language=).

British and other EU police have to cooperate to get intelligence on these varied but linked criminal operations. In Britain the Serious Organised Crime Agency (SOCA) has set up links with Europol. There are also joint investigation teams set up with police in other countries (e.g. the Netherlands) to tackle crime which affects both countries.

Impact of plans for increase in powers of courts to try offences across Europe

Increased coordination of European criminal courts is being achieved by an organisation called Eurojust, which is an agency of the EU government. The aim is for courts to be able to help each other across the EU with exchanges of information and in order to carry out **extradition** requests. Previously countries were unwilling to extradite (i.e. send to another country) people who were wanted in that other country on criminal charges. But the cooperation through Eurojust and the success of European arrest warrants which enable people to be arrested in one EU country for crimes which they committed in another EU country is helping the courts across Europe to deal more effectively with organised crime.

> **remember**
>
> EU countries have traditionally been less willing to cooperate on security matters than many other matters (e.g. the environment) because they risked losing independence. However, the fear of terrorism and international crime is drawing them together.

Figure 8.3 International cooperation is needed to tackle cross-border crime

case study 8.4 — The Hague, the Netherlands, 15 December 2005

More than 30 addresses of a wide range of people suspected of being involved in the clandestine smuggling of thousands of illegal immigrants into the EU were searched yesterday morning. In total, 53 main suspects were arrested in France (22), Italy (18), the United Kingdom (7), Greece (3) and Turkey (3). Subsequently, 56 illegal immigrants were arrested in France, mainly in the region of Calais but also in Paris.

The police operation, which was explained today in a press conference in Paris, was the largest international police operation ever supported by Europol within this crime area. Raids were carried out and arrests were made simultaneously across 5 countries and suspected members of an international criminal network responsible for the facilitation of the illegal entry of immigrants into a variety of EU Member States were successfully targeted.

The immigrants smuggled by the network were spread all over Europe.

The United Kingdom was the main destination country, although immigrants were also smuggled to the Scandinavian countries, Belgium, the Netherlands and Germany.

This long planned operation, codenamed 'PACHTOU', was led by the French Central Office for the Repression of Illegal Immigration and Employment of Foreigners without Residence Permits (*Office Central pour la Répression de l'Immigration Irrégulière et de l'Emploi d'Etrangers Sans Titre*[OCRIEST]). This organisation has provided the majority of the evidence focusing on dismantling a criminal network facilitating illegal immigrants, mainly from Iraq and Afghanistan, into the EU.

Due to the fact that the actions of this criminal organisation had **ramifications** in a variety of countries and also that there were certain constraints in multilateral operational cooperation, OCRIEST requested support from Europol in this matter.

Europol supported the exchange of information, provided intelligence analysis and assisted with operational support at OCRIEST in Paris, France during this day of action.

Eurojust was also involved in this investigation. The French leading magistrate (an investigation judge) issued a European Arrest Warrant to request help from Greece for the surrender of a person arrested in Greece.

Source: Europol Annual Report 2005

activity — GROUP WORK

What kinds of difficulties need to be overcome to achieve international police cooperation on this scale?

European Defence Force

The EU does not have a permanent EU army, navy or air force. Instead, member countries contribute forces as required. For open warfare there is a European Rapid Reaction Force (see page 11 above). Otherwise European defence is carried out by a system of 'Civil-Military Co-Military Co-cordination (CMCO)'. This includes military operations, security support organisations (e.g. at Gaza/Egypt and Ukraine/Moldova borders), training and 'security reform' such as peacekeeping, disarmament of militia, demobilisation, policing etc. and other forms of conflict prevention, management and reconstruction (e.g. Bosnia, Congo). British forces and police are involved from time to time in all these EU 'civil-military' activities.

activity
GROUP WORK
8.1

P2

Give a presentation suitable for a Britain-Europe friendship society outlining the organisation and decision-making systems of the EU, and describing five key EU decisions that have affected UK public services. (Back up your presentation with notes, handouts and visual aids showing that all group members have fulfilled the grading criteria.)

activity
GROUP WORK
8.2

M2

In a presentation to a Britain-Europe friendship society give a detailed explanation of how the EU has influenced the work of a uniformed public service. (Back up your presentation with notes, handouts and visual aids showing that all group members have fulfilled the grading criteria.)

NATO

NATO stands for the North Atlantic Treaty Organization.

Membership

In 2007, NATO had the following member countries:

Belgium	Germany	Luxembourg	Spain
Bulgaria	Greece	Netherlands	Turkey
Canada	Hungary	Norway	United Kingdom
Czech Rep	Iceland	Poland	United States
Denmark	Italy	Portugal	
Estonia	Latvia	Romania	
France	Lithuania	Slovakia	

Structure and institutions

NATO was set up by the North Atlantic Treaty of 1949. Its primary aim, though this is not stated in the Treaty, was to protect the western powers against the Soviet Union (USSR) – the **communist** bloc of countries then led by Russia which was seen by the west as a threat to the **capitalist** system and to world peace.

Figure 8.4 NATO structure

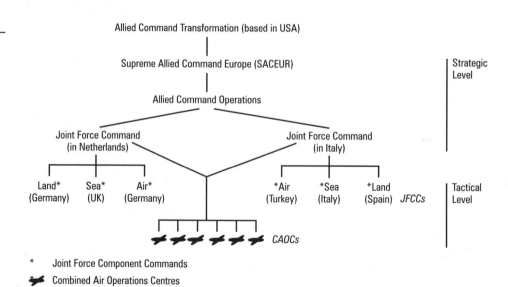

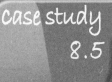

Article 5

The key article in the Treaty states:

> The Parties agree that an armed attack against one or more of them in Europe or North America shall be considered an attack against them all and consequently they agree that, if such an armed attack occurs, each of them, in exercise of the right of individual or collective self-defence recognised by Article 51 of the Charter of the United Nations, will assist the Party or Parties so attacked by taking forthwith, individually and in concert with the other Parties, such action as it deems necessary, including the use of armed force, to restore and maintain the security of the North Atlantic area.

> Any such armed attack and all measures taken as a result thereof shall immediately be reported to the Security Council. Such measures shall be terminated when the Security Council has taken the measures necessary to restore and maintain international peace and security.

Source: NATO

activity
GROUP WORK

In what ways do treaties like this make the world a safer place, and in what ways do they make the world more dangerous?

The leading member of NATO is the US. Europe needed protection in 1949 because it had been weakened and devastated by World War II. The Treaty is drawn up in such a way that it gives special protection to NATO's member states without openly undermining the authority of the United Nations.

Political and military

NATO has a political role firstly by backing up member states in their disputes by non-member states. The possibility of NATO military action if disputes are not resolved enables member states to strengthen their political position by the threat (or possibility) of force. NATO also carries out diplomatic activity in countries which wish to 'deepen their relationship with NATO', e.g. Georgia, Kazakhstan, Moldova and Ukraine.

Political activity of a different sort exists between NATO and the EU. The two organisations are close allies but have different priorities. Their current aims are to create a shared European Security and Defence Policy (ESDP) and sort out a suitable role for the European Rapid Reaction Force which will fit in with, but not overlap with, the NATO Response Force.

In 2007, NATO was heavily involved in military activity in Afghanistan and Iraq. It also cooperates closely with the Organisation for Security and Cooperation in Europe (OSCE) in conflict-prevention, crisis management and anti-terrorism.

Post Cold War role

The period of history from 1945 to the end of the 1980s is known as the **Cold War**. It was the Cold War that prompted the US and its allies to form NATO. In fact, there was no direct fighting between the US and the USSR, but there was always the fear (both in the west and in the USSR) that nuclear war could break out and the world might be destroyed in the third, and last, world war.

After 1989 Russia switched from a communist to a **free-market** democratic system. The Union of Soviet Socialist Republics broke up into a number of independent countries such as Ukraine, Belarus, Kazakhstan, etc. For a time it was thought that NATO might dwindle away into nothing. But that has not happened, and NATO is now active as far afield as Afghanistan, where in 2007 it was supporting the pro-western Afghan government by carrying out counter-insurgency operations against the Taliban.

remember

There was no direct fighting between the US and USSR in the Cold War, but there were wars in Korea, Vietnam and elsewhere which were linked to the Cold War.

Effects on UK forces (e.g. rapid deployment forces, peacekeeping and policing roles)

NATO can request the British government to provide UK forces for NATO operations – and for various reasons the government tries to say yes to such requests. This is why over 7000 British troops were fighting and/or carrying out reconstruction work in Afghanistan in 2007. Since 2001, when British troops were also involved in the invasion of Afghanistan to oust the Taliban, more than 50 soldiers have died there, and this figure will increase the longer they stay there and the more troops that are supplied to NATO forces. There are concerns that the armed forces are becoming overstretched by having such heavy commitments in Afghanistan on top of those in Iraq and elsewhere.

Security issues at world summits

Security at world summits is not a direct NATO responsibility, except in so far as many of the world's richest nations are members of NATO. NATO itself holds summit meetings of its leaders, at which they review the world situation and the strategies of NATO to meet various challenges. As was stated at NATO's Riga Summit of 2006:

> for the foreseeable future, the principal threats to the Alliance are terrorism and proliferation, as well as failing states, regional crises, misuse of new technologies and disruption of the flow of vital resources.

(www.nato.int/home.htm)

Having said that, security issues at world summits are of great importance to the public services of the country where the summit takes place. The Gleneagles Summit, in Scotland, took place in July 2005 and involved the leaders of the G8 countries (the world's richest countries). Some 11,600 police were needed for the occasion to boost security in the area. The total cost of the event in police overtime alone was £72 million! Of that, £52 million was paid by Scottish taxpayers and £20 million was paid by the Treasury (i.e. the central government in London).

Other institutions

European Court of Human Rights

This court was set up in 1959. Its purpose was to uphold the rights and freedoms listed in the European Convention on Human Rights. These are the same human rights which are now listed in the Articles of the Human Rights Act 1998.

The cases which appear before the court usually concern individuals who feel that their rights have been infringed by an EU government, and who have exhausted all appeals in their own country. However, EU countries can take other EU countries to this Court. In the 1970s the Irish government brought a case in the Court against the UK, alleging that the British were infringing human rights at the time in Northern Ireland.

The number of cases dealt with by the European Court of Human Rights doubled between 1999 and 2005, rising from 22,600 to 45,500. Judges are elected by the Parliamentary Assembly of the Council of Europe, and they serve for six-year terms which can be renewed. Though candidate judges are put forward by governments, they do not represent any EU member country when in the Court. There are around 50 judges in all. Many of the cases are dealt with in writing, but those which are heard in court are usually heard publicly.

The relevance of the European Court of Human Rights to the British public services is that cases brought by British people to the court are likely to involve **complaints** of, or allegations about, public service employees, even though the complainant is really complaining about the government. This is because the government acts at a grass roots level through public services such as the NHS and the police.

World Bank

The World Bank is an organisation based in the US which works closely with the UN and exists to help the economies of countries which ask it for economic help. It was founded in 1944. It is run as a company and many national governments have bought shares in it. The World Bank has two sections which do different kinds of work. The International Bank for Reconstruction and Development (IBRD) works to reduce poverty in middle-income countries such as the countries in North Africa. The other main section of the World Bank – the International Development Association (IDA) – helps the economies of the very poorest countries, such as Burkina Faso in West Africa. Both sections of the World Bank lend money to countries at favourable rates, but there are strings attached: the countries receiving loans have to restructure their economies where necessary to encourage **free enterprise** and **privatisation**. This benefits the countries financially and appears to improve the standard of living, though it also westernises them.

The relevance of the World Bank to British public services is that it makes the countries more accessible to foreigners, and this includes aid workers, uniformed public services giving training and advice to local armies, police, etc., companies and their security staff and people such as teachers who might want to go and work there.

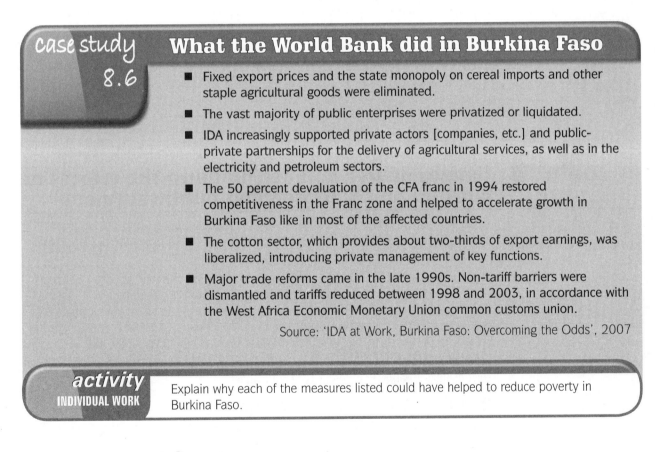

case study 8.6

What the World Bank did in Burkina Faso

- Fixed export prices and the state monopoly on cereal imports and other staple agricultural goods were eliminated.

- The vast majority of public enterprises were privatized or liquidated.

- IDA increasingly supported private actors [companies, etc.] and public-private partnerships for the delivery of agricultural services, as well as in the electricity and petroleum sectors.

- The 50 percent devaluation of the CFA franc in 1994 restored competitiveness in the Franc zone and helped to accelerate growth in Burkina Faso like in most of the affected countries.

- The cotton sector, which provides about two-thirds of export earnings, was liberalized, introducing private management of key functions.

- Major trade reforms came in the late 1990s. Non-tariff barriers were dismantled and tariffs reduced between 1998 and 2003, in accordance with the West Africa Economic Monetary Union common customs union.

Source: 'IDA at Work, Burkina Faso: Overcoming the Odds', 2007

activity
INDIVIDUAL WORK   Explain why each of the measures listed could have helped to reduce poverty in Burkina Faso.

Greenpeace

Greenpeace is an international environmental pressure group. It campaigns to protect the environment, fight global warming, prevent the use of genetically modified plants and animals, and get rid of nuclear weapons and nuclear power.

Greenpeace is a non-violent organisation but its protests often involve daredevil stunts which attract media attention. Where it tries to prevent the lawful work of, say, a nuclear submarine base or an oil installation, or destroy fields of genetically modified maize, the military authorities or the police have to take action.

www.greenpeace.org.uk/

Amnesty International

Amnesty International (AI) is a worldwide organisation campaigning for human rights.

It publicises and campaigns against human rights abuses that are often carried out by the uniformed public services in those countries where the abuses take place. Its work is not directly relevant to the work of British uniformed public services unless they deny human rights – in which case AI will publicise the case and campaign for action to be taken to stop the abuse.

www.amnesty.org/

activity

INDIVIDUAL WORK 8.3

P1

M1

Produce a fact-sheet suitable for reservists likely to be sent on peacekeeping missions. It should outline the key international organisations and show how their decisions affect the UK public services. Your fact-sheet should also contain an analysis of how their (and other international) decisions affect UK public service operations.

Causes of war and conflict and the effects of conflict on UK uniformed public services

War is a situation where countries, or ethnic or religious groups, carry out large-scale attacks on another country or group with the aim of inflicting maximum casualties and achieving a permanent victory, e.g. World War II; the Iraq War.

Conflict is a state of hostility or enmity between countries or ethnic or religious groups. There is likely to be fighting, but it tends to be less systematic and organised, or on a smaller scale, than in war. The word is used vaguely to describe any fighting which is less than a full-scale war, e.g. the Falklands conflict; the Palestinian conflict.

Spectrum of conflict

This means the range of different types of conflict.

From minor terrorism to nuclear war

These are the two extremes of the spectrum. Minor terrorism includes things like:

- Death threats.
- Damage to property.
- Letter bombs.
- Packets of anthrax spores sent through the post.
- Ricin plots, etc.
- Hijackings that do not result in many casualties.
- Use of home-made rockets fired at random.
- Occasional kidnappings.

All of these are very serious crimes in peaceful society, but compared with what happens in all-out war they are minor.

Nuclear weapons were used by the US on Japan in 1945 at the end of World War II. An atomic bomb was dropped on Hiroshima killing around 140,000 people outright. A second atomic bomb was dropped on Nagasaki killing about 74,000 people immediately. After both of these bombings radiation burns and sickness claimed many lives, so that by 1950 the total death toll (immediate and delayed deaths) at Hiroshima was 200,000. The 1950 figure for Nagasaki was 140,000 deaths.

Though these were acts of nuclear war, it was not nuclear war in the true sense because only two bombs were dropped and it was one-sided. Furthermore the atomic bombs of 1945 were feeble compared with modern nuclear weapons, which can be thousands of times more powerful. The US alone has 10,000 nuclear warheads. A full-scale nuclear war, with modern nuclear missiles fired by both sides, would probably result in mutually assured destruction (MAD) and could, in theory, kill every person on the planet and most other life-forms. Weapons known as neutron bombs could kill all of the people while leaving buildings and infrastructure largely intact.

> **remember**
>
> Full nuclear war is the most devastating type of war possible, which is why it is put at the top end of the spectrum.

Low-intensity conflict

Most conflict is low intensity. The fighting is not continuous and is not conducted by full-scale, professional or national armies. Death tolls are in the tens or hundreds rather than thousands. In many cases the conflict covers a limited area and is not well understood by the rest of the world.

Conflicts of this type are not always reported in the news unless they are near to Britain or involve British people in some way. The recent case (March 2007) of British nationals being kidnapped by an armed gang in Ethiopia and turning up some time later in Eritrea was linked to an ongoing low-level conflict between Ethiopia and Eritrea. The disappearance and reappearance of the British people was widely reported. But the conflict as a whole (and the fact that the Ethiopian escorts of the British were not released) gained less news coverage.

Northern Ireland

This low-intensity conflict began (in its recent phase) in 1970 and petered out around the time of the Good Friday Agreement in 1998. During this period over 3000 people died as a result of the conflict. The causes of the conflict were complex and rooted in history, but in essence it was a power struggle between Protestant and Catholic communities, with a background of long-term discrimination against Catholics by the British government and by Northern Ireland protestants. The effects of the conflict on uniformed British public services were enormous, since the army had to maintain a large presence in Northern Ireland over a long period of time. Many British soldiers were killed.

The Royal Ulster Constabulary, which never gained the trust of the Catholic community, was reconstructed as the Police Service of Northern Ireland. The level of distrust of the police in Northern Ireland is shown by the existence of the Northern Ireland Police **Ombudsman** (there is no police ombudsman for the rest of Britain, because the relationship between the public and the police is better). The prison service in Northern Ireland also had to face unique difficulties in running Long Kesh (the Maze) where IRA activists were imprisoned and where they held famous hunger strikes, resulting in their deaths in 1981.

The army are gradually leaving Northern Ireland, as the risk of renewed violence decreases, even though it seems that full political reconciliation has not yet been completed. The experience in peacekeeping and police-style duties which the army gained in Northern Ireland has since (it has been claimed) proved useful in places like Basra.

Yugoslavia

In the 1980s and 1990s a violent civil war erupted in Yugoslavia, which had been a communist **dictatorship** under President Tito until his death in 1980. This war resulted eventually in the formation of a number of different countries: Bosnia-Hercegovina, Croatia, Macedonia, Montenegro, Serbia and Slovenia. These countries had their own long histories but became lumped together as provinces against their will under Tito's communism.

With different ethnicities and religions (some Muslim, some Christian) they fought not only for freedom from Serbia (where Slobodan Milosevic, a brutal but cunning dictator later put on trial for war crimes by the UN, still ruled), but also to get more land from their neighbours. The phrase 'ethnic cleansing' was used to describe the terrorism which took place in these countries during the 1990s, the purpose of which was to get rid of certain communities so that their land could be settled by other communities. Atrocities including mass killings were carried out against Muslims. UN and EU peacekeepers are still operating in the region.

There is also unfinished business in Kosovo, a part of southern Serbia which has been settled by Albanians who want Kosovo to be independent. In the late 1990s Kosovo was terrorised by Serb militia who were driven out by NATO bombing of Kosovo and Serbia. Kosovo is at present under the protection of UN peacekeepers (British forces have been involved). It is likely that the region will remain unstable at least until Kosovo achieves some sort of independence from Serbia.

Middle East

This region has been unstable since 1948 when the state of Israel was created by the withdrawal of Britain from Palestine and the Israel war of independence. Many Palestinians – and many people in the surrounding countries, including the leaders of some countries (e.g. Iran) – do not believe to this day that Israel has a right to exist.

Israel, strongly backed by the US and Britain and backed slightly less strongly by the EU in general, has armed itself and has a policy of universal conscription so that all Israelis have some military training. In two wars (the 1967 Six-day War and the 1973 Yom Kippur War) Israel was attacked by its neighbours. Israel won both wars decisively and extended its area considerably. Even without the conflict between Israel and the Palestinians this is enough to ensure that the area remains unstable.

The Palestinians live as second-class citizens on Israeli land in the West Bank and other areas which the Palestinians believe belongs to them. Over the years, stoning of Israeli troops (the 'intifada'), suicide bombings and the firing of rockets have resulted in Israel bombing the houses and headquarters of people identified as Palestinian terrorists. Israel has settled the West Bank illegally, building on Palestinian land. Since 2002 Israel has been building a huge concrete security 'fence' between Palestinian and Israeli communities.

Also in 2002 the US, Russia, the UN and the EU agreed on a Road Map for Peace – a timetable for building peace between the Israelis and the Palestinians. Although neither the Israelis nor the Palestinians have totally condemned the road map, no obvious progress has been made.

In 2005 Israel and 5000 Israeli settlers pulled out of another disputed area, the Gaza Strip, between Israel and Egypt, leaving it (in a devastated condition) to the Palestinians. The Palestinians welcomed this, though it fell far short of what they really wanted. Then Israel's prime minister, Ariel Sharon, suffered a severe stroke and his post was taken over by the present PM, Ehud Olmert.

Meanwhile, in 2006, Hezbollah, an Iranian-backed organisation, began firing rockets at Israel from Southern Lebanon. Olmert organised an invasion of southern Lebanon in 2006 which caused massive destruction, killing around 1100 Lebanese, but not beating Hezbollah. International peacekeeping forces now occupy southern Lebanon, but Lebanon itself has been seriously destabilised, with many people calling for the resignation of the government.

The nearness of Iraq (which is close to civil war and where there are 150,000 or more US troops) and of Syria and Iran (both deeply hostile to Israel), and potential instability from Saudi Arabia (the birthplace of Osama bin Laden) all add to the dangerous mix. A further problem is the development of 'peaceful' nuclear energy by Iran. This has been condemned in a UN resolution, and will probably lead to UN sanctions if not bombing by Israel or the west.

High-intensity conflict

These are wars where there is more or less continuous fighting and heavy death-tolls.

Falklands

This short conflict (it was never officially called a war) was between Britain and Argentina and happened in 1982. Britain claimed that Argentina had illegally occupied the Falkland Islands. Argentina claimed that the islands were the Islas Malvinas and had always belonged to them. (There was some historical backing for their argument, but all of the 1800 inhabitants of the Falkland Islands were of British descent, spoke English and wished to remain a British colony.)

In 1981 a new military government took power in Argentina as a result of a **coup**, and occupying the Falkland Islands seemed an easy way for them to get popularity. For the previous 16 years, the British had been negotiating with Argentina over the future of the islands, so the Argentineans were able to claim that they really thought Britain wanted to hand them over. When the Argentineans invaded in April 1982 the British set up a large naval task force which arrived at the Falklands in May 1982. There was a short war lasting about six weeks, at the end of which the Falklands were back in British hands. Two hundred and fifty-five British service personnel were killed, and 649 Argentineans died. The president of Argentina, General Galtieri, resigned, EEC sanctions against Argentina were quickly lifted, and Britain restored full diplomatic relations with Argentina in 1990.

For the British armed forces the Falklands conflict was, of course, a major event, and they were praised for their performance. The Thatcher government gained a lot of popularity from the victory, though some argued that it was the government's poor diplomacy in the years before that led to the conflict happening in the first place.

Chechnya

This conflict was between Russia and a breakaway region on the north side of the Caucasus mountains. It started when Chechnya declared independence in 1991. There was fighting between Russian troops and Chechens between 1994 and 1996, after which the Russians withdrew. After this there were a number of terrorist bombings around Moscow, and Russian troops re-entered Chechnya in much greater numbers in 1999. The fighting, some of the most violent and devastating in recent times, destroyed the capital city of Grozny. There is continuing instability in the region, with the Muslim Chechens receiving support from **Islamist** fighters, but a referendum in 2003 allowed more **autonomy**. A number of leaders have been assassinated. The present leader, Ramzan Kadyrov, has had some success in reconstructing the region, which is rich in oil.

Gulf War

This war between Iraq and a western coalition led by the US was triggered by Iraq's attack on Kuwait in 1990. After a successful bombing campaign from the air around 540,000 coalition troops, some of them British, entered the country and got to within 150 miles of Baghdad before turning round and leaving the country. This left Saddam Hussein in power and able to claim victory, at least to the Iraqi people. For the west the conclusion was unsuccessful in that it left Saddam Hussein in power.

In the 1990s around 100,000 **Shiite** rebels were killed by Hussein's troops in an uprising. The UN applied sanctions against Iraq which caused widespread hardship and starvation. The Kurds in the north of Iraq were protected by a no-fly zone patrolled by the US; later the same protection was given to Shiites around Basra. In 1998 Iraq was bombed by the US and the UK for failing to cooperate with UN weapons inspectors who were looking for **weapons of mass destruction** (WMD).

In 2001 George W Bush became US president and he had a plan to finish the Iraq business of 1991. Iraq was blamed by some for the 9/11 attacks, and Bush named Iraq as part of an 'axis of evil' of terrorist-**sponsoring** countries. In 2002 Iraq and the UN began negotiating on Iraq's disarmament. A month later, Bush told the UN to take action against Iraq. The UK produced a **dossier** making alarming (and untrue) claims about Iraq's WMD. The US Congress approved military action if Iraq did not disarm. In November 2002 the UN passed Resolution 1441 sending arms inspectors back to Iraq, and threatening serious consequences if Iraq did not cooperate. (The wording was such that the US and Britain were able to claim it gave permission for war, but in 2004 Kofi Annan, Secretary General of the UN, described the war as illegal.) In December the US sent a huge build-up of troops to the region, and Britain sent 26,000 more the following January. In January 2003 the UN inspectors said Iraq was not cooperating properly. Colin Powell, US Secretary of State, argued for war at the UN. In March 2003, France, Germany and Russia issued a statement opposing war in Iraq. The US, UK, Spain and Portugal told the UN that war was necessary. Bush warned Hussein to leave Iraq or face war. Hussein didn't leave and on 19 March 2003 the invasion of Iraq began.

> **remember**
> Information about wars is often biased or untrue. Always try to make your own judgement based on the evidence available.

Areas of instability and risk

There are many areas in the world where there is a threat of conflict or even war breaking out.

Kashmir

This territory, long disputed between Pakistan and India, lies north of Rawalpindi at the western end of the Himalayas. In recent years there have been peace moves and the fighting appears to have died down.

Afghanistan

Since the invasion of Afghanistan in 2001 by western forces the country has been unstable. The area round Kabul is ruled by the pro-western government of Hamid Karzai. The extreme laws of the previous Taliban government (e.g. that it was illegal for women to get educated) have been reversed. The country is thought to be (or have been) a hiding place of Osama bin Laden, the US's most wanted man and head of Al-Qaida, the terrorist network.

British forces, under the overall control of NATO, are fighting in the southern Helmand province against Taliban Islamist guerrillas. Afghanistan is a country that has been in a state of almost continuous unrest since 1947, and despite their bravery and good training the British forces are finding it hard to create conditions peaceful enough for reconstruction to begin. Matters are made worse by the fact that Afghanistan is a poor country and that help promised by the international community to pay for rebuilding the economy has not arrived. The main source of wealth is the opium crop, and there has been disagreement between the US and Britain about how this should be dealt with.

Korea

> **remember**
> Conflicts are changing and developing all of the time. Old ones end and new ones start. Keep an eye on the news.

The problem in Korea is that since the Korean War of 1954 the peninsula has been split into two. South Korea is a prosperous and industrialised western-style democracy. North Korea is one of the very last of the old, hard-line communist dictatorships. North Korea has a nuclear weapons programme which is a threat to peace and stability in the region. North Korea is thought to have developed missiles which could go as far as Canada and the US. Recent negotiations (in 2006/07) give some hope that the situation may be resolved peacefully.

Causes of conflict

This highly complicated subject is dealt with very briefly here.

Politics

Since 1945 the main political conflict has between left-wing and right-wing politics. Put very simply, left-wing politics, which includes socialism, communism, Marxism,

radicalism, etc. believes that the rich exploit the poor, that there is a class war (or potential class war) between the rich and the poor, and that the rich should be heavily taxed so that the poor can be helped. Right-wing politics believes in free enterprise, minimum taxation, privatisation rather than public or government ownership, and not giving money to the poor because if they get benefits they will not work. The wars or conflicts in Korea, Nicaragua, Peru, Mozambique and Vietnam have been essentially of a political nature. Before 1989 the USSR used to support militant left-wing rebel groups in many parts of the world. Since the break-up of the USSR in 1989, Russia has become relatively democratic and this type of conflict is now less likely.

Nationalism

Conflicts due to nationalism are linked to ethnic conflicts. To put it simply, they are based on the belief that one's own country is the best, and it must be fought for, if necessary to the last drop of blood. Nationalism is a powerful emotion and it becomes particularly intense when a region such as Chechnya feels that it is a nation and should become independent. The most famous example is World War II, where extreme German nationalism caused the deaths of 20 million or more people. Of course countries such as Britain which defended themselves against attack were also, in their way, being nationalistic. Today nationalism is evident in the Israel/Palestine conflict, where the Israelis are determined to protect their national security and boundaries (e.g. by erecting a huge concrete 'fence' round the West Bank) and the Palestinians are equally determined to have their own independent Palestine.

> **remember**
> Patriotism and nationalism describe similar feelings and loyalties. Patriotism puts them in a good light; the word nationalism implies criticism.

Religion

Religions preach peace, yet seem to cause wars. Perhaps it is not the religion itself that causes the wars, so much as the persecution of believers of one religion by believers of another religion. In addition, religion is linked to **ethnicity**, and religious differences are often used as an excuse to justify what is really an ethnic conflict (as happened in the former Yugoslavia). Religion, or the persecution of believers of other religions, is involved in the Israeli-Palestinian conflict, in the **Sunni**-Shiite violence in Iraq, and in the 2007 invasion of Muslim Somalia by Christian Ethiopia.

Ideology

An **ideology** is a set of beliefs and is therefore related to politics or religion. The word is normally used in a pejorative (i.e. critical) way to mean a narrow system of beliefs which everybody is expected to stick to – and if they do, the theory goes, there will be no problems.

The ideology of the political right (capitalists) is that 'everything will be fine if we leave it up to the market', or 'Let's have "small government" and privatise the public services'. The ideology of the left (socialists) is, 'Let's set government targets,' or '**Nationalisation** works better than privatisation' or simply 'There should be more equality'. The ideology of supporters of Al-Qaida is, 'A war against the west and western values is a holy war'.

> **remember**
> Ideologies tend to be extreme, to explain everything with reference to a single system of beliefs, and to encourage violence.

Ideology expresses itself in slogans, rather than detailed thinking, and it does not admit that there may be exceptions to a general rule. Ideologies normally oppose diversity, though 'choice' itself can become an ideology if carried to an extreme. Because ideology is oversimplified and is used in **propaganda**, it can be dangerous and a cause of war.

Land and resources

The German Nazis justified their expansion to the east (e.g. Poland and the then Czechoslovakia) by saying they had a need for 'lebensraum' (living space) – in other words they needed the land for the German people. Arab-Israeli conflicts have centred on the fact that Israel is perceived as having stolen land which rightfully belongs to the Arabs. An additional problem for Palestinians is that Israelis control their water supplies in a land where water is a scarce resource. In countries such as Ukraine, Georgia and Belarus there is tension because gas and oil supplies, which come by pipeline from

Russia, can be cut off by the Russians and only reconnected after a price hike which the smaller countries can do nothing about. Civil war in southern Sudan before 2004 was partly about control of oil in that region (though religion and ethnicity were also factors). Many people argue that the invasion of Iraq in 2003 was a war about oil, though this has not been admitted by the US or British governments. However, the media now say that the present unrest in Iraq is because the three main groupings – Sunnis, Shiites and Kurds – all want their fair share of the country's oil wealth.

www.globalsecurity.org/

Going to war is expensive. In the first two years of the invasion/occupation of Iraq, Britain spent £6 billion on that war alone. In the same period of time the Americans, who committed far more resources to the war, spent $148 billion (£77 billion). Between 2003 and 2007 the Americans spent $456 billon (£237 billion) on the war in Iraq. Countries do not like to throw vast amounts of taxpayers' money down the drain, and for this reason wars have to result in a gain of land and resources for the victors. Wars are sometimes great business opportunities for oil companies and similar organisations. They can make fortunes by investing in, and rebuilding, countries which have been destroyed by war.

Historical rivalry

This is the idea that wars and conflicts happen because countries have always been enemies. This may have been a factor in Europe's two world wars. The idea is linked to nationalism. Historical rivalry in itself is not likely to lead to war unless some other factor (e.g. ethnicity, land, resources or ideology) also applies.

Ethnic conflict

For reasons which are not always clear (and may have their roots in human nature) different populations (ethnic groups) tend to dislike or distrust each other. This is on the level of collective rather than individual feeling. Whatever the cause, most conflicts are between people of different ethnic groups. The **genocide** in Rwanda (1994) was between the Hutu and Tutsi peoples. In this case there was a link with historical rivalry, because for many years the Tutsi had been a kind of ruling class in Rwanda, and the Hutu resented it. The conflict in the Balkans (former Yugoslavia) discussed above was ethnic in nature, though religion was also a factor. It is worth remembering that ethnicity expresses itself in things like lifestyle, language, customs, etc. as well as people's physical appearance. Participants in ethnic conflict think that they are always able to recognise the enemy. Ethnic conflict therefore leads to the killing of civilians, 'ethnic cleansing' (driving people of a particular ethnic group out of a region) and genocide (as in the Holocaust).

> **remember**
>
> Some people believe that the **Holocaust** was the only true genocide in modern times.

Superpower rivalry

This was a major cause of conflict before 1989 when the Soviet Union finally broke up. Though it was always hard to prove, it was alleged that many small conflicts (e.g. independence struggles) were financed either by the west or the communists, who were using these wars to expand their sphere of influence in the world. The Vietnam War, for example, was between the communists of the north and the capitalists of the south. Russia and China supported the north, and the US supported the south. In the short term the communists gained influence by winning that war, but as Vietnam becomes more capitalist in its economy the balance is now tilting the other way, with more western influence in Vietnam.

The balance of world power

This is the idea of 'divide and rule', and that a world with stable power blocks (groupings of friendly countries such as the EU) will avoid having 'power vacuums' – weak, disorganised countries which get attacked. Some wars have been encouraged by the superpowers on the grounds that the result will improve the balance of power. The

Figure 8.5 War – who benefits?

classic recent case is the Iran-Iraq war of the 1980s. Western countries supported and armed Iraq so that Iraq would reduce the power of Iran and there would be a better balance of power in the Middle East. Around a million people died, and the region became less stable than ever.

Effects of conflict on UK uniformed public services

If there was no conflict in the world, presumably armed forces would not exist, so the essential effect of conflict is that it is necessary for countries to have armed forces in case of attack. Nearly all countries claim that their armed forces are for defensive purposes only, which is one reason why Britain has a Ministry of Defence but not a Ministry of War.

Britain spends around £30 billion a year on defence. If nothing is done, the money is wasted. The uniformed public services, and especially the armed forces, therefore take active roles in the country's defence. These roles are outlined below.

Peacekeeping (e.g. Bosnia, Sierra Leone)

Peacekeeping duties are many and varied. They include:

- Preventing fighting.
- Stopping insurgents from operating.
- Protecting borders.
- Enabling infrastructure to be repaired and developed.
- Enabling industry and commerce to be re-established.
- Supporting aid agencies.
- Encouraging community support activities.
- Preventing ethnic and inter-community conflict.
- Preventing and fighting crime.
- Training personnel in all the public services.
- Assisting new governments.
- Allowing elections to take place.

The nature of peacekeeping depends on the situation in the country. For example, peacekeeping in Afghanistan includes a good deal of fighting, because peace (in 2007) has not yet been established in some parts.

It is essential for peacekeepers to try not to take sides where there has been inter-ethnic conflict. Peacekeepers often have special **rules of engagement** which make it hard for them to defend themselves when under attack. The job is a difficult one, and peacekeepers get a lot of criticism when things go wrong – as they sometimes do.

Training (e.g. Kosovo, Iraq)

Peacekeeping in Bosnia, Kosovo and other Balkan areas is more to do with setting up the systems and institutions needed for a democratic and peaceful country.

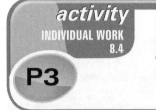

activity

INDIVIDUAL WORK 8.4

P3

Produce a wall chart, suitable for a training centre for new uniformed public service recruits, outlining briefly but clearly the main causes of war and conflicts. Your chart should show the range of possible conflicts, and the various ways in which the uniformed public services can be affected by them.

activity

INDIVIDUAL WORK 8.5

M3

D1

Write a report, suitable for new recruits, about an officer's training course. Your report, divided into sections, should contain:

- An explanation of the spectrum of conflict.
- A detailed comparison of the causes of low-intensity and high-intensity conflict.
- A comparative study of the effects of such conflicts on the uniformed public services.
- A closer analysis of the causes of two recent conflicts and how they have involved and affected UK uniformed public services.

Security and evacuation of UK nationals

The Foreign and Commonwealth Office is the government department with first responsibility for the safety and security of Britons abroad. One of its main functions is to issue travel warnings, which are frequently updated, about the potential dangers of travelling to any country. These can be found on their website.

Foreign and Commonwealth Office
(www.fco.gov.uk)

Security for British nationals who are already in another country is the responsibility of the British **Consulate** in that country.

In the event of a major catastrophe or the sudden outbreak of war, as happened in Lebanon in 2006, it may be necessary to evacuate UK nationals. Such help is dependent on the Foreign Secretary declaring that the government will allocate public funds to help these people. The **evacuation** will not necessarily be done by the British – anyone who has the facilities will carry out the evacuation if the emergency is great enough and if conditions make evacuation possible. In the Lebanon case many British citizens were evacuated by the French simply because there were more French nationals trapped in Lebanon than British nationals, so the French arranged the main airlift.

Individual British citizens can be evacuated in medical emergencies if they are correctly insured.

In extreme cases, as in mass kidnappings, the armed forces may consider a special rescue mission – but this rarely happens.

case study
8.7

Peacekeeping – police role – in the Balkans

The following text forms part of the objectives of the European Union Police Mission (EUPM) in Bosnia and Herzegovina:

- developing police independence and accountability by: de-politicising the police; strengthening the role of directors of police/police commissioners; monitoring performance of these officials; promoting transparency;

- fighting organised crime and corruption by carrying out a joint **strategy** with the Office of the High Representative (OHR); supporting the local police with operational capacities; strengthening the investigative capacity of the local police; supporting the establishment of a state level police agency (SIPA);

- financial viability and sustainability of the local police by: supporting the efficiency and effectiveness of the local police; carrying out a financial audit of the affordability of local police forces; supporting efforts which lead to increases in police officers' salaries;

- institution and capacity building by: focusing on management capacity; supervising the establishment of local recruitment and promotion procedures; consolidating state-level agencies such as the SBS and SIPA.

Source: Assembly of WEU

activity
GROUP WORK

What are the main difficulties and rewards for this kind of police work?

case study
8.8

Travel warning – Nigeria

We advise against all travel to the riverine areas of Bayelsa, Delta and Rivers States. Riverine areas are generally regarded as being those accessible only by boat. This is because of the high risk of kidnapping, armed robbery and other armed attacks in these areas.

We advise against all but essential travel to Akwa Ibom State and the rest of Bayelsa, Delta and Rivers States, including Port Harcourt, because of the high risk of kidnapping, armed robbery and other armed attacks in these areas. On 18 December 2006, two bombs exploded in Port Harcourt, one in a Shell residential compound and the other at Agip's headquarters. On 23 January 2007 a British and a US national were taken hostage while driving to work in Port Harcourt.

Source: Foreign and Commonwealth Office

activity
GROUP WORK

Think of as many possible causes of these attacks as you can.

Disaster relief

The British armed forces sometimes carry out disaster relief work after hurricanes and earthquakes and other major disasters. Usually they travel to the disaster area in small groups and assist in rescues, provide urgently needed shelter, and work with road and bridge repair. Their role is not military on these occasions.

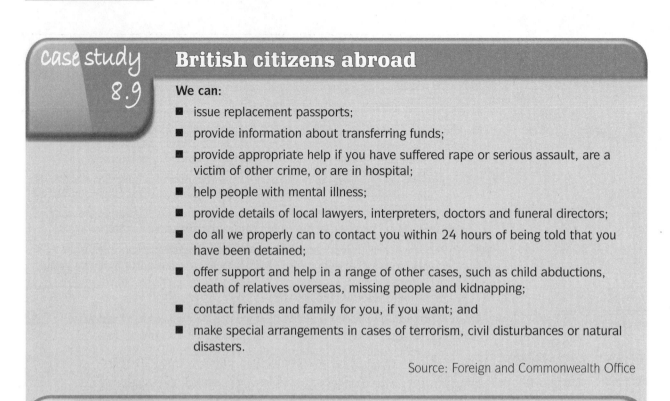

case study 8.9

British citizens abroad

We can:

- issue replacement passports;
- provide information about transferring funds;
- provide appropriate help if you have suffered rape or serious assault, are a victim of other crime, or are in hospital;
- help people with mental illness;
- provide details of local lawyers, interpreters, doctors and funeral directors;
- do all we properly can to contact you within 24 hours of being told that you have been detained;
- offer support and help in a range of other cases, such as child abductions, death of relatives overseas, missing people and kidnapping;
- contact friends and family for you, if you want; and
- make special arrangements in cases of terrorism, civil disturbances or natural disasters.

Source: Foreign and Commonwealth Office

activity

INDIVIDUAL WORK

What factors could limit the power of a consulate to help a British citizen abroad?

Refugees

Refugees, who can be displaced from conflict areas such as Iraq and Sudan in huge numbers, are temporarily housed, if possible, in refugee camps and cared for either by the UN or international aid organisations. Often the pressure of supporting the refugees overwhelms the countries concerned. For example, Jordan has received around 700,000 refugees from Iraq and (in 2007) has apparently closed its borders to further refugees because it can no longer cope with them.

www.un.org/
www.unhcr.org/

War crimes investigation

There are many organisations which try to identify and track down war criminals. Some are official peacekeeping forces, e.g. of the UN and the EU. Some are national governments, such as the governments of the US and of Iraq. Some are human rights organisations which document abuses and try to identify the perpetrators. There are also independent groups, such as the one led by the late Simon Wiesenthal to track down Nazi war criminals, though these are now less effective in the modern world.

People accused of war crimes can be tried in national courts, but there is some doubt as to whether they can get a fair trial under those conditions, especially where the national court is in the country where they are accused of committing their crimes. For these reasons some prominent **war criminals** are tried at the International Criminal Court, the Special Court for Sierra Leone and the Sarajevo War Crimes Chamber. These are independent courts, working under the umbrella of the United Nations.

www.icc-cpi.int/about.html (International Criminal Court)
www.humanrightsfirst.org/
http://hrw.org/
www.amnesty.org/

War crimes are crimes committed during wartime. Examples listed by the International Criminal Court include:

- 8(2)(b)(xix) War crime of employing prohibited bullets.
- 8(2)(b)(xx) War crime of employing weapons, projectiles or materials or methods of warfare listed in the Annex to the Statute.
- 8(2)(b)(xxi) War crime of outrages upon personal dignity.
- 8(2)(b)(xxii) 1 War crime of rape.
- 8(2)(b)(xxii) 2 War crime of sexual slavery.
- 8(2)(b)(xxii) 3 War crime of enforced prostitution.
- 8(2)(b)(xxii) 4 War crime of forced pregnancy.

How the public services deal with the problem of international and domestic terrorism

Terrorist organisations and areas of instability

The Home Office publishes a list of **proscribed** (banned) international groups. These are changed and added to from time to time. The present list was brought in with the Terrorism Act 2000 and added to in the Terrorism Act 2000 (Proscribed Organisations) (Amendment) Order 2005. In all there are 58 banned terrorist groups (2007 figure).

http://security.homeoffice.gov.uk/

National and regional terrorist groups

Nearly all of the banned groups listed by the Home Office are based in the Middle East. They are either **secessionist** groups, that want to create their own state using violence, or Islamist groups, which want to impose their own version of Islam by using violent methods.

Hamas

This is a Palestinian organisation formed in the 1980s as a branch of the Egyptian Muslim Brotherhood. Its original identity and aims are explained in the Hamas Charter of 1988.

Hamas has gained in strength since the 1980s, and early in 2006 it won a democratic election over the previous ruling Palestinian political party, Fatah. It won the election because it was more efficient, less corrupt and did more good works, including educational works, than Fatah. The problem with Hamas as far as western countries are concerned is that it is an organisation with two faces:

- It carries out bombings and rocket attacks against Israelis, and part of its constitution is the elimination of Israel.
- It is prepared to operate cease-fires and carries out well-documented good works, and is effective in local government.

It is impossible for western countries to cooperate with any organisation which refuses to recognise the right of Israel to exist. That, after all, was what Hitler meant when he

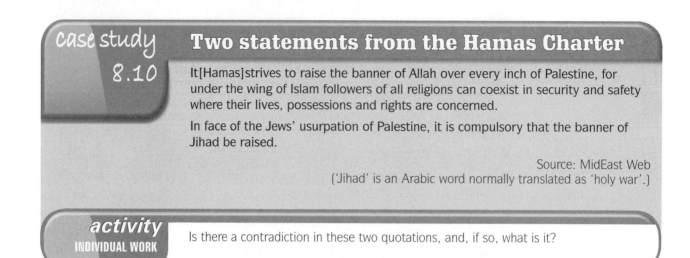

case study 8.10 — **Two statements from the Hamas Charter**

It[Hamas]strives to raise the banner of Allah over every inch of Palestine, for under the wing of Islam followers of all religions can coexist in security and safety where their lives, possessions and rights are concerned.

In face of the Jews' usurpation of Palestine, it is compulsory that the banner of Jihad be raised.

Source: MidEast Web
('Jihad' is an Arabic word normally translated as 'holy war'.)

activity
INDIVIDUAL WORK

Is there a contradiction in these two quotations, and, if so, what is it?

organised the extermination of the Jews. The Palestinian Authority (the government of Palestine) used to be supported financially by the west, especially the EU, but this support stopped the day Hamas was elected. Terror attacks against Israel have recently become less, but there has been fighting between supporters of Fatah and Hamas. This led in 2007 to Hamas taking over the Gaza Strip. The leader of Fatah, Palestinian President Mahmoud Abbas, dismissed the Hamas Prime Minister, Ismail Haniye, Abbas is now receiving funds from the west and from Israel. Hamas and the Gaza Strip are excluded from international help.

US Patriots

This terrorist group is apparently no longer active. Timothy McVeigh, a neo-Nazi, and Terry Nichols planted a truck-bomb in Oklahoma in 1995 which killed 168 people.

Real IRA

This is one of a number of banned Irish republican organisations which are still considered capable of terrorist attacks.

Euskadi Ta Askatasuna (ETA)

This is the Basque **separatist** movement which operates in part of northern Spain and (to a lesser extent) in part of southern France. Its violent campaign has killed around 800 people over the years.

Global terrorist groups

At present there are few global terrorist groups.

Al-Qaida

Al-Qaida is the main global terrorist group, led but not directed by Osama bin Laden from a hideout thought to be in the border region between Pakistan and Afghanistan. Al-Qaida was responsible for the attacks of 11 September 2001 in the US which caused over 2500 civilian deaths and, due to the intense media coverage and the responses of western governments (wars in Afghanistan and Iraq), changed 'the rules of the game' as Tony Blair, the British Prime Minister at the time, put it. It is not very clear what kind of organisation Al-Qaida is: is it close-knit or is it a loose network, or is it really a collection of ideas followed by regionally based terrorist groups? Unlike, say, Hezbollah, which in 2006 carried out a sustained rocket campaign against Israel, it does not seem to have much military capability. There appear to be links with the Taliban of Afghanistan, because Bin Laden lived relatively safely in Afghanistan while the Taliban were in power. Al-Qaida has been blamed for the Bali bombings (2002, 202 dead) and the Madrid train bombings (2004, 191 dead), but they seem to have been the inspiration rather than planners. Al-Qaida releases taped messages from time to time from Bin Laden or his fellow group leaders stating the group's aims – which are anti-American and Islamist.

remember

'Islamic' relates to the Muslim religion; it is better to use the word 'Islamist' when discussing the ideology of Al-Qaida.

remember

State support for terrorists includes money, weapons, propaganda, and providing a 'safe haven'.

States sponsoring terrorists

These are countries which – officially or unofficially – support terrorist groups. It is likely that the secret services of many countries have, in the past, worked with or even supported terrorist organisations for their own reasons, For example, in the 1980s the US was accused of supporting right-wing rebels called Contras in Nicaragua. Today the main states accused of sponsoring **terrorism** are Iran and Syria. Syria is thought to support Hezbollah, and Iran is thought to support many terrorist organisations, though the support is not official. Sudan is accused of supporting the Janjaweed militia who have been accused of killing 200,000 people in Darfur. Under Saddam Hussein many Kurds were gassed in the 1980s – around 5000 in Halabja – and Hussein himself was executed for ordering mass killings in Dujail. Serbia under Milosevic also sponsored terrorism through its militia who attacked Muslims in Kosovo and Bosnia, most notoriously in the Srebrenica Massacre of 1995.

Areas of terrorist activity (e.g. Middle East, Northern Ireland, Kashmir)

Terrorism happens in areas where:

- There is a power struggle within a particular territory.
- Particular ethnic groups feel they have been unjustly treated by their neighbours or by the international community.
- An ethnic group wants independence and has little realistic chance of getting it.
- There are huge inequalities of power and wealth between the people who feel oppressed and the perceived oppressors.

The terrorist groups, and the people they claim to represent, do not have the resources to form a disciplined and effective army. They feel that the international community ignores and despises them and their concerns. The aim of terrorism is to be noticed, and to use the media reporting of their acts as publicity for the terrorists' usually unachievable aims. In this sense, although terrorism causes death, devastation and suffering, it is also a sign of powerlessness – the powerlessness of the terrorists and their supporters and, probably, the unpopularity of their cause.

Terrorism in the Middle East has resulted from:

- The creation of Israel without the consent of the Palestinians and other Arab peoples.
- The failure to give 27 million Kurds the self-government they desire.
- The **destabilising** impact of oil wealth, and the dependence on oil as a source of income.
- The support of Israel by the US, which has made it militarily vastly more powerful than neighbouring countries.
- Brutal **repressive** policies of Israel towards Palestinians.
- Instability in Lebanon, a country with a long history of civil war.
- A perception that the Christian or materialistic west disrespects Islam.
- The existence of pro-western Arab governments such as that in Saudi Arabia which are out of step with many of their own people, especially the poor in those countries.
- The failure of the west to work consistently and meaningfully for peace.
- The victory of Hamas in the Palestinian elections of 2006 and the cutting off of international aid as a result.
- The invasion, occupation and **regime change** in Iraq.
- The exploitation of the situation by Al-Qaida and other groups.
- The poor relations between Sunni and Shiite communities.
- The financing and supporting of terrorist groups by Iran and Syria.

In Northern Ireland and Kashmir, terrorist activity has recently declined. Ireland and Britain are working together to develop the peace process in Northern Ireland, and India and Pakistan are cooperating to reach peace in Kashmir (though there is still a risk of war in that region).

Methods used by terrorists

These include the following:

- Bombings, e.g. Madrid 2004. Bombs are left in trains, markets, etc.; there is death and devastation, and wide media reporting and government condemnation – which give the terrorists and their cause 'the oxygen of publicity'.

- **Assassinations**, e.g. of Rafiq Hariri in Lebanon in 2005. A UN report blamed this on Syrian agents, and accused Syria of sponsoring this act of terrorism. Since the death of Hariri there have been several other bombings in Lebanon, and an apparent upsurge in support for Hezbollah.

- Suicide attacks, e.g. in Iraq, where suicide bombers drive trucks loaded with explosives to police and other recruitment centres and then blow up themselves and recruits standing nearby. The attacks in the US on 11 September 2001 were also suicide attacks. Suicide attacks are used by terrorists because they are hard to prevent and because they gain wide publicity. Defending against them has become a major expense for governments and public services alike.

- Hostage taking, etc. This involves false imprisonment and making demands – either political or for money. The political demands are rarely fulfilled, and the financial demands, if paid, are done so secretly. The UK and US governments have a policy of never paying ransoms, but some other governments, e.g. the Italians, are thought to do so. Hostages are sometimes taken for publicity. The Beslan School siege in Russia in 2004, where 1200 were held hostage in a school which was wired up with explosives, led to the deaths of 340 people, of whom 186 were children.

- Biological and chemical threats. These have rarely been carried out due to the technical difficulties involved. After 9/11, anthrax spores (which can cause a fatal lung disease) were sent through the post in the US. There are fears in Britain of 'dirty bombs' – non-nuclear bombs which can spread radioactive dust. There have also been rumours of terrorist threats to poison water supplies, etc.

- Hijackings. The taking over of aircraft or trains by terrorists used to be more common in the 1980s than it is now. Better airport security has made this crime more difficult to carry out.

Counter-international terrorism

After 11 September 2001, the US launched a 'war on terror'. To some extent this has been a conventional war, in Afghanistan and Iraq.

But the war on terror has also been an unconventional war, using the civilian uniformed services as well as the armed forces, and using new laws and public education (propaganda) to get the anti-terror message across.

> **remember**
> Iraq under Saddam Hussein seemingly did not sponsor terrorist groups, but it had used weapons of mass destruction against Iran and the Kurds in the 1980s.

(i) Countering International Terrorism: The United Kingdom's Strategy, July 2006 (www.cabinetoffice.gov.uk/)

Methods and their effectiveness

The methods of fighting international terrorism are many and various. They include:

- Fighting wars in Afghanistan and Iraq, the Ethiopian invasion of Somalia, etc.
- Passing laws against funding, supporting, encouraging or glorifying terrorism.
- Major diplomatic efforts to isolate Iran, Syria and Sudan.

- US and western foreign policy, which builds alliances with all countries pledged to combat international terrorism, especially countries seen to be in the 'front line' such as Turkey and Israel.

- Media reports and propaganda designed to discourage terrorism and rob it of any popular support it may have.

- Proscription and refusal to communicate with listed terrorist organisations such as Hamas.

- Government measures to reduce **social exclusion** and Islamophobia in many western countries.

- Worldwide security efforts by police and security organisations such as MI5.

- The activities of the EU, the UN, NATO and the OSCE.

- Sanctions and trade embargoes against countries such as North Korea and Iran.

- Attempts to control the illicit world trade in arms, and to secure stocks of nuclear, chemical and biological materials which could be used for terrorism.

- Major monitoring of world communication networks, mobile phones, the internet, foreign broadcasting, etc.

- Massive research and development into monitoring and communications technology such as 'smart dust' and the miniaturisation and digitisation of cameras and transmitters.

- Various ways of trying to cut off terrorists from their money supply.

- Increasing civilian awareness of the threats through setting up **resilience**-based organisations in governments and in local communities (in Britain and many other countries).

The effectiveness of these and other methods is hard to judge. International terrorism has been a threat for many years (e.g. the blowing up of flight Pan Am 103 over Lockerbie, Scotland in 1988), but despite all of the efforts made since then the threat is now much greater. In 2007 MI5 were allegedly monitoring over 2000 suspects in the UK (25% up in six months) and in 2006 the US State Department recorded 14,000 terrorist attacks worldwide compared with around 11,000 in 2005.

Some people (e.g. anti-war protesters) argue that some of the methods being used to combat terrorism are encouraging rather than deterring the problem. In any case, it is hard to assess the effect of measures when there are so many of them, when they are hard to test reliably, and when there are no valid controls to determine what might have happened if the measures had not been put into place.

As long as measures against international terrorism can be justified by governments and have popular support, they are likely to continue. Some are discussed in more detail below.

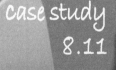

case study 8.11 — Financial measures against terrorists

In the wake of the 11 September 2001 terrorist attacks in the United States, the United Nations Security Council unanimously adopted resolution 1373, which, among its provisions, obliges all States to **criminalise** assistance for terrorist activities, deny financial support and safe haven to terrorists and share information about groups planning terrorist attacks.

activity
INDIVIDUAL WORK

Find resolution 1373 at the website below, and identify the main points.
www.un.org/Docs/journal/asp/ws.asp?m=S/RES/1373(2001)

Financial measures

The United Nations led these measures in 2001.

Many actions have been taken by the UN, the Organisation for Security and Co-operation in Europe (OSCE), the EU and the British government. Recent British measures include:

- Consultation with the charitable sector to keep it safe from terrorist exploitation.

- Increasing asset-freezing powers by creating a new Treasury Asset Freezing Unit.

- More asset freezing in response to advice from law enforcement and security agencies.

- More data-sharing between the public and private sectors, and better pooling of intelligence.

- Tackling the abuse of money service businesses (e.g. loan companies).

- A new action plan for HM Revenue and Customs (HMRC) to identify terrorist funding.

- Revised **Money Laundering** Regulations.

- Changes to the consent and tipping-off rules.

- Fresh international action, using the Financial Action Task Force (part of the UN) to identify and tackle the most serious financial threats to international security.

It is hard to judge the effectiveness of measures within Britain in combating international terrorism. Britain is thought to be a major centre for money-laundering and other abuses of its banking system because of its banking expertise and light regulation. The banking industry is a major money earner for the UK. Banks benefit from having minimal government prying (as in Switzerland), so it is hard to open them up to government checks on terrorist funds and money laundering. The links between terrorist funding and crime in general can make the money easier to find, but there are still legal difficulties in getting access to suspected terrorist accounts. Millions of pounds of terrorist funding have been confiscated in Britain, but it is hard to know how much terrorist money is left or how much money is kept by terrorists overseas (or how it is invested). In any case, terrorist money is not necessarily banked: it can be invested in businesses, either criminal (e.g. drugs trading) or legitimate (e.g. property). Britain by itself cannot cut off all terrorist funding – international organisations such as the UN, the EU and their agencies also have a major role to play.

www.osce.org/atu (Organization for Security and Co-operation in Europe)

www.fatf-gafi.org (Financial Action Task Force)

Sanctions

This is the agreed cutting of trade by the international community (e.g. through a UN Security Council resolution) to countries which appear to support terrorism. Sanctions can be targeted (e.g. bans on military equipment or materials which could be used for developing nuclear power) or more general. They have been carried out in the past against Serbia, North Korea, Iran and Iraq. If they involve things like food and medicine, or if they prevent the country from earning money by trade, they are liable to cause great hardship to ordinary people. The defenders of sanctions say that they are better than war; opponents say they are a 'blunt instrument' which cause suffering and breed long-term resentment, therefore encouraging terrorism.

Direct retaliation

The war in Afghanistan, which started in 2001 and lasted for six weeks during which there was intensive bombing, was a direct **retaliation** for the 9/11 attacks on the US. After the bombing campaign, coalition (mainly US and British) troops moved in and the central area round Kabul was occupied. A provisional council of Afghan elders chose

Hamid Karzai as leader in 2002, and his position was confirmed in 2004 with the first free elections in Afghanistan for some years.

In this case direct retaliation appears to have brought some positive results, at least for the west, in that central Afghanistan is opened up to education, investment and business in a way which might bring more wealth and a higher standard of living into an impoverished country. Other parts of Afghanistan are still highly unstable, and though Karzai is considered in the west to be a highly competent leader, there is at present no certainty that he will be able to unite the country in the long term.

However, generally speaking retaliation is an ineffective policy as it builds grudges and resentment, as in the case of the endless retaliatory attacks which have taken place over the years between Israel and Palestine. These seem to have brought the area no nearer to a lasting peace.

Extrajudicial killing of suspects

This happens when countries like Israel kill suspected terrorist leaders, usually by missile strikes on their homes, without making any effort to arrest them or bring them to trial. Case study 8.12 states the legal problems of such actions.

---

case study 8.12

Targeted killings in Israel

The April 18th killing in Gaza of Hamas leader Abdel Aziz Rantisi, following on the heels of the killing of his predecessor, Sheik Yassin, provoked an international outcry about Israel's policy of targeted killing. Such tactics have been widely condemned as unlawful under international law. In contrast, the United States, while occasionally uncomfortable with Israel's policy, has acknowledged that Israel has a right to self-defense that could be used in some circumstances to target leaders of terrorist groups – much as the United States has asserted its own right to target Osama Bin Laden. From a legal standpoint, there are three critical issues that determine the validity of this policy: the law of self-defense; international humanitarian law; and the principle of proportionality.

Source: American Society of International Law

activity
GROUP WORK

What are the arguments for and against killings of the type described above?

The US-led war on terrorism

Many books will be written on this subject in years to come. The war on terror is not over yet – and it may never be over. It seems likely that technology, intelligence, surveillance and other sophisticated methods will make terrorist plots easier to detect and prevent at an early stage. Whether outright war in countries like Iraq and Afghanistan can reduce terrorism is very doubtful. The British view, put forward by Tony Blair, is that it is possible to 'win the argument' against terrorists. But this may be contradicted by the fact that nobody even wants to talk to them (at least not publicly). Certainly education, propaganda and the media all have a big part to play in combating terrorism, but they may (intentionally or otherwise) encourage terrorism as well. Frank Gardner, the BBC Security correspondent, has argued that the 'rhetoric' (i.e. propaganda) of the war on terror is 'incredibly counter-productive'. If this is so, in parts of the war on terror the west is busy shooting itself in the foot. It is hard to know what will happen in the future. Terrorism may spread and be used by other groups, e.g. anti-globalisation. Or people may get tired of the subject and the war on terror, even if it continues, may no longer be big news.

Measures to prevent domestic or international terrorism in the UK

Since 2001 there has been increasing government and public awareness of the terrorist risk in the UK. After the London bombings of July 2005 this awareness intensified.

Training for biological and chemical attack

Biological and chemical terrorist attacks are rare. The worst such attack by a terrorist organisation (as opposed to a government) in recent years was carried out in 1995, in Tokyo subways, by the Aum Shinrikyo cult. This gas attack, on 20 March, killed 12 people, injured 3800, and 1000 had to go to hospital.

Some scientific expertise is needed to carry out biological and chemical attacks, but they are feasible and could be as dangerous as bombs or more so.

Hospitals are places where such attacks could be particularly deadly, and the NHS gives staff training on what to do if such an attack happens.

Training points include:

- Risk assessment.
- Communications.
- Command and control.
- Utilities – what happens if they fail?
- Evacuation plans.
- Infection control.
- Protective equipment.
- Major incident roles.
- Local support.
- Action plans/practices.

On a bigger scale, the government's Civil **Contingencies** Secretariat has a 'capabilities programme' to develop responses to possible terrorist attacks. One of their **workstreams** devises ways of dealing with chemical, biological, radiological and nuclear (CBRN) attacks. By 2006, 7000 police officers had received CBRN training.

Legal backing for the necessary emergency powers is contained in the Civil Contingencies Act 2004. The Home Office runs a national programme of counter-terrorist exercises using the CBRN skills that have been developed. The government expects to spend £2 billion on counter-terrorism measures by 2008.

10 Downing Street
www.number-10.gov.uk

Cabinet Office
www.cabinetoffice.gov.uk

Foreign Office
www.fco.gov.uk

Security Service
www.mi5.gov.uk

Secret Intelligence Service
www.sis.gov.uk or www.mi6.gov.uk

Threat assessments

Prior to July 2006, terrorist attack threat levels (which were publicised in the US) were not publicised in Britain, but the Home Office now issues and publicises its own threat-level assessment. The threat levels are:

■ Low – an attack is unlikely.

■ Moderate – an attack is possible, but not likely.

■ Substantial – an attack is a strong possibility.

■ Severe – an attack is highly likely.

■ Critical – an attack is expected imminently.

The points considered when making the threat-level assessment are:

■ Available intelligence.

■ Terrorist capability.

■ Terrorist intentions.

■ Timescale.

The body making the decisions is the Joint Terrorism Analysis Centre (JTAC), which was started up in 2003.

Threat Levels: The System to Assess the Threat from International Terrorism, July 2006

www.cabinetoffice.gov.uk/

Control of immigration and asylum seekers

Immigrants and **asylum** seekers usually do not like terrorism any more than anybody else, and asylum seekers may have left their home countries for fear of terrorist attacks. Nevertheless, in the past, Britain has been accused of allowing asylum seekers who are really terrorists to stay in the country.

A number of laws have been passed to tighten up asylum procedures. However, it is not legally possible to stop asylum seekers from coming altogether because Britain

Figure 8.6 Asylum seekers

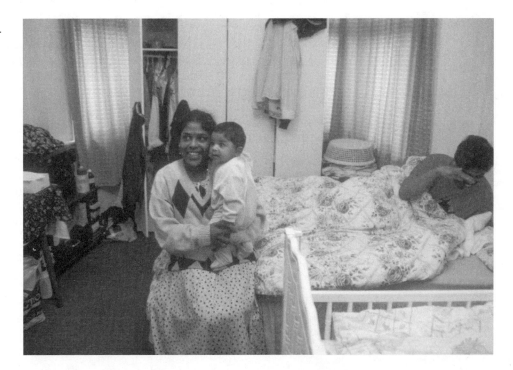

has signed the Geneva Convention, the international law giving people who are being persecuted in their own country the right to seek asylum in another.

The Asylum and Immigration Act 1996 made it more difficult for illegal immigrants to get work in Britain, and required employers to check people's papers before giving them work. The Immigration and Asylum Act 1999 made it easier to bar and remove people from the country. The Asylum and Immigration (Treatment of Claimants, etc.) Act 2004 strengthened the powers of immigration officers to arrest people and gave them greater control over who came into the country. The Immigration, Asylum and Nationality Act 2006 further strengthened border controls and made it possible to remove people on national security grounds without the right of appeal until *after* they had been deported.

There are also technological measures being brought in, including **biometric** passports and identity cards. Both of these are intended to tighten national security by making it more difficult for known or suspected terrorists to enter the country, and to protect against passport fraud and false identities. Project Semaphore electronically captures the details of travellers coming in and out of the country, and the information is sifted by the UK Immigration Service, the Police Service, UK Visas and HM Revenue and Customs – who can then issue alerts if it seems that a person is a potential threat.

The British government now liaises with other governments and agencies to tackle illegal immigration. The agencies include Europol, Interpol and the OCSE. Immigration liaison officers work with the immigration departments of other countries to track down international criminals and people who are a security or terrorist risk.

Security of public buildings

Terrorist attacks typically occur in places where large numbers of people gather, and the risk appears greater in London than elsewhere, perhaps because of its symbolic importance as a capital city and because the media are based nearby. Airports, train, bus and tube stations, sports grounds, nightclubs and large shopping malls are the kinds of buildings most at risk. Such places are increasingly equipped with large numbers of CCTV cameras in an effort to take clear pictures of everyone who passes through. Radiation detection equipment is installed at air and sea ports. The private security industry plays a major role, and public buildings are heavily staffed with trained security personnel. Since the 1980s there has been a zero-tolerance policy towards unattended luggage and suspect packages, and even litter bins are designed to make them less suitable for planting bombs.

Large public buildings have evacuation plans, and staff are trained in dealing with chemical attacks. The fire and rescue and ambulance services provide **decontamination** expertise and equipment. There are systems for communicating the emergency to those who need to know about it, and for recording details of casualties. Good detailed information is available on local NHS websites.

Freedom of speech and other human rights issues contrasted with anti-terrorist measures

All anti-terrorist measures involve some reduction in people's human rights and, under recent UK legislation, limitations on freedom of speech. The Terrorism Act 2006 makes it illegal to make a public statement (e.g. speech, pamphlet, newspaper article, website) 'that is likely to be understood by some or all of the members of the public to whom it is published as a direct or indirect encouragement or other inducement to them to the commission, preparation or instigation of acts of terrorism'.

Apart from free speech, there are other human rights issues linked to terrorist legislation.

Detention without trial
The main human rights issue relates to locking people up on suspicion of terrorist involvement and then keeping them locked up without charging them. Under the Terrorism Act 2006 suspects can be detained without charge for up to 28 days. This

case study 8.13 — Freedom of speech

A statement is illegal if it:

(a) **glorifies** the commission or preparation (whether in the past, in the future or generally) of such acts or offences; and

(b) is a statement from which those members of the public could reasonably be expected to infer that what is being glorified is being glorified as conduct that should be emulated by them in existing circumstances.

Source: Terrorism Act 2006, section 1(3)

activity — GROUP WORK

1. Why might the Terrorism Act 2006 be hard to enforce?

2. When this law was brought in there was a lot of disagreement about including this section. What are the arguments for and against limiting freedom of speech in this way?

3. Are there, in your opinion, any circumstances in which an act of terrorism *might* be justified?

---

is much less than the 90 days that many people wanted. The US have locked up terror suspects in the Guantanamo Bay detention centre, near Cuba, for years without trial.

Failure to bring suspects to proper trial

Both in the US and Britain it is argued that terrorist trials in open court will bring unacceptable risks to the participants, and that making evidence gathered by security services public will put the members of those services, and their effectiveness, at risk. For these reasons terror suspects are having their human right to a fair trial infringed.

Deportation

Some suspects are, like failed asylum seekers, being deported to countries where there is no guarantee that they will not be tortured or killed by the authorities.

> **remember**
>
> The government has a 'white list' of countries which it considers it is safe to **deport** people to.

---

case study 8.14 — What the public can do

Members of the public can help by:

■ Working in their own community, particularly with young people, to encourage community engagement and to counter those who seek to promote radicalisation and terrorist violence.

■ Being alert to their surroundings and identifying and reporting unusual or suspicious activities. Any suspicious activity should be reported to the Anti-Terrorist Hotline on 0800 789321.

■ Consulting FCO travel advice (www.fco.gov.uk) before travelling abroad.

■ Reading the *Protecting Against Terrorism* booklet. It is not just for government and big businesses. It contains clear, general security advice about how to help make a community safer. It is available on the internet at www.mi5.gov.uk.

activity — GROUP WORK

Imagine that somebody you know has expressed sympathy or support for a terrorist act. What arguments would you use to persuade them – through reasoning – that they were wrong?

Awareness/vigilance campaigns/advertisements

The government encourages ordinary people to be vigilant in security matters, and to report cases where they think there may be terrorist encouragement, education or planning going on.

Centre for Protection of National Infrastructure
www.cpni.gov.uk/

Build relationships with communities, education

Public services such as the police and prison service have extensive community and diversity awareness training to make them better able to communicate and coordinate with minority groups. The Home Office has carried out research on contacting hard-to-reach groups, and this includes radicalised groups who might consider supporting terrorism. The government has been keen to win the argument against terrorist groups who use education and/or propaganda to convince their listeners of the rightness of their cause. Since the government sees the main danger as lying in the Muslim community, they have tended to concentrate on them with 'Scholars' Roadshows', and similar events, where influential Muslim lecturers and experts talk to communities to persuade them that terrorism is un-Islamic. In order to contest the belief held by some that British foreign policy has been unfairly targeting Muslim countries such as Afghanistan and Iraq, the government has produced documents explaining all the things that Britain has done overseas (e.g. in Kosovo) to help Muslims.

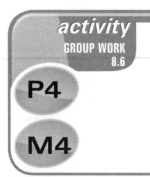

activity
GROUP WORK
8.6

P4

M4

Give a presentation suitable for trainee security staff on terrorism and counter-terrorism, explaining the methods used both by terrorists and by those who combat terrorism. (Back up your presentation with notes, handouts and visual aids showing that all group members have fulfilled the grading criteria.)

Understanding human rights and human rights violations, showing how UK uniformed public services are used in a humanitarian role

Human rights

Human rights are the entitlement that we all have to be treated fairly and equally by those in power.

Universal Declaration of Human Rights (1948)

This definitive statement of human rights, which all modern statements of human rights follow, was produced by the United Nations. It can be found in full on the internet.

www.un.org/Overview/rights.html

Historical background

The Universal Declaration was written shortly after World War II, which saw the worst ever recorded abuse of human rights in the state-sponsored murder of 6 million Jews under Hitler. The prime aim of the United Nations was to provide peace for a world that badly needed it. The people who drew up the Declaration believed that a shared respect for human rights in all countries was an essential prerequisite for a lasting peace.

Key features

The Universal Declaration of Human Rights begins with a preamble (i.e. introduction) which states that human rights should be made law so that there can be friendship, justice and freedom among people and nations.

The rest of the Declaration, which is about 1750 words long, consists of 30 articles, or paragraphs, each stating an essential human right.

Right to life, not subject to torture

These are two of the rights laid down in the Declaration. Others include the right to freedom, equality before the law, the right to fair trial, freedom of movement, the right to asylum, freedom of thought, religion and expression, the right to vote, the right to work, trade unions, holidays, a decent standard of living, education, culture and a government which respects all of these rights.

activity
INDIVIDUAL WORK 8.7
P5

Write a campaign leaflet for a local human rights group describing the key features of the Universal Declaration of Human Rights and explaining how human rights have been violated in a country other than Britain.

Geneva Convention

The Geneva Convention is a UN agreement made in 1949 which most countries have signed. There are in fact four separate Conventions:

- First – treatment of sick and wounded members of armed forces on land.
- Second – treatment of sick, and wounded members of armed forces at sea.
- Third – treatment of prisoners of war.
- Fourth – protection of civilians in times of war.

There is also a 1951 Refugees' Convention which was produced by the UN and, like the Geneva Convention, is part of international law and aims to protect human rights.

The extract from the Geneva Convention below deals with prisoners of war.

The **convention** is often flouted, for prisoners of war are often brutally treated, humiliated or killed by their captors. The worst recent recorded case was the Srebrenica Massacre, when 7000 Bosnian Muslims were slaughtered by Serb militia in 1995. Even disciplined armies such as those of Britain and the US occasionally break the rules – for example when Saddam Hussein was shown on television having a dental examination, and in the maltreatment of prisoners at Abu Ghraib Prison in 2004.

European Convention on Human Rights

This statement was produced in 1950 by the Council of Europe – a body formed in Europe after World War II to help build peace. (The Council of Europe still exists but

case study 8.15

Prohibited acts

The following acts are and shall remain prohibited at any time and in any place whatsoever ...

(a) Violence to life and person, in particular murder of all kinds, mutilation, cruel treatment and torture;

(b) Taking of hostages;

(c) Outrages upon personal dignity, in particular, humiliating and degrading treatment;

(d) The passing of sentences and the carrying out of executions without previous judgment pronounced by a regularly constituted court affording all the judicial guarantees which are recognized as indispensable by civilized peoples.

activity
GROUP WORK

1. Using the internet or other sources of information find examples where these prohibited acts have been reported as taking place over the last year.

2. Why is it important that British forces follow the Geneva Convention?

is entirely separate from the EU.) The Convention is very similar to the UN Universal Declaration of Human Rights, though it goes into more detail. Britain signed acceptance of the Convention in the early 1950s, but some of it was never formally added into UK law. However, it was incorporated into the constitutions of most EU countries, and in 1998 it was also fully incorporated into British law through the Human Rights Act 1998.

Human Rights Act 1998

This Act compels public authorities, such as the police and other uniformed and non-uniformed public services, to act in accordance with the human rights which were originally set down in the European Convention.

Book 1, Unit 6, page 243

Violations

More detail in Book 1, Unit 5, page 194

Violations by regimes

'Regimes' means governments. The word is normally used in a pejorative sense, to refer to non-democratic governments, i.e. dictatorships.

All governments sometimes violate human rights, but the violations are usually worse in non-democratic countries where there is no proper legal system and where the government is not open and accountable. Violations also tend to be worse in developing countries because there is not enough money to set up properly regulated government systems and to have a legal system that will protect the people. Countries with particularly poor human rights records include Zimbabwe, Myanmar, North Korea, Sudan and Liberia.

> **remember**
>
> Detailed information on human rights abuses by regimes is available on the websites of Human Rights Watch and Amnesty International.

http://hrw.org/
www.amnesty.org/
www.ohchr.org/

Torture

The purpose of torture is to extract information from people by the threat or application of pain or fear. It is practised, officially or unofficially, in many countries. Torture is a violation of human rights. It is also an unreliable way of getting information because people will say anything if they are frightened enough. Information gained through torture is not admissible in any proper court of law.

Extrajudicial killings

This means killing criminal or terrorist suspects without putting them on trial. The aim is to get rid of people who are believed (but not proved) to be dangerous. As a means of justice it is ineffective because it causes anger (leading to civil disobedience or terrorist attacks) and fails to get useful information about criminal or terrorist networks.

Ethnic cleansing

This means clearing people of a certain ethnic group out of their land, either by terrorising them and driving them away or by massacring them on the spot. **Ethnic cleansing** was first used during the fighting in Bosnia and it bears some resemblance to crimes of genocide. Recently it has been happening in Darfur, western Sudan.

Genocide

This is the organised attempt to exterminate a particular race. It has happened at various times in history and, more recently, in World War II with the extermination of European Jews.

UK public services humanitarian role

Several UK public services carry out humanitarian work overseas from time to time.

Humanitarian aid programmes

This general term covers much of the work done by UK public services in relation to education, peace, human rights, famine relief, medical aid, etc. British government humanitarian aid is normally channelled through the Department for International Development (DFID). The actual relief work tends to be done by charities or in partnerhip with the EU, UN, etc. Contributions from DFID for flood relief in Mozambique in 2007 included donations to Save the Children, Oxfam, the Red Cross, CARE and the provision of a logistics expert to the Government of Mozambique's National Institute (INGC) for Disaster Management. The DFID also works with the Ministry of Defence and the Foreign and Commonwealth Office through partnerships called Conflict Prevention Pools which combine 'development, diplomacy and defence'. The armed forces are actively involved in these cases in the development and the defence – the former by urgent reconstruction work and the latter through peacekeeping duties.

www.dfid.gov.uk/

Disaster relief abroad

The armed forces have been active in a number of disasters, notably the Pakistan earthquake in 2005 and the 2004 tsunami. They save lives, provide food and shelter and do heavy reconstruction work. The fire and rescue service also do humanitarian work, especially in earthquakes. Information about such activities can usually be found on public service websites.

activity
INDIVIDUAL WORK
8.8

P6

Write an article for a children's newspaper or magazine describing the humanitarian work done by UK uniformed services in a named international crisis or disaster.

Peacekeeping

This is discussed on page 5 above.

www.un.org/
www.mod.uk
www.fco.gov.uk
www.nato.int/home.htm
http://ec.europa.eu/

Progress Check

1. What are the roles of the UN Security Council?
2. Outline what the EU Commission, the Council of the EU and the European Parliament do.
3. What is the role of NATO?
4. What are the roles of the World Bank?
5. What do peacekeepers do – and how do they do it?
6. How can British consulates help British citizens?
7. What are war crimes and how can war criminals be brought to justice?
8. Why is the Middle East unstable?
9. List the methods used by terrorists.
10. What steps can make it more difficult for terrorists to get the money they need?
11. Give arguments for and against the **extrajudicial** killing of suspects.
12. What are threat assessments?
13. Name the organisations and measures taken which reduce illegal immigration into the UK.

UNIT 10

Skills for Land-based Outdoor and Adventurous Activities

This unit covers:

- Different land-based outdoor and adventurous activities
- How risks are managed in land-based outdoor and adventurous activities
- Participating in land-based outdoor and adventurous activities
- Personal skills development in land-based outdoor and adventurous activities

This unit enables you to explore the theory and practice of land-based outdoor and adventurous activities such as mountain walking, orienteering, rock-climbing, caving, skiing and snowboarding. It begins by looking at the organisations which provide these activities, the kinds of people who can take part, the places where they are done and the purposes of the activities.

The unit then goes on to examine the risks of land-based outdoor and adventurous activities – and how these risks can be limited without taking the adventure out of the activity.

A large section of the unit is practical. You will be expected to take part in land-based outdoor and adventurous activities, and become as good at them as you can in the time available.

The final section of the unit shows how you can build on your achievements and progress, if you wish, to higher and more demanding qualifications in land-based outdoor and adventurous activities.

grading criteria

To achieve a **pass** grade the evidence must show that the learner is able to:	To achieve a **merit** grade the evidence must show that, in addition to the pass criteria, the learner is able to:	To achieve a **distinction** grade the evidence must show that, in addition to the pass and merit criteria, the learner is able to:
P1 describe four different land-based outdoor and adventurous activities Pg 56	**M1** compare and contrast four different land-based outdoor and adventurous activities Pg 56	**D1** evaluate the skills and techniques required to successfully perform in two different land-based outdoor and adventurous activities Pg 76
P2 carry out risk assessments for two different land-based outdoor and adventurous activities Pg 67	**M2** compare and contrast the skills and techniques required for two different land-based outdoor and adventurous activities Pg 76	**D2** demonstrate advanced skills and techniques in two different land-based outdoor and adventurous activities Pg 78

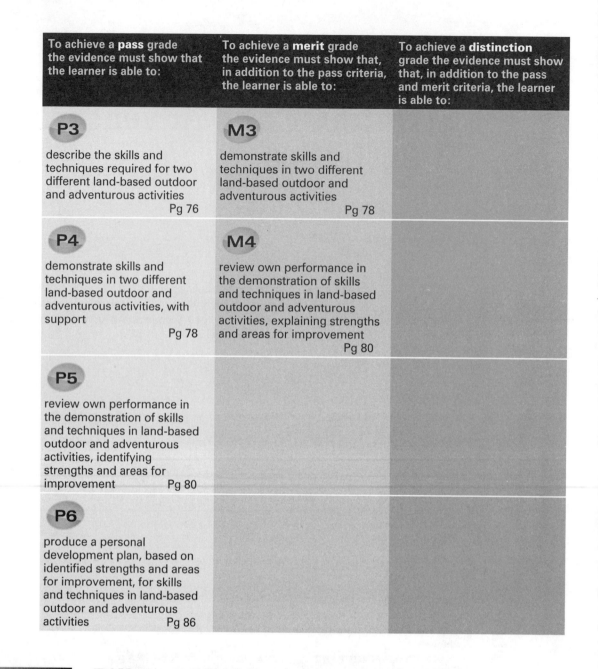

To achieve a **pass** grade the evidence must show that the learner is able to:	To achieve a **merit** grade the evidence must show that, in addition to the pass criteria, the learner is able to:	To achieve a **distinction** grade the evidence must show that, in addition to the pass and merit criteria, the learner is able to:
P3 describe the skills and techniques required for two different land-based outdoor and adventurous activities Pg 76	**M3** demonstrate skills and techniques in two different land-based outdoor and adventurous activities Pg 78	
P4 demonstrate skills and techniques in two different land-based outdoor and adventurous activities, with support Pg 78	**M4** review own performance in the demonstration of skills and techniques in land-based outdoor and adventurous activities, explaining strengths and areas for improvement Pg 80	
P5 review own performance in the demonstration of skills and techniques in land-based outdoor and adventurous activities, identifying strengths and areas for improvement Pg 80		
P6 produce a personal development plan, based on identified strengths and areas for improvement, for skills and techniques in land-based outdoor and adventurous activities Pg 86		

Different land-based outdoor and adventurous activities

Land-based outdoor and **adventurous** activities are physical activities carried out for pleasure, training and competition which use natural (or simulated) **terrain** and settings as a necessary part of the activity. They can use equipment such as bicycles, ropes and climbing gear but (for the purposes of this unit) exclude motorised transport and ball games played in a simulated natural setting, such as golf.

Activities

Land-based outdoor and adventurous activities include:

- Biking – off-road.
- Caving/potholing.
- Rock-climbing.
- **Mountaineering**.

- Mountain walking.
- Fell running.
- Hill walking.
- Horse-riding.
- Orienteering.
- Paintball.
- Skiing.
- Snowboarding.

Mountain walking

Mountain walking is walking on mountains for pleasure, recreation, training purposes or sport. It ranges from strolling up hills to long treks over wild, rugged terrain, mountaineering and fell-racing.

In Britain a mountain could be loosely defined as a hill over 1500 feet (about 457 metres), preferably with rock outcrops or cliffs on it. In other countries the height limit may be different, and a mountain might be any hill whose summit is, say, 450 metres or more above the surrounding countryside. Alternatively, a mountain could be described as any hill which is hard to climb, or which requires special clothing or equipment to get up it.

Orienteering

Orienteering is a competitive sport originally developed in Scandinavia. It tests map-reading and **navigation** skills, and fitness. The **aim** is to navigate yourself around a pre-planned course in rough terrain as quickly as possible, visiting 'control points' marked on a map on the way. There are four main types of orienteering:

- Foot orienteering, where the course (which usually is without tracks) is travelled on foot.
- Mountain-bike orienteering, which follows the same principles but the course has tracks which are followed on mountain bikes.
- Ski orienteering, where participants use ski-tracks and have to plan and follow the fastest route between control points.
- Trail orienteering. This is a form of orienteering for people of limited mobility, and the test is to identify the **control points** rather than visit them all. The activity has been a recognised competitive sport since 1999.

Rock-climbing

This sport involves climbing rocks, cliffs and indoor climbing walls. There are a huge variety of approaches and techniques, reflecting the differences between different types of rock, cliff and climbing conditions, and the different physical fitness and aims of participants. It ranges from climbing small boulders to long routes in the Alps and beyond which can take several days and involve ice-climbing as well.

Caving and mines

These activities involve going into natural and human-made holes, tunnels and shafts in the ground. Caves are natural; mines have been dug by miners, either by hand or using machinery, to extract minerals from underground. Caving is a sport which has been going on for a hundred years or more (and, of course, prehistoric people lived in caves, sometimes deep underground). Mine exploration has been going on for less than 50 years, and is often linked to research in industrial history, as disused mines frequently date from the nineteenth or twentieth centuries, and in some cases from even earlier. Caving and mine exploration are rather different, but much of the equipment is the same.

Skiing

Skiing is a sport where people slide over snow or artificial snow on special strips called skis. It is a major winter sport and a multi-million pound industry. People ski for fun, recreation, training and competition. There are two main kinds of skiing:

- Downhill skiing, where the aim is to go down a steep slope as fast as possible.
- Cross-country skiing, where the aim is to cover a long distance over fairly smooth, snowy terrain.

Snowboarding

This resembles skiing but uses a single board, like a skateboard without wheels, instead of a ski attached to each foot. Though the speeds reached are not as high as those in conventional downhill skiing, snowboards can be steered in tight curves and are very manoeuvrable. The sport is acrobatic and technical, and requires agility and balance.

Providers

Providers are organisations or companies which can enable people to take part in an activity. Some are publicly funded, others are charities and many are private businesses.

One land-based outdoor activity can be done without a **provider** – mountain walking. In Britain anybody who is properly equipped and experienced can walk up and over mountains as often as they like, with or without other people. However, for people who are not experienced, or who like their mountain walking to be sociable, there is a lot to be said for going with a provider.

> **remember**
>
> Most outdoor adventurous activities now have governing bodies which regulate the safety of the activity and train and award qualifications to instructors. These bodies are providers in a sense because they arrange competitions and train the providers.

Table 10.1 Summary of types of providers

Activity	Providers	Possible clients	Comments
Mountain walking	1. Clubs such as the Ramblers' Association	Families; single or older people who like walking	Also campaigns for better countryside access
	2. Local clubs and societies	Varied; mainly older people	Mainly recreational, but some are ambitious and even organise expeditions
	3. Local authorities	Young people	Partnerships with youth service, schools, etc.
	4. Educational institutions	Young people	These often use other providers, e.g. the army
	5. The army (and, sometimes, other uniformed public services)	Young people, potential recruits – and army personnel themselves	Work with schools and colleges through Army Youth Teams, etc.
	6. Charities supported by the client	Young, relatively well-off people looking for adventure holidays	Outward Bound for example
	7. Charities supported by the public and volunteers	May help disabled and/or economically disadvantaged people	Some have specially equipped centres and staff trained to work with disabled
	8. Private providers (sometimes in partnership with local authorities, etc.)	Various client groups	May link mountain walking, etc. with teamwork and management training
	9. Other organisations	Mainly young people	Duke of Edinburgh's Award; Scouts, etc.
Orienteering	1. Local authorities	Families, young people, orienteering groups	Local authorities may set up their own orienteering areas
	2. Private providers	Families, young people, orienteering groups	Can act in partnership with local authorities or receive extra funding

Activity	Providers	Possible clients	Comments
Rock climbing	1. Local authorities	Mainly fit people	Set up climbing walls, etc.
	2. Private providers	Mainly young people	Work in partnership with schools and colleges
	3. Climbing clubs	Mainly dedicated climbers	They buy and share their equipment
Caving and mine exploration	1. Caving clubs	For enthusiasts. Often set up at universities. High standards needed	Equipment costs included in club membership fees
	2. Private-sector providers	For educational parties and adventure holidays	The client usually pays
	3. Army	Young people	They give a first experience of caving
Skiing	1. Local authorities with ski slopes	Families, young people and others	To prepare people for skiing on snow, or to keep fit
	2. Informal groups arranging to holiday together, using commercial providers at their destination	Skiing holidays for families and adults	Many different people, e.g. instructors, hotels provide for the needs of the skiers: there is no single provider
	3. Private providers (there could be several providing different ski-related services)	A wide range of clients	May be travel firms arranging skiing holidays
	4. Schools, colleges and universities arranging skiing trips	Young people	Many of their needs probably covered by the private sector at the ski resort
Snowboarding	As with skiing, but on a more limited scale	Mainly young people	Similar arrangements to skiing

remember
For many, particularly young people, family and friends can act as informal providers.

Public providers

These are providers such as schools, local authorities and the army who are mainly paid for through taxation (public money).

Private providers

These are commercial organisations aiming to make a profit. They run holidays and outdoor centres or give training and instruction to participants. Some private providers are individuals or couples who have the expertise and equipment to lead parties up mountains or down caves. More usually they work in teams with both men and women in them. Some private providers are registered as charities but still have to make enough money to cover their salaries and **overheads**.

Voluntary

Voluntary providers usually work for organisations such as the Scouts or the Duke of Edinburgh's Award. They give instruction, advice and other care and may work alongside paid staff.

remember
It is sometimes hard to get details of partnerships – since businesses do not always like to give the public too many details of their finances.

Partnerships

A simple example of a partnership is when teachers accompany schoolchildren on a day out with the army. Some of the costs are paid by the pupils or the school, but much of the cost is covered by the army (which gets its money from the taxpayer). The army staff are responsible for the activities, including safety, organisations and skills training, while teachers are responsible for the general order and well-being of the children, especially when they are not taking part in activities.

In a partnership, responsibilities and/or costs are shared.

Many providers work in partnership – for example a local authority might give a grant to a privately run charity which provides adventurous activities to disabled young people. Both the authority and the charity are essential in providing the activity for the clients.

Target groups and participants (e.g. children, young people, people with disabilities)

Providers of land-based outdoor and adventurous activities, like other organisations, specialise in the work they do. This specialisation is seen in the activities they offer and in the kinds of people they cater for.

---

case study 10.1 — Avon Tyrell (Hampshire)

4.1 Avon Tyrell is the National Activity and Residential Centre for Youth Clubs UK, an organisation that provides outdoor education and environmental opportunities for school students and adults across Hampshire. Last year's funding was used to further develop their classroom, barn and outdoor areas and new equipment was purchased for the development of new environmental activities.

4.2 This year the centre would like to update their teaching materials to ensure they meet the National Curriculum, update computer equipment and implement more audio visual equipment.

4.3 With regard to corporate objectives, Avon Tyrell works with a variety of groups from 'hard to reach' backgrounds, including Hampshire Youth groups, local play schemes and a number of `young offenders' groups. They contribute to 'maximising **life opportunities**' for these young people, and deliver an environmental message consistent with aims within '**stewardship** of the environment'. In addition, the partnership funding will enable them to 'improve services'.

Source: Hampshire County Council

activity
INDIVIDUAL WORK

1. Which groups does the Avon Tyrell Centre cater for, according to the extract?
2. What advantages will group members gain from going to the centre?

---

case study 10.2 — Kepplewray (Cumbria)

What do we do at the Kepplewray Centre?

We provide superb accommodation, food and activity instruction for people of all backgrounds and ages including those with disabilities. Most of our guests are schools on 'residentials' (field courses to the rest of us), groups (e.g. Scouts, Church groups, **Phab**), and families and individuals. We can also accommodate training courses, small business conferences and one-day meetings.

Source: The Kepplewray Project

activity
GROUP WORK

What kinds of people attend the Kepplewray Centre and what sorts of activity would you expect them to specialise in?

Figure 10.1 Factors determining choice of provider

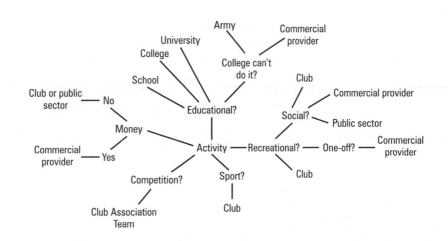

Many centres specialising in particular target groups and participants are charities or private companies set up to fill a 'niche' (business opportunity) in the market. Having a private sector is beneficial because it can raise standards by competition for clients, and bring new ideas into the adventure holiday industry. As clients pay, private providers cost the taxpayers less money than a publicly funded project. In practice, however, many organisations and charities rely on a mixture of public (local council grants) and private funding (including charging customers) to pay for their services. In outdoor activities, as in many other public service related fields, partnerships are becoming more and more important.

Locations

These are the areas or places where outdoor and adventurous activities are carried out.

Natural

Britain is a country with varied scenery and landscape, and as a result of this there are many places which are naturally suitable for outdoor and adventurous activities. The mountains in Scotland, Wales and the Lake District, though not high by world standards, are often rocky and provide natural playgrounds for people who like adventurous outdoor activities. Climbing is carried out on particular cliffs where the rock is hard and the cliffs themselves are high enough to provide a challenge. Examples are the cliffs on the Cuillin Hills in Skye, the east side of Ben Nevis, the north side of Scafell in the Lake District, and Clogwyn Du'r Arddu – a cliff on the side of Snowdon which is 600 feet (183 metres) high. Mountain walking is done in the Scottish Highlands, the Southern Uplands, the Pennines, the Lake District, Wales and on Dartmoor. Caving is practised, in Britain, in limestone regions such as the Yorkshire Dales, the Peak District, part of South Wales and the Mendip Hills in Somerset. Mine exploration is done mainly in Wales.

The natural potential for skiing and snowboarding in Britain is patchy, since snow is not dependable. Good downhill skiing is possible at Aviemore and a few other centres in the Highlands of Scotland – but snow can be in short supply in a mild winter. There are good places for cross-country skiing – mainly around the Cairngorm Mountains and Lochnagar. From time to time cross-country skiing is possible in some other hilly areas of Britain. But for both skiing and snowboarding people usually prefer to go to the Alps, Norway or North America.

The natural setting for orienteering is woodland or heathland, which is fairly widely distributed throughout the UK. However, orienteering courses are not completely natural, since the areas have to be managed and control points and courses set up by people who know what they are doing.

remember
Most outdoor activities providers are based close to the mountains, caves, etc. where their activities are practised.

remember
The best way to understand orienteering, or any other adventurous activity, is to have a go at it!

Figure 10.2 Outdoor
activities in the UK

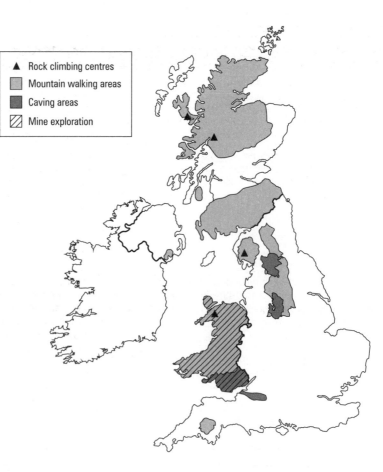

Manmade (artificial)

There are no man-made mountains or areas for mountain walking. Mines are man-made caves and are in areas where metals or slate have been mined in the past. Disused mines are dangerous environments especially if they have been dug in soft, layered rock (e.g. coal mines).

Caves are always natural features and there are no artificial ones.

There are, however, plenty of indoor artificial rock-climbing facilities, with routes of varying difficulty. In some parts of Britain there are quarries which are artificial and which provide steep, sound rock-faces for climbing on. They are also good places to practise **abseiling**, because the faces are often vertical.

Orienteering courses are artificial because they have to be laid out and mapped – in a natural environment. They do not have to be made professionally, but it takes time to lay the course and prepare maps that contestants can use. If the same course is used too often, tracks form which make the course less of a challenge.

For skiing and snowboarding there are artificial ski slopes in various British towns and cities (e.g. Sheffield and Edinburgh) which provide a useful training facility for skiers and snowboarders.

Fixed and competition courses

A fixed course is a place where an activity can always be practised. A competition course is one where competitions in the relevant adventurous activity can be held.

Table 10.2 outlines the main points on fixed and competition courses.

remember Even in Britain new venues for rock climbing and caving are still being discovered.

Table 10.2 Main points on fixed and competition courses

Activity	Fixed courses	Competition courses
Mountain walking	There are many paths on British mountains which are fixed courses. But some walkers like to leave the paths and take different routes, which they plan themselves, in order to see different places and views	There are mountain-walking competitions, for example on the 'Welsh Three-Thousands' (15 tops over 3000 feet or 914 metres). Fell races where competitors run up and down mountains are more common
Orienteering	For mountain-biking and ski and trail orienteering there are semi-permanent courses often with clearly marked tracks. For orienteering on foot, trackless terrain can be used	There need to be additional practice courses for 'model' events in a major championship. Water and plastic cups are provided. There are refreshment places, helpers, arrangements in case of illness and injury. A timed or electronic punch-starting system is used. Courses must be fair but difficult. Controls must be in place so as not to give an unfair advantage to later runners
Rock climbing	Natural rock climbing is on cliffs whose features only change slowly, with erosion or the breaking off of lumps by frost or climbers. Weather changes conditions but not the shape of the rock. Climbing routes are usually illustrated in climbing books, showing the way climbers should go. Routes are graded according to difficulty. Indoor rock climbing can be on fixed courses, but they can usually be rearranged to give variety	Most competition rock climbing is done on indoor walls, where there is less risk of injury and less unfairness due to changing conditions caused by the position of the sun or changes in weather. Bouldering (short route, high strength), speed climbing and red point (amassing points by climbing different routes of graded difficulty) are some formats for climbing competitions. There are local, regional, national and world cup competitions
Caving	Caves are fixed courses in that caves which have been explored are of a fixed length, formed naturally in solid and mainly unchanging rock. However, caving clubs do dig and tunnel for new caves, and in this sense caves grow and develop as new passages are explored	The competitive element in caving is that of finding newer and deeper caves. The biggest cave in Britain is Titan, discovered in 2005 – a vertical shaft in Derbyshire 459 feet (140 metres) deep. The world's biggest is Krubera, in the Caucasus, 6824 feet (2080 metres) deep
Mines	Mines are fixed courses, but new ones are being rediscovered and explored all the time	Mine exploration is not a competitive sport
Skiing	Downhill skiing has fixed courses, unless you ski **off-piste**. The same is true of cross-country skiing. The courses are fixed, but of course the snow changes all the time	There are competitions at every level in many kinds of downhill skiing and in ski-jumping. These reach their high point in the Winter Olympics, which take place every four years. Cross-country skiing is also an Olympic event as part of the biathlon
Snowboarding	Snowboarding is downhill, but with fixed and sometimes artificial courses, suitable for the acrobatic moves of this sport	As with skiing, there are plenty of competitions, all the way up to Winter Olympic Level. Some competitions are judged rather than based on speeds and distances

Aims

If we consider human history from prehistoric times, it appears that we developed in a nomadic way, spreading all over the world from a point of origin. Most of this movement must have been done on foot or on the backs of domesticated animals. The ability to walk great distances, to cross mountain ranges and all types of terrain, and to adapt to different environments, is, it seems, a quality that has helped to ensure our survival and success as a species. It may be that we hardly need an aim or an excuse to carry out adventurous outdoor activities – a love of adventure is part of human nature.

Nevertheless, we also tend to do things for a reason, and outdoor and adventurous activities are no exception. On the following pages are some reasons why people go out and do the things that are the subject matter of this unit.

Recreation

Recreation is pleasure, enjoyment and amusement for its own sake. Throughout the world, millions of people take part in land-based outdoor and recreational activities because they enjoy them. This enjoyment comes from the sense of freedom in being out of the towns and cities, the pleasure of tackling a challenge such as a difficult rock climb, the sense of exploration that comes from caving and going down old mines or the excitement of rushing headlong down a snowy hillside in sub-zero temperatures. It is a combination of the pleasure of free movement, the pride in being able to do something that not everybody can do, and a feeling of closeness to nature and interacting with the natural world in a way which is so much more involving and satisfying than simply seeing it on television.

Skills development

Outdoor and adventurous activities develop two main categories of skills.

Technical skills These are skills and techniques are to do with the activity itself. Table 10.3 indicates technical skills linked with different activities.

Table 10.3 The technical skills linked with different activities

Activity	Technical skills
Mountain walking	Map reading, compass use, navigation, walk planning, route cards, safety awareness, contingency planning, getting help, first aid, judging best walking speeds, dealing with awkward or dangerous terrain, weather knowledge, understanding boots and other walking equipment, what to carry, eating and drinking on the mountains
Orienteering	Running/cycling/skiing/walking skills; navigation skills, including map reading, setting map, bearings, transferring bearings from map to ground and from ground to map; using catching features, handrails, aiming off, attack points, collecting features; pace counting
Rock climbing	Fitness, strength, balance; knowing and understanding equipment – rope, helmet, harness, rock boots, belay/karabiner; recognising the qualities of different kinds of rock; knots and rope work; use of **prusik** knots; belaying; commands; **camming**, wedging; foot techniques, e.g. edging, **smearing**; hand techniques, e.g. jamming; getting down: abseiling (rappelling), lowering
Caving	Fitness, strength, balance; understanding and care of cave environment; route selection; cave map reading, navigation, e.g. draughts; equipment – helmet, lights, clothing, boots, food, drink, first aid; ropes – knots, belays, rigging ropes, ladders; emergency procedures; other techniques – squeezes, cave climbing; recognising and dealing with hazards, e.g. water hazards, cold, fatigue, loose terrain, mud, slippery surfaces, risk of falls, contingency and escape plans; getting help
Skiing	Fitness, strength, balance; skiing equipment and clothing; skiing techniques, steering, edging, controlling pressure; ski-lifts, rope tows, gondolas; types of skiing, e.g. downhill (Alpine), cross-country (Nordic), **telemark**; judging weather and snow; off-piste skiing; risks, hazards, safety procedures, first aid, getting help; how to avoid endangering other skiers or being endangered by them
Snowboarding	Fitness, strength, balance; stance, edge control, unweighting, side slipping, correct falling technique, jumps, toe-turns, heel-turns, grabs, spins

Personal skills

All of the above activities are likely to improve the following skills:

■ Learning skills – since starting activities and becoming good at them involves gathering knowledge and remembering it.

■ Planning and problem-solving skills – each activity requires preparation, and all of them involve decision making and problem solving.

■ Communication skills (e.g. cooperating on a task, shouting warnings, giving advice, reaching decisions through consultation).

■ Personal qualities such as confidence, determination, sense of responsibility.

Figure 10.3 Caving: plenty of skills – and plenty of thrills

Team development

All the above activities can be carried out by teams, and if they are, the teams will be strengthened by their shared experience, their practice in cooperation, and the feedback that team members can give each other during the activity and afterwards when reviewing it (formally or informally).

Personal development

As well as the skills learned, many people feel they develop through these activities because they are in a natural environment, doing something they have chosen to do. They develop insight into the natural world, and they find the experience excellent for getting rid of the stresses of work or of everyday life.

People with real interest and **aptitude** can make a career in outdoor activities. Excellent training is available through Mountain Leader Awards, etc., and increasing numbers of the public want to be taught and want to spend their leisure time doing outdoor pursuits. This means that, independently or as part of a partnership or in a uniformed public service, people who love outdoor activities can make a living through them.

The public services are generally more interested in whether you have teamwork skills and personal qualities than whether you have technical skills. If you need technical skills, the public services will give you the training after you have been accepted.

www.mltw.org/
www.mlte.org/
www.thebmc.co.uk

See below, page 76 (Advanced skills and techniques) for more

Objectives

Objectives in this case are reasons for doing something – reasons which go beyond enjoyment, skills development or personal development. Objectives can be both group and personal. For example, a group of keen walkers who also like a bit of rock climbing can traverse the Cuillin ridge, in Skye, from end to end. The group objective is to complete the traverse of the ridge from one end to the other, taking in all of the tops. But the group members may have individual objectives such as, for example, taking photographs, studying rock formations, or developing their personal fitness. These are important to the individuals concerned, but not to other group members whose individual interests are different.

Journey

Travel is an objective, and mountain walking, caving and skiing all involve journeys, first to where the activity takes place, and then during the activity itself. Travel to the activity base involves planning, meeting people, perhaps sampling other cultures, or using a foreign language, etc. On the mountains or down the caves, the scenery constantly changes and develops – whether it is the beauty of rock or ice, or of cave formations.

Environmental

This relates to a point made above, that land-based outdoor activities tend to take place in areas of natural beauty. This is a major motive for some people to do such activities.

Discovery

Every new place that we visit is a new discovery. Equally, every new experience is a discovery. We learn about the world, and other people, and we learn about ourselves. Discovery is a learning experience, where that which was unknown is revealed, but it is also an emotion of wonderment. Since emotions are intensely personal, there is little point in generalising about them – but we should be open to these emotions, and try to recognise them in ourselves, because they are part of the meaning of life.

As for discovery in the old sense, 'to boldly go where no man has gone before', this is difficult in a world which has been fully surveyed and mapped by satellites as well as people. In caving, however, it is still possible – even in Britain – to find places that no one has ever visited since the beginning of time.

http://news.independent.co.uk/uk/this_britain/article1961469.ece
http://w01-0504.web.dircon.net/pdc/caveguides.htm
www.timesonline.co.uk/article/0,,2-2440041,00.html
www.caves.org/

Educational

Many people get their first serious experience of land-based outdoor and adventurous activities through education. Sometimes the experience is a formal part of a course, as it will be when you do outdoor activities for this unit. Sometimes it contributes to a qualification which is extracurricular but still valued by employers and higher education, for example the Duke of Edinburgh's Award. Outdoor pursuits have been done traditionally by Scouts and Guides, both as fun and as character-building exercises.

Education is linked to training, and in the armed forces outdoor and adventurous activities are part of training. They are part of gaining experience in things like mountain warfare. Through doing mountain walking and other activities people in the armed forces can also get qualifications such as Mountain Leader which enable them to take part in army-sponsored mountaineering and exploring activities. And there are growing opportunities in the private sector for mountain leaders, ski instructors etc., who are much in demand in a world where tourism of all sorts is booming.

remember
The countryside is heavily used by visitors. Take care of it.

remember
Universities are great places to find climbing and caving activities.

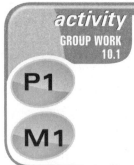
activity
GROUP WORK 10.1
P1
M1

Produce a display for an outdoor pursuits exhibition describing, comparing and contrasting four different land-based outdoor and adventurous activities. (Include notes and documentation demonstrating that each person in the group has described, compared and contrasted the activities.)

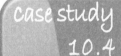

Hangman's Hole

We concluded our week's caving with an ill-advised trip down the aptly named Hangman's Hole. My first mistake came at the bottom of the entrance climb and squeeze where I found the way on silted up … I accidentally dug it open! My reward for this was a wave of cold dark water that had hitherto been happily dammed. The way on is called Unprintable Passage and consists of a flat out, tight, wet crawl. Rather perversely this is the most pleasant part of the cave. Dave eventually joined me at the head of the first pitch but only after he had put his foot (and several large boulders) through where the floor was supposed to be. The rigging in this cave is entirely off naturals, presumably because none of the walls are strong enough to take a bolt! Nevertheless, we got to the bottom safely. We had been warned that the third pitch, in particular, had no belays. It now has two less. Apparently you are supposed to rig off some loose boulders and rely on the friction from as many rub points as you can make to reduce the load on your belay! Now why didn't we think of that?

Source: Oxford University Cave Club

activity
GROUP WORK

This account was written by a student. What do you think the two cavers gained from the experiences described?

How risks are managed in land-based outdoor and adventurous activities

Land-based outdoor and adventurous activities are *potentially* dangerous. Some people (usually sitting at home in their armchairs) argue that if all the risk is eliminated, all the adventure is eliminated as well – and therefore risk is something we should not get too steamed up about. This is not the view of people who get injured, or the friends and relatives of people who get killed.

Mountain deaths in the UK

Table 10.4 Mountain incidents in the UK, 2000–04

Year	Incidents	Fatalities	Injured	Persons assisted
2004	609	25	376	804
2003	597	33	391	742
2002	655	23	438	824
2001	421	18	274	518
2000	679	19	435	916

activity
GROUP WORK

What factors could cause the differences in the figures in individual years?

Nor is it the view of providers and most participants. The people who provide outdoor adventurous activities are becoming skilled at providing adventure with safety, and the accident rate is very low. For example, in 2005 the British Cave Rescue Council recorded two underground deaths (a cave diver and a schoolboy on an organised visit) and six fatalities above ground (not all of which were due to adventurous activities).

Risk assessment

Organised trips for outdoor and adventurous activities are often a form of work, and are therefore covered by the Health and Safety at Work Act 1974. There are **procedures** which have to be followed to ensure safety 'as far as is reasonably practicable'. These are called risk assessments.

Figure 10.4 indicates the main points to be considered when making a risk assessment for land-based outdoor and adventurous activities.

The **risk** is only present when the hazards and human beings come together, which is why a risk assessment has to take into account not only the hazards themselves, but the experience and the competence of people likely to be exposed to them. Thus a steep slope which would be a minimal risk for an experienced and well-equipped walker could become a serious risk for an inexperienced walker with the wrong footwear.

Information on **risk assessments** and how they should be carried out comes from the **Health and Safety Executive**. In their leaflet *Five Steps to Risk Assessment* they suggest five stages:

Step 1: What are the hazards?

Step 2: Who might be harmed and how?

Step 3: What are you already doing?

      What further action is necessary?

Step 4: How will you put the assessment into action?

Step 5: Review date

www.hse.gov.uk/

Each of these stages should be recorded in writing, and the resulting document should be kept and used until the next assessment is made.

Figure 10.4 Carrying out a risk assessment for land-based outdoor and adventurous activities

For a risk assessment to be complete, all five stages have to be completed. Identifying the hazards is not enough: actions to reduce or eliminate the risk have to be carried out, and recorded. Finally (and this is especially true of adventurous activities where weather and conditions vary and the people taking part may change frequently) the assessment has to be reviewed and updated from time to time.

Details of risk

To carry out a risk assessment it is necessary for the organiser to visit the place where the outdoor activity will happen, and look carefully at it in relation to the people who are going to use the site. The visit should take place long enough beforehand to change the activity plans in any way which might be necessary.

Natural (rocks, water temperature)

Natural settings of the kind used for land-based outdoor and adventurous activities have typically developed over millions of years. The hazards they present may be hard to detect, and the person carrying out the risk assessment should be experienced in both the activity itself and the natural setting in which the activity takes place.

Rocks Directly or indirectly rocks play a part in most outdoor adventurous activities. They are particularly important in mountain walking, rock climbing, caving and mine exploration.

Rocks vary in age from thousands of millions of years right down to less than one million years. They are not all formed in the same way, which is one major reason why their physical characteristics (e.g. hardness, roughness and chemical behaviour) vary so much. Having been formed, rocks are baked, compressed and changed by earth movements, mountain building and other complex processes which have been going on for many millions of years. All of these differences in the formation of rock mean that hardly any two types of rock are exactly alike.

On the other hand, rocks can be roughly classified into types, and these types are linked to their suitability for outdoor activities and also to the hazards they pose. The table below gives very basic details about rocks.

Rocks can be dangerous when they are slippery, loose, crumbly, sharp, covered with moss, slime, vegetation or **lichen**, too high, too steep or overhanging, with too few handholds and footholds, or with cracks that can trap ropes, feet, etc. The condition of rock varies with the weather, so it can also be too cold, too hot, too wet or icy. Rocks can be safe with some kinds of shoes/boots and not others. They are unpredictable and their nature can change halfway up a climb. It also makes a difference which direction they face in. If they catch the sun they are drier and warmer, but many British cliffs face north.

Risk assessments on rocks must be done by an experienced climber who knows what rocks can be like in different weather conditions. Furthermore, they must be done for the exact climbs which a party is going to do since conditions on one part of a rock face may be very different from the conditions a few feet away.

Water Land-based activities are not always dry. Mountains have heavier rainfall than other parts of the country, and swollen streams are a serious hazard in wet weather. Caves, which are made by water, often have underground streams and rivers running in them. These can rise suddenly if there is heavy rain outside the cave, and cavers have sometimes been trapped, washed away or drowned. Swollen streams, both inside and outside caves, are the main cause of accidental death for people doing land-based outdoor and adventurous activities in Britain.

Risk assessments of water hazards must be based on a worst-case scenario, and if there is heavy rain people should not go down caves where there is the slightest risk of flooding. The same risks are there if it is necessary to ford a stream while mountain walking or orienteering. Mines too can become flooded in wet weather.

remember

A **hazard** is something that might cause harm, e.g. loose stones, climbing high above the ground, a river that could rise in heavy rain.
A risk is the chance that someone could be harmed by these hazards.

remember

If you like climbing, learn a bit about **geology** – and find out about the different qualities of different kinds of rock.

Table 10.5 Rocks and outdoor activities

Rock type	Name(s) and qualities	How formed	Area found	Mountain walking	Climbing and hazards	Caving/mines
Igneous The name given to rocks which were originally hot and liquid, and formed deep under the Earth's crust. Some come out of volcanoes, others never escape and cool slowly underground, baking the rocks around them	Granite. Whitish or pinkish crystalline rock	Large amounts of liquid rock cooling slowly deep underground	Dartmoor SW Scotland Arran Cairngorms Mountains of Mourne	Good walking country – mountains or hills with tors or cliffs	Good – rock sometimes crumbly and short of holds	Some big quarries but few mines
	Gabbro. Black or dark grey crystalline rock	As with granite, but the chemistry is different	Skye Rhum St Kilda	Forms very rocky mountains. Tough walking	Excellent – the best in Britain. Long, difficult routes	None
	Basalt. Grey smooth rock; can form columns	Solidified lava, poured out of ancient volcanoes	Skye Mull Eigg Arran Antrim	Forms hills and moorlands. Good walking	Big sea cliffs, but soft, loose and wet for climbing	Big sea caves – hazardous to go in
	Tuffs, rhyolite, etc. Hard dark-coloured rock	Other old volcanic rocks	Highlands Lake District Wales	Forms rocky mountains with cliffs. Excellent hard walking	Very good for rock climbing, e.g. on Ben Nevis. High dangerous cliffs	Few mines
Sedimentary These rocks were formed in layers either from the shells of plankton, old coral reefs, or deposits of sand and mud. Millions of years of compression has hardened them into rock, but they have not been altered very much by heat	Chalk. White or cream; soft, powdery	Formed in the deep ocean from countless microscopic shells	East and SE England (Downs, white cliffs of Dover, etc.)	Low rolling hills good for gentle upland walking	Big sea cliffs, but the rock is soft, loose and dangerous	Mines and tunnels, often unsafe
	Limestone. Pale grey, smooth, with fossils	Similar to chalk, but older and harder. Soluble in rain water	N Pennines Yorkshire Dales, Peak District; N and S Wales Mendips	Excellent walking – some risks from holes and cliffs	Good for technical climbing, but can be loose	By far the best rock for caves
	Sandstone. Made of sand, sometimes with layers and striations	Formed in the deltas of ancient rivers, along old coastlines and in ancient deserts	Many areas around the Pennines, the NE, Midlands, Cheshire, Kent, etc.; S Wales	Variable walking, but usually low-lying (except in a few parts of the Scottish Highlands)	Some climbing, e.g. in Kent. Very good climbing in Torridon, Scotland	Few caves. Some mines
	Millstone grit. Hard, made of coarse sand	As with sandstone	Yorkshire Lancashire Derbyshire	Good moorland walking	Very good 'safe' climbing rock	Deep cracks which cavers explore
	Shale. Soft, dark, breaks into flat layers	Formed in shallow seas from mud and silt deposits	Many low-lying areas, coalfields, etc.; SE England	Too soft to form hills	Shale sea cliffs are too soft and dangerous to climb on	Coal mines (usually dangerous when disused)
Metamorphic These are former sedimentary rocks which have been heated and compressed so much that they have been partly melted and re-crystallised.	Marble. Hard white rock with faint sparkle	Limestone, heated and compressed deep underground	Fairly rare in Britain. Some in N Pennines and Isle of Purbeck	Forms good rocky mountains, but not in Britain	Good climbing rock but not in Britain	Forms caves
	Schist. Flat or folded rock with glistening surface	Sandstone heated and compressed	Scottish Highlands	Excellent walking country	Big cliffs but the rock is unreliable, wet and covered in plants	Few caves – some small mines
	Slate. Flat, hard, dark grey; splits well	Shale, heated and compressed	Scotland Lake District N Wales	Forms rounded hills, good for walking	Cliffs usually slabby and risky	The best rock for mines and quarries
	Gneiss. Hard greyish rock	Extremely ancient rocks – formation not very clear	NW Scotland Outer Hebrides	Very good walking country – low rocky hills	Lots of low cliffs, but often wet and covered in plants	Some sea caves

remember

Hyperthermia
= too hot;
hypothermia
= too cold.

Temperature It is possible to get too hot or too cold doing adventurous outdoor activities. Hazards of heat or cold, in summer or winter, must be included in the risk assessment. Hyperthermia (heatstroke) is possible on British mountains in summer, as is severe sunburn (the sun is stronger on a mountain top than in a valley). However, more lives have been lost through cold, especially in the Scottish Highlands where temperatures are the lowest in Britain in winter. Risk assessment for winter walking, climbing, orienteering or caving must take this hazard into account.

Human

Conditions which cause mild discomfort for experienced and well-equipped outdoor adventurers can be deadly for inexperienced, unfit and poorly equipped people. Deaths or accidents while carrying out land-based adventurous activities are more likely to happen to the following categories of people:

- Young, inexperienced people.
- People who are poorly led.
- People who are badly clothed, shod or equipped.
- People who are ill.
- People who are injured.
- People who are seriously unfit.
- People who have recently been ill or are sickening for something.
- Older people who are out of training and risk heart attacks.
- People who take risks, fool about or push themselves too hard.
- People under the influence of alcohol.
- People who know nothing about navigation.
- Parties which split up without good reason.
- People who have not told anybody where they are going.
- People who plan the activity badly and get caught out after dark.

Obviously, if no people did an activity there would be no risk at all, so the people taking part are an essential element of a risk assessment. Leaders of activities must know about the people they are leading if they are to carry out a meaningful risk assessment rather than a pointless paper exercise.

Instructors have to be skilled, experienced and qualified.

Equipment related

It is very risky carrying out adventurous activities without the necessary equipment, with poor equipment or with equipment which is not understood by the user. The rules are:

- The equipment which is needed must be used.
- Equipment must be properly stored and maintained.
- Equipment must be used correctly by participants.
- The equipment such as top ropes, ladders, etc. must be correctly set up by the organisers so that they can be used safely by unskilled people.
- The equipment must be of good quality.

Also important are clothing and footwear. Sometimes participants in outdoor activities have to wait around in chilly conditions. Whoever carries out risk assessments must be aware of this problem, and do everything possible to eliminate it by

- organising activities in such a way that people do not have to wait
- ensuring that participants are properly dressed if they do have to wait around.

remember

If you borrow equipment, check it out first to make sure that there's nothing wrong with it and that you know how to use it.

case study 10.5

Instructor abilities (rock activities)

The following skills/attributes are required by climbing or caving instructors:

- Climbing skills.
- Knowledge of site-specific hazards.
- Ability to lead a group (including identifying the competencies within the group).
- Knowledge of instruction techniques.
- Communication skills.
- Experience of rescue and emergency techniques.
- First aid skills.
- Knowledge of equipment needed (including emergency equipment).
- Knowledge of weather conditions.

activity
GROUP WORK

1. Explain why each of these abilities is needed for a climbing or caving instructor.
2. Which abilities are also needed for other activities, such as orienteering and skiing, and why?

Food and drink are like equipment in that people cannot function safely in adventurous activities without them. Hunger and thirst are risks, and they should be included in a full risk assessment.

Who might be affected

Anybody who takes part in a land-based outdoor and adventurous activity is potentially at risk.

Instructors

In the educational and commercial sectors instructors are at risk because they work outdoors for long periods of time supervising activities, fixing ropes and other equipment, etc. Although instructors are almost always highly skilled and well qualified, the job is demanding and tiredness or carelessness together with treacherous weather or conditions can lead to fatal accidents (though this is rare).

Participants

Participants in outdoor adventurous activities are often school or college parties, or members of the public who want an adventure holiday or a team-building experience. They vary in fitness, motivation, age, discipline, thinking ability and experience. Some may have medical conditions or even be disabled. Very often they are mixed-ability groups, so that keen competent people are mixed with people who have little aptitude and commitment. Participants are at risk if activities are organised which are too demanding for some of them. They are also at risk if the activities are too easy, so that those who are potentially good get bored, begin messing about or taking risks. Major factors in ensuring the safety of participants are:

- Assessing participants' abilities and motivation.
- Pitching the activities at the right level of difficulty.
- Having a good ratio of staff/instructors to participants so that participants can be monitored and any who are getting into difficulty can be helped before a problem turns into a crisis.

It is also important to train and equip participants adequately before they do the activity so that they can enjoy the experience and be less likely to make dangerous mistakes.

For some activities, especially skiing or snowboarding, a programme of training on artificial slopes or practice areas – or, indeed, full instruction over a period of time – may be a necessary preparation.

Remote surveillance

In armed forces exercises or training using outdoor adventurous activities, and for the Duke of Edinburgh's Gold Award, participants are watched from a distance or met at checkpoints during the activity. This is more difficult than monitoring participants from close quarters, especially in bad weather, and this should be taken into account when carrying out a risk assessment of a remotely surveyed activity.

Other parties

People who go mountain walking, caving, orienteering or mine exploring in clubs or informal groups for their own recreation should still carry out risk assessments, even if they are not as formal as those carried out by people who do adventurous activities for a living. If they are going down a cave they should find out about it, assess the dangers, make sure their equipment is suitable, check the weather forecast, etc. And if climbers are going up a known route on a cliff, they should (and almost always do) find out from a guidebook or other climbers what the climb is like before they attempt it. People who do adventurous activities for fun are often dedicated and highly safety aware – which is just as well, since they do not have the back-up of a commercial or educational organisation if anything goes wrong.

Likelihood of occurrence

Accidents during adventurous activities are rare, but that has more to do with the skill and care of most organisers and participants than with the activities themselves which are always potentially unsafe.

The likelihood of an occurrence is often judged on a five-point scale (see Case study 10.6 on page 65).

The nature and severity of risks varies with the activity, the season and other factors, as Table 10.9 shows.

Severity

Severe risks are life-threatening. They are, on the whole, less common than minor risks, but they have to be taken very seriously because of their possible fatal consequences. Severe risks should never be taken, especially by people who are inexperienced or ill-equipped. People who explore deep caves, climb the highest mountains or ski the most difficult slopes put themselves in positions of greater risk than the average land-based adventurer, but they should have the skills and equipment to minimise those risks. They should also have the knowledge and judgement to know when something is impossible, and cancel their plans (see case study 10.8).

Risk rating

A **risk rating** is a figure giving the degree of risk in an activity. It takes into account both the likelihood and the seriousness of a possible accident. There are various ways of calculating risk. A straightforward one is the method used in Case Study 10.6 (Blackland Farm), where the likelihood (1–5) is multiplied by the consequence (severity) (1–5).

Table 10.6 Risk rating

Level (1 to 5)	1	2	3	4	5
Likelihood	Unlikely	Possible	Quite possible	Likely	Very likely
Severity	No injury	Slight injury	Injury over 3-day duration	Death or serious injury	Multiple death
	1	2	3	4	5

Thus an activity where a slight injury was very likely (e.g. running as fast as possible down a steep stony hillside) would get a risk rating of 10 (2 × 5). An activity where 'multiple death' was 'possible' (e.g. exploring a mine which had a slightly loose ceiling) would get the same risk rating. Risk rating, however, is not scientifically accurate, and the HSE (Health and Safety Executive) simply says that activities should be 'as safe as reasonably practicable'. Using the calculation above, any risk rating over 8 would normally be unacceptable.

Risk rating can be expressed also in the difficulty of an activity. Climbs, caves, orienteering courses and ski runs are graded according to difficulty, and difficulty is linked to risk.

UK rock-climbing grades are as follows:

- Moderate.
- Difficult.
- Very difficult.
- Hard very difficult.
- Mild severe.
- Severe.
- Very severe.
- Hard very severe.
- E1–E8 (extremely severe grades).

> **remember**
>
> The system of risk rating is different in other countries, e.g. France, the US, Australia.

Risk controls

These are **measures** which can be put in place before an adventurous activity to reduce the risk, or to limit the severity of an accident if it does happen. Table 10.7 relates to caving.

Table 10.7 Risk controls for caving

Problem	Risks linked to problem	Measures to reduce risk and prevent worsening situation
Injury Any incapacitating injury underground is extremely serious and potentially fatal. Greatly increased risk of hypothermia to victim and team	1. Exhaustion 2. Hypothermia 3. Light failure 4. Carelessness 5. Rock fall 6. Personal fall 7. Equipment failure 8. Poor personal technique	Personal fitness Experience Avoid injury First aid training First-aid kit carried and more extensive kit above ground Appropriate group size Appropriate call-out time

case study 10.6

Risk assessment

Table 10.8 Blackland Farm risk assessment

Activity being assessed	Climbing at rocks
Assessor	Martin Robinson
Date	2/1/07
What is the hazard?	Fall from height
Who is at risk?	Staff and customers
How likely is an accident? 1 unlikely; 2 possible; 3 quite possible; 4 likely; 5 very likely	2
If an accident occurs, what is the consequence? 1 no injury; 2 slight injury; 3 injury over a three-day duration; 4 death or serious injury; 5 multiple death	4
Likelihood × Consequence score	8 (i.e. 2 × 4)
Current control measures	Equipment checked prior to use and weekly. Radio contact is made with the office. Other sessions are held to demonstrate how to obtain help in an emergency. Correct ratio of instructors to pupils is essential. Equipment used is suitable for use. Climbers tied to safety rope while climbing, told to keep away from edge of rock and advised of safe route down. Instructors trained in safe procedures at rocks
Are these adequate?	Yes
What other measures are necessary?	None
What monitoring is needed?	Sessions checked for safety
Any other information	To be reviewed Jan 08
Signature of assessor	Bryn Beach

Source: Girlguiding UK

activity
GROUP WORK

If you were a health and safety inspector, would you feel that the system for assessing risks at Blackland Farm was a good one? Give your reasons.

case study 10.7

Risk table

Table 10.9 Risk table for mountain walking

Activity	Risks	Likelihood	Severity
Mountain walking	Getting lost	3	1
	Suffering from hypothermia	Depends on season	Depends on severity of case and weather
	Breaking a leg	2	3
	Fall from height	1	4
	Drowning	1	4

activity
INDIVIDUAL WORK

Produce a similar table for risks in another land-based outdoor adventurous activity.

case study 10.8

Climbing Hornbein Couloir

Even at its best, the Hornbein Couloir is treacherous. At a relentless 45 degree angle, it is filled with crumbling, flaky rock and exposed to ferocious winds ... but the climbers found something even more dangerous: wind slab!

It was time for an agonising decision but this is exactly the sort of situation where Army training excels: Dave Bunting weighed up the glory of reaching the summit with the dangers posed by that final stretch and concluded that the risk was simply too great. The expedition wasn't just about climbing Everest; it was also about bringing every single climber home safely.

Source: Army on Everest, MOD

activity
GROUP WORK

What factors – in your view – make the difference between an acceptable and an unacceptable risk?

All written risk assessments should include a section for risk controls, and checks should be made to ensure that these controls, when suggested, are put in place.

www.hse.gov.uk/risk/
www.hse.gov.uk/risk/fivesteps.htm

Contingencies

Contingencies are unforeseen happenings which create danger. Examples are injuries, bad weather, nightfall on a mountain or a sudden rise of water in a cave.

Contingency plans are plans which anticipate (i.e. prepare for) such problems. In fact they are a kind of emergency planning used for outdoor adventurous activities. There should always be a contingency plan for any land-based outdoor or adventurous activity.

Contingency plans include:

- Plans for getting off a mountain safely, in case of injury, illness, nightfall or bad weather.

- Plans for getting out of a cave if water rises or someone is injured.

For mountain walking, contingency plans should be written into a **route card** if possible. Back-up teams should know what the contingency plans for each group (if there are several) are. Failing that, if the walk is done for recreational purposes walkers should know the terrain and know the easiest ways off the mountain at any time. It is best if contingency plans are agreed by a group in advance to avoid confusion and argument.

Sometimes, when conditions are really bad, a planned activity has to be cancelled for the day before it has even started. There should be contingency plans for this too, e.g. climbing on an indoor wall if the weather is unsuitable for outdoor climbing.

remember

Route cards can be created on a standard form (which saves time and effort).

activity
INDIVIDUAL WORK 10.2

P2

Visit the venues for two different land-based outdoor and adventurous activities and carry out a risk assessment for each one.

Participating in land-based outdoor and adventurous activities

For this unit you should aim to take part in as many land-based outdoor and adventurous activities as you can. To get high grades you will need to show some proficiency and understanding in at least two acceptable activities. The unit is practical. Useful as it is to read about and study adventurous activities, it is not enough!

To maximise participation you could:

- Go on all outdoor pursuits organised by your centre or college.

- Consider doing the Duke of Edinburgh's Gold Award in an outdoor adventurous activity.

- Arrange to go on days out (or longer) with the army to get expert tuition in caving, rock climbing, etc. (it is not necessary to join the army afterwards).

- Join the Territorial Army (TA).

- Work with cadets, guides or scouts.

- Join a mountaineering, orienteering or caving club in your area.

- Go skiing on a regular basis.

- Consider the options available with Outward Bound and other commercial providers of adventurous activities.

- Do a good deal of mountain walking with your friends, informally.

If you do other activities which are not offered by your course or covered in this book, and you think these would count towards your grades for this unit (e.g. pony trekking, mountain biking, paragliding or bungee jumping) discuss them with your tutor so that they can count towards either your assessment or accreditation.

In any event, if you do adventurous activities outside college, get your tutor's advice about obtaining witness statements or other evidence if you want the activities to count towards your unit grades.

Skills and techniques

These are the abilities needed to carry out an adventurous activity successfully and with enjoyment. Skills and techniques are by definition learnable, so you should not be put off if you seem painfully unskilled when you do an activity for the first time. Skills and techniques are learned by:

- Understanding.
- Imitation.
- Practice.

As far as possible you should learn your skills and techniques in a practical setting, taught by a skilled instructor.

Personal technical abilities

Technical abilities in adventurous outdoor activities are closely linked to the components of fitness.

Table 10.10 Components of fitness

Health-based components of fitness	Skill-based components of fitness
Aerobic capacity	Speed
Cardiovascular fitness	Reaction time
Strength	Agility
Muscular endurance	Balance
Flexibility	Coordination
Body composition	Power

Link See Book 1, Unit 7, pages 299–308 for more on components of fitness

The advantages that these components can give in adventurous activities is indicated in Table 10.11.

Table 10.11 Advantages of various aspects of fitness

Component	Adventurous activities
Aerobic capacity	Important in mountain walking, orienteering and cross-country skiing. Useful in all other activities too. Aerobic capacity is linked to stamina
Cardiovascular fitness	Important in mountain walking, orienteering and cross-country skiing, but needed for all activities. Linked to stamina
Strength	Important in climbing, caving, skiing and snowboarding
Muscular endurance	A big advantage for all adventurous activities. Linked to both strength and stamina
Flexibility	Especially useful in climbing, skiing, snowboarding and caving
Body composition	An ideal **body mass index** (18.5–24.9) is a physical advantage for all adventurous activities. A low body mass combined with strength is an advantage for climbers and cavers. (It is a help for cavers to be on the small side.)
Speed	Particularly useful in skiing and snowboarding, but a benefit for all land-based adventurous activities

Component	Adventurous activities
Reaction time	Used most in skiing and snowboarding, but a quick reaction time is an asset for all adventurous activities – and can save lives (e.g. in climbing)
Agility	Very important for climbing, skiing and snowboarding, but useful for all activities
Balance	As for agility
Coordination	Vital for skiing and snowboarding; good coordination is useful for other activities too
Power	Needed in climbing, caving, skiing and snowboarding

It should be stressed that though you may need to be super-fit to excel in these activities, especially at competition level, you do not need to be super-fit to enjoy them or to benefit from them. All land-based outdoor and adventurous activities can be done to a certain level by most people – including disabled people.

Efficient movement

Efficient movement is different for different activities. For mountain walking:

■ Experiment with your stride until you find the one that suits you.

■ Shorten your stride when going up steep hills.

■ Walk at the fastest pace you reasonably can, yet still be able to talk to somebody without getting short of breath.

■ Go up steep hillsides diagonally or in zig-zags.

■ Do not run down steep hills.

■ Do not walk with your feet sticking outwards.

■ Walk steadily and try not to rest too often.

■ Watch where you put your feet on rough ground.

Figure 10.5 What components of fitness are needed?

Grades climbed

See page 66 above for a list of rock-climbing grades. Do a few easy climbs to develop confidence and technique before attempting more difficult ones.

Level of proficiency

This rises with increased fitness, skill, motivation and interest. As with most sporting activities you can expect to reach a peak, if you practise consistently and strive for improvement, at the age of about 30. The secret is to know what your level of proficiency is, but to want to get better. Do not attempt things which you know are well outside your capabilities – this is a recipe for an accident.

Technical skills particular to activity

There are far too many of these to go into detail here. In any case, most people need to learn technical skills in a hands-on manner.

Figure 10.6 Simplified learning cycle

Technical skills involve making the best and safest use of equipment. Adventurous activities are becoming more technical all the time as new equipment is invented and old techniques are changed and refined. Every activity has many technical skills associated with it. Some are essential to know and practise, even for beginners. Others are used only by advanced practitioners.

The following is a list of technical skills for people who are beginners at caving:

- Use and care of helmet, light, spare light and emergency lighting, protective clothing, footwear, first-aid kit.

- Emergency procedures.

- Knots – e.g. bowline.

Figure 10.7 Bowline knot

Source: www.iland.net/~jbritton/ bowline.htm#PageTop

Step 1
Arrange the rope as shown, with a small loop in the standing part and the end going around the object the loop is to be tied around.

Step 2
Insert the end through the loop.

Step 3
Pull the end around and behind the standing part.

Step 4
Insert the end back through the loop.

Finished Bowline – Front View
Press and set the knot.

- Belays.
- **Handlines**.
- Body belay on a hand line.
- A ladder climb.
- Abseiling.
- Fit **harness**, attach to rope.
- Controlled descent.
- Cave navigation.
- Maps: symbols, features, horizontal scale, cross-section.
- Navigation using draught, tape.

Placing protection

Protection in climbing is the use of ropes and/or belays to prevent yourself and/or another climber from falling. A belay is a device to attach yourself or another person to the rock or sometimes a hand line. If a person who is belayed falls, he or she is stopped (sometimes in mid air). Belays can be tied with rope alone, but it is more usual now to use a belay device which – through the use of friction – can enable a climber to stop another climber from falling. To fix a belay it is necessary to use a bulge or other rock feature which will hold the rope (or an arrangement of anchoring devices) so that the climber attached to the belay cannot fall.

A hand line is a rope fixed on steep rock to which climbers or cavers can hold on or attach themselves while moving across a rock face.

There are a large number of devices, e.g. cams, used to place protection (a safe anchor for ropes, belays, etc.).

Appropriate use of rope and knots

Rope is used for climbing and caving, in order to:

- Protect people from falling;
- Enable people to reach places that would otherwise be unreachable.

The correct use of rope allows parties of climbers and cavers to protect each other from falling, whether on British rock faces or in the world's highest mountains and deepest caves.

In caving, ropes are used as hand lines, to enable people to hold onto something while crossing a difficult section, and to attach rope ladders to the tops of **pitches** (vertical drops). The ladders, which in extreme cases can be 100 feet long or more, are used for descending and ascending vertical sections of a cave. While climbing or descending ladders cavers are attached by a harness and rope to a person belaying them at the top of the pitch, so that if they slip they can be held, and can get back on the ladder again.

Different knots are used for different purposes in climbing and caving. These need to be learned and practised until you can do them in the dark or without looking. It is possible to cut yourself short sections of cheap rope to use as practice pieces for learning and practising knots (e.g. while sitting on the bus).

remember
Belaying is a technical subject. It must be learned properly before you try it.

www.massey.ac.nz/~sglasgow//nzss/knots.htm ('It's Knot Homework')
www.en.wikipedia.org/wiki/List_of_knots
www.geocities.com/Yosemite/7944/knots.htm
www.42brghtn.mistral.co.uk/knots/42ktmenu.html
www.tollesburysc.co.uk/Knots/Knots_gallery.htm

Belaying

Belaying means securing or protecting a climber against falling. A typical belay involves a rope, harness and a belay device. The harness is made of webbing that goes round the climber's trunk and legs, and to which clips, etc. can be attached. A belay device usually consists of a kind of lockable clip, called a **karabiner**, and a metal plate. When a climber's rope is threaded through the device, friction is generated and if the climber falls, the weight can be held fairly easily. The climber operating the belay must be tied to an anchor (e.g. a projecting rock) for self-protection. Using proper belaying techniques a climber can hold a heavier climber who is falling.

Belaying is a technique which must be learnt through proper training, and thoroughly practised, as lives can depend on it.

www.princeton.edu/~oa/climb/belaywal.shtml

Use of compass for direction finding

Figure 10.8 Compass with base-plate

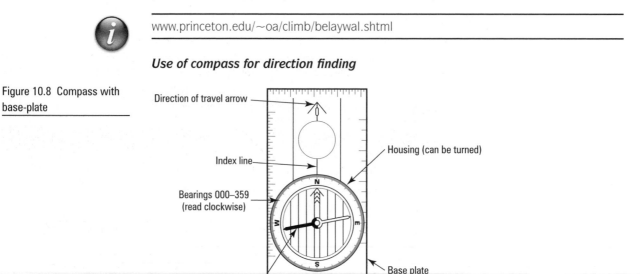

A compass is a device which uses the Earth's natural magnetic field to tell the direction. In Britain it is the easiest and most reliable way to find out the direction. The magnetised needle points about 4 degrees west of north (which is the same as north for most practical purposes).

Direction finding On a map it is possible to find directions by pointing the map north (setting the map) and then using the compass in conjunction with the map to read off the directions of landmarks when you are planning a walk or writing a route card.

 Link

Book 1, Unit 9, page 343

A compass is also used for finding direction when you are out on a mountain walk.

Method:

1. Hold the compass close to your chest, where you can keep it steady and see it properly.

2. Point the direction of travel arrow in the direction you want to go.

3. Turn the compass housing so that the north end of the magnetic needle is at N on the housing.

4. Read off the bearing of the direction you want to go in at the **index line** below the housing.

> **remember**
>
> There are 360 **bearings** which are used to describe direction on a map or a compass; 000 is north, 090 is east and so on. You go round the compass face clockwise till you get to 359.

Personal fitness

As stated above, fitness matters when doing land-based adventurous activities.

 Link   Table 10.10 (Advantages of various aspects of fitness), page 68

Strength, stamina, flexibility

These health-related components of fitness are discussed on page 68 above.

Generic skills and knowledge

These are skills and knowledge which are useful for all land-based outdoor and adventurous activities.

Weather forecasting

Weather forecasts can be obtained from many sources, e.g. the internet, the BBC, the Coastguard, radio stations, local newspapers. It is essential to know the weather forecast before you go out on an adventurous activity in the open air. Relevant weather is shown in Table 10.12.

Table 10.12 Weather and adventurous activity

Activity	Favourable weather	Unfavourable weather
Mountain walking	Bright, medium temperatures, dry, little wind	Heavy rain, strong winds, thick fog, extremes of temperature, powerful sunshine (if unprotected), snow (if unprepared), storms
Orienteering	As for mountain walking	As for mountain walking
Climbing	Dry, warm, settled	Any bad, uncomfortable or very cold weather (except for ice climbing)
Caving and mines	Dry, settled	Heavy rain, sudden downpours (can cause cave flooding)
Skiing	Heavy snow followed by cold clear weather	Thaws, avalanche conditions, lack of snow
Snowboarding	As for skiing	As for skiing

Experienced people can forecast the weather themselves, but they can get it wrong. It is best to rely on a proper forecast.

Figure 10.9 Orienteering – the sport of navigation

Navigation

Navigation is the art or science of finding your way around in a strange environment. It is used in mountain walking, climbing, caving and cross-country skiing and it is the main skill used in orienteering.

For mountain walking and orienteering it is necessary to be able to use a map and compass. Experienced navigators also use a number of little tricks which help to save time and effort.

See Book 1, Unit 9, pages 343–346 and 350–351

- **Catching feature**: A catching feature is something easily recognisable which is beyond your destination. If you reach it, you know you have gone too far.

- **Handrail**: A handrail is something like a track, road, stream or wall which you can follow, and which will take you near where you want to go. It saves you the bother of checking the map or the compass at frequent intervals.

- **Aiming off**: If your destination is hidden but near a handrail, you deliberately aim for one side or the other so that you can meet the handrail and follow it knowing that you are going towards, and not away from, your destination.

- **Attack point**: This is a visible point near your destination. You head towards it, then when you reach it (or get near it) you take another bearing to your destination.

- **Collecting features**: These are features that you know you have to pass before you get to your destination. You check them off in your mind as you approach your destination. In the example in Figure 10.10 you know you have to pass the quarry, stream, rocky hill and track before you are near your destination.

The advantage of these tricks is that they save you the trouble of checking your map and compass, while reducing the likelihood of getting lost.

> **remember**
>
> There are ways to navigate – e.g. using the sun, stars, the lie of the grass, land forms and cloud movement – which do not require a compass. They are less reliable than a compass but better than nothing.

Figure 10.10 Navigation techniques (on land)

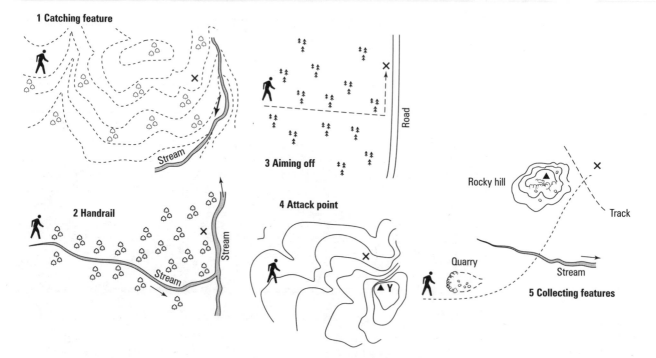

Communication

For team activities such as climbing and caving, communication is very important – especially in an emergency or while carrying out a difficult manoeuvre.

An example of cave communication is given in Table 10.13.

Table 10.13 Cave communication

Climber	Lifeliner
'Stop'/one shout or whistle	Holds climber on belay and waits
'Take in'/two shouts or whistles	Takes in any slack lifeline through belaying device
'Slack!'/three shouts or whistles	Give climber more lifeline through belaying device
'Falling!'/any great anguished shout	Holds climber on belay and braces to hold fall
'Resting'	Takes in any slack lifeline through belaying device, gives partial support to climber
'Climbing' (after 'resting')	Lifelining resumed
'Rope free' (having reached end of climb, found a place of safety and untied from lifeline)	Retrieves lifeline

> **remember**
>
> Your instructors will probably teach you the necessary shouts and communications for difficult **manoeuvres**. Write them down and memorise them if necessary.

Instructions can be given either by shouts or whistles. Obviously the lifeliner (belayer) must pay close attention and listen at all times.

If you are in trouble on a mountain, the International Distress Signal is six shouts or torch flashes or whistle blasts repeated at one-minute intervals. The reply is three shouts, flashes or blasts repeated at one-minute intervals.

Technology is changing communication on mountains. Mobile phones have saved lives and are often used to call for help. In caves, communication is possible using a device called a **heyphone**.

http://bcra.org.uk/creg/heyphone/index.html

Conservation of energy

See 'Efficient movement', page 69 above

Calculating distance

This is best done using the map. The main thing to remember about British walking maps (1:25000 and 1:50000) is that they are divided into 2 km blue squares, and these can be used as a guide for working out distances on the map. More detailed advice on calculating distance is given in Book 1 page 345. Experience will teach you how to calculate distance roughly by looking at the ground, hills, etc. in front of you and by comparing what you see from a viewpoint with a map of the same area. Calculating distance in caves is very difficult without a scale map of the cave, and it takes practice. The best way to do it is by pacing (if you can walk upright) or by using a tape or cord of known length and recording distances measured.

Planning emergency procedures

The main rules are:

- Always fill out or produce a route card and leave a copy at base.
- Make contingency (emergency) plans and note them on your route card (e.g. the easiest and quickest ways to get off a mountain if someone is hurt or the weather turns bad).
- Know how to summon help and/or carry a phone on which to dial 999 in an emergency. (This will get the police, who may pass you on to mountain or cave rescue.)
- Carry spare clothes, food, drink, first aid, a torch and a loud whistle.

> **remember**
>
> Keep track of the time spent in a cave, since it can take longer to get out than it took to get in.

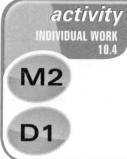

activity

INDIVIDUAL WORK
10.3

P3

Write a leaflet suitable for distribution at an outdoor centre for young people. Your leaflet should outline the main skills, moves and methods used in two different adventurous, outdoor, land-based activities.

activity

INDIVIDUAL WORK
10.4

M2

D1

You are an instructor working for a team which provides land-based outdoor and adventurous activities. Write a piece for a promotional booklet or your company website, including illustrations where appropriate. Your piece should compare, contrast and evaluate the skills and techniques needed in two different land-based outdoor and adventurous activities.

Advanced skills and techniques

The kinds of advanced skills and techniques needed by professional instructors in land-based outdoor and adventurous activities are now the responsibility of the activities' governing bodies. These skills focus on moving fluently and safely in the activity concerned.

Bodies such as Mountain Leader Training UK organise training in advanced skills and techniques, and they issue qualifications recognised by the army and used by army instructors. The qualifications are also used by providers in the private sector.

case study
10.9

Mountain Leader Training UK

MLTUK is directly responsible for the Mountaineering Instructor Award (summer), Mountaineering Instructor Certificate and European Mountain Leader Awards and works closely with four home nation boards (MLTE, MLTNI, MLTS and MLTW (Mountain Leader Training England, Northern Ireland, Scotland and Wales respectively)) and the Association of British Mountain Guides (BMG), who are responsible for the other awards. Also, MLTUK has direct links with the mountaineering councils (the British Mountaineering Council (BMC), the Mountaineering Council of Ireland (MC of I) and the Mountaineering Council of Scotland (MC of S)), enabling the training schemes to support the needs of the sport as a whole. Finally MLTUK also represents the UK internationally in matters related to mountain training, and it works to secure national and international recognition of the awards.

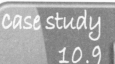

activity

GROUP WORK

What are the advantages and disadvantages of having a unified system of training and accreditation for instructors of adventurous activities?

As prescribed by governing bodies, as required by competition

There is at present a desire on the part of the government and others to encourage people – especially young people – to be more actively involved in adventurous activities. In addition a number of outdoor adventurous activities have governing bodies. These act as information centres, encourage participation, uphold safety standards, run training courses, award qualifications (in some cases), organise competitions, and liaise with international associations which have similar aims. Examples of such bodies are The British Mountaineering Council, the British Caving Association and the British Orienteering Association.

The law controlling adventurous activities is the Activity Centres (Young Persons' Safety) Act 1995. The main point was that centres providing instruction in adventurous activities to people under 18 had to be licensed. This led to the Adventure Activities Licensing Regulations 1996 (where the details of the Act are spelt out) and the Adventure Activities Licensing Regulations 2004 (which changed the licence fee).

Adventurous activities as a whole are overseen by the government through the **Adventure Activities Licensing Authority**.

Local Cave and Mine Leader Assessment Scheme Handbook (latest edn), British Caving Association

---

case study 10.10 — Adventure Activities Licensing Authority (AALA)

The Adventure Activities Licensing Authority is an independent, cross-departmental public authority, sponsored by the Department for Work and Pensions, and operating under the written guidance of the **Health and Safety Commission**. In effect it is an independent watchdog that polices the delivery of outdoor adventure activities for young people.

activity
INDIVIDUAL WORK

Note down as many reasons as you can why adventurous activities need to be licensed by the government

---

Some useful organisations:

www.aala.org/index.php

www.thebmc.co.uk/

www.fellrunner.org.uk/

www.scottish-orienteering.org/

www.skiclub.co.uk/

www.basi.org.uk/

http://members.aol.com/britboard/

www.ramblers.org.uk/

www.britishorienteering.org.uk/index.asp

www.meto.gov.uk/

www.ordsvy.gov.uk/

www.bluedome.co.uk/

www.caving.uk.com/

www.british-caving.org.uk/

activity
INDIVIDUAL WORK
10.5

P4

Participate in two different land-based adventurous activities, with guidance or help where needed.

activity
INDIVIDUAL WORK
10.6

M3

D2

Carry out two different land-based adventurous activities, without help and using the relevant skills to the best of your ability.

Fluency and competence under environmental or time-pressured situations
This means performing with skill, confidence and care in a range of settings. This can only be achieved by:

- Good training.
- Enthusiasm.
- Practice.
- Safety awareness.

> **remember**
> Speed is not the same thing as hurrying, and **fluency** is not the same thing as rushing.

The experience must be gained in a variety of conditions and types of weather (environmental situations). People taking part in adventurous activities have to do so confidently, safely, skilfully and at a reasonable speed.

Personal skills development in land-based outdoor and adventurous activities

To become good at adventurous activities you have to develop a range of learnable skills. Your assessment in this unit will be based partly on your practical demonstration of the skills needed in adventurous activities.

The skills used fall into two types:

1. Practical skills related to the techniques, methods, equipment and natural settings used in land-based outdoor and adventurous activities.
2. Learning, thinking, leadership and teamwork skills which are developed as a result of working in teams in demanding settings.

The development of these skills comes through tuition and practice. It is made easier by having:

- A structured approach which follows the learning cycle (see page 70 above).
- The opportunity to measure, monitor and **review** progress.
- A good provision of equipment and training facilities.
- Good-quality instruction.
- An enthusiastic and committed attitude on the part of the learner.

Review

A review is an investigation of what has been done in a given project or activity, with recommendations for the future. Reviews are used throughout public service work as a way of **mapping progress** and planning what has to be done next.

The advantages of having a review system are that:

- Progress can be seen.
- Proper records of progress can be kept.
- Objectives and targets can be met.
- Health and safety problems can be recognised and acted upon.
- Problems are noticed and dealt with at an early stage.
- Development can be adapted to changing pressures and conditions.
- Teams and individuals can be motivated by them.
- The system is **accountable**.
- The team's efforts can be recognised.

The disadvantages of reviews are that:

- If conducted clumsily or inefficiently they can be annoying and demotivating.
- They create paperwork (but if they are done well the paperwork should be useful).
- They may, at times, interrupt team activities.

> **remember**
> A review is not the same as monitoring (a process of fairly frequent checking) or evaluation (judging the success of a project by comparing costs and benefits).

Figure 10.11 Elements of a review

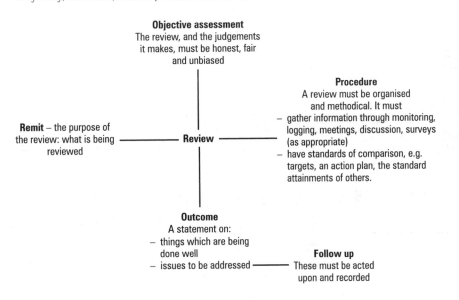

Objective assessment
The review, and the judgements it makes, must be honest, fair and unbiased

Remit – the purpose of the review: what is being reviewed

Review

Procedure
A review must be organised and methodical. It must
– gather information through monitoring, logging, meetings, discussion, surveys (as appropriate)
– have standards of comparison, e.g. targets, an action plan, the standard attainments of others.

Outcome
A statement on:
– things which are being done well
– issues to be addressed

Follow up
These must be acted upon and recorded

Formative and summative

A **formative** review is a review which takes place while a project (e.g. learning to ski) is ongoing.

A **summative** review takes place at the end of a project or process (e.g. at the end of an orienteering event).

Strengths

Strengths are things we are considered to be good at. They might be practical or technical skills (e.g. tying knots, navigating in fog). They might be teamwork skills (e.g. giving an effective briefing before going down a cave). In a review strengths should be acknowledged by the team leader (and by peers too, when appropriate).

Though strengths are strengths, we should always try to build on them. If we are very good at something we should try to be even better for the following reasons:

- It is easier to get better at things we are already good at than to get better at things we are bad at.
- The things we are good at are more likely to be useful in our careers than the things we are bad at.

Areas for improvement

These are not necessarily things that we are bad at, though they might be. They should be identified against some valid standard of comparison, which is not always easy. The need for improvement might be based on a missed target, the performance of other people or an opinion of the instructor. Areas for improvement might be fitness, an aspect of **technical competence** (e.g. jumps in snowboarding, or a need to practise **belays**), or some teamwork skill (e.g. the ability to take criticism without getting annoyed).

Having identified areas for improvement in a review, it is necessary to follow up with an action plan to carry out the improvements within a realistic period of time. The action plan should have a clear description of the actions (training, etc.) to bring about the desired improvement, and a target date. The action plan will be more effective if it includes some effective plans for monitoring progress.

Feedback (e.g. from observers, peers, coaches, supervisors)

This takes the form of comments from other people. Feedback is a major source of information about our performance and an essential part of any review. You have a right to get feedback on your performance and progress in adventurous activities. Feedback can be either formal or informal, written or spoken. You should consider it carefully and (where appropriate) act upon it.

Whoever it comes from, feedback should be thought about. The people who know most about adventurous activities may not know you very well. The people who know you best – your friends – may not know very much about adventurous activities. But most feedback will tell you something that is worth knowing. Likewise, you too should be prepared to give feedback to others.

Recording (e.g. log, diary)

You should keep a record of your training, planning and participation in outdoor pursuits. Normally this will be a written record, which should be open for inspection by other people. The format is probably a matter of choice – but it should be one which is convenient for you and may be in note form provided you can understand it when you come to re-read it. Every entry should contain:

- Date.
- Times of activity.
- Team (if relevant).
- Description of what was done/seen/experienced.
- Note on equipment used.
- Comment on own performance, including strengths/areas for improvement.
- Any other points of interest.

activity
INDIVIDUAL WORK
10.7

Carry out a review of your performance in land-based outdoor and adventurous activities, identifying and explaining your strengths and areas for improvement.

P5

M4

Development plan

A **development plan** is a plan showing how you intend to improve your skills and performance in a given activity over a period of time. For educational purposes it should be a written plan which can be looked at and commented upon by tutors, instructors and anybody else who may be interested.

Personal development plans are used in the uniformed public services as a way of helping people to plan their careers, and to identify the kind of help (e.g. courses, financial back-up) they may need. Figure 10.12 is an example of how a plan can be designed.

www.british-caving.org.uk/
www.learning-forces.org.uk/

Aims

A statement of aims usually begins with the word 'To …'. It states the basic purposes of your development plan, e.g.:

- To become a competent rock-climber.
- To learn mountain navigation skills to a good standard.

Objectives

Objectives are more exact statements of what you will do in order to achieve your aims, e.g.:

- Do toeside J-turns down a snow slope.
- Do heelside J-turns down a snow slope.
- Attach a rope to a harness using a figure-of-eight knot.

> **remember**
> Many people make development plans and do not write them down. But a written plan is more likely to be carefully thought out and to be taken seriously and followed.

Figure 10.12 Personal development plan

Name Clinton Potts				
Title of plan Caving skills (LCMLA Level 1 and 2 onwards)				
Start date	12/09/09	**End date**		12/09/11
Date plan written	05/05/09	**Date plan reviewed**		07/05/10
Brief outline of aims of plan To develop my caving skills and learn something about instructing others in caving To get a qualification in caving and cave instruction (LCMLA Level 1 and 2 awards)				
How the plan will benefit me It will enable me to spend time doing something I enjoy It will develop my fitness and coordination It will improve my caving skills It will give me a qualification which may enable me to earn money from doing something I like It may help me to get a job as a firefighter (my second choice of career after being a cave instructor)				
	Objectives	**Date started**	**Date finished**	**Comments**
Short-term objectives	To do as much caving as possible	05/05/09	12/09/09	This will give me a firm basis at the start of the course.
Medium-term objectives	To do Level 1 (Module 1: Core Skills; Module 2: Group Skills and Local Knowledge)	12/09/09	12/09/10	This is the first half of the course. It has to be completed in one year
Long-term objectives	To do Level 2 (Module 3: Vertical Skills; Module 4: Group Vertical Skills and Local Knowledge)	12/09/10	12/09/11	This completes the qualification, though there are two more modules I can take later if I wish

Targets

These are highly specific, quantifiable or measurable objectives, which are to be achieved by a particular date, e.g.:

- Come fifth or better in the Wuthering Heights Orienteering competition in June 2010.
- Be able to lead mild severe rock climbs by August 2009.
- Climb 20 Scottish mountains over 914 metres (3000 feet) in the next 12 months.

Specific

Targets must be exact and refer to a single achievement or a group of closely related achievements.

Measurable

A target must be countable, measurable or quantifiable. It must not depend on somebody's judgement or opinion.

Achievable

A target must be within a person's capabilities. The person must have the mental and physical qualities needed to reach the target.

Realistic

There must be the time, money and facilities needed.

Time based

A target always has a time limit, or deadline.

A target is usually agreed with other people, so that there is an obligation to meet it. This is especially the case in the uniformed public services where police targets, for example, may be set by the government or by the local police authority. However, individuals can (and should) set targets for themselves, and should make all reasonable efforts to meet them.

SMART

This is an acronym and also a mnemonic. See the five previous sub-headings.

Milestones

A **milestone** is an intermediate target – often halfway to the final target. If a person's target is to climb 20 mountains in 12 months, the milestone might be to climb 10 mountains in six months.

Opportunities

Opportunities are chances to develop. They might be favourable circumstances, e.g. living in a place like Sheffield which is near to a good rock-climbing area. Or an opportunity might be something that has happened, e.g. a new orienteering area has been set up near your home, or someone has invited you on a skiing trip.

Potential obstacles

These are things that stand in the way of your development in a particular adventurous activity. They could include:

- Pressures at work or on your course.
- Lack of fitness and/or strength.
- Illness or injury.
- Lack of motivation.
- You would rather do something else.
- A time-consuming relationship.
- Family problems.

remember

A target should not be too easy, and it should not be impossible. It should be difficult enough to be a challenge – a motivation to greater effort.

remember

A target is **achievable** if you have enough ability. A target is realistic if you have enough money, etc. It would be achievable for a good mountaineer to climb Mt Cook in New Zealand, but it would not be realistic if they could not afford the air fare to New Zealand.

A method suggested by the RAF when planning personal development is to do an analysis, on paper, using the format shown in Table 10.14.

Table 10.14 Planning personal development

What am I good at	What do I need to work on?
What could help me along?	What might stop me?

This is a modern version of the 'SWOT analysis', where a person looks at 'strengths, weaknesses, opportunities and threats' in relation to their planned personal or career development.

Resources (e.g. human, physical, fiscal)

Resources in this context are the things you need in order to succeed in a programme of planned personal development. The needs are obviously different in each individual case, but they come under the following three headings.

Human resources

This category splits into two parts:

1. Your own personal qualities, e.g. likes and dislikes, strengths, abilities, motivation and so on. These are your personal resources, which you will use to achieve your aims in life. Every individual has a different mix of personal qualities.

2. Other people who can help you achieve your personal development plan. This includes friends who motivate you, your family, teachers, instructors, the local public services and training organisations.

Physical resources

This category also splits into two parts:

1. Your own physical fitness, health and strength. Knowing these will influence your personal development plan.

2. The places and facilities where you can develop your skills and abilities in land-based adventurous activities. They include things like mountains, rocks, caves, rough land and ski slopes. (On the whole these are more plentiful in the north and west of Britain. But other countries, such as France, also have excellent physical resources for adventurous activities.) There are also helpful artificial facilities such as old mines, indoor climbing walls and assault courses.

Fiscal resources

This refers to money. The cheapest source of expert instruction in adventurous activities is the army. Clubs – especially college or university clubs (if they exist and if you can join) – are also a way of getting adventurous experience without paying too much. Your own college may also arrange good activities at a reasonable cost – and some activities will be done during the course of this unit.

> **remember**
> The cheapest adventurous activity is mountain walking.

Do not spend money on buying your own equipment unless you can afford it and you really need the equipment. If you are buying equipment for adventurous activities for the first time, get impartial advice.

Employer's requirements

Employment for land-based outdoor and adventurous activities is available through the army (but that means joining the army) or through the private sector, i.e. working with companies which provide outdoor and adventurous experiences to the public, or to schools and colleges.

Qualifications are not always required, especially if the work is with younger children.

case study
10.11

Robinwood

If this would be your first work in the outdoors; as long as you have some experience working with children, an interest in adventure activities, the right personal qualities and commitment, we can provide all the training you need, to become an excellent adventure activity instructor.

Source: Robinwood

activity
GROUP WORK

Choose a public service career which interests you. Then list as many ways as you can in which a season's work as an outdoor instructor would:

1. Help you with that long-term career plan.

2. Not be so helpful.

For indoor climbing walls the SPA (see below) is often a required qualification.

Personal attributes

The main personal attributes (qualities) for work in adventurous activities are:

- Liking people.
- Fitness.
- Energy and enthusiasm.
- Interest in adventurous activities.
- Safety awareness and a sense of responsibility.

remember There are plenty of outdoor and adventurous jobs advertised on the internet; there is also work of this sort in various kinds of summer camp.

Rewards

The work is interesting, and it is excellent experience for a young person. As a career it is competitive in that many people want to work in adventurous activities in beautiful surroundings. Rates of pay tend to be low, the work is often seasonal, and contracts are usually for fixed periods only.

Governing body awards, qualifications

A governing body is an organisation that regulates a sport and sets up the training and assessment of people who wish to be instructors in that sport. The awards are qualifications which in many ways resemble BTEC qualifications, only they are more practical and qualify the holder only for a clearly defined and limited range of activities.

The trainee has to pay (unless training is subsidised by an employer).

Outdoor activity qualifications are complex and there are several of them. For mountaineering they include:

- Association of Mountaineering Instructors:
  - Mountaineering Instructor Certificate MIC (qualifies in all aspects of mountaineering).
  - Mountaineering Instructor Award MIA (mountaineering and rock climbing in non-winter conditions).
  - Winter ML (Winter Mountain Leader Award) (walking only on British mountains in winter conditions).
- British Association of International Mountain Leaders:
  - UIAGM/IVBV/IFMGA Mountain Guide's qualification.
  - UIMLA International Mountain Leader's qualification.

- Mountain Leader Training.
- Mountain Leader Award.
- Single Pitch Award (SPA).

www.mltuk.org/

For caving, qualifications include:

- Local Cave and Mine Leader Assessment Scheme.

www.british-caving.org.uk/

For orienteering, organisations and qualifications include:

- British Orienteering Federation.
- Orienteering Awards 1–5.
- Orienteering Young Leader Award.

www.britishorienteering.org.uk/

For skiing and snowboarding, organisations and qualifications include:

- BASI (British Association of Snowsport Instructors).
- CSIA (Canadian Ski Instructors' Alliance).
- CASI (Canadian Association of Snowboard Instructors).
- NZSIA (New Zealand Snowsports Instructors Alliance).

www.peakleaders.com/

- Fédération Française de la Montagne et de l'Escalade:
  - Initiateur ski de montagne.
  - Moniteur ski de montagne.

www.ffme.fr/

- Guide de haute montagne.
- ENSA (different levels of ski instructor).

www.ensa.jeunesse-sports.fr/

Governing body requirements (e.g. experience, registration, evidence, good practice)

To achieve a qualification in an adventurous activity from a governing body it is normally necessary to go through a number of stages.

Mountain Leader Award

The trainee should have at least 12 months experience of hill walking before registering and be 18 or over. After registration it is necessary to achieve, and **log**, 20 'quality days' of mountain walking. This has to be inspected by a registered training course provider who gives the training course. The training course is about leading groups on the mountains and assumes that people are competent mountain walkers. Consolidation experience involves at least 40 quality days of mountain walking, including at least eight

Mountain Leader Award stages

3.1 Gain personal hill walking experience.

3.2 Register and be issued with a logbook.

3.3 Attend a training course.

3.4 Consolidate experience.

3.5 Attend an assessment course.

3.6 Continue to gain and record experience and any relevant additional training.

activity
GROUP WORK

Discuss the advantages of this kind of training for someone who wants to work in a uniformed public service.

nights camping on the hills. Candidates must have a current first-aid qualification. The assessment course consists of 60 guided learning hours (the same as this BTEC National unit). Results come at the end of the assessment course and can be Pass, Defer or Fail. The Defer grade means that performance has been generally good but there is a lack of evidence that at least one of the required **competences** (e.g. the walking experience, or first aid) has been achieved.

Good practice

Good practice by leaders includes:

- Good planning.
- Responsibility towards the group being led.
- Providing a safe, healthy, worthwhile experience.
- A suitable leadership style.
- Competent navigation.
- Conveying an understanding of mountains and the mountain environment.
- Ensuring that they and their parties respect the environment and follow the countryside code.

The Countryside Code contains advice for the public:

- Be safe – plan ahead and follow any signs.
- Leave gates and property as you find them.
- Protect plants and animals, and take your litter home.
- Keep dogs under close control.
- Consider other people.

www.naturalengland.org.uk/

activity
INDIVIDUAL WORK
10.8

P6

Produce a personal development plan, based on your strengths and areas for improvement, to build up your skills and techniques in land-based outdoor and adventurous activities.

Progress Check

1. List five types of organisation that provide land-based outdoor and adventurous activities.

2. Outline the types and levels of competition which take place in land-based outdoor and adventurous activities.

3. Choose any two land-based outdoor and adventurous activities and name five technical skills needed for each one.

4. Explain the difference between a hazard and a risk.

5. Give three reasons why rock climbing can be dangerous.

6. Give five categories of people who are more likely than most to get into difficulties on a mountain. Say why in each case.

7. How are the risks of an outdoor activity calculated?

8. What grading system is used for rock climbs?

9. State the components of fitness which are particularly useful for any two land-based outdoor and adventurous activities.

10. What is a belay?

11. How do you find directions using a compass?

12. How are whistles used in land-based outdoor and adventurous activities? (Give details.)

13. What laws and official bodies govern land-based outdoor and adventurous activities in Britain?

14. What is a review and how should it be carried out?

15. Name the British governing body(ies) and awards for any two land-based outdoor and adventurous activities.

Crime and its Effects on Society

This unit covers:

- The effects of criminal behaviour on communities
- How the public services support victims of crime
- Legislation relating to crime and disorder, including the sentences and orders
- The approaches used to reduce crime, disorder and antisocial behaviour

This unit is about crime, its effects on the public, and the ways in which the police and others tackle crime.

The opening section looks at the roots of criminal behaviour. It also examines the effects of crime on people and their living environment, the way people see crime, the effect of crime on people's lifestyles and the cost of crime.

The next part of the unit looks closely at victims of crime and the kinds of support crime victims get from the public services, voluntary groups and the community.

After this the unit covers the laws and penalties used to deal with crime and offenders.

Finally there is a section outlining the various ways in which the police, the criminal justice system and a wide range of other agencies work together to reduce crime, disorder and antisocial behaviour.

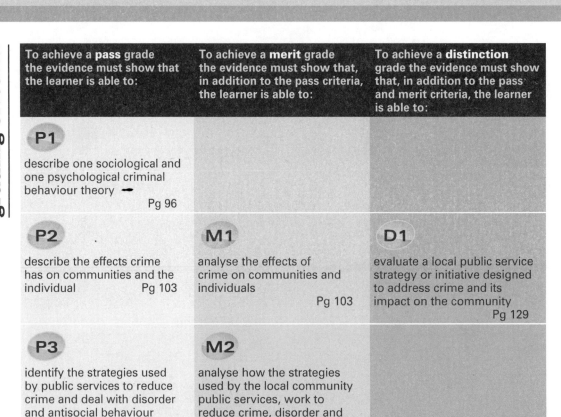

grading criteria

To achieve a **pass** grade the evidence must show that the learner is able to:	To achieve a **merit** grade the evidence must show that, in addition to the pass criteria, the learner is able to:	To achieve a **distinction** grade the evidence must show that, in addition to the pass and merit criteria, the learner is able to:
P1 describe one sociological and one psychological criminal behaviour theory ➤ Pg 96		
P2 describe the effects crime has on communities and the individual Pg 103	**M1** analyse the effects of crime on communities and individuals Pg 103	**D1** evaluate a local public service strategy or initiative designed to address crime and its impact on the community Pg 129
P3 identify the strategies used by public services to reduce crime and deal with disorder and antisocial behaviour Pg 129	**M2** analyse how the strategies used by the local community public services, work to reduce crime, disorder and antisocial behaviour Pg 129	

To achieve a **pass** grade the evidence must show that the learner is able to:	To achieve a **merit** grade the evidence must show that, in addition to the pass criteria, the learner is able to:	To achieve a **distinction** grade the evidence must show that, in addition to the pass and merit criteria, the learner is able to:
P4 describe the role of three different public services in assisting and supporting victims of crime Pg 111		
P5 outline current crime and disorder legislation Pg 116	**M3** analyse the implications of two pieces of crime and disorder legislation Pg 118	**D2** evaluate the implications of two pieces of crime and disorder legislation Pg 118
P6 describe the main sentences and orders the courts can impose Pg 118		

The effects of criminal behaviour on communities

A crime is an act which violates a law and for which the person or people doing it can be punished by law.

For practical purposes 'criminal behaviour' can be seen as conduct or actions which are against the law.

Communities are groups of people who share geographical, social, economic and cultural characteristics. In this unit, 'communities' can also mean 'the general public' – especially the public who live or work in places which are affected by crime.

Criminal behaviour

Even people who do not study the law and do not know much about it recognise criminal behaviour when they see it. They know it is wrongful behaviour which harms or threatens their person, property, security and quality of life – or which would do if it was directed against them. But for the many people who rarely if ever break the law (or do so in minor ways which they think no one will notice, or which do not seem to matter), the reason why some people's behaviour is so much more criminal than others' is – and perhaps always has been – something of a mystery.

Originally people tended to use religious explanations for the existence of crime. They believed in evil spirits, witchcraft, the devil, original sin and many similar ideas which seemed to explain why some people committed crimes and others did not. These beliefs still exist, and plenty of intelligent people believe in them all over the world. But they are not used in the uniformed public services, or by anyone connected with the uniformed public services, such as the government, the Home Office, the Department for Constitutional Affairs, Crime and Disorder Reduction Partnerships, or the **criminology** departments of universities where the causes of criminal behaviour are studied. Individual police or prison officers may describe certain people as being 'evil', but on the whole such emotive language is thought to get in the way of understanding what criminal behaviour is really about.

> **remember**
> Communities often live in a particular area; they may have a shared social life; they may have similar jobs and standard of living; and may share the same culture and ethnic origin.

Theories

Researchers and academics have put forward various theories about what criminal behaviour is and what its causes are.

A theory is a set of ideas which attempts to explain things that are not obvious. Some researchers try to support their theories by carrying out experiments or surveys which might tell them whether the theories are true or false. Since it is easier to prove that a theory is false than that it is true, theories tend to remain theories even when everybody seems to accept them.

Theories about criminal behaviour usually come under one of two headings: **sociological** and **psychological**. The sociological theories claim that crime is caused by society and the way it is organised. Psychological theories claim that crime is caused by something in human nature.

Sociological

Social disorganisation theory This is an old theory but a modern form of it is widely believed today. The originators were Park and Burgess in 1925. Social disorganisation theory is based on the belief that cities evolve like ecosystems (groups of plants and animals) in nature, with people of different types colonising different parts of a city and moving about, just as animals and plants might colonise a new island. When organised areas are invaded by new populations there is disruption and **deviant behaviour**.

Park, R., Burgess, E.W. and McKenzie, R.D. (1925) *The City*. University of Chicago Press, Chicago

Social disorganisation theory also sees a cause of crime in people from settled rural communities coming to the city and finding that their social **norms** (traditional patterns of behaviour) fall apart in a disorganised modern western urban society. Examples could include the people from rural Italy who emigrated to the US and formed the Mafia. Violence in Belfast during the 'troubles' in Northern Ireland has also been blamed on this process. More recently the Yardies of Jamaica were people from rural communities on the island who took to crime in Kingston, and were accused of spreading crime and gang culture later in parts of the UK, such as Manchester. Society permits crime to exist in these pockets because:

- The effort and expense of trying to stop it could not be justified politically.

- Certain influential and corrupt business people benefit from activities such as drug dealing and prostitution.

This theory was first fully put forward in the US by Sutherland (1934).

Sutherland, E.H. and Van Vechten, C.C. Jr. (1934). The reliability of criminal statistics. *Journal of criminal law and criminology*, 25 (May–June): 10–20

Shaw and McKay (1942) said high inner-city crime rates were the normal result of ordinary people being put in a strange social setting. Policing from outside such 'zones' is ineffective, and inner-city society is not cohesive enough to police itself. Shaw and McKay said high crime rates were linked to the area people lived in (the **inner city**) and not the culture the people originally came from (e.g. if they were immigrants). Faris (1955) extended the theory by linking criminality to other inner-city social problems such as suicide, mental illness and mob violence.

Shaw, C. and McKay, H. (1942). *Juvenile Delinquency and Urban Areas*. Chicago University Press, Chicago

Faris, R.E.L. (1955) *Social Disorganization*, 2nd edn. The Ronald Press Company, New York

Sampson and Wilson (1995) linked high inner-city crime rates with racism, arguing that black people in inner cities were rejected by white society and cut off from their rural roots. These two problems acting together explained the high crime rate among black people in US cities at the time they were doing their research.

Sampson, R.J. and Wilson, W.J. (1995) Toward a theory of race, crime, and urban inequality. In: *Crime and Inequality* (ed Hagan J. and Peterson, R.). Stanford University Press, Stanford

Modern measures by the British government to build '**cohesive**' communities in inner cities, and in the old, impoverished industrial towns of Yorkshire and Lancashire, suggest that politicians and civil servants broadly accept the truth of the social disorganisation theory.

Strain theory This sociological theory was first suggested by Emile Durkheim in *The Rules of Sociological Method* in 1895. Durkheim said the main cause of crime is the difference between what society seems to offer people and what it actually does offer people.

Durkheim, E. (1982) *The Rules of the Sociological Method* (ed. Lukes, S.). Free Press, New York

An example of this is advertising which presents an **idealised** image of wealth and success, which is different from the very limited levels of success that society offers most people.

The theory was developed further by Robert King Merton (1910–2003). He claimed that strains on society made people evolve in different ways, some of which could lead to criminal behaviour. He classified the different ways in which people responded to social strain and identified five main types:

1. Conformity – trying to achieve success by accepted methods.
2. Innovation – like conformity but prepared to break the rules.
3. Rebellion – the system is no good and should be replaced, violently if necessary.
4. Retreatism – dropping out, drug-taking, etc.
5. Ritualism – following society's norms, but with neither hope nor belief in their chances of success.

Apart from those people that fall into type 1, all are at risk of criminal behaviour. Even ritualists, who are rule-followers, could be attracted to racism and other patterns of thought and behaviour which can lead to crime.

Labelling theory states that *saying* people are bad *makes* them bad.

Labelling *theory* This theory states that criminals are labelled as criminals by society, and they and their criminal acts are defined as criminal by those in power. This stigmatisation pushes them into a criminal subculture (i.e. a group of people with shared criminal norms and values who think crime is acceptable).

Becker, H. (1963) *Outsiders: Studies in the Sociology of Deviance*. The Free Press, New York. (www.criminology.fsu.edu/crimtheory/becker.htm)

Conflict theories These theories state that the fundamental causes of crime are the great inequalities of wealth and power within society. Conflict theories argue that crime is an understandable (some even say justifiable) response to the injustices of society. They view the police and the law as agents of the rich operating against the oppressed poor. These theories (there are a number of them) have their origin in the influential writings of Karl Marx (1818–83).

Psychological

Social learning theory This is a psychological theory because it attempts to explain crime by looking at the ways in which people learn and, in particular, looking at the ways they learn criminal behaviour.

Social learning is seen as a process which happens in stages. These are:

1. Attention – the learner observes what is happening.

2. Retention – the learner remembers what happened.

3. Reproduction – the learner reproduces what happened either in his/her imagination or by copying the action.

4. Motivation – these are the rewards and punishments which make the learner act, in the future, on the basis of what has already been learned.

Social learning theory argues that behaviour is encouraged by rewards or the expectation of rewards. This process is called **reinforcement**. Reinforcement takes three main forms:

■ Past reinforcement. If an action is done which appears to have a positive consequence, the memory of that positive consequence causes the action to be repeated. If a young person steals a bottle of whisky from a shop, gets a 'buzz' out of stealing it, gets 'respect' from their friends and the 'pleasure' of drinking the whisky, each of the items in quotation marks acts as a past reinforcement associating the action with pleasure and a sense of achievement.

■ Promised reinforcement. If stealing the whisky gave excitement, gained status and resulted in pleasure on a previous occasion, this can encourage either a repeat of the offence or a more serious offence which gives a bigger buzz, gets more respect, and gives greater pleasure. The experience of the past promises reinforcement (the expectation of rewards) in the future.

■ **Vicarious** reinforcements. The process of social learning through reinforcement works vicariously as well as through our own experience. 'Vicarious' means 'through another person' or 'imagining ourselves in someone else's shoes'. Thus if a person (A) has a friend (B) who steals a bottle of whisky and finds the experience worthwhile, A is impressed and B becomes a role model to be imitated. Research suggests that films of crime are a form of vicarious reinforcement. A person watching the film experiences the buzz vicariously, and can learn through this reinforcement that crime may be worth doing.

As well as reinforcement, social learning theory puts forward 'negative motivations' which are the opposite of reinforcements (though they work in a similar way). These are punishments or discouragements which warn us against doing or repeating certain actions. As with reinforcements they take three forms: past, promised and vicarious. If a person commits a crime and gets a sentence, the sentence is punishment, which is 'negative motivation'. But repeated negative motivation, according to social learning theory, causes low 'self-concept' (**self-esteem**). This may itself lead to criminal behaviour in order to gain esteem (respect) from admiring peers who also have criminal tendencies.

Bandura, A. (1986) *Social Foundations of Thought and Action*. Prentice-Hall, Englewood Cliffs, NJ

Bandura, A. (1977) *Social Learning Theory*. General Learning Press, New York

Psychoanalytic theory **Psychoanalytic** theories of crime are based on the famous teachings of Sigmund Freud (1856–1939). Freud believed that everybody has unruly and possibly criminal forces in their unconscious mind (especially the 'id') which the 'super-ego' (the conscience) struggles to keep under control. Events in early childhood, he believed, could destroy the balance of personality and make people criminal.

http://psy.ucsd.edu/~hflowe/intheory.htm

Cognitive theories These are based on learning theory (social learning theory, mentioned above, is partly cognitive and partly **behaviourist**). Kohlberg (1964) put forward the theory that children go through three stages of moral development (i.e. awareness of right and wrong).

Kohlberg, L. (1964) *Development of moral character and moral ideology*. In: Hoffman, L. and Hoffman, L.W. (eds), Review of Child Development Research, I, 381–431

Table 12.1 Stages of moral development in children

Age	Name of stage	Meaning
Early childhood	Pre-conventional	Moral reasoning is based on fear of punishment
Late childhood	Conventional	Moral reasoning is based on satisfying the expectations of their family and friends
Adolescence	Post-conventional	It is now possible to question **morality** – which may lead to deeper understanding or to the abandonment of morality which shows itself in criminal behaviour

Opportunity theories of crime These recent theories of crime look not so much at the causes within the criminal as the causes of individual crimes. They are psychological in that they assume that criminals are rational human beings who weigh up the advantages and disadvantages of an action before doing it. But they argue that the real cause of crime is the opportunity rather than the criminal.

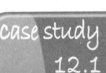

case study 12.1 — Ten principles of opportunity and crime

1. Opportunities play a role in causing all crime.
2. Crime opportunities are highly specific.
3. Crime opportunities are concentrated in time and space.
4. Crime opportunities depend on everyday movements.
5. One crime produces opportunities for another.
6. Some products offer more tempting crime opportunities.
7. Social and technological changes produce new crime opportunities.
8. Opportunities for crime can be reduced.
9. Reducing opportunities does not usually displace crime.
10. Focused opportunity reduction can produce wider declines in crime.

Source: Felson, M. and Clarke, R.V. (1998) Opportunity Makes the Thief: Practical theory for crime prevention. *Police Research Series*, Paper 98. Home Office, London

activity — GROUP WORK

Why do you think many police officers regard **opportunity theories** of the causes of crime as far more useful than most sociological and psychological ones?

Victim-centred theories These theories are based on the findings that some people are much more likely to become victims of crime than others.

case study 12.2 — Victims of crime

[T]he key reasons for repeats are believed to be the presence of good, and lack of bad, consequences of the first crime for the offender, and the stability of the situation which presents itself to an offender on the first and subsequent visits to the scene of his or her crime. The failure to change circumstances which led to crime may be a result of many factors; poverty (Wojcik et al., 1997), lack of motivation to prevent crime (as colleagues of the writer found among many small businesses), lack of awareness that a crime has taken place (as in **embezzlement** and fraud, for example) and perception of the crime as the lesser of two evils (as in domestic violence where escape also means removing from one's children their father's economic support and their removal from a home to the nobly provided but inadequate conditions afforded by refuges).

Source: Pease, K. (1998) Crime Detection and Prevention Series, Paper 90, *Repeat Victimisation: Taking Stock*. Home Office, London

activity
INDIVIDUAL WORK

What useful conclusions might police officers draw from this kind of research?

Causal factors

Every theory of criminal behaviour identifies different causal factors. Sociological theories usually suggest that the causes of crime lie in the organisation of society. They often take the view that crime results from the inequality of people, or from a clash of cultures. Some take the view that crime is partly caused by our definition of crimes (e.g. criminalising or decriminalising an activity) or of criminals. Psychological theories look for abnormalities in individual criminals, which may be innate, or arise from upbringing, or have causes in mental illnesses, **psychopathy**, etc. Opportunity theories say crime is caused by the chance of committing a crime successfully and getting away with it.

Crime theories are often seen by the public as an attempt to 'go soft' on crime, and to somehow excuse criminals for their actions. The idea that someone commits crimes because society is unfair takes away the blame from the criminal. Equally, if someone commits crimes because of a mental condition, then it takes the blame away from them and instead blames their abnormality (or their parents who brought them up wrongly). Moreover, if people's crimes are caused by something outside themselves, why should they be punished for something they cannot help? Theorists say that there are causes of crime such as a damaging family background, or unjust political and economic systems. But judges, magistrates and juries are expected to blame the offender, and sentence them.

Family influences

These are often blamed for criminal and antisocial behaviour. However, Case study 12.3 below shows results from a Home Office survey of young offenders aged 16–25.

The statements in the left-hand column show characteristics linked to offending. The statements in the right-hand column show other characteristics which those in the left-hand column contrast with.

The figures to the right show that for all the characteristics mentioned in the left-hand column there is a greater likelihood of offending. Some characteristics are more strongly

Home Office survey of young people and crime

Table 12.2 Young people and crime

Factors showing association	Reference category	Odds ratio*
Victim of personal crime	Not been victim of personal crime	3.7:1
Committed antisocial behaviour in last 12 months	Not committed antisocial behaviour in last 12 months	2.6:1
Friends/siblings have been in trouble with the police	Friends/siblings have never been in trouble with the police	1.7:1
More likely to agree criminal acts are OK	Less likely to agree criminal acts are OK	2.5:1
Taken any drug in last 12 months	Not taken drug in last 12 months	2.2:1
Male	Female	1.5:1
Highly impulsive	Not impulsive	1.7:1
Ever been expelled or suspended	Not been expelled or suspended	1.5:1
Age 16 to 19	Aged 20 to 25	1.4:1
Have been drunk once a month or more in last 12 months	Have been drunk less than once a month in last 12 months	1.4:1
Parents have been in trouble with police	Parents have never been in trouble with police	1.4:1

*Odds ratios with values above one indicate higher odds of offending in relation to the reference category.
Source: Young People and Crime: Findings from the 2005 Offending, Crime and Justice Survey, Home Office

activity

GROUP WORK

Through discussion, compile a list of other characteristics which you think might make it more likely for a young person to commit offences. Having made your list, rank them in agreed order of importance.

associated with offences than others. For example, a young person who has been a victim of personal crime is 3.7 times more likely to be a perpetrator of offences than a young person who has not been a victim of personal crime. But a young person whose parents have been in trouble with the police is only 1.4 times more likely to commit offences than a young person whose parents have not been in trouble with the police. Of the items listed in the table only two are directly to do with family influences. The conclusion from the evidence given is that though some family influences can make offending more likely, family influences are not the strongest factors in making offending more likely. Factors such as having taken drugs, or been expelled from school, are also important. But information of this sort is limited by the scope of the survey, which did not focus only on family influences.

Political and socio-economic climate

This is a complex subject and there is little agreement on it, least of all among politicians! Crime figures are officially falling, but that may be partly due to recent differences in the way that they are collected through the National Crime Recording Standard. There is thought to be a connection between crime figures and the state of the **economy**. Crime against property goes up when the economy is doing badly and it goes down when the economy is doing well. The opposite is true of crime against the person, which goes up when the economy is doing well. The probable reason is

remember

Statistics can tell us things that we cannot find out by any other method – but they may not be true of every individual. For example, not all young offenders have themselves been the victim of personal crime.

that everybody is (or feels) poorer when the economy is doing badly, so there is more temptation for people to steal. But as everybody feels richer when the economy is doing well, they go out more often, meet more people, and are more likely to get drunk – which are risk factors for violent crime.

Since 1997 there has been a greater emphasis on punishing criminals and looking after victims than there was before that. In 2007, 80,000 people were in British prisons. This may reduce crime to some extent because criminals are locked up; it may also act as a deterrent and put people off offending. Equally, difficulties in sentencing and the cost of dealing with people in both custodial and non-custodial sentences may make the courts less willing to convict at all.

activity

GROUP WORK 12.1

P1

Produce a wall-chart, suitable for police cadets, describing two criminal behaviour theories – one based on psychology and one based on sociology.

Effects of crime

Table 12.3 The effects of crime

On the victim(s)	On the rest of society
Physical harm – sometimes severe injury or death.	Financial harm: the criminal justice system – police, prison, courts, etc. cost the taxpayer a lot.
Financial harm – money and possessions stolen and damaged; replacement, repairs and preventive measures for the future; time off work; time wasted dealing with the aftermath of the crime.	Costs: preventive and deterrent measures such as locks, catches, fences, CCTV, burglar and car alarms; costs added to goods and all transactions by companies having to pass on anti-crime costs to the customer; the reduction of property values in areas of high crime.
	Emotional: a public fear of crime, especially among people who feel vulnerable, which stops some people from going out and reduces their quality of life; mistrust among communities.
	Intellectual: a general obsession with crime and criminals which shows itself in TV programmes, newspapers, films, government policy, political activity, etc.
Emotional harm – trauma, fear, stress and depression that can all result from being a victim of crime; effects on family members.	Employment: many jobs – police, security, prisons, courts, social work and insurance – are linked to crime and crime reduction.
	Environmental: crime degrades the environment (a) by criminal damage and graffiti, and (b) by the barriers, installations and architectural ugliness of 'designing out crime'.

Antisocial behaviour (e.g. damage, graffiti, violence against the person)

This is the name given to a range of criminal activities which (without necessarily being very serious in themselves) combine to undermine the quality of life in many parts of Britain.

Figure 12.1 How worried should we be about antisocial behaviour?

Public perception of crime

This is the awareness and concern which ordinary people (e.g. people who do not work in the media, politics or the criminal justice system) have about crime. In practice the public perception is taken as a majority opinion: it is the majority perception that politicians and the police have to act upon.

Own experience

An individual's perception of crime can be influenced by many different things. Figure 12.2 below indicates some of them.

Figure 12.2 Factors influencing an individual's perception of crime

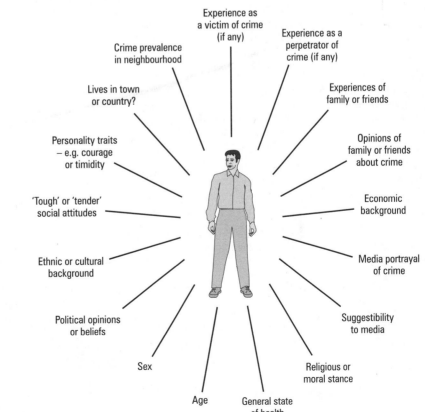

Experience as
a victim of crime
(if any)

Experience as a
perpetrator of
crime (if any)

Crime prevalence
in neighbourhood

Experiences of
family or friends

Lives in town
or country?

Opinions of
family or friends
about crime

Personality traits
– e.g. courage
or timidity

Economic
background

'Tough' or 'tender'
social attitudes

Media portrayal
of crime

Ethnic or cultural
background

Suggestibility
to media

Political opinions
or beliefs

Religious or
moral stance

Sex

Age   General state
of health

case study 12.4 — Home Office categories of antisocial behaviour

Table 12.4 Categories of antisocial behaviour

Misuse of public space	Disregard for community/personal well-being	Acts directed at people	Environmental damage
Drug/substance misuse and dealing	Noise	Intimidation/harassment	Criminal damage/vandalism
Taking drugs	Noisy neighbours	Groups or individuals making threats	Graffiti
Sniffing volatile substances	Noisy cars/motorbikes	Verbal abuse	Damage to bus shelters
Discarding needles/drug paraphernalia	Loud music	Bullying	Damage to phone kiosks
Crack houses	Alarms (persistent ringing/malfunction)	Following people	Damage to street furniture
Presence of dealers or users	Noise from pubs/clubs	Pestering people	Damage to buildings
Street drinking	Noise from business/industry	Voyeurism	Damage to trees/plants/hedges
Begging	Rowdy behaviour	Sending nasty/offensive letters	Litter/rubbish
Prostitution	Shouting and swearing	Obscene/nuisance phone calls	Dropping litter
Soliciting	Fighting	Menacing gestures	Dumping rubbish
Cards in phone boxes	Drunken behaviour	*Can be on the grounds of:*	Fly-tipping
Discarded condoms	Hooliganism/loutish behaviour	Race	Fly-posting
Kerb crawling	Nuisance behaviour	Sexual orientation	
Loitering	Urinating in public	Gender	
Pestering residents	Setting fires (not directed at specific persons or property)	Religion	
Sexual acts		Disability	
Inappropriate sexual conduct	Inappropriate use of fireworks	Age	
Indecent exposure	Throwing missiles		
Abandoned cars	Climbing on buildings		
Vehicle-related nuisance and inappropriate vehicle use	Impeding access to communal areas		
Inconvenient/illegal parking	Games in restricted/inappropriate areas		
Car repairs on the street/in gardens	Misuse of air guns		
Setting vehicles alight	Letting down tyres		
Joyriding	Hoax calls		
Racing cars	False calls to emergency services		
Off-road motorcycling	Animal-related problems		
Cycling/skateboarding in pedestrian areas/footpaths	Uncontrolled animals		

activity
INDIVIDUAL WORK

1. Which of these problems exist in your own local area?
2. Which of them do you consider most annoying?
3. How important is it to tackle antisocial behaviour?
4. List 10 ways of tackling antisocial behaviour which might be acceptable to the general public.

Victims and perpetrators are likely to have strong feelings about crime. As many criminals are '**volume offenders**' there are more victims than criminals. Victims' views on crime are more influential than the views of perpetrators, because we sympathise with victims and fear becoming victims ourselves. The crime-related experiences of family, friends and neighbours have a big influence on people's perceptions of crime. People's perceptions of crime are also influenced by the opinions of people they meet.

People's personal circumstances affect the way they think and feel about crime (see below). Their personal social attitudes matter as well:

■ Some people have 'tough' attitudes about crime (e.g. in favour of bringing back the death penalty or posting up the names and addresses of paedophiles on the internet).

■ Others have 'tender' attitudes (e.g. feel that criminals tend to be treated too harshly, that fewer people should be sent to prison, and that 'restorative justice' is better than severe punishment).

Perceptions of specific crimes vary with social group. For example, women have much stronger feelings about rape as a crime than men, and people from ethnic minorities are, on average, more concerned about racially **aggravated** crime than white people. There are also differences between age groups and their perceptions of crime. Moreover, people in **socio-economic** groups 1 and 2 ('professional' classes) worry less about crime and are more 'tender' towards criminals than people in groups 5, 6 and 7 ('manual workers').

Interestingly most individuals believe that crime rates are going up, even though, according to official statistics, they are going down. This may be due to the prevalence of antisocial behaviour which often goes unreported to the police, or to increased crime coverage in the media.

www.statistics.gov.uk/ **National Statistics: the site for socio-economic groups**

Media influence

At a less personal level people are strongly influenced by the portrayal of crime on television and in the media generally. The strength of the influence is shown through market research and TV viewing figures, and by the fact that there is so much coverage of crime (both factual and fictional) in the media. News portrayal helps to reinforce public attitudes about the relative seriousness of crimes – for example there is more coverage of the murder of a police officer than of the murder of a suspected drug dealer. This in turn is linked to the politics of crime. Law and order is seen as a major vote-winner by political parties, and if they feel they have a strong law and order policy (e.g. 'tough on crime and tough on the causes of crime') it is in their interest to generate a public fear of crime in order to get more votes at a general election.

> **remember**
>
> Different kings of newspaper have different attitudes towards crime and influence people in different ways. The influence of the *Sun* or the *Daily Mail* is not the same as the influence of the *Guardian* or The *Independent*.

It should perhaps be mentioned that the attitude of the media to crime is slightly two-faced. Usually it reflects the public dislike of crime, but it has been accused of glamorising it by sensational and prolonged coverage of horrific or disturbing crimes, e.g. the killing of five women in Ipswich at the end of 2006, the mysterious murder of Alexander Litvinenko and the 2007 disappearance of Madeleine McCann.

Fear of crime

Many people are afraid of crime, and since people's fear of crime affects the way they vote, fear of crime has been studied by the government. According to the **British Crime Survey** 2005/06, 17% of people worry about violent crime, 14% worry about car crime and 13% worry about burglary. These figures have been falling over the years. In 2000 24% were worried about violent crime, 21% were worried about car crime and 19% were worried about burglary.

Different social groups have different levels of worry about crime. These are outlined in Table 12.5.

Table 12.5 Fear of crime in different social groups

	Violent	Car	Burglary
Women	More than twice as likely as men to be worried about violent crime – especially among younger age groups	Same level of worry as men about car crime	More worried than men about burglary
Younger people	More worried than older people 12% of young men (16–24) worry about violent crime while only 7% of older men (65–74) worry about it	More worried than older people	Little variation with age
Non-white groups	More than twice as likely as other groups of people to have significant worries about all three types of crime		
People in social rented accommodation	Higher levels of worry than the average for all three categories of crime		
Readers of national tabloid newspapers, e.g. *Sun, Mirror*	Around twice as worried about all three types of crime as readers of the national broadsheet papers, e.g. *The Times, Guardian*.		

Source: Information from *Crime in England and Wales 2005/06*, Home Office

Impact of crime on the victim

Except for so-called 'victimless' crimes such as drug use and illicit consensual sex, crime has a direct impact on victims. This impact varies according to the severity and nature of the crime, and the kind of person the victim is. In the most serious crimes such as murder, the victim is killed and family and friends may be emotionally devastated. In minor crimes such as petty theft, the effect may be no more than inconvenience or mild annoyance, but if the crime is repeated or likely to be repeated the emotional effect could be much greater.

The impact of crime on an individual can be physical, emotional or material and could well be a mixture of all three. In addition, a crime may have a number of victims, not all of whom have been direct targets.

Figure 12.3 Who is the victim?

Table 12.6 Impact of crime

	Physical effects	Emotional effects	Material effects
Murder	Death of victim Pain of victim before death	Fear of victim before death Shock and bereavement of friends and family Shock and fear in community	Loss of property if motive for murder was robbery. Likely loss of earnings for relatives
Rape	Suffering of victim Risk of pregnancy and disease Risk of psychological effects such as depression	Shock, fear and many other probably long-lasting and intensely painful emotions	Perhaps relatively few immediate material losses, but psychological and other long-term effects could cause loss of earnings
Burglary	No immediate physical effects	Feeling of violation and insecurity	Loss of property (may be covered by insurance but that has to be paid for in increased premiums)
Shoplifting	No immediate physical effects	Annoyance and concern if it threatens the business	Depends on the amount of property stolen. Could be severe if business finally closes as a result
Graffiti	No physical effects	Could cause stress by abusing individuals, and by lowering the quality of life in a neighbourhood	Lowers property values in areas where it is a problem – therefore may have many victims

The financial (monetary) impact on victims has been calculated by the government. Their estimate of costs for different types of crime is given in Table 12.7.

Table 12.7 Estimated average cost of crimes against individuals and households in 2003/04 by crime type and cost category (£)

	Offence category		
	Homicide	Robbery	Criminal damage
1. Defensive expenditure	145	0	13
2. Insurance administration	229	21	36
3. Physical and emotional impact on direct victims	860,380	3,048	472
4. Value of property stolen	–	109	–
5. Property damaged/destroyed	–	12	212
6. Property recovered	–	19	–
7. Victim services	2,102	16	2
8. Lost output	451,110	1,011	6
9. Health services	770	483	–
10. Criminal justice system	144,239	2,601	126
Average cost (£)	1,458,975	7,282	866

Source: Home Office

Items 1 and 2 are costs in anticipation of crime. Items 3–9 are all costs as a consequence of crime, while item 10 is a cost in response to crime.

Impact on lifestyle

Crime affects both the lifestyle of victims, who may stay at home for fear of getting mugged in the street, and (to a lesser extent) the lifestyle of the whole community. Without crime we would have little reason to fear other people and would probably not even have to lock our doors at night. Taxes would be lower and it might be that the whole appearance of the environment would be different, especially in built-up areas which are often uglier than they ought to be because of the need to **design out crime**. Absence of crime would have a strange effect on the media, however, perhaps leaving us with thin newspapers and television dramas in which nothing dramatic ever happened. There would also be a serious lack of careers in the public services.

'Real' and perceived crime figures

It is impossible to know exactly how many crimes take place, so by 'real' we mean either police figures or the figures collected by the British Crime Survey. The British Crime Survey used to be done every two years, but since 2001 it has been done every year. In 2005/06, 47,796 face-to-face interviews were carried out among people aged 16+ in private households. Using advanced methods of sampling and by processing the figures, a picture which is thought to be representative of the situation in the whole country is obtained. The police do not record every crime that is reported to them, so what the public interpret as crimes will not always be the same as what the police consider to be crimes following the **National Crime Recording Standard** on which police crime figures must be based by law.

Whether police or British Crime Survey figures are used, there is a gap between what the public think is the crime rate and what the statisticians think.

Between 2004/05 and 2005/06, crime in England and Wales went down in six out of nine categories, and it went down overall, but Figure 12.4 shows that nearly two-thirds of people thought crime rates had gone up nationally, while over 40% thought crime levels had gone up in their local area.

According to the British Crime Survey 2005/06, women, older people, less-educated people, those living in social rented housing and readers of national tabloid newspapers were all more likely than average to think that crime had increased 'a lot'.

Figure 12.4 Public perceptions of changing crime levels, BCS, 2004/05–2005/06

Source: Home Office

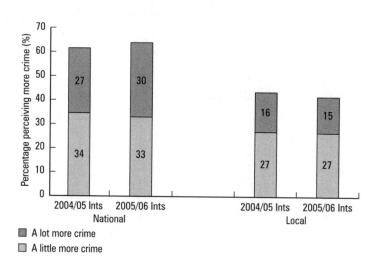

Collective costs to community (e.g. health service, police service)

It is hard to estimate the costs of crime to the community (whether community means the whole country or a local area), but there is no doubt that the costs are very high.

The collective costs of crime are all of the costs to victims of the type outlined on page 101, together with all the taxes paid by individuals and businesses which go towards:

- All types of crime prevention.
- Crime fighting.
- Insurance against crime.
- The proportion of health service money spent on crime victims.
- Prison.
- Probation.
- Most of the cost of the Home Office and the **Ministry of Justice**.
- Some of the cost of Parliament and MPs.

Costs of the police for 2007 are estimated at about £15 billion, while costs for the law courts are £6 billion and the prison service about £4 billion. Health service costs linked to individual crimes are quite high, with the average cost of a serious wounding amounting to up to £150,000, but an overall figure for all health service costs linked to crime is not available. As a standard of comparison, total government spending on *all* services and other publicly funded activities is around £550 billion.

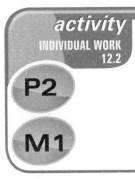

activity

INDIVIDUAL WORK 12.2

P2

M1

Write an article for a local newspaper both describing and explaining in depth how crime affects communities and individuals.

How the public services support victims of crime

Victims of crime

There is a feeling among many voters that governments ever since the 1960s have been trying to make life too easy for criminals, and in recent years there has been increasing emphasis on the rights of the victim. Although a few lucky people may never be direct victims of crime, most of us are victims of some sort of crime at some time in our lives.

One of the main features of crime victims is that many of them, once victimised, are victimised again. For example, if a shop is broken into once, it is statistically likely to be broken into again. This is called '**repeat victimisation**'. The possibility that crime can be better understood and controlled by studying and tackling repeat victimisation is one of the factors leading to the more 'victim-centred' approach to crime that both governments and the police have been using in recent years.

Businesses

Businesses suffer from a wide range of crimes. Obvious ones are theft, fraud, intimidation, embezzlement, arson and criminal damage. They also suffer from repeat victimisation, as the following figures (taken from 1997) show.

A study of small businesses in parts of Leicester carried out for Crime Concern showed that:

17% of businesses suffered 69% of burglaries

11% of businesses suffered 76% of criminal damage

17% of businesses suffered 83% of fraud

9% of businesses suffered 92% of threats, abuse and intimidation

8% of businesses suffered 65% of transport losses

3% of businesses suffered 81% of violent attacks

2% of businesses suffered 60% of employee theft

1% of businesses suffered 45% of robbery

(Wood et al., 1997, quoted in Pease, K. (1998) *Repeat Victimisation: Taking Stock* Home Office, London (www.homeoffice.gov.uk/rds/index.html))

Communities

Communities, which are large groups of people living in defined geographical areas, are likely to suffer (as individuals) from every type of crime. Crimes suffered by communities as a whole depend on the people living in the community and the opportunities for crime within the community, and are often linked to socio-economic factors such as:

■ Inequality.

■ Poor environment.

■ Cultural and ethnic tensions.

■ The lack of facilities for young people.

■ Poor education.

■ Drugs.

■ Unemployment.

Different types of crime are prevalent in different communities and affect communities in different ways. It is hard to generalise about it except to say that crime always has a negative effect on communities and degrades people's quality of life.

Minority groups

Many non-white ethnic minority groups, especially black African and black Caribbean groups, are **over-represented** in prisons and also over-represented as victims of crime. The same is true, to a lesser extent, of people of Pakistani descent. According to the British Crime Survey, people from minority ethnic groups feel more worried about crime, on average, than people from other ethnic groups.

Vulnerable members of the community

The very old, the very young, the disabled and the mentally ill are vulnerable members of the community from the point of view of ill-health, poverty, etc. They are likely to fear crime more than the average. But they are not as likely as less vulnerable people to actually be victims of crime. Recent figures are hard to come by, but in 1998 the British Crime Survey found that the risk of burglary was highest in inner-city areas, that young people, especially men, were at the highest risk of being victims of violent crime and that people over 65 had the lowest risk.

Individuals

Individuals are the usual victims of crime, and it is individuals who suffer most as a result of crime. They are more likely to be victims in urban areas than rural. There are big regional variations: according to the BCS 2004/05, the risk of being a victim in household crime is much greater in Manchester than in Essex. Antisocial behaviour and burglary rates are higher in London, so there are more victims of these crimes in London than elsewhere in England and Wales.

Role of public services

Crime victims often receive support, both emotional and financial, from friends and family. The insurance industry gives **private-sector support** for crime victims, enabling people to protect themselves against financial loss and medical costs in advance by paying premiums and taking out insurance policies. The public services, both **statutory** and voluntary, also have a major, and increasing, role to play in supporting the victims of crime.

Police

The police, who are in the front line against crime, are also in the front line in helping victims of crime. Their roles are to:

1. Get information from the victim so that the crime can be dealt with.
2. Pass the victim's details to relevant victim support services (if the victim agrees).
3. Provide family liaison officers when someone has died, and give all relevant literature to help them.
4. Keep the victim (or a representative, if the victim is incapacitated) informed of the progress of the case.
5. Notify victims about suspects' bail conditions, etc.
6. Give advice about compensation and how to apply for compensation in personal injury cases to the **Criminal Injuries Compensation Authority**.
7. Liaise with the press, either to protect the victim from press coverage or to encourage it in the hope of solving the crime.
8. Offer crime prevention advice, to reduce the risk of repeat victimisation.
9. Implement measures to protect victims from being identified in court.
10. Provide information about appeals and any involvement of the **Criminal Cases Review Commission**.

Social services

The main role of social services is to protect victims who are vulnerable to attack – for example abused women or children who have to be given a place of safety from an abuser or his/her associates.

Probation service

The probation service, now part of the **National Offender Management Service** which also includes the prison service, has a duty under the Domestic Violence, Crime and Victims Act 2004, to protect the victims of abusive husbands, partners and others who have been sentenced to prison for 12 months or more for a violent or sexual offence. The **Act** gives victims the right to have a say on what kind of supervision and licence conditions the offender has on release. This enables the probation service to make arrangements which do not put former victims at increased risk of being victimised by a former abuser.

Local authority

In conjunction with social services, a local authority is expected to set up safe houses for people who have been victimised or abused.

Education service

The role of the education service is to detect signs of abuse among children, report them to the police or social services, and ensure that schools and colleges are as secure as they can reasonably be against abusive adults who may attempt to victimise the young people in their daytime care.

Voluntary agencies

The most well known of these is Victim Support (see page 110).

Agencies bound by code of support for victims of crimes

The code of support referred to here is the Code of Practice issued under section 32 of the Domestic Violence, Crime and Victims Act 2004 which states the services to be provided in England and Wales by a range of organisations to victims of criminal conduct which occurred in England and Wales. The Code of Practice was issued in 2006.

The following organisations are required under the Victim's Code of Practice to provide help to victims of crime:

■ The Criminal Cases Review Commission.

■ The Criminal Injuries Compensation Authority.

■ The Criminal Injuries Compensation Appeals Panel.

■ The Crown Prosecution Service.

■ Her Majesty's Courts Service.

■ The joint police/**Crown Prosecution Service Witness Care Units.**

■ All police forces for police areas in England and Wales, the British Transport Police and the Ministry of Defence Police.

■ The **Parole Board**.

■ The Prison Service.

■ The probation service.

■ **Youth Offending Teams**.

A crime is defined as 'an allegation of criminal conduct … which would be recorded under the National Crime Recording Standard (NCRS)'.

The full Victim's Code of Practice can be found at: www.homeoffice.gov.uk/

A useful Victim's Guide to the Code of Practice is available on the same website

---

Multi-agency cooperation and partnerships

The doctrine of '**joined-up government**' is particularly useful where victims of crime are concerned. The aim is to ensure that all victims receive the care and support they need both in the short and the long term, and to limit the risk of repeat victimisation, especially in cases of physical and sexual abuse. It seems that the best way to give this kind of all-round protection is by ensuring that victim support agencies work closely together, for example in partnerships, sharing information and providing the various kinds of care that victims need.

Figure 12.5 indicates some of this **multi-agency** cooperation.

Advice

Advice for victims depends on the agency giving the advice, the circumstances, and the kind of crime the victim has suffered. The purpose of the advice is usually:

■ To help the victim cope with problems arising directly out of the crime.

■ To limit the risk, and fear, of repeat victimisation.

Counselling

Where victims have suffered trauma or depression they will receive counselling (which is not the same thing as advice) through the NHS, the **Samaritans** or through organisations which they can be referred to by their doctor or by Victim Support.

Figure 12.5 Cooperation to support victims of crime

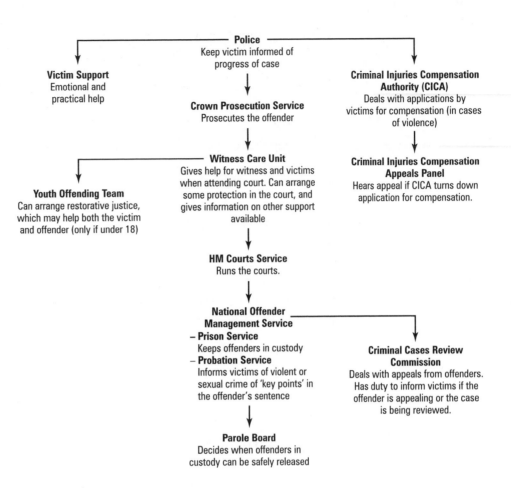

Police
Keep victim informed of progress of case

Victim Support
Emotional and practical help

Crown Prosecution Service
Prosecutes the offender

Criminal Injuries Compensation Authority (CICA)
Deals with applications by victims for compensation (in cases of violence)

Witness Care Unit
Gives help for witness and victims when attending court. Can arrange some protection in the court, and gives information on other support available

Youth Offending Team
Can arrange restorative justice, which may help both the victim and offender (only if under 18)

Criminal Injuries Compensation Appeals Panel
Hears appeal if CICA turns down application for compensation.

HM Courts Service
Runs the courts.

National Offender Management Service
– Prison Service
Keeps offenders in custody
– Probation Service
Informs victims of violent or sexual crime of 'key points' in the offender's sentence

Criminal Cases Review Commission
Deals with appeals from offenders. Has duty to inform victims if the offender is appealing or the case is being reviewed.

Parole Board
Decides when offenders in custody can be safely released

Initiatives

An **initiative** is a project or new idea set up to solve a problem or improve people's lives. In most parts of England and Wales there are initiatives to help victims of crime. These are often partnerships between public services, including the police and local authorities, and the voluntary sector.

Victims of crime are sometimes not in a position to fend for themselves, especially if they are abused, and if their abusers, for whatever reason, have not been arrested or charged with any crime. Liverpool Social Services, for example, lead an integrated scheme for protecting vulnerable adults.

case study
12.5

Vulnerable adults

Since 2001 Liverpool City Council has worked with partners in the Police, health, the voluntary and independent sectors to protect adults who may be at risk.

In partnership with Sefton Borough Council and the executive Safeguarding adults boards we have produced a new set of safeguarding adults protocols which can be viewed here.

Source: Liverpool City Council

activity
INDIVIDUAL WORK

Research a similar initiative in your own area.

City of Liverpool and Borough of Sefton, Safeguarding adults: a framework for action 2006 (www.sefton.gov.uk/PDF/SOC_Safeguarding_Adults_2006.pdf)

Reducing the fear of crime

The following measures help to create a feeling of order and security which many people find reassuring:

- Visible policing.

- Patrols by community support officers.

- The installation of vast numbers of CCTV cameras.

- Brighter street lighting and the redesigning of town centres to give better lines of sight and fewer dark corners.

- Environmental clean-up campaigns including the removal of graffiti and the tidying of waste land.

Organisations such as Neighbourhood Watch, and the notices they put up, also help to reduce the fear of crime (as well as actual levels of crime in their patch). The media have a part to play in reducing fear of crime by publicising the advances made by the police and the government in reducing crime levels – though some newspapers and TV programmes are accused of increasing our fear of crime by negative or sensational reporting. Finally, new approaches such as **restorative justice** (see page 116) appear to have some success in reintegrating offenders into society by making them see in direct human terms what the consequences of their crimes have been.

Victim support

Victim support is any activity which helps or comforts the victims of crime.

The victim's charter

This is a document which originated with the Conservative government in 1990 and indicated the beginning of a shift of interest in the criminal justice system from the rights of the **defendant** to the rights of the victim. Originally it was a statement of intent designed to send out a message to the people that it was time to start protecting victims more. Later it got a new lease of life with the passing of the Domestic Violence, Crime and Victims Act of 2004. The Victim's Charter is a 32-page booklet, written in simple language and addressing the general public, which 'aims to explain, as clearly as possible, what happens after the offence has been reported to the police and the standards of service you should expect.'

case study 12.6 — The code of practice for victims of crime

All victims, including relatives of victims who have died as a result of relevant criminal conduct, should have access to a range of support services in their area. While no organisation has an obligation under this Code to ensure appropriate support services are available for every victim, the Government aims to ensure that every victim has access to appropriate support services in their local area. Such support needs to be timely and of sufficient quality to meet the individual needs of every victim, including victims who require specialist support.

Source: Home Office

activity
GROUP WORK

What skills and abilities do you think public service workers need if they work in the field of victim support?

Code of support

As mentioned on page 106, this document sets out the support that a range of organisations should give to victims of crime. These organisations are bound by the Domestic Violence, Crime and Victims' Act 2004 to give this support.

Victim protection

The need for victim protection has been based on:

- Evidence of repeat victimisation found by criminology research.

- Experience in the courts of the difficulties of getting witnesses to testify against abusers (e.g. wives against abusive husbands).

- Crimes, including murder, against people who have testified against criminals (especially gang leaders) in courts.

These problems have existed not only in Britain but also in many other countries such as the US and Italy which have a history of violent and organised crime.

For many years victims and witnesses have been protected by the police, courts and other organisations using informal or semi-formal arrangements. In a sense, all victims are witnesses (unless killed or too disabled to testify), and many witnesses who are not direct victims are indirect victims because they have seen shocking events and been emotionally or psychologically affected by them. The Youth Justice and Criminal Evidence Act 1999 made legal requirements for the courts to protect witnesses, including a range of 'special measures'. These include arrangements for protecting witnesses from intimidation by associates of the accused, restrictions on cross-examination by the defendant, and the provision of video '**live links**' so that victims and witnesses can be questioned by a court without having to be there in person.

Victim protection is also done by the police, who can do 'whatever needs to be done' to protect people who are under death threats – up to and including (in very extreme cases) the construction of a new identity. They are also able to supply or organise security as they did in the case of the author Salman Rushdie while he was under a death threat from the government of Iran.

Extreme measures like these, of course, are rare. Much more widespread is the kind of victim protection given by local authorities and social services, who provide hostels and secure houses for people who have been abused at home by their partners and others. Children thought to be at risk of abuse are put on an **at-risk register** and can be removed from their families and put in foster care if it is clear that they are being victimised. Victims of special crimes, e.g. rape, have special arrangements, such as those put in place by the Metropolitan Police under Project Sapphire.

www.met.police.uk/sapphire/index.htm (**Project Sapphire**)

www.opsi.gov.uk/acts.htm#acts (**Government Acts since 1988**)

Tackling repeat victimisation

Repeat victimisation is the occurrence of two or more crimes against the same person or property, often in a relatively short period of time (such as two weeks). The problem was closely studied in the US and Britain in the 1990s. The causes are thought to be:

- 'Flags' otherwise known as 'risk heterogeneity' – attributes which make a place or person inherently vulnerable to crime. Examples are a wealthy and unprotected house near a poor estate, or a person who makes an enemy who is prepared to attack them physically.

- 'Boosts' otherwise known as 'event dependence'. This is a situation where a successful outcome or some other factor makes a criminal want to repeat the same offence against the same person or property. For example, if a burglar gets into a house and discovers that it contains more valuables than can be removed in one trip, he or she makes a return visit to steal the rest of the valuables.

remember

MO, also known as 'method of operation' or 'modus operandi' (the 'trademark' or recognisable ways in which some criminals operate), is now recorded in crime reports and helps to detect repeat and prolific offenders and protect potential victims.

Repeat victimisation is tackled by a range of methods, including:

- An immediate response to reduce the risk of repeat (e.g. firmly securing a property that has been broken into).

- Detection methods such as installation of CCTV in crime hot spots where repeat victimisation is suspected.

- More proactive and intelligence-led policing, where crime prevention and detection are more closely linked.

- The introduction of data storing and sharing methods which enable crime patterns to be identified, e.g. the **National Intelligence Model** and the National Crime Recording Standard.

- Closer police contact and awareness of victims and any behaviour patterns which have led to increased risk of victimisation.

There is more about the National Intelligence Model on page 118

Pease, K. (1998) *Repeat Victimisation: Taking Stock*. Home Office, London

Voluntary and statutory agencies (e.g. Victim Support)

Victim Support is 'the independent charity which helps people cope with the effects of crime'. It is the most well known of a number of organisations which support victims. The very useful work of such organisations is well documented on their websites.

www.victimsupport.org.uk/

www.samaritans.org.uk/

Counselling and support

Counselling, which can be provided under the NHS, is a way of helping people to overcome depression, post-traumatic stress disorder and other conditions which can be caused or worsened as a result of being a victim of crime. Cognitive-behavioural methods of counselling and therapy are the most widely used in helping victims understand and deal with the fear, anxiety and low self-esteem which can result from being a victim.

Support covers a wide range of activities, from protection to financial help and companionship, which can benefit victims. Some is informal, provided by family and friends. Some can be accessed through the police or through local authorities, or obtained through churches, charities and self-help groups.

The 2002/03 British Crime Survey, which examined the support issue, found that the kinds of support that crime victims wanted were as shown in Table 12.8.

Table 12.8 Support wanted by victims of crime

Type of support	% of respondents wanting and getting it	% of respondents wanting and not getting it
Someone to talk to	48	52
Practical help	29	71
Security advice	28	72
Insurance/compensation help	22	78
Help in reporting	19	81
Help from police	19	81
Protection from further victimisation	13	87

Preventative measures

Crime against property can be reduced by taking steps to secure the property and making it less attractive to burglars, vandals, etc. Limiting the risk of becoming a victim of personal attack may involve lifestyle choices, where risks of attack are balanced against the need to live a free and unrestricted life.

Personal safety

Simple measures such as meeting people for the first time in safe public places, or keeping an eye on a drink that could be spiked, reduce the risk of becoming a victim. Police websites give good advice on personal safety.

case study 12.7 — Personal safety

- Think ahead and plan your journey, avoiding deserted areas.
- Try to avoid walking alone at night, and keep to well-lit main roads where possible. You should try to avoid short cuts like alleyways, waste ground and wooded, bushy areas.
- Stay alert: be aware of what's going on around you.
- It is always worth letting someone know where you are going, the route you intend to take and when you expect to return.
- Consider investing in a mobile phone. There are various services available for light users. (see also **Mobile Phone** safety)
- Try to avoid wearing headphones – your ability to hear traffic, strangers or potential trouble is severely restricted.

Source: Metropolitan Police Service

activity
INDIVIDUAL WORK

You have a pen friend who is going to visit you for the first time. Make notes on the personal safety advice you would give your pen friend as regards your local area, entertainment, etc.

Household security

remember
Police crime prevention officers are the experts in this field: it is worth talking to them.

In a private house or flat there are as many risks of becoming an accident victim as a victim of crime. From a crime point of view it is important to have good locks, bolts and chains on the door and secure windows. Chains should be left on when answering the door. The area around the house should be free of shrubs, etc. where people can hide. Dogs are said to be a deterrent to burglars.

activity
GROUP WORK 12.3

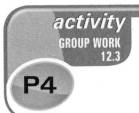

Do a presentation for local Neighbourhood Watch members outlining how three other public services help crime victims.

P4

Legislation relating to crime and disorder, including the sentences and orders

Legislation means laws, and **disorder** is mainly antisocial behaviour, though it includes larger-scale disturbances such as rioting as well. A **sentence** is a punishment given by a court, usually lasting for a period of time and involving some loss of freedom, or, at the very least, a criminal record. An **order** is an instruction by a court telling someone that they must either do, or not do, a particular thing (e.g. they must not visit someone they have been harassing).

Crime and disorder legislation

In recent years a large number of new laws have been passed by Parliament to tackle crime and disorder. The main reasons for all the new laws have been:

- A general belief among the public that crime is increasing.

- The fact that law and order is a political issue which can gain or lose votes.

- Evidence of high levels of crime blighting some communities and being part of a 'cycle of disadvantage'.

- Fears of cross-border and international crime, and the need to align Britain with Europe in the fight against crime.

Current legislation

This includes any laws that can be used at the present time.

Crime and Disorder Act 1998

This law deals with a variety of types of crime all of which are related to antisocial and disorderly behaviour on the streets.

See below, under 'Sentences and orders', for a more detailed discussion.

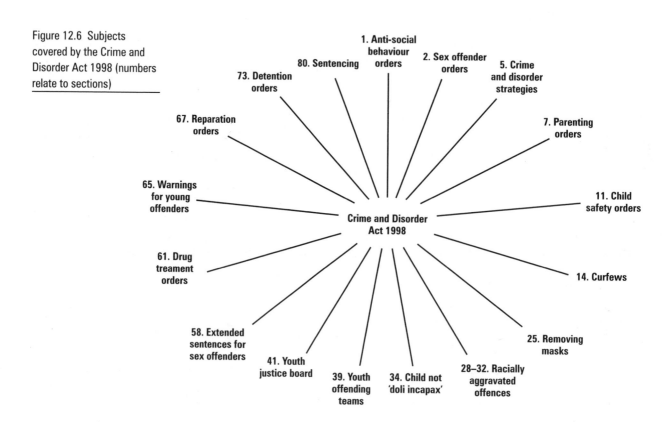

Figure 12.6 Subjects covered by the Crime and Disorder Act 1998 (numbers relate to sections)

Theft Act 1968

Theft is the most common of all recorded crimes, and the Theft Act 1968 is the current law that deals with it. The Theft Act 1968 states that 'A person is guilty of theft if he dishonestly appropriates property belonging to another with the intention of permanently depriving the other of it'. Then it lays down maximum prison sentences for different kinds of theft. The main ones are:

■ Theft – seven years.

■ Robbery – life.

■ Burglary – 14 years.

■ Aggravated burglary – life.

■ Blackmail – 14 years.

Since 1968 some changes have been made through the Police and Criminal Evidence Act 1984, the Criminal Justice Act 1991, the Aggravated Vehicle Taking Act 1992 and the Youth Justice and Criminal Evidence Act 1999 (and several others). This means that although the date of the Act is 1968 it is constantly being reviewed and kept up to date.

> **remember**
>
> Government Acts keep their original date, however much they have been changed in later years. (If an Act is repealed, however, it is taken off the law books and replaced by another Act.)

Sentences and orders

As indicated above, these are legal penalties and restrictions placed upon people who are found guilty of offences by the courts. Sentences are 'large' punishments involving a restriction of freedom or a criminal record. Orders can be attached to sentences, and may be connected with civil law rather than criminal law.

General

The system of sentencing and orders is linked to age. There are differences between the sentences available for people in different age groups under the age of 18. However, there are also similarities, e.g. an order such as an **antisocial behaviour** order (ASBO) can be given to anybody over the age of 10.

Youth

Under the Crime and Disorder Act 1998, crime and disorder by children and young people is covered by parenting orders, child safety orders, curfew notices and various measures for dealing with truants.

Parenting orders

These are given to parents of a child when their child receives:

■ A child safety order.

■ An ASBO.

■ A criminal conviction.

■ A conviction in a truancy offence.

Under a parenting order a parent or guardian has to ensure that the child under their care does not repeat the offence which they have been punished for. The parent can also get counselling or guidance for up to three months (once a week) aimed at making them more effective parents. The parenting order is supervised by a probation officer, a social worker or a member of a youth offending team. Parents who do not comply with the order may be fined. Appeals against parenting orders can be made to the High Court.

Child safety orders

These are issued when children of 10 or younger have committed what would have been an offence if they had been older, have broken a curfew or have caused 'harassment, alarm or distress' to people outside the household. The order lasts three months (but can, exceptionally, last a year), it places the child under a 'responsible officer', and makes requirements designed to give a child care, protection, support and control, and prevent a repetition of the offending behaviour.

Child curfew schemes

These can be run by local authorities and prohibit children under 10 being out in a public place between 9 p.m. and 6 a.m. unless under the control of a responsible adult. The notice announcing the curfew can be posted up in the street and may fix different time limits for children of different ages.

Pre-court measures

The courts have some new powers under the Crime and Disorder Act 1998 designed to make them work faster, especially with young offenders. These are given in Sections 46–53 of the Act. Non-legal staff can carry out some procedures, and district judges can sit alone in youth and magistrates' courts, which was not the case before. Courts can fix early administrative hearings to sort out paperwork relating to the case, or vary bail conditions in the period before the case is heard.

Antisocial behaviour measures

The most well known of these are antisocial behaviour orders (ASBOs). They are described in Sections 1–4 of the Act.

www.crimereduction.gov.uk/

---

case study 12.8 — Antisocial behaviour orders

An ASBO prohibits a named individual from committing specific antisocial acts, and/or entering a specified area, and/or associating with named individuals.

Interim ASBOs are effective immediately, last for a specified period and cease when the application for the full order is determined. They can be made without notice to the defendant where there is an urgent need to protect the community.

activity — GROUP WORK

1. What do you think the advantages and disadvantages of antisocial behaviour orders are?
2. Find out how much antisocial behaviour orders are used in your local area, and how effective the police, community support officers, etc. consider them to be.

ASBOs can be issued by a magistrates' court after an application from either a local authority or a chief police officer. ASBOs last two years, and if the specified conditions are broken the person may be imprisoned (for six months by a magistrates' court or five years by the Crown Court) or fined.

Other antisocial behaviour measures have been added under the Antisocial Behaviour Act 2003 ranging from powers to disperse groups of people or close premises used for drug dealing to the service of fixed-penalty notices and the removal of hedges by local authorities.

Sentences (financial penalties, community sentences, with orders attached, custodial sentences)

Financial penalties

Financial penalties are normally known as fines. These are a convenient form of penalty and are less expensive to the taxpayer than other kinds of penalty. On the other hand they are not appropriate for all kinds of offence, and many offenders do not have the money to pay them anyway. Fines, especially in the magistrates' court, follow a **standard scale** which was fixed in the Criminal Justice Act 1982 and updated in the Criminal Justice Act 1991.

Table 12.9 Fines

Level on the scale	Amount of fine
1	£200
2	£500
3	£1000
4	£2500
5	£5000

Source: Criminal Justice Act 1991, Section 17(2)

> **remember**
>
> Some offences can be tried in either the magistrate's court or the Crown Court – and the sentencing in the two courts can be very different.

These figures were still the same in 2006, despite the big increase in most people's disposable income since 1991. The fine for breaking an antisocial behaviour order is anything up to £5000, i.e. it can be any of those listed above. On the other hand if a parenting order is breached, according to the Crime and Disorder Act 1998, the parent will be liable to pay a fine not exceeding level 3 – £1000. As a generalisation, and provided cases are tried in a magistrates' court, fines for offences under the Crime and Disorder Act 1998 do not exceed £5000.

Community sentences

Community sentences are used for persistent offenders who have had three or more convictions since the age of 16. They can consist of:

'1. Unpaid work 2. An activity requirement 3. A programme requirement
4. A prohibited activity 5. A curfew requirement 6. An exclusion requirement
7. A residence requirement 8. A mental health requirement 9. A drug rehabilitation requirement 10. An alcohol treatment requirement 11. A supervision requirement
12. If the offender is aged under 25, an attendance centre requirement

Source: Rizer

Requirements are things that the offender has to do. For example, an exclusion requirement means the offender has to keep away from certain places. A prohibited activity is something the offender must not do, e.g. attend football matches. Requirements 8, 9 and 10 above can only be carried out with the consent of the offender.

www.rizer.co.uk/ (A very useful government-backed website!)

With orders attached

The word 'order' is sometimes used rather loosely. Requirements (as listed above) are orders if they are orders of the court which sentenced the offender. They are usually decided on the basis of pre-sentence reports and other advice from social workers and probation officers. Their aim is to limit opportunities for reoffending and to encourage rehabilitation – constructive activities which will enable the offender to lead a useful and law-abiding life in the future.

A community sentence itself can be called a community order, and often several carefully chosen requirements are attached to it, relevant to the individual needs of the offender.

Custodial sentences

Custodial sentences are sentences in prison or in a young offenders' institution. They are the most serious kind of sentence used by the courts. As there is a massive problem with prison overcrowding (over 80,000 people were in prison in 2007), and because the punishment is unpleasant, expensive and of doubtful benefit to many prisoners, custody is only used as a last resort, i.e:

■ For a very serious offence.

■ For refusal to do a community order.

- For a dangerous sexual or violent offence.

- For the maximum prison sentence allowed by law for that particular offence.

www.opsi.gov.uk/acts.htm#acts. **Check out dangerous offender provisions under the Criminal Justice Act 2003**

If a non-dangerous offender (e.g. for a fairly major fraud) has a custodial sentence of over 12 months, they can be let out on licence after only half of the sentence has been served. The licence (a permit to be 'free') may have conditions attached and if these are broken the offender will go back to prison.

Short periods of imprisonment, from 14 to 90 days, followed by a time on licence lasting to the end of the sentence period given by the court, are called 'intermittent custody'. In certain circumstances people can spend part of the week in prison, and part outside.

'Dangerous' offenders serving long sentences are not automatically released on licence. They have to be passed as safe to the public by a parole board before they can be released on licence, and they may be heavily supervised after that.

Youth custody arrangements consist of:

- Secure Training Centres for vulnerable young people. Education, welfare and rehabilitation are all provided on site. At the time of writing there were only four of these centres.

- Local Authority Secure Children's Homes. These have 40 beds or less and are run by local authorities.

- Young Offender Institutions. These are prisons for people aged 15–21.

activity

INDIVIDUAL WORK 12.4

P5

Plan and design a web page, handout or poster naming and giving the main points of the laws on crime and disorder.

Restorative justice

This is a relatively new idea in the modern English justice system, though it has some parallels in traditional religious justice systems – for example in Christianity, in Islam and in the traditions of North American Indians and Maoris. In restorative justice the offender meets the victim of the crime, with the consent of both and under carefully arranged circumstances. The offender apologises for the crime and may well carry out some kind of reparation, e.g. charitable work which 'atones' for the offence. The victim in turn forgives the offender. Modern western interest in restorative justice may have been inspired by Pope John-Paul II when he went to a prison in Rome and publicly met and forgave his would-be assassin, Mehmet Ali Agca. The shooting took place in 1981 and the forgiveness in 1983.

A definition of restorative justice accepted in England is: 'Restorative justice is a process whereby parties with a stake in a specific offence collectively resolve how to deal with the aftermath of the offence and its implications for the future' (Marshall, T. (1999) *Restorative justice: an overview*. Home Office, London).

The term originated in the US in 1977 and was used by Barnett to describe principles used in mediation between victims and offenders.

Barnett, R. (1977) Restitution: a new paradigm of criminal justice. Ethics, 87(4), 279–301

Restorative justice is said to have a number of strengths. It:

■ Attends to the needs of the victim.

■ Reintegrates offenders.

■ Enables offenders to assume responsibility for their actions.

■ Recreates a working community.

■ Prevents escalation of legal processes.

Since 1990 there have been many initiatives both in Britain and elsewhere to try to develop restorative justice techniques. The three main difficulties are:

1. Getting the **criminal justice system** to provide a regular stream of suitable candidates, rather than relying on other systems involving schools, telephone hotlines, housing agencies, etc.

2. Sorting out the relationship between criminal justice and restorative justice: is restorative justice bolted on to the criminal justice system after sentencing, etc., or is it to some extent an alternative to the criminal justice system?

3. Relating the principles and ideas of restorative justice to those for criminal justice, e.g. shared moral values, etc.

These difficulties are both practical and theoretical. Restorative justice has been practised by a number of pilot schemes such as CONNECT, the Justice Research Consortium and by more well-established organisations such as the probation service and Nacro, but its effectiveness in terms of discouraging reoffending and satisfying the needs of victims is still unclear from a statistical point of view.

Figure 12.7 **Stakeholders** in restorative justice

Marshall, T. (1999) *Restorative justice: an overview*. Home Office, London

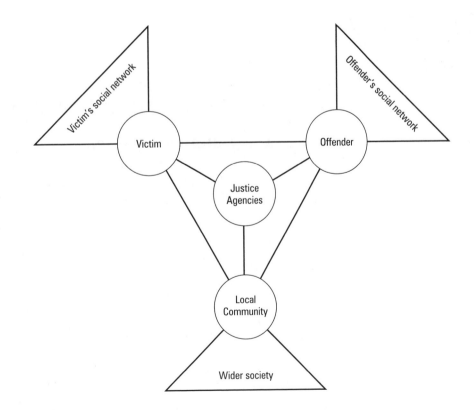

'Implementing restorative justice schemes (Crime Reduction Programme), A report on the first year', Home Office Online Report 32/04

www.homeoffice.gov.uk/rds/index.html

www.crime-reduction.gov.uk/

www.restorativejustice.org/

www.youth-justice-board.gov.uk/PractitionersPortal/PreventionAndInterventions/RestorativeJustice/

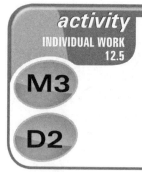

activity

INDIVIDUAL WORK 12.5

M3

D2

You work for a community action group. Prepare and give a presentation for a volunteers' training session explaining in detail the purpose and effects of two crime and disorder laws. You should also consider their advantages and drawbacks, their cost-effectiveness, their impact on offenders and victims and their possible long-term effects on the community.

activity

INDIVIDUAL WORK 12.6

P6

You work for an organisation which helps offenders. Produce a fact-sheet for your colleagues outlining clearly the usual sentences and orders that courts impose for a range of common offences.

The approaches used to reduce crime, disorder and antisocial behaviour

National Intelligence Model

The National Intelligence Model (NIM) was introduced in 2005 by Centrex, the National Centre of Police Excellence, now called the National Policing Improvement Agency. The National Intelligence Model is described as a business plan for policing. Its aim is to reorganise the gathering of intelligence on all matters relating to crime and policing, and to do it in such a way that intelligence can be processed and shared much more effectively. The purpose is to identify and predict crime patterns so that policing can be more '**intelligence-led**' and '**proactive**'. This means that instead of waiting for a report to come in and then acting on it, the police can take active steps to disrupt and prevent crime before it happens. The approach brings crime prevention and crime detection closer together. Other aims linked to the NIM are developing people's skills, managing information sources (both human and electronic), devising and spreading more advanced techniques of '**tasking** and coordination' (solving problems and working with others) and more effective neighbourhood policing. The overall aim is for the police to know much more than before about what is going on, and to be able to act on that knowledge much more effectively.

case study 12.9 — NIM assets

- Knowledge assets – Knowing the business of policing and understanding law, policy and guidance …;

- System assets – Having appropriate systems and structures in place, including secure environments and practices …;

- Source assets – Ensuring information is effectively gathered and managed from as many sources as possible …;

- People assets – Establishing a professional personnel structure with trained and suitably skilled staff to carry out the required functions within the model ….

Source: Guidance on The National Intelligence Model © ACPO Centrex 2005

activity
INDIVIDUAL WORK

Explain in your own words, with as many examples as you can, what is meant by 'knowledge assets', 'system assets', 'source assets' and 'people assets'.

Identification of crime trends or problem areas

The Association of Chief Police Officers (ACPO) defines a **crime trend** as 'the direction or pattern that specific types or general crimes are broadly following'. To give a simple example, if the number of burglaries in Anytown was 14,807 in 2007 and 12,016 in 2008, there is a downward trend. In practice, trends may be much more complex than this, so under the NIM the police use sophisticated computer modelling techniques called crime pattern analysis. For this to be possible all forces have to use the same methods, headings, etc. when inputting crime information, so that the information gathered by Force X is compatible with that collected by Force Y. Modern criminals are mobile, and do not confine their activities to one area. This is why it was necessary, before NIM got underway, to set up the National Crime Recording Standard in 2002. As it says in Guidance on the National Intelligence Model 2005 (page 55):

> Inaccurate information such as incorrect postcodes, non adherence to national crime recording standards and limited or incorrect detail regarding stolen property will lead to the development of imprecise intelligence products.

Equally (page 107):

> In order for the National Intelligence Model to function effectively at all levels, chief officers must ensure that there is consistency and compatibility of records and data sets. Forces will have in place the National Crime Recording Standard, and a standardised intelligence recording system as recommended by the Association of Chief Police Officers.

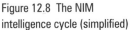

Figure 12.8 The NIM intelligence cycle (simplified)

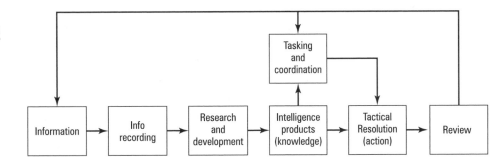

Targeting of prolific and priority offenders

Studies of repeat victimisation have highlighted the importance of catching prolific offenders, who may carry out hundreds of, say, burglaries in one year. Priority offenders are people who must be caught quickly – for example because they are highly dangerous and may offend again. The NIM says (page 124):

> Collecting as much information as possible about the activities of priority and prolific offenders enables offender profiling, improves tasking and enhances the effectiveness of analytical products.

According to the NIM such people, when caught, should be fully interviewed as they are valuable sources of intelligence which could be used in catching similar offenders. They can also be interviewed later on, when they are in prison. What is learnt about their methods, motivation and psychology adds up to a modus operandi (method of working) which may be personal but which may also be shared by other criminals of their type. An understanding and identification of MOs from stored information on crimes by offenders who have not yet been identified provides valuable information which may enable them to be caught by intelligence-led policing.

Tasking and coordination to encourage problem sharing

Tasking means setting somebody a job to do, but not telling them how to do it. Normally the best policing, like the best military work, comes when commanders have well-trained subordinates who can be given responsibility, told what they have to do and why, and then be allowed to get on with it (with monitoring carried out in a way that does not hamper their freedom of action).

Unit 13, page 149

Coordination means working with others, or in communication with others, so that actions can happen at the right time and in the right order, and be carried out at a speed which will disrupt the activities of criminals.

Coordination for the police often involves working with neighbouring forces. But increasingly it also involves working with different agencies, as happens in neighbourhood policing, where **Basic Command Units** work with community support officers, schools and local community groups, or where Crime and Disorder Reduction Partnerships involve the police, the fire and rescue service, local authorities, housing associations, voluntary organisations and so on. Here the police have to be able to share their problems and coordinate with their partners. As it says on page 139 of the NIM:

> Local forces and BCUs must ensure access to other law enforcement agencies, government regulated organisations, business and company data. This should be achieved centrally through agreed gateways and authority protocols. Locally, access to external data can be achieved through CDRP agreements, particularly in planning preventative measures.

Creating problem-solving policing initiatives

This is done by profiling areas where there is a particular crime problem. The profiling involves identifying all of the opportunities and security weakness which put the area under threat. As NIM says on page 91:

> A rigorous assessment of these factors will inform crime reduction initiatives and highlight the most appropriate agencies or departments to address the issue.

The development of the initiative follows the path shown by arrows in Figure 12.8. The profile of the area where crime is a problem is the 'intelligence product'. 'Tasking' involves deciding what to do about it and making mission statements (saying what needs doing and why) which the teams on the ground can then act upon ('tactical resolution').

Safer communities and multi-agency partnerships

For many years there has been a political movement in Britain towards developing communities and giving them more of a say in their own affairs. This is because 'community' in the old sense has declined, and the population moves around more than it used to. Crime benefited from the lack of community as people stopped 'looking out for' their neighbours; antisocial behaviour increased because people felt unwilling or unable to tackle antisocial people on their own, for fear of getting abused or even attacked. Increased diversity, both ethnic and cultural, brought mistrust which showed itself eventually in inner-city disturbances in the late 1990s and early 2000s in places such as Oldham and Bradford. There were problems with so-called 'sink estates' where a cycle of petty crime and social disadvantage made life a misery for the inhabitants. Attempts by individuals to take the law into their own hands (e.g. the farmer Tony Martin in Norfolk who shot and killed a teenage burglar in 1999) caused massive publicity and made it clear that the government should keep a guiding hand on community safety. These and other issues have led to large-scale investment and development in community schemes designed to reduce crime and improve the quality of local life. These developments have been mainly overseen by the Home Office and the Department for Communities and Local Government, both of which have plenty of information about them (and useful links) on their websites.

www.homeoffice.gov.uk/

www.homeoffice.gov.uk/rds/

www.communities.gov.uk/

www.crimereduction.gov.uk/

www.communitysafety.gov.uk/toolkits/vc00.htm

www.nacro.org.uk

> **remember**
>
> There are lots of strategies and initiatives of this type around. Many are linked to local authorities, and information can be obtained about them from your council offices, on local authority websites and on the national websites listed in the information point above.

'Safer communities' is the name of a government-run scheme. Multi-agency partnerships are groups of public services, private organisations and voluntary services working together, usually under some kind of formal arrangement. Often they are linked to, and funded by, local government. A partnership usually has a name, holds meetings, carries out projects and initiatives and so on. Many of them produce annual reports and publish plans for the future.

Strategies and initiatives (to reduce fear of crime, improve community safety, prevent crime, reduce crime)

A strategy is a long-term plan. An initiative is a new project, scheme or idea – usually for tackling a social problem of some sort.

Some of these strategies and initiatives are outlined below.

Neighbourhood policing

Neighbourhood policing, the policing of local areas such as suburbs, estates and villages, changed with the passing of the Police Reform Act 2002. This was because the public felt that local needs were being ignored due to the pressure on the police of serious crime, and many people were complaining that there was not enough visible police presence on the streets. The Act introduced Police Community Support Officers (see below).

Neighbourhood policing is organised into groups called Basic Command Units (BCUs). They are a combination of members of what is sometimes called the 'police extended family', which includes not just police officers and PCSOs (police community support officers) but also special constables, civilian police employees and even traffic wardens. BCUs are typically split into a number of smaller areas, called neighbourhoods.

The work of neighbourhood policing involves a range of partnership activities of varying levels of formality. It is also intelligence-led, and is part of the National Intelligence Model.

Table 12.10 Example of neighbourhood policing organisation

Neighbourhood	Population	Inspector	Neighbourhood Action Group	Sgt	NSO*	PC	PCSO	Wardens
Nerdly	19,000	1	A	1	2	4	1	3
Anytown Centre	N/K		B	1	1	2	0	0
Toffbury/Geekton	21,000		C		1	2	1	0
Loamshire North	8,000		D	1	1	1	0	0
Loamshire South	13,000		E			1	0	0

*NSO = Neighbourhood Specialist Officer (often a police constable)[/footnote]

The aim of neighbourhood policing is both to reassure the public and obtain information which might lead to the reduction or detection of crime. Neighbourhood Specialist Officers have to be approachable, easy to talk to and have the well-being of the community at heart, as the following extract shows.

case study 12.10 — Neighbourhood Specialist Officers

Neighbourhood Specialist Officer for Deepcut, Mytchett, Heatherside and St Pauls, PC Michaela Canning has been making a big impact since she took up the post over four months ago.

PC Canning's open and friendly approach has gone down well amongst local residents and she has built up great trust with the local youngsters. PC Canning explains: 'I got a call late one evening from a local teenager who was worried about a friend taking drugs and he didn't know what to do about it or who to talk to. I went round to visit the teenager's friend to make sure she was OK and offered her advice and support. This is just one incident where I was able to help and there have been many more like this. People are starting to trust me and look on me as a friend and I feel honoured. When I'm out on the beat I often have little children running over to me to say hello and find out what all my equipment does. I am always very happy to stop and chat with them.'

Source: Surrey Police

activity
INDIVIDUAL WORK

With a friend, draw up an action plan for things you could do to help you develop the qualities that PC Canning shows in her work.

Link
There is more about Basic Command Units in Unit 13, page 161

Figure 12.9 Policing for the future

Neighbourhood Watch

This is an organisation which dates from the 1980s. The organisation has three main aims:

- To cut crime and the opportunities for crime.
- To help and reassure those who live in fear of crime.
- To encourage neighbourliness and closer communities.

The schemes are not started by the police: they have to be started by volunteers, though the police are keen to give encouragement and support. They receive information from the police about crime risks and development in their area through a computerised message system called Ringmaster. The role of Neighbourhood Watch is:

- Identifying issues of local concern.
- Becoming involved in community problem solving, agreeing regularly which problems to target and what actions to take.
- Getting involved in crime and disorder and antisocial behaviour prevention initiatives.
- Providing volunteer administrators/coordinators who assist paid Neighbourhood Watch staff to effectively run Neighbourhood Watch.
- Monitoring and reporting on Antisocial Behaviour.

Neighbourhood Watch Purpose Statement, ACPO, www.acpo.police.uk/
(A must-see website!)

Safer community initiatives

'Safer communities' is an initiative launched by the Home Office in 2004. It received £20 million to begin with to support the 376 Crime and Disorder Reduction Partnerships (CDRPs) which were set up under the Crime and Disorder Act 1998. The initiative is a 'framework' to supply money where it is needed so that CDRPs can organise themselves properly (drawing up action plans and strategies) and carry out full audits of what they achieve. The money is given out by Regional Crime Reduction Teams (one for each of the nine regions) which consult with the CDRPs and assess their needs.

Link   See page 126 below

Crime reduction and prevention initiatives (implementation, funding, evaluation)

Crime reduction and prevention initiatives come mainly from:

- The Home Office.
- The Department for Communities and Local Government.
- Some other government departments such as the Department for Transport and the Treasury.
- The police themselves.
- Local authorities.
- Volunteer groups or community organisations.

Some initiatives, such as those from the Home Office and the police, are targeted only at crime. Other initiatives, such as those that come from the Department for Communities and Local Government, join crime up with other social problems such as inequality, ethnic tension, poor environment and so on.

Local strategic partnerships and other initiatives linked to the Department of Communities and Local Government also work towards creating 'cohesive' and 'sustainable' communities.

remember

You should consult your local police for the latest crime reduction initiatives. Things are changing quickly in this field!

www.communities.gov.uk/ **(There is a huge range of initiatives on this site, all to do with building communities.)**

Implementation

Statutory initiatives are included in new laws and the implementation (i.e. putting into practice) of the initiatives is also organised by the government, who draw up a timetable and pass laws or **regulations** saying when the initiatives have to start. The more detailed planning, tasking and implementation is carried out by organisations such as the police, probation officers, social workers and others who actually work with offenders or in crime reduction.

Funding

Funding, the supply of money needed to start the initiative and keep it going, usually comes from central or local government or a mixture of the two. In some cases local industry and other interested groups such as Rotary Clubs may give some added financial support. Central government money comes mainly from national tax – income taxes, VAT, business taxes and customs and excise duties. Local government money comes mainly from council tax. Police money – whether from local or national government – is channelled through police authorities, local bodies made up mainly of elected councillors who set police budgets and priorities and therefore have a major role in deciding how and where police money is spent.

Non-police initiatives such as safe houses for abused people usually get money from the local authority. Organisations such as Childline, which are charities, get money from a range of sources including charitable donations from other organisations or members of the public.

Evaluation

The use of money and getting value for money are reviewed by the organisations which spend the money (they have to keep accounts and make them public). It is also inspected by bodies such as the **Audit Commission** to make sure that money is being

> **remember**
>
> See the annual reports of your local police force for more information on how the police spend money and evaluate their performance.

well spent and in the public interest. In the case of crime reduction, statistics are gathered about crime rates, and there are consultations with the public through forums and focus groups. In addition, police authorities and other bodies evaluate spending against results to ensure that local people, as well as the nation as a whole, are getting value for money.

Community action teams

'Community action team' can mean different things. In Cardiff, for example, a community action team is an organisation which draws up and then works towards a long-term community action plan, which should last at least 10 years. The team should have goals which include: business and jobs, education and training, environment, health and well-being, community activities and community safety.

---

i www.cardiff.gov.uk/

In the Nottingham area community action teams consist of civilians who are concerned about crime, driving, street-cleaning, vandalism, road signs, waste recycling and planning applications. They work with the police and local councillors.

In South Cambridgeshire a community action team is a group of police officers who tackle crime within particular communities. The work they do is neighbourhood policing and includes specialised knowledge of types of crime prevalent in that community, e.g. to do with horses and equestrianism.

Community action groups

As with community action teams, there are many kinds of community action group.

Community Action Groups Oxfordshire is a network of organisations concerned with recycling waste. They are made up of concerned members of the public and are supported by a number of local authorities. Skelmanthorpe Community Action Group in Yorkshire is a citizens' pressure group which lobbies local councils about planning, building and other issues which have a bearing on the long-term future of the community. Winchester Area Community Action is a group which runs an advice centre dealing with issues ranging from transport and volunteering to legal help and rape and sexual abuse counselling. Groups are slightly different from teams in that they tend to be formed by members of the public and created by the communities they serve rather than services, local governments and other official organisations. But the distinction is not clear cut.

Public and community involvement

There is plenty of public and community involvement in all sorts of groups working to reduce crime, disorder and antisocial behaviour. The best way to research this is to talk to your local council, collect their leaflets on community groups or visit their website.

Police community support officers (PCSOs)

See Unit 16, page 288

Community wardens

Community wardens can be appointed under the 'neighbourhood renewal' schemes which are run through the Department of Communities and Local Government. Though uniformed they have no powers of arrest and aim to present an image which is different from that of the police. They are a 'help point' for intimidating and antisocial behaviour, especially by children and young people.

Partnerships (Crime and Disorder Reduction Partnerships (CDRPs) and Community Safety Partnerships (CSPs))

These organisations are essentially the same thing, and were set up by the Crime and Disorder Act 1998, Sections 6, 7 and 8 (headed 'Crime and disorder strategies'). There are 367 of them in England and Wales. They are part of the 'Safer Community' initiatives mentioned on page 123. They are organised as in Figure 12.10.

www.opsi.gov.uk/

www.youth-justice-board.gov.uk/

Under the Crime and Disorder Act 1998 membership of these partnerships must include the local authority, the police, the probation service and the local health authority. Others are included by special orders of the Home Secretary, or by the strategic group running the partnership. The partnership has to review levels and patterns of crime in the area, analyse the results, publish a report on the analysis and collect local opinion on the crime problem. They then have to formulate a strategy with agreed objectives and long- and short-term targets for crime and disorder reduction. Developments must be monitored and strategies and targets modified where appropriate.

Charities (e.g. Nacro)

Nacro is a charity with a very long history, going back over 200 years. In its present form it was set up in 1965 as the National Association of the Care and Resettlement of Offenders. It is a pressure group and was originally set up to criticise government policy. Having grown over the years to an organisation with an annual turnover of close to £60 million, it is now more likely to work in partnership with the government and other agencies in educating, employing, resettling and housing ex-prisoners, and in setting up and running community-based projects for young offenders. Some of its work is linked to probation work and includes **intensive supervision and surveillance programmes** (ISSPs) for young offenders who have just missed having a custodial sentence. Nacro also runs mediation and reparation schemes, and is interested in restorative justice. It also works in the fields of combating racial discrimination, and organising care and treatment for ex-offenders with mental health problems.

Figure 12.10 Partnerships

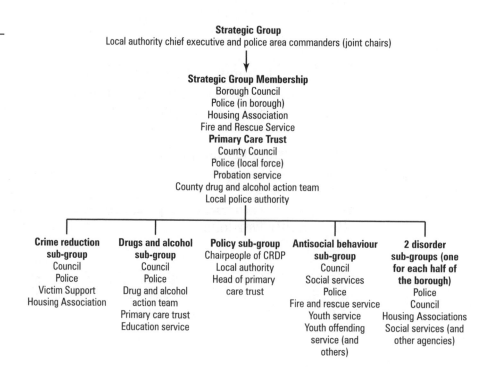

www.nacro.org.uk/ A very useful site!

Criminal justice agencies

These are the organisations, mainly statutory and official, which apply the law and deal with offenders.

Prisons

Prisons are places where offenders, mainly adult, are kept in secure custody. There are over 139 prisons in England and Wales, 16 in Scotland, five in Northern Ireland and one each in the Isle of Man, Jersey and Guernsey. The most common reasons why people are in prison are for drug offences, theft and handling, and crime against the person. In July 2007 there were nearly 80,000 prisoners in custody in Britain: over 75,000 men and over 4,000 women.

Together with the National Probation Service, prisons have recently moved from Home Office control to the Ministry of Justice. They are run by the National Offender Management Service (NOMS). The aims of prisons are those of NOMS itself: to protect the public, reduce reoffending, give the opportunity for lawbreakers to lead 'law-abiding, productive and healthy lives', and to treat offenders fairly and with decency.

The great majority of prisons are run by Her Majesty's Prison Service, but around 11 are privately run.

www.hmprisonservice.gov.uk

Courts

See Unit 17, pages 344–346

Crown Prosecution Service

See Unit 17, page 340

Youth Justice Board

The **Youth Justice Board** (YJB) is an 'executive non-departmental public body'; in other words it is set up by the government, is statutory because it is set up by law (in this case the Crime and Disorder Act 1998), but is fairly independent, despite being under the overall control of the Ministry of Justice. The aims of the YJB are:

- 'preventing crime and the fear of crime;
- identifying and dealing with young offenders;
- reducing re-offending'.

Source: Crime Reduction website

The YJB was set up to develop a youth justice system in England and Wales. It was tasked with developing community penalties which would be a meaningful and constructive alternative to custody (which is expensive and has a high rate of reoffending with young prisoners). It is keen to work with other agencies and has 'core principles' of leadership, partnership, teamwork, openness, respect and trust. The YJB concerns itself with such matters as accommodation and resettlement, custody and alternatives to custody, education, training, employment, crime prevention, research and work with victims.

Youth offending teams and their key members

Youth offending teams (YOTs) are a good example of how partnerships are used to tackle crime.

case study 12.11 — Youth Offending Teams

There is a YOT in every local authority in England and Wales. They are made up of representatives from the police, probation service, social services, health, education, drugs and alcohol misuse and housing officers. Each YOT is managed by a YOT manager who is responsible for co-ordinating the work of the youth justice services.

Because the YOT incorporates representatives from a wide range of services, it can respond to the needs of young offenders in a comprehensive way. The YOT identifies the needs of each young offender by assessing them with a national assessment. It identifies the specific problems that make the young person offend as well as measuring the risk they pose to others. This enables the YOT to identify suitable programmes to address the needs of the young person with the intention of preventing further offending.

Source: YJB

activity
INDIVIDUAL WORK

Outline the various ways in which justice for young offenders is different from justice for adult offenders. Explain each difference that you identify.

remember

YOTs provide pre-sentence reports for young offenders, advising courts on the best ways to deal with them.

YOTs liaise with their partner agencies and also with the courts to ensure that the youth court and Crown Court cases involving young people are supplied with all of the information they need about sentencing and facilities overseen by the YOT.

Police

YOT liaison with the police is close. The Youth Offending Team typically contact the local police each morning to find out if any young people are in custody and are at risk of custodial remand. It is normally in the interests of the young people and the police that young people are not kept in police custody or, worse still, sent to a remand prison.

Probation service

The probation service provides members to YOTs and supplies information to youth offending teams by giving them access to their databases on young offenders. The service works with the team and supervises sentencing and reparation. Inspectors' reports on YOTs appear on the HM Inspectorate of Probation website.

http://inspectorates.homeoffice.gov.uk/hmiprobation/recent-reports.html/

Social services

Social services have an important role in safeguarding young people who are referred to a YOT. They carry out assessments and reviews, and make sure that the diversity of offenders is taken into account.

Education service

The education service:

- Assesses children with special educational needs.
- Promotes good behaviour, attendance at school and educational achievement.
- Reintegrates excluded children into mainstream education.
- Supports the young people's further education, training and employment.
- Keeps records of achievement.

There is close liaison between YOTs and educational establishments.

Health services

The health service has a major role in:

- Identifying possible physical and mental health problems.
- Making appropriate referrals.
- Carrying out specialist assessments.
- Discouraging substance misuse.
- Recording changes in young offenders' health.

The work that YOTs do is complex and, of course, not always successful. The best way of getting further information, apart from meeting the people who work in YOTs, is to read about them on the internet – especially in their inspection reports.

www.probation.homeoffice.gov.uk/ (This url may change for more recent reports as the National Probation Service, and the Youth Justice Board, is now part of the Ministry of Justice, not the Home Office.)

www.justice.gov.uk

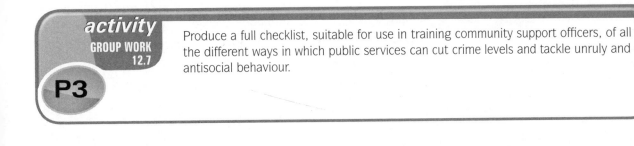

activity

GROUP WORK 12.7

P3

Produce a full checklist, suitable for use in training community support officers, of all the different ways in which public services can cut crime levels and tackle unruly and antisocial behaviour.

activity

INDIVIDUAL WORK 12.8

M2

D1

Write a report investigating how local public services work to bring down crime, disorder and antisocial behaviour. Having examined how the different plans, systems and methods work, choose one of them and assess its success in achieving what it sets out to do.

Your report should be suitable for use by an organisation which trains community support officers.

Progress Check

1. Outline briefly three theories of crime. Explain why criminologists and the police are now most interested in opportunity theories.

2. Are people to blame for the crimes they commit? Give arguments for and against.

3. Do the media encourage or discourage crime? What is your view and why?

4. Outline the costs of crime:

    (a) to the victim and

    (b) to the rest of society.

5. Why do you think there is a difference between real and perceived crime figures?

6. How do the police, the probation service and social services help or protect victims of crime?

7. What is the difference between the Victim's Charter and the Code of Practice for Victims of Crime?

8. State four ways in which the police can deal with 'repeat victimisation'.

9. Think of as many ways as you can in which people can increase their personal safety.

10. What is the difference between sentences and orders?

11. State four ways of dealing with young offenders under the Crime and Disorder Act 1998.

12. What is the standard scale of fines?

13. Under what four circumstances are custodial sentences commonly given?

14. What are the advantages and disadvantages of restorative justice?

15. Explain the importance of the National Intelligence Model in the fight against crime.

16. Describe the organisation of neighbourhood policing.

17. Who would you expect to find in a community safety partnership?

18. What does a youth offending team do?

UNIT 13

Command and Control in the Uniformed Public Services

This unit covers:

- How the principles of rank, responsibility and the chain of command relate to the command structures of the uniformed public services
- The skills and personal qualities required for command and control
- How an individual can exercise command and control
- Demonstrating command and control skills through command task activities

Unit 13 introduces the concepts of command and control and shows how they operate in the uniformed services.

The unit begins by examining the rank structures in a range of uniformed services. It shows what the ranks mean and how rank is reflected in people's duties and responsibilities. The way ranks fit into an overall chain of command, and how this chain ties in with the government is also examined.

The second part of the unit deals with the personal skills and qualities needed for effective command and control. You will learn how to motivate people and develop your authority.

The third part of the unit outlines techniques and principles used in effective command and control. These techniques include planning, briefing, monitoring and other ways of ensuring that a task is done to the best of everyone's ability.

Finally you will carry out your own command and control tasks, using a range of skills in a number of testing situations.

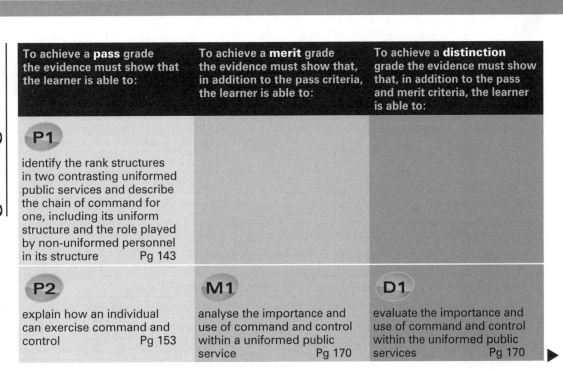

grading criteria	To achieve a **pass** grade the evidence must show that the learner is able to:	To achieve a **merit** grade the evidence must show that, in addition to the pass criteria, the learner is able to:	To achieve a **distinction** grade the evidence must show that, in addition to the pass and merit criteria, the learner is able to:
	P1 identify the rank structures in two contrasting uniformed public services and describe the chain of command for one, including its uniform structure and the role played by non-uniformed personnel in its structure Pg 143		
	P2 explain how an individual can exercise command and control Pg 153	**M1** analyse the importance and use of command and control within a uniformed public service Pg 170	**D1** evaluate the importance and use of command and control within the uniformed public services Pg 170

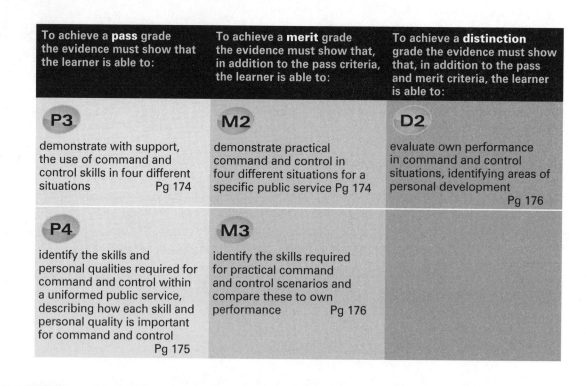

To achieve a **pass** grade the evidence must show that the learner is able to:	To achieve a **merit** grade the evidence must show that, in addition to the pass criteria, the learner is able to:	To achieve a **distinction** grade the evidence must show that, in addition to the pass and merit criteria, the learner is able to:
P3 demonstrate with support, the use of command and control skills in four different situations Pg 174	**M2** demonstrate practical command and control in four different situations for a specific public service Pg 174	**D2** evaluate own performance in command and control situations, identifying areas of personal development Pg 176
P4 identify the skills and personal qualities required for command and control within a uniformed public service, describing how each skill and personal quality is important for command and control Pg 175	**M3** identify the skills required for practical command and control scenarios and compare these to own performance Pg 176	

How the principles of rank, responsibility and the chain of command relate to the command structures of the uniformed public services

Rank is a system of levels of power or authority in an organisation. The word 'rank' is defined as: 'An official position or grade: the rank of sergeant'. It is a way of ordering and labelling people according to their responsibilities and their power to make decisions.

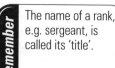

The name of a rank, e.g. sergeant, is called its 'title'.

Rank is always based on a **hierarchy**, a sort of ladder of increasing responsibility and authority. Higher ranks have different roles and responsibilities from lower ranks, roughly along the lines indicated in Table 13.1.

Table 13.1 Differences between ranks

Higher ranks ('senior')	Lower ranks ('junior')
Fewer members	More people in these ranks
Make decisions affecting large numbers of people	Make decisions affecting small numbers of people, or no decisions affecting other people at all
Give commands	Receive commands
Receive feedback	Give feedback
Control others	Are controlled by others
Make plans and set tasks	Implement plans and carry out tasks
Lead teams	Belong to teams
Impose discipline	Receive discipline
Give permission	Ask permission
Have high status and visibility in an organisation	Have lower status and less visibility in an organisation
Leadership and management roles	Operative, hands-on roles
Well paid with better conditions of service	Less well paid with worse conditions of service

Rank, or command, structures are a feature of the uniformed public services, but there are significant differences between the armed forces and the civilian uniformed public services. Civilian non-uniformed public services (such as colleges, schools or the civil service) also have rank structures of a sort, but these structures are usually organised in a way which makes the differences in rank much less obvious than they are in the armed forces.

Rank structures

Rank structures are the ways in which people of different rank are organised within a uniformed service. The structures can be represented diagrammatically in two ways:

- As a list (i.e. hierarchy), with the 'top' ranks at one end of the list and the 'bottom' ranks at the other.
- As a tree diagram (organogram) which outlines more clearly the working relationships between people of different rank within an organisation.

Identifying which uniformed public services have a rank structure

Basically, all uniformed services have a rank structure of some sort, but the word 'rank' is more popular in the armed forces than in the civilian uniformed services. In 2004 the fire and rescue service, which up until then had a rank structure, changed to a **role structure** in order to give the whole service a more civilian, family-friendly and community-based image.

Rank structures in the uniformed public services are given in the two case studies below.

www.homeoffice.gov.uk (police, Border and Immigration agency)

www.justice.gov.uk (prison and probation services and the courts)

www.communities.gov.uk (fire and rescue service)

www.royal-navy.mod.uk (Royal Navy)

www.raf.mod.uk (RAF)

www.army.mod.uk (army)

www.mod.uk (all the armed forces)

www.mcga.gov.uk (Maritime and Coastguard Agency)

www.londonambulance.nhs.uk (useful ambulance site)

www.hmrc.gov.uk (HM Revenue and Customs)

www.hmprisonservice.gov.uk (prison service)

Police, RAF

Right from the time it was set up by Sir Robert Peel in 1829 the police service has been seen as a civilian organisation. Their uniform was designed from the start not to look military, and until recent years the British police were almost unique in being unarmed. The only rank with a military-sounding title is that of Sergeant. The others, such as Superintendent and Inspector, suggest watching and patrolling rather than direct action, and have a distinctly civilian sound.

The Royal Air Force has more military-sounding titles (e.g. Flight Lieutenant, Wing Commander) but with references to the 'air' to distinguish officer ranks from their near (but not exact) equivalents in the army.

remember

Civilian employees of uniformed public services are not part of the service rank structure, though they have role and management structures of their own.

case study 13.1

Military rank structures

Table 13.2 Military rank structures

NATO Code	RN	Army and Royal Marines	Air Force
OF-10	Admiral of the Fleet	Field Marshal	Marshal of the Royal Air Force
OF-9	Admiral	General	Air Chief Marshal
OF-8	Vice-Admiral	Lieutenant-General	Air Marshal
OF-7	Rear Admiral	Major-General	Air Vice-Marshal
OF-6	Commodore	Brigadier	Air Commodore
OF-5	Captain	Colonel	Group Captain
OF-4	Commander	Lieutenant-Colonel	Wing Commander
OF-3	Lieutenant-Commander	Major	Squadron Leader
OF-2	Lieutenant	Captain	Flight Lieutenant
OF-1	Sub-Lieutenant (but junior to military and air force ranks)	Lieutenant	Flying Officer
	Midshipman (but junior to army and air force ranks)	Second Lieutenant	Pilot Officer Acting Pilot Officer (but junior to Second Lieutenant)
OR-9	Warrant Officer	Warrant Officer Class I	Warrant Officer Master Aircrew
OR-8		Warrant Officer Class 2	
OR-7	Chief Petty Officer	Colour Sergeant, RM	Flight Sergeant Chief Technician
OR-6 OR-5	Petty Officer	Sergeant	Sergeant
OR-4	Leading Rate (but junior to army ranks of corporal and bombardier)	Corporal Bombardier	Corporal
OR-3		Lance Corporal Lance Bombardier	
OR-2 OR-1	Able Rate Rating	Private Marine	Junior Technician Senior aircraftman/woman Leading aircraftman/woman Aircraftman/woman

Source: Annex B, Armed Forces Act 2006

activity
GROUP WORK

1. Why is there a NATO code on the left-hand side of the table?
2. Where is the 'glass ceiling' between officers and **non-commissioned** officers (NCOs)?

case study 13.2

Civilian rank structures

Table 13.3 Civilian role/rank structures (ascending order – junior roles at top)

Ambulance	**Fire and Rescue**
(Role structures)	(Role structures)
Ambulance care assistants	Firefighter
Ambulance technicians	Crew Manager
Call handlers	Watch Manager
Emergency care practitioners	Station Manager
Emergency medical dispatchers	Group Manager
Paramedics	Area Manager
Patient transport services controllers	Brigade Manager
Police	**Prison Service**
(Rank structures)	(Rank structures)
Constable	Prison auxiliary
Sergeant	Assistant storeman
Inspector	Storeman
Chief Inspector	Night patrol
Superintendent	Operational support grade
Chief Superintendent	Prison officer
Assistant Chief Constable	Senior officer
Deputy Chief Constable	Principal officer
Chief Constable	Manager G
Ranks above Chief Superintendent in the Metropolitan Police	Manager F
	Manager E
Commander	Senior manager D
Deputy Assistant Commissioner	Senior manager C
Assistant Commissioner	Senior manager B
Deputy Commissioner	Senior manager A
Commissioner	
HM Revenue and Customs	**Maritime and Coastguard Agency**
(Role structures)	(Role structures)
Administrative Assistant	Station Officer
Assistant Officer	Coastguard Watch Assistant
Officer	Coastguard Watch Officer
Higher Officer	Sector Manager
Senior Officer	
Graduate trainee	
Grade 7	
Grade 6	

activity
GROUP WORK

Rank structures in civilian uniformed services are often arranged in ascending order of importance. Why do you think this might be?

Similarities and differences between public services

Table 13.4 Public services, similarities and differences

Similarities	Differences
All have rank or role structures which also serve as chains of command	Chains of command are more formal and traditional in the armed forces than in the civilian uniformed services
The idea of 'command' exists in all uniformed services, and is needed for them to be disciplined and effective	Command is often described as 'leadership' or 'management' in the civilian public services, reflecting more democratic leadership styles
Rank badges are worn on the shoulders so that rank can be recognised at a glance by other members of the service. Rank badges in the armed forces are all conspicuous (chevrons/stripes, etc.) and can be seen from a distance	Police wear rank badges; constables and sergeants also have numbers. Fire service have rank badges (changed since 2004). Prison officers have compulsory numbering system but no compulsory rank badges

Rank badges

Both the police and the army have similar rank badges but they have different titles and mean different things. The best way to understand the badges of rank in the army, the police or any other public service which has them, is to study the examples given on official websites.

www.firesafe.org.uk/html/fire&resc/ranks.htm#index

www.royal-navy.mod.uk/

www.army.mod.uk/

www.met.police.uk/

www.hmprisonservice.gov.uk/

Prison Service Order 8805, Identification of Prison Staff when on duty

Badges of rank (e.g. identifying a badge and relating it to a title)

In a uniformed public service which has a rank structure it is essential to be able to recognise people of different rank. This is because people who 'take **precedence**' (have a higher rank) have the **authority** to command a person of lower rank. If they do not have a higher rank, they have no such authority.

It would be a recipe for confusion or worse in an organisation such as the army if people did not know whose commands to obey. It would be equally chaotic if people gave commands without knowing the rank of the people they were giving commands to. The recognition of badges of rank, and the constant acknowledgement of rank through saluting and other gestures, acts as a permanent reminder of the importance of rank.

In fact, badges of rank have an important training function. Raw recruits who may not have been used to discipline before joining the army learn the habit of prompt and willing obedience through the repeated ritual of salutes, and repeatedly following orders, for example in drill and many other activities. Badges of higher rank are also symbolic in that they can be seen as a reward for good work. They have a motivating effect and encourage subordinates to see the wearer of the rank badge as a role model.

Responsibilities

The word 'responsibilities' can refer to:

1. The job or the work that a person is supposed to do.

2. The way they are supposed to do it.

The meaning used in this section is that shown in point 1. In the armed forces, rank is linked to the number of people or the size of the group that the person commands. A person of higher rank commands more people, or a bigger group of people.

remember

Military rank structures are a longstanding British tradition. But the rank structures of some civilian uniformed public services are changing because they are seen as less appropriate for a diverse, changing society, and a deterrent to applicants from minority groups.

remember

Badges of rank sometimes used to be called 'stripes'.

In the army, for example, soldiers fight in groups. These groups have different names, such as **divisions**, **brigades**, **battlegroups**, **regiments**, **battalions**, **squadrons**, **platoons**, **troops** and **sections**.

Army personnel are divided into two categories – officers and non-commissioned ranks.

The officers are sometimes called '**commissioned** officers'. They are chosen and trained from the start to be leaders and managers, and their responsibilities are mainly responsibilities of command and control. In Table 13.1 above, officers are people of the rank of second lieutenant (sometimes called 'subaltern') and above. Officers lead groups of soldiers. High-ranking commissioned officers lead large groups, such as divisions, brigades and regiments. The lower-ranking commissioned officers lead small groups such as squadrons and platoons.

Non-commissioned ranks are people in the army whose rank is lower than second lieutenant. They are chosen and trained as soldiers and begin their army careers as privates, infantry soldiers, etc. Their responsibilities at this stage are not to lead but to develop and use their warfare skills. They can be promoted up through the ranks to Warrant Officer Class I. As they get promoted they become non-commissioned officers (NCOs) such as corporals and sergeants, and take on leadership responsibilities. They can lead small groups of, say, 10 soldiers, or bigger groups when assisting commissioned officers.

It is very rare for a soldier or non-commissioned officer to become a commissioned officer. The responsibilities of the non-commissioned ranks are mainly practical; the responsibilities of officers are mainly managerial. The educational and training requirements are so different that if someone wants to become an officer, they should work towards that goal from the start.

What would normally be expected of a particular rank

Table 13.5 indicates the levels of control and command which can be expected of particular ranks in the army.

Table 13.5 Levels of control and command in the army

Rank	Control/command	Civilian equivalent
General; Lieutenant General; Major General	Can command a division (20,000)	Senior manager, chairman, chief executive
Brigadier	Can command a brigade (5000)	Managing director of company up to 10,000
Colonel; Lieutenant Colonel	Can command: an armoured battlegroup a battalion (600) a regiment (600)	Middle-senior manager of large company
Major	Can command: a company (100) a squadron (100)	Departmental head – in charge of 100–200
Captain; Lieutenant	Can command a platoon (30)	Assistant manager/team leader
Second Lieutenant	Can command a troop (16)	Team leader
Warrant Officer Class I and II	Can assist officers	Middle manager – could be responsible for up to 600
Colour Sergeant; Sergeant	Can assist officers	Supervisor-junior manager responsible for 30-200
Corporal	Can command a section (6–10)	Team leader
Lance Corporal	Can command a small team (4)	Shift leader
Private	No formal command	Skilled operative

Relationship between posts and ranks (e.g. the commander of an RAF aircraft is not necessarily the senior rank on board)

A **post** is not the same thing as a rank. A post carries specific duties and has a job description which sets out in writing what the post holder has to do – or may have to do – in the course of the job. A rank is a level of command and control and refers to leadership and management roles, not skill or ability at performing a particular job. A post often includes special responsibilities and requires special skills which come with special training and experience. Just as, in a college, your principal would not be able to teach public services as well as your own public service tutor, so in the uniformed services a person of senior rank does not claim to have the skills and abilities needed to do the work of post holders of lower rank. A lieutenant or sergeant leading a platoon would not be able to operate and fire an artillery gun as well as the lead gunner in that platoon.

Chain of command

A **chain of command** is a sequence of people or teams in rank order, organised in such a way that commands can be passed down from the highest to the lowest rank, and be acted on.

Organisations that operate within the command structure

Because uniformed services are so huge – sometimes with well over 100,000 employees – they are divided into smaller organisations which are much more manageable and adaptable and can be used to tackle the vast range of tasks which faces any uniformed service at any given time. The police, who have about 140,000 officers in England and Wales, are divided into 43 forces, and each force is divided up into departments and teams which either specialise in the type of work they do or are responsible for a geographically limited area such as a local district or community.

Figure 13.1 shows a simplified version of the chains of **command** existing in Gwent police. Only the chief constable is attached to all three of the main chains of command. The chief constable therefore has overall responsibility for what goes on in Gwent police in a way that no other person has.

The lines in a chain of command do not only show who is boss or who gives the orders. They also show paths of responsibility and accountability. They connect up the **subsidiary** organisations in a way which involves all of them in the success of the whole service. In this sense the chains of command are also chains of **control**, passing information and feedback as well as orders. They are also routes through which people and smaller organisations can absorb the **ethos** or spirit of the organisation, and share its aims and values in a wider sense.

Within the army

The army, the RAF and the Royal Navy are not identical organisations, but they tend to mirror each other. To gain detailed information about their organisation, control and command you are strongly advised to visit them, or arrange visiting speakers who will be able to give you a wealth of detail on the points you want to know about.

The army, like the RAF and the Royal Navy, has to operate in many places at once, and its organisation is designed to ensure that it is mobile and can send troops to any part of the world at reasonably short notice. Since the world is a very diverse place, the army also needs to be able to train its personnel in many different kinds of work, in different environments and among people whose attitudes and cultures vary enormously. This is only possible if the army is itself divided up into linked but distinct organisations, which can both specialise in the work they do and be able to operate in widely separated geographical areas yet without losing identity or cohesiveness in the process.

Regiment

A regiment (or a battalion, which is similar) traditionally consists of around 500–600 people, though with recent mergers some of them are currently much bigger than this.

Figure 13.1 Police command structure

Source: Gwent police

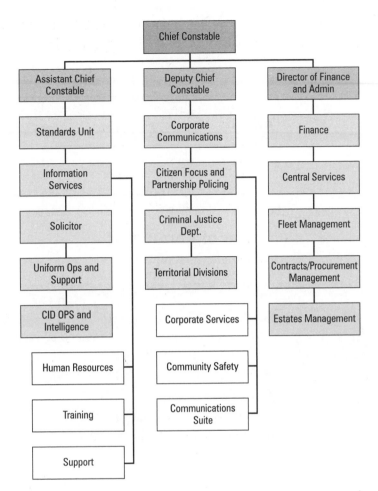

Brigade

A brigade consists of about 5000 people and is organised as shown in Figure 13.3.

Division

A division is the biggest internal organisation in the army.

The army contains five divisions:

- 1st (UK) Armoured Division and 3rd (UK) Mechanised Division. These two are fully operational.

- 2nd Division (Scotland and the north of England); 4th Division (East Midlands and south-east England); 5th Division (Wales, West Midlands and south-west England). These divisions have, at present, a command and training function.

There are two more divisional level bodies: Headquarters Northern Ireland and London District.

Figure 13.2 Organisation of a battalion and its chain of command

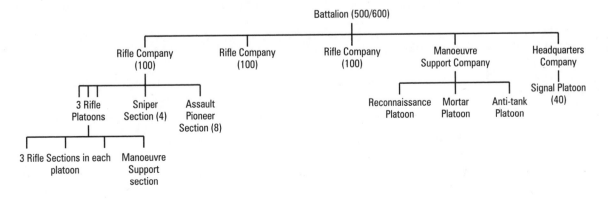

Figure 13.3 Organisation of a brigade

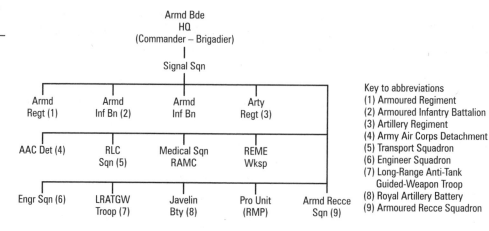

Key to abbreviations
(1) Armoured Regiment
(2) Armoured Infantry Battalion
(3) Artillery Regiment
(4) Army Air Corps Detachment
(5) Transport Squadron
(6) Engineer Squadron
(7) Long-Range Anti-Tank Guided-Weapon Troop
(8) Royal Artillery Battery
(9) Armoured Recce Squadron

case study 13.3 — One (UK) armoured division

Figure 13.4 shows one (UK) armoured division as it was in 2005. At that time it contained the following:

- Army personnel: 17,000.
- Challenger 2 MBT: 150.
- Warrior armoured fighting vehicles: 450.
- Other tracked vehicles: 1,100.
- Artillery guns: 66.
- Armoured vehicle launched bridges: 18.
- Helicopters (Army Aviation): 24.

Figure 13.4 Organisation of a division

Source: The Online Global Defence Marketplace (www.armedforces.co.uk/)

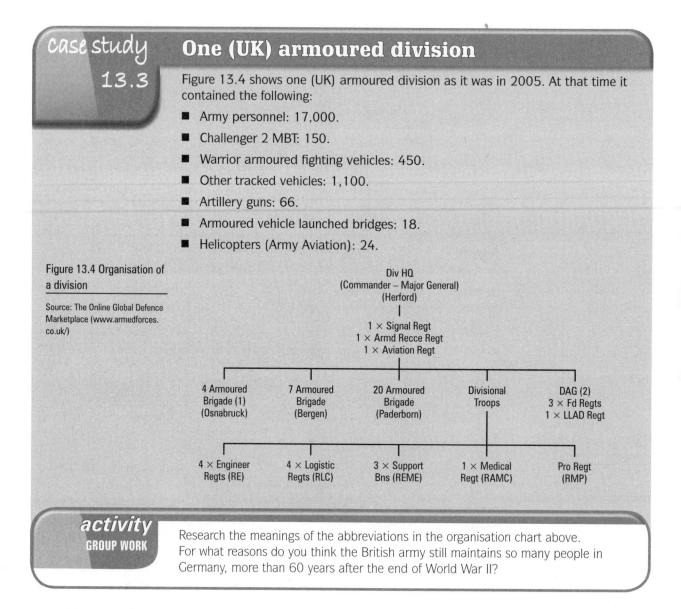

activity
GROUP WORK

Research the meanings of the abbreviations in the organisation chart above. For what reasons do you think the British army still maintains so many people in Germany, more than 60 years after the end of World War II?

'Battlegroup' is a relatively new command structure, more flexible than some others and more adaptable to modern joint or functional command techniques.

Divisions, like the other command structures or organisations in the army, are arranged in such a way that they can act flexibly. In major wars the whole division could be involved in an action, whereas in minor wars, such as the ones taking place at present, only certain battalions, regiments or other battlegroups need to be involved at any one time.

Their relative level of control (e.g. what individuals would be responsible for)

The ranks of the people in control of the different organisations in the army are given in Table 13.5 on page 137. The main principle is that the bigger the organisation the higher the rank of the person at the head of it.

These individuals have a wide range of responsibilities depending on circumstances and on the number of people and type of organisation under their command. The responsibilities include:

- Overall organisation.
- Identifying and setting objectives.
- Conveying intent (strategies and **tactics**) and making mission statements.
- Setting the 'ethos' and 'tone' of the organisation.
- Encouraging discipline and initiative among **subordinates**.
- **Monitoring** and reviewing performance.
- Effective **delegation** of tasks and responsibilities.

Twenty-first century warfare is a high-speed, high-tech activity carried out in chaotic, rapidly changing surroundings. For this reason modern military command is not the centralised and inflexible affair it sometimes was. Instead it is a system of empowering and enabling each unit to act fast, give of its best and achieve dominance over an enemy.

Control of the public services by non-uniformed organisations (e.g. Ministry of Defence, Home Office)

'Control' in this context is not the strict issuing of orders and instructions by one organisation to another. Government departments such as the Ministry of Defence and the Home Office certainly have responsibility for the armed forces and the police respectively, but the control is of a rather 'hands-off' type. The Ministry of Defence does not 'tell' the army what to do except in the broadest sense. Its job is more to set a budget for the army (in consultation with the army and with the Treasury – the government department which controls spending), agree certain targets (e.g. for staffing, training and equipment) and to ensure that the army is carrying out the broad strategic aims of the government and its partners such as NATO, the US and the EU. The Ministry of Defence is not supposed to interfere with the day-to-day running of the army or the other armed services.

The organisation of the Ministry of Defence and its relationship with the armed forces is outlined in Figure 13.5.

NB: TLB means 'Top Level Budget-holders'.

These groups (e.g. Strike Command, for the RAF) have powers to spend money on the parts of the armed forces which are their responsibility.

www.mod.uk/DefenceInternet/AboutDefence/

The relationship between the Home Office and the police is similar to that of the MOD and the armed forces. There are layers of **management**. The 'top' layer is Parliament, the Home Secretary and the Home Office Ministers, who are MPs elected by their constituency and chosen by the prime minister and advisers linked to the ruling party for

Figure 13.5 MOD and armed forces

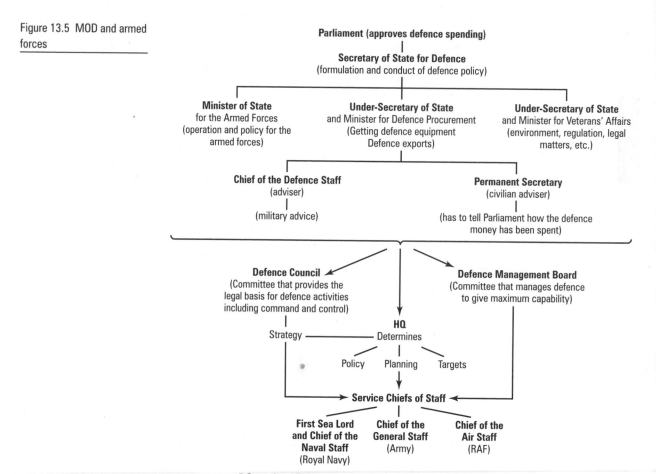

5 Operational TLBs – (Plan and manage military operations and spend the money)

those posts. The second layer is composed of senior civil servants who have substantial experience and understand nearly all there is to know about the running of the Home Office. The third layer, as far as the police are concerned, are the chief constables including the Metropolitan Police Commissioner. The top government layer is the most powerful because:

- They supply a good deal of the money needed by the police.

- They have been **democratically elected** and are part of the government. They can therefore claim to 'speak for the wishes of the people' if they want something done.

However, it would be misleading with the Home Office (as with the Ministry of Defence) to think that it simply tells the police what to do. Most of the information that politicians and civil servants have about policing comes from the police themselves. If the politicians have the money, the police have the knowhow. If the government wants the police to do something, they need to have some cooperation from the police themselves. The Home Office is not expected to command the police, but it has a political duty to control them. This means, for example, inspecting the police, setting targets, issuing Home Office Circulars (a kind of ongoing code of practice), standardising training, cooperating on strategies and new initiatives – and, of course, plenty of less formal communication between the Home Office and the police.

Note that, for the Home Office as much as for the Ministry of Defence, the 'chain of command' is not really a chain, and there is not a huge amount of 'command' in it. The Home Office aims to control the police with a light touch. This reduces any resentment that the police may feel at possible interference from above, and enables the police to be more creative and effective in their responses to new challenges. In addition the 'light touch' control protects the government against political or media accusations of being too controlling or even of trying to turn the country into a '**police state**'.

remember

Civil servants exist to carry out the work that ministers tell them to do. They are not supposed to make **policy** decisions or to show their political feelings.

remember

In major emergencies such as flooding, the emergency services' overall strategy is decided by a government committee called COBRA (Cabinet Office Briefing Room A).

Figure 13.6 Home Office and the police

		Home Secretary			
	Minister of State for Security, Counter-terrorism, Crime and Policing		Minister of State for Borders and Immigration		
Under-Secretary of State for Crime Reduction		Under-Secretary of State for Security and Counter-terrorism		Under-Secretary of State	
		Permanent Secretary			
Home Office Board					
Policing and Counter-terrorism	Criminal Justice Reform (Linked to Minstry of Justice)	Border and Immigration	Financial and Commercial	Human Resources	Performance and Reform
Strategic Centre					
Delivery Groups: 1. Office for Security and Counter-terrorism 2. Crime Reduction and Community Safety Group				Delivery Agencies 1. Criminal Records Bureau 2. Border and Immmigration agency 3. Identity and Passport Service	
Delivery Partners				Communication	
1. Counter-terrorism partners	2. NDPBs including Serious Organised Crime Agency; National Policing Improvement Agency	3. Local partnerships and police forces (communicated with through Chief Constables and Police Authorities)		Circulars e-bulletins Briefings Setting targets and priorities	

activity
GROUP WORK
13.1

P1

Produce a wall chart suitable for a careers exhibition showing the rank structures in two contrasting uniformed public services.

Then produce a handout describing the chain of command for one uniformed public service. Include the uniform structure and the role played by non-uniformed personnel in the structure of the chain of command.

The skills and personal qualities required for command and control

Everybody has the potential to command and control to some degree. We can see it in the way babies and toddlers quickly learn to control, if not command, their parents and relatives, and in the command and control elements of children's games. The development of these **skills** should therefore be approached with optimism and confidence – they are easily learnable for people who want to learn them.

Skills and qualities

Skills and qualities are not exactly the same thing. A skill is an ability which has to be learned – e.g. writing, driving or playing a musical instrument. A **quality** is an attribute or characteristic which we have naturally, but which can be developed if we want to (e.g. a sense of humour).

Technical skills

These are skills which are to do with techniques, methods, procedures and equipment. They are all about putting theory into practice. They are the kind of skills which uniformed service recruits learn in basic and later training – the kind of skills which distinguish the professional from the non-professional.

Every job, from welding to teaching, has its **technical skills**. In welding the technical skills are to do with understanding and using metal and equipment. In teaching, the technical skills are to do with things like fair assessment or organising a class so that it is fun and yet work gets done. Command and control is more similar to teaching than to welding, but the skills are still technical even though they relate to people rather than hot metal.

Technical skills used in military command and control include:

- Understanding military doctrine (British defence doctrine (BDD)).*
- Understanding the **components of fighting power.***
- Leadership.
- Motivation.
- Maintenance of morale.
- Conveying intentions.
- Encouragement.
- Admonishment.
- Management skills (not leadership, but knowing how to make the best use of resources).
- Training, mentoring and skills development.
- Knowing when to act and when not to.
- Knowing how to delegate responsibilities.

*These are the only technical skills in this list which are specifically military. All the rest could apply to any other kind of uniformed public-service work.

Few if any technical skills of the mechanical or technological type are needed in command. It is not necessary to be good at computing, for example, or to be able to mend a piece of equipment. In some services, that kind of background may be useful in gaining the approval of subordinates – which is one reason why police officers always start as constables even though they may be aiming for higher management roles. But that may change.

> **remember**
>
> Some technical skills involve handling equipment; others involve handling people.

Specialist skills

Specialist skills are skills which are only used in certain types of work and which do not have a general application. Non-specialist, generic or general skills are skills used in a wide variety of work.

Many jobs, both inside and outside the uniformed public services, involve an element of command and control, so in this sense command and control are not specialist skills.

However, officers in the armed forces and in the higher ranks of the police are different. The main element of their work is command and control. Their skills become more highly developed and specialised because they use them in demanding fields of work which are not like other kinds of work.

For such people, command and control are specialist skills because they have to fit the exact needs of:

- The service.
- The situation and tasks being carried out.

Figure 13.7 Bomb disposal uses both technical skills and command skills

- The rank and post of the person commanding and controlling.
- The people being commanded and controlled (especially in relation to their motivation and how much understanding and training they already have).

The specialist skills of others are an important factor in command and control. In a military context it is vitally important for a commanding officer to know about the specialist skills and abilities (e.g. level of training and fitness) of the people being commanded, since these can influence military planning and the likelihood of success.

Military command and control are specialised skills because they involve understanding and harnessing all of the elements of the war effort in order to have a maximum impact on the enemy. Command and control are used to bring together what military planners call the 'components of fighting power' (see Figure 13.8 below).

'Components of fighting power' are all the aspects of thinking and planning, of people and military hardware, which have to be brought together and made to act effectively in a military conflict or, indeed, a peacekeeping operation.

For specialist police skills, visit the following website, which states all of the **national occupational standards** (specific skills) for the police:
http://ukstandards.org.uk/default.aspx (Skills for justice)

Other specialist skills are not normally needed for command and control, except in small teams (a typical one being a surgeon's team, where the surgeon's specialist skills in particular operations are closely linked to the command and control of the team).

Personal qualities

Here is a list of personal qualities which are useful in command and control:

- A refusal to be dominated by circumstances.
- Having an open mind.
- Being able to make firm, timely decisions.
- The ability to keep calm.
- Moral and physical courage.
- Being stress free.

case study 13.4

Fighting power

Figure 13.8 The components of fighting power

Source: From *Joint Warfare Publication 0-01, British Defence Doctrine* (2nd edn), Ministry of Defence, 2001

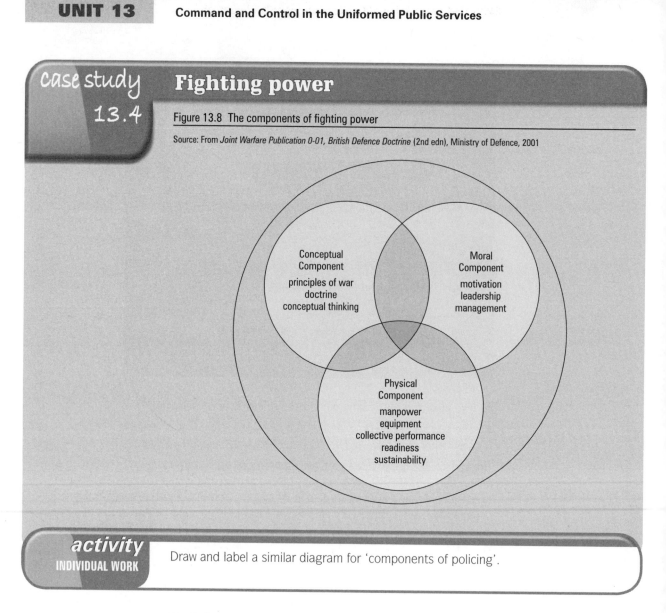

Conceptual Component
principles of war
doctrine
conceptual thinking

Moral Component
motivation
leadership
management

Physical Component
manpower
equipment
collective performance
readiness
sustainability

activity
INDIVIDUAL WORK

Draw and label a similar diagram for 'components of policing'.

- Endurance.
- Steadiness of purpose.
- The ability not to be discouraged or distracted by bad news.
- Being able to explain things clearly.
- Boldness and **audacity**.
- The ability to think in a logical, organised manner.
- A readiness to accept responsibility.
- Being able to generate trust, respect and confidence in subordinates.
- Persuasiveness.
- A sympathetic understanding of people, their strengths and weaknesses.
- The confidence to delegate responsibility and tasks to others.
- A sense of humour.
- The ability to instil discipline, cooperation and teamwork.
- Being able to apply free thought responsibly.
- Self-protection (avoid overwork, keep healthy, know how to relax and sleep well).
- Avoiding immersion in detail (leave detail to staff).

Role model

A **role model** is a person who is admired by others and who acts as a good example to them. The effect of role models on their admirers is that the admirers try to act and behave in the same way. In civilian life role models may be sportspeople, film stars, musicians or other glamorous people, and members of the public who admire them may imitate their hairstyles, clothing, the way they talk, etc. But we also meet people we admire and feel we can learn from in our ordinary lives – friends and colleagues – and they too are role models. In uniformed service life commanders and commanding officers can be role models to the people they command, setting examples and standards which their subordinates follow not because they are told to, but because they want to.

Courage

There are two kinds of courage – physical courage and **moral courage**.

Physical courage is the ability to overcome the fear of pain, hardship, injury or death and do dangerous or physically difficult things. A firefighter who enters a burning building to rescue someone shows physical courage; so does a fighter pilot, or a soldier who is being fired at by the enemy but does not run away.

Moral courage is the ability to make difficult or unpopular decisions because they are right in the long run. However, it is quite difficult to identify moral courage in practice because actions are ambiguous. What can seem brave or moral to one person may seem cowardly or immoral to another. To take a well-known political example, did the British government's decision to take part in the war in Iraq in 2002 show moral courage or moral cowardice? The moral courage argument is that Saddam Hussein was threatening the peace of the region and ill-treating his own people, therefore it was right for the West to do an unpopular and unselfish thing by moving in before the UN had finished its **WMD** inspections and getting rid of the source of the problem. The moral weakness argument was that Britain did it under pressure from the US, and that Britain was politically afraid to do anything else. Opponents of the war argued that fighting an unjust war would demoralise British forces. Whether they were right or not is too early to say. But for good command and control it is certainly important that commanders are perceived by their followers to have moral courage, for nobody wants to follow a moral coward.

> **remember**
>
> Courage is not the same thing as recklessness or fearlessness. Courage means using reason, a sense of purpose and determination to overcome fear.

Confidence

Confidence is being able to trust yourself and other people. Commanders should have confidence in:

- Their own abilities and commitment.
- The abilities and commitment of their subordinates.
- Their equipment and resources.
- Their mission, aims and objectives.
- Their understanding of the wider situation and strategies.
- Their own superior officers.
- The support of their own superior officers.

They should be able to communicate this confidence to those they command in order to raise and maintain their confidence too.

Integrity

This is a form of moral courage and also a professional code of conduct. It means being fair, honest and incorruptible. Good commanders should not show favouritism, nor should they discriminate unfairly against anybody for any reason. They should treat their own subordinates fairly, and they should treat the wider public, or the people among whom they work (e.g. in peacekeeping) fairly as well. 'Fairly' means without brutality, without discrimination and without taking bribes or accepting gifts and favours from local people.

> **remember**
>
> Integrity is one of the most important qualities in any public-service work. Without high standards of integrity no public service can operate successfully.

Determination

Determination means sticking to an aim until it has been achieved. This is important in warfare or any other difficult and long-lasting operation. Determination is a combination of physical and emotional endurance and the ability to keep the mind focused on the essentials which must be achieved. Leaders and commanders need determination:

- To achieve their aims.

- To inspire effort and raise morale among their subordinates.

Decisiveness

Decisiveness is the ability to make the best possible decisions in the most suitable time frame. In other words, if there is the need to make a decision quickly, the decision is made quickly. But if the decision will benefit from extra time and thought, a decisive person will give it that extra time and thought before making the decision.

Good command decisions have the following characteristics:

- The decisions fit the situation. They take into account relevant conditions, problems and (in war) the will and aims of the enemy.

- They are made quickly if need be. In war it is important to make and carry out decisions faster than the enemy can.

- Good decisions are not just calculations of probability; they need to be intuitive and creative yet practical.

- Effective commanders use their experience, education, intelligence, boldness, perception and character to make decisions. The decisions should come as a result of their total understanding of the situation, and not be based on some narrow formula or system.

- Good wartime decisions are unlikely to be perfect, they are simply the best available. They give a promising course of action with an acceptable degree of risk, and can be carried out before the enemy is ready.

- Decisions should be made as low down as possible on the chain of command. This means that they are based on more practical knowledge, and can be put into action more quickly, without the delay of going right up and down the chain of command.

In any emergency service work, it is important that commanders can make quick decisions – they may save lives, or prevent serious destruction. A habit of good, fast, clear decision making builds confidence and morale among subordinates.

Mental agility

This is a very important quality in a commander in the uniformed public services. The process of command is a complex one, involving the interpretation of strategic, large-scale intentions and their application to the real situation faced by a commander and the troops. In warfare the real situation is often chaotic and fast changing, so for a commander it is hard enough to understand the information coming in, let alone use it in important decision making. Mental agility is needed because commanders have to bring together huge amounts of information, understand it, reduce it to practical problems, and then devise a solution to those problems which can be communicated to the troops and acted upon.

Each stage of the command process requires different thinking skills. Some parts – for example collecting information and making sense of it – are **analytical**. Other parts – such as making mission statements, statements of intent and setting tasks – are **creative**. Military strategy and tactics are **theoretical**, based on study, knowledge and the understanding of principles of warfare. Addressing real problems here and now, using troops whose strengths, weaknesses and equipment are known (but which keep changing), is a **practical** activity. Analytical, creative, theoretical and practical thinking are all carried out by different parts of the brain, and most of us are much better at some types of thinking than others. Commanders have to be good at all four types of

Figure 13.9 The command process

Intelligence about enemy and other dangers, risks or problems

Strategic intent from government and top commanders

Activities and needs of coalition partners (or NATO, UN or EU troops)

↓

Command process begins

↓

Derive mission through analysis

↓

Identify tasks and purposes

↓

Prioritise

↓

Make mission statement
(clear, concise, proportional)

↓

Consider constraints
(e.g. resources, infrastructure, rules of engagement)

↓

Identify specific, realistic, clear objectives
(a) Physical – destroying enemy units and strongholds
(b) Functional – destroying enemy's ability to command and control

↓

Make a statement
(a) of intent – the strategic, operational or tactical aim
(b) setting tasks or assigning missions ⟶ Subordinate commands

↓

Delegate further command tasks where
possible to subordinate commands. Disseminate.
Ensure that 'tempo' (speed of decision and action) is maintained.
Monitor developments and prepare further command actions.

thinking, and they have to be able to think under pressure, because time is always short and there is a great deal at stake. In addition, modern military communication opens up wider possibilities for collecting intelligence and making decisions, but makes the time available for making decisions and issuing commands even shorter. For all of these reasons mental agility is essential for an effective commander.

Qualities instilled by a good commander

Modern command is often **decentralised**. In warfare, peacekeeping, policing or in a large-scale emergency many things are happening at once, and it is unrealistic and ineffective for commanders to try to command everything at once. Delegation, which at one time was seen as a sign of weakness, is now seen as a sign of strength. Effective delegation, which allows subordinates to command and control, is good for motivation and increases the speed and adaptability of the response. But delegation can only work if subordinates have the skills and understanding to accept the extra responsibility and act on it. This is why commanders must not only command and control; they must also instil in subordinates the qualities they need to take on the delegated responsibilities and carry out their work to the highest possible standard.

Trust

Trust is a belief in the commander's soundness of judgement, leadership skills and professional abilities. Where trust has been instilled, followers (subordinates) believe their commander is likely to bring them success, will treat them fairly, will not show weakness or cowardice, will listen if there is a problem, understands the situation they are in and will make the best decisions possible in the circumstances.

A commander instils trust by being:

■ Dependable.

■ Successful.

- Fair-minded.
- Dedicated to the job.
- Determined.
- Unselfish.
- Able to give clear messages.
- Well-informed.
- Good at problem solving.

Loyalty

People who are loyal support their team-mates, colleagues, commanders and the service they work for. In the armed forces they are proud of their units and traditions; they show esprit de corps; they are patriotic towards their country and they believe in the cause they are working or fighting for. There is some difference between personal **loyalty** (pride, respect and support for a particular commander, for example), and loyalty to the service as a whole. Commanders may try to instil both kinds of loyalty, since they are good for morale.

Disloyalty can be extremely dangerous, for example if it leads to selling secrets to an enemy during wartime or leaking classified information. Until 2002, such actions were sometimes classified as treason and technically punishable by death. This is why commanders have always placed emphasis on the importance of loyalty in their subordinates.

Discipline

Discipline has a number of definitions which you can find listed in any good dictionary.

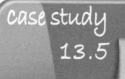

remember

Loyalty is a good kind of faithfulness to the team. If it goes too far and leads, for example, to the covering up of human rights violations by fellow soldiers during peacekeeping operations, it then stops being loyalty and becomes a crime.

Link

Book 1, Unit 5, page 183

In the armed forces it means obedient, self-controlled, orderly behaviour and also any systems used to train or enforce such behaviour. In addition it can refer to systems of punishments for lack of discipline.

---

case study 13.5 — Discipline in the army

[T]he essence of sound military organisation is achieved by instilling in people a discipline based on cooperation and teamwork

British defence doctrine

The Army's doctrine of discipline is founded in its doctrine of command which places the responsibility for maintaining discipline on commanders. In order to fulfil their disciplinary responsibilities, commanders are granted appropriate authority.

...

[the army has] a special code of discipline and a special system for enforcing it. Such special provision is necessary in order to maintain, in time of peace as well as war, and overseas as well as at home, the operational efficiency of an armed force.

Source: *Army General Administrative Instruction*, Volume 2, Chapter 67

---

activity — GROUP WORK

What are the advantages of having a system of discipline which is the direct responsibility of commanding officers?

Commanding officers instil discipline by giving clear statements of the rules and of the behaviour they expect. In addition they demonstrate good discipline and self-discipline themselves, thus leading by example. They organise practice activities such as drill and exercises which constantly reinforce the principles of discipline and obedience. They are also able, by praise or blame, reward or punishment, to encourage good discipline and deter bad discipline. Their long-term aim is to develop self-discipline so that their subordinates can be trusted to use their own initiative and take up command and control roles themselves if necessary. The development of self-discipline among subordinates can lead to a great increase in a troop's flexibility, efficiency, effectiveness and speed of response.

Morale

This is a combination of confidence, enthusiasm, optimism, self-belief and team spirit. A major aim of a commander is to develop high morale. This is good for subordinates because it helps them to enjoy their work. People with high morale perform at a higher level, with more determination and more attention to detail than people with low morale. So high morale is good for the service as a whole.

Respect

This is an aspect of discipline and self-discipline. Shared respect among subordinates for each other (mutual respect) makes for good order and job satisfaction. Respect for the commander, and respect from the commander to subordinates, are necessary in a command and control situation. This respect is most effective if it is earned by good performance on both sides. If it is established, it makes the command and control process easier and more effective.

Motivation

Motivation is the process of making people actively want to do what the commander wants them to do. It is an essential aspect of good command and control. Motivation is achieved by a range of strategies (methods) which are associated with particular leadership styles.

> **remember**
>
> Many aspects of effective command and control take training and practice to achieve. There has to be a good shared understanding, built up over time, between the commander and the people being commanded.

Link

See Book 1, Unit 2, pages 53 and 65

Motivational strategies

This is a complex issue because different people are motivated in different ways in different situations and for different reasons. A number of theories of motivation have been put forward in an attempt to clarify what really causes people to work well. Marx (1818–83) argued that people are motivated by the needs for money and power. Maslow (1908–70) claimed that people are motivated by different needs: poor people are motivated by food, shelter and security while people who are more well off are motivated by the esteem and approval of their peers and other social factors. McGregor (1906–64) stated that people are motivated by the opportunity to develop their skills and potential in their work. According to Herzberg (1923–2000), what motivates people are the 'negative' factors of pay and working conditions on the one hand, and the 'positive' factors of recognition, responsibility and advancement on the other. The negative factors make people work; the positive factors make them work to a high standard.

Effective commanders often use a range of strategies depending on who is being commanded and on the circumstances under which they are working.

Table 13.6 Motivational strategies and their effectiveness

Motivational strategy	Effectiveness; points for and against
Threats	Mainly effective with people who have no commitment or who are hostile to the commander. Has little educational function, especially if frequently repeated
Reward and punishment	These are useful techniques with people during the early stages of motivation, before they are fully motivated by peer group, team leader, commander, etc. They have little training value, but may help discipline and conformity in the short term
Approval of commander	Approval is a form of reward. It is the job of a commander to approve good performance, and it associates good work with pleasure and raised self-esteem for the subordinate. It works well if the right things are approved, and if it does not lead to favouritism and discrimination
Peer group approval	This is a powerful motivator, but it is only useful if the peer group approves the things the commander wants them to approve. Peer group approval is very effective with teams that are already well motivated and disciplined, and it helps to bond the group
Delegation of authority	This means passing on command functions for subordinates. This is a powerful motivator if the delegation is to the right kind of person and if that person has the skills and training needed to do the command function that has been delegated to them. When command is delegated, there should be monitoring and review to ensure that the delegation is working well
Transformational leadership	This is an excellent motivator as it makes people want to be commanded by the leader, who is seen as gifted and able to change the subordinates into 'better' people. This style of command should be linked to delegation to avoid seeming like a **personality cult**, and to avoid fatigue and disillusionment setting in among followers

Instigate and maintain command

Instigating command means establishing command in the first place. It is the things the commander says and does when meeting new subordinates. The aim in these early meetings is to establish authority, or at least the conditions under which authority can develop. Authority is the power and right to enforce obedience, and commanders need to have this kind of authority even if they rarely want to use it. Individual commanders have different visions of the kind of relationship they wish to have with their subordinates (though whatever happens they must not undermine the overall ethos of the service). What all commanders want is a good working relationship which brings out the best in the people being commanded.

Command is maintained by being committed to the role of commander and the tasks which have to be done. Effective command is divided between tasks – for example preparing **mission statements** and analysing strategy – and the leadership and management of people. Commanders must care about the success and well-being of the people they command. Although they are working for a uniformed public service which, in the end, may demand people to risk their lives, they must do everything possible to protect and support their troops, teams or whoever they command. Commanders must keep people busy with interesting, purposeful and meaningful work, and must pay attention to people's personal and professional development. They should be willing to delegate and give responsibility to others. If there are discipline problems they must deal with them fairly and effectively, according to the rules, and in a way which is in the best interests of the unit. Commanders should never turn a blind eye to bullying, harassment, discrimination or human rights abuses.

Inspire loyalty and obedience

Commanders who are loyal to their subordinates, and who stick up for them when they need or deserve it, are likely to receive loyalty in return. They are also likely to instil a culture of loyalty among their subordinates.

remember

Leadership has been defined as 'the art of motivating people towards a common objective'.

Inspiring obedience is a balancing act. Ill thought out commands, or too much emphasis on minor rules, may inspire disobedience or disrespect. On the other hand, slackness will not achieve obedience either.

Obedience is linked to discipline, and commanding officers in the armed forces always have wide disciplinary powers which have been restated in the Armed Forces Act 2006. They can practise '**summary justice**' (quick disciplinary action for minor infringements). This has to be done fairly and consistently, but without malice, and once the matter is over it should be over. Obedience should in any case not only be achieved by punishment or **reprimands** – appreciation should be shown for good performance or conduct. The aim is not simply obedience, but self-discipline, and commanding officers should be able to lead by example in this.

activity

GROUP WORK 13.2

P2

Give a short presentation suitable for a group of cadets, scouts, guides (or similar) explaining how a person can carry out command and control.

Maintenance of authority

A commanding officer has authority through being of a given rank in the hierarchy of a uniformed public service. But there is much more to authority than showing a rank badge, as Figure 13.10 shows.

Figure 13.10 Where the commanding officer's authority comes from

Where the commanding officer's authority comes from

Maintaining authority is achieved in a general sense by the same methods as those outlined above, under 'Instigate and maintain command'. Positive authority comes through being a good role model and a person whom others wish to be like.

Negative or coercive authority is imposed through sanctions (discipline or punishments). As stated above, using summary justice (for relatively minor disciplinary breaches) the commanding officer can impose the discipline required. For more serious offences there are legal systems and procedures which can, in the armed forces, lead to a **court martial**. In the civilian public services similar offences would be tried in a civilian criminal court.

remember

In the long run, positive methods of maintaining authority work better than negative methods – but most commanders have to use a combination of the two.

Need for authority

Without authority – or with authority which has been abused (as has been clear over the years in places such as Rwanda, Bosnia, Iraq and Sudan) – armies can become instruments of brutality and even genocide. The need for authority is:

- To enable people to be commanded.
- To protect human rights (both within and outside the service).

Failure to obey orders promptly undermines authority

If somebody fails to obey an order in a uniformed public service and gets away with it, it is seen as the beginning of 'a slippery slope' – so in general there is a zero-tolerance attitude to this sort of disobedience. As it says in *Army General Administrative Instruction*, Volume 2, Chapter 67:

> acts or omissions which in civil life may amount to no more than breaches of contract (like failing to attend work) or, indeed, mere incivility (like being offensive to a superior) become in the context of army life punishable offences.

This is because respect for authority is essential for the smooth working of all uniformed public services (and, indeed, non-uniformed public services). Questioning or even disagreeing with a person in authority is permissible and may be a sign of good working relationships if it leads to a worthwhile outcome and is not done in a negative, disrespectful spirit. But there should still be respect for authority itself. Lack of such respect is a recipe for endless arguments, hassle, stress, poor teamwork and general underperformance.

Practical consequences of orders not obeyed

Under certain circumstances – especially in danger – the practical consequences of orders not being obeyed might be serious injury or death, either for the person who does not obey or for his or her colleagues. More often, the effect is the waste of time and general annoyance caused by disobedience in an organisation where people are busy. Disobedience to reasonable orders is bad for discipline as a whole, and undermines morale and team spirit.

Course of action if orders not obeyed

The course of action taken if orders are not obeyed depends very much on:

- Whether it happens in the armed forces or in a civilian uniformed service.
- The kind of order.
- The circumstances in which the order is given.
- The rank and experience of the person disobeying the order.
- The way in which it is disobeyed.
- The reason why it is disobeyed.
- The effect of the disobedience.

---

case study 13.6 — Disobedience to lawful commands

1. A person subject to service law commits an offence if:

   (a) he disobeys a lawful command; and

   (b) he intends to disobey, or is reckless as to whether he disobeys, the command.

2. A person guilty of an offence under this section is liable to any punishment mentioned in the Table in section 164, but any sentence of imprisonment imposed in respect of the offence must not exceed ten years.

Source: Armed Forces Act 2006

activity
GROUP WORK

What does (b) mean and how do you think it could be proved?

Disobedience to lawful commands can lead to trial in a court martial. The range of penalties available in the army if orders are not obeyed extends from imprisonment to minor punishments.

Credibility as a commander

Credibility means authority, respect or the ability to be taken seriously. There are a number of things that commanding officers must be able to do in order to gain and keep this credibility.

Be fair

Commanders must treat the people they command equally. For example, if two subordinates commit the same offence they should receive the same administrative or disciplinary action.

Do not favour individuals

It is inevitable that commanding officers will like some of the people they command more than others. But they should not show it, especially when it comes to giving any kind of reward or favourable treatment. Favouring an individual may please the individual being favoured, but it will upset other individuals who notice that they are not being favoured – therefore the effect is counterproductive. In any case, favouritism is a form of discrimination, which has no place in the modern uniformed public services.

Know the strengths and weaknesses of direct reports and managers

'**Direct reports**' means 'immediate subordinates'.

Commanding officers must be interested in people – especially the people they command. They should know their strengths and weaknesses because these will be a factor in the decisions they make. Commanding officers cannot tell their own commanders that they will undertake a project or operation if they know that their team is not up to it.

Managers are people who have a command responsibility delegated to them by the person in command. Managers themselves therefore have to be capable of command and control as well. However, commanding officers cannot delegate to people whom they know to be unsuitable for the role they are being told to carry out. When they give responsibilities to people, they must know (through their own previous observation, appraisal and monitoring of the person) that the person is capable of doing the job.

Understand the group's role or function

New commanding officers have to learn about the people they are commanding and the work they do. This means they have to be able to listen to their subordinates, and learn from them, without losing their own authority in the process. This quick understanding uses the mental agility which, as we have seen, commanders need to have.

Understanding the group's function is necessary so that appropriate command and control can be carried out. Commanders cannot monitor, review or improve performance if they do not know what the performance is supposed to be!

Demonstrate confidence

Commanders demonstrate confidence by:

- Setting ambitious but realistic and **achievable** objectives and targets for their teams.
- Being able to delegate, in order to improve performance and develop team skills.

Delegation spreads the burden of command and allows decisions to be made lower down the chain of command. This leads to quick, **realistic** responses to problems, since it is the people low on the chain of command who know most about what is happening 'on the ground'. It also leaves the commanding officer with more time and energy to carry out other command and control tasks. Overall, the unit's productivity increases if there is effective delegation to people who have earned the commander's confidence.

> **remember**
> You should talk to people who work in the uniformed services about the importance of obeying orders – and find out what they really think.

> **remember**
> In the army, **administrative action** is a mild form of corrective behaviour such as a verbal warning or official reprimand. Disciplinary action is more serious, involving definite punishments and, perhaps, sentencing under military law.

> **remember**
> Commanding officers have a duty to train their subordinates to develop their strengths and reduce their weaknesses.

> **remember**
> 'Confidence' sometimes means 'feeling fairly sure of success', and sometimes means 'trust'. Both are important in command and control.

Ensure information is shared and orders disseminated

Commanders deal in information. Their job is to receive it, process it and pass it on.

Sharing simply means giving information to all those who need it. Dissemination means passing information or orders to a number of people, teams or units.

In the command process, a commander receives information (called '**intelligence**'), processes it into an intent, mission, strategy, plan or series of orders, and **disseminates** it.

Figure 13.11 The process of dissemination

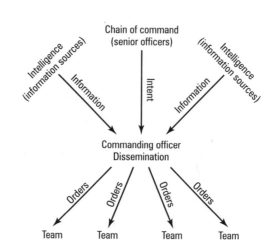

'Dissemination' comes from an old word which means scattering seeds. The orders disseminated are the 'seeds' of actions which will be carried out by the operational teams acting under the command of the commanding officer.

When commanding officers process information they add to its value, rather like an industry adding value to raw material by processing it into a manufactured, usable product. Dissemination spreads the product (in this case, commands) to the people who need them. Under a system of delegation the teams receiving the orders will be able, within limits, to use their initiative to adapt the orders to their situations and tactical needs.

How an individual can exercise command and control

Individuals exercise command and control by using:

- Intelligence about the operation they are involved in.
- Strategy from their superior officers.
- Their communication and leadership abilities.
- Their experience.
- Their planning and thinking skills.
- Their knowledge of the people they are commanding.
- Their knowledge of the resources available.

Command and control

Command and control is a cyclical process. It goes through a series of phases, then begins again where the last cycle left off.

The command and control cycle is called the '**OODA Loop**' or the 'Decision and Execution Cycle'.

Figure 13.12 The OODA loop

Source: Developed by Col. John R. Boyd, USAF (Ret) (1987) 'An Organic Design for Command and Control', *A Discourse on Winning and Losing*. Quoted in www.nwdc.navy. mil/Library/Documents/NDPs/ndp6/ ndp60002.htm

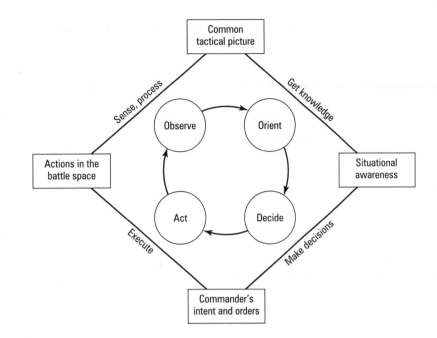

The OODA loop is both a basis for action and a learning curve. The sequence of learning activities which the commander has to go through in order to complete the loop and cause commands to be carried out is shown in Figure 13.13.

Who is responsible for assuming control and how they would do it?

The person who assumes control is the commanding officer of a given operation. In the armed forces or any other British uniformed public service, commanding officers are promoted, either through a competitive exam (such as **OSPRE** in the police) followed by interviews and other assessments, or (in the armed forces) through qualifying at the appropriate level of the Junior Officer Training and Education Scheme, plus interview and assessment of candidates by the appropriate selection board.

In the case of the emergency services the situation is different. At the scene of a serious road accident the first service to arrive will assume temporary control, but once the police arrive overall control will be assumed by them. Whoever arrives first at the scene of an accident or emergency the procedure followed is the one using the initials SAD CHALET.

Unit 15, page 241, SAD CHALET

Comparison of the methods used by the services

The command and control theory used by the different uniformed public services is very similar. The OODA loop is used at crime scenes, road traffic accidents, major fires and any other challenging event which needs a serious level of command and control. The sequence of observe, orient, decide and act is always used.

Figure 13.13 The learning curve (cognitive hierarchy) of command

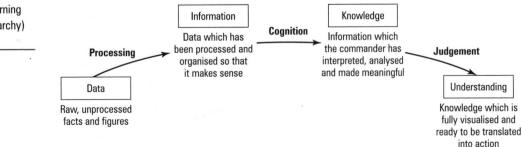

remember

You should learn the OODA loop and apply it to planning your own command and control exercises.

Wartime and peacetime situations often present comparable problems, requiring speed, decisiveness and flexibility. When firefighters arrive at an industrial fire, the fire is the enemy and they have to predict and prevent its development, just as British commanders in Afghanistan have to try to predict what the Taliban plan to do next and prevent it. Nevertheless, there are major differences in the methods of command and control used by different services – or even by the same service when the situation is different.

Emergency services

The command and control responsibilities for the emergency services in major incidents are laid down by law in the Civil Contingencies Act 2004. A great deal of command and control goes into setting up systems for emergency responses in the first place, as Table 13.7 indicates.

Table 13.7 OODA loop, planning phase

OODA loop	Emergency command and control (planning phase)
Observe	Observe history of emergencies, e.g. in other countries
	Observe history of British emergencies
Orient	Assess risk of emergency happening in UK
	Assess the readiness of the emergency services to deal with the emergency if it happens
Decide	Draw up draft emergency plans
	Discuss ways for different services to work together
	Devise monitoring and review systems
	Plan a new law giving emergency powers to government and local authority in a major disaster
Act	Pass the law in Parliament
	Implement the law
	Draw up finalised emergency plans
	Delegate duties to local authorities and emergency services
	Carry out joint emergency service training and practice – followed by reviews and more exercises
	Advise the public (through leaflets, media, etc.)

At a major incident, command and control follows the pattern shown in Table 13.8.

Table 13.8 Command and control at a major incident

First attendance	Initial control by whoever gets there first. Start to carry out SAD CHALET, preserve the scene, disseminate information to get more back-up – and rescue people
Gold command (strategic)	Gold command, which can be single or (more often) multi-agency, decides the overall response strategy and records a strategy statement. Usually based at a police station, Gold monitors and reviews strategy as the incident (or its response) develops.
Silver command (tactical)	Silver, based near but not at the incident, plans the tactics to be used by each service to carry out the strategy set by Gold.
Bronze command (operational)	Bronze will control and deploy the resources of their respective service at the incident scene, carrying out specific roles and implementing the tactics defined by Silver
Later stages	Senior managers are fitted into the Gold, Silver and Bronze command structure to increase the level of supervision – which is important during the complexities of incident investigation

Note that the main control function is carried out by Gold.

Figure 13.14 Control
– easier said than done

Practice Advice on Tasking and Coordination 2006, Association of Chief Police Officers, National Centre for Policing Excellence (www.acpo.police.uk/)

Armed forces

Command and control in the armed forces is carried out under difficult conditions. Warfare, or peacekeeping for that matter, takes place in an unstable, risky and rapidly changing environment where it is important that forces can act or react quickly in order to impose their will on the situation. This means that a type of command and control is needed which gives maximum freedom and flexibility to subordinates, so that they can respond quickly and effectively to challenges without having to seek orders and advice from higher up the chain of command.

To deal with these situations command and control is of the 'mission' type. This means that commanding officers tell their teams, or troops, what they have to do and why they have to do it. But they do not tell them how to do the job. They delegate responsibility for this kind of tactical decision to people lower down the chain of command.

The advantages of this method are that:

- Troops can act faster because they do not have to wait for orders.

- Command is delegated, which frees the commanding officer for strategic planning and for monitoring.

- Subordinates to whom command is delegated can use their initiative and creativity to solve problems by making their own decisions and giving their own commands.

The weakness of this method is that it only works with troops who have high levels of self-discipline, motivation and expertise at their job. (Inexperienced troops may need 'detailed' control, which is more authoritarian and gives them less freedom to make their own decisions.) But if the troops are well trained and prepared to take the responsibility handed down to them, 'mission command and control' in the armed forces enables troops to disrupt enemy preparations and activities, and gain the upper hand in a conflict.

remember

Strategic is to do with long-term overall planning.

Tactical is to do with medium-term and more specialised or detailed planning.

Operational is to do with the practical details of the work (NB: in military planning the word has a slightly different meaning).

Other uniformed public services

Command and control in neighbourhood policing may seem very different from the mainly military control discussed in many parts of this unit. But it follows similar principles of delegation, with tactical and operational decisions made as low as possible in the chain of command. Since 2003, neighbourhood policing has been organised around basic command units (BCUs). The units are assigned to areas as big as the average town (50,000–100,000 people) but are broken up into sectors, which themselves are broken into **beats**, each of which is coordinated by a **beat manager**. The system is outlined in Figure 13.15, with the roles of the beat manager shown at the bottom of the diagram.

The BCU system promotes flexibility and responsiveness to community needs, and provides policing which is visible and approachable.

case study 13.7 — Command and control (fire and rescue)

The **Incident Commander** of the first attendance will take all necessary measures to:

- Assess the effectiveness of fire fighting or other measures carried out before his/her arrival.
- Identify the risks associated with the location, including those details held on the Brigade's Central Risks Register.
- Form a plan of action to deal with the developing situation.
- Decide on appropriate additional resources.
- Take effective command and issue instructions to effect the plan of action.
- Maintain operational command of the fire fighting and rescue operations within the Inner Cordon.
- Evaluate the situation and any potential for development, preparing to brief a more senior officer on the incident, the police and Ambulance Service officers attending.
- Liaise with other emergency service incident officers at the earliest opportunity.
- Provide a safety **briefing**.

Source: London Emergency Services Liaison Panel (2004) *Major Incident Procedure Manual*, 6th edn. TSO, London

activity
INDIVIDUAL WORK

How far does this sequence of command and control actions fit in with the OODA Loop discussed above?

Levels of command and control: tactical, operational, strategic

The levels of command and control are described differently in military and civilian contexts. The armed forces use the definitions provided by NATO which are:

- The **grand strategic**.
- The **military strategic**.
- The operational.
- The tactical.

Figure 13.15 Levels of command in a basic command unit. Strategic decisions are made at the top, tactical decisions in the middle and operational decisions at the bottom.

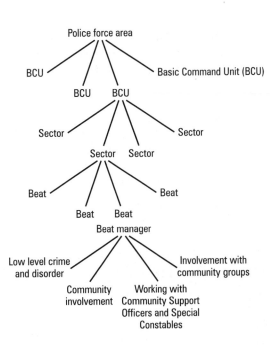

Grand strategic

This level of command is mainly carried out by the prime minister and the cabinet. It is to do with political, economic and military decisions which advance the security and prosperity of Britain and British interests in the world. Grand strategy is linked to the aims of other friendly Western industrialised nations and to organisations such as NATO. It is important to military commanders because it determines the operations they are involved in, and who their allies and enemies are.

Military strategic

This level is carried out by the Ministry of Defence and the chiefs of staff of the three armed services. It involves making military decisions which will support the political aims of Britain's grand strategy.

Operational

This level is carried out by joint task force commanders. The operational level of command plans all major military actions, campaigns, peacekeeping operations, etc. Operations are designed to put military strategy into practice.

Tactical level

This is carried out by people who are actually fighting, peacekeeping or carrying out humanitarian work. The joint task force commander, component commanders (of the different armed forces in the operation) and all the other commanders in the field are responsible for tactical decisions. Tactical command is to do with deploying troops, logistics, communications and all of the day-to-day planning, deciding and execution of battle plans.

Civilian public services

The civilian uniformed public services name their levels of command: strategic, tactical and operational (**Gold**, **Silver** and **Bronze**). These levels of command are used particularly in serious or major incidents, such as fatal car crashes, explosions, terrorist attacks, floods, large industrial fires and disease epidemics. Strategic command organises and controls the whole operation from a distance. Tactical command directs the operation on site but is not hands on. **Operational command** is to do with practical actions such as rescue, triage of casualties and organising the details of any investigation.

Planning

The planning process includes the following elements:

- Setting objectives.
- Gathering information and intelligence.
- Assessing risks.
- Making contingency plans to counter or avoid the risks.
- Liaison with partners.
- Resources.
- Drawing up the plans.
- Getting authority.
- Keeping records.

Clear objectives

An objective is a statement of intention.

Usually objectives are written down. An example of a written objective is 'deal with individuals in an ethical manner, recognising their needs with respect to race, diversity and human rights'.

Objectives must be worded very carefully and examined to make sure they say exactly what you want them to say.

Specific

An objective should relate to one clearly defined activity or action. It should have fixed limits. For example, in 'gather and review all the available information and intelligence in relation to the operation' the fixed limits are *available* and *in relation* to the *operation*.

Measurable

This means that you should be able to see, measure or test whether the objective has been achieved. For example, 'conduct a risk assessment in relation to the operation' is an objective because the risk assessment by definition is written down, and it can be checked and evaluated by someone else, in relation to risks that have been recorded in writing. On the other hand, 'be aware of possible risks' is not an objective, because awareness is inside the mind. It cannot be measured, tested or evaluated in the way that a written risk assessment can.

Achievable

This means there is no logical reason why the objective cannot be carried out. In 'conduct a risk assessment in relation to the operation', it is clear that a person who knows about risk assessments and knows about the operation could do it. On the other hand, a statement such as 'eliminate every risk in relation to the operation' would not be an achievable objective, simply because it is logically impossible for all risk to be removed from any operation.

(Quotes from 'Skills for Justice' (www.ukstandards.org.uk))

Realistic

This is to do with time, money and other constraints which might make an objective impossible to carry out. For example, if a police force had an objective to 'charge all people found writing graffiti', this would be achievable, but it would not be realistic because the amount of time and money needed would waste police resources, bearing in mind the more serious crimes they have to tackle, and the fact that other crime reduction strategies would be a more effective way of dealing with the problem of graffiti.

Time based

To be useful, objectives should have a time limit in which they must be achieved. Targets which are set by or for the uniformed public services usually have a deadline by which a certain level of success should be reached. For example, West Yorkshire police had the following as one of their objectives to be achieved in 2006/2007: 'Implement drug testing on arrest so that offenders can be directed into drug treatment in order to reduce their offending'. This looks realistic and achievable since it will not require vast resources and drug testing is technically possible. Directing offenders into drug treatment is clearly feasible within the time scale. (Whether offenders complete the treatment or reduce their offending is largely outside police control, but this part of the objective is an explanation, not the objective itself.)

SMART

This word is an acronym (a word made from the initials of other words) which will help you to remember the five principles given above for effective planning.

Briefing

Briefing is the process of:

- Explaining situations and assigning tasks to teams or subordinates before they carry out a **mission**, project or other activity.
- Monitoring or controlling an ongoing project using a briefing meeting to review progress that has been made so far, what still needs to be done and any problems which need to be dealt with.

Methods

Briefings can be given to groups or individuals, and can be done either face to face or in writing, or by a combination of the two.

In practice, most briefings are given by a leader to a team or group (4–15 people). They:

- Are face to face.
- Begin with a situation summary.
- Explain the tasks that subordinates will do.
- Give reasons for the tasks.
- Allow time for questions, answers and clarification.
- May include a handout, or notes.

Briefings should not last any longer than necessary. Commanders or team leaders should prepare the briefing properly in advance, thinking about:

- The best way to present information (talk, PowerPoint presentation, etc.).
- The amount of questions, answers and discussion that might be needed.
- The individuals present at the briefing.
- Any problems that might arise.

Situation

The situation is the background to the briefing, the team's work, and any mission or project which is going to take place. It includes:

- The context, including relevant intelligence.
- The strategic aims.
- Progress so far.
- Difficulties, dangers or obstacles.
- Resources.
- Legal and other issues (e.g. rules of engagement).

The more complex issues such as strategic aims, the difficulties and dangers and legal and other issues will have been communicated to the team, where necessary, at an earlier date. The success of briefings depends very much on a shared understanding of the strategic position and of the main intentions of higher command (in a military setting).

Mission

The mission is a statement of what the commander wants subordinates to do. It consists of a task and a purpose. 'I want you to search the area for a murder weapon' is a simple example of a mission statement. It gives the task and the purpose of the task.

The mission should be made clear at the briefing itself. Objectives of a mission should be clearly defined, **specific** and realistic. Written information giving key points may be useful to increase clarity and help ensure full understanding. But the most important thing about a mission statement is that it does not tell subordinates how the task should be done. It gives them the responsibility and the initiative to decide this themselves.

> **remember**
> Briefing is a useful skill – you should try to practise it whenever you get the chance.

---

case study 13.8 — Briefing and tasking

- Conduct briefings.
- Determine and assign tasks.
- Assign tasks commensurate with an individual's skills and development needs.
- Amend tasks.
- The importance of maintaining an ongoing evaluation of progress.
- Identify and deal with welfare needs of individuals.
- Communication methods and techniques.

Source: Adapted from 'Conduct briefing and tasking (Customs)', Skills for Business

activity
INDIVIDUAL WORK

This adapted extract comes from the National Occupational Standard on how customs officers should give briefings. Write notes on each of the above points, then get someone to look through your notes and give their comments.

Execution

Execution means 'doing' or 'carrying out'. It includes tactical decisions – how to carry out the task. Such decisions should not be made at a briefing. Tactical decisions are made by the people carrying out the task or their immediate team leaders. Under modern systems of command, tactical decisions are delegated as far down the chain of command as possible. This has the effect of:

- Speeding up decision making.
- Making it more responsive to real situations.
- Making actions more difficult for an enemy to predict.
- Using the intelligence, creativity and leadership talents of lower commanders to the full.
- Motivating the teams who carry out tasks.
- Reducing the dependence on time-consuming communications and feedback up and down the chain of command.
- Reducing the risk of orders being misunderstood.
- Increasing security by cutting down the number of messages which can be intercepted.
- Making commanders more free to develop wider strategies.

Under the modern '**manoeuvrist**' system of delegated command it is possible to raise the tempo (rapidity) of operations and respond very quickly – an important consideration not only in warfare but also in responding to major civilian incidents such as fires, motorway pile-ups, terrorist attacks, floods and other large-scale emergencies.

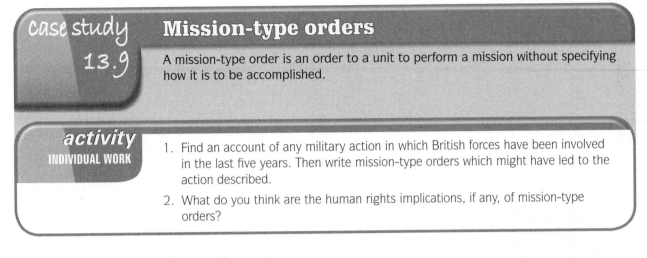

case study 13.9

Mission-type orders

A mission-type order is an order to a unit to perform a mission without specifying how it is to be accomplished.

activity
INDIVIDUAL WORK

1. Find an account of any military action in which British forces have been involved in the last five years. Then write mission-type orders which might have led to the action described.

2. What do you think are the human rights implications, if any, of mission-type orders?

Any questions

For briefings to be worth doing, they have to be understood. It is frustrating and dangerous for people to attend a briefing and then realise afterwards that they are not sure what it was about. Equally, for delegated leadership to work, the delegated leaders have to be clear about their roles and responsibilities. So questions can be important. It is therefore essential that they are dealt with clearly and fully by the person running the briefing. For this reason the team leader should:

- Before the briefing, think about questions that might arise, and come prepared with the relevant information.

- Think about possible answers to questions in advance.

- Leave enough time for questions.

But the team leader should not:

- Allow questioning to drag the briefing out.

- Get involved in public arguments.

- Be impolite about questions which seem stupid.

- Claim to be able to answer something which they cannot.

If particular individuals have lengthy questions which are not relevant to the briefing as a whole, the matters should be discussed afterwards when people have dispersed, to avoid wasting everybody's time.

Check understanding

It is not easy to be sure what people have understood and what they have not. Asking people in public if they have understood is ineffective, and may well embarrass or antagonise them (if they have not understood they will not want to be shown up in public).

Understanding can be checked by:

- Monitoring reactions during the briefing (e.g. body language and the kinds of questions people ask).

- Questioning people individually after the briefing.

- Distributing questionnaires which can be answered and returned privately.

- Checking with subordinate commanders to ensure that they understand their mission.

- Monitoring, controlling and reviewing the mission once it gets under way.

SMEAC

This is an acronym to help you remember the five stages of a briefing, as above.

Importance of clarity

Clarity means expressing facts and ideas in such a way that people hearing or reading them will receive the same facts and ideas that the speaker or writer gives out, without any omissions or distortions.

A clear briefing leaves people sure of what they are supposed to do and why they are doing it. An unclear briefing may cause people to make wrong or dangerous decisions, and causes frustration, annoyance, misunderstanding, wasted time and lowered morale.

Lack of clarity in a briefing may arise from:

- Muddled strategic or preparatory thinking.
- Lack of necessary or accurate information.
- Failure to announce in advance what the briefing will be about.
- Lack of structure or planning in the briefing.
- Poor command of language.
- Poor **diction** or voice production (too quiet).
- Weak self-presentation and body language.
- Starting the briefing before people are ready.
- Lack of useful visual aids or handouts.
- Use of language inappropriate for the audience.
- Bad time management.
- Poor understanding of the concerns, skills, thinking or culture of subordinates.
- Bad handling of questions.
- Failure to find a suitable (quiet and comfortable) place for the briefing.

> **remember**
>
> If you feel your written or spoken English is letting you down, see your tutor and arrange for extra tuition or learning support.

Being accurate and concise

Being accurate means giving facts which are true and sufficiently detailed. Being concise means expressing facts in a way which is clear and does not waste words.

Effective control

Two types of control can be used:

1. **Detailed control**. This means centralised command and control. An example of detailed control is the control of a convoy of ships passing through a sea area where they could be attacked. Detailed control works well when time is not a problem, when the people being controlled are untrained or inexperienced, and when safety has to be maximised.

2. Mission control. This is the system used in warfare and emergency situations where speed and flexibility of response are needed, and when the people being controlled are self-disciplined, knowledgeable, competent and motivated. Under this system control is delegated and is much less tight.

Receiving and giving orders

These procedures depend on good training and practice. They also depend on good communication skills and, sometimes, equipment.

Receiving orders promptly and without misunderstanding requires good listening skills and an ability to distinguish key points. It also requires good short-term memory and perhaps long-term memory as well. All of these skills and abilities can be developed by training and practice.

Giving orders clearly and with authority demands a good knowledge and understanding of the reasons, strategy and background to the orders, and clear expression of a kind which will be understood by the people receiving the orders. People giving orders must know what to put in and what to leave out, since orders with too much or too little detail can be ineffective. Giving orders in a professional manner is also a skill which requires plenty of training and practice.

Direct and monitor teams effectively

Direction and monitoring are aspects of control. Under situations requiring detailed control the direction and monitoring are more frequent. Teams can be more effectively monitored if some kind of written record, such as a logbook, is kept. This will remind the commander what to check, it will enable notes to be kept about the team's performance, and will record the team's learning and development. If the team is being monitored against targets or milestones, the log can be used to guide the team and let them know whether they are on course to achieve their targets or not.

For detailed control the control should include risk assessments and other preparations which are done before the activity being controlled begins.

Under situations requiring mission control, direction should be kept to a minimum since it will undermine the authority, self-reliance and initiative of junior commanders. Monitoring may be best done at a distance, since the presence of the person monitoring may hamper or distort the team's performance. Nevertheless it is important that some form of monitoring is done, and that it is done in a systematic and conscientious way, so that problems can be detected and acted upon before they become too serious.

Maintain a physical position of control

When personally controlling an inexperienced team it may be important for the commander to be physically present at all times. He/she should be positioned where it is possible to see what is going on and intervene if necessary. This is particularly the case where the command involves young, inexperienced people in situations which may be dangerous.

Issue clear orders and commands

Orders should be spoken or shouted clearly and loudly enough for the people they are directed at to hear easily. They should not be too long or contain too much information to be absorbed at once. Spoken commands should avoid slang, **jargon** which will not be understood by the team, or any language which may be offensive or discriminatory. If orders are written, they should be in clear English and set out so that they can easily be distinguished and understood.

Maintain a strong command presence

This is to do with 'looking the part'. Commanders who are on the spot should show by their body language and tone of voice that they are taking command, and that they expect all reasonable commands to be obeyed. They should be dressed in a manner suited to the conditions. In mission command (e.g. sections and platoons in enemy territory) commanders tend to lead from the front. In detailed command this is less likely, because people cannot lead from the front and monitor and control people closely at the same time.

Influence the tempo

The **tempo** is the speed at which actions are done or objectives are achieved. Tempo is a very important concept in warfare. Having a faster tempo than the enemy disrupts enemy plans and communications, and helps to degrade their efforts and gain initiative over them. The best way to increase the tempo, with experienced teams, is to delegate command to subordinates. This motivates them and cuts down time spent giving and receiving orders from higher up the chain of command.

> *remember*
>
> Study the techniques used by your teachers, lecturers or instructors to gain attention, keep control, manage the class and motivate students. The methods that work can be adapted and used in your own command tasks.

'More haste, less speed!'

In detailed command the tempo can be increased by giving orders more quickly, and by encouraging people to 'get a move on' – but the more often this is done, the less effective it is, and if the team rushes too much, it becomes a safety risk and the quality of work done goes down. A better way of increasing tempo in detailed command may be to plan actions on paper first, bearing in mind which will take a long time and which will not, using a flow chart or a chart like the one in the link below, explaining road accident management.

Link   Unit 15, page 232

Delegate

'Delegate' means to give power and responsibility to people lower down in the chain of command. Where the people lower down have motivation, self-discipline, knowledge and training, this is effective and efficient, especially in military operations such as warfare or in major incidents such as chemical spillages or terrorist attacks. Delegation is also useful where someone has special expertise which is needed and which the commander does not have.

Delegation should be monitored and controlled, but with a light touch. If it becomes purposeless and uncontrolled, it degenerates into laissez-faire leadership – ineffective and demoralising for people who are poorly briefed or are used to strong, purposeful command.

Functional command methods

Functional command is command based not on geographical areas or on particular armed services but on the role, purpose or function of the command. A functional command is therefore a joint or unified command with different forces operating together to carry out a shared and coordinated strategy. The present NATO operations in Afghanistan where the armies and air forces of several countries are working together

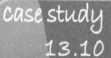

case study 13.10   **Functional command**

11. The functional command is Allied Command Transformation (ACT) in Norfolk, Virginia, formerly Supreme Allied Command Atlantic (SACLANT). Its role will be to harmonise capabilities and assist in the transformation of allied armed forces to more mobile and integrated units. Part of this will be training joint multinational forces to operate together with interoperable communications equipment. It has a subordinate command in Stavanger, Norway (Joint Headquarters North).

12. In large part ACT will become a centre for the development of doctrine and training. As the last Supreme Allied Commander Atlantic Admiral Ian Forbes said, 'The key point for us is the possibility of a technical gap (between US and European forces) being accentuated by a widening intellectual imbalance.' By co-ordinating training and doctrine as well as the use of **transformational** technology, ACT aims to prevent a further widening of this gap in the Alliance.

Source: NATO

activity
GROUP WORK

1. What does this extract from a NATO document suggest about the future military relationship between the US, NATO and Britain?

2. What does it suggest about the importance and future of functional command?

under the umbrella of NATO is an example of functional command. Functional command makes it easier to work in alliances and have 'interoperability' (coordination between different services, often from different countries and continents). It requires new approaches, but fits in well with western aims of having a globalised military presence to fight terrorism.

Plan
This is carried out first at the grand strategic level of world governments forming political plans, then at the military strategic level. The key military strategic organisation at present is called the Allied Command for Transformation, and the result so far is the NATO Response Force, which NATO countries including Britain agreed to set up at the Prague Summit in 2002. Planning consists first of military theory, called '**doctrine**', then of strategy, which is military theory applied to a country's political and economic needs.

Initiate
Initiation of functional command is through a statement of intent – basically saying that something must be done about a particular problem which demands a (usually military) solution. The idea that British troops would occupy Helmand Province in Afghanistan in 2006, pacify the Taliban, and carry out reconstruction was a statement of intent which initiated the British actions which have taken place there since then.

Control
'Control' (in functional command) means:

■ To analyse the situation and the strategic needs.

■ To devise missions and make mission statements.

■ To set tasks and the reasons for those tasks.

■ To delegate command powers.

■ To monitor and review what happens.

Support
This involves supplying teams with the resources they need to carry out their tasks, and giving support from other services following the methods of 'interoperability'.

Inform
Apart from delegated command tasks and the reasons for them, information is intelligence about the problem that needs to be solved. In war it is about the numbers, movement, equipment and intentions of the enemy. It may also be about the local population, their attitudes, culture, beliefs, political loyalties and so on. Information such as maps, or any back-up that might be available, is important too. In functional command it is important to be able to disseminate this knowledge, as well as commands, to the people who need it. In addition, information may take the form of feedback (e.g. requests for more material or support) moving up the chain of command.

Evaluate
Evaluation should take place during and after a mission. The main questions to be asked in an evaluation are 'Was it worth doing?' or 'Did we get more out of it than we put into it?'. Evaluation therefore takes the form of a **cost/benefit analysis**, followed by a consideration of the lessons learned. The lessons learned include appraisals and self-appraisals of individual performance, and an assessment of the performance and success of the team as a whole. An important factor in assessing functional command is how well people communicated with each other and worked together, since functional command often draws together team members from very different backgrounds.

PICSIE
This acronym can help you to remember the above sequence of actions used in functional command.

case study 13.11

Information

There are two basic uses for information. The first is to help create an understanding of the situation as the basis for making a decision. Information serving this purpose can be described as *image-building information*. This type of information primarily supports the orientation and decision phases of the decision and execution cycle. Image-building information consists of information about the enemy, the surrounding environment, and the status and disposition of our own forces. The second basic use for information, equally important, is to make it a means of coordinating actions in the execution of the plan after the decision has been made. Such information can be described as *execution information*, and primarily supports the action phase of the decision and execution cycle. Execution information may take several forms, e.g. orders or guidance issued to subordinates, execution coordination or requests of one unit for support by another. Execution information refers not only to instructions or plans; it also means disseminating the commander's vision and intent.

Source: NDP 6 (U), Chapter 3 The naval command and control system, Navy Warfare Development Command

activity
INDIVIDUAL WORK

1. What factors might make image-building information unreliable?
2. What factors might make execution information unreliable?
3. What are the dangers of having:
   (a) too little information and
   (b) too much information?

activity
INDIVIDUAL WORK 13.3

M1

D1

You are a member of a volunteer organisation such as Mountain Rescue or a group of reservists. Research and write a report for your organisation:

1. Analysing the importance and use of command and control within a chosen public service.

2. Evaluating the importance and use of command and control within the uniformed public services in general.

Demonstrating command and control skills through command task activities

For this section you will need to carry out your own command tasks, showing skills you have learned and practised.

Command and control skills and qualities

The skills you need include:

- Gathering intelligence.
- Making decisions.
- Devising mission statements, tasks and reasons.
- Carrying out risk assessments and acting on them.
- Delivering briefings.

- Communication skills: listening, reading, speaking, writing.
- Understanding strategic and tactical planning.
- Setting tasks and objectives.
- Being inclusive of team members.
- Effective delegation.
- Disseminating information.
- Checking understanding.
- Motivational skills.
- Supplying equipment.
- Recording decisions, actions, etc.
- Identifying **welfare** needs.
- Monitoring and evaluation.
- Flexibility to change tasks if necessary.
- **Debriefing**.
- Giving feedback and appraising performance.

<table>
<tr><td>*remember*</td><td>Everybody has some personal leadership qualities. They can be developed through practice, studying how other people lead, getting advice from other people and putting yourself in leadership situations.</td></tr>
</table>

Personal qualities

The qualities you need include:

- Initiative.
- Confidence.
- Self-discipline.
- Imagination.
- Decisiveness.
- Commitment.
- Sympathetic interest in other people.
- Fair-mindedness.

Effective control

You must first decide whether you are going to use detailed control or mission control (see above, page 166).

Table 13.9 Control

Detailed control – main points to remember	Mission control – main points to remember
Plan the activity and the control process in advance	Devise the mission using information and strategic background
Give clear briefings which contain clear-cut tasks	Give a briefing which sets tasks or objectives and gives the reason for them
Give information on how tasks should be carried out.	Do not say how the tasks should be done
Do *not* delegate command	Delegate command to other people
Play an active role in commanding while tasks are being carried out	Do not play an active role in commanding – leave it to the people you have delegated command to
Monitor all activities closely	Allow team(s) to make all tactical decisions
Aim for obedience to commands at all times	Monitor activities carefully, but from a distance if possible
Remember that safety is the main criterion, and that time is not the most important issue	Do not aim for obedience – aim for speed, initiative and effectiveness
Your aim is to control all tasks, and the tasks must be done correctly	Only intervene directly if you think safety is being put at risk
Carry out a debrief at the end	Record the way the tasks are done and run a debrief at the end

For guidance on evaluating your own performance in command and control, see the principles outlined in Book 1, Unit 2, pages 79, 86–87

Effective communication

The rules are:

- Be clear.
- Speak loudly.
- Plan what you are going to say, and rehearse it.
- Avoid reading aloud to your listeners.
- Use visual aids if need be.
- Make eye contact with listeners.
- Be relaxed and confident – you are the boss!

Types of command task activities

Command tasks are projects, missions or activities where problems have to be solved by groups, and where the successful resolution of the problem depends on command skills and teamwork.

In real life, command tasks are used in warfare, emergency, crime-fighting and other challenging situations where teamwork, initiative, imagination and quick thinking are needed. The experts at command tasks are the armed forces and the emergency services, though any large and potentially risky enterprise (e.g. organising the 2012 Olympic Games or setting up a major business deal) has elements of the command task about it.

Command tasks are also used in training – in schools, colleges and business as well as the uniformed services – and for entertainment. Educational command tasks do not have the same risks as real-life command tasks, but they use and develop the same kinds of ability.

Combat

Any fighting involving groups of people, including large-scale warfare, is combat. Warfare is an interlocking succession of command tasks all working towards the strategic objective of victory. In a war both sides have chains of command and mission control, and if both sides are equally well equipped and have similar numbers of combatants, victory will go to the side that has better command and control procedures, and carries out its command tasks more effectively.

In combat, command tasks should be carried out in a way that:

- Surprises the enemy.
- Disrupts enemy communications and strategy.
- Upsets the tempo of the enemy's activities.
- Reduces the enemy's flexibility and options.
- Degrades enemy capabilities by killing people, destroying equipment and infrastructure, and weakening morale.

remember

Warfare is a mental battle as well as a physical battle – good command enables one side to out-think the other.

Rescue

Rescue often has to be carried out quickly under dangerous conditions (e.g. snatch rescues from burning buildings). Rescues are command tasks because:

- There is a problem to be solved.
- There is a task and a reason for carrying out the task.
- Initiative and improvisation may be needed.

- Teamwork is used.
- Speed matters.
- There are risks to be assessed and overcome.
- Responsibility is delegated by higher command to the person or people doing the rescue.
- Conditions are likely to be chaotic, so decisions have to be made on the spot and as low down the chain of command as possible (e.g. by the person actually carrying out the rescue).

Containment

This word describes what is done to prevent a bad situation from getting even worse. In a major fire, containment is activities such as cooling surrounding buildings with water to stop the fire from spreading; in a chemical leak containment is, literally, containing the chemical so it cannot escape.

Situation control

In conditions of mission control, where the situation is rapidly changing, this means:

- Giving subordinates to whom the command has been delegated the information, power and freedom they need to get on with the job.
- Monitoring the command task and reviewing its progress with a light touch – not interfering with the tactical decisions made by the person in charge of the command task unless something is going seriously wrong.

remember

If you want to learn more about military control, read the material on British defence doctrine on the MOD website, and also the material on 'doctrine' on US armed forces websites.

http://atiam.train.army.mil

www.mod.uk/DefenceInternet/AboutDefence/

Accident

Accidents are command task activities because command task skills and methods are used to carry out rescues, investigate the accident and restore the scene to normality. Mission command and control methods are well suited to dealing with chaotic and unpredictable situations and achieving results quickly. This style of command also makes

Figure 13.16 A real-life command task

it easier for different services, which are under different commands, to communicate and work together at a tactical or operational level since immediate, one-off decisions on inter-service cooperation can be made by people who are on the scene and low in the chain of command. Under functional command (the type which happens at accident scenes) interoperability is easier and more effective. It allows, for example, paramedics to tend accident victims while firefighters are releasing them from crashed vehicles.

Accident simulations provide good training scenarios for practising command task skills.

Recovery

These are activities which involve searching, finding or retrieving people or equipment – as for example in mountain rescue or dealing with drug smuggling and people trafficking. International policing and customs activity is increasingly run on systems of functional command. Training in this sort of work, and in the command and control skills required, is given through simulations and live exercises which develop and test these skills through realistic command task activities.

Recovery can also mean returning to normality after a disaster, emergency or major incident. Recovery work is carried out by a variety of agencies. Command and control in such situations (in Britain) is the responsibility of local authorities, their emergency planning units, and the local resilience forums based in each local police force area.

Lead and support people to resolve operational incidents

Operational incidents are any happenings associated with warfare, peacekeeping, emergency-service work, policing or anti-terrorism which might need a rapid response of the type made possible through 'mission control' techniques of delegation. The theory of this kind of command and control is outlined in the OODA loop shown on page 157 above.

To link theory and practice, training and exercises in command task activities based on realistic scenarios are used to develop skills in leading and supporting people to deal with such incidents. These skills are essential in the concept of '**resilience**' – the ability of a country or community to withstand and recover from disasters or major incidents.

www.ukresilience.info/preparedness/exercises.aspx#content. Useful site on resilience exercises

activity
INDIVIDUAL WORK
13.4

P3

M2

Carry out four practical command and control tasks in four situations related to the work of a particular public service. Keep a log of what you did, examining and commenting on your performance.

Problem-solving techniques

These are useful in the planning stages of command and control, when strategies, the intent of higher command, and intelligence (information) are brought together and need to be translated into mission statements, statements of tasks and reasons for the tasks.

---

remember

It is relatively easy to prepare simulations and role-plays which train and test command task activities. These can be based on events which appear in the news, and role slips and a scenario can be given to participants.

Define the problem

This is done by making a clear statement of a problem, e.g. 'The street price of heroin is going down, therefore more people are becoming addicted and the crime rate is going up'.

(Some statements will be much longer and more detailed than this one.)

Gather all of the relevant information

In the example given this might include:

■ Data, statistics and evidence on the current heroin street prices.

■ Evidence from drug rehabilitation centres.

■ Crime figures.

■ Information from HM Revenue and Customs, from the police, from Europol, etc. about drug trafficking and drug seizures (including estimates).

■ Information on world heroin production levels.

List the possible solutions

This should be done, at first, as rapidly as possible, without pausing to think whether the solutions would actually work or not. The listing can be done individually or as a group exercise of the brainstorming type.

Test the possible solutions

Tests can either be theoretical or practical.

Theoretical tests might include:

■ Researching or surveying attitudes, previous attempts at drugs control, etc.

■ Surveys among drug users or drug rehabilitation organisations.

■ **Computer modelling** and other methods to project likely scenarios which could result if certain solutions were tried.

Practical tests might include:

■ Pilot policing/social work/voluntary projects carried out in certain areas and closely monitored.

■ New approaches tried and tested as pilot schemes by Customs, Europol, etc. to disrupt heroin supply routes.

■ Experimental schemes to deter opium production in countries such as Afghanistan.

Select the best solution

It is, perhaps, unlikely that a serious problem will have only one solution. However, it may be that one of the solutions on offer is more effective than any of the others.

The best solution can be achieved:

■ By consensus (agreement between the group) following consideration of test results.

■ By analysing the results of trials, pilot schemes or experiments which give verifiable evidence that they solve the problem.

---

activity

INDIVIDUAL WORK 13.5

P4

Write a leaflet suitable for cadets outlining the skills and qualities needed for carrying out command tasks in a uniformed public service. In your leaflet show how each skill or quality is needed in command and control situations.

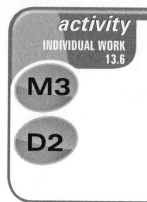

activity

INDIVIDUAL WORK 13.6

M3

D2

Write a self-appraisal of your performance in specific command and control situations. Your self-appraisal should include:

■ The skills and personal qualities needed for the kind of command and control you carried out.

■ Accounts of the command and control tasks you did and a careful review of how far your own skills satisfied the requirements of those tasks.

■ An evaluation of your own command and control performance, identifying the personal development achieved, and ways in which your skills and qualities could be developed further in the future.

Progress Check

1. What are the main differences in rank structure between military and civilian uniformed public services?

2. What is the importance of badges of rank in the armed forces?

3. Outline the command structure of two uniformed public services.

4. Explain the relationship between government departments and the uniformed public services.

5. What skills are used in military command and control?

6. What is moral courage, and what is its place in uniformed public service work?

7. Explain the characteristics of good decision making.

8. Describe four ways of motivating people.

9. Why is the OODA loop useful for understanding command and control?

10. Explain Gold, Silver and Bronze command.

11. Compare the levels of command and control used in the armed forces and in the emergency services.

12. What is an objective and what are its characteristics?

13. Describe the process of giving a briefing.

14. Why is it a good thing for tactical decisions to be made low down on the chain of command?

15. Explain the difference between 'detailed control' and 'mission control'.

16. When, and why, is mission control more effective than other types of control?

17. What is tempo and why does it matter?

18. What are:

    (a) the requirements and

    (b) the advantages of effective delegation?

19. What personal skills are needed for effective command and control?

UNIT 14

The Planning for and Management of Major Incidents

This unit covers:

- The effects of recent major incidents
- The type of work carried out by the public services during major incidents
- The considerations for **emergency** planning and preparation for possible major incidents
- Preparing for a particular major incident by using tabletop scenarios

This unit outlines large-scale incidents such as floods, major fires and terrorist attacks, and the ways in which the public services deal with them. It begins by examining the causes, effects and long-term aftermaths of such incidents.

The unit then explores the ways in which the public services and other agencies deal with major incidents, covering both their individual roles and the ways in which they work together. It also looks at emergency planning law – and how this affects the way the public services work.

Planning for major incidents before (or in case) they happen is essential, and the unit examines aspects of emergency planning, and the ways in which risks can be minimised. It includes an outline of the nature and role of both the professional and volunteer services involved.

The final section of the unit covers the emergency planning process, using the techniques of '**tabletop scenarios**'. These planning exercises show how information received is processed into practical actions that can be used to deal with a real-life **major incident**.

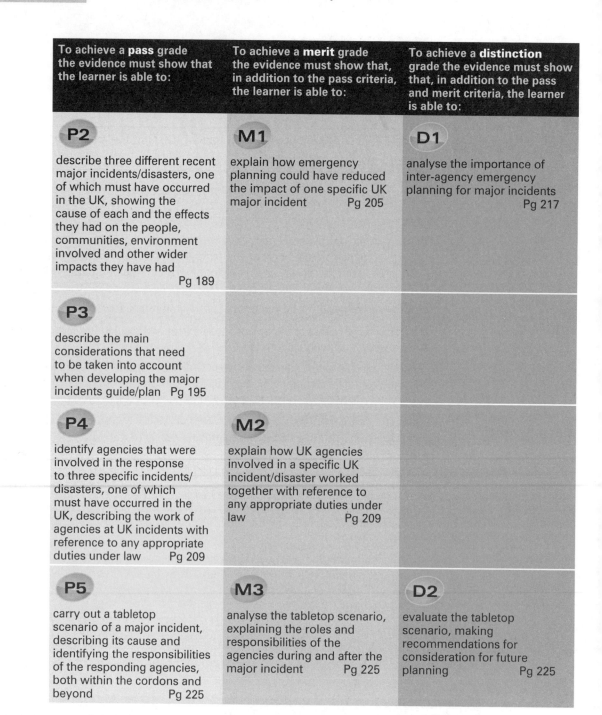

To achieve a **pass** grade the evidence must show that the learner is able to:	To achieve a **merit** grade the evidence must show that, in addition to the pass criteria, the learner is able to:	To achieve a **distinction** grade the evidence must show that, in addition to the pass and merit criteria, the learner is able to:
P2 describe three different recent major incidents/disasters, one of which must have occurred in the UK, showing the cause of each and the effects they had on the people, communities, environment involved and other wider impacts they have had Pg 189	**M1** explain how emergency planning could have reduced the impact of one specific UK major incident Pg 205	**D1** analyse the importance of inter-agency emergency planning for major incidents Pg 217
P3 describe the main considerations that need to be taken into account when developing the major incidents guide/plan Pg 195		
P4 identify agencies that were involved in the response to three specific incidents/disasters, one of which must have occurred in the UK, describing the work of agencies at UK incidents with reference to any appropriate duties under law Pg 209	**M2** explain how UK agencies involved in a specific UK incident/disaster worked together with reference to any appropriate duties under law Pg 209	
P5 carry out a tabletop scenario of a major incident, describing its cause and identifying the responsibilities of the responding agencies, both within the cordons and beyond Pg 225	**M3** analyse the tabletop scenario, explaining the roles and responsibilities of the agencies during and after the major incident Pg 225	**D2** evaluate the tabletop scenario, making recommendations for consideration for future planning Pg 225

The effects of recent major incidents

remember 'Recent' means different things to different people. According to the Specification, a 'recent' incident is one that occurred 'within the last five or six years'. However, if you choose to study incidents which are too recent, it may be that the full effects will not yet be clear.

Major incidents

Definition

The *Major Incident Procedure Manual* (7th edn, 2007) produced by the London Emergency Services Liaison Panel defines a major incident as shown in case study 14.1.

London Emergency Services Liaison Panel (2007) *Major Incident Procedure Manual*, 7th edn. TSO, London

---

case study 14.1

What is a major incident?

A major incident is any emergency that requires the implementation of special arrangements by one or all of the emergency services and will generally include the involvement, either directly or indirectly, of large numbers of people. For example:

- the rescue and transportation of a large number of casualties;
- the large scale combined resources of the police, London Fire Brigade and London Ambulance Service;
- the mobilisation and organisation of the emergency services and support services, for example local authority, to cater for the threat of death, serious injury or homelessness to a large number of people; and
- the handling of a large number of enquiries likely to be generated both from the public and the news media usually made to the police.

Source: London Emergency Services Liaison Panel (www.leslp.gov.uk/LESLP_Man.pdf)

---

activity
GROUP WORK

1. Identify each of the main points in this definition.
2. Choose five major incidents which have taken place in the past five years. (Three should have taken place in Britain.)
3. For each incident you have identified, discuss and reach agreement on how well it fits in with this definition.

British major incidents

Britain has fewer major incidents than many countries which have similar populations – but we hear about them because the media (and the public) tend to be more interested in major incidents which happen in the UK than overseas. Table 14.1 shows a summary of some recent major incidents which happened in Britain.

Report of the Official Account of the Bombings in London on 7th July 2005 (2006) ordered by the House of Commons. TSO, London (www.official-documents. gov.uk/document/hc0506/hc10/1087/1087.asp)

Intelligence and Security Committee, *Report into the London Terrorist Attacks on 7 July 2005* (www.cabinet-office.gov.uk)

Report of the 7 July Review Committee, London Assembly Greater London Authority 2006 (www.london.gov.uk)

Addressing Lessons from the Emergency Response to the 7 July 2005 London Bombings, What we learned and what we are doing about it (22 September 2006) Cabinet Office (http://security.homeoffice.gov.uk/news-publications/publication-search/general/lessons-learned?view=Binary)

Table 14.1 Major incidents in the UK

Incident details	Date	Casualty numbers	Causes	Why it was a major incident
Widespread severe flooding in central and south-west England	July 2007	1 direct death; 2 indirect deaths	Slow-moving low pressure over southern England	Affected millions; posed severe health risk; 3 deaths. Political issues: planning regulations about building on land at risk from flooding; possible climate change link
Huge explosion at fuel depot, Buncefield, Hertfordshire	11 December 2005	No deaths; 43 injured	300 tonnes of fuel spilled from full tank; vapour cloud ignited	The biggest peacetime explosion in western Europe since World War II. Many injuries; pollution risks. Political issues: public health and safety
Terrorist bombings in London	7 July 2005	52 deaths; hundreds injured	'Fierce antagonism to perceived injustices by the West against Muslims'*	Deaths, injuries, major terror attack. Investigation involved over 10,000 police. Political issues: public security; UK foreign policy
Boscastle flood	August 2004	No direct casualties	2½ inches of rain in two hours	Alarming and dramatic – a miracle people were not killed
Reading train crash	6 November 2004	6 died; 5 seriously injured	Train collided with a car at an **unstaffed** level crossing	Deaths and injuries. Political issues: questions on safety of unstaffed level crossings were raised again
Cockle-pickers drowned in Morecambe Bay	February 2004	21 died	Tide came in while they were working at night	Deaths. Political issues: exploitation of illegal migrant workers; illegal immigration
Foot-and-mouth epidemic	Spring–summer 2001	No direct human casualties	Viral infection originating in infected pig food	7 million livestock killed. Total cost over £8 billion. Serious economic damage to tourism and farming. Political issues: government mismanagement
Selby train crash	20 February 2001	10 killed; many more injured	Driver asleep at the wheel: car came off the motorway and ended up on the train track – a train crashed into it	Deaths and injuries. Political issues: health and safety
58 Chinese illegal immigrants found suffocated in a lorry	19 June 2000	58 dead; 2 taken to hospital	Suffocated in a sealed lorry while being brought illegally into the UK from the Netherlands	High death toll. Political issues: illegal immigration; the seriousness of the crime of people trafficking; international police liaison

*Report of the Official Account of the Bombings in London on 7th July 2005

Boscastle

This major incident was a flash flood which tore through the Cornish village of Boscastle on Monday, 16 August 2004.

London terrorist bombings

On the morning of 7 July 2005, in London, four terrorist suicide bombings killed 52 people and injured around 700 others. Three of the bombs went off on underground trains at 8.50 a.m.; the fourth bomber blew himself up on the top deck of a bus at 9.47 a.m. The emergency services' immediate response included:

■ Wide deployment of police, SO13 (anti-terrorist) officers and other specialist officers.

■ 240 firefighters with 42 'front-line' appliances at the sites of the four explosions.

■ 400 ambulance staff with 200 vehicles.

- 1200 hospital beds made available.
- A major effort by volunteer organisations.
- Setting up a **Gold** coordinating group at 10 a.m. the same morning.

Ministers and officials of COBRA ('Cabinet Office Briefing Room A' – formerly COBR), the government's crisis management centre, also met the same morning at 10 a.m. to determine overall strategy and consider the wider implications.

 Link

More on the London bombings and terrorism below. Also see Unit 8, page 29

---

case study 14.2

Boscastle

Around 1000 residents and visitors are believed to have been affected in this devastating event. They witnessed the largest peacetime rescue in the history of mainland Britain.

- Miraculously, there were no fatalities, with only 1 reported casualty – a broken thumb.
- 7 helicopters airlifted 100 people (including 6 firefighters) to safety.
- 29 out of the 31 Cornwall County Fire Brigade stations were involved in the incident. They remained at Boscastle for 7 days, assisting in the clean-up operation.
- 58 properties were flooded, 4 of which were demolished, The Visitor Centre, Clovelly Clothing, Things and the Harbour Light.
- A further 40 properties were flooded in Canworthy Water, Bude, Helebridge and Crackington Haven with severe flooding at Otterham, Week St Mary, Marshgate, Millook and Camelford.
- 4 footbridges along the Valency Valley were washed away.
- 84 wrecked cars were recovered from Boscastle's harbour and streets, 32 could still be out at sea.
- The significant infrastructure damage to buildings and services, could cost North Cornwall District Council up to £2 million.
- A National Appeal was set up and administered by local trustees, with help from North Cornwall District Council. Over £200,000 of donations had been received by November 2004; £100,000 of which has already been distributed.

Source: *Boscastle: the flood 16:08:2004*, North Cornwall District Council 2004 (www.ncdc.gov.uk)

activity
GROUP WORK

1. Suggest as many reasons as you can why there were so few casualties.
2. What are the arguments for and against flood prevention work in places like Boscastle?

Foot-and-mouth

Foot-and-mouth is a viral disease which can affect all 'cloven-hoofed' animals – especially pigs, sheep and cows. Except in some very young or weak animals it is not deadly, and infected animals normally make a full recovery. The symptoms are mouth ulcers, drooling and sore feet.

Foot-and-mouth is one of the most easily spread of all diseases. It can be transmitted by water (e.g. drainage from one field to the next) and wind for a distance of up to 60 miles. It can also stick to car tyres, mud on boots and remain in meat and dairy products. The practice of moving sheep and cattle around the country by road – to markets or to other parts of the country for fattening or for slaughter – caused much of the country to become infected during the disastrous outbreak in 2001.

The importance of the disease is that it affects the market value of the animals (interfering with weight gain and meat production). This is of major **economic** importance, since Britain's export trade in meat and dairy products (worth £1.9 billion before 2001 but only £1.1 billion in 2002 and £1.5 billion in 2005) is dependent on Britain being officially **designated** as a country free of foot-and-mouth. If foot-and-mouth disease became endemic (widespread or permanent) in the country Britain would lose its 'disease-free' status, and many farmers would go out of business. The 2001 outbreak of foot-and-mouth cost Britain between £8 billion and £10 billion, of which about £3 billion was a loss to agriculture and the rest was a loss to tourism and the rural economy in general. This was because, in 2001, the public were banned from large areas of the countryside in an effort to control the spread of the disease, and the loss of trade by hotels, campsites, outdoor centres and other organisations added up to nearly twice as much as the loss of trade by farmers. In addition over 4 million livestock were slaughtered and incinerated in huge open fires in the countryside.

Foot-and-mouth poses no danger to humans, though people can get it and suffer mild flu-like symptoms which quickly pass. However, the scale of the 2001 epidemic, and the stress and misery it caused farmers, together with the horrific images of burning sheep and cattle, are thought to have resulted in significant increases in mental illness such as depression and even post traumatic stress disorder (PTSD) among the farming community.

Rail crashes

Rail crashes are not common in Britain, and though they are shocking and can be fatal, the death toll on Britain's railways is nothing compared with the number of road deaths (3201 in 2005). The worst rail crashes between 2000 and August 2007 were at Selby, Yorkshire in 2001 and Reading, Berkshire in 2004. In both cases trains collided with vehicles which should not have been on the track. Rail crashes make the news headlines because they are horrific and visually dramatic, and because they have some political importance (railways are not owned by the government, but the government is closely involved in the way they are run and in overall transport policy).

Figure 14.1 Spread of foot-and-mouth in 2001

Source: BBC website (http://news.bbc.co.uk/1/hi.html)

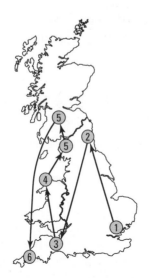

1. 19 February 2001
2. 23 February 2001
3. 24 February 2001
4. 27 February 2001
5. 1 March 2001
6. 3 March 2001

Train Derailment at Ufton Level Crossing, Near Ufton Nervet, Berkshire Saturday, 6 November 2004. HSE interim report, 9 November 2004 (www.hse.gov.uk/ railways/index.htm)

Causes and types

World-wide there are a huge variety of major incidents (often called 'disasters'). Their causes are usually clearly defined though not always fully understood. In many cases they have causes *and* contributory factors. The contributory factors are circumstances which make the incident more serious than it might otherwise have been.

Natural causes

Natural causes of major incidents are causes over which human beings can have little or no influence. These events are caused either by the physical structure and behaviour of the Earth, or by **climatic** or weather factors.

Earthquakes

The Earth consists of a solid crust of rock about 30 miles thick floating on a base that is semi-liquid and very hot. The crust is divided into enormous natural rafts called tectonic plates. Where these plates meet there are zones of stress and earthquakes can happen.

The force of earthquakes is measured on the Richter scale, using information based on seismograph readings (a seismograph is an instrument for measuring vibrations in the ground). The scale is '**logarithmic**' – which means, for example, that an earthquake measuring 7 on the Richter scale of magnitude is roughly 100 times more destructive than an earthquake measuring 5 on the Richter scale.

The destruction and death caused by earthquakes is not dependent only on the force of the quake itself. It also depends on the population of the area affected, the building methods used, and whether most people were indoors at the time. In 1994 an earthquake in Los Angeles measuring 6.6 on the Richter scale killed 60 people and injured 7700. In 2003 an earthquake at Bam, Iran, also measuring 6.6 on the Richter scale, killed 26,000 people. The reason for the difference was that in Los Angeles for many years buildings have been built to be earthquake-proof. Bam, by contrast, was a medieval city built of stone in an area where earthquakes were not expected, so many thousands of people were crushed under falling rubble.

A further feature of earthquakes is that if they occur under the sea they can cause **tsunamis** – waves which can travel thousands of miles across the ocean and may cause massive loss of life and destruction when they hit land. The 2004 tsunami in the Indian Ocean, which killed over 250,000 people (mainly in Indonesia and Thailand but also in Sri Lanka and as far away as Somalia), was caused by an undersea earthquake off Sumatra measuring 9.0 on the Richter scale.

Volcanic eruptions

Volcanic eruptions, like earthquakes, occur where there are cracks in the Earth's crust caused by movements of the **tectonic** plates. They are most common in countries like Iceland, Japan or Indonesia which are situated on these lines of weakness. Sometimes earthquakes and volcanic eruptions are linked.

Every volcano is different. Some, such as Mount Etna in Sicily, erupt frequently but with only mild intensity and they are not particularly dangerous. Others explode violently and can kill hundreds of people (though volcanoes are less deadly, on the whole, than earthquakes). Unlike earthquakes, volcanic eruptions often give clear warnings before they happen and the warnings may take the form of earth tremors, escapes of steam or minor eruptions. Volcanoes can be classified according to the type of eruption: some pour out lava (liquid rock), but the more dangerous ones spew out hot gas and ash which can run down the slopes faster than people can escape it. These rushes of hot toxic gas and dust are called 'pyroclastic flows' – and they are the most dangerous kind

---

> **remember**
> Climate relates to average weather in a place over a period of years. Weather relates to conditions (e.g. rain, snow, frost, sunshine, temperature, etc.) from day to day.

> **remember**
> Places which are not near where the tectonic plates meet, such as Britain, are unlikely to experience severe earthquakes. However, minor ones do happen from time to time, usually along old fault lines (cracks in the Earth's crust) such as the Great Glen in Scotland.

> **remember**
> Volcanoes come in three types: active, which erupt fairly frequently; dormant ('sleeping'), which erupt very rarely; and extinct, which will never erupt again.

of volcanic eruption. Dangerous volcanic eruptions usually come from volcanoes which have been dormant for some time. The biggest since 1912 was the eruption of Mount Pinatubo on Luzon Island in the Philippines in 1991. Scientists now think the volcano had been dormant for 500 years.

Pinatubo began showing signs of life in 1990, after a major earthquake in the region. Experts warned that an eruption was imminent and most of the surrounding area was evacuated. Two large US military bases within 50 miles of the mountain helped in the evacuation. In July 1991 a series of gigantic explosions destroyed the mountain and forced the military bases to be abandoned. There are no photographs of the biggest explosions because they happened during a typhoon. Ten cubic kilometres of rock were blasted into the stratosphere, up to a height of 32,000 feet, in the form of fine dust – enough to make blue skies look pale and milky even in Britain for the next two years. Thanks to the evacuation tens of thousands of lives were saved. Three hundred people were killed directly by the eruption, but many hundreds later died as a result of poor sanitation in the relief camps to which they were evacuated.

Other disasters

Apart from tsunamis, the natural disasters mentioned above are not as devastating as climatic ones, i.e. floods and droughts. The worst floods are caused by hurricanes and similar storms (they are famous for their winds, but the floods that they bring kill more people). They occur only in certain tropical and sub-tropical parts of the world and are graded on a scale of 1–5 in severity, with 5 being the most severe. Hurricane Katrina (which passed directly over New Orleans in 2005 as a Category 3 **hurricane**) killed 700 people, even though clear warnings had been given and the US is a wealthy and well-prepared country.

In other parts of the world hurricanes are called cyclones or typhoons. A cyclone of the same violence as Hurricane Katrina (Category 3) killed 300,000 people in Bangladesh in 1970 and an even more violent one (Category 4) killed 138,000 Bangladeshis in April 1991. The death toll in Bangladesh was high because 10 million Bangladeshis live in the delta of the River Ganges on land which is only one metre or less above sea level. Floodwaters coming down the Ganges met 'tidal surges' (exceptionally high tides caused by storm-force winds and low atmospheric pressure) and the people in the middle were drowned.

Hostile acts

In terms of death and destruction, not to mention overall cost, hostile acts cause worse disasters than the forces of nature. A million died in the Iran–Iraq War in the 1980s, 800,000 died in the Rwanda genocide of 1994, and more than 200,000 died in the ongoing unrest in Darfur, Sudan. Deaths are caused not only by the fighting and massacres, but also by hunger and disease.

For much more about hostile acts and their effects see Unit 8, page 18–44

Terrorism

> It is more difficult to get a true figure for deaths caused by hostile acts than it is for deaths caused by natural disasters.

The biggest single terrorist act of recent years was the attack of 11 September 2001 on the World Trade Center in New York and the Pentagon (the US Ministry of Defence) in Washington. Passenger planes were hijacked and flown into the World Trade Center (WTC) 'twin towers' and the Pentagon building in a suicide attack. One plane crash-landed in a field. Total deaths were 3030 (approximate figure). This was carried out by **militants** inspired by the 'Islamist' ideology of the Al-Qaida organisation which aims to overthrow the west and bring about a new world order based on teachings which they claim come from the Qur'an.

www.september11news.com/911Art.htm

Terrorism happens in many parts of the world. The attacks in Madrid in 2004 and London in 2005 are the most well known in Britain, but there have also been major terrorist attacks in recent years in Russia, Turkey, Indonesia, India, Pakistan and in other Middle East countries. Following the invasion of Afghanistan in 2002 and of Iraq in 2003, deadly terrorist attacks in those countries have become an almost daily event, killing many thousands of people.

Civil wars

These are wars fought between hostile groups belonging to the same country. The fighting between Shia and Sunni communities in Iraq is considered by some to be a civil war. The 1994 killings in Rwanda were inter-ethnic conflict between the Hutu and Tutsi people, following a long-running struggle for control of the country. Civil wars are not usually 'declared' (i.e. officially recognised or admitted) like wars between one country and another. It is extremely hard to get accurate casualty figures for this kind of war.

Technological

Disasters such as train and plane crashes caused by the malfunctioning of parts, metal fatigue, signals or systems failure, etc., and explosions caused by chemical leaks and poor storage methods can be classified as 'technological'. Disasters in shipping, mines and oilfields come broadly under this heading too. Improved manufacturing methods and safety standards are reducing the size and frequency of this kind of disaster. In this kind of incident technological failure is often linked with other problems such as human or management error and adverse weather conditions.

Plane crashes

As with other technological incidents, plane crashes may not be wholly technological. The crash of an Air France Concorde at Gonesse outside Paris on 25 July 2000 killed 114 people. It was caused by a splinter of metal, possibly a spanner, left on the runway after the servicing of a DC 10. The metal burst a tyre of the Concorde as it ran over it, then shot upwards and ruptured a fuel tank in a wing, which then caught fire. However, the investigation showed that there was a weakness in the wing design of the Concorde which had contributed to previous accidents involving this type of plane. The judge in charge of the inquiry at Pontoise into the causes of the incident claimed that a previous French minister of transport had known about this weakness yet had never ordered anything to be done about it.

Crash du Concorde: le champ des responsabilités prend forme, 24 July 2005, France 2 (www.france2.fr/)

> **remember**
>
> Many disasters do not have a single cause; there are a number of causes and contributory factors that come together at the same time.

case study 14.3 — Buncefield

Monday marks the first anniversary of the giant explosion that ripped through the site near Hemel Hempstead, sending clouds of black smoke high into the atmosphere and causing chaos on the ground. An investigation revealed that a faulty **gauge** allowed thousands of gallons of unleaded petrol to be pumped into a full tank at the depot. More than 300 tonnes of fuel gushed unnoticed for 40 minutes from the top of the tank and the resulting vapour cloud ignited. The blast injured 43 people, two of them seriously.

Source: Buncefield a year on: clean-up continues, 9 December 2006, *Guardian*

activity — GROUP WORK

From the facts as they are given, to what degree would you say the Buncefield explosion was a technological incident, and to what degree would you say it was caused by human error?

Figure 14.2 Buncefield – technological failure or human error?

Radiation emissions

Nuclear radiation consists of high-energy sub-atomic particles (e.g. neutrons, protons and gamma rays) which can pass through living organisms and cause serious cell damage. With the exception of Chernobyl in 1986, nuclear power stations have not put out huge amounts of radiation, but there have been a number of significant leaks causing potential emergencies. The Chernobyl disaster led directly to the deaths of 56 people, and indirectly to another 4000 deaths (i.e. cancer deaths over and above the expected level), according to a report published for the Chernobyl Forum by the International Atomic Energy Agency.

Health-related and epidemics/pandemics

The number of deaths caused by illness is very much higher than all other causes, including war, put together.

However, a distinction has to be made between illness as a fact of life and illness as a major incident. The NHS and ambulance services deal with illnesses every day as an ongoing process. But illnesses vary in frequency, and when they increase over a period of a few years, or appear out of nowhere as HIV/AIDS did in the 1980s, or take the form of epidemics and pandemics (worldwide epidemics) they become major incidents in their own right.

Avian flu

This is a disease which affects birds – especially poultry and migratory birds such as geese, ducks and swans. It is becoming more common in the Far East and in some African countries. Birds die of avian (bird) flu, and if humans catch it they are likely to die too. According to the Department of Health, of 319 people known to have caught the deadly H5N1 strain worldwide, 192 have died. H5N1 is a virus, related to ordinary flu, which can be caught by people in close contact with infected birds. The fear is that the virus will **mutate** so it can pass directly from person to person like ordinary flu does. If this happens the only way to prevent widespread deaths will be a massive programme of vaccination, perhaps coupled with a **state of emergency** which limits travel and movement. But no vaccine can be made until the avian flu virus has already mutated into a form which can be passed from person to person.

> **remember**
>
> HIV/AIDS is the most serious **epidemic** of modern times. Since 1981, when the disease was identified, over 25 million people worldwide have died from it.

 www.dh.gov.uk/en/PandemicFlu/index.htm (Department of Health)

SARS

Severe Acute Respiratory Syndrome (SARS) is a viral disease which is believed to have originated from animals (possibly cats or ferrets) in China in 2002 and 'crossed the species barrier' so that it became a disease which humans could pass from one to another. The virus caused 8098 SARS cases in 26 countries, with 774 deaths, before the outbreak was declared over in summer 2003. SARS produces flu-like symptoms, but the ratio of infections to deaths suggests that it is not as deadly as bird flu. SARS was successfully eliminated by a concerted international effort, based mainly on the **dissemination** of information and measures to recognise, isolate and treat individuals who had it.

www.who.int/csr/resources/publications/WHO_CDS_CSR_ARO_2004_1.pdf

Produce a wall display or similar, suitable for informing volunteers in an organisation such as the Red Cross, outlining what major incidents are. Your display should outline three different causes of major incidents and give examples of each.

Effects

The effects of major incidents are serious, varied and widespread. The arrows between the three boxes in Figure 14.3 indicate that many of these effects overlap and can be felt by individuals, members of rescue services and the community as a whole. Rescue workers are also individuals and are often part of the community they serve.

Figure 14.3 Effects of major incidents

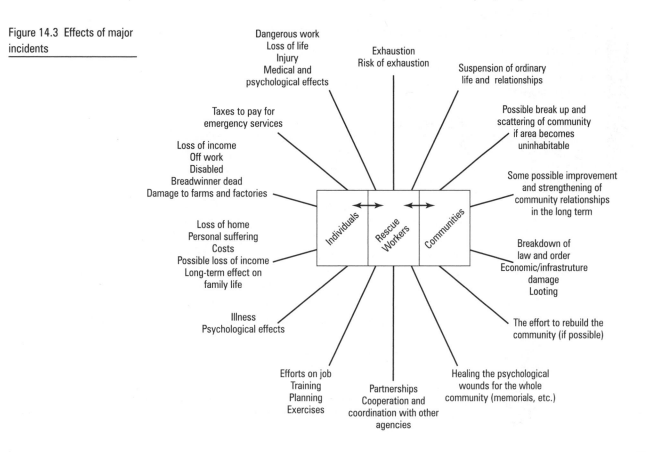

On individuals

Loss of income

If people suffer a major incident it is likely they will lose income as a result. This can happen through injury, illness, disability, death of a breadwinner or through the damaging psychological after-effects. The loss may or may not be compensated (partly) through health or life insurance, or – for needy people – through the government's Social Fund.

www.jobcentreplus.gov.uk **(see the Social Fund)**

Loss of income can also result from the loss of the means to make money – as case study 14.4 shows.

Loss of home

The loss of a home in a disaster can be temporary (for example evacuation for two nights during a flood alert) or permanent (as happens in floods or wars in some countries). The effects range from a period of inconvenience to a total change of living environment and lifestyle.

On rescue workers

In Britain and other developed countries rescue workers are mainly paid professionals, highly trained and skilled and with a good deal of equipment and back-up to protect them from the dangers and stresses of rescue work. Nevertheless, rescue work is dangerous, and may depend on taking a calculated risk. In the US such a risk led to the deaths of 343 firefighters during the destruction of the World Trade Center in 2001.

The other side of the coin is that rescue workers save lives in major incidents, and they are rightly admired for their bravery and professionalism when this happens.

case study
14.4

Effects of flooding, summer 2007

'Disaster zone'

According to NFU [National Farmers' Union] vice-president Paul Temple, the effect on flooded farms is 'phenomenal in terms of productivity'.

... In the West Midlands alone, the NFU estimates losses will run into tens of millions of pounds.

Among the crops worst hit are potatoes, broccoli, cauliflower and peas.

One NFU member in north-east Herefordshire is believed to have lost £500,000 worth of potatoes.

In Hereford and Worcester, dairy farmers have had to pour away thousands of pounds worth of milk because delivery tankers couldn't reach them through the floods.

Source: Floods spell 'crisis' for farming, 26 July 2007, http://news.bbc.co.uk/

activity
GROUP WORK

1. How will news like this affect ordinary people and why?
2. Discuss ways in which food production in Britain could be protected from the risk of flooding.
3. What role could the public services have in preventing or reducing flood losses for farmers?

Post-traumatic stress disorder

This condition, often called PTSD, can be suffered by people who have undergone shocking or traumatic events in their private or working lives. According to the American National Institute of Mental Health it takes the form of 'flashbacks or bad dreams, emotional numbness, intense guilt or worry, angry outbursts, feeling "on edge", or avoiding thoughts and situations that remind them of the trauma. In PTSD, these symptoms last at least one month'.

PTSD sometimes affects emergency service workers, and it is well-known in soldiers. Back in the 1914–18 War it was called 'shell shock' and thought, quite wrongly, to be a sign of cowardice. Now it is better understood, and most sufferers can be cured.

www.nimh.nih.gov/publicat/post-traumatic-stress-disorder-research-fact-sheet.cfm

On communities

Serious disasters can destroy whole communities, or cause social and economic damage which may take decades to recover from. The worst community effects are seen in countries where there has been a civil war, such as Iraq, Afghanistan, Sudan, Liberia and Somalia.

http://hrw.org/ (Human Rights Watch)

www.amnesty.org/ (Amnesty International)

Non-political disasters, which cannot be blamed on other people, are easier for communities to recover from. For example, New Orleans is rebuilding after the disaster of Hurricane Katrina – and this means rebuilding the community's social, cultural and economic life as well as the **infrastructure** and buildings.

Loss of law and order

During and immediately after Hurricane Katrina there was looting and civil disorder after a million people had fled, including many of the police. Other police had to abandon search and rescue in order to control the looting. Nevertheless, it does not appear to have been complete chaos.

Disease

Disease is a problem after hurricanes, tropical storms, droughts and other natural disasters. Rotting rubbish, abundant water, lack of sanitation and the weakened immune systems of disaster victims mean that water-borne diseases such as diarrhoea, **dysentery** and even **cholera** can flourish and spread if precautions are not taken. In the case of Hurricane Katrina only a handful of people are thought to have died from water-borne diseases.

> **remember**
>
> In countries such as India, Bangladesh, Mozambique and others which have suffered severe flooding, water-borne diseases are a much greater threat than they are in Europe or the US.

activity

GROUP WORK 14.2

P2

Research and make notes on three different major incidents, including one from the UK, showing their causes and their effects on people, communities and the environment – and any other short- or long-term effects they had. Using these notes, put together a presentation about at least three major incidents, with visual aids, then give the presentation, which should be suitable for volunteers in an agency such as the Red Cross. (NB: Keep your notes, to show that each group member has individually researched and described three major incidents.)

Wider impact of incidents
Reviews of disasters

A review of a disaster usually consists of:

- An account of the disaster.
- An account of the emergency service responses.
- An assessment of the effectiveness of those responses.
- An exploration of the causes of the disaster.
- A consideration of who (if anyone) is to blame for the disaster.
- A consideration of how such events can be prevented in the future.

The exact form of the review depends on:

- Who is carrying it out.
- The nature of the disaster.
- The format of the review (e.g. government-only review, **public inquiry**, etc.).
- The public interest (what is best for the public and also for the people/organisations, etc. involved).

Public inquiries

A public inquiry is an investigation which:

- Is initiated or permitted by a government minister, and announced in Parliament.
- Is open to the public and the media.
- Is not broadcast, e.g. on radio or TV.
- Is chaired by a judge, some other impartial expert, or a panel of people.
- Can have 'assessors' to assist the panel.
- Is intended to be as free and fair as possible.
- Is allowed to take evidence on **oath**, or not on oath, according to the decision of the chairperson.
- Is designed to seek causes and solutions (**inquisitorial**, not **adversarial**).
- Is not intended to lead directly to prosecutions ('not to determine any person's civil or **criminal liability**').
- Is followed up by a published report, which may lead to government action or changes in the law.

The main limitations to the freedom of public inquiries are that they can be prevented from **disclosing** information which would damage the British economy, and they can be prevented from publishing legally confidential material in the inquiry's report.

A public inquiry can lead indirectly to prosecutions, since the evidence it uncovers can form the basis of a further investigation by a **prosecuting authority**, such as the Health and Safety Executive – which can then take the people who are blamed for the disaster to court. This happened as a result of the Ladbroke Grove (Paddington) train crash in 1999 in which 31 people died and over 400 were injured. The public inquiry was carried out by Lord Cullen in 2000 and two reports were brought out in 2001, containing 163 recommendations, mainly about rail safety and safety management.

In 2003, after sifting through the evidence, the Health and Safety Executive decided to prosecute Thames Trains under the Health and Safety at Work Act 1974. The company pleaded guilty and, after the court hearing at the **Old Bailey** in 2004, they were fined £2 million, and the HSE were awarded costs.

Public inquiries are hugely expensive to run. They can also be politically embarrassing. As they can only be held with the consent of the government, it is possible for a government to refuse permission for a public inquiry – as happened in 2005 after the London bombings.

Inquiries Act 2005 (www.opsi.gov.uk/)

Debriefs of incidents by agencies

After major incidents the agencies (e.g. emergency services, Highways Agency, local authorities) all hold debriefings with their staff. Such debriefs typically come in two stages:

1. Individual agency '**operational debriefs**'.

2. **Multi-agency debrief** – may include findings from non-emergency services involved.

Purpose of debriefs

Debriefs aim to discover areas for improvement in procedures, equipment and systems.

They should not criticise others or interfere with ongoing investigations. Debriefs are not confidential: they can be disclosed in legal proceedings if, for example, the major incident leads to prosecution of the emergency services or anyone else linked to the incident or its aftermath.

Prevention

This complex subject is too wide to go into here in much detail. In technological disasters prevention is theoretically possible by, for example, maintaining aircraft and airports to such a high standard that this sort of incident cannot happen. Health-related incidents can be prevented by vaccination or avoiding contact with infection. Natural disasters cannot be prevented, but their effects can be limited, e.g. by not building on floodplains, by building earthquake-proof buildings in earthquake zones and by evacuating areas near volcanoes when the signs are that they are about to erupt.

Incidents involving human activity (e.g. terrorist attacks) cannot be prevented, but the threat may be reduced by a range of security measures coupled with social and political action to reduce discrimination and – perhaps – changes in foreign policy.

Better planning

This means planning:

■ To prevent preventable disasters.

■ Better emergency responses.

■ Better research, collection and dissemination of disaster information to agencies worldwide.

Some preventative aspects of planning are indicated in Table 14.2.

Table 14.2 Preventative aspects of planning

Hazard	Prevention
Flooding	Not building on floodplains (low-lying land near rivers which is known to get flooded from time to time)
Major fires	Building factories, etc. so that they have safe storage for flammable materials, and are constructed with fire risks in mind
Earthquakes	Building regulations which ensure buildings are resistant to earthquakes, e.g. with diagonal ties across the foundations
Aircraft terrorism	Good security at airports, coupled with intelligence about known terrorist groups and sympathisers

Improved technology

This includes vehicle and aircraft safety features, improved plant for chemical and other industrial processes and improved control and communication facilities so that a quick and appropriate emergency service response can be made when a major incident happens.

Better funding

This means more money for the emergency services and for any organisations (e.g. universities) which research into the causes or prevention of major incidents. The level of **funding** of the emergency services in Britain depends partly on the state of the economy, partly on the level of taxation, and partly on the **political climate** (e.g. can the government get more votes in the next general election if they give more funding to the emergency services?).

Environmental initiatives

Local environmental initiatives include things like flood defences, tree planting or measures to cut **firebreaks** (e.g. in Mediterranean countries) so that buildings are not threatened by forest fires. Recycling of household and other waste, and reducing our '**carbon footprints**' may (if everybody does it) help to slow down global warming which is blamed for extreme weather conditions in many parts of the world. Renewable energy schemes such as wind farms may help to limit global warming (though at an environmental cost of industrialising the countryside). Political initiatives include inter-government agreements to limit carbon dioxide emissions, 'carbon-trading' schemes, increased taxes for airports and other polluting industries, and Kyoto-style agreements to set strict targets for limiting carbon emissions. How effective these (and other) measures are in reducing environmental or weather-related disasters remains to be seen.

Education by authorities

Teaching people to recycle their rubbish will help to reduce pollution – but since environmental and climate/weather-based disasters depend on the entire world's climatic balance (e.g. pollution from the US, China or India, the burning of the Amazon rain forests, or the triggering of the **El Niño** ocean current in the Pacific), education may not be able to do much to tackle such problems in the short term unless it can change public opinion drastically.

Costs

The costs of major incidents are always enormous. As an example, according to insurance assessors the flooding in England in the summer of 2007 is expected to cost up to £3 billion. Britain has had to take the unusual step of asking for special help from the EU – a donation from the **Solidarity Fund** which could amount to £125 million. The costs include the following.

Damage

Damage to buildings and other property, farm crops, businesses, roads and other infrastructure, rivers and other flood defences.

Rebuilding

For a British flood disaster the buildings do not usually need rebuilding, but internal plastering will need to be replaced as will floors, carpets, furniture, etc., and flood defences, embankments, **levees**, etc. will have to be rebuilt.

Compensation

People who are privately insured will usually get compensation for flood damage. However, this is not true for farmers, who have difficulty insuring their crops. The government offers no compensation to victims of floods or coastal erosion, though it will compensate people whose land is compulsorily purchased for flood defences.

www.defra.gov.uk/environ/fcd/policy/strategy/comp.htm

Insurance

Private insurance poses problems for repeated flood-damage victims, who either have to pay high premiums or cannot get insurance at all. Furthermore, some less well-off people are unable to insure their houses or belongings properly. Such people may have to apply for grants or crisis loans from the government's Social Fund to get the help they need.

Grants and loans from the Social Fund, www.jobcentreplus.gov.uk

New investment (e.g. by governments and private companies for rebuilding)

Investment involves putting money into a project which will be of value, or will save money, in the future. Sometimes the investment needed is huge, because a disaster can highlight a danger which will cost the country an enormous amount of money to put right. This was the case with the Hatfield train derailment in 2000, in which four people died because the train ran over a cracked rail. It was followed by massive investment in track renewal – the high point being £6 billion spent in 2003/04. Though railways are partly self-funding they also receive around £7 billion per year from the government for normal maintenance and reinvestment costs. Annual expenditure on maintaining and renewing the tracks and signals alone (as opposed to the railways as a whole, including stations and rolling stock) has slowly declined since 2003/04 and is expected to be about £4.3 billion in 2008/09. In the case of the railways, reinvestment in track is the responsibility of Network Rail, a private company which is closely monitored by the government.

As is the case with many things in Britain, reinvestment after disasters often involves partnerships between public and private sectors. The government's role is biggest in things which are of strategic importance – such as railways.

Resultant legislation (e.g. new terrorism laws, new criminal offences)

Where major incidents are caused by human wrongdoing – terrorism or crime – it is possible to pass new laws to make it more difficult for terrorists or criminals to operate.

Since 1997 the Labour government has passed many laws which are designed to be 'tough on crime'. Table 14.3 outlines some which are relevant to dealing with emergencies or reducing the risk of major terrorist incidents.

Table 14.3 Laws designed to be tough on crime

Date	Law	Major incident risks addressed
1999	Statutory Instrument (SI) 1999/743	*Chemical spillages, explosions and other major industrial accidents.* The regulations give strict instructions on the safe storage of specific chemicals and list a range of dangerous substances
	The Control of Major Accident Hazards Regulations 1999	*Terror attacks.* Some of the substances listed can be used for making bombs; regulations to ensure that such materials are kept very secure will make it more difficult for would-be terrorists to obtain them
2000	Terrorism Act 2000	*Terror attacks*
		Lists and bans organisations considered to cause or support terror either in the UK or in other friendly countries
		Makes it an offence to raise money for a terrorist organisation
		Gives powers to seize money thought to belong to, or to be used by, terrorists

Date	Law	Major incident risks addressed
	The Anti-Terrorism, Crime and Security Act 2001	*Risk of terrorism* Cuts off terrorist funding Improves security of nuclear and aviation industries Improves security of dangerous substances Some increases in police powers
2004	Civil **Contingencies** Act 2004	*Any large-scale national emergency – especially floods, war, major terrorist attack, etc.* Emergency services and others (Category 1 and 2 Responders) have a duty to make risk assessments and draw up emergency plans Places a legal obligation on the 'responders' to deal with major emergencies Defines and clarifies emergency powers Defines and gives duties to Category 1 and Category 2 Responders (see page 206)
2004	Fire and Rescue Services Act 2004	*Major incidents* Strengthens the role of fire and rescue authorities so that they can either combine or set up **'reinforcement schemes'** to cooperate with other fire and rescue authorities and so become more effective at dealing with major incidents Defines the **'core duties'** of the fire and rescue service, placing a new emphasis on fire safety and prevention Gives the fire and rescue service a duty to deal with large-scale emergencies which it was not obliged to deal with before (though it did)
2005	Serious Organised Crime and Police Act 2005	*Civil disorder and risk to security of Parliament* Restricts processions and demonstrations within one mile of Parliament (Palace of Westminster) Gives extra powers of arrest
2006	Terrorism Act 2006	*Terrorist attacks* Creates offences of encouraging terrorism and of disseminating terrorist-related literature Creates terrorist training offences Creates offences relating to the misuse of radioactive material Bans groups that 'glorify' terrorism Allows terrorist suspects to be detained for up to 28 days without charge

Also see Anti-terrorism, Crime and Security Act 2001, www.opsi.gov.uk/ Police Reform Act 2002 (National Intelligence Model and extra powers for police employees) The Prevention of Terrorism Act 2005 (Control orders – suspected terrorists)

Procedures (e.g. new police powers)

Procedures are systems used when doing a job, and much police work consists of following procedures designed to ensure that justice is done, that criminals can be prosecuted and that evidence will stand up in court.

Most police powers are laid down in the Police and Criminal Evidence Act (PACE) 1984. However, new police powers have been brought in – mainly in the Criminal Justice Act 2003, the Serious Organised Crime and Police Act 2005 and the Terrorism Acts of 2000 and 2006.

New bodies such as the **National Policing Improvement Agency** (set up in 2004) and initiatives such as the National Intelligence Model improve the recording and communication of information and help the police to counter the threats of terrorism and organised crime. Criminal intelligence is stored and processed in the Police National Computer, National DNA Database and IDENT1, the national fingerprint and palm print system. Other procedures include gathering and sharing intelligence internationally through Europol, Interpol and international policing and political agreements.

Processes (e.g. secure airport check in)

Ever since the 1980s (especially after the Lockerbie bombing of 1988) there has been increasing awareness of the need for security in airports, on planes, in ferry terminals, etc. With the events of 9/11 the risks became even more obvious. Airport security has been increased, and there are plans to introduce national identity cards and **biometric passports** (which are thought to be impossible to fake). There are restrictions on the carrying of liquids, aerosols and other things that might (or look as if they might) be used in carrying out hijackings or terrorist attacks on a plane. The US has introduced requirements for passenger registration for all people visiting the US. Immigration processes have been tightened under the Immigration, Asylum and Nationality Act 2006 as a result of fears that potential terrorists are entering the country under the pretence of being asylum seekers.

Improvements (e.g. communication systems)

It is possible to obtain a good deal of information through the electronic and satellite monitoring of mobile phone messages. Millions of these are routinely scanned for '**chatter**' about terrorism and terrorist-related subjects, and are used for, among other things, fixing threat levels for terrorism in Britain and elsewhere. Within the emergency services new communications technology, called 'Airwave' (a secure digital mobile radio service) is replacing the older systems, which can become overloaded (as they did in the 2005 London bombings).

Addressing Lessons from the Emergency Response to the 7 July 2005 London Bombings, What we learned and what we are doing about it, 22 September 2006, http://security.homeoffice.gov.uk/news-publications/publication-search/general/lessons-learned?view=Binary

activity
INDIVIDUAL WORK 14.3

P3

You work for a Local Resilience Forum. Write a short leaflet to be given to new delegates to the forum explaining the main points that have to be considered when drawing up an emergency plan.

The type of work carried out by the public services during major incidents

Inter-agency cooperation

An agency is any organisation (e.g. the police, the fire and rescue service, the Health and Safety Executive, the Red Cross) which acts for the government or the public. Agencies can be statutory or non-statutory, uniformed or non-uniformed, professional or voluntary. Cooperation means working and planning together (sometimes closely coordinating activities; sometimes working independently but on the same site).

Agencies involved in major incident/disaster recovery

Different agencies specialise in dealing with different aspects of a major incident. In the biggest emergencies many agencies can be involved. The following appear in the latest edition of the London Emergency Services Liaison Panel's *Major Incident Procedure Manual* 7th edition, 2007.

Table 14.4 Roles of agencies in a major incident

Agency	Roles in major incident
Air Accident Investigation Branch	Investigates plane crashes
Ambulance	See under 'London Ambulance Service'
Borough Emergency Control Centre (BECC)	Coordinates the local authority response
British Association of Immediate Care (BASICS)	Gives primary care and first aid; assists ambulance service
British Red Cross Society	Assists ambulance service; helps to run care centres
Central Government	Decides overall strategy and gives financial aid through COBRA
Coroner	Establishes identity and cause of death
Counter Terrorism Command	Specialist branch of Metropolitan Police working against terrorism
The Environment Agency	Monitors weather (using the Met Office) and river levels
	Issues warnings through automatic voice-messaging for registered users, loudhailer, volunteer flood wardens, sirens, the media and the internet
	Helps deal with and prevent floods; also concerned with air quality and waste disposal
Fire and rescue service	Search and rescue
	Fire fighting and prevention
	Humanitarian services
	Identifying and dealing with hazards
	Safety management
First Aid Nursing Yeomanry (FANY)	Assist police; carry out first aid
Forensic specialists	Assist **pathologist** in carrying out post mortems and establishing causes of death
	Help police collect evidence of crime
Health Advisory Team	Strategic group chaired by NHS; advises police, etc. on health aspects of major incident
Health and Safety Executive	Investigates causes and blame for major incidents
Helicopter Emergency Medical Service (HEMS)	Emergency evacuation of casualties – especially to distant hospitals. Emergency life support
HM Coastguard	Coordination of search and rescue (sea or estuary)
	Identify casualty landing points
Home Office pathologist	Post mortems to find out causes of deaths
Interpol	Information on international crime and terrorism
Joint Emergency Services Control Centre (JESCC)	HQ of the emergency services at Silver command level, based at or near the scene of the incident. Makes tactical decisions

Agency	Roles in major incident
Local authority	Supports emergency services
	Supports community
	Sets up rest and emergency centres
	Activates emergency plans (which it has already drawn up)
	Staffs Gold, Silver and Bronze commands
	Leads recovery stage – rebuilding, caring, etc.
London Ambulance Service	Saves lives with the other emergency services
	Treats people at scene
	Sets up casualty clearing station for assessment, treatment, triage and evacuation/removal to hospital of casualties
	Evacuates vulnerable people
	Supports the local authority
	Alerts hospitals to receive casualties
London Resilience Team	Overall coordination of disaster response in London area. Works with Gold command
Marine Accident Investigation Branch	Investigates major shipping incidents
Media relations	Police take the lead and follow arrangements laid down in emergency plan; other agencies can comment on their areas of expertise. The aim is to avoid 'contentious' and 'contradictory' statements
Military	Helicopter rescues (RAF Search and Rescue)
	Special Security duties (authorised by Ministry of Defence)
	General duties help by unarmed military personnel in widespread emergencies such as major floods
	Military help is usually requested only if the emergency is too great to be coped with by non-military services
NHS	Makes special arrangements to deal with casualties and health threats to the community
Police	See page 202 below
Private industry recovery specialists	Dealing with wreckage, clearing roads, etc. after investigation of incident is finished
RAF Search and Rescue (SAR) Helicopters	See under 'Military'
Rail Accident Investigation Branch	Investigates rail crashes
RAYNET	Voluntary government-licensed radio operators who are able to provide emergency radio communications to the emergency services, local authorities and central government departments
Salvation Army	Humanitarian help, especially at care centres, etc.
St John Ambulance	First aid (works with ambulance service)
Utility companies (e.g. gas, water, electricity, telephones)	Can supply or cut off water, gas, electricity as required and provide communication facilities
Victim recovery and identification teams	Disaster Victim Recovery and Identification Teams (DVRITs) are specially trained police who find and identify victims
Women's Royal Voluntary Service (WRVS)	Helps the police (humanitarian work)

London Emergency Services Liaison Panel's *Major Incident Procedure Manual* 7th edn, 2007 (www.leslp.gov.uk)

www.environment-agency.gov.uk/ (Environment Agency)

www.defra.gov.uk/ (DEFRA)

www.metoffice.gov.uk/ (Met Office)

> **remember**
>
> The Department for Environment, Food and Rural Affairs (DEFRA) gives help, advice and guidance on pollution, animal disease and waste disposal.

Local authorities

Local authorities have a major and often extended role in dealing with major incidents.

Figure 14.4 shows the how the role evolves during and after the emergency.

Summary of local authority duties

Immediate stage:

- Support emergency services.
- Care for local and wider community.
- Mitigate (limit) effects of emergency.
- Coordinate agencies other than the emergency services.
- Give advice and information to the affected communities.

Transitional stage:

- Take over increasing responsibility from the emergency services.
- Give advice and help to the community.
- Give humanitarian assistance.
- Temporary and urgent rebuilding.
- Tackling homelessness in the short term.

Recovery stage:

- Continued advice, support, humanitarian help.
- Manage appeal fund (if any).
- Handle VIP visits.
- Repair to property, infrastructure and environment.
- Handle any memorial service.
- Debrief.

> **remember**
>
> 'Emergency' is the word used in the Civil Contingencies Act; 'major incident' is the term often used by the emergency services; 'disaster' is a more sensational word preferred by the media. All three mean roughly the same thing, but the professionals tend to prefer 'emergency' or 'major incident'.

Figure 14.4 Stages of local government (county council) involvement in an emergency

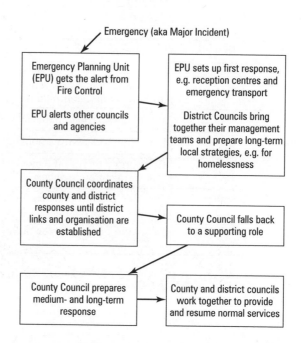

Lincolnshire County Council Emergency Plan 2007, www.lincolnshire.gov.uk/

Lincolnshire Emergency Planning, www.lincolnshire.gov.uk/emergencyplanning.

Several good emergency plans

Emergency services

Table 14.4 on page 196 outlines the role of all the emergency services except that of the police, which is slightly more complex.

Red Cross

The Red Cross backs up the fire and rescue service and the ambulance service in responding to major incidents such as transport accidents, evacuations, floods and fires. It trains first aiders, gives advice on workplace safety and gives assistance to asylum seekers. Overseas it plays a major role in relief work for natural disasters and in war zones. In some Muslim countries the organisation is called the Red Crescent.

www.redcross.org.uk/39992

Military

Military help in large-scale emergencies is called Military Assistance to Civil Authorities (MACA). It is available under three schemes:

- Military Aid to the **Civil Power** (MACP).
- Military Aid to other Government Departments (MAGD).
- Military Aid to the **Civil Community** (MACC).

MACC is requested by local authorities and involves things like relief work in floods. MACP is requested by the police, since it involves duties relating to law and order or security and is politically sensitive.

Central government can also ask for military aid in an emergency. In 2003 the military were called in by the then prime minister, Tony Blair, to reinforce security at Heathrow and other sites in London after a security alert warning of an attack by Al-Qaida or its sympathisers.

Figure 14.5 It would be chaos, but for the planned response

case study 14.5 — Duties of the police in a major incident

- The saving of life together with the other emergency services.

- The coordination of the emergency services, local authorities and other organisations acting in support at the scene of the incident.

- To secure, protect and preserve the scene to facilitate the work of the Emergency services.

- The management of cordons to protect the public, property and survivors.

- The criminal investigation of the incident; **collation** of evidence and the facilitation of investigation by the responsible accident investigation bodies where applicable.

- The collection and distribution of casualty information.

- The identification of the deceased on behalf of Her Majesty's (HM) Coroner.

- The coordination of search activities on land.

Source: Lincolnshire Resilience Forum Emergency Procedures Manual 2006

activity
INDIVIDUAL WORK

1. The police response is carried out in the order shown. Explain, in relation to each activity, why this is so.

2. Which other agencies or services could be involved in each of the roles given and how?

Other aspects of the role of the military in major incidents and emergencies are outlined on page 197 above.

Interaction between emergency and other services (e.g. knowledge of objectives as laid down in emergency plans, joint training)

Interaction is a growth area in emergency service work because:

- Disasters are complex and require several different types of expertise to deal with them.

- In the past, the rescue services have sometimes hampered each others' work.

- Different services have different structures, chains of command, communication systems and emergency response equipment. They need to be able to coordinate effectively in a crisis, and know when and how to call on each others' help.

- Major incidents are rare and unexpected, so people do not learn about them from experience – they need special training.

- There is a legal requirement under the Civil Contingencies Act 2004 for agencies to work together in the preparation of and training for emergency plans.

- The public is more 'emergency-minded' following recent terrorist attacks, floods, etc.

Emergency plans produced by central government, local government, the NHS and other organisations need to be disseminated and practised just as fire drills and evacuation procedures do in a college – and for the same reason. Unless people are informed and trained in emergency response they do not know what to do and lives can be lost because the response was either too slow or the response was wrong. In addition there is the safety and well-being of emergency service workers to consider: for their own protection they need to know in advance what dangers they can face and the best procedures for facing those dangers.

Emergency plans produce objectives: clear statements of what different agencies should do in an emergency, and how strategy, tactics and operations should be organised.

Link

For more on chains of command see page 207

Interaction between the emergency services happens all the time, at many levels. It can be divided into **multilateral** interaction, such as meetings of the Local Resilience Forum (LRF), where many agencies are involved, and **bilateral** interaction, which is more informal links, usually between two services, for example the police and the fire and rescue service. Interaction takes the form of phone calls, emails, visits, seminars, secondments, joint training sessions and simulations where a whole range of agencies are involved in a large-scale 'live exercise' based on a disaster **scenario**. The interaction also happens at different levels of the chain of command, ranging from formal agreements such as 'protocols' and 'memoranda of understanding' between, say, the Association of Chief Police Officers and the fire and rescue service, to interaction between people who work together operationally (at the incident scene) under **Bronze command**. A wide range of training which people from different agencies can attend is carried out at places such as the Emergency Planning College at Easingwold, near York.

> **remember**
>
> Emergency plans are easily downloaded from the internet and contain much of the material you need to cover this unit. They can be found on many local authority websites.

Responsibilities at the scene

Common objectives

Common objectives are objectives (purposes) which are shared by all of the emergency services attending a major incident scene. They are outlined in Figure 14.6.

Figure 14.6 Common objectives of emergency services at the scene of a major incident

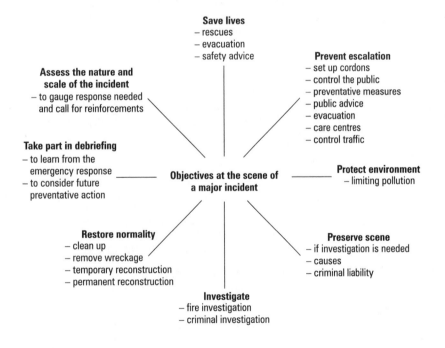

Agency-specific objectives

This is the specialised work which is done by each of the individual emergency services.

Link

See page 197 and Unit 15, pages 241–246

Local authority

Local authorities have more different functions than any of the emergency services. The more major and long-lasting the incident, the greater their duties are likely to be. In the early stages one of their main roles is to facilitate the emergency services' response – for example by helping them to close roads, by warning the public, by contacting and employing specialised services, etc. Once the investigation is over and the clean-up begins (if it is that kind of major incident) the emergency services withdraw and allow the local authority services to restore normality.

Maintenance of normal community services

Major incidents such as train crashes, foot-and-mouth disease or explosions in oil storage depots may be national headline news, but people who are not directly affected usually want (and need) to get on with their lives as if nothing had happened. Thus, even at the height of the emergency, the local authority has a duty to try to see that the lives of most people are not disturbed more than necessary.

Evacuation

The local emergency plan should indicate who evacuates people and where they should be evacuated. Evacuation usually happens on the instructions of the fire and rescue service (Silver command) and it is carried out by local authority staff helped by volunteers. Local authority buildings such as schools and community halls can be set up as rest centres.

Emergency telephone numbers

These are set up by a central **casualty bureau** to answer enquiries from the public about missing relatives and friends. They are publicised over local and sometimes national radio, television and other media. As the enquiries diminish, the local police area may then deal with them.

Accommodation and rest/reception centres

Depending on the size of the need, these are usually in community halls and other places where there is shelter, heating, security, welfare, communication, catering and medical facilities – and where disruption to the rest of community life is minimised.

Creation of a unified response procedure

This comes about through:

- The **Local Resilience Forum** (based in a local police area – also called a 'local **resilience** area') which coordinates multi-agency planning and may publish an emergency plan. This plan outlines duties of all the emergency services and the local authority (Category 1 and Category 2 responders) in the event of a major incident.

- The **Emergency Planning Unit** (run by the local authority) which produces both generic and specific emergency plans with the active collaboration of local emergency services.

- Training, practice and coordination in emergency procedures now carried out by all emergency services, following the Civil Contingencies Act 2004.

Support to emergency services

The local authority will try to support the emergency services in any way they can – especially by facilitating transport (e.g. to hospitals) and communication, assigning staff to clean-up and other duties, and getting help either from nearby local authorities or from specialist organisations (e.g. scientific bodies or clean-up services).

Police

Collate and distribute casualty information

The police have a role at major incidents to collect **casualty** information, collate it (i.e. put it together in lists) and distribute it to those who need it.

Information about injured people is needed:

- By primary care trusts, GPs and hospitals if they are receiving them.

- By their relatives and friends.

- For statistical and media information.

---

remember

A Local Resilience Forum is an arrangement (set up under the Civil Contingencies Act 2004) for ensuring that all the Category 1 and Category 2 responders (i.e. all emergency services) in a police area are able to meet, liaise and plan together on a regular basis. LRFs are usually chaired by a Chief Constable.

remember

An Emergency Planning Unit is a local authority department which produces, updates and reviews major incident response plans. It coordinates council departments and emergency services.

remember

The word 'casualty' is ambiguous, in that sometimes it means injured people and sometimes it means dead people.

Information about fatalities is needed by:

- The **coroner**, so that the cause of death can be determined and a decision made as to whether the death(s) is(are) the result of criminal activity.
- Relatives and friends.
- The media.

The media are given a special phone line for their inquiries. Care is taken not to release the names of victims to the media until the victims' families have been told.

The police set up a casualty bureau for collating information about deaths, casualties, survivors and evacuees. This is a temporary office full of telephones and computer links. The role of the bureau is to:

- Trace, identify or obtain information about people involved or potentially involved in the incident.
- Assess and process that information.
- Provide accurate information to relatives and friends, the investigating and identification officers and HM Coroner.

Preserve crime scene

If the major incident (e.g. a train or aircraft crash, an explosion, a major fire) may be the result of a crime, the police have to preserve the scene so that forensic and other investigators can get valid evidence about the causes of the incident, and about possible criminal actions.

Unit 15, page 247

Investigate cause

All emergencies and major incidents are investigated. The police have to do what they can to facilitate the investigation, and preserve evidence, even if they are not the main people carrying out the investigation. For that reason the **Senior Investigating Officer** at the scene of a major incident is likely to be a police officer, even if he or she is not directly in charge of the main investigation. Different kinds of incident may be investigated by different groups of investigators, as Table 14.5 shows.

Table 14.5 Incidents and the investigating bodies

Type of major incident	Probable investigating body(ies)
Fire	Divisional fire investigation teams
Explosion	Police
	Health and Safety Executive (HSE)
Air crash	Air Accident Investigation Branch (AAIB)
Capsize of boat	Marine Accident Investigation Branch
Floods	Environment Agency
	Local authorities
Chemical leak	Health and Safety Executive
Rail crash	Rail Accident Investigation Bureau
Radiation leak	HSE's Nuclear Safety Directorate

www.hse.gov.uk/nuclear/thorpreport.pdf

Identify dead

The police appoint a Senior Identification Manager to coordinate the task of identifying casualties and collating casualty information at a major incident. Identities of deceased persons are needed by the coroner.

Ensure access and egress at incident

The police are responsible for ensuring that all emergency services, inspection teams, etc. have access to the incident scene. They establish holding areas, where ambulances can load up with casualties, or conduct triage (sorting) to determine priority cases. A **rendezvous point** (RVP) is set up where information can be exchanged between the different services working on the site (e.g. about casualties).

Control cordons

A cordon is a barrier (often made of tape) indicating an area around an incident scene where access is controlled. Major incident scenes often have three concentric cordons, arranged as in Figure 14.7.

Crowd control

This may be needed for the following reasons:

■ To protect people from the incident or its effects.

■ To protect the incident scene from contamination or disturbance by members of the public.

■ To enable emergency workers to get on with their job without distraction.

■ To organise decontamination of members of the public after a major chemical incident.

■ To enable casualties and dead bodies to be dealt with efficiently and decently.

■ To control looting, disorder and lawlessness after a major incident.

Control is by use of cordons, loudhailers, media announcements to discourage sightseers, or even the strategic parking of public service vehicles to make an improvised barrier. For wider disasters such as major flooding, extra policing or deployment of community support officers, etc. can help prevent problems of looting and vandalism.

> **remember**
>
> The **marshalling area** is used as a vehicle park, a rest area for emergency workers, and a place for briefing and debriefing.

Figure 14.7 Control cordons

Source: London Emergency Services Liaison Panel

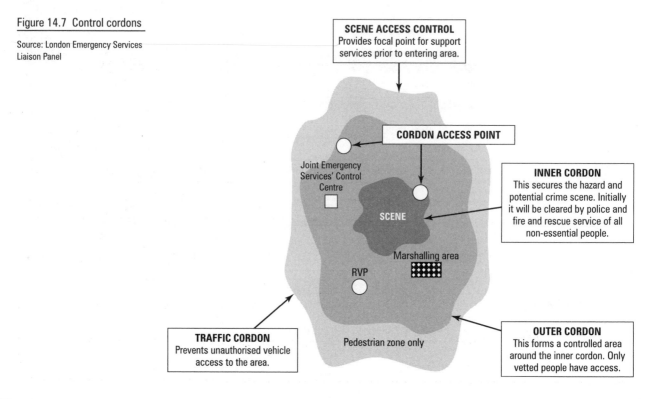

SCENE ACCESS CONTROL
Provides focal point for support services prior to entering area.

CORDON ACCESS POINT

Joint Emergency Services' Control Centre

SCENE

INNER CORDON
This secures the hazard and potential crime scene. Initially it will be cleared by police and fire and rescue service of all non-essential people.

Marshalling area

RVP

TRAFFIC CORDON
Prevents unauthorised vehicle access to the area.

Pedestrian zone only

OUTER CORDON
This forms a controlled area around the inner cordon. Only vetted people have access.

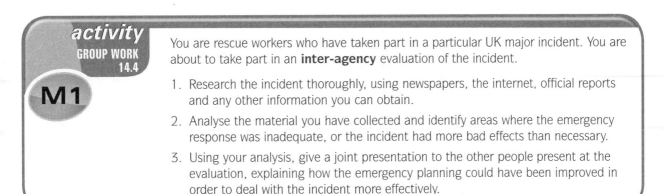

You are rescue workers who have taken part in a particular UK major incident. You are about to take part in an **inter-agency** evaluation of the incident.

1. Research the incident thoroughly, using newspapers, the internet, official reports and any other information you can obtain.

2. Analyse the material you have collected and identify areas where the emergency response was inadequate, or the incident had more bad effects than necessary.

3. Using your analysis, give a joint presentation to the other people present at the evaluation, explaining how the emergency planning could have been improved in order to deal with the incident more effectively.

Duties under law

remember

A contingency is any major unexpected incident, danger or emergency.

Civil Contingencies Act 2004

The Civil Contingencies Act 2004 is the main law governing large-scale emergency response in Britain.

The Act describes a 'contingency' as an 'emergency' rather than a 'major incident' and defines emergency as shown in case study 14.6.

---

case study
14.6

Definition of 'emergency'

An event or situation which threatens serious damage to human welfare [or] to the environment of a place in the United Kingdom [including] war, or terrorism, which threatens serious damage to the security of the United Kingdom... if it involves, causes or may cause:

- loss of human life
- human illness or injury
- homelessness
- damage to property
- disruption of a supply of money, food, water, energy or fuel
- disruption of a system of communication
- disruption of facilities for transport
- disruption of services relating to health
- contamination of land, water or air with biological, chemical or radio-active matter...
- disruption or destruction of plant life or animal life.

The event or situation... may occur or be inside or outside the United Kingdom.

Source: Adapted from Part 1(1) of the Civil Contingencies Act 2004

---

activity
INDIVIDUAL WORK

Read the definition carefully, then:

1. Make a list of all the major emergencies which have happened in Britain in the last five years.

2. Go through each of the bullet points and decide which emergencies satisfy each point.

The Civil Contingencies Act:

1. Defines 'emergency' (see case study 14.6 above).

2. Defines Category 1 and 2 responders (see Table 14.6).

3. Outlines Category 1 duties:

   (a) duty to assess, plan and advise;

   (b) duty to give advice and assistance to enable commercial activities to continue;

   (c) to take account of what voluntary organisations can do.

4. Includes rules on information-sharing between responders.

5. Allows for government monitoring of Category 1 plans and performance of functions.

6. Lays down rules for declaring a state of emergency (must be within the Human Rights Act 1998).

7. Gives provision for regional and emergency coordinators in a nationwide state of emergency (coordinators are attached to the nine regional development agencies).

Table 14.6 Responders

Category 1 responders	Category 2 responders
Local authorities (including county councils, district councils, borough councils)	Utilities: gas, water, electricity, sewerage and telephone companies/providers
Chief Constables (i.e. the police)	Public transport operators
Fire and rescue authorities (i.e. the fire and rescue service)	Airport operators
	Port authorities
NHS trusts (including ambulance services)	Secretary of State for Transport
Environment Agency	Health and Safety Executive
Secretary of State for Transport (maritime and coastal emergencies only)	

Subsequent amendments

The Civil Contingencies Act 2004 is a major law outlining the main national arrangements for emergency planning. More exact and strictly defined legal guidelines are provided by the Civil Contingencies Act 2004 (Contingency Planning) Regulations 2005.

Cabinet Office (2005) *Emergency Preparedness, Guidance on Part 1 of the Civil Contingencies Act 2004, its associated Regulations and non-statutory arrangements* (www.ukresilience.info/preparedness/ccact/eppdfs.aspx)

Cabinet Office (2005) *Emergency Response and Recovery, Non-statutory guidance to complement Emergency Preparedness* (www.ukresilience.info/)

Civil Contingencies Act 2004 (www.opsi.gov.uk/)

The Civil Contingencies Act 2004 (Contingency Planning) Regulations 2005 (SI 2005/2042) (www.ukresilience.info/upload/assets/www.ukresilience.info/finalregs.pdf)

Emergency powers

Emergency powers are special powers given to the police, courts and other public authorities in order to deal with serious emergencies such as a major epidemic, the risk of civil war, or some other situation which could not be dealt with under normal arrangements or normal legal processes. They can be applied to a region of Britain, or to the whole country. Under the Civil Contingencies Act 2004 there are various limitations (see sections 22 and 23 of the Act). For example, people cannot be compelled under emergency powers to undertake military service against their will. The Human Rights Act 1998 has to be respected as far as possible, and the state of emergency must be lifted as soon as it is safe to do so.

Duties of cooperation placed on agencies by law

By going to the High Court, government ministers or Category 1 or 2 responders can legally force others to cooperate. Secondary legislation (sometimes known as Regulations or Statutory Instruments) can be used to define the types of cooperation which should be given by other agencies.

Chains of command

Chains of command are organisational structures designed to make it easy for orders to be given and for feedback to be received. In an emergency these chains of command are 'role' related, not 'rank' related, and do not necessarily follow the official chains of command of the service(s) involved.

Operational (Bronze)

In an emergency, Bronze command, based on the incident scene, is likely to be the first tier (level of command) established.

Bronze command is made up of people who are at 'operational supervisor' level (e.g. police sergeants). Bronze command is based at a 'forward control point' – often a large vehicle parked at the scene.

The role of Bronze is to command and control tasks such as casualty identification or chemical monitoring.

Tactical (Silver)

Silver command, which is normally based near the incident scene, is usually activated shortly after Bronze command has been established. Silver is made up of 'middle managers'. A multi-**agency** Silver command is normally coordinated by the police. The roles of Silver are shown in case study 14.7.

---

case study **14.7** **Silver command**

The roles of Silver command are as follows:

- Determine priorities for allocating available resources.
- Plan and coordinate how and when tasks will be undertaken.
- Request additional resources if required.
- Assess significant risks and use this to inform tasking of Bronze commanders.
- Ensure the health and safety of the public and personnel.

---

activity
INDIVIDUAL WORK

What is 'tasking' and how is it done?

Strategic (Gold)

Gold command is used only for the biggest emergencies, and is usually not based at the incident but at the nearest police headquarters.

Gold command (headed by someone of chief officer level) is in overall charge of the strategic management of the emergency. Sometimes a multi-agency Gold Strategic Coordination Group is formed.

The roles of Gold command are outlined in case study 14.8.

case study 14.8 — Gold command

The roles of Gold are to:

■ Determine and **promulgate** a clear strategic aim and objectives within which Silver will work, and to review this regularly.

■ Establish a **policy framework** for the overall management of the incident.

■ Prioritise the demands of Silver and allocate personnel and resources to meet requirements.

■ Formulate and **implement** media handling and public communication plans.

■ Direct planning and operations beyond the immediate response in order to facilitate the recovery process.

activity
INDIVIDUAL WORK

1. What is a review and what is its purpose?
2. What is a policy framework and why is it needed?
3. Write out a list of rules which you think should apply to media briefings by the emergency services at a major incident.

Organisation of the local authorities and emergency services

Each of the nine regions in England and Wales has a Regional Resilience Forum – a body which coordinates local authorities in the region and sets up a regional (large-scale) framework for inter-agency planning and response to a major incident. The Forum organises the sharing of resources if the incidents are so big that a number of local authorities have to work together to deal with it.

The local authority response is overseen by a partnership between the local authority and the emergency services called a Local Resilience Forum (LRF; see below for a list of members of an LRF). At the early stages of the emergency the LRF coordinates closely with Gold command, especially if Gold command takes the form of a Strategic Coordination Group taking charge of the multi-agency management of a large-scale emergency. Indeed, the Strategic Coordination Group can be seen as an extension of the LRF.

Local authorities have their own emergency planning units and contingency plans. In the event of an emergency they set up traffic cordons. They also usually have a civil protection unit which will help organise evacuation, rest centres, family assistance centres, family and friends' reception centres (for members of the public), etc. The local authority may provide rest and recuperation facilities for emergency workers since dealing with emergencies is exhausting work which may carry on non-stop over several days or even longer.

remember

Local Resilience Forum (LRF) is defined as a 'process for bringing together all of the Category 1 and 2 responders within a local police area for the purpose of facilitating cooperation in fulfilment of their duties under the Civil Contingencies Act'.

remember

In smaller emergencies there may not be a Gold command, only Silver and Bronze.

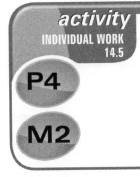

activity

INDIVIDUAL WORK 14.5

P4

M2

Choose three major incidents, at least one of which must have been in the UK. List the agencies which took part in the emergency response to each incident. For the UK incident(s), show and explain how the duties carried out by the emergency and other services fitted in with the laws which lay down those duties. Put your information into a leaflet for emergency service recruits headed 'Emergency Response and the Law'.

The considerations for emergency planning and preparation for possible major incidents

Main considerations

The main considerations when making emergency plans are based on risk assessments carried out in the area covered by the Local Resilience Forum. The risks identified depend on the nature of the local area, for example:

- The topography (coast, main rivers, access to different parts of the area, risk of floods and landslips, towns built close to rivers, developments on flood plains, etc.).

- The main industries carried out there (especially potentially hazardous industries such as mining, fishing and forestry, chemical works, major dams and reservoirs, oil refineries, fuel storage depots, power plants, nuclear power plants – but also farming and poultry-rearing which might be at risk of disease).

- Strategic or terrorist targets (airports, sea ports, ferry ports, military bases or communication centres, sports stadiums, major train and bus stations).

- Communications and infrastructure (motorways, railways, reservoirs, water supplies, high-tension electricity pylons).

- People living in the area (are there people or communities who might be sympathetic to terrorism; large organised events and festivals etc.?).

- The past history of emergencies or major incidents in the area (or in similar areas elsewhere).

Assessment – identification of possible incidents (e.g. large-scale road traffic collisions, possible plane/train accidents, terrorist activities, flooding, diseases)

Assessment of risks is based mainly on an analysis of historical emergencies matched with the hazards of the type listed above which are present in the local area. The assessments can be done by the emergency services, any other Category 1 or Category 2 responders, Emergency Planning Units or Local Resilience Forum working groups. A Local Resilience Forum typically involves a range of knowledgeable organisations.

case study 14.9

Membership of Lincolnshire Resilience Forum

The following are members of the Lincolnshire Resilience Forum:

- Lincolnshire Ambulance Service
- Lincolnshire Fire and Rescue
- Lincolnshire Police
- Maritime and Coastguard Agency
- Lincolnshire County Council
- Lincoln City Council
- North Kesteven District Council [and five other]
- The Environment Agency
- Health Protection Agency
- East Lincs **Primary Care Trust** (on behalf of Lincolnshire PCTs)
- Anglian Water (on behalf of the Critical Infrastructure Group)
- The Red Cross (on behalf of the Voluntary Sector)
- Government Office for the East Midlands
- The Armed Forces

Source: Lincolnshire Resilience *Forum Emergency Procedures Manual 2006*

Lincolnshire Resilience Forum Emergency Procedures Manual 2006
www.lincolnshire.gov.uk/section.asp?catid=2341

activity
GROUP WORK

What expertise do you think each of the listed organisations could bring to emergency planning?

Table 14.7 outlines possible incident hazards.

Table 14.7 Potential incident hazards

Type of incident	Potential hazard
Large-scale road traffic collisions	Motorways – especially overloaded motorways in areas prone to fog
Plane/train accidents	The presence of airports and railways; unstaffed level crossings
Terrorist activities	Air terminals; public transport; military installations; any place or event which attracts huge numbers of people and publicity
Flooding	Rivers with a history of flooding; low-lying built-up areas; places subject to deforestation or large-scale change in land use
Diseases	Animal diseases such as bird flu which could cross the 'species barrier'; animal diseases such as BSE and foot-and-mouth; **legionnaires' disease**; **E-coli**; immigration from countries where diseases, e.g. tuberculosis, are not controlled

Hazard prevention options

Preventing emergencies from happening is cheaper and more effective than dealing with them once they have happened. Prevention saves huge numbers of lives: this shows up in statistics (e.g. of fire deaths since the invention and widespread installation of smoke alarms).

Table 14.8 Hazard prevention/minimisation

Type of incident	Hazard prevention options	Hazard minimisation options
Large-scale road traffic collisions	Closing all roads with more than two lanes	Closing motorways and major roads in fog Educating drivers on safe procedures Good road marking Effective policing, etc.
Plane/train accidents	Abolishing planes and trains	Strict maintenance of planes International controls Better airport and runway design Improved air traffic control equipment and working practices Upgrading of trains, track and signalling Redesigning or abolishing unstaffed level crossings
Terrorist activities	Probably none	Security; intelligence; monitoring suspected groups; eliminating causes of terrorism by changing foreign policy; improved respect and/or integration for disaffected communities; changing the law; military action overseas
Flooding	Not building or carrying out commercial work (e.g. farming) on any land which has ever been flooded Designing buildings and roads which are equipped with huge storm drains Building flood barriers which are physically too big and strong for floodwaters ever to cross	Properly planned and researched flood control schemes; limiting or controlling building on flood-prone land; climate control measures (perhaps); planting trees to reduce surface run-off in heavy rain; building reservoirs to stabilise river flows; providing more sandbags and better flood warnings; better insurance and other help for flood victims
Diseases	Universal vaccination for viral diseases so that the disease (like smallpox) becomes extinct Genetic modification of some other organisms that cause or carry disease	Hygiene; health awareness; safe sex; proper inspection and control of farm animals; scientific research (e.g. into causes of bovine TB – a serious threat to cattle and to the livelihoods of cattle farmers) and into diseases such as bird flu which threaten humans

Hazard minimisation options

As Table 14.8 shows, not all emergencies are preventable. The best we can do is to minimise the risk of them happening. Usually the best we can do is minimise the risk of them happening or try to limit their bad effects. For example, heavy snow can cause emergencies, but it is not worth buying expensive snow-blowers if they are only going to be used once every 10 years.

Preparedness – plan for known hazards as well as for unforeseen events

Known hazards are potential dangers which are well recognised. Often they are linked to installations such as chemical works, or to natural features such as rivers which are liable to flood. Large organisations such as major companies, hospitals and colleges have evacuation and other emergency plans because where there are many people the risks of an emergency are greater. Advice about hazards of this type can be obtained from the fire and rescue service or the Health and Safety Executive.

www.hse.gov.uk/ (Health and Safety Executive)

Responses (by emergency services, by local authorities, by voluntary organisations)

Responses are the actions taken by the authorities when it becomes clear that there is (or that there is going to be) an emergency. Responses by emergency services and local authorities are outlined on pages 196 and 201–204 and in Unit 15, pages 241–246.

Recovery – activities required to return to normality

All major incidents have to be followed by a period of recovery, when the emergency is over and the priority is to get things back to normal. In incidents such as industrial fires or major road traffic accidents the recovery period begins once the on-site investigation (e.g. by fire investigation teams) to discover the causes of the incident is complete. In incidents such as major flooding, the recovery period begins when people are able to return to their homes or workplaces and the clean-up begins.

Recovery after fires, crashes, explosions, etc, is a dangerous technical job which has to be carried out by specialist agencies and companies. Some initial clearing up, to remove immediate hazards, can be done by the fire and rescue service if they have suitable equipment, otherwise specialised firms must be called in.

See more on this in Unit 15, pages 246, 261–263

Types of plans (e.g. local authority major incident guide)

There are different types of emergency planning guides which are studied and used by the emergency services and by local authorities. The basic theory comes in a guide produced by the Cabinet Office in central government. This is called *Central Government Arrangements for Responding to an Emergency: Concept of Operations* (2005). It 'sets out the arrangements for the response to an emergency (irrespective of its cause) requiring co-ordinated UK central government action'. It defines 'levels' of emergency as shown in Table 14.9.

Table 14.9 Levels of emergency

Level	Name	Examples
1	Significant emergency	Local emergency not requiring COBRA
2	Serious emergency	Major terrorist attack or serious outbreak of animal disease requiring COBRA
3	Catastrophic emergency	9/11-scale attack or Chernobyl-scale incident requiring COBRA

Central Government Arrangements for Responding to an Emergency: Concept of Operations (2005) Cabinet Office (Arrangements for emergency planning), www.ukresilience.info/upload/assets/www.ukresilience.info/conops.pdf

remember

Your local authority should have a detailed emergency plan or manual available either on their website or by contacting them by phone or in person. These emergency plans give clear and detailed information on the responses to emergencies by the emergency services and the local authority.

remember

COBRA is the government's emergency committee which meets in Cabinet Office Briefing Room A (hence its name).

Local authority major incident guides take two main forms. One is an emergency plan which states the main responsibilities of all the bodies that could be involved in an emergency response.

Local authorities also produce emergency procedures manuals which give more detailed guidance and advice on the best responses to major incidents. They outline what the emergency services do, and give checklists and other information to guide local authority responders.

Institutions such as health authorities, hospitals, factories and colleges also have written emergency plans dealing with evacuation and giving the responsibilities of named individuals and departments.

Organisations involved in planning

Relevant organisations and their involvement in planning are dealt with briefly in Table 14.10.

Table 14.10 Organisations involved in planning for an emergency

Organisation	Role	Responsibilities	Objectives
Local authorities	Maintain an emergency planning unit and participate in a local resilience forum. Collect information for and facilitate the writing of emergency plan(s); initiate the plan; disseminate the plan; update the plan from time to time as necessary	Ensure that the plan fits in with the law (Civil Contingencies Act 2004); ensure that details are correct (by writing drafts and distributing them for corrections); publish and disseminate the plan to all who need it	To produce a useful emergency plan which will form the basis of training and exercises of emergency and volunteer services, and which will guide responders in the event of a real-life emergency
NHS	Incorporate their role and facilities into the plan; check for accuracy; inform local authority when updates are needed	Ensure that the information about their role is accurate; disseminate the plan to the ambulance service and to hospitals and GPs; arrange for feedback and changes when needed	To maximise the efficiency and effectiveness of the ambulance service and other branches of the NHS in an emergency response
Inter-faith groups	Advise the planning committee or LRF on the religious and moral requirements which should be taken into account in the planning process	Uphold the ethics and morals of local people's religious moral religions while facilitating agreement on such issues in the planning process	To achieve an emergency plan which respects the local people's religious moral and spiritual needs of the community without risking safety
Department for Environment, Food and Rural Affairs (DEFRA)	Ensure that flood planning is in place in the regions and in local authorities. The Environment Agency, attached to DEFRA, monitors weather (using the Met Office) and river levels and issues flood warnings Liaise with police and the emergency services where necessary (as a Category 1 responder the Environment Agency has a legal obligation to liaise with emergency services under the Civil Contingencies Act 2004)	Ensure that planning for floods, etc. is carried out in accordance with the principle of subsidiarity, with planning and decisions made at the lowest possible level Ensure through the Environment Agency that pollution and waste issues are planned for	To prevent or reduce flooding To reduce effects and damage caused by flooding To forecast and warn, through the Environment Agency, about flooding To prevent pollution and/or minimise its effects To assist with the aftermath of flooding

▶

Organisation	Role	Responsibilities	Objectives
Fire	Contribute actively to the emergency planning process through the Local Resilience Forum and/or the local authority's Emergency Planning Unit Liaise formally and informally with other emergency services in planning and training activities	Carry out risk assessments for emergencies linked to fire, chemical accidents, traffic accidents, etc. and use these to inform the planning process Update plans in the light of new risks and technologies	To advise, inform and liaise with other bodies involved in emergency response To involve and train volunteers where appropriate To participate in training exercises based on the emergency plan, and to change the plan if the exercises indicate weaknesses
Police	As with the fire and rescue service, take a major role in overall organisation and the logistics of the emergency response	Perform the duties of a Category 1 responder to 'assess, plan and advise' for the best possible emergency response	To help create a definitive, clear and usable plan To disseminate, publicise and support the plan so that its provisions are known and understood by all who may be involved in emergency response
Ambulance	Plan the ambulance service response and ensure that the emergency plan takes all ambulance needs into account	As with the police, but focusing on the roles and needs of the ambulance service, and the requirements for giving primary care and getting casualties to hospital	To ensure that the plan enables the service to provide the best possible emergency response in the event of an emergency
Military	Ensure that local authorities and other emergency planners know what facilities they can provide Devise their own large-scale emergency response plans	Disseminate information about their possible role in major emergencies	To back up local authorities and the emergency services when requested, in the event of a really major threat or emergency
Red Cross and Red Crescent	Study draft versions of the emergency plans and make suggestions	Make plans themselves so that their service, when called on, can be of the highest possible quality	To support the emergency services in providing prompt and effective primary care, first aid or humanitarian help
Radio Amateur's Emergency Network (RAYNET)	Publicise their communication services to planning groups	Ensure that they are licensed and that their skills are kept up to date by exercises, etc.	To support the emergency services in communication, especially in rescue situations
Coroner	Ensure that their role is well understood by the emergency services	Carry out their work carefully, accurately and efficiently Communicate their findings to the police	To investigate violent or unexplained deaths To determine whether there may have been a criminal cause
Salvation Army	Plan for emergencies	Review and develop their skills	To inform planners of their skills and facilities for humanitarian work
Casualties Union	Take the part of casualties in emergency simulations and training exercises	Follow instructions and appear and behave as real-life casualties would	To help the emergency services to practise and improve their emergency response procedures and skills
Mountain and cave rescue teams	Inform emergency planners of their skills, equipment and role	Train and practise mountain rescue skills	To carry out search and rescue, especially on mountains or in caves

Organisation	Role	Responsibilities	Objectives
Utilities	Give emergency planners the technical information they need about gas, water, electricity, sewage, etc.	Make themselves available to help in an emergency in any way they reasonably can Plan ways of restoring supplies when they are cut	To supply the public with power, water and other needs To vary, cut or change supplies to help an emergency effort To limit the risk of disease and accidents resulting from sewage, gas, etc.

Home Office/Cabinet Office (2005) *The Needs of Faith Communities in Major Emergencies: Some Guidelines* (www.cabinetoffice.gov.uk/)

Regional resilience (www.communities.gov.uk/index.asp?id=1123755)

Multi-agency involvement in real-life exercises

Large-scale live exercises are carried out from time to time so that the emergency services can test their planning, training and skills. Afterwards they analyse what happened in debriefing sessions, producing reviews and evaluations which let them know what they are doing well and where improvements can be made. Using what they have learned from their reviews and evaluations they are able to improve their future planning, training and skills development.

www.co-ordination.gov.uk/preparedness/exercises.aspx

www.gnn.gov.uk/ Government News Network (accounts of exercises)

www.co-ordination.gov.uk/preparedness/exercises/nationalcasestudies.aspx (examples of large-scale exercises)

Other organisations involved in prevention

Health and Safety Executive

The work of the Health and Safety Executive is discussed in some detail in Unit 15, pages 248–250.

Large and small businesses

Businesses have obligations under the Health and Safety at Work Act 1974 to do what is 'reasonably practicable' to prevent accidents and emergencies. They have to produce a written safety policy outlining the safety arrangements in force in the workplace, and bring it to the attention of employees. There must be arrangements for training and equipping workers so that dangers are minimised. Dangerous substances must be stored safely, and risk assessments must be carried out periodically and acted upon.

Media agencies

These include the press, television companies, local radio, and news agencies such as Reuters that **syndicate** stories.

Local authority and other emergency plans include guidance for how to deal with the media.

The emergency services use the media to:

- Warn the public of dangers, delays, etc. caused by an emergency.
- Present them to the public in a favourable light.

remember

Not all emergency planning is multi-agency. The police, fire and rescue service, NHS, etc. have their own emergency plans which are focused on their own roles and responsibilities.

case study 14.10   Milford Haven Oil Refinery

Emergency response: The refinery has detailed contingency plans to deal with major incidents such as oil spills and fires. These take into account local emergency plans drawn up by the County Council and Port Authority. The plans are tested regularly at emergency response exercises.

Source: www.texaco.co.uk/Education.htm

activity
GROUP WORK

1. What differences would you expect to find between contingency plans drawn up by an oil refinery, a local authority and a port authority?

2. In what ways could the refinery 'take into account' the local emergency plans?

But the media can cause problems, for example:

- Getting in the way of rescues, e.g. by parking in the wrong place.
- Getting past the **cordon** and interfering with work or contaminating evidence.
- Putting out stories which are alarmist, contradictory or false.

To maximise the benefits of media involvement and minimise the problems, emergency plans give guidance on how the media should be treated.

Joint press briefings
Media liaison is often planned so that the public relations (PR) managers for the main emergency services give a joint briefing at which they make statements and answer questions from journalists.

Figure 14.8 Media handling – planning considerations

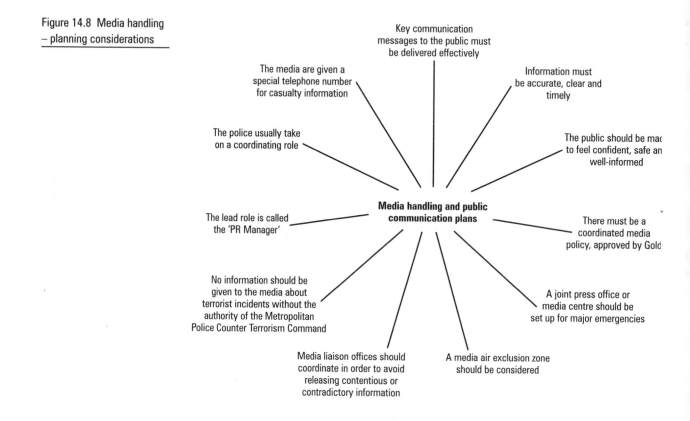

Key communication messages to the public must be delivered effectively

Information must be accurate, clear and timely

The media are given a special telephone number for casualty information

The public should be mad to feel confident, safe an well-informed

The police usually take on a coordinating role

Media handling and public communication plans

There must be a coordinated media policy, approved by Gold

The lead role is called the 'PR Manager'

A joint press office or media centre should be set up for major emergencies

No information should be given to the media about terrorist incidents without the authority of the Metropolitan Police Counter Terrorism Command

A media air exclusion zone should be considered

Media liaison offices should coordinate in order to avoid releasing contentious or contradictory information

case study 14.11
Who covers what at a joint press briefing

- Police – Overall response to the incident; the number of casualties; how the Emergency services coped/are coping; Casualty Bureau telephone number (if issued); any criminal investigations (except incidents on the railway); local disruption (past and continuing); praise for local people who may have assisted in rescue operations; commendable actions by Police Officers.

- Fire and Rescue Service – The rescue operation; how many people were trapped and in what circumstances; the level of its response in terms of appliances and personnel; what equipment was needed to free people and (where relevant) specific information related to flooding, fires or chemical incidents; commendable actions by Fire Officers.

- Ambulance Service – The nature and seriousness of those injured; where casualties were taken; how many ambulances and medical staff were involved; commendable actions by ambulance personnel.

Source: Lincolnshire Resilience Forum *Emergency Procedures Manual 2006*

activity
GROUP WORK

1. What are the advantages and disadvantages of having joint press briefings of the kind outlined here?

2. Choose a disaster or other major incident and role-play a joint **press briefing**, following agreed plans of procedure similar to those outlined in a local authority emergency plan of the kind that this case study comes from.

Emergency planners make policies for dealing with interviews with relatives of victims, etc. to ensure that they are properly supervised and do not put too much stress on the interviewee. The plan should also state how and by whom casualty figures will be released. Names of victims are not released until next-of-kin have been told.

Overall relations between emergency services and the media are often organised and overseen by Regional Media Emergency Forums.

www.ukresilience.info/mef/index.htm **(Media Emergency Forums)**

activity
INDIVIDUAL WORK 14.6

D1

Write an article for an in-house journal for one of the emergency services explaining in depth why it is so important that agencies work closely together when planning their joint responses to a major incident.

Possible future disasters:

Emergency planning takes into account disasters which might happen. Emergency planning by local bodies such as local authority Emergency Planning Units and Local Resilience Forums focuses on emergencies that could happen in their areas. These bodies do not plan for, say, volcanic eruptions because they cannot happen in Britain for geological reasons. Response to emergencies that do not happen in Britain but might happen elsewhere, such as serious earthquakes, is considered by the fire and rescue service (and the armed forces) which have sent relief teams to give help in overseas earthquakes.

Volcanoes erupting, earthquakes

There are no active volcanoes in Britain, and experts say there is no realistic possibility of them in the foreseeable future. Earthquakes are rare and mild.

Floods, drought, coastal erosion

The Department for Environment, Food and Rural Affairs (DEFRA) coordinates and advises on these hazards, as indicated on page 213 above.

www.defra.gov.uk/environ/fcd/default.htm

Terrorism

Overall planning is carried out by the Cabinet Office in the form of COBRA – the government's top emergency committee. The specialist agency for emergency planning against terrorism is the Metropolitan Police's Counter Terrorist Command. Although based in London this command is headed by Britain's National Coordinator of Terrorist Investigations. The aim is to disrupt and prevent terrorist plans and attacks before they are carried out.

www.mpa.gov.uk/ (Metropolitan Police Authority)

Preparing for a particular major incident by using tabletop scenarios

Tabletop scenarios

Definition

Tabletop exercises or seminar exercises are a kind of emergency planning exercise which involves using a realistic scenario (outline of a major incident), giving people information and roles, and allowing them to act out their roles and so plan their response to the emergency given in the scenario.

A scenario may be based on a real emergency which has happened (e.g. Buncefield oil depot explosion), or it may be based on an imagined emergency which could happen in the future (e.g. epidemic of **avian** flu). A scenario has to have a setting – which is normally the town or area in which the emergency planners operate.

For this unit you will be expected to devise and carry out your own tabletop exercises. You should use your own locality as a setting for these, in order to gain more understanding. Talk to police, your local emergency planning unit, safety officers and security staff to gain an in-depth insight into the issues.

> **remember**
>
> When creating tabletop scenarios for BTEC, use the resources in your own area. Shopping centres, local motorways, large production areas, airports, etc. are all excellent settings. Visit them, study them, make plans of them and work out a scenario that could happen!

www.co-ordination.gov.uk/preparedness/exercises.aspx (Introduction to tabletop planning; UK Resilience)

Agencies that may be involved

Any agencies involved in emergency response can carry out tabletop exercises. Such exercises can be carried out by individual agencies, several agencies or by voluntary organisations involved in emergency response.

Emergency services such as the police, fire and rescue service and ambulance service carry out tabletop exercises both individually (to help them understand their own roles better) and on a multi-agency basis (since in real life they will probably be working together when responding to a major incident).

Multi-agency groups which use tabletop exercises include Local Resilience Forums and **Regional Resilience Teams**.

www.co-ordination.gov.uk/preparedness/exercises/nationalcasestudies.aspx (Case studies – national exercises)

Types of tabletop scenarios

Tabletop scenarios can be classified according to the type of emergency they relate to. Case study 14.12 shows some examples.

Chemical/fuel spillage, train/plane crash, building collapse, terrorist attacks

These are all events which could be used as the basis for constructing scenarios for tabletop planning exercises. The kinds of information about them which ought to be included in scenarios for your own tabletop emergency planning exercises are outlined below and up to page 222.

HAZCHEM Guide, www.the-ncec.com/

Signs warning of chemical hazards on tankers, lorries, etc.

---

case study 14.12

Tabletop scenarios

Examples of tabletop scenarios are as follows:

- Chemical, biological, radiological or nuclear.
- Chemical hazards.
- Coastal pollution.
- Dam or reservoir failure.
- **Downstream oil**.
- Environmental health emergencies.
- Failure of major utilities: electricity, gas, telephone, water.
- Foot-and-mouth disease.
- Influenza **pandemic**.
- Prolonged freezing weather.
- **Rabies**.
- Rail crash.
- Refugees.
- River and coastal flooding (general).
- Schools emergencies.
- Severe weather.
- Smallpox.

remember

A scenario is a setting for a simulation or role-play. It can be based on a real incident/ situation, or it can be imaginary. The purpose of a scenario is to outline the problem that has to be 'solved' in a tabletop exercise.

---

activity
GROUP WORK

Discuss which of these could happen in your area, and plan a rough scenario for one that would interest you.

Issues for consideration in the scenario

The overriding aim is to create a scenario which enables participants in the tabletop planning exercise to gain the maximum amount of insight and knowledge into the emergency response for the major incident described.

This means that participants must be briefed with:

- Relevant information.
- In a form in which it can be understood and assimilated.

The minimum level of information to be contained in an emergency plan is outlined in *Emergency Preparedness* as shown in case study 14.13.

---

case study 14.13

Essential elements of a specific emergency plan

Aim of the plan, including links with the plans of other responders

Information about the specific hazard or contingency or site for which the plan has been prepared

Trigger for activation of the plan, including alert and standby procedures

Activation procedures[1]

Identification and roles of multi-agency strategic (gold) and tactical (silver) teams

Identification of lead responsibilities of different responder organisations at different stages of the response

Identification of roles of each responder organisation

Location of joint operations centre from which emergency will be managed

Stand-down procedures

[1]The Civil Contingencies Act 2004 (Contingency Planning) Regulations 2005 (SI 2005/2042), part 24 (www.ukresilience.info/upload/assets/www.ukresilience.info/finalregs.pdf)

Source: *Emergency Preparedness*, Annex 5C

---

activity
INDIVIDUAL WORK

Note down information about the above in relation to a specific major incident scenario.

In a scenario for a tabletop exercise the following kinds of information relating to a specific emergency are also needed.

Cause of incident

Emergencies can have more than one cause. The 'cause' may therefore have to be separated into a 'trigger' which is the immediate cause, and contributory factors. For example, the immediate cause of the 2001 foot-and-mouth emergency was apparently the importation of infected pig-food. But contributory factors were lack of awareness of the risks in some parts of the farming community, the practice of moving animals around the country for commercial reasons and a faulty government response.

Likely agency response

This is determined by:

- The nature of the emergency.
- The size and urgency of the required response.
- Legislation on how agencies should respond to emergencies.
- The different agencies available or involved.
- Staffing factors.
- Skill/training factors.
- Equipment available.
- 'Reinforcement' (liaison or back up) arrangements with other local services and agencies.
- Weather and other factors at the time.
- Decisions by the local authority, regional or central government, linked to the scale and seriousness of the emergency.

Resources that may be required

Resources means people and equipment. The resources required vary enormously according to the scale of the incident, its duration and the kind of threat it presents.

Table 14.11 Resources required during an incident

Incident	Resources
Security, G8 Summit, Gleneagles, Scotland, 2005	11,600 police officers including 7950 brought from south of the border (England and Wales). Ministry of Defence made food and accommodation available on journeys there and back
Reading train crash, 2004	20+ ambulances and 14 fire engines (immediate response); 61 people taken to hospital
Buncefield	650 firefighters from 16 brigades put the fire out after 59 hours of firefighting
7 July 2005 bombings, London (52 died; 700 injured): Piccadilly bomb (21 died) Bus bomb (13 died) Ambulance service total for 4 bombings Police investigation Casualty Bureau (police)	Some of the resources used are given below: 60 firefighters; 12 fire engines 20 firefighters; 4 fire engines 250 ambulance staff; 100 ambulances 10,000 police officers involved 200 officers brought in from 21 forces worked round the clock to answer phones (over 100,000 calls in first day)

Inner and outer cordons

Outer cordons are used to protect areas which are being investigated by forensic teams. Inner cordons are safety areas which may only be entered by people wearing protective clothing.

 Link

See page 204 above

Casualty clearing stations

These are set up when there are large numbers of casualties. The aim is to ensure:

- That people get the treatment they need as quickly as possible.
- That the most urgent cases are identified and get priority treatment.
- That proper information is collected and records kept.

Rendezvous points and marshalling areas

See page 204 above.

Press information centre

See pages 216–217 (under 'Press information centre') above.

Command and control

This follows the system of Gold, Silver and Bronze outlined on page 207 above. The aim is to separate strategic, tactical and operational planning so that they do not become confused or interfere with each other. The principle of 'subsidiarity' is used. i.e. that decision making is delegated as far as possible down the chain of command. This means that operational decisions about actions needed at the scene are taken by Bronze command, who are on the spot, know what the problems are, and have been well trained in their role through participation in tabletop and live exercises.

Communication network

Communication in an emergency is a rapidly developing field. Mobile phones have been widely used but are not considered reliable or secure enough. The fire and rescue services are being provided with new regional control centres, and a digital system called Airwave is gradually being adopted by all of the emergency services to facilitate inter-service communication and increase security of communication (prohibiting eavesdroppers).

Environmental considerations

These mainly involve pollution – which can take many forms. Flood pollution is very different from the specific kinds of pollution that result from a fire, explosion or chemical leak for example. The Environment Agency is the main government body dealing with pollution, but the fire and rescue service will clear up small-scale pollution from spillages, leaks and firefighting foam, etc. if it can be done reasonably quickly and safely. The Health and Safety Executive is also concerned with pollution especially if it is likely to affect people. Debris and waste is dealt with either by local authorities or by private waste disposal and processing companies such as Biffa.

Buncefield a year on: clean-up continues, 9 December 2006, *Guardian* (www.guardian.co.uk/)

www.environment-agency.gov.uk/

Common and agency-specific responsibilities at the scene

Common responsibilities are responsibilities which are shared by all the agencies and individuals working at the site of a major incident. Agency-specific responsibilities are those which are carried out by single agencies. Examples are shown in Table 14.12.

Post-incident responsibilities

Debrief of situation by all agencies

Initial debriefs take place during or immediately after the incident – perhaps in the marshalling area inside the outer cordon. The aim is not to blame people, but to gather information which will be of use in training and preparing for future emergencies. First debriefs are within each agency. Later there is a multi-agency debrief so that each agency can learn from the experiences of the others. Some debriefs are also used as stress-relieving activities.

Table 14.12 Responsibilities at the scene

Common responsibilities	Agency-specific responsibilities
Preserving the scene	Fighting fire (FRS)
Risk assessment	Assessment and sorting of casualties (A)
Following health and safety laws	Cutting people out of wreckage (FRS)
Relieving suffering	Criminal investigation (P)
Limiting the spread of the emergency	Coordination of emergency services and local authority at the early stages (P)
Facilitating investigations	Collection and distribution of casualty information (P)
	Pumping out floodwater, etc. (FRS)
	Dealing with chemicals (FRS)
	Transport to hospitals (A)

A = ambulance service; FRS = fire and rescue service; P = police

remember

Emergencies are rare – another reason why experiences must be shared.

Reviews of response procedures

These are analyses of the debrief findings. They may well be published and disseminated throughout the country, posted on the internet, or sent to overseas emergency services, so that as many people as possible can benefit from the lessons learned.

Scene investigation

See Unit 15, page 252.

ACPO (2005) *Practice Advice on Core Investigative Doctrine*

ACPO (2007) *Practice Advice on the Policing of Roads*

ACPO (2006) *Policing Motorways*

www.acpo.police.uk

Long-term social service and NHS aftercare of victims and relatives

Events such as the London bombings of 2005 leave lasting physical, mental and emotional effects. Survivors reported a need for:

■ Protection from the media.

■ Contact with other-survivors.

■ Financial assistance and advice.

■ Legal advice.

■ Support for psychological trauma.

■ Advice on long-term health risks such as **post-traumatic stress disorder**.

According to the Health Protection Agency the most common long-term effects were post-traumatic stress disorder and hearing loss.

Aftercare has been patchy and there is an ongoing dispute about compensation. Most sufferers are being treated by their GPs. The public health effects are being overseen by a steering committee, which has members from the Department of Health, the NHS, the Health Protection Agency, the emergency services and London Transport.

www.hpa.org.uk/

Criminal and inquest proceedings support

This is financial, legal and emotional support provided to casualties and other living victims of disasters. The government offers some support through the Criminal Injuries Compensation Authority if the event had a criminal cause. Private solicitors also represent disaster victims. They are overseen by the Law Society of England and Wales and the Solicitors' **Pro Bono** Group.

Criminal Injuries Compensation Authority www.cica.gov.uk

Clear up of scene and/or environment

The nature of the clear-up depends on the scale and nature of the incident and the kind of wreckage or environmental damage it leaves. Depending on circumstances it is carried out by the fire and rescue service, the local authority, the Highways Agency, the Environment Agency, private contractors, the army and – in the case of floods – by private individuals as well.

Evaluation

Evaluation is a process using monitoring, debriefing and review procedures to arrive at a judgement of how well an emergency has been dealt with. Who does the evaluation depends on the scale and nature of the disaster. For 'smaller' disasters the local authority and the emergency services carry out the evaluation. A final evaluation must include not only an evaluation of the contribution of all the individual services involved in the response, but also on their 'interoperability' – how well they communicated and worked together. For larger disasters, public inquiries are used. Where there is a security

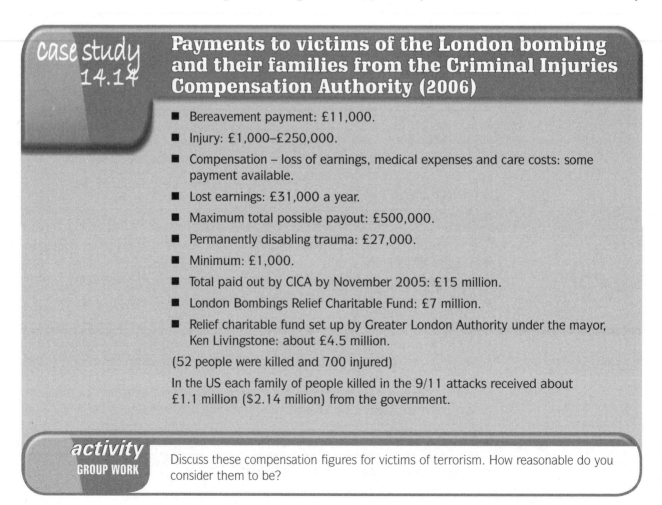

case study 14.14

Payments to victims of the London bombing and their families from the Criminal Injuries Compensation Authority (2006)

- Bereavement payment: £11,000.
- Injury: £1,000–£250,000.
- Compensation – loss of earnings, medical expenses and care costs: some payment available.
- Lost earnings: £31,000 a year.
- Maximum total possible payout: £500,000.
- Permanently disabling trauma: £27,000.
- Minimum: £1,000.
- Total paid out by CICA by November 2005: £15 million.
- London Bombings Relief Charitable Fund: £7 million.
- Relief charitable fund set up by Greater London Authority under the mayor, Ken Livingstone: about £4.5 million.

(52 people were killed and 700 injured)

In the US each family of people killed in the 9/11 attacks received about £1.1 million ($2.14 million) from the government.

activity
GROUP WORK

Discuss these compensation figures for victims of terrorism. How reasonable do you consider them to be?

risk, or where a public inquiry is thought to be too expensive or politically **contentious** (as after the 2005 London bombings), Parliamentary committees and other bodies write evaluations and have them published in the form of reports.

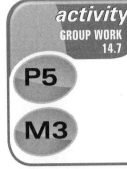

activity
GROUP WORK
14.7

P5

M3

Using local settings, work out a scenario for a major incident. Then take part in a group tabletop exercise to work out how the responding agencies should deal with the incident. In your exercise you should decide what the agencies involved should do, both close to the incident and in all the wider areas or communities that might be affected. Take notes or keep other records during the exercise, then hold a group debriefing session (which should be recorded in writing or in some other appropriate way) analysing and reviewing what you have discovered about the emergency response and the way it should be (or should have been) done.

activity
INDIVIDUAL WORK
14.8

D2

Write a report suitable for your line manager evaluating the tabletop exercise (together with any monitoring, debriefing or review), making an assessment of the success of the exercise, and giving reasoned recommendations on how the planning could have been developed or improved.

Progress Check

1. List as many causes of disasters, worldwide, as you can.
2. Outline the effects of emergencies on:
   (a) rescue workers;
   (b) communities.
3. Explain how reviews and debriefs are used during and after an emergency.
4. State 10 features of a public inquiry.
5. What are the costs of an emergency? Outline as many of them as you can.
6. Name four recent laws which have affected the ways in which the emergency services deal with major incidents. Then give the two main measures contained in each of those laws.
7. Name five professional services and four voluntary services which could cooperate in tackling a major incident.
8. Explain the roles of a local authority in dealing with a major incident.
9. State the main duties of the police, ambulance and fire and rescue services at a major incident.
10. Name five agencies that can investigate the causes of major incidents.
11. Explain the uses of an inner and an outer cordon.
12. List four Category 1 responders and four Category 2 responders.
13. In emergency response, what are Bronze, Silver and Gold?
14. What is a Local Resilience Forum and what does it do?
15. Give examples of hazard prevention and hazard minimisation.
16. Explain the roles of three contrasting organisations in emergency planning.
17. Describe how the emergency services liaise with the media in a major incident.
18. What is a tabletop exercise and what is it used for?

UNIT 15

Responding to Emergency Service Incidents

This unit covers:

- The use of incident grading and the importance of responding to emergency incidents safely in response vehicles
- The roles and responsibilities of key services when attending the scene of an emergency response incident
- The necessity for scene preservation and the service provisions of specialist units at emergency incidents
- The health and safety considerations when attending the scene of an emergency response incident.

This unit is about the actions of the emergency services when attending an incident such as a serious road traffic accident, crime scene or fire.

It begins with how incidents are handled in control centres after 999 calls are received, how the incidents are graded, and all of the things taken into consideration when the services hurry to the scene.

The next part of the unit covers what happens when the emergency services reach the scene of the incident, what their priorities are, and how they work together.

After this the unit deals with the preservation of the scene and the techniques of investigation that are used to find out the cause of the incident and who – if anybody – is to blame. This section also looks at the help and care which can be given in emergency situations by the voluntary services.

The final part of the unit is about the steps the emergency services take to protect themselves and others from any dangers at the scene, and the health and safety laws which need to be followed.

grading criteria

To achieve a **pass** grade the evidence must show that the learner is able to:	To achieve a **merit** grade the evidence must show that, in addition to the pass criteria, the learner is able to:	To achieve a **distinction** grade the evidence must show that, in addition to the pass and merit criteria, the learner is able to:
P1 describe how emergency incidents are graded by a selected public-service control room Pg 230	**M1** explain the roles and responsibilities of the key services attending an emergency incident Pg 235	**D1** evaluate the interagency cooperation of the emergency response services Pg 235
P2 identify the initial actions, roles and responsibilities of the key services when attending at the scene of an emergency incident Pg 235		

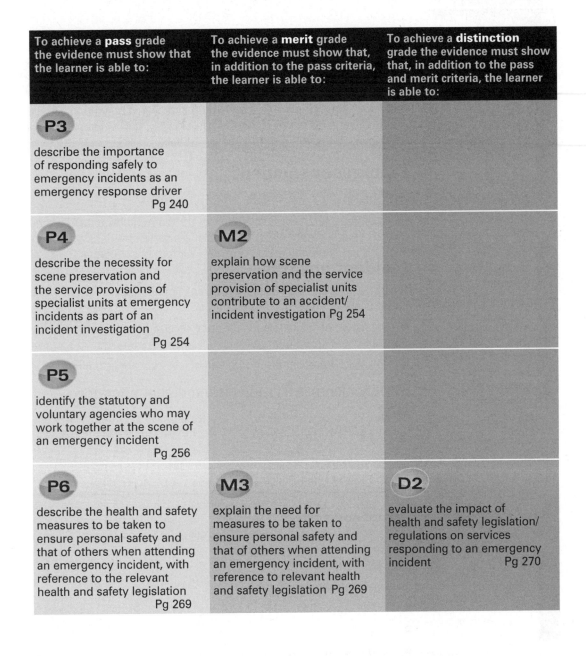

To achieve a **pass** grade the evidence must show that the learner is able to:	To achieve a **merit** grade the evidence must show that, in addition to the pass criteria, the learner is able to:	To achieve a **distinction** grade the evidence must show that, in addition to the pass and merit criteria, the learner is able to:
P3 describe the importance of responding safely to emergency incidents as an emergency response driver Pg 240		
P4 describe the necessity for scene preservation and the service provisions of specialist units at emergency incidents as part of an incident investigation Pg 254	**M2** explain how scene preservation and the service provision of specialist units contribute to an accident/ incident investigation Pg 254	
P5 identify the statutory and voluntary agencies who may work together at the scene of an emergency incident Pg 256		
P6 describe the health and safety measures to be taken to ensure personal safety and that of others when attending an emergency incident, with reference to the relevant health and safety legislation Pg 269	**M3** explain the need for measures to be taken to ensure personal safety and that of others when attending an emergency incident, with reference to relevant health and safety legislation Pg 269	**D2** evaluate the impact of health and safety legislation/ regulations on services responding to an emergency incident Pg 270

The use of incident grading and the importance of responding to emergency incidents safely in response vehicles

An **incident** is an event or happening. It is usually sudden, unexpected and unwelcome. The characteristics of an incident are:

- It can cause loss of life or injury and/or damage or loss of property.
- Neither victim(s) nor emergency services know about it in advance.
- It involves human beings.

'Incident' does not mean the same as 'accident'. An incident may or may not be caused deliberately, while an accident is – by definition – not caused deliberately. All accidents are incidents, but not all incidents are accidents.

The emergency services use the word 'incident' because it says as little as possible about the real nature of what happened, and enables them to keep an open mind.

For example:

■ A truck crashes into a jeweller's shop because the road is icy. For the driver, who had no intention of crashing, this is an accident. For the police, who receive a 999 call, it is an incident.

■ A truck crashes into a jeweller's shop and a large quantity of jewellery is stolen. For the driver, who rammed the shop deliberately, this is not an accident. For the police, who receive a 999 call, it is still an incident.

Emergency incident

Definition

An emergency service incident is any event that requires a rapid attendance at the scene by the police, fire and rescue or ambulances services – or all three of them.

Incident grading

This is the process of deciding how urgent or important an incident is. The grading used depends on:

■ The nature of the telephone message received at the control room or **control centre** (sometimes called Central Communications Command).

■ Any revised grading given when more is known about the incident.

How incidents are graded by emergency services

Police

Calls received at a police control centre are graded as 'emergency' or 'non-emergency' contacts.

Association of Chief Police Officers (www.acpo.police.uk/)

Fire and rescue service

Calls in the fire and rescue services are all treated as emergency if a fire is in progress or an accident has just happened. The aim is to get to the incident as quickly (but safely) as possible.

Incidents are categorised into six types:

■ Rescue.

■ Fire.

■ Hazardous material.

■ Alarm.

■ Explosion.

■ Civil disturbance.

Figure 15.1 Incidents and accidents

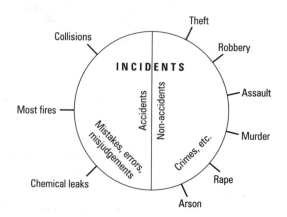

case study 15.1 — Incident grading

Operators must be aware of local policies on incident grading. The ACPO (2005) *National Call Handling Standards* defines how to classify calls from the information provided as **emergency** and **non-emergency**.

An emergency contact

An emergency contact will result in an immediate emergency police response. It is where an incident is taking place and in which there is, or is likely to be, a risk of:

- Danger to life;
- Use, or immediate threat of use, of violence;
- Serious injury to a person; and/or
- Serious damage to property.
- Where the contact relates to a traffic collision, it will be dealt with as an emergency if:
- It involves, or is likely to involve, serious personal injury;
- The road is blocked or there is a dangerous or excessive build up of traffic.

A non-emergency contact

A contact will be classified as a non-emergency if the above criteria are not met.

A non-emergency contact means that the police response may not be immediate. There are three levels of initial response for this type of call.

- **Priority** – The police contact handler acknowledges that there is a degree of importance or urgency associated with the initial police action, but an emergency response is not required. A priority response typically arises in circumstances where:
  - There is genuine concern for somebody's safety;
  - An offender has been detained;
  - A witness or other evidence is likely to be lost;
  - At a road collision there are injuries or a serious obstruction;
  - A person involved in an incident is suffering extreme distress or is otherwise assessed as extremely vulnerable.

- **Scheduled** – Some priority calls can be dealt with as scheduled where the following applies:
  - The response time is not critical to apprehending offenders;
  - The matter is service-oriented and a better quality of initial police action can be taken if it is dealt with by either
    - a pre-arranged police response by a police officer or by other appropriate resource, or
    - attendance at a police clinic or a surgery.

- **Resolution without deployment** – This is where the needs of the caller are adequately met through telephone advice or the helpdesk, access to a database of frequently asked questions, the involvement of another and more appropriate agency or service, or through some other method.

Source: www.sussex.police.uk/foi/ UploadFolder

activity
GROUP WORK

What are the advantages, disadvantages and dangers of having an **incident grading** system?

Ambulance service
See page 234 below for the grading of calls.

activity
GROUP WORK 15.1

P1

Produce a leaflet for a citizenship class for adults explaining how to call the emergency services in an emergency, and explaining how the emergency services grade their response. Each person in the group should research one emergency service, and the leaflet should be a team production.

Interagency approaches/agreements

Different agencies (especially the police, the fire and rescue service and the ambulance service) have to work together in serious incidents where people have been injured or are at risk of injury. This has happened for many years with serious road traffic accidents, for example, where all three 'blue-light' services have attended the scene.

In the most serious incidents which come under the headings of 'resilience' or '**civil contingencies**', the emergency services are obliged by law (Civil Contingencies Act 2004) to work together in the planning, organisation and implementation of a joint response.

Such incidents which include big industrial fires, floods, chemical leaks, etc. have a system of grading which does not describe the scale of the incident itself as much as the levels of command within the emergency services dealing with the incident. These are called Gold, Silver and Bronze commands.

Gold command is the person in charge of the strategy of each blue-light service dealing with the incident. This means that normally the police, ambulance and the fire and rescue services will each have a Gold command. The job of Gold command is to liaise with other Gold commands to make a strategy (overall plan) for tackling the major incident.

Silver command has a tactical role concerned with making decisions and plans which affect their particular service and which enable the Gold strategic plans to be carried out.

Bronze command has an operational role and organises the ongoing work by their service at the major incident site.

Link

For much more on this see Unit 14, especially pages 195 and 206

remember

Your local government area will have a disaster or emergency plan which will have a lot to say on cooperation between agencies. Check it out.

Some agreements are worked out at government level. For example, following the advice of the three emergency services, the Department of Communities and Local Government has developed an agreement which facilitates (makes as easy as possible) communication between Bronze commands of the police, fire and rescue and ambulance services. This agreement was publicised to the fire and rescue service in FRS circular 51-2006 *Emergency Services Radio Communications – Interoperability at Bronze Levels*. The circular, sent to all fire services, explained that the new **Airwave** radio technology used for command and communications would be specially adapted so that it could ease communications between the three services. The lead role in this type of **interagency cooperation** would be taken by the police.

www.communities.gov.uk

Role of call centres and incident managers

This is a rapidly changing area of public service work. **Call centres**, also called control centres, are places where telephone calls reporting incidents (especially 999 or 112 calls) are received, and information is processed and sent out to the emergency teams nearest the incident. Call-centre work can be difficult and stressful and the people who work in the centres are highly trained in procedures designed to get all of the information required from each emergency call. People who report emergency incidents are often confused and in a state of shock when they do this, and will certainly not be experienced at reporting emergencies.

The primary role of a call centre is to get accurate information about an incident, as quickly as possible, so that the best possible response can be given to the incident in the shortest possible time.

The secondary role of a call centre is to give a good impression of the service to the person who has telephoned them about the incident. This includes dealing with the call in a polite and efficient manner, and assuring the caller that something is indeed being done.

Call centres are open 24 hours a day, every day of the year. They are increasingly being modernised and **centralised**, with a trend towards bigger centres covering wider areas. In the past the service they gave, and their efficiency, varied from region to region and service to service, and their effectiveness depended on the equipment installed and the skill and local knowledge of their switchboard operators. Schemes are now in place to standardise and regionalise communications, and big new control centres are being built, especially for the fire and rescue service, under the 'FiReControl Project'. For the police, the National Policing Improvement Agency (NPIA) includes plans for standardising and upgrading police control rooms and systems.

www.npia.police.uk/en/index.htm

www.acpo.police.uk/

Incident manager

The **incident manager** is the person in overall charge, on the site, for example, of a motorway crash, serious fire, etc. Figure 15.2 shows the incident-related tasks that the incident manager is in charge of.

Policies and procedures for dealing with incidents

A policy for dealing with incidents is a planned approach. Policies are usually **standardised**, written down, used as a basis for training, and followed. They have systems built into them to make them flexible enough to cover the wide range of incidents that can happen, and the big differences between them. Usually they are based on the experience of the emergency services over many years, together with research into the practices and experience of other countries (e.g. the US). In Britain strategic policies are produced by government departments, but the more practical policies which are actually followed by the emergency services are produced by people within the uniformed public services. Many police policies are now being produced by the Association of Chief Police Officers (ACPO).

Road Death Investigation Manual, Version 2, Centrex 2004

www.acpo.police.uk/ **(top site!)**

www.cfit.gov.uk/mf/index.htm

The policy can be defined as a grouping or sequence of tasks (as in Figure 15.2).

Case study 15.2 shows incident management simplified into its essential processes.

Figure 15.2 Incident-related tasks that the incident manager is in charge of

Source: Motorists' Forum

Main task	Time in minutes (0–95, then 0–20)
Awareness of incident	0–15
Location of incident	0–15
Mobilisation of emergency services	5–17
Guidance of emergency service	5–30
Getting to incident	5–30
Operational liaison	15–end
Initial assessment at scene	5–13
Create safe work environment	5–20
Make secondary assessment	18–30
Act on secondary assessment	23–38
Manage traffic flow	5–30
Make tertiary assessment	20–33
Act on tertiary assessment	28–43
Manage initial arrival of FRS	20–40
Manage members of public	(intermittent across timeline)
Construct infrastructure	33–end
Make quaternary assessment	33–43
Act on quaternary assessment	35–48
Main phase – police	55–
Main phase FRS	43–
Accident investigation	45– and later
Clearance	later
Inspection	later
Declare road open	later
Open road	later
Manage distal effects	later

case study 15.2

Incident management

■ Phase A – Initial arrival and making and acting on primary assessment.

■ Phase B – Setting up a sterile area, making and acting on secondary assessment.

■ Phase C – Setting up, developing and maintaining a working infrastructure, making and acting on tertiary assessment.

■ Phase D – Post-emergency phase management.

activity
INDIVIDUAL WORK

1. What is meant in this context by 'sterile area'?

2. What is a 'working infrastructure'?

As with most managed tasks in the uniformed public services, reviews and progress assessments are important. The purpose of such assessments is to ensure, as far as possible, that the incident is being dealt with in the best way and that nothing of vital importance is being overlooked.

www.acpo.police.uk/

Definitions of emergency response

The word 'emergency' is used in two separate but overlapping senses. The Civil Contingencies Act 2004 defines 'emergency' as:

> An event or situation which threatens serious damage to human welfare in a place in the UK, the environment of a place in the UK, or war or terrorism which threatens serious damage to the security of the UK.

However, the police define emergency as:

> an incident … in which there is, or is likely to be, a risk of:

- Danger to life;
- Use, or immediate threat of use, of violence;
- Serious injury to a person; and/or
- Serious damage to property.'

The first definition suggests that an emergency has to be on a national scale; the second suggests that there is imminent serious danger and that something has to be done about it very quickly.

An emergency response can be defined as:

- An urgent attendance at a serious incident using blue lights, sirens, etc. to get there quickly.
- Any large-scale or high-speed action to deal with a major incident.
- Any urgent action to deal with an incident which poses an immediate danger or threat.

The flashing blue lights and sirens may be only part of the overall emergency response. Some very large-scale possible emergencies – such as an outbreak of **avian** (bird) flu or even of foot-and-mouth disease (as in 2001 and 2007) – may cause all of the relevant authorities to take on the emergency powers they need, for example setting up exclusion zones. But there may not be many flashing blue lights.

Response times

It is important for the emergency services to get to an emergency as quickly as possible. Every passing minute can mean a fire spreading beyond control, or an injured person losing more blood. Moreover, the public want and expect a quick response to 999 calls.

The police have targets for response times:

- For answering 999 calls.
- For attending an emergency incident.

To give an example, the targets used in West Yorkshire in 2006 were to answer 999 calls within 15 seconds, and to attend 'immediate' incidents (the most urgent category) within 15 minutes.

Initial response services

An initial response service is the quantity of vehicles, equipment and people sent on a first attendance to an incident. This applies mainly to the fire and rescue service, which, in urban areas, traditionally sent two or even three pumps (fire engines containing water and equipped with hoses) on every 'shout' to an emergency incident. These standards

case study **15.3** — **Response times, London Ambulance Service**

When a 999 call is received in our Emergency Operations Centre, our highly trained call takers use our call-prioritisation software to ask a series of questions and determine the urgency of the patient's needs. Each incident is categorised as follows:

- Category A – immediately lifethreatening incidents
- Category B – serious incidents
- Category C – neither serious nor lifethreatening

The Government-set performance targets require us to reach patients within nationally agreed timescales. They stipulate that we must reach 75 per cent of Category A calls within eight minutes and 95 per cent within 14 minutes, and that we must respond to 95 per cent of Category B calls in 14 minutes.

activity
GROUP WORK

What is the purpose of 'call-prioritisation software'?

What are the advantages and disadvantages of the government setting targets for ambulance response times?

remember

Fire and rescue initial responses vary from place to place.

of cover, which had been laid down by central government, were abolished in 2004 and replaced by initial response services set by the local fire and rescue authority.

Initial response services are based on the 'levels of risk' of particular places (the likelihood of fires or accidents in those areas, calculated on the basis of past evidence). They are also linked to distance from fire stations, which are usually situated in built-up areas.

The ambulance service

The initial response from the ambulance service is based on the information gathered from 999 calls. Highly trained staff categorise the calls according to how serious or urgent the patient's needs are. They use what they call the 'Advanced Medical Priority Dispatch System' to get the best use of resources and ensure that the most urgent cases receive the most specialised help.

For very urgent calls the ambulance service have Motorcycle Response Units and Rapid Response Units. Where a high degree of medical help is likely to be needed on the spot, paramedic motorcycles and cars can also be sent. Many ambulance services now have a Helicopter Emergency Medical Service (HEMS) for the most urgent cases or for places which would be slow or difficult to reach by road. For less urgent cases which may be emergencies, such as people who are very drunk, for the first attendance they use alternative **response vehicles** which are not fully equipped ambulances.

The initial emergency response service for ambulances is linked to other schemes such as the setting up, in London, of nine heart-attack centres around the city, and **defibrillating** equipment installed in 410 different public places in the city – with more than 2500 people trained to use it.

Additional public services offering specialist knowledge

Bomb disposal

Bomb disposal, sometimes called **explosive ordnance disposal** (EOD) involves dismantling explosive devices or making them harmless with the help of a 'robot' which detonates suspect packages. Most bomb disposal is carried out by the armed forces – for example the Royal Engineers – but the Metropolitan Police in London also have bomb disposal experts attached to the Counter Terrorism Command. The Counter

remember

Your local police can tell you what they do about bomb disposal and underwater searches.

Terrorism Command was formed out of the old Anti-Terrorist Branch and Special Branch when they were merged in 2006.

case study 15.4

Response standards

Table 15.1 Shropshire's response standards for life risk incidents

	Life risk fires		Road traffic collisions		
Risk areas	Minimum of 5 firefighters in:	Minimum of 8 firefighters in:	Minimum of 5 firefighters in:	Minimum of 8 firefighters and Rescue Pump in:	Rescue Tender arrives within:
High	10 minutes	13 minutes	10 minutes	13 minutes	30 minutes
Medium	15 minutes	18 minutes	15 minutes	18 minutes	30 minutes
Low	20 minutes	20 minutes	20 minutes	20 minutes	30 minutes
Target 2006/07	75%	95%	77%	77%	85%

Source: *Putting S rops ire's Safety irst* (p. 51), April 2006, Shropshire Fire and Rescue Service

activity
INDIVIDUAL WORK

What are the meanings of the percentages in the bottom row?

activity
INDIVIDUAL WORK
15.2

P2

Write a leaflet suitable for an adult citizenship class stating what each of the main emergency services does when attending an emergency incident. Your leaflet should say what the services do, who does what, and what their duties are.

activity
INDIVIDUAL WORK
15.3

M1

D1

Write a feature article for a local newspaper explaining the work and duties of the emergency services at emergency incidents, and examining and assessing how well they work together.

Underwater search

This is carried out by the police. They wear dry-suits to protect them from polluted water and are fully inoculated against disease-carrying organisms. For communication they use radio and attached lines. The job is not a full time one, so they are seconded to other units when there is no underwater searching to be done.

Accountability

Accountability is the process of:

- Making an activity open to checking and inspection.
- Having measurable systems to improve **quality** and **productivity**.
- Making it clear where the responsibility lies if things go wrong.

It involves:

- Keeping clear, honest and full records of activities.
- Setting targets and **performance indicators**.
- Measuring and recording performance and trends in performance against records and targets.
- Monitoring, reviewing and **evaluating** activities.
- Making information public unless it is legally confidential.
- Having complaints and grievance systems.
- Having a system where people are legally responsible for their actions.

Accountability covers all aspects of an organisation's work, from its core duties (e.g. fighting crime) and its financial affairs to its record on discrimination and safety.

Accountability is difficult to achieve in emergency service work. It involves keeping full records and statistics of incidents and their outcomes. In work where decisions have to be made very quickly, under stress, serious errors can be made, yet these have to be recorded openly and honestly. In extreme cases such as the killing of Jean Charles de Menezes (an innocent Brazilian who was mistaken for a terrorist) by Metropolitan Police anti-terrorist officers in 2005, factors such as political pressure and the rapidity of events made it very difficult to get a clear picture of what actually happened.

All three blue-light services are locally accountable through their fire and rescue authorities, their police authorities and their local ambulance trusts. They have to show how they spend the public's money, and their success rate. In incidents such as road traffic accidents (RTAs) the **senior investigating officer** (SIO) has to keep a 'policy file' recording in writing all of the main (strategic) decisions and choices made in the emergency services' response and any investigation. If the investigation goes wrong, the policy file becomes a valuable tool for finding out where it went wrong and who is responsible. Accountability in the police has been greatly improved by the setting up of the **Independent Police Complaints Commission** in 2004 (under the Police Reform Act 2002) which can investigate complaints independently and recommend the prosecution of police officers if they are seriously at fault.

Emergency response

An emergency response has to be fast and effective. This means the emergency services require suitable:

- Vehicles.
- Equipment.
- Personnel.

> **remember**
>
> Without accountability a uniformed service could do whatever it liked – which would not always be a good thing.

Figure 15.3 Internal, local
and national accountability

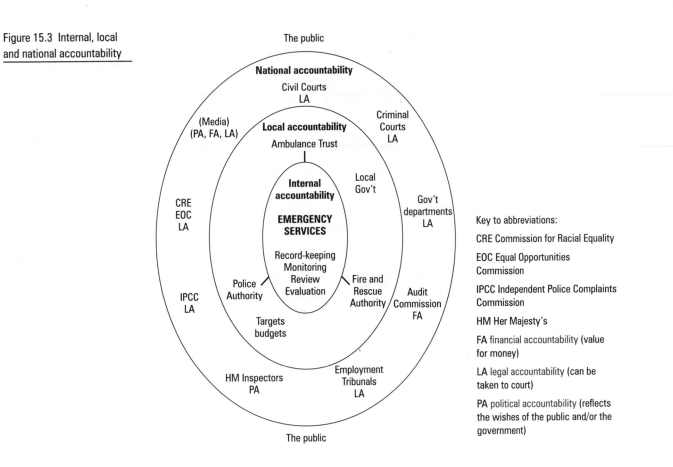

Key to abbreviations:

CRE Commission for Racial Equality

EOC Equal Opportunities
Commission

IPCC Independent Police Complaints
Commission

HM Her Majesty's

FA financial accountability (value
for money)

LA legal accountability (can be
taken to court)

PA political accountability (reflects
the wishes of the public and/or the
government)

Emergency vehicles and equipment

Every child can recognise emergency vehicles. They have special designs, bright colours, flashing lights and loud sirens and hooters. They are made to be noticed and to be easily identifiable.

The best way to find out about emergency vehicles is to visit your local emergency services and get the officers there to show you the vehicles and explain their features. The same is true of equipment. Open days and other occasions are also opportunities to see the emergency services' hardware and find out what the equipment is used for.

In 2005, the Somerset Fire and Rescue Service fleet had about 145 vehicles in it. This included pumps, **hydraulic** platforms, a water carrier, a rescue **tender**, a command unit, Land Rovers, specialist vehicles for upland fires, and plenty of others. Fire and rescue services have a lot of equipment for dealing with collisions, especially cutters and spreaders which can be used to release trapped people. They also carry equipment for primary care of accident victims.

In recent years ambulance equipment has become more sophisticated as paramedics try to perform more primary care as soon as possible after an accident, heart attack or other emergency. The sooner people can be treated, the higher the survival rate.

Driver training and driving standards for emergency response vehicles

Answering 999 calls and other emergencies needs special driving skills that have to be taught, learned, practised and updated. Errors can be costly – leading to the deaths of emergency service personnel and other road users or failure to save members of the public. Accidents that happen during emergency responses also lead to public outcry and serious problems for the rescue services in general – which depend on the goodwill and cooperation of the public.

Figure 15.4 Emergency
vehicles need to be noticed

Emergency drivers have to have the right physical abilities and eyesight. Police drivers
are trained to three standards: basic, standard and advanced.

Emergency driving skills are assessed against a national competency framework (national
occupational standards). Training records are kept to ensure an 'audit trail' (so that there
is clear written evidence that the driver has been trained for the job and is up to it).

www.skillsplus.gov.uk

case study 15.5 Standards of emergency driving

- Basic – Training to fulfil a patrol function within the constraints of the Highway
  Code.

- Standard – Extending basic training to include emergency response driving,
  night response driving and, most importantly, attitudinal training. A pragmatic
  introduction to pursuit incidents and pursuit management in line with standard-
  level car control skills.

- Advanced – Achieving a high level of all round driver skills, enabling pursuits
  and high-speed response driving, as well as a full understanding of the effects
  of attitude and associated stress.

activity
GROUP WORK

1. What is 'attitude' in a driver, why does it matter in the emergency services and how
   can it be trained?

2. What does 'pragmatic' mean in this context?

Public perception and reaction to emergency response vehicles

Perception refers to what people see, hear and feel. When most people hear an emergency service vehicle rushing to an incident they want to keep out of the way and not impede or delay its progress. In some areas, emergency response vehicles are sometimes regarded as 'fair game' by antisocial people who throw stones at them. The garish appearance of emergency response vehicles may be a factor in complaints about excessive police response to, for example, terrorist-related reports (e.g. Forest Gate, June 2006).

On the other hand, the conspicuous appearance of police vehicles means that they are in themselves a deterrent to bad driving, e.g. speeding. An experiment took place a few years ago whereby cardboard images of police cars were placed on motorway bridges, and it was discovered that even these reduced speeding on those sections of motorway.

Other road users' behaviour

The Highway Code gives clear instructions on what pedestrians should do if an emergency response vehicle approaches with lights flashing and/or siren going:

> **29: Emergency vehicles**. If an ambulance, fire engine, police or other emergency vehicle approaches using flashing blue lights, headlights and/or sirens, keep off the road.

Instructions for drivers are:

> **194: Emergency vehicles**. You should look and listen for ambulances, fire engines, police or other emergency vehicles using flashing blue, red or green lights, headlights or sirens. When one approaches do not panic. Consider the route of the emergency vehicle and take appropriate action to let it pass. If necessary, pull to the side of the road and stop, but do not endanger other road users.

Roadcraft – *The Essential Police Driver's Handbook* (1994) TSO

Roadcraft – *The Police Driver's Course on Advanced Driving* (2005) TSO

www.tsoshop.co.uk/

Emergency service driver accountability

The Road Safety Act 2006, Section 19 gives exemption from speed limits to emergency vehicles being driven in emergency response by properly qualified people.

---

case study 15.6 | **Speed limits**

No statutory provision imposing a speed limit on motor vehicles shall apply to any vehicle on an occasion when–

- it is being used for fire and rescue authority purposes or for or in connection with the exercise of any function of a relevant authority as defined in section 6 of the Fire (Scotland) Act 2005, for ambulance purposes or for police or Serious Organised Crime Agency purposes ... if the observance of that provision would be likely to hinder the use of the vehicle for the purpose for which it is being used on that occasion.

Source: Road Safety Act 2006, Section 19

activity
INDIVIDUAL WORK

Study the wording. Does this allow emergency service drivers to break the speed limit whenever they want during working hours? Justify your viewpoint.

According to the Independent Police Complaints Commission, road traffic accidents involving police vehicles are the biggest single cause of death 'following police contact'.

Table 15.2 Fatalities following police-related road traffic incidents – England and Wales

Financial Year	Pursuit related	Emergency response	'Other incidents'	Total fatalities
2002/03	26	3	11	40
2003/04	18	9	9	36
2004/05	23	6	15	44

Source: Teers, R. and Bucke, T. (2005) *Deaths during or following police contact: Statistics for England and Wales 2004/2005*

The Police Reform Act 2002 makes it compulsory for the police to refer all fatal accidents involving police vehicles to the IPCC for an independent investigation. This provides a measure of accountability, but there is no certainty that police officers who, say, kill people during a car chase will end up in court.

Media coverage when mistakes are made

The media coverage of cases where people are accidentally killed by emergency vehicles is relatively low-key. This is in contrast to incidents such as drink-driving offences by the police which, when they happen, are widely publicised.

case study 15.7 — The media

Kevin Clinton, head of safety at the Royal Society for the Prevention of Accidents, added: 'We and the public have the right to expect the police to set the right example in the way they behave as drivers and if they drive badly or break the law, they are treated in exactly the same way as other drivers by the police and the courts.'

During the trial, the court was told that PC Dunning was spotted driving his van at 2am at high speed near his home in Milton-under-Wychwood, Oxfordshire, in March last year. Marked police cars gave chase with their blue lights flashing and sirens sounding.

PC Robert Stubley, who was driving one of the vehicles, told the jury how PC Dunning refused to stop.

Source: 'Policeman free after 2am car chase', *The Times*, 10 February 2007

activity
GROUP WORK

1. Judging by the comments of Kevin Clinton, what do you think happened in this case?
2. What are the arguments for and against Kevin Clinton's point of view?

activity
INDIVIDUAL WORK 15.4

Give a presentation suitable for cadets describing how emergency response drivers get to emergency incidents and showing why it is important that they drive safely.

P3

The roles and responsibilities of key services when attending the scene of an emergency response incident

The key emergency services are usually the police, fire and rescue and ambulance service. Their roles are what they do (at the scene of an incident). Their responsibilities are:

■ To do those tasks which are within their **remit** (job description) and their expertise.

■ To carry out their work professionally and to the best of their ability.

The scene of an emergency response incident could be – among other things – a car crash, a fire, a fight outside a pub, a person having a heart attack or an offence in the process of being committed.

Initial actions of first in attendance

When a 999 call is made – especially for a road traffic accident – all three blue-light services may attend. Any of the three may arrive first – and they may find a scene of chaos and carnage. What do they do about it?

Information update

There is a standard procedure to follow on first attendance at an incident such as a road traffic accident. It is summed up in the mnemonic SAD CHALET.

Table 15.3 SAD CHALET

Consideration should be given to the following when approaching an incident:	
Survey	Survey the scene from a distance having regard to your personal safety
Assess	Assess the incident
Disseminate	Disseminate the information below to your force control room and others as necessary
Casualties	Approximate number of casualties – fatal, injured and not injured
Hazards	Present and potential, e.g. fuel spillage, debris, weather and road conditions, terrain, gas, chemicals, fire or danger of explosions
Access	Best routes for emergency vehicles and suitable provisional RVP (rendezvous point)
Location	Exact location (road junction or map reference to pinpoint the scene)
Emergency services	Emergency services present and required
Type and Timescales	Type of incident with details of types and numbers of vehicles involved

This is a checklist of information which must be obtained, preferably in the order listed. 'Dissemination of information' is informing other emergency services and agencies of what has happened and what they need to do.

Roles and responsibilities of key emergency services attending incidents

Different emergency services have different skills, equipment, jobs and duties when attending incidents. This 'division of labour' ensures that people do what they are best at and avoids confusion as to who does what, and when. At the same time, there has to be a level of communication between the three services so that they can help each other when help is needed and coordinate their response in a way which gives the best help to the victims and which aids (where necessary) the investigation of the incident.

Practice Advice on the Policing of Roads (2007) published by NPIA for ACPO (www.acpo.police.uk/policies.asp)

Guidance on Policing Motorways (2006) ACPO Centrex (www.acpo.police.uk)

Police

The roles and responsibilities of the police when attending an incident such as a road traffic accident (RTA) are as follows:

- Secure and protect the scene, and preserve the life of those present;
- With other emergency services, to save life;
- Coordinate the emergency response with other emergency services and support agencies;
- To preserve the scene and maintain control of it to ensure the integrity of it for any subsequent investigation;
- Investigate the incident, including obtaining and securing the evidence in conjunction with other investigatory bodies where applicable;
- Act as the agent for HM **Coroner**;
- Family liaison.

Source: *Guidance on Policing Motorways* (2006) © ACPO Centrex

> **remember**
> Other things being equal, the police are 'in charge' at a road traffic accident.

The coroner is a kind of judge whose work involves sudden or unexplained deaths (such as the deaths that take place in road accidents). The job of the coroner is to determine:

- The identity of a dead person.
- When, where and how the person died.
- The cause of death.

Clearing access and exit routes

Access here means ways of getting to the site of an accident. The police have to do what they can to clear traffic which blocks the way to an accident, either because of a tailback building up or because damaged vehicles are blocking the way as in the case of a motorway pile-up.

However, much of the actual work is not done by the police themselves but by the Highways Agency (run by the Department for Transport). The police and the Highways Agency work in close cooperation in the event of a serious road traffic accident – especially on a motorway. The police direct the Highways Agency to do what is necessary to clear access and exit routes. The Highways Agency's job is to manage traffic at the scene and beyond the scene, by setting up diversions, etc.

The effect of this work is to:

- Make it easier for emergency vehicles such as fire appliances and ambulances to reach and leave the scene of the accident quickly and safely
- Reduce delays for other road users.

In extreme cases specialist contractors have to be hired to improve access to an accident site – for example at Grayrigg in Cumbria in 2007 where Cumbria police arranged for a temporary road using 2500 massive steel panels to be built across fields to the site of a train crash.

Directing traffic

This is organised by the police, but for larger incidents, especially on motorways, it is often carried out by the Highways Agency. The Highways Agency have vehicles called

Incident Support Units which can carry out signing and coning to redirect traffic in the vicinity of a serious incident. The police can also direct traffic in person, using traditional hand signalling or by placing a wide range of diversion signs for minor roads.

Providing clear information

Information provided by the police about road traffic accidents which are likely to disrupt traffic flow is regularly given out over local and national radio, so that drivers can be kept up to date with accidents in their area. In major incidents where people have been killed the police are in charge of:

- Informing the coroner.
- Informing relatives.
- Talking to the media.

In very major incidents such as train crashes the police set up helplines which are broadcast by the BBC and other services, and information is given to callers who fear that their relatives or friends might have been casualties. In the long run, the police also give information to local authorities about accident hazards (e.g. blind corners) on local roads, so that roadworks can be done to reduce the hazards if necessary.

Public order

As a rule the police like to keep the public well away from major incidents because:

- The public can obstruct rescue and **salvage** operations.
- They can 'contaminate' the scene and reduce its value as evidence of a possible crime.
- They can put themselves and others at risk.

Using signs, loudhailers, taped cordoning and other methods, the police exclude, control or manage the public so that they cannot interfere with rescues or investigations.

Crowd control, cordons

For peaceful demonstrations, football matches and other crowds where the majority of people wish to act peacefully, crowd control is normally achieved by lines or cordons of police maintaining a firm, friendly and visible presence and keeping the crowd in the area which is designated for them. Occasionally mounted police are also used: they have the advantage of visibility, and the horses probably have a mild and acceptable deterrent effect.

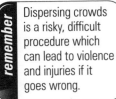

remember

Dispersing crowds is a risky, difficult procedure which can lead to violence and injuries if it goes wrong.

Under the Antisocial Behaviour Act 2003 the police have the power to disperse a crowd, but only if they have the authorisation of an officer of the rank of superintendent or above and with the official agreement of the local authority. Sometimes community groups and local businesses are involved in the authorisation to disperse a crowd. For the police this has the advantage of making the dispersal less of a police matter and therefore reduces accusations of 'police heavy-handedness' or '**officiousness**' in the media. Directions to disperse can be done orally, and people who do not comply can be arrested.

Fire service

There are four main roles at an emergency incident:

- Saving life.
- Dealing with fires.
- Freeing trapped casualties.
- Dealing with hazardous loads.

remember

What the fire and rescue service does sounds simple – but it is not. Contact your local firefighters and get the low-down on what they do at emergency incidents.

Extinguishing fires

Fires are powerful chemical reactions requiring three ingredients: fuel, heat and oxygen. Firefighting robs the fire of one or more of these so that the reaction stops and the fire goes out.

remember

Fuel, heat and oxygen are often called the 'fire triangle'.

For many fires (e.g. in buildings and forests) water is the perfect medium for extinguishing them. It is cheap, easy to get, can seal the fire off from its oxygen supply, absorbs heat better than almost any chemical, and cools potential fuel so that the fire cannot spread. Where water is unsuitable (e.g. for petrol or electrical fires) other **extinguishing media** such as foam, powders or CO_2 can be used. The fires that can occur in road traffic accidents are usually extinguished with foam.

Fire Service Manuals, www.ife.org.uk/

Rescuing casualties

Firefighters rescue casualties from road traffic accidents by extricating them when they are trapped in crashed vehicles. The first step is often to stabilise the condition of the casualty, giving **rehydration**, painkillers, etc. even before they are released from the wreckage. Firefighters sometimes work in conjunction with paramedics in these situations, so that maximum use is made of the 'golden hour' (and the 'platinum 20 minutes') when critically injured people are most likely to be saved. When the victim has been 'stabilised' (or while this is going on) cutters and spreaders are used to release the trapped person. This is a risky process – for example, the victim may have a broken back and be in danger of paralysis. Once the person is released paramedics usually take over and the victim is rushed to hospital.

remember

Your college library should have up-to-date copies of the Fire Service Manuals, published by the Institution of Fire Engineers (IFE). They give clear, in-depth information on all aspects of fire and rescue service work.

People overcome by smoke or panic, or people who are simply trapped, also have to be rescued from house fires. This is dangerous for the firefighters, who may have to wear breathing apparatus and crawl around searching for people – in conditions of zero visibility and intense heat in buildings which could well collapse – and then drag the people out without getting trapped themselves.

Removing harmful by-products of combustion

Fire chemistry is complex, and when things burn they can often leave harmful chemicals behind. Firefighters cannot remove these from the fire or accident site until the causes of the incident have been investigated, because investigators have to take photographs and collect samples to create an evidence record which may be needed in court.

However, firefighters can decontaminate themselves and others by using decontamination units – cubicles where showers and other equipment get rid of potentially dangerous chemicals from their clothes and bodies. These chemicals are then either stored or disposed of as safely as possible.

remember

The fire and rescue service often deal with chemicals, and if you want to work with them it is useful to learn the basics of chemistry yourself.

When the time comes to clear up the site of an accident or fire, firefighters are able to take measures to protect the environment. Methods used include placing **booms** across the road to channel toxic run-off away from grates and sewers and into places from which it can be pumped into tankers and then taken away to be disposed of safely.

Diluting or neutralising harmful chemicals

Diluting means making a chemical less harmful by mixing or dissolving it in water. This can be done with some acids, alkalis and some soluble salts. It is what happens if a road is hosed down after a chemical spillage or other accident. Sometimes, however, dilution can cause environmental harm. For example, if acid which is dangerous to humans is diluted by hosing down the road, it may run into the local sewers and drains and end up by killing all the fish in a nearby river.

Very concentrated acids and some other chemicals can sometimes react violently with water – so firefighters have to know what they are diluting before they try it. **Hazchem** codes and other warning panels seen on tankers provide the necessary information.

See page 262 below

Ambulance service

Where there are casualties or suspected casualties, the ambulance service has vital roles and responsibilities at the scene of an emergency response incident. The main ones are:

- Paramedic services and emergency casualty treatment on site for the purposes of saving life and minimising injuries.
- Casualty evacuation.
- Alerting hospitals.

In a major incident the ambulance service has to assess the needs of a number of casualties and **prioritise** them by a system known as 'triage' (sorting). This is to ensure that the most urgent cases get the most urgent treatment, and to maximise the saving of life and the recovery prospects of victims.

Providing emergency aid

Emergency aid is any primary medical care that can be given by paramedics at the incident site or in an ambulance on the way to hospital. It includes **resuscitation** and administering drugs, fluids, drips and painkillers. Ambulances are increasingly well equipped, and paramedic training schemes are developing to include more skills, so that full advantage can be taken of the period immediately after an incident when medical help is most likely to bring about full recovery.

Resuscitation

Resuscitation is the process of 'bringing people back to life' when they are unconscious or close to death. A variety of resuscitation skills are used by paramedics, such as mouth-to-mouth and cardiopulmonary (heart and lungs) resuscitation, which is highly effective in saving heart attack victims. The London Ambulance Service has an interesting and effective scheme in which members of the public are taught these skills – and lives have been saved as a result.

> **remember**
>
> Everybody who wants to work in a uniformed public service should learn about first aid and resuscitation.

Transportation of casualties

This is the most well-known function of Accident and Emergency (A&E) ambulances. The first stage is getting the casualty safely into the ambulance, which requires specialised handling skills and ambulance equipment. The next stage is transporting the casualty to hospital, normally by road but occasionally by helicopter. Further **stabilisation** and medical care can be carried out in the ambulance on the way to hospital.

---

case study 15.8 — Saving lives

A number of factors have contributed to the improved survival rate, one of these being effective bystander cardiopulmonary resuscitation (CPR), which is known to double a person's chance of survival.

During 2005/06 the London Ambulance Service Community Resuscitation Training team taught 8,500 people this simple life-saving technique, and this has improved the public's ability to help people in a cardiac emergency whilst our crews are on the way.

Source: London Ambulance Service

---

activity
GROUP WORK

What are the arguments in favour of compulsorily teaching paramedic and first-aid skills (up to a certain level) to everybody?

Other statutory or voluntary agencies

Besides the blue-light emergency services a number of other services have roles to play at the scene of an emergency response incident. The main ones are as follows.

Highways Agency Traffic Officers

The Highways Agency is a national statutory agency (executive agency of the Department for Transport) set up by the government in 1994. Its jobs are:

■ To keep the traffic moving.

■ To minimise congestion and disruption.

■ To limit danger to road and motorway users.

■ To prevent damage to the road and its immediate surroundings.

Its work is done on major motorways and trunk roads. Since 2005 the role of the agency has evolved and it now has new duties helping the police to deal with serious traffic accidents. The agency's police-related roles are clearing debris, removing damaged vehicles, providing mobile and temporary road closures, helping to coordinate other emergency services and reopening routes.

Highways departments

These are local government departments which maintain non-trunk roads and repair them after accident damage.

Hazardous materials clean-up services

These are provided by specialist companies such as Biffa. In major cases the Environment Agency is also involved.

www.biffa.co.uk/

Health and Safety Executive

The HSE has an investigatory role in some major accidents, especially rail accidents and road traffic accidents which directly involve police drivers.

www.hse.gov.uk/

Towing and recovery companies

These private-sector companies help the Highways Agency and others to clear roads after the investigation of a serious accident has finished.

Local radio to advise of traffic problems or evacuations

Various radio services give traffic information in Britain to help motorists decide their routes or to avoid congestion.

See Case study 15.14 below.

www.bbc.co.uk/Cambridgeshire

Bomb disposal to investigate suspicious packages

See above (page 234).

The necessity for scene preservation and the service provisions of specialist units at emergency incidents

Scene preservation is the protecting of the scene of an incident or crime so that it can be investigated before anyone can disturb the evidence. For example, if vehicles which have been involved in a collision are moved too soon, the sequence of events which led to the collision may never be known – so they have to be left in place until investigators have been able to take all of the necessary photographs, measurements and other records.

Service provisions are the things done by experts, such as forensic officers, and other helpers at the scene of an incident. They collect and examine evidence in order to get a clear picture of what really happened – and why.

Scene preservation for scene investigation

The principles of preserving the scene of an incident so it can be investigated are much the same whatever the type of incident. They are outlined in Figure 15.5.

Identifying the scene means deciding upon the area to be protected (in other words, the area which is likely to contain useful evidence). In some cases there may be a central area (e.g. where a body has been found) which can be protected by a tent, and then an outer area which can be protected by taping, temporary fencing, etc. The initial aim of securing and protecting the scene is to prevent people from trampling all over it or even to prevent criminals or their associates from coming back and moving evidence or planting misleading evidence. Evidence from the scene of an incident can take the form of photographs, drawings, measurements, CCTV footage, mobile-phone records, foot and tyre prints, body fluids, dust, marks and fingerprints, potential weapons, paint flakes, soot deposits, chemical residues, burnt materials, melted materials and many other things depending on the kind of incident being investigated. (There are other kinds of evidence such as witness evidence, etc. which are not directly linked to the scene but may corroborate (back up) evidence retrieved from the scene.)

www.crime-scene-investigator.net

Need for accident investigation (e.g. serious and fatal road traffic collisions)

Incidents need to be investigated. The three main reasons are:

- Whatever caused the incident may cause similar incidents and pose a significant health and safety risk to many people in the long term. For example, there may be design faults in a building or vehicle, and if the design fault is in something that is mass produced, many thousands of people might be at risk. Road accidents are sometimes caused by faults in the design, lighting, signing or surfacing of a road; these danger spots can be changed if the hazard is identified.

> **remember**
>
> There are some interesting US websites about crime scene investigation. These are well worth checking out to get the basics of the procedure.

Figure 15.5 Scene preservation

Source: Adapted from Road Death Investigation Manual, ACPO

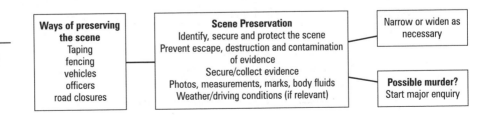

- Negligence or some criminal act may be involved. In the interests of the public, crimes have to be investigated and the perpetrators brought to justice. Scenes of crime are investigated by forensic teams to try and find out who committed the crime. Incidents which might at first sight appear to be accidents (e.g. buildings burning down) may turn out, after investigation, to be arson (the purpose of which may be murder, or to conceal a murder or other crime that has already been committed). A substantial number of road traffic accidents are linked to criminality (e.g. drugs or joyriding) and the identification of these and the prosecution of offenders is needed for public safety. There is a legal obligation for all violent and unexplained deaths, such as road accident deaths, to be reported to the coroner in order to determine whether the circumstances are suspicious and whether a full police investigation is needed.

- Knowledge of the cause of an incident is needed for insurance and compensation purposes. The costs involved in serious or fatal road accidents and their aftermath is enormous. In 2002 the average fatal road accident cost £1,447,490. In the same year serious road accidents cost, on average, £168,260. The figures will have risen since then.

Need for fire investigation (e.g. malicious and suspicious ignitions)

Arson, the deliberate starting of fires with criminal intent, is not mentioned as such in police law, but is covered by the Criminal Damage Act 1971, section 1(2).

Lorton, R. (2001) *A–Z of Policing Law*, 2nd edn. The Stationery Office, London

Reasons why fires need to be investigated are as follows:

- They are often caused by faulty electrical equipment or installation, and it may be that manufacturers or builders are to blame. For the sake of public safety these causes need to be identified, and the risk of further fires can be reduced by recalling faulty goods or inspecting buildings which might have similar defects.

- **Malicious ignitions** cause immense damage and some loss of life in countries where forest or 'brush' is deliberately set alight in dry seasons such as Australia, the US, France, Spain, Portugal, etc. In Britain there are occasional tragedies where people are killed by arsonists who set fire to their homes. Arsonists sometimes have a habit, even a kind of addiction to lighting fires, and it is therefore important for the police to be able to find and arrest them before they repeat the offence too often.

Arsonists who start fires to hide thefts or murders, or who light fires out of revenge, often do not realise that a deliberately started fire is easy for fire investigators to recognise, and leaves many clues as to the identity and purpose of the person(s) who did it. The use of '**trailers**', '**plants**' and **accelerants** is easily detected, and the seat(s) of a fire can be found from soot deposits and other signs. Therefore, investigation is well worth doing because it brings results.

Role of the Health and Safety Executive

The Health and Safety Executive is a body of inspectors, set up by law under the Health and Safety at Work Act 1974, and overseen by a governing body called the Health and Safety Commission. It has wide powers to enforce safe and healthy practices in the workplace. The aim is to protect not only the workers but also the public who use such workplaces as well.

One of the jobs of the Health and Safety Executive (HSE) is to investigate dangerous incidents, including major events such as train crashes. Deaths caused by the police are also investigated by the Health and Safety Executive.

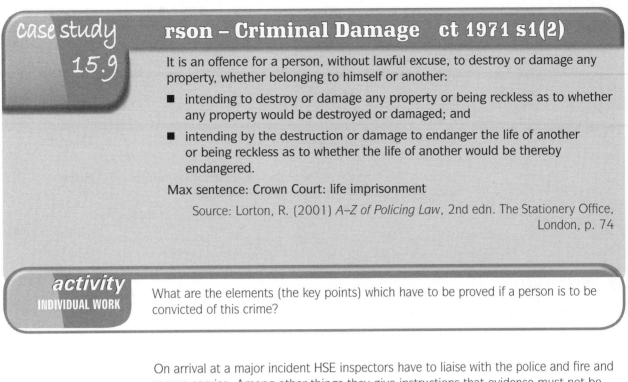

case study 15.9

rson – Criminal Damage   ct 1971 s1(2)

It is an offence for a person, without lawful excuse, to destroy or damage any property, whether belonging to himself or another:

■ intending to destroy or damage any property or being reckless as to whether any property would be destroyed or damaged; and

■ intending by the destruction or damage to endanger the life of another or being reckless as to whether the life of another would be thereby endangered.

Max sentence: Crown Court: life imprisonment

Source: Lorton, R. (2001) *A–Z of Policing Law*, 2nd edn. The Stationery Office, London, p. 74

activity

INDIVIDUAL WORK

What are the elements (the key points) which have to be proved if a person is to be convicted of this crime?

remember

Nearly everything you need on health and safety is freely available on the HSE website.

On arrival at a major incident HSE inspectors have to liaise with the police and fire and rescue service. Among other things they give instructions that evidence must not be disturbed, and start collecting evidence under appropriate headings such as: precise location, using the grid reference if necessary, casualties (numbers, severity, deaths, injuries, persons trapped, etc.); hazards (spillages, leaks, fire, safety of buildings, machinery, etc.); type of incident (chemical release, explosion, fire, structure collapse, etc.). The full investigation may be carried out by a large team of expert inspectors who will set up a special office. The team liaises with Silver command, but under exceptional circumstances HSE inspectors can overrule and issue **prohibition notices** against the police, the fire and rescue service and the Ministry of Defence. At all times the investigation team keeps its independence from any of the other bodies connected with the major incident because it is vital that their investigation is as honest and unbiased

Figure 15.6 How did it start? A job for the fire investigators

Major incidents

The HSE's definition of a major incident includes these words:

The event may either cause, or have the potential to cause, either:

- multiple serious injuries, cases of ill health (either immediate or delayed), or loss of life, or

- serious disruption or extensive damage to property, inside or outside the establishment

Events which, taken in isolation, may not warrant classification as major incidents, may do so when considered together.

Source: HSE, Major incident response and investigation and major incident policy and procedure review

activity
GROUP WORK

Can you think of any major incidents which would not be covered by this definition?

as possible. A body is set up to review, coordinate and direct the investigation of a major incident: this is called the Major Incident Investigation Board (MIIB). With the help of the Legal Adviser's Office the MIIB decides what action should be taken after the investigation is over. If a large company is at fault there may be a major court case resulting in a fine of millions of pounds, and a great deal of bad publicity.

Accidents in the workplace

These are not necessarily considered to be major incidents, according to the HSE definition, but they can still result in HSE prosecutions. These are posted up on the HSE's website, following their 'name and shame' policy. One example among many is the prosecution of Nexen Petroleum UK Ltd in 2005.

Figure 15.7 HSE prosecution of Nexen Petroleum UK Ltd, 2005

Source: HSE

Summary	Gas release on 5/8/05. Incident occurred when a pressure safety valve that was connected to the live HP flare system was being removed. Gas release was approximately 8.1 tonnes.	
Offence date	05/09/2005	
Total fine	£400,000.00 **Total Costs Awarded to HSE** £0.00	

Work Related Deaths – Investigators Guide (www.hse.gov.uk/enforce/investigators.pdf)

British Transport Police (e.g. accidents on the railways, trains and the underground network)

Serious accidents on Britain's railways make the news when they happen, but in fact they are rare. The British Transport Police, which police the rail network, are mainly concerned with routine crimes such as mobile-phone theft and antisocial behaviour, though robberies and obstructions to railway tracks are also a significant part of their work. Their role is essentially the same as other police services.

In the London bombings of 2005 they played a valuable role in the aftermath. They used both their underground radio system and the new Airwave digital radio system (which is in the process of being adopted by other uniformed services as well) to help coordinate evacuation and rescue from the London Underground. During security alerts, British Transport Police try to ensure security while minimising disruption: they work with railway management, the Counter Terrorism Command of the Metropolitan Police, the Ministry of Defence, London Resilience and the Security Service to ensure the safety of rail users and staff and to minimise disruption to people's journeys as a result of security alerts. They also have a unit which deals with suspect packages – most of which can be cleared without calling in explosives experts.

  www.btp.police.uk/

Security for scene preservation; use of cordons

The main methods used by the police are:

- Using tape to prevent access to or from the scene.
- Deploying officers to guard the scene (care should be taken to ensure that officers only attend individual scenes in order to prevent cross-contamination).
- Using vehicles as barriers to prevent entry.
- Road blocks to protect wider scenes.
- Temporary fencing.
- Road diversions.
- Ensuring that persons entering the scene are wearing suitable protective clothing to prevent contamination of the scene and to ensure that they are protected from any hazards present.
- Logging those who enter and leave the scene.

Source: Practice Advice on Core Investigative Doctrine, © ACPO Centrex 2005

> **remember**
>
> It might be worth studying and photographing signs, cordons, barriers and any other devices used to control traffic around accidents and hazards.

Scene preservation for evidence collection

Scene preservation is the first thing that a police team must ensure on reaching the scene of an incident. It should take priority over rescues and casualties – which, if possible, should be done by the fire and rescue and ambulance services.

Methods of preserving the scene are outlined above. The purpose of preserving the scene is to protect evidence which needs to be collected or examined by accident investigators or the police. The Association of Chief Police Officers (ACPO), whose *Road Death Investigation Manual* provides full guidelines for the police response to fatal road accidents, has a mnemonic for things which must be *prevented* if the scene is to be properly preserved:

M – movement of exhibits

E – evidence being **obliterated**

A – additional material being added

L – loss of evidence

An 'exhibit' is anything which can show information about how or why the incident happened. It includes debris (bits of vehicle, etc). Some exhibits may be collected and used in presenting a court case. Obliteration is the covering or destruction of marks on the road, streaks of paint indicating contact between vehicles, or the trampling of significant tyre marks. Material added might – for example – be mud or dust from some other place, brought in on the boots of an emergency worker. (This is why forensic examiners now wear white suits and special footwear – to minimise the risk of contamination of evidence with material from outside the crime scene.) Evidence can be lost if, for example, a contractor comes and starts to clear the road before the accident investigators have finished their job.

As well as all of these things, evidence (including samples, video, photographs, notes and sketches) has to be properly catalogued and stored so that it can, if necessary, be studied in greater detail (e.g. down a microscope) away from the scene, and used eventually by the Crown Prosecution Service if a criminal case needs to be prepared.

Crime scene investigation

Crime scene investigation is a complex process, and the priorities vary according to the type of scene, and the type of crime. Nevertheless, all crime scene investigation (or examination) follows certain principles and procedures. The stages are:

1. Identifying and securing the scene. This establishes a boundary inside which evidence can be expected to be found, and where special rules have to be followed to avoid losing or destroying that evidence.

2. Preliminary survey.

3. Evaluating the possibility of finding physical evidence.

4. Preparing a narrative description of the scene (this could be a tape recording).

5. Photographing/videoing the scene.

6. Preparing a diagram/sketch of scene.

7. Detailed, systematic searching and collection of evidence.

8. Carrying out the final survey in case anything has been missed.

9. End of investigation.

Note that the early stages of the examination are less invasive, in that things do not have to be moved, and there is little tramping around. The last stage – a detailed, perhaps fingertip, search – is the most invasive because it has the greatest physical impact on the scene of crime.

Some kinds of evidence need to be collected and preserved quickly because they are perishable, e.g. blood, fingerprints.

Use of photographs

Photographs of crime scenes are taken in a systematic way, starting with photographs of the crime scene from outside, then of the entire crime scene. The next stage is to photograph all the parts of the crime scene, at medium distance and afterwards in close up. All of the main items of evidence are then photographed while they are still in place, and from a number of angles if necessary. Close-up photographs are taken of all relevant marks, and smears are taken of other evidence before it is moved or '**lifted**'. All photographs are logged and identified in a systematic way. The photographs will be used in later forensic work, in the preparation of a case against anyone who is accused, and as evidence in court.

Video

Video can be used to create a visual record of the crime scene and a narrative (diary or log) of the crime scene examination showing what was done and how it was done at each stage. Video has an important role to play at later stages of an investigation – in the interviewing and identifying of witnesses and suspects, as court evidence, and as a way of interviewing or cross-questioning vulnerable witnesses.

Forensics

Forensics is the scientific examination of crime and crime scenes. Many branches of science have relevance to solving crimes, e.g. biochemistry, organic chemistry, physics and psychology. Figure 15.8 shows some of the branches of forensics and the kinds of science they are related to.

remember

Police and forensic investigators usually record their findings about evidence on special forms.

remember

The aim is to get as much information from the crime scene as possible, with minimum effort and minimum damage to evidence.

remember

Locard's Principle: 'Anyone who enters the scene both takes something of the scene with them and leaves something of themselves behind.'

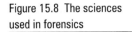

Figure 15.8 The sciences
used in forensics

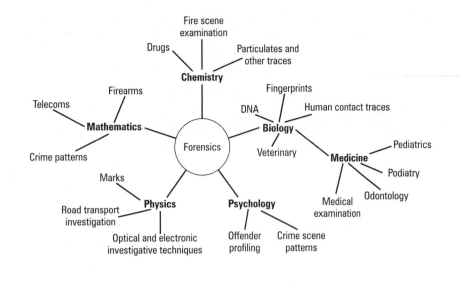

www.crfp.org.uk/
www.forensic.gov.uk/forensic_t/index.htm

Forensics is based on the idea that criminals leave traces of their method of working and their identity at the scene of the crime. Some crimes have two scenes. For example, if someone is murdered in a coal cellar and their body is dumped in a wood, both the coal cellar and the place where the body was found are scenes of crime. In this example there would be a forensic link if grains of coal were found on the body in the wood.

In Britain forensic work is mainly carried out by the Forensic Science Service – a government-funded body which will also do private work (e.g. DNA tests to determine paternity). Materials found at the scenes of crimes, fatal road accidents or unexplained fires can be examined in laboratories at one of a number of Forensic Science Service centres around the country. If the materials turn out to be possible evidence of a crime the details go to the Crown Prosecution Service, which prepares the police prosecution of offenders.

remember

Testimony is anything that a witness says – to the police or in a court – about a crime.

Witness testimony

Though witnesses are human, and therefore in some ways less reliable than forensic evidence, they have a necessary role in most criminal cases. Interviewing witnesses and finding out as accurately as possible what they have seen, or what they know, is an important part of criminal investigation.

The police have databases giving information about types of witness, what to expect from different types of witness, and the effects of culture, language, social needs, ethnicity and other factors that will help to determine how witnesses should best be interviewed.

All victims (if they are alive and able to speak) are witnesses, but not all witnesses are victims.

Finding witnesses is not always easy. Methods that can be used by the police to locate witnesses or encourage them to come forward include:

- Viewing CCTV.
- Media appeals.
- House-to-house enquiries.
- Interviews with victims and other witnesses.
- Interviews with suspects.
- Anniversary appeals.

case study 15.11 — Witnesses

Witness is defined as one, who sees, knows or vouches for something. One who gives testimony under **oath** or **affirmation**, in person, by oral or written deposition or by affidavit.

A witness must be legally competent to testify.

Source: *Black's Law Dictionary*, 8th edn (2004)

activity
INDIVIDUAL WORK

What is meant by 'legally competent to testify'? Give two examples of kinds of people who would not be legally competent to testify.

Witnesses are often vulnerable people – if not in themselves, then because they are witnesses to crime or some other traumatic incident – and their concerns should be understood and respected. Risks and threats to potential witnesses should be assessed and acted on. Fast-track interviews are used to establish the basics of an investigation, or help to determine which way an investigation should go. Witnesses can be interviewed through video link if this seems appropriate because they are, say, young or vulnerable.

Police interviews of witnesses (and victims and suspects) follow the guidelines shown in case study 15.12.

> **remember**
> The police have to balance the need for information with the human rights and welfare of the witness.

From a police point of view, witness testimony often takes the form of a statement which is written down on a special form and signed by the witness. If the case later goes to court and the witness is needed, the witness's testimony will be what he or she says in court in response to questions asked by lawyers.

Provisions made to each emergency service

The emergency services which carry out investigations of the scenes of crime and other incidents are:

- The police (crime scenes and most road accidents where there has been no fire).
- The fire and rescue service (scenes of fires, chemical spillages, some explosions).

Non-emergency services which carry out investigations include:

- The Health and Safety Executive (train crashes, industrial accidents and fatalities, police-related deaths).
- Air Accidents Investigation Branch (AAIB) (civil aircraft accidents and serious incidents within the UK).

Usually it is the responsibility of the police to create the conditions in which investigation can take place by the fire and rescue service or any other non-police organisation.

activity
INDIVIDUAL WORK 15.5

P4

M2

Write an article for a local newspaper showing how the emergency services investigate incidents. Include material on how and why scenes are preserved, and how specialist units work together on an investigation.

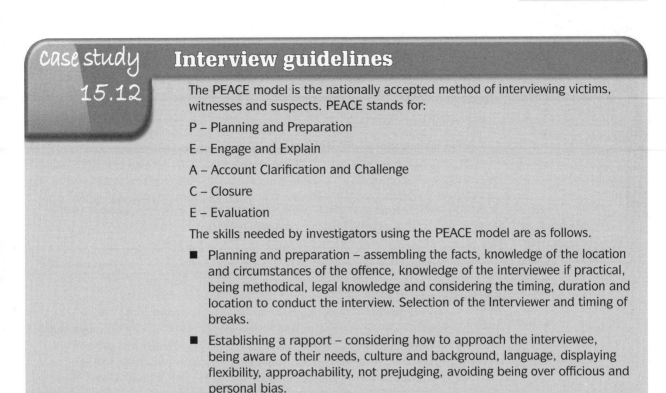

case study
15.12

Interview guidelines

The PEACE model is the nationally accepted method of interviewing victims, witnesses and suspects. PEACE stands for:

P – Planning and Preparation

E – Engage and Explain

A – Account Clarification and Challenge

C – Closure

E – Evaluation

The skills needed by investigators using the PEACE model are as follows.

■ Planning and preparation – assembling the facts, knowledge of the location and circumstances of the offence, knowledge of the interviewee if practical, being methodical, legal knowledge and considering the timing, duration and location to conduct the interview. Selection of the Interviewer and timing of breaks.

■ Establishing a rapport – considering how to approach the interviewee, being aware of their needs, culture and background, language, displaying flexibility, approachability, not prejudging, avoiding being over officious and personal bias.

■ Listening skills – developing the ability to listen actively, displaying **empathy**, consideration and tolerance. Using silence to obtain further information.

■ Questioning skills – asking the right questions at the right time, use of appropriate language and perseverance.

Source: Practice Advice on Core Investigative Doctrine, © ACPO Centrex 2005

activity
GROUP WORK

Design a role-play in which you can question a 'witness' or 'suspect' practising the principles outlined in this extract.

This means that they themselves preserve the scene until the other investigative service arrives. Normally the investigative team liaises closely with the police over the practicalities of access, etc., while keeping their independence as far as the techniques and findings of the investigation are concerned.

Voluntary agencies

In large-scale incidents involving many casualties and/or evacuation, the professional emergency services are helped by a number of voluntary organisations.

Other agencies who can offer assistance in the event of an emergency incident

There are several large voluntary organisations which can help in emergency incidents – especially if people have to be evacuated from their homes. Some are described below.

St John Ambulance

The St John Ambulance, which has branches in many countries, has 43,000 volunteers in the UK and runs a fleet of volunteer-staffed ambulances. The organisation offers a range of first-aid and health and safety courses for the workplace, for the general public and for children and people who work with children. Its aim is to train as many people in first aid as possible. Its members act as health and safety stewards at major sporting and other events at which there are likely to be large crowds. In addition it runs patient transport services for out-patients who attend hospitals on a non-emergency basis. It also has a 'neighbourhood first responder scheme' to help out the ambulance service.

British Red Cross

The British Red Cross is an organisation which encourages and trains people to become skilled in first aid. It is linked to a large international charitable organisation and has a sister organisation, the **Red Crescent**. It supports overseas charitable and investigative work in parts of the world which are at war or suffering from disasters and emergencies (e.g. Iraq) and produces influential human rights documents. The British Red Cross has many trained volunteers who help in British emergencies such as floods, transport accidents and major fires. Like the WRVS (Women's Royal Voluntary Service), they organise and staff emergency shelters and rest centres.

> **remember**
> The bigger the incident, the more need there will be for volunteers.

www.redcross.org.uk/

Victim Support

Victim Support is an organisation which helps victims and witnesses of crime. It runs the witness service in criminal courts. The main purpose of the service is to help and reassure witnesses who are, inevitably, going through a demanding and stressful experience. Though it is an independent organisation, it works in liaison with the police, who will themselves support witnesses or victims who feel that they are under threat from the associates of criminals that they may have helped to convict. Victim support will also visit crime victims in their home and offer reassurance and advice – sometimes working in conjunction with police crime prevention officers.

www.victimsupport.org.uk/

Women's Royal Voluntary Service

The WRVS, as it is now often called, has about 60,000 volunteers and mainly works with old or isolated people to help improve their quality of life and give them social support. It also has a special role in major incidents such as floods to provide evacuation facilities, welfare and rest centres for people who have been temporarily made homeless. As well as this the WRVS staff helplines, run casualty bureaus and give emergency response training – for example on how to organise and run an emergency support centre.

www.wrvs.org.uk/

Summary

The above are some of the best known of a wide range of charitable, social or religious organisations which do similar work, formally or informally, to help the victims of crime, accidents and other misfortunes.

activity
INDIVIDUAL WORK 15.6

P5

Produce a poster for a police reception area showing the statutory and voluntary agencies who may work together at the scene of emergency incidents.

The health and safety considerations when attending the scene of an emergency response incident

Incidents such as house fires, motorway pile-ups, chemical leaks and explosions are neither healthy nor safe, and they can have very dangerous after-effects. The emergency services who attend such scenes have to take serious steps to protect their own health and safety and the health and safety of the general public.

Self-preservation

The emergency services are rightly praised for their 'heroic' response to major or life-threatening incidents, but their preferred aim is the slightly less dramatic one of doing a professional, effective job of rescuing and protecting people at minimum risk to themselves. It does not benefit the public if emergency service personnel are injured or killed in the course of duty. Increasingly, therefore, the emergency services are protected with clothing, equipment and other measures which reduce the personal risks that come with the job.

Specialist clothing

Much emergency service work is done in a hostile environment. The dangers include:

- Being hit by traffic.
- Being hit by falling objects.
- Slips, trips, cuts and falls.
- Heat (and hyperthermia).
- Hyperthermia (and hypothermia).
- Chemicals and poisons.
- Dusts.
- Radioactive materials.
- Bacteria, **pathogens**, etc. (including HIV).
- Aggression from other people.

The emergency services have specialist clothing, footwear and equipment which can protect against all of these (to varying degrees).

High-visibility clothing

High visibility (sometimes called 'high conspicuity') is important, especially when working on roads and motorways when there is risk from traffic. It also reassures the public who like to see 'a visible police presence'. When working in the dark or in artificial light, such clothing makes workers more visible to their colleagues and reduces the risks of accidents (e.g. caused by heavy lifting gear and other machinery).

High-visibility clothing uses bright colours and reflective or fluorescent qualities to maximise conspicuity. Colours are chosen:

- To make the type of worker instantly recognisable (ambulance staff wear different colours from the police).
- To be visible in fog, smoke or darkness (reds and yellows are better).

Reflective (**reflectorised**) strips, using tiny transparent beads which focus and reflect light back in the direction it came from, gleam brightly in headlights and torch beams. Fluorescent colouring is colouring which changes ultraviolet light – which is invisible – into visible light, and therefore has a dazzling Day-Glo effect.

Figure 15.9 Specialist
clothing, styled for safety

Footwear

High-tech footwear is used, which gives full protection to feet and lower legs. Depending on the type used it can be crush-proof, heat-proof, cut-proof, non-slip and retain its effectiveness in oil or chemicals. In addition it has to be comfortable, well-fitting and not too heavy – people in the emergency services often have to spend a long time on their feet.

Eye protection

Goggles, eye-guards, transparent helmets and shields are used to protect the eyes of firefighters and other emergency workers. In highly dangerous environments such as wreckage on railways or motorways, dust, splinters and shards of metal, smoke, fumes and gas emissions can cause permanent damage to unprotected eyes.

Head protection

Breathing apparatus is used by firefighters when working in thick smoke or toxic fumes.

A wide range of headwear and helmets is used by the emergency services to protect against impacts from falling or thrown objects, or banging their heads against projections in a shifting and unfamiliar environment. Firefighters' helmets are fireproof and have good insulating properties. Protection is also needed against cold in certain circumstances, e.g. mountain rescues in winter, where hoods and balaclavas are more necessary than hard helmets. Ear protection against loud noise is used as well.

Gloves

As with other protective clothing, the emergency services now use high-specification gloves. Some of the materials used in gloves made for the emergency services are indicated in case study 15.13.

Scene safety measures

One of the main hazards for the emergency services when attending road traffic accidents is the risk of collisions with other drivers. Therefore the emergency services put up safety warnings and other measures as quickly as possible to reduce or eliminate this danger.

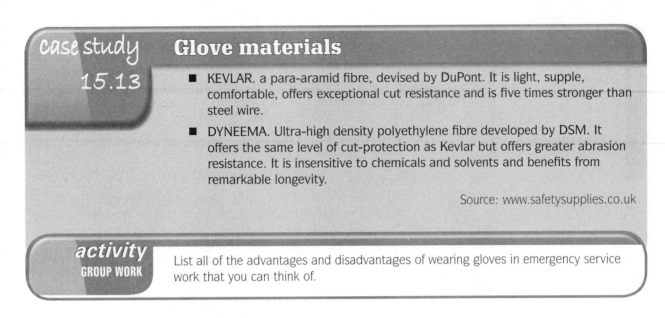

case study 15.13

Glove materials

- KEVLAR. a para-aramid fibre, devised by DuPont. It is light, supple, comfortable, offers exceptional cut resistance and is five times stronger than steel wire.

- DYNEEMA. Ultra-high density polyethylene fibre developed by DSM. It offers the same level of cut-protection as Kevlar but offers greater abrasion resistance. It is insensitive to chemicals and solvents and benefits from remarkable longevity.

Source: www.safetysupplies.co.uk

activity
GROUP WORK

List all of the advantages and disadvantages of wearing gloves in emergency service work that you can think of.

Warning signs

The rules for warning signs are laid down in the *Traffic Signs Manual* which is published by the Department for Transport. They follow the Traffic Signs Regulations and General Directions of 2002. Warning signs are used sparingly so that drivers pay attention to them when they do see them. There are five prescribed sizes ranging from 1500 mm downwards. The Department for Transport recommends distances at which warning signs should be placed from the obstruction or hazard they refer to. They should be placed on the left-hand side of the road, at heights between 900 mm and 1500 mm (lower edge). Signs should either be directly lit or 'reflectorised'. Warning signs can be either permanent or temporary. Temporary ones should be removed as soon as the hazard (e.g. flood) is no longer there.

Two official hazard warning signs are shown in Figure 15.10.

In Figure 15.10 the thick black line round the panel indicates a hazard sign.

On motorways, electronically operated signs such as matrix signals or **variable message signs** are used to give advance warning of hazards. The messages can be changed easily, but there are limits on the number of characters that can be used and on the amount of information an approaching driver can take in.

Other warning devices include:

- Motorway Incident Detection and Automatic Signalling System (MIDAS). This sets automatic mandatory speed limits.

- Controlled motorways. These systems use subterranean vehicle detector loops to monitor traffic flow and then control the flow to reduce congestion.

Figure 15.10 Hazard warning signs

Source: DfT (2004) *Traffic Signs Manual*, Chapter 4

600
(750)
(900)
(1200)
(1500)

562 Other danger ahead

May only be used in combination in diagram 563, 563.1 or 7022 'JOINING TRAFFIC NOT SIGNAL CONTROLLED'

62.5
(75)
(100)
(125)
(150)
(200)

563 Nature of other danger

May only be used in combination in diagram 562, or when varied to 'Road liable to flooding' with diagram 554. 'Accident' may be varied to 'Ambulance station', 'Blasting', 'Blind summit', 'Census', 'Dust cloud', 'Fallen tree', 'Fire station', 'Frost damage', 'Hidden dip', 'Overhead cable repairs', 'Pedestrians crossing', 'Runners in road', 'Smoke' or 'Walkers in road'. A distance, an arrow or both may be added

- Active traffic management. This system uses overhead gantries to regulate traffic flow – sometimes in relation to incidents that have taken place ahead.
- Rolling roadblocks. This is a police technique in which they use their own vehicles to slow traffic in advance of an accident which has just happened. It uses police or highway agency vehicles to move with the traffic and obstruct the flow by slow degrees, to reduce the risk of subsidiary accidents or pile-ups ahead of a fresh serious incident.

Barriers

These can be made of plastic sections or traffic cones. They will not bring a vehicle to a complete stop, or cause injury to a driver, but they are clearly visible and will make any driver aware that they have hit something. Impact with a barrier is noisy and warns workers at a site of potential danger. Barriers can be used for demarcating contraflow and other traffic redirection systems which operate around accident sites on motorways and dual carriageways.

Cones

The purpose of traffic cones is to guide traffic along a temporary route around roadworks or an accident site.

- Category A Traffic Cones are fully compliant with BS873: Part 8.
- They are supplied with a Designation 2 reflective sleeve for extra night-time safety.
- They are designed and constructed for maximum strength and stability and will give long-life performance.
- Cones can be stacked for greater space economy.

Road closures

Warning signs for road closures should comply with Chapter 8 of the *Traffic Signs Manual* and the *Safety at Street Works and Road Works Code of Practice*.

www.dft.gov.uk/ (the Traffic Signs Manual is published by the Department for Transport and is downloadable)

Diversions

The police, sometimes in conjunction with the Highways Agency, set up diversion signs when an accident is likely to obstruct traffic on a motorway or major road for a long time. This benefits drivers who would otherwise get caught in tailbacks, but it may cause additional hazards or problems for people living on the diversion routes if the routes are not built for large volumes of traffic.

Consideration for public welfare

Major incidents such as serious road traffic accidents or house fires are disastrous to those involved, but they also cause problems for other people – often because of traffic congestion and sometimes because of pollution or environmental damage. Though the primary tasks of the emergency services are to rescue casualties, limit damage and investigate the cause of the incident, they are also responsible for minimising the public inconvenience and the environmental effects. They carry out this public welfare duty in a number of ways.

Use of the media to warn the public, warning the public about possible delays to public transport, warning the public about congestion

On the whole the media are a nuisance at the scene of a road traffic accident. The police discourage them from entering, and place strict controls on their behaviour if they do allow them on the scene. However, they expect the media to warn the public of severe traffic congestion and other possible results of major incidents.

For major roads and motorways, media reports on traffic conditions come through the Highways Agency. Up-to-date traffic information – especially about blocked carriageways and congestion – is available on the Highways Agency website and on BBC websites. Traffic news is also broadcast through local radio.

www.highways.gov.uk/traffic/traffic.aspx

case study 15.14 · Traffic information

Get the latest traffic and congestion news for the region. For regular reports tune in to BBC Radio Cambridgeshire on 96FM, 95.7FM, 1026AM or listen online.

Source: bbc.co.uk

activity
INDIVIDUAL WORK

Listen to your local radio station and make a note of the first three traffic announcements that you hear. Are any of them about accidents?

www.highways.gov.uk/business/13090.aspx

Ensuring the scene is safe and will not affect the local environment and its citizens

Emergency incidents involving the fire and rescue service – fires, traffic accidents and industrial accidents – are often bad for the environment. Because of the need to investigate causes it is not always possible to clean up immediately, and sometimes the clean up can be a very big operation indeed.

The agency involved in the Buncefield clean-up was the **Environment Agency** (linked to the Department for the Environment, Food and Rural Affairs). This agency has responsibility for the biggest clean-ups and spillages.

www.environment-agency.gov.uk/subjects/waste/

The legal basis for clearing up hazardous waste from industrial accidents is The Control of Major Accident Hazards Regulations 1999 and The Control of Major Accident Hazards (Amendment) Regulations 2005.

For clean-ups after major road accidents the Highways Agency has the main role. They work in partnership with the Environment Agency, fire and rescue services and local authorities. When a road accident takes place on a minor road, local authorities clear up wreckage and debris (sometimes together with the fire and rescue service). Problems can be caused by liquid wastes or spillages dissolved in water: these cannot be released into local sewers or streams, and have to be contained until they can be pumped and transported elsewhere for safe disposal. This itself is not easy as there is a risk of toxic materials soaking down into reserves of ground water and appearing in wells, boreholes, streams or drinking-water supplies elsewhere.

case study 15.15   Environmental clean-up

Buncefield a year on: clean-up continues

…

David Adam, environment correspondent

Saturday December 9, 2006

The Guardian

Engineers are still working to clean up millions of litres of water polluted by the blaze at the Buncefield oil depot in Hertfordshire nearly a year ago, the Environment Agency said yesterday. The toxic legacy of the disaster is expected to linger well into the new year, with some 26m litres of contaminated water not expected to be safely disposed of until February.

Senior managers and key staff at the oil companies responsible for the depot are being interviewed by the agency and the Health and Safety Executive, with a view to possible prosecutions.

Source: Guardian Unlimited

activity
INDIVIDUAL WORK

Research the Buncefield fire. What measures do you think could be taken to reduce the risk of a similar disaster in the future?

Dangers at the scene

Accident scenes are dangerous. Some of the main dangers are discussed briefly below.

Chemical spillage

Modern high-tech industry uses a wide range of chemicals and these have to be transported around the country. Despite the much-improved design of tankers, lorries and other vehicles and increased safety awareness, the sheer amount of chemicals being transported increases the risk of accidents. If chemicals are spilled in road accidents the driver of the vehicle, road users, the emergency services and people living nearby may all be at risk.

Hazardous chemicals (HazChem warning system)

Hazchem is the name given to a system of codes used to identify dangerous substances which are being transported in bulk. These codes are printed in large letters on panels at the back of tankers and other bulk transport vehicles. The codes give information on:

- The fire-extinguishing media to be used.
- The level of personal protective equipment (**PPE**) required.
- Whether the spillage should be contained or may be diluted.
- Whether there is a possibility of violent reaction.
- Whether the substance poses a Public Safety Hazard.

Figure 15.11 Who does the clean up?

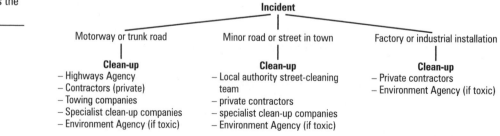

Hazchem codes protect the emergency services from the hazards of bulk chemicals which can be:

- Toxic.
- Oxidising.
- Explosive.
- Flammable.
- Violently reactive with water.
- Liable to release toxic gases on contact with water.
- Harmful to the environment.

Hazchem codes are easy to learn and understand.

www.the-ncec.com/ **(There is a good hazchem guide on this site.)**

Electricity cables

Live electricity cables are a risk for emergency workers in fires, industrial sites, buildings and some roadworks, and in gales and storms where they may have been blown down. The main dangers are:

- Shock and burns (the usual mains voltage of 230 V can kill).
- Fires caused by electrical faults (poor connections or damaged insulation).
- Fire or explosion caused by electrical sparks igniting a flammable or explosive mixture (e.g. gas and air or dust and air).

Railways and railway crossings

Accidents on the rail network have a number of causes:

- Equipment failure, e.g. points failure, cracks in the line, signal failure, mechanical failure of the train itself.
- Human error, e.g. driver not seeing signal, safety checks not carried out properly, errors made by car drivers, pedestrians or cyclists at level crossings.
- Criminal activity, e.g. children playing on tracks, people placing obstructions on the line.

Railways are potentially dangerous for anyone who goes on the track, which includes rescue workers. Some tracks are electrified and there is also a risk from trains and runaway wagons. In tunnel incidents there are dangers from fumes, smoke or intense heat if trains or freight are on fire. Railways and trains can also be targets for terrorists (Madrid 2004, London 2005). The main dangers for emergency services are jagged, broken metal, unstable wreckage, electric shocks, fires, explosions and accidents with cranes and lifting gear.

www.networkrail.co.uk/

Fires (e.g. persons trapped, smoke inhalation, evacuation)

In 2006 there were 57,100 house fires, 34,400 other building fires and 63,100 vehicle fires, and 473 people died in fires. (This compares with 3,200 road deaths in 2005.)

Burned buildings are dangerous places for the rescue services too.

Persons trapped

These people have to be rescued:

- By getting them out of windows and carrying or helping them down ladders.
- By getting into the building and leading them or dragging them to safety (perhaps through thick smoke and intense heat).

- In hospitals, old people's homes etc., by getting people out in beds or on stretchers.
- By persuading them to jump from the building, preferably onto something soft.

Firefighters always minimise risk, but they are trained and able to do 'snatch rescues' in burning and smoke-filled buildings. There are great dangers in getting trapped by fire, lost in smoke and overcome by fumes.

Smoke inhalation

This can cause suffocation, poisoning and burning of the airways. Firefighters wear breathing apparatus to try to avoid these dangers.

Evacuation

In public buildings there should be frequent and stringent fire drills, so that people know how to get out in case of fire and where they should muster afterwards for a head count. The head count is vital because it may be the only way of discovering if someone is still trapped in the building.

Dangers in evacuation include stampedes, people getting lost or people getting stuck in lifts – which should never be used if there is a fire. There are special risks for disabled people and the people who help them to get out. They may get trapped or delayed if the building is badly designed or the evacuation is badly organised.

> **remember**
>
> The safety officer at your college or workplace may well be able to talk to you about evacuation and other emergency arrangements.

Bombs and explosive devices

A bomb is a container with violently reactive materials inside it which can be detonated either by impact, heat, a timer or electronically. Death and destruction are caused by the shock waves that result from the suddenness and violence of the explosion, the impact of flying fragments or by the collapse of buildings, etc. **Explosive devices** are similar, but tend to be home-made or designed to be incendiary. This means that instead of destroying by shock waves they destroy by causing sudden, violent fires.

Bombs have been a danger to the emergency services ever since World War II, when large numbers of bombs that were dropped on Britain failed to explode, only to turn up years later on demolition sites, beaches or other places. Many of these were made safe by army bomb disposal units. Terrorist bombs have been a danger since the 1970s. The risk to the emergency services is mainly secondary – that of injury from weakened buildings or broken glass. A further risk with organised terrorist attacks is that bombs go off, and then a second wave of bombs is timed to explode after the emergency services have rushed to the scene.

It is theoretically possible to make explosive devices which have chemical, biological, radiological or nuclear contents. At the time of writing, these had not been used in Britain, but if they were, they would pose serious dangers to the emergency services.

The biggest and most dangerous terrorist bombs are vehicle bombs, where a large volume of explosives is packed into a car, van or lorry. They can destroy buildings and kill large numbers of people, and they are hard to detect.

The events of July 2005 have shown that there is a now a risk of suicide bombing in Britain. This affects the emergency services because:

- Bombings give them a huge amount of rescue and investigation work to do, which may have long-term effects (e.g. post-traumatic stress disorder).
- They could themselves be targets.

Bomb warnings

Bomb warnings can either be hoaxes, in which case there is either no bomb or there is an imitation bomb which cannot explode, or they can be warnings of real bombs which have actually been planted. The warnings are almost always made by telephone.

> **remember**
>
> Even a hoax bomb warning can be made for terrorist purposes.

It is important to try to get as much information from the caller as possible. This includes impressions of the caller's voice, age, state of mind, etc. The police must be informed.

Normally buildings are evacuated when there is a bomb warning (see page 266 below).

MI5 (www.mi5.gov.uk/)

Targets

Terrorists usually target places where there are large numbers of people. In recent years, in the world as a whole, targets have included business centres, banks, nightclubs, cafés, tourist centres, trains, buses, markets, airports, stations, hotels and ports.

They also prefer to choose capital or large cities, probably because they get more publicity in the world media as a result.

By choosing busy places in big cities, terrorists maximise the involvement of the emergency services. In places such as Baghdad police and police recruits have been heavily targeted. In the attacks on the World Trade Center in 2001, 343 firefighters died. The emergency services have not yet been targeted in the UK, but it must be assumed that there is a risk.

Terrorist activity

Deaths from terrorism in the UK are not high compared with the figures for other violent deaths, but it is thought that a number of terrorist plots are being hatched at any given time. The government publishes official threat levels giving the risk of terrorist attacks based on available intelligence. The levels are: Low, Moderate, Substantial, Severe and Critical.

See Unit 8, page 29 onwards (International perspectives)

The threat is monitored by MI5 and the Joint Terrorism Analysis Centre, which is a branch of MI5.

Terrorist activity in the UK is thought to be mainly linked to Islamist groups. In 2007 these formed the majority of organisations banned by the Home Office:

■ 42 international terrorist organisations are currently proscribed under the Terrorism Act 2000, which means they are outlawed in the UK.

■ 14 organisations in Northern Ireland are proscribed under previous legislation.

■ Under powers introduced in the Terrorism Act 2006, two organisations are currently proscribed as glorifying terrorism.

http://security.homeoffice.gov.uk/

Thirty of the banned organisations have Islamist aims according to the Home Office. However, at present there is no clear evidence that the London bombers of 2005 belonged to any banned organisation.

Dangers for emergency services at the scene of a terrorist attack include the risk of further bombs, gas and other explosions, falling masonry and debris, broken glass, electrocution, fumes, exposure to toxic dusts, possible exposure to chemical, biological, radiological or nuclear material, and risks linked to human panic and disorder. There are also serious long-term psychological risks such as post-traumatic stress disorder.

Searching

In a public-service run building, searching for bombs should follow a search plan which has been produced by safety officers or other qualified people, and approved by police counter-terrorism security advisers (who can be contacted through local police forces).

The following is a summary of MI5 advice:

■ Have a search coordinator.

■ Divide the building into search sectors.

■ Prioritise the vulnerable areas (those open to the public).

■ Have a system for starting searches.

remember

Terrorists target busy places where the uniformed public services tend to be. Overseas they target police and army recruits, and there are similar risks, potentially, in Britain.

- Give clear instructions to searchers (look for unusual objects; do not touch; report to police).
- Practise the search plan regularly.

Evacuation

Evacuation after a bomb warning should follow a security plan which has been drawn up in advance and has been practised from time to time. People should be moved well away from the building and a head-count should be carried out – as in a normal fire drill. The fire and rescue service, or other trained people, then search the building, looking in particular for things which should not be there.

Legislation and regulations

Legislation means laws, especially Acts of Parliament. Regulations are also laws passed by Parliament, but they are much more limited – and exact – in the way they are applied.

Impact of legislation and regulations

Prevention is better than cure, and laws about health and safety have done a great deal to reduce dangerous incidents. Thousands of lives have been saved, and the workload of the emergency services – especially the fire and rescue service – has been enormously reduced.

Fire and Rescue Services Act 2004

A new law which is likely to have a big impact on fire and rescue service work for a long time to come is the Fire and Rescue Services Act 2004. This replaces the Fire Service Act of 1947. It is of major importance because:

- It sets out a revised legal basis for what the fire and rescue service do.
- It gives the fire and rescue service legal obligations to carry out prevention and safety work, and to plan for and tackle major emergencies.
- It encourages the growing trend of partnership working between the fire and rescue services, other emergency services, and other non-emergency public services.

The main points of the Act are as follows:

1. The Act 'puts prevention at the heart of what the Fire and Rescue Service does'. There is a 'shift towards a more prevention-based and risk-assessed approach, thereby helping to save more lives by reducing the number of fires occurring in the first place'.

2. All fire and rescue authorities must promote fire safety.

3. The fire and rescue service has new powers to help create safer communities.

4. The Act gives the fire and rescue services a legal basis for carrying out road traffic accident rescues. This duty was not laid down under the Fire Services Act 1947.

5. It gives the fire and rescue service a legal duty to plan for and respond to other serious incidents such as flooding and terrorist threat.

6. The Act allows flexibility for the fire and rescue service to expand or change its role in response to future challenges.

7. Fire and rescue services must update and use their integrated risk management plans to respond to the specific local needs which the plans identify.

8. Services must set up 'co-responder schemes'. These enable fire and rescue services to carry out, by agreement, duties which might normally be done by another emergency service. An example is arranging to carry out some primary care if the ambulance service is not present, or if the emergency is too great to be covered by any one service.

9. The Fire and Rescue National Framework, which was originally an advisory document, will be put on a statutory footing. The FRNF gives 'national and strategic guidance and support to the service'. The FRNF must be monitored and brought up to date at least every two years.

10. Fire authorities will be encouraged to combine into bigger regional organisations. The aim is to give faster and bigger emergency responses where needed, and to fit in with the new system of regional control centres.

11. Public safety, economy, efficiency and effectiveness will be the four criteria against which fire and rescue services will be judged.

12. The Act allows the government to impose uniformity of approach on fire and rescue services, and to have a greater role in the buying of equipment.

13. The Act establishes the Fire Service College at Moreton in Marsh as a national centre of excellence and supports the Integrated Personal Development System of fire service training and staff development.

14. The fire and rescue service now has an obligation to carry out rescues and other measures in the event of a chemical, biological, radiological or nuclear attack.

15. It widens the power of firefighters to cover situations where fires are imminent, and involves them in a wider range of operational activities.

16. It increases the power of fire and rescue services to delegate authority (e.g. for fire safety) to other bodies.

17. The fire and rescue service cannot employ police officers, but they can employ special constables or community support officers.

To put this Act and other related measures into effect firefighters are undergoing extra training, especially in fire safety measures and in ways of involving the community more actively in fire safety. They are supported in this through:

- Integrated Risk Management Plans (IRMPs). These were introduced in 2004. They are written plans produced by fire authorities in collaboration with 'stakeholders' such as the Health and Safety Executive, local industry and local authorities. IRMPs aim to:
  - Reduce the number and severity of fires, road traffic accidents and other emergency incidents in the local area.
  - Reduce the severity of injuries in fires, road traffic accidents and other emergency incidents.
  - Reduce the commercial, economic and social impact of fires and other emergency incidents.
  - Safeguard the environment and heritage (both built and natural).
  - Provide value for money.

- Fire and Rescue Service Circulars, which come from the Department for Communities and Local Government. These give guidance on a wide range of fire prevention and emergency response issues.

- A timetable of 'milestones' for the fire and rescue service to ensure that they make swift progress in these and other reforms. Over a million home fire-risk checks must be carried out between 2004 and 2008.

- Changes in the building regulations to enable the fire and rescue service to have more say on building materials and construction.

- An ambitious series of safety campaigns, some of them targeting ethnic minority groups.

www.opsi.gov.uk/ (See the full text of Fire and Rescue Services Act 2004)

http://communities.gov.uk/ (FRS circulars, explanations of the Act; The Fire and Rescue National Framework 2006/08, etc.)

www.somerset.gov.uk/somerset/fire/irmp.asp (Integrated Risk Management Plan)

Health and Safety at Work Act 1974, including any subsequent amendments of legislation

This major law has to be followed in all workplaces, including the uniformed public services. Its main points are as follows.

Employers must:

■ Ensure 'so far as is reasonably practicable' the health, safety and welfare at work of their employees.

■ Consult employees or their safety representatives on safety matters and the planning of health and safety.

■ Provide a safe workplace with adequate welfare facilities.

■ Give information, instruction, training and supervision necessary for employees' health and safety.

■ Assess, in writing, the risks to employees' health and safety.

■ Carry out improvements recommended in the risk assessment.

■ Draw up a **health and safety policy statement** showing health and safety arrangements, and bring it to their employees' attention.

■ Appoint a safety officer.

■ Set up emergency procedures.

■ Provide first-aid facilities.

■ Provide free protective clothing or equipment.

■ Provide appropriate safety signs.

■ Report certain injuries, diseases and dangerous occurrences.

Employees must:

■ Take reasonable care of their own health and safety and that of others.

■ Cooperate with their employer on health and safety.

■ Use correctly all work items and personal protective equipment provided by the employer.

■ Not interfere with or misuse anything provided for their health, safety or welfare.

The Health and Safety at Work Act 1974 also set up the Health and Safety Commission and the Health and Safety Executive (HSE) – official bodies which regulate and inspect workplace safety.

www.hse.gov.uk/

Subsequent amendments of legislation

Amendments are changes, clarifications or updates of the Health and Safety at Work Act since it first came out in 1974. The main reasons for these amendments are changes in working practices, changes in technology, higher expected standards of health and safety, and the influence of the EU.

The Reporting of Injuries, Diseases and Dangerous Occurrences Regulations (RIDDOR)

These regulations made by Parliament require employers to notify certain occupational injuries, diseases and dangerous events. The following must be reported to the HSE's Incident Control Centre:

- Deaths.
- Major injuries.
- Injuries whose effect lasts longer than three days.
- Injuries to members of the public.
- Some work-related diseases.
- Dangerous occurrences – where someone could have got injured but did not.

The Control of Substances Hazardous to Health (COSHH)

These regulations compel employers to assess the risks from hazardous substances and take appropriate precautions. This covers potentially dangerous substances which are used, stored or produced in a workplace, and sets out a system for limiting their bad effects. The following is a bullet-point summary of the COSHH system:

- Assess risks.
- Decide on precautions.
- Prevent or control exposure.
- Ensure continued control.
- Monitor exposure.
- Do health checks.
- Make emergency plans.
- Train and supervise employees.

 www.hse.gov.uk/ (*COSHH: A brief guide to the Regulations. What you need to know about the Control of Substances Hazardous to Health Regulations 2002* (COSHH))

Hazard Analysis Critical Control Points (HACCPs)

This is a system for ensuring the safety of manufactured or processed foods. It is a form of risk assessment based on identifying the points in food production where hazards (e.g. the appearance of bacteria, or contamination of some sort) might lead to the food becoming a danger to health. The system also requires food producers to prevent things going wrong at these critical points, and keep full records of the steps, monitoring and reviews they take to ensure that the system works.

The procedure is now required by law: Regulation 852/2004 of the European Parliament on the Hygiene of Foodstuffs (2006).

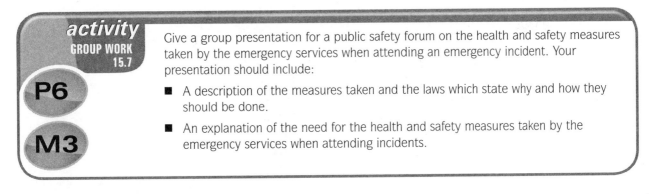

activity
GROUP WORK
15.7

P6

M3

Give a group presentation for a public safety forum on the health and safety measures taken by the emergency services when attending an emergency incident. Your presentation should include:

- A description of the measures taken and the laws which state why and how they should be done.
- An explanation of the need for the health and safety measures taken by the emergency services when attending incidents.

activity

INDIVIDUAL WORK 15.8

D2

You are working as a researcher for a health and safety organisation. Write a report assessing in detail the effect of health and safety laws on emergency services attending a serious incident. Your report should include:

■ An assessment of the effectiveness of the laws in protecting emergency service workers from the dangers they can face.

■ An assessment of any delays or difficulties these laws may cause, either for the emergency services or the people they are trying to protect or rescue.

■ Any cost implications which you feel are relevant to an evaluation of the effects of health and safety laws on emergency service workers.

Progress Check

1. Explain how and why incidents are graded by the emergency services.
2. What happens at emergency service call centres?
3. Under what four circumstances is a police response classified as an emergency response?
4. State the three main aspects of accountability.
5. What is the legal position with regard to emergency-service vehicles and speed limits?
6. What does SAD CHALET stand for?
7. State the main roles of the police, fire and rescue and ambulance services at a road traffic accident.
8. What does the Highways Agency do and where does it do it?
9. State the three main reasons why accidents have to be investigated.
10. What is the role of the HSE at the scene of a serious accident?
11. Outline the stages of a crime scene investigation.
12. What is the relevance of Locard's Principle to forensic work?
13. Outline the PEACE model for interviewing witnesses.
14. Who are the bodies responsible for cleaning up after emergency response incidents?
15. State eight requirements of the Health and Safety at Work Act 1974.

Uniformed Public Services Employment

This unit covers:

- The purpose, roles and responsibilities of a range of uniformed public services
- A range of jobs and conditions of service within the uniformed public services
- The application and selection process for a given uniformed public service
- The initial training and opportunities for career development within a given uniformed public service

Many hundreds of thousands of people are employed in Britain's uniformed public services. For example, there are over 100,000 uniformed people working in the British Army, more than 40,000 in the Royal Navy, and more than 50,000 in the RAF. In 2005 there were over 141,000 police officers and 70,000 civilian staff working for the police. There are around 48,000 prison officers and 33,000 firefighters.

The aim of this unit is to introduce you to a variety of uniformed public service careers, and to give guidance on choosing and applying for a public service job.

The unit begins by examining what the public services do. Then it looks at conditions of service. After this it moves on to application and selection procedures, including tests, simulations and interviews.

The final part of the unit examines initial training and the ways in which a person's career can develop after they have joined a uniformed public service.

Unit 16 is a Level 2 unit, unlike all the other units in this book which are Level 3.

grading criteria

To achieve a **pass** grade the evidence must show that the learner is able to:	To achieve a **merit** grade the evidence must show that, in addition to the pass criteria, the learner is able to:	To achieve a **distinction** grade the evidence must show that, in addition to the pass and merit criteria, the learner is able to:
P1 describe the roles, purpose and responsibilities of two contrasting uniformed public services Pg 284	**M1** explain the role, purpose and responsibilities of two contrasting uniformed public services Pg 284	**D1** evaluate the role, purpose and responsibilities of a uniformed public service Pg 284
P2 describe the type of work done in three different jobs within a named uniformed public service Pg 288	**M2** explain in detail the work of a job within a uniformed public service Pg 289	

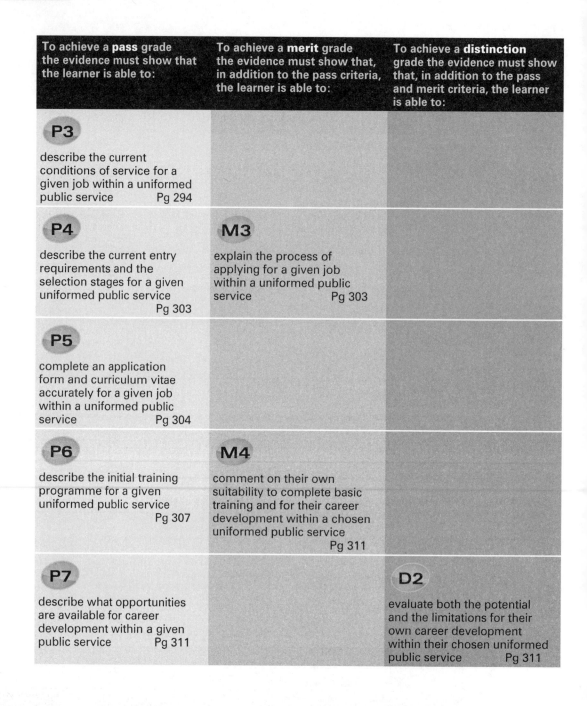

To achieve a **pass** grade the evidence must show that the learner is able to:	To achieve a **merit** grade the evidence must show that, in addition to the pass criteria, the learner is able to:	To achieve a **distinction** grade the evidence must show that, in addition to the pass and merit criteria, the learner is able to:
P3 describe the current conditions of service for a given job within a uniformed public service Pg 294		
P4 describe the current entry requirements and the selection stages for a given uniformed public service Pg 303	**M3** explain the process of applying for a given job within a uniformed public service Pg 303	
P5 complete an application form and curriculum vitae accurately for a given job within a uniformed public service Pg 304		
P6 describe the initial training programme for a given uniformed public service Pg 307	**M4** comment on their own suitability to complete basic training and for their career development within a chosen uniformed public service Pg 311	
P7 describe what opportunities are available for career development within a given public service Pg 311		**D2** evaluate both the potential and the limitations for their own career development within their chosen uniformed public service Pg 311

The purpose, roles and responsibilities of a range of uniformed public services

The purpose of a uniformed service is its aim: what it was set up to do. The purpose of a service is outlined in its mission statement and, in many cases, defined by law.

The roles of a uniformed service are the actual work the service does. This is outlined in its **job descriptions**.

The responsibilities of a uniformed service are to do the work as well as possible, fairly, honestly, as openly as possible and without wasting money. These responsibilities can be found in plans, annual reports, inspection reports, the relevant government Acts (laws about how that service does its job) and documents to do with accountability.

Emergency services

The main emergency services in Britain are the police, the fire and rescue service and the ambulance service. They are called emergency services because they are equipped, trained and tasked to deal with emergencies. An emergency is an incident which threatens life or property and demands an urgent response.

The police

Figure 16.1 Purpose, roles and responsibilities of the police

Source: Adapted from West Yorkshire policing plan 2005/06

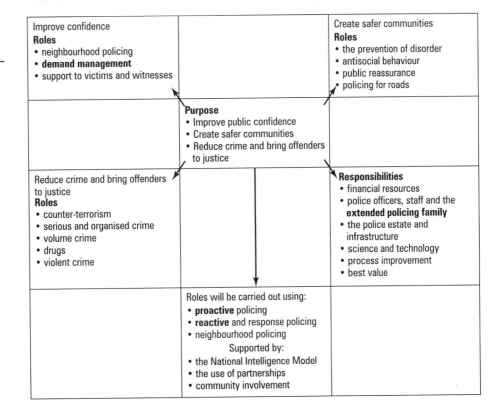

Improve confidence
Roles
• neighbourhood policing
• **demand management**
• support to victims and witnesses

Create safer communities
Roles
• the prevention of disorder
• antisocial behaviour
• public reassurance
• policing for roads

Purpose
• Improve public confidence
• Create safer communities
• Reduce crime and bring offenders to justice

Reduce crime and bring offenders to justice
Roles
• counter-terrorism
• serious and organised crime
• volume crime
• drugs
• violent crime

Responsibilities
• financial resources
• police officers, staff and the **extended policing family**
• the police estate and infrastructure
• science and technology
• process improvement
• best value

Roles will be carried out using:
• **proactive** policing
• **reactive** and response policing
• neighbourhood policing
Supported by:
• the National Intelligence Model
• the use of partnerships
• community involvement

Fire and rescue service

Under the Fire and Rescue Services Act 2004, the former fire service was renamed the fire and rescue service. Its purposes, roles and responsibilities as laid down in the Act are given in Table 16.1.

Table 16.1 Fire and rescue service: purposes, roles and responsibilities

Purposes	Roles	Responsibilities
Promote fire safety	Fire inspections	Recruit, train and organise suitable staff
Fire fighting	Fire prevention	
Protect life and property	Attending fires	Have call systems and methods of getting information
Limit damage to property	Putting out fires	
Rescue people from road traffic accidents	Rescuing people from fires and crashed vehicles	Prepare for major emergencies
Other rescues	Educating the community about fire safety	Organise reinforcement schemes and partnerships
Protect the community in major emergencies	Encouraging fire safety	Be accountable
	Investigating fires	Give value for money
		Be an equal opportunities employer

Ambulance service

Table 16.2 Ambulance service: purposes, roles and responsibilities

Purposes	Roles	Responsibilities
Give care in emergencies, serious cases and less serious cases Take people to hospital	Rescues (with fire and rescue service) Resuscitation Urgent primary care Other paramedic duties Accident and emergency and **patient transport service** roles	To meet targets for response times and the saving of lives To be accountable To give cover at all hours on every day of the year To drive safely

The armed forces

These consist of the army, the Royal Navy (including the Royal Marines) and the Royal Air Force.

Table 16.3 Armed forces: purposes, roles and responsibilities

Purposes	Roles	Responsibilities
To deliver security for the people of the United Kingdom and the overseas territories by defending them, including against terrorism; and to act as a force for good by strengthening international peace and stability	Peacekeeping – UN, NATO and Coalition Fighting – Iraq and Afghanistan Supporting police in Northern Ireland Disaster relief Humanitarian aid	To achieve public service agreement target (military objectives set by UK government) To maintain and develop skills and fitness for action To recruit personnel To update weaponry

Source: Ministry of Defence Defence Plan 2007, 'The Defence Aim'

Under systems of joint command (operations involving all of the armed services, as in Iraq and Afghanistan) the purposes, **roles** and responsibilities of the armed forces are increasingly similar to each other.

However, their areas of operations remain technically separate. The army are involved in land operations, the Royal Navy in sea operations and the RAF in air operations. The Royal Marines, though a branch of the Royal Navy, operate both on water and on land.

Other uniformed services

Like all uniformed services, these specialise in particular activities. Each has different purposes and roles. However, their responsibilities are in some ways identical:

- To give the best possible service at the lowest possible cost.
- To be accountable so that both the government and the public know what they are doing and how they are spending public money.

The prison service

**case study
16.1**

HM Prison Service

Her Majesty's Prison Service serves the public by keeping in custody those committed by the courts. Our duty is to look after them with humanity and help them lead law-abiding and useful lives in custody and after release.

Our Vision

■ To provide the very best prison services so that we are the provider of choice

■ To work towards this vision by securing the following key objectives.

Objectives

To protect the public and provide what commissioners want to purchase by:

■ Holding prisoners securely

■ Reducing the risk of prisoners re-offending

■ Providing safe and well-ordered establishments in which we treat prisoners humanely, decently and lawfully.

In securing these objectives we adhere to the following principles:

Our Principles

In carrying out our work we:

■ Work in close **partnership** with our commissioners and others in the Criminal Justice System to achieve common objectives

■ Obtain **best value** from the resources available using research to ensure effective correctional practice

■ Promote **diversity**, equality of opportunity and combat unlawful discrimination, and

■ Ensure our staff have the right leadership, organisation, support and preparation to carry out their work effectively.

Source: HM Prison Service

activity
GROUP WORK

In pairs, decide which of these are purposes, which are roles and which are responsibilities.

HM Revenue and Customs

HM Revenue and Customs was formed in 2005 by the merging of the Inland Revenue (the government body which collected income tax) and Her Majesty's Customs and Excise which collected import duty, tax on things like tobacco and petrol and VAT.

Table 16.4 HM Revenue and Customs: purposes, roles and responsibilities

Purposes	Roles	Responsibilities
Collect national taxes	Collecting taxes	Collect taxes fairly and honestly, according to the law
Prevent smuggling and other forms of illegal trade	Inspecting luggage and freight at ports	
	Cooperating with the police and others to combat cross-border crime	Treat the public with consideration and respect
		Be accountable

Coast guard

Table 16.5 Coast guard: purposes, roles and responsibilities

Purpose	Roles	Responsibilities
Keep watch over Britain's coastline Coordinate sea rescues Promote safety at sea Protect the marine environment	Checking ships for safety Reporting incidents Advising users of Britain's inshore waters, both recreational and commercial	Be accountable Give value for money for the taxpayers Work in partnership with the Met Office, the RAF, police, etc.

Private security services (e.g. local government)

Table 16.6 Private security services: purposes, roles and responsibilities

Purposes	Roles	Responsibilities
Protect people from crime, terrorism, etc. Protect property Reassure the public Help members of the public who are in difficulty	Patrolling hospitals, colleges, etc. Installing alarm systems Monitoring CCTV Airport security Door staff Cash in transit	Work legally, honestly and conscientiously Be licensed by the Security Industry Authority Be professional and polite in dealings with the ordinary public

Purpose

Most uniformed public services are statutory, i.e. their purpose is laid down in laws made by Parliament. However, though they have laws to follow, organisations such as the police and the fire and rescue service are also locally based. This means that their purposes must follow local needs as well as national laws.

For this reason the police, fire and rescue and ambulance services set themselves objectives which are slightly different in different forces in different places.

The objectives are set by bodies called 'authorities', e.g. police authorities and fire and rescue authorities. These are committees of about 15–20 local councillors, chosen to reflect the political mix of the area.

Organisational objectives

Objectives are statements of what an organisation wishes to do, usually within a given time limit.

Mission statements

These are statements of aims. They say what the organisation wishes to do, but they do not say how they are going to do it.

The purpose of a mission statement is:

- To focus the service on its key aims.
- To show the public in clear and memorable language what the purpose of the service is.

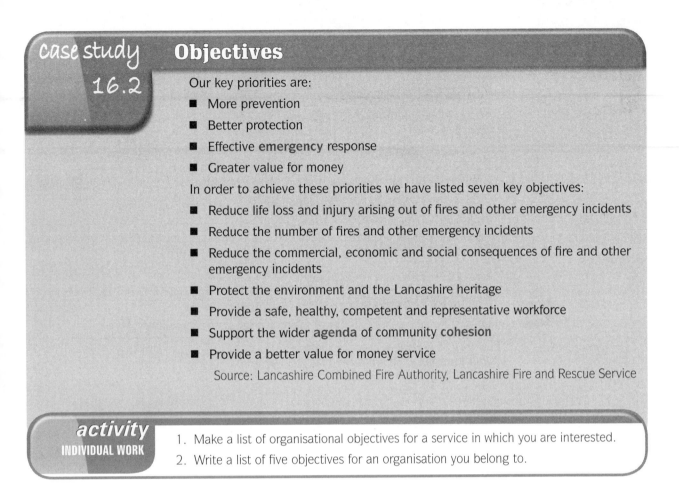

case study 16.2

Objectives

Our key priorities are:

- More prevention
- Better protection
- Effective **emergency** response
- Greater value for money

In order to achieve these priorities we have listed seven key objectives:

- Reduce life loss and injury arising out of fires and other emergency incidents
- Reduce the number of fires and other emergency incidents
- Reduce the commercial, economic and social consequences of fire and other emergency incidents
- Protect the environment and the Lancashire heritage
- Provide a safe, healthy, competent and representative workforce
- Support the wider **agenda** of community **cohesion**
- Provide a better value for money service

Source: Lancashire Combined Fire Authority, Lancashire Fire and Rescue Service

activity
INDIVIDUAL WORK

1. Make a list of organisational objectives for a service in which you are interested.
2. Write a list of five objectives for an organisation you belong to.

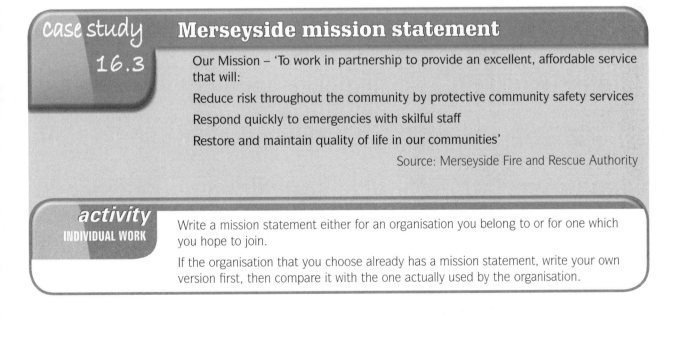

case study 16.3

Merseyside mission statement

Our Mission – 'To work in partnership to provide an excellent, affordable service that will:

Reduce risk throughout the community by protective community safety services

Respond quickly to emergencies with skilful staff

Restore and maintain quality of life in our communities'

Source: Merseyside Fire and Rescue Authority

activity
INDIVIDUAL WORK

Write a mission statement either for an organisation you belong to or for one which you hope to join.

If the organisation that you choose already has a mission statement, write your own version first, then compare it with the one actually used by the organisation.

Legislation

These are laws passed by Parliament in London. In the case of laws about the public services, they state what the government requires the public services to do. There are two kinds of legislation:

1. **Primary legislation**. These are the 'big' laws that say what the uniformed public services must do, e.g. Fire and Rescue Services Act 2004.

2. **Secondary legislation**. These are 'little' laws which say in detail how the uniformed public services must carry out certain tasks, e.g. the Disability Discrimination (Public Authorities) (Statutory Duties) (Amendment) Regulations 2007. (Police and many other public services have to publish a disability equality scheme and update it at intervals.)

There are also other documents such as codes of practice, which give instructions on how jobs should be done, and 'national frameworks', which set out aims and policies. Failure to carry out such instructions is normally a disciplinary rather than a legal matter.

PACE Codes of Practice (police) http://police/homeoffice.gov.uk

Fire and Rescue Service National Frameworks www.communities.gov.uk

Main laws for each uniformed service

The main laws for the army used to be:

- Army Act 1955.
- RAF Act 1955.
- Naval Discipline Act 1957.
- Armed Forces Act 2001.

These have all been replaced by:

- Armed Forces Act 2006.

The main law for the fire and rescue service used to be:

- Fire Services Act 1947.

This has been replaced by:

- Fire and Rescue Services Act 2004.

The main laws for the police are:

- Police and Criminal Evidence Act 1984.
- Criminal Justice and Public Order Act 1994.
- Criminal Justice and Police Act 2001.
- Police Act 1997.
- Anti-Terrorism, Crime and Security Act 2001.
- Terrorism Act 2000.
- Prevention of Terrorism Act 2005.
- Terrorism Act 2006.
- Police Reform Act 2002.
- Police and Justice Act 2006.
- Regulation of Investigatory Powers Act 2000.

The main law for HM Revenue and Customs is:

- Commissioners for Revenue and Customs Act 2005.

The main law for the emergency services is:

■ Civil Contingencies Act 2004.

The main law for private security is:

■ Private Security Industry Act 2001.

Roles

For this section of the unit you are strongly advised to visit as many public services as possible and get direct information about the different roles (jobs) carried out by each service.

Dealing with accidents and emergencies

In accidents and emergencies the police are usually in overall charge, the fire and rescue service carry out rescues and release people who are trapped, while the ambulance service give **primary care** and transport people to hospital.

Link

Unit 15, pages 241–246

i

www.acpo.police.uk/ (One of the best websites listed in this book. Look up 'Policies'.)

Routine work

This is work that people do every day – non-emergency work that can be planned in advance.

Peacekeeping activities

This is what the armed forces do when they are posted to places where there have recently been wars or conflict. Peacekeeping ranges from protecting politicians and journalists to building bridges, sorting out water supplies, training people in the occupied community to making sure that children get safely to school, etc.

remember

Work placement or shadowing can be very valuable if you can arrange it. Visiting speakers are also a useful source of information.

remember

The fact that work is routine does not mean it is not important. Fire prevention, as carried out by the fire and rescue service, for example, is routine work but it saves many lives.

Figure 16.2 An emergency services control centre. Routine work – but you never know what is going to happen next!

British peacekeeping forces are often under the overall command of the UN or NATO.

www.britishembassy.gov.uk/
www.fco.gov.uk/
www.nato.int/home.htm
www.un.org/

remember

There is formal
and informal
cooperation with
the police and other
agencies in many
other western and/
or allied countries.

remember

The Metropolitan
Police's Counter
Terrorism Command
is the main police
organisation fighting
terrorism in the UK.

Other roles (e.g. anti-terrorist and anti-smuggling roles)

To tackle complex problems such as terrorism or smuggling, uniformed public services often work in partnerships. The police, the armed forces and HM Revenue and Customs work with **MI5** (internal security), **MI6** (external security) and other security services. They also work with international organisations such as Europol, Interpol, the Organization for Security and Cooperation in Europe (OSCE), the North Atlantic Treaty Organization (NATO) and the European Union (EU).

Defence roles of the armed forces

The main role of the armed forces is to defend Britain, Britain's allies and British **interests** against attack. Allies are nations such as the US, NATO members, European Union countries and other countries with which Britain is friendly or has treaties. British interests include sources of oil, gas and other essentials, industries owned by Britain or Britain's allies, etc.

The armed forces defend Britain:

- By acting as a **deterrent**. Many countries will not attack Britain simply because they know we have a strong army, Royal Navy and RAF.

- By backing up British political action with a real or implied threat of force. This is believed to increase Britain's influence in the world and help Britain to negotiate more effectively with other countries.

- By fighting enemies (usually helping the US, NATO, the UN or the EU). At present these enemies are mainly classed as '**insurgents**' – groups such as the **Taliban** in Afghanistan which are not governments but which are attacking friendly governments (such as the NATO-backed Hamid Karzai government in Afghanistan).

- By peacekeeping activities which prevent warfare or unrest which could threaten Britain's allies or interests.

Humanitarian work

This is work to reduce large-scale human suffering, e.g. after major disasters such as the 2004 Indian Ocean tsunami and the 2005 Pakistan earthquake. British forces carried out relief and reconstruction work in Sri Lanka, Indonesia (Banda Aceh) and Pakistan (Muzzafarabad).

Disaster relief

This is a form of **humanitarian** relief. It includes building infrastructure such as temporary bridges and roads so that food aid and shelter can reach stricken populations.

Conflict

Conflict means low-intensity fighting, where there are small operations and outbreaks of fighting rather than continuous warfare.

Working in prisons

The main service doing this is the prison service. Most British prisons are government run, but there are an increasing number of private prisons (where pay and conditions for prison officers are said to be somewhat worse).

The first job of prison officers is to prevent escape. Other than this, they try to treat prisoners humanely and prepare them for release, so that they are less likely to reoffend.

case study 16.4 — Counterinsurgency

Because the small-war environment (counterinsurgency) seems likely to be prevalent for the foreseeable future, one military expert's observations about the British Army are germane: the promotion of the values of decentralization, lightness, quality of training, and unit cohesion are no less important for the small wars of the future than they have been for the small wars of the past.

Source: Cassidy R.M. (2005) *The British Army and Counterinsurgency: The Salience of Military Culture*, Military Review, May-June 2005.
www.army.mil/professionalwriting/volumes/volume3/november_2005/11_05_2.html

activity
GROUP WORK

This is a US view of the British army. What is it saying – and do you agree with it based on your own knowledge?

> **remember**
>
> The aim of privatisation is to save taxpayers' money.

Transporting prisoners

This is done by private companies such as Group 4 Securicor. Like many kinds of public service work, transporting prisoners has been privatised (sold off by the government to private businesses) in recent years.

Patrolling the coast

This is the work of the HM Coastguard. The main purposes of the patrols are to ensure that vessels are safe, to detect pollution, to prevent people trafficking and carrying out other forms of **illicit** trade.

Operating CCTV

This is done by private security companies. In 2007 there was said to be one **CCTV** camera for every 14 people in Britain – one of the world's highest concentrations. CCTV has been a major factor in reducing town-centre and vehicle crime, though civil liberties campaigners see it is as an infringement of our right to privacy.

Working with local communities

The three emergency services are all community based. There are 43 police forces in England and Wales and almost all are local, named after the area they serve, e.g. Avon and Somerset. The introduction of police Basic Command Units in 2003 strengthened local policing, especially with the introduction of community support officers who back up the police and provide a visible police-type presence on the streets which the public find reassuring.

Link

Unit 13 pages 160–161

There are 47 fire and rescue authorities (each in charge of a fire and rescue service) in England alone. Some fire stations are called community fire stations, and the fire and rescue services have many outreach centres where they can work more closely with the community in order to spread life-saving knowledge about fire safety.

Responsibilities

Accountability

Accountability means taking responsibility. The uniformed public services have increased their accountability greatly since 1984 when the Police and Criminal Evidence Act was brought in and began the process of making the police more accountable.

Accountability depends on keeping records and making them public or at least available for independent inspection.

Legal accountability

Legal accountability is the ability to take a public service to court, or to investigate thoroughly and openly whether it has broken the law.

Professional accountability

Professional accountability ensures that the uniformed service is going about its job in a way which is fair and honourable both to its own employees and to the general public. This means having an **equal opportunities** policy and making sure that it works. It also means having proper complaints and **grievance** procedures, and the right for complainants to go to an independent system if they are not satisfied with the service's internal system. This is why there is an Independent Police Complaints Commission, and why there is a Prisons Ombudsman: both of these bodies investigate complaints without the police or prisons being involved.

Political accountability

Political accountability means having political systems in place which ensure that uniformed public services are run according to the genuine wishes of the people they serve. In the **civilian** services this is achieved by having 'authorities' (e.g. police authorities) made up mainly of local councillors who set budgets for local policing and ensure that local policing priorities fit in with the wishes of local people.

The armed forces are politically accountable to Parliament and the prime minister.

Performance indicators – what they are, examples of, effect on work

Statutory Performance Indicators (SPIs) are a government measure of how well an organisation is doing in meeting a particular target. They are used for local government and the police. In the police, the performance indicators are based on a framework which is shown in Figure 16.3.

The government requires all uniformed public services to set targets for improvement. These include things like average response times for the emergency services, and clear-up rates for reported crimes.

Case study 16.5 shows an example of a performance indicator used by the police.

The measuring of performance using the statutory performance indicators appears under 'Best Value' in some public service annual reports. Similar information is collected by Her Majesty's Inspectors of Constabulary when they inspect Basic Command Units and other police organisations.

The intended effect of performance indicators on police work is to improve performance year on year. The actual effect may be to increase police paperwork and increase the cost of policing.

> **remember**
> If there is no valid and consistent record of what a service has been doing, it can never be accountable.

> **remember**
> An ombudsman is an independent investigator of complaints against a public service.

> **remember**
> Political and public disagreements about British activities in Iraq and Afghanistan have led some people to question whether there is enough political accountability for the armed forces.

> **remember**
> Best Value is a scheme for improving the performance of public bodies, introduced in the Local Government Act 1999. Best Value performance indicators also appear in the Fire and Rescue National Framework.

Figure 16.3 Policing performance assessment framework

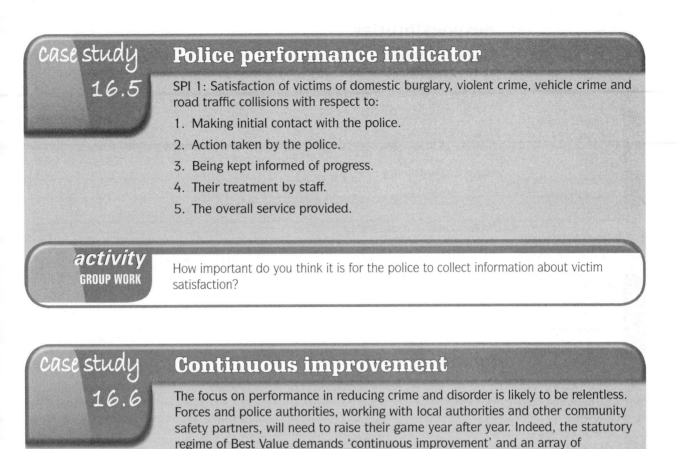

case study 16.5 — Police performance indicator

SPI 1: Satisfaction of victims of domestic burglary, violent crime, vehicle crime and road traffic collisions with respect to:

1. Making initial contact with the police.
2. Action taken by the police.
3. Being kept informed of progress.
4. Their treatment by staff.
5. The overall service provided.

activity — GROUP WORK

How important do you think it is for the police to collect information about victim satisfaction?

case study 16.6 — Continuous improvement

The focus on performance in reducing crime and disorder is likely to be relentless. Forces and police authorities, working with local authorities and other community safety partners, will need to raise their game year after year. Indeed, the statutory regime of Best Value demands 'continuous improvement' and an array of sanctions exist if authorities fail to deliver this.

Source: Inspection of Tendring BCU, Essex Police, May 2005

activity — INDIVIDUAL WORK

What are the advantages and problems of having a 'continuous improvement' requirement for police forces?

case study 16.7 — Performance

Table 16.7 Performance indicators

Crime category	Visits	Force average
Burglary, dwelling	90.75%	86.97%
Burglary, other	46.03%	46.21%
Theft of motor vehicle	51.91%	51.17%
Theft from motor vehicle	41.79%	24.14%

*Figures show the percentage of reported burglaries or thefts that are attended by an officer. Figures in the Visits column are for the BCU inspected; figures in the Force average column are for the whole force, i.e. Essex police

Source: Inspection of Tendring BCU, Essex Police, May 2005

activity — GROUP WORK

Why do inspectors of police want to know how often police attend the scenes of crime?

activity
GROUP WORK
16.1

P1

M1

You are staffing a public service stand at a careers exhibition for school leavers. Produce charts or leaflets to be put up or distributed at the stand. Your materials must outline to the public the jobs, purpose and duties of a range of uniformed public services. Each individual must produce materials relating to one military service and one civilian service, or to one professional public service and one voluntary public service.

activity
INDIVIDUAL WORK
16.2

D1

Write an in-depth article for a student magazine assessing the work, aims and duties of a uniformed service. The title of the article is: '(Name of public service): Are they as good as they say they are?'

Public service work

Information under this heading is available elsewhere in this book and in Book 1. It is also available from the public services themselves, through visits, visiting speakers, work placement or shadowing, or through talking to anybody who works in the uniformed public services.

Range of emergency and routine work undertaken

This is to do with urgent responses to emergency incidents on the one hand, and ordinary daily routine on the other. Firefighters, for example, follow a daily routine of exercises, training, inspections, etc., but if an incident is reported they attend it.

> **remember**
> Incidents range from false alarms (malicious or non-malicious) all the way up to major emergencies.

Daily work routine

Routine is non-emergency work. It has to do with things such as planning, organisation, fire and crime prevention, training, record-keeping, monitoring and accountability.

Administrative work

This is paperwork, work at a computer, or management tasks such as telling people what to do, and checking that they are doing it. It is normally done in an office, and some of it is done by civilian (i.e. non-uniformed) employees.

Work with other public services

This is an increasingly important aspect of public service work. A typical example, relatively easy to research, is crime and disorder reduction partnerships (CDRPs). In these the police form multi-service teams with local authorities, fire and rescue services, schools, primary care (health) trusts, housing associations, local businesses and so on, so that they can have a '**joined up**' response to local crime, disorder and antisocial behaviour.

Link

Book 1, Unit 12, pages 123 and 126

Community work

This is work with local people, or people belonging to a specific social or ethnic group. It includes neighbourhood policing, now carried out by Basic Command Units and community support officers. Very often it involves liaison with social services and voluntary and community groups.

Implications of working in the public services on a personal level

These are the effects of public service work on the individual, and on his or her health, happiness, social and family life. They vary greatly with the service, the work done, the individual, etc.

Positive and negative aspects of working in the services

Table 16.8 Good and bad points of working in the services

Good points	Bad points
In the armed forces you can see the world, develop character, fitness, teamwork and self-reliance and do a difficult job which requires courage and initiative	There is a risk of getting killed or seriously injured, of having to kill others, of stress, homesickness and hardship
Public services offer good career prospects, better than average job stability and plenty of variety	The work gets only moderate pay at lower levels, and it does not suit everybody
In public service you are contributing to society, doing a necessary job, which allows other people to go about their lives in reasonable security and comfort. Many people deeply appreciate what you do	You often have to deal with people who are hostile, difficult, mentally or physically ill, stressed or bereaved Not everybody is pleased to meet you!
Your work gets you out and about, and you see life	There are traumatic and distressing incidents
There are reasonable holidays, occupational health and pensions	There is plenty of shift work, and your social life can get messed about

Examples of recent peacekeeping activities and humanitarian work

In 2005/06 the armed forces carried out peacekeeping work in Cyprus, the Democratic Republic of Congo, Georgia, Liberia and Sierra Leone. The work protects British interests, creates security and stability and allows reconstruction to take place in countries where there has recently been fighting. Peacekeeping is often done in partnership with other countries or organisations such as the US, the UN, NATO, the EU and the African Union.

Recent humanitarian work included sending survey vessels and food aid to help with the aftermath of Hurricane Katrina in 2005, and a reconstruction team of Royal Engineers (army) and Royal Marines to earthquake-hit areas of Pakistan, also in 2005.

Roles at major incidents

The roles of the uniformed services at major incidents are shown in Figure 16.4.

http://news.bbc.co.uk/

Figure 16.4 Emergency service roles – major incidents

Fire and rescue service	Police	Ambulance service
• Search and rescue • Life-saving • Fire fighting/prevention • Humanitarian services • Managing hazardous materials • Protecting environment • Salvage • Safety management of scene	• Coordination of services at scene • Protecting/preserving scene • Controlling traffic/public • Investigation of scene • Collecting/distributing casualty information • Identifying dead; telling the coroner • Family liaison • Helping to restore normality	• Saves lives • Treatment, stabilisation and care of injured • Transport to hospital, etc. • 'Triage' – sorting and prioritising casualties • Coordination/communication for NHS • Alert hospitals to receive injured

In very major disasters, or large-scale terrorist threats, the armed forces are involved (e.g. Heathrow, February 2003).

Examples of activities in recent conflicts

In Iraq British forces (as part of the US-led coalition) are working to stabilise the southern part of the country, around Basra. Their activities include fighting and deterring 'insurgents' (armed groups who oppose the occupation). British troops are also attempting to create conditions for rebuilding the infrastructure (water, electricity, etc.) and, when possible, training Iraqi police, soldiers, security workers, etc.

In Afghanistan British forces are fighting Taliban insurgents in Helmand Province, southern Afghanistan. They are part of a NATO-led **multinational force** supporting the government of Hamid Karzai.

A range of jobs and conditions of service within the uniformed public services

Range

A range of jobs is simply a variety of jobs – and in the uniformed public services there is an enormous variety of different jobs. **Conditions of service** are things such as pay, working hours, holidays, pensions, sick pay and other welfare arrangements that come with a job.

It is not possible to describe in this book all of the jobs or conditions of service in the uniformed public services. Furthermore, for people who want to work in the public services there is no substitute for meeting public service employees and – best of all – seeing them at work.

The following points may help you to make useful public service contacts:

- Never miss an arranged visit to a public service.
- Ask questions and talk to visiting speakers after they have given their talk.
- Inquire about work placement, if you are interested.
- If you apply for work placement, pay great attention to the quality of your application and your CV.
- Individually, or with course-mates, contact the public services that interest you and see if you can talk to anybody about the work, to get a real idea of what it is like.
- If you make appointments, make sure you keep them.
- Show interest, enthusiasm, good manners and gratitude if you get advice, information or help from anyone who works in a public service.
- If you are interested, find out if there are volunteer opportunities.
- If a group of you want the same information, arrange to get it at the same time – it saves time and effort for the service concerned.

Different operational jobs

Operational jobs are hands-on (non-managerial) jobs where people do the work rather than tell other people what to do. Some jobs, such as that of a **paramedic** (see below), while being mainly operational, are also managerial in that paramedics have to guide and oversee ambulance **technicians** in their work.

Ambulance service, patient transport services, technician and paramedic

The ambulance service is a general name for a branch of the National Health Service. Within the service different people do different jobs. Patient transport services take out-patients to hospital for routine treatment such as dialysis. Ambulance technicians assist paramedics with life-saving treatment at accident and emergency scenes. Paramedics diagnose casualties, give immediate health care at accidents and emergencies, and brief doctors at Accident and Emergency units when casualties have been rushed to hospital. All of these people are also trained as ambulance drivers.

www.nhscareers.nhs.uk/details/Default.aspx?Id=468

Royal Navy, operator mechanics, engineering technicians and writers

The Royal Navy is a complex high-technology organisation. Many of the operational jobs are for technicians or mechanics. Their work involves regulating, repairing, replacing and maintaining equipment. The word 'mechanic' is not used so much in relation to modern ships and aircraft. 'Technician' is preferred because the work is of a technical nature requiring advanced skills and a high degree of specialisation, e.g. in electronics.

Writers are office staff who look after the administration of a ship or submarine. Their responsibilities include keeping accounts, dealing with pay and keeping personnel (staff) records.

Civilian support roles

The uniformed public services, especially the police, are employing increasing numbers of civilian (non-uniformed) staff.

Police control-room operators Police control-room operators (communications staff) play an essential role in linking the police to the public and determining what tasks the police carry out. They work on the phone and on computers to record information given to them by the public, and they then take appropriate action.

Scenes of crime officers These are people who work at scenes of crime, investigating the scene and collecting, processing and storing evidence. Some are police officers, e.g. the senior investigating officer (SIO) who manages the crime scene. Others are civilian specialists, e.g. the **forensic** staff. Forensic staff collect fingerprints, dust, fibres and other items which can be examined microscopically and used as evidence. Some have special expertise in examining computers and mobile phone data. Most forensic scientists have science degrees, and then undergo further training in the Serious Crime Analyisis Section of the National Policing Improvement Agency (NPIA).

www.npia.police.uk/en/index.htm

remember

There are many interesting police-related jobs which do not require you to pass the fitness test!

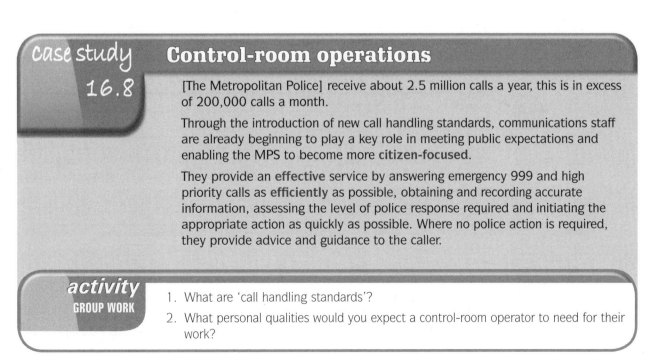

case study 16.8   Control-room operations

[The Metropolitan Police] receive about 2.5 million calls a year, this is in excess of 200,000 calls a month.

Through the introduction of new call handling standards, communications staff are already beginning to play a key role in meeting public expectations and enabling the MPS to become more **citizen-focused**.

They provide an **effective** service by answering emergency 999 and high priority calls as **efficiently** as possible, obtaining and recording accurate information, assessing the level of police response required and initiating the appropriate action as quickly as possible. Where no police action is required, they provide advice and guidance to the caller.

activity
GROUP WORK

1. What are 'call handling standards'?
2. What personal qualities would you expect a control-room operator to need for their work?

Community support officers

Police community support officers are uniformed staff who work with the police on visible patrols. Their role is to help reduce antisocial behaviour and 'street crime', deal with minor offences, collect intelligence and liaise with the community. They have fewer powers than the police: they cannot arrest people, question or deal with prisoners or investigate serious crime.

Your Guide to becoming a Police Community Support Officer, Home Office, 2006

Management and administrative

Management means organising, motivating and monitoring staff. **Administration** means carrying out organisation and paperwork to ensure the smooth running of an organisation.

Uniformed services management is mainly done by officers within the service. Higher management is combined with leadership (e.g. decision-making and planning) roles.

Administration is increasingly carried out by civilian employees – though some has to be done by service members as well.

Part-time opportunities (e.g. special constables, retained firefighters, Royal Navy Reserve, Territorial Army)

These part-time organisations are usually recruiting. If you have the time and interest they are well worth joining.

These people are either volunteers (unpaid) or part-timers. Special constables are volunteers who work with the police, wear uniform, receive training and have the same powers as the police. They are expected to work 200 hours a year. Retained firefighters are paid a 'retainer', a sum of money which is not directly linked to the amount of work they have to do. They are well trained and work with full-time firefighters on any kind of incident, but they are typically only called out two or three times a week. The Royal Naval Reserve is a trained group of part-timers who are available to add to the full-time Royal Navy in wartime or on other occasions when there is a clear need for extra personnel. The Territorial Army is similar to the Royal Naval Reserve but there are many more of them.

Jobs undertaken by the private sector

The public services are not as 'public' as they used to be. Many people now doing public service work are actually employed in the private sector. This is most obvious in the prison service where there are now 11 'privatised' prisons run by companies such as Group 4 Securicor. The work done by officers in private prisons is essentially the same as that done by officers in the government-run prisons.

www.hmprisonservice.gov.uk/
www.g4s.com/uk.htm

Other public service jobs done by the private sector include security work, private nursing, health-care and some patient transport work. In addition, some large firms have their own firefighters.

activity
INDIVIDUAL WORK
16.3

P2

Research three jobs in a uniformed public service and then explain what they involve as if you were describing them to a job-seeker at a careers office.

activity

INDIVIDUAL WORK 16.4

M2

You now work in a uniformed public service. Write a letter to a former teacher with whom you have kept in touch explaining in detail what you are doing and what the purpose of the job is.

remember

Conditions of service, especially salary, change in the public services from year to year. For up-to-date information, check on official websites, or phone or visit the recruitment sections/offices of local public services.

Conditions of service

Starting salary

Salaries, especially in the armed forces, can have hidden extras. These include free or low-cost accommodation, and the X factor – a 13% add-on to the basic salary to compensate for the difficulties and inconvenience of military life.

Holiday entitlement

Workers in the civilian uniformed public services have holidays fixed by national agreements. In the police the standard holiday is 24 days a year. In the armed forces the statutory entitlement is 30 days a year.

In the armed forces there are other kinds of leave which are not holiday. An example is relocation leave, which lasts 10 days in the army and allows people to sort out their affairs before going on a new posting.

In some careers holiday allowances increase with length of service. For example, in the prison service the increase is from 22 days a year to 30 days a year for senior staff.

Benefits (e.g. gym use, private medical insurance)

These benefits vary from service to service. In some jobs, e.g. firefighter, working out in the gym can be part of a normal day's routine. Private medical insurance may be available as a recognition of the fact that good health and fitness are needed for uniformed public service work. Fire and rescue services, for example, have occupational (workplace) health schemes, and police forces have police doctors and even police

case study 16.9

Salaries

Table 16.9 Starting salaries for a number of public service careers in 2007 (£/year)

Army*	Royal Navy*	RAF*	Police	Fire and rescue	Ambulance Technician	Prison Service	Ministry of Defence Police
15,677	15,677	15,677	21,009	19,918	16,405	17,744	18,663
21,880	21,880	21,880					

*Figures recommended by the Armed Forces Pay Review Body. The top line refers to other ranks; the bottom line refers to officers. The officers are graduate officer cadets. On completion of training their salaries rise to about £26,000.

All figures can be expected to rise by about 3% each year in line with inflation, but should be checked if you want to be accurate.

activity

INDIVIDUAL WORK

1. How would you account for the differences in starting salary in the different services shown?

2. Find out the equivalent present figures. Are there any changes in the *relative* amounts?

case study 16.10 — Police constable salaries

Table 16.10 Annual salary for police constables, with effect from 1 September 2006

On starting service	£21,009
On completion of initial training	£23,454
2	£24,813 (*)
3	£26,331
4	£27,159
5	£28,029
6	£28,830
7	£29,544
8	£30,489
9	£32,334
10	£32,985 (**)

(*) All officers attain this salary point on completion of two years' service as a police constable.
(**) Officers who have been on this point for a year will have access to the competence related threshold payment of £1,095 a year.
Source: police-information.co.uk

activity
GROUP WORK

1. Why do salaries for constables go up each year for 10 years? Give as many reasons as you can.

2. How important do you think salary is when considering a job?

psychiatrists to help ensure good heath. In addition services such as the fire and rescue service have annual fitness checks.

Retirement age

Retirement age in most professions is covered by the Employment Equality (Age) Regulations 2006. Retirement from the uniformed public services takes place earlier than in many private sector jobs – but nevertheless retirement ages tend to be later than they used to be.

In the fire and rescue service, for example, the minimum age at which a firefighter can receive a full pension rose in 2006 from 50 with 30 years' service to 60 with 40 years' service. There is now no compulsory retirement age for firefighters.

Army officers have to work for 34 years in the army to get a full pension, and must retire at 60. Other ranks have to retire at 55.

Pension arrangements

Pension arrangements have recently altered in a number of public services, and more alterations may be in the pipeline. Pensions are incredibly expensive – 25% of total expenditure on the fire and rescue service goes on pensions. Members of the firefighters' pension scheme who joined before 2006 contribute 11% of their pay. For this they can expect to be able to retire at the age of 50, if they have done 30 years' service, with a pension equal to two-thirds of their take-home pay before retirement. But under the new scheme introduced in 2006, firefighters contribute 8.5% of their pay to the pension scheme. They will have to work to age 60 and have 40 years' service to get a pension worth two-thirds of their take-home pay before retirement. If they retire earlier

remember

State pensions (old age pension) come from the government; occupational pensions come from the employer or a private pension scheme.

Figure 16.5 Firefighters in the gym: fitness benefits them and it benefits the fire and rescue service

or with fewer years' service they have an 'actuarially reduced' pension based on their individual case.

New entrants to the armed forces join the Armed Forces Pension Scheme 05. It is possible to opt out. Armed forces personnel get no occupational pension until they have done at least two years' **reckonable service**'. People who retire at 55 and over get a pension immediately plus a lump sum equal to three times their annual pension. After 25 years the armed forces pension is approximately one-third of the person's salary in the last three years of working.

Prison officers use one of two Civil Service pension schemes. One of these schemes is called 'nuvos'; the other is called a 'partnership pension account'. For nuvos the officer pays 3.5% of earnings and receives a pension at 65. Life assurance and the possibility of a lump sum are included in this scheme. The maximum possible nuvos pension is 75% of pensionable earnings. These pensions increase annually to take into account inflation (i.e. the rise in the cost of living). Under the partnership scheme the officer may pay optional contributions up to 3% (but need not pay anything). Pension money is invested and therefore the pension received on retirement depends on how well the investments have done over the years. In both cases the employer pays money towards the pension.

The latest police pension scheme (2006) requires officers to pay 9.5% of their salary during their working years. Their maximum pension comes after 35 years. It consists of 50% of their final salary, and a lump sum of four times the final salary.

Public service pension arrangements are considered to be generous (and secure!) compared with most of those in the private sector.

Sick pay

Sick pay in the civilian public services follows the government system of 'statutory sick pay'.

Figure 16.6 Conditions for statutory sick pay

Off sick for 4 days or more in a row (including weekends, bank holidays and other non-working days)

Notify employer of sickness within 7 days of start of sickness

Average weekly earnings of at least £84 (2006/07)

May have to fill in a self-certificate form for 7 days' illness or less

You work at least one day a week

Standard weekly rate of SSP (statutory sick pay) = £70.05 (2006/07)

The armed forces do not have statutory sick pay. They receive pay as usual when sick. For injuries, illness or death caused after April 2005 there is the Armed Forces Compensation Scheme, run by the Veterans' Agency, part of the Ministry of Defence.

Maternity/paternity provisions

For civilian public services these are set by the Work and Families Act 2006. Statutory maternity pay lasts 39 weeks. For the first six weeks the mother gets 90% of her salary. For the next 33 weeks she gets £112.75 a week. Fathers can get two weeks' statutory paternity pay of £108.85 a week, or 90% of their average weekly earnings, whichever is less.

The same rights to maternity pay exist for women in the armed forces, though some other civilian legal rights (e.g. to time off for pre-natal care) do not exist.

Minimum length of service

There are no minimum lengths of service in the civilian uniformed services, but for the armed forces people have to stay for what is called a 'term of engagement' or 'term of service' after 'attestation', i.e. the end of the recruitment period. (During the recruitment period, including initial training, it is fairly easy to leave.) These rules are likely to become less strict following the Armed Forces Act 2006.

www.parliament.the-stationery-office.com **(Defence Select Committee report 2005 Part 3: Recruitment). This is an interesting report on social and moral issues connected with recruitment**

Postings

Posting is being sent to work in a particular place, for a particular length of time. In the armed forces, posting to other parts of the country, or other parts of the world, is to be expected – typically for periods of about six months. Officially, people have little choice but to go to where they are posted.

Posting is less of an issue in the civilian uniformed public services, but there is still a better chance of getting a job if you are prepared to go anywhere you are needed.

Shift patterns

Shift patterns in most uniformed public services are complex and may include night shifts, working unsocial hours or working during public holidays. Rules for fire and rescue service shifts are shown in case study 16.12.

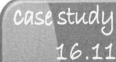 **Enlisting**

case study 16.11

From the point of view of an under-18 recruit, the army, the largest recruiter, has the harshest terms of enlistment of the three armed forces. All recruits to the army are required to enter on a 22-year open engagement, but with a right to give 12 months notice to resign at any time after completing the first three years, making a four-year minimum engagement. In the case of recruits enlisting under the age of 18, however, the period between the date of enlistment and the 18th birthday does not count towards either the 22-year full engagement or the four-year minimum. This means that a recruit enlisting on or soon after his/her 16th birthday is liable to a minimum six-year term, as against the minimum four years required of an adult entrant. This is described by critics as the 'six-year trap'. The navy used to have a six-year trap, and the air force a five-year one, but they were both abolished in 2001, the minimum engagement for under-18s being aligned in each case with that for adults.

Source: UK Coalition to Stop the Use of Child Soldiers

activity
GROUP WORK

What are the arguments for and against having these terms of engagement in the armed forces?

Contracted hours

These are the number of hours a person has to work during a week, a fortnight, or any other specified period of time. In civilian services the hours are fixed by agreement between the employers and the personnel. For example, firefighters work a basic 42-hour week.

Things are different in the armed forces.

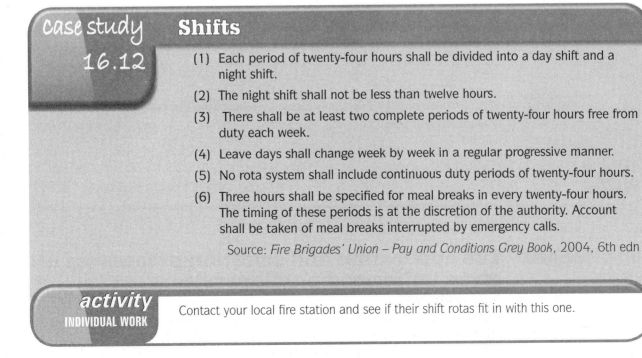

case study 16.12 **Shifts**

(1) Each period of twenty-four hours shall be divided into a day shift and a night shift.

(2) The night shift shall not be less than twelve hours.

(3) There shall be at least two complete periods of twenty-four hours free from duty each week.

(4) Leave days shall change week by week in a regular progressive manner.

(5) No rota system shall include continuous duty periods of twenty-four hours.

(6) Three hours shall be specified for meal breaks in every twenty-four hours. The timing of these periods is at the discretion of the authority. Account shall be taken of meal breaks interrupted by emergency calls.

Source: *Fire Brigades' Union – Pay and Conditions Grey Book*, 2004, 6th edn

activity
INDIVIDUAL WORK

Contact your local fire station and see if their shift rotas fit in with this one.

case study
16.13

Working hours

The Armed Forces are exempt from the flexible working provisions of UK employment legislation because of the overriding requirement to maintain operational effectiveness and the unique nature of military life. When joining the Regular Armed Forces, personnel accept an open-ended commitment to serve wherever and whenever they are needed. This means that they may be redeployed at short notice and a firm expectation to work regular hours cannot be relied upon.

activity
GROUP WORK

Give as many reasons as you can think of why people in the regular armed forces are prepared to accept this 'open-ended commitment' with regard to working hours and postings.

Access to training

In most public service careers, military or civilian, training has become part of the job. This is due to:

■ Technological change, which requires frequent updating of IT and other skills.

■ Legal changes, which need to be understood by public service workers (implementing new laws).

■ Social and political changes, which cause changes in work priorities (e.g. public attitudes to immigration).

■ Changes in management systems and ways of working (e.g. partnerships).

■ Responses to new conditions and threats (e.g. terrorism).

Education

Firefighters and army personnel are expected to take NVQs and other qualifications which link up with their on-the-job training.

Increasing numbers of graduates are going into the uniformed public services. It has been estimated that 25% of all police officers have degrees. (The figure is about 5% for the fire and rescue service.) Some people in the public services continue their education, e.g. by working towards an Open University degree.

activity
GROUP WORK
16.5

P3

Produce a poster advertising work in a uniformed public service, focusing on the benefits and conditions of service which go with the job.

The application and selection process for a given uniformed public service

Uniformed public services are choosy about who they have working for them. They want the right people, and they want them to stay. For these reasons the application and selection processes are demanding and thorough.

Application process

This starts when the applicant writes off for an information pack and a form, and ends when the applicant is either invited or not invited to tests and an interview. For details see below.

Entry requirements – educational, physical, medical and other requirements

Table 16.11 shows a summary of the entry requirements for some uniformed public services. These may change, so always check the latest information.

Table 16.11 Entry requirements for some uniformed public services

	Prison	Police	Fire	Paramedic	Army officer
Age	18–62	18½–51	18–NUL	Not stated	Not stated
Nationality	British/EU/ Commonwealth With indefinite leave to stay in UK	British/EC/EEA Commonwealth or foreign with no restrictions on stay	Right to reside or work in UK	Right to reside or work in UK	UK, Common-wealth or Irish citizen
Education	No fixed requirement, but taken into account	No fixed requirement	No fixed requirement 'Literacy/numeracy skills'	IHCD Paramedic award IHCD Technician 'Stable education record'	Usually graduates, though 180+ UCAS points can be considered
Character	Must not be bankrupt	Financial vetting. Must have been non-bankrupt for 3 years	Able to work at heights	Hygienic; professional appearance	Good: much officer training is character training
Fitness	Must pass fitness test	'Physically fit'	Good level of all-round fitness; good hearing	Not stated	Must be very good
Health	Must pass medical	No height restrictions	Medical test Medical records will be inspected No height restrictions	Must pass medical assessment	Excellent all-round health needed
Eyesight	6/12 or better in each eye if corrected (i.e. with glasses or lenses if used)	Good unaided vision	6/9 6/9 + good colour vision without glasses or lenses	Standard for Group 2 licence holders	Not stated
Racism	'Must not be a member of a group or organisation that the Prison Service considered to be racist'	No racially motivated or **homophobic** offences	'Commitment to diversity'	'An understanding of and commitment to equal opportunities'	Armed forces are equal opportunities employers
Criminal record	Will be checked if working with under-18s	All cautions and convictions including military must be disclosed	Declare 'unspent' convictions	Must be declared	Must be declared
Other		Full UK driving licence	No tattoos above collar	Communication, interpersonal skills Full manual driving licence for 2 years	Good knowledge of current affairs and service matters useful

Application forms

To understand fully the application forms for uniformed public services you need to get examples. Some can be downloaded from the internet, e.g. from police forces which are recruiting at the time. Others can only be obtained by writing off for an applicant's pack and application form.

Types of forms

The application forms for each public service differ. They vary in length and the questions they ask, and although they are often similar from one service to another, they are not exactly the same. In addition the form for each service is divided into parts so, in effect, there may be several different forms in one application pack. Police forms, for example, have sections similar to those shown in case study 16.14.

Requirements on completing forms

The main feature of public service application forms, especially for the police, is that they are long and difficult to fill in. Advice for filling in the forms includes:

---

case study 16.14

Sample sections of a police application form

Table 16.12 Police application form

Section 1 About you	Section 2 About your employment	Section 3 About your education and skills
Force you wish to apply to	Present or most recent employment	Your qualifications and training
Disability	Previous employment	Your other activities (e.g. driving; language skills)
Nationality	Referees	
Convictions and cautions	HM Forces	
Tattoos	Previous applications to, or service with, a police force	
Membership of **BNP** or similar		
Health, eyesight and disability		
Business interests		
Financial position		
Previous addresses		
About your family		
Section 4 Competency Assessment (9 questions) • Please answer truthfully as you may be asked to expand on these examples at assessment. • Do not use continuation pages. Continuation pages will not be scored.	Equal Opportunities Marketing form	Section 5 Declaration (... all the statements I have made in this application are true ...)

---

activity
GROUP WORK

List and discuss all of the factors mentioned in Section 1 which might lead to an applicant not being accepted into the police. Give reasons where possible.

- Photocopy the entire form so you can give yourself a practice run before completing the real thing.

- Read, understand and *follow to the letter all instructions* (however trivial and pointless they may seem).

- Never rush the form. It may take many hours' work to get it right.

- Get your form checked carefully for spelling and punctuation by someone who knows what they are doing.

- Where you are asked to give your own experience or views, think carefully and discuss what you should write if you are not sure.

- What you write must always be honest, truthful and expressed to the best of your ability.

- Check your facts before you fill in the final form (you can be sure the police will check them!).

- If you are asked about any cautions or criminal convictions, and you have them, they must be stated because they will be checked anyway, and because failure to disclose a conviction would make your application null and void. Minor convictions will no longer bar you from most public services.

Personal statements and supporting information

Forms such as the police and prison service forms expect you to make personal statements about experiences relevant to the work.

On the police application form there is advice on answering the sort of question shown in case study 16.15:

- Be clear and concise, and pay attention to handwriting, spelling and grammar.

- Write in sentences.

- Cover all prompts (parts of the question).

- Use examples 'from situations you found challenging or difficult'.

- Use examples from a work setting where possible.

- Try to use a different example for each question.

---

case study 16.15

Respect

Give an example of when you have shown respect for someone with a deep-rooted belief. This may be a religious, cultural, ethical or moral belief or some important aspect of their lifestyle. You will be assessed in this question on your understanding of, and sensitivity to, the differences you and this particular person had, and on how you adapted what you said or did.

(i) Tell us how the situation arose.

(ii) Tell us in detail what you did.

(iii) Which aspects of the difference did you find most difficult to deal with?

Source: Could You? Police

---

activity
INDIVIDUAL WORK

Tackle this question – then show it to someone whose opinion you trust and get their feedback.

Curriculum vitae

A curriculum vitae (CV) is a document listing the facts about yourself, your education, your qualifications, your work experience and any qualities or abilities which might interest a prospective employer.

Different formats

Most colleges have computer programs which help people to write well laid-out, attractive CVs. Take advice from your tutors or employer.

Essential information

The information normally expected on a CV is listed below. It should be in the order shown:

- Names: first name; other (family) name.
- Date of birth.
- Address.
- Telephone number(s).
- Email.
- Nationality.
- Educational history (schools, colleges attended, qualifications obtained, dates).
- Present employment if applicable (name and address of employer, date started, job title, nature of work, main duties and responsibilities).
- Past employment starting with the most recent, giving name and address of employer, starting and finishing dates, nature of work, main duties and responsibilities.
- Work placements, etc.
- Any special skills or abilities, e.g. driving, languages, computer skills, etc.
- Sports and recreation.
- Any other relevant achievements.
- Names and addresses of two referees.

CVs are rarely used for job applications for the uniformed public services. But they are needed:

- When applying for some private sector jobs.
- When applying for work placement in a uniformed public service (sometimes).
- As a record which you can consult when filling in application forms.

Good practice

Keep an up-to-date CV, preferably on disk. It will help you to remember things such as the starting and finishing dates for jobs and courses.

Use a format which is concise and tidy, make sure you include all relevant information.

If you are applying for a job using a CV, make sure the information on the CV is relevant to the job and will maximise your chances of getting an interview.

Bad practice

Scruffy, inaccurate, badly-spelled, badly laid-out CVs give a poor impression. Never leave gaps in your life history. Avoid self-praise.

Selection process

The selection process is all the tests and interviews you undergo before being finally accepted or rejected by the employer.

remember

Performance on psychometric tests can be improved through practice. Try to get samples or tests similar to the ones you will have to take when applying to the service of your choice, and test yourself against the clock.

Types and purpose of psychometric tests

Psychometric tests are tests of job-related mental abilities. They may test language and number skills, thinking skills, and 'practical' skills such as checking lists, awareness of shapes and simple rules of mechanics. Psychometric tests have to be done by applicants for those public services which do not have specific educational entrance requirements, e.g. the armed forces (other ranks), the police, the prison service and the fire and rescue service. Most are multiple-choice tests, where the best answer is indicated as instructed in the appropriate space on a computerised form. Psychometric tests have a time limit. (See case study 16.17 page 301 – items 2 and 3 are psychometric tests, sometimes called Police Initial Recruitment (PIR) tests.)

www.npia.police.uk/en/5224.htm

www.fireservice.co.uk

www.hmprisonservice.gov.uk/careersandjobs/becomingaprisonofficer/selection/post/

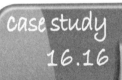

remember

To get the best results in fitness tests, build up your fitness well in advance, and lead a healthy lifestyle!

Physical fitness tests

Most uniformed public services require applicants to take a fitness test. These vary in difficulty according to the service. They test health-related fitness through a bleep test, and job-related fitness through tests linked to the physical work done in the service.

Link

See Book 1, Unit 7, pages 295–296 for more information

Public service fitness tests keep changing, and you should contact the services direct to be sure of getting up-to-the-minute information.

Other types of selection tests

For services such as the police and the armed forces it is necessary to attend an assessment centre for a variety of tests and assessments.

---

case study 16.16

West Midlands Police fitness test

1. CIRCUIT

The circuit covers a total distance of 300 metres.

From the starting line, candidates must complete 3 laps of the course in under 3 minutes and 45 seconds. Each lap contains 8 activity stations, which must be completed sequentially. The activities are as follows:

1. Crawl for 3 metres across a gym floor.

2. Jump 1 metre 20 cm over a mat.

3. Stair climb up a small flight of steps across a vaulting box and down steps on the other side for a total of 5 metres.

4. Balance across a 2 metre 80 cm beam.

5. Gate climb over a 1 metre 20 cm gate.

6. Weave in between cones for a total of 6 metres.

7. Carry 2 cones 8.2kg each for a total of 2 metres.

8. Drag a life size 35kg dummy for 2 metres and 40 cm.

2. PUSH PULL MACHINE

After the circuit, candidates will be asked to complete a test of pushing and pulling. This device has been purpose built and scientifically validated to simulate struggling with an assailant. The test is of 20 seconds duration during which time you must perform successive maximum pushing and pulling strokes. The force exerted is measured by computer during this period.

Source: West Midlands Police

Police entrance fitness test – Could You?

Expect to be tested on two key fitness requirements:

■ dynamic strength – involves performing five seated chest pushes and five seated back pulls on the Dyno machine to measure your strength.

■ endurance – you will be asked to run to and fro along a 15 metre track in time with a series of bleeps, which become increasingly faster.

Source: Could You? Police

activity
GROUP WORK

Compare the West Midlands and Could You? police tests. Which do you think is better:

1. For testing abilities needed in police work?

2. For giving an objective measure of a person's fitness?

3. For encouraging a more diverse intake into the police?

Suggest reasons in each case.

Types of interview

Interviews for the uniformed public services are carefully structured to identify the abilities the services are looking for in their applicants. For the police, interviews last 20 minutes and are designed to assess candidates on the basis of the following competencies:

■ Personal responsibility.

■ Resilience.

■ Teamworking.

■ Respect for race and diversity.

■ Effective communication.

The interviews are linked to the part of the application form where you describe a difficult situation which you experienced – and how you responded to that situation. You are likely to be asked to discuss such experiences in more depth, giving details and suggesting how such experiences relate to the work of the service you are applying for.

Approaches

The more interviews you have, the better you become at being interviewed. You should therefore arrange, and take part in, practice interviews whenever you can. In addition, if you apply for a job or course and get invited to the interview, always go and do the interview even if you are not sure that you are keen on the course or the job. In this way you will overcome any feelings of fear and dislike which you may feel at the prospect of interviews, and you will develop a positive approach.

remember

There are courses on interview skills. It is also possible to arrange practice interviews with police officers, etc. especially if a group of people are interested.

case study 16.17

Police selection tests 2007

Table 16.13 Police selection tests

Item number	Number of tests	Type of test	Time	Number of questions
1	1	Competency-based interview	20 minutes	4 questions
2	1	Numerical test	12 minutes	25 questions
3	1	Verbal logical reasoning test	25 minutes	31 questions
4	4	Interactive role-plays	10 minutes each	Not applicable
5	2	Written exercises	20 minutes each	Not applicable

The purpose of the interview and interactive tests is to assess 'core **competencies** relevant to the role of a police constable'. Core competencies are abilities which are needed in order to be able to train and work successfully in a given job.

activity
GROUP WORK

1. Collect examples of numerical and verbal logical reasoning tests from police recruitment websites.

2. Arrange with your tutor to practise any or all of these tests in the times allowed, using material from internet sources or any practice tests prepared by your tutor.

3. Arrange to visit a public service recruitment office and carry out their tests or assessments in order to practice.

case study 16.18

Core competencies

- Community and customer focus
- Effective communication
- Personal responsibility
- Problem solving
- Resilience
- Respect for race and diversity
- Teamworking.

Source: Could You? Police

activity
INDIVIDUAL WORK

1. Describe (in two sentences for each competence) a time in the past year when you have shown each of these competencies.

2. For each of these competencies, list two things you could do in the next six months to improve your own abilities.

case study 16.19   Dealing with conflict

You will come across prisoners who are in conflict, perhaps arguing or even fighting. You will have to be able to find out what is wrong, calm them down and help sort out their differences. Please describe one situation when you had to help resolve a conflict between two people.

What was the situation?

How did you help to resolve the conflict?

And why did you do it this way?

Source: Prison Officer Skills Assessment Form

activity
INDIVIDUAL WORK

Describe a situation of this type, and answer the three questions that follow it.

Dress code

Ask your teachers and people who work in public services what you should wear (and not wear) at public service interviews. Arrive at the interview clean, smart, well-groomed and with clean fingernails.

Preparation for interview (e.g. arrangements, potential questions, research)

It is worth preparing seriously for an interview. If you prepare well you will feel more confident and do yourself justice. If you prepare well and they do not accept you, you can say to yourself, 'It is their loss!' And it probably is.

Checklist

Long term:

- Get a clear idea in your mind of the sort of person your favourite public service are looking for – and be that sort of person.

Medium term:

- Learn about the organisation and the job you are applying for. Read leaflets, brochures, the application pack, etc. Trawl the internet. Keep an eye on the news.
- Write down all of the questions you think you may be asked.
- Write down what you will say if you are asked those questions.
- If you do not know what you will say, do some research and ask other people what they think.
- Make sure that you know what competencies the interviewers are looking for, and why.
- Give some thought to how you could demonstrate or discuss those competencies.
- Think through questions and answers until you feel comfortable with them.
- Find out how to get to the assessment centre/interview place (including transport, etc.).
- Have a haircut and make sure you have some decent clothes.

Short term:

- Lead a healthy life in the days before the interview, getting enough sleep, food, etc.
- Get to the interview place with plenty of time to spare.
- Do not worry about interview questions and answers at the last minute.

Interview skills

These include being able to:

- Talk about yourself in an interesting and honest way.
- Show a genuine interest in the job or career and what it involves.
- Answer questions in a relevant and thoughtful manner.
- Give a pleasant, competent, sincere impression.

Figure 16.7 Nothing to be afraid of – as long as you are well prepared

There are many 'technical' interview skills such as speaking clearly, not using slang, sitting up straight, making eye contact, etc. These can be practised at mock interviews and in other situations. In the interview itself, focus your mind on the key aims. You want to show that you are a person that others can work with, and that you are willing and able to learn. Your interviewers will make allowances for nerves if they can see that, underneath the nervousness, you are the kind of person they are looking for. They do not want someone who knows everything before they have even started the job. What they want is a person with **potential**, who is open-minded, enthusiastic, motivated, and willing and able to learn.

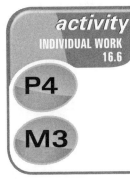

activity
INDIVIDUAL WORK
16.6

P4

M3

You work in a recruitment office or at the front desk of a civilian uniformed public service. Explain to a would-be applicant:

1. The kind of person the service is looking for.
2. The stages that applicants have to go through.
3. The reasons behind each part of the application and selection process.

activity

INDIVIDUAL WORK
16.7

P5

You are applying for a uniformed public service. Produce a CV and, using the information on the CV and other information when needed, complete the application form. The form should be of a standard high enough to be considered seriously by the service concerned.

The initial training and opportunities for career development within a given uniformed public service

For this part of the unit you will be expected to research one particular public service and study the training and career opportunities in that service. You should therefore contact services you are interested in and try to get as much information from them as you can, either in written form (leaflets, annual reports, websites, job descriptions, etc.), or by meeting them and getting them to talk to you.

Initial training

Initial training is the first period of general training for new recruits in a uniformed public service. The skills developed in initial training are called '**generic** skills'. These are skills which are used in a whole range of jobs throughout the service. In later training you will specialise in particular knowledge and skills which you will develop to a higher, more technical level.

Preparation suggested for new recruits prior to their basic training (e.g. physical fitness, background knowledge)

Basic training (which is the same as initial training) means basic training. It starts with the essentials and does not need a huge amount of **prior** knowledge. If new recruits try to learn too much before their basic training they may have to 'unlearn' it once the basic training starts. Furthermore, basic training is hard work. New recruits should therefore have a holiday and build up their fitness before basic training starts.

If anybody has been accepted into a public service and cannot drive, they should immediately start to learn.

remember

In some areas there is collaboration between police basic training and BTEC public service courses, enabling BTEC students to take part in role-plays and other activities linked to the IPLDP. If you are interested, talk to your tutors or contact your local police and make enquiries.

Duration and content of basic training programmes (e.g. theory/practical mix)

The length and content of basic training programmes depends on the service and, in some cases, the role in the service. For new police constables the programme and system is similar throughout the country, but the content of basic training still differs from force to force because it contains an element of community awareness, and all communities are different.

Initial training in the uniformed public services includes both theory and practice. There is most theory in those services which are traditionally more 'academic', e.g. officers in the armed forces, paramedics and the police.

Skills and abilities developed during basic training (e.g. technical skills, teamwork skills, communication skills)

Technical skills are skills which are specialised and linked to a particular job. They may look easy, but in fact they have to be done in a special, professional way.

case study 16.20

Part of the syllabus for police basic training (2006)

Common induction modules Phase 1

1. Underpinning ethics/values of the police service.
2. Foster people's equality, diversity and rights.
3. Develop one's own knowledge and practice.
4. Develop effective relationships with colleagues.
5. Ensure your own actions reduce the risk to health and safety.
6. Assess the needs of individuals and provide advice and support.
7. Develop effective partnerships with members of the community and other agencies.
8. Operation of information technology systems.
9. Administer first aid.
10. Use police actions in a fair and justified way.
11. Social, community issues and neighbourhood policing.

Source: National Centre for Applied Learning Technologies

activity
INDIVIDUAL WORK

Imagine you have just been accepted into the police. What preparation could you do for each of these modules?

case study 16.21

Technical skills learned by police recruits

1. Deal with aggressive and abusive behaviour
2. Obtain, evaluate and submit information and intelligence to support local priorities
3. Respond to incidents, conduct and evaluate investigations
4. Participate in planned operations
5. Search individuals and premises
6. Prepare, conduct and evaluate interviews
7. Arrest and report suspects
8. Escort suspects and present to custody
9. Prepare and present case information, present evidence and finalise investigations

Source: Accessing IPLDP Materials on the Managed Learning Environment (MLE), Centrex (now NPIA)

activity
GROUP WORK

Analyse any five of the above points, showing how technical skills can enable an officer to do the job in an effective and professional manner.

Table 16.14 Basic training

Service/job	Duration of basic training	Content of basic training
London Ambulance Service/Emergency medical technician	Total duration: 16 months Including: 3 weeks' induction 3 weeks' advanced driving 9 weeks' intensive immediate aid course 5 weeks' operational training (working) 1 year probationary period with continual supervision, monitoring and assessment At end: Practical assessments and exams	Includes: Cardiopulmonary resuscitation Ambulance-related law Driving Patient care, ambulance equipment, anatomy and physiology, major emergencies and childbirth
West Yorkshire Fire and Rescue Service/Trainee firefighter	13 weeks' intensive training Training uses national occupational standards This is the start of an NVQ Level 3 qualification completed after 1½ years	Breathing apparatus Ladder safety Dealing with road traffic collisions Chemical incidents Hose running Fire safety
Police constables	Training follows the Initial Police Learning and Development Programme (IPLDP) Methods of training include: Role plays and simulations Placements and attachments Independent patrol Problem-solving projects Partnership and leadership experience Community engagement activities Use of tutor constables and mentoring Reflective exercises (self-appraisal)	22 National Occupational Standards Core learning goals: 1. Understanding and engaging with the community 2. Enforcing the law and following police procedures 3. Responding to human and social diversity 4. Positioning oneself in the role of a police officer inside the police organisation 5. Professional standards and ethical conduct 6. Learning to learn and creating a base for career-long learning 7. Qualities of professional judgement and decision making

Source: Initial Police Learning and Development Programme, Central Authority Practitioner Guidance, 'Community Engagement and Professional Development Units'

See Book 1, Units 2 and 4, and in this book, Unit 13, for more on teamwork and communication skills

Main reasons for recruits not completing basic training

The uniformed public services do not accept people unless they feel they have the capabilities to pass the initial training and go on to become successful employees. This is why the selection procedure is so demanding – to reduce the risk of '**wastage**' later on.

Injuries

If injuries are serious, they could prevent recruits from completing their initial training. However, the armed forces and others carry out careful risk assessments of all activities to try to prevent this from happening.

Personal problems

Again, the police in particular conduct inquiries into applicants' family backgrounds – and one reason for this is to reduce the risk of personal or family problems interfering with a recruit's training and later success. However, if personal problems between recruits are not addressed and sorted out in a fair and lasting manner, this can be a reason for people dropping out.

Culture

Every effort is made in all uniformed public services to prevent recruits leaving for culture-related reasons. As equal opportunities employers they take steps to prevent **discrimination**, harassment and activities that might cause a person from an ethnic or other minority to leave.

Wrong perception of the service

During initial training new recruits in any service are finding their way around. In this period they might discover that the career they had set their hopes on is not what they thought.

Fitness

This too is tested before entry to a service and should not normally be a problem. However, in some services such as the Royal Marines standards of fitness have to be so high that inevitably this is a problem for some recruits. Another problem noted by the armed forces is the 'fading' of fitness in recruits as soon as initial training is over.

Assessment

In police initial training this is done using policing action checklists and a portfolio called the Student Officer Learning and Assessment Portfolio. The assessment is done both in the workplace and during training. There is also an NVQ system. Assessment sets out to be 'rigorous and standardised' and is based on the 22 competencies which form the initial training curriculum. It aims to balance knowledge and problem-solving skills.

Lincolnshire **Police Authority** Personnel Committee (IPLDP)

However, the IPLDP has been criticised for the quality of assessment in some forces.

Errors in assessment, inconsistent or unfair assessment, and assessment which fails to motivate the trainee could all lead to people leaving in their probationary period.

activity
INDIVIDUAL WORK
16.8

P6

Write a handout for new recruits to your uniformed service, giving an outline timetable for their initial training programme.

Career development

Career development is the changes of job and rank which happen if a person works for a long time with the same uniformed public service. It takes two forms: promotion and specialisation.

case study 16.22

Adult Learning Inspectorate report on the evaluation of IPLDP

The forces plan their own assessments, but these are inconsistent. Months into their programme, many student officers are still awaiting their first assessment. The forces recognise this issue and have requested further support and guidance. Currently, assessment practices are insufficiently thorough, with few checks on the appropriateness of the assessment method, the quality of feedback during the daily debrief, and the consistency of judgements between assessors. Actual performance is not always observed. **Competence** is based on student officers' reflective accounts and these are used to develop subsequent action plans. There are few plans to use witness testimony from other experienced officers.

Source: Home Office, Police

activity

GROUP WORK

1. Which of these criticisms do you think are most serious and why?
2. How do you think trainee police officers should be assessed?
3. Contact the training sections of other public services and find out how they do assessment.

Promotion

This means moving up the rank structure. It is achieved by different methods in different services. The police have to take exams, among other things, in order to be promoted from constable to sergeant and from sergeant to inspector. The army method is described in case study 16.23.

case study 16.23

Promotion in the army

Soldiers are selected for promotion at special boards convened annually for that purpose and held according to individual MCM [Manning and Career Management Division] requirements. Each promotion board, normally comprising 5 members, will review the files containing the Confidential Reports (CR) of every person eligible for promotion. The number of vacancies available from that board will be determined by the predicted number of established posts in the higher rank the MCM will have to fill in the coming year.

Source: Soldier Management

activity

GROUP WORK

1. The confidential report system is being replaced by a 'Servicepersons' Joint Appraisal Report (SJAR)'. What do you think are the advantages and disadvantages of using a confidential report system for selecting promotions?
2. Discuss what qualities would lead soldiers to be promoted. Make notes, then contact the army and find out if you were right.

Soldiers are carefully appraised by their commanding officers, who keep a written record of their performance. If the records show good work and leadership qualities, the soldier is likely to be promoted.

Police promotion follows the pattern below:

1. The officer applies through his/her line manager.

2. The officer must have completed their probationary period.

3. The officer must be competent (as assessed by current Performance Development Review).

4. Application to OSPRE Force Examination Officer to take an exam called OSPRE (Objective Structured Performance-Related Examination). This rather difficult exam is in two parts:

    (a) Part I: tests knowledge of criminal law and policing procedures.

    (b) Part II: a series of work-**simulation** exercises, which test whether the applicant has the necessary skills to perform at a higher rank.

5. Further assessments take place after the applicant has passed the exam. These take the form of 'competency based application forms, structured interviews, presentations, group discussions, in-tray exercises, psychometric tests and assessment centres'.

6. When there is a vacancy the successful applicant takes up work at the new grade, but on **probation** for the first year.

Operating Manual for Police Promotion to the Rank of Sergeant and Inspector Incorporating Work-Based Assessment, June 2006

Specialisation

Specialisation means choosing an area of work where there is less variety but more depth and expertise.

Specialist police roles include:

- Police dogs handlers.
- Traffic police.
- Criminal Investigation Department (CID).
- Special Branch.
- Firearms units.
- Drugs Squad.
- Serious Organised Crime Agency.
- Air Support Units.

Although these types of work may be no more highly paid than working on the beat, and they require special training and expertise, they are popular and there is plenty of competition for them. There are no examinations; selection is done through interviews.

Rank structure

See Unit 13, pages 134–135.

Competition for promotion or specialisation

All promotion or specialisation is competitive if there are more candidates than posts.

Minimum service required

This varies, especially in services which offer accelerated promotion schemes (High Potential Development Schemes), as some police forces do. In the police it is not possible for 'ordinary' constables to apply to become sergeants until they have completed their probationary two years.

The time scale for promotions in 'other ranks' in the army is shown in Figure 16.8.

Personal skills and qualities required

It depends on the job and the rank, but for promotion some of the skills and qualities shown in Table 16.15 are needed.

Table 16.15 Personal skills and qualities needed in order to be promoted

Ability to think strategically	Good health*	Personable: presents a good image
Ability to talk well to groups of people	Good teamwork skills*	Problem-solving skills*
Ability to write reports*	Good track record at present job*	Reliable*
Commitment to the organisation	Initiative and originality	The desire to lead or manage
Courage	Interest in the work*	Tough – able to hold people to account
Easy to get on with*	Leadership skills	Understands other people (empathy)*
Good at paperwork	Loyalty	
	Management training	

*These qualities would not only help in promotion, they might well be looked for in people wishing to specialise

Link

See Book 1, Unit 2, pages 61–66. Also (this book) Unit 13, page 143–156

Promotion or specialisation process including details of training and examinations

This topic is complex and the best way to find out about it is to ask people in a public service that interests you. Training is a feature of all uniformed public service work, at every level. It stops at, or shortly before, retirement! Training in the fire and rescue service, and in the armed forces, is often linked to NVQs (National Vocational Qualifications). Specialised police training ranges from learning to use new equipment to topics to do with sociology, psychology and criminology.

Figure 16.8 Time scale for promotions in the army

Source: British Army

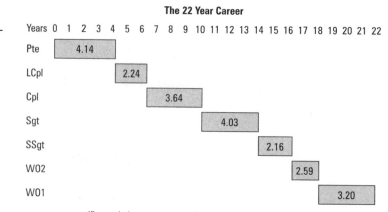

(figures in boxes represent the average number of years spent in each rank)

To be promoted in the police up to inspector it is necessary to pass exams. These are called OSPRE (Objective Structured Performance-Related Examination). OSPRE is divided into two parts.

Table 16.16 OSPRE

Part	Questions	Time
OSPRE I	150 multiple-choice questions mainly on law and police procedures	3 hours
OSPRE II	7 work-based role-plays each lasting 5 minutes, done in front of an assessor	45 minutes' preparation allowed 35 minutes in the test

Main roles and responsibilities of supervision (e.g. leading paramedics, leading fire fighters, police sergeants, non-commissioned officers or specialist staff)

Visiting speakers, or visits to a uniformed public service, are needed if you are to research the jobs and duties of people in supervisory posts. Even within similar jobs different supervisors or managers will have different ideas of their roles.

Supervisors have roles which are at least partly managerial. This means they have to organise, motivate, monitor and evaluate the people under their supervision, control or command. They may also have to be team leaders, taking tactical decisions at the scene of a major incident or even on the field of battle. In addition they may have administrative work to do: to record progress and ensure that work is done in an efficient, cost-effective and accountable manner which can be audited or inspected if necessary.

Modern supervisors are also expected to be human beings, able to understand the people under their supervision and to identify with their needs, aspirations and difficulties.

remember

Promotion to higher levels requires the development of communication, managerial and leadership skills, and an increasing role in planning and decision making.

Design and produce a flow chart or other diagram showing how a person's career can develop once they have joined a particular uniformed public service. The diagram should be annotated indicating the kinds of qualities that might be looked for in people whose careers progress along the paths indicated.

activity
GROUP WORK
16.9

P7

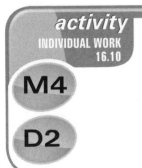

You are a new recruit in a uniformed public service. Write a self-**appraisal** of your future career potential, explaining your present strengths and weaknesses in relation to **initial** training and future career development in your service. Also examine any ways in which you think a career in that service would particularly suit you, and any problems it might cause at some time in the future.

activity
INDIVIDUAL WORK
16.10

M4

D2

Progress Check

1. Explain the difference between roles, purposes and responsibilities.
2. List four roles each for the armed forces, the police, the fire and rescue service and the ambulance service.
3. Explain the differences between legal, professional and political accountability.
4. What is a performance indicator?
5. Outline the roles of each of the emergency services at a major incident.
6. What is meant by the words 'management' and 'administration'?
7. Give as many examples of conditions of service as you can.
8. List the entry requirements of one uniformed public service.
9. Why are uniformed public service application forms so long and difficult to fill in?
10. State two reasons why it is a good idea to have a CV.
11. Explain three types of selection test.
12. What are the main purposes of initial training?
13. Explain the differences between promotion and specialisation.
14. Give three duties of supervisors.

UNIT 17

Understanding the Criminal Justice System and Police Powers

This unit covers:

- The requirements of a lawful arrest and the regulations regarding detention of suspected offenders
- The regulations regarding the search of people and premises
- Pre-trial procedure in criminal courts
- How the criminal trial process works in both magistrates' courts and the Crown Court

This unit is of particular relevance to people who want to work with the police or the **criminal justice** system. The first half of the unit deals with police **powers**: the things the police are allowed to do when investigating crimes. These include arresting, questioning and detaining people and searching for evidence.

The unit then looks at criminal offences, the granting of bail and the ways in which prosecutions are carried out.

The last part of the unit covers criminal trials in both the magistrates' courts and the Crown Court, including sentencing and appeals.

grading criteria

To achieve a **pass** grade the evidence must show that the learner is able to:	To achieve a **merit** grade the evidence must show that, in addition to the pass criteria, the learner is able to:	To achieve a **distinction** grade the evidence must show that, in addition to the pass and merit criteria, the learner is able to:
P1 outline the difference between arrest with and without a warrant Pg 318	**M1** analyse the requirements of lawful arrest and detention Pg 318	**D1** evaluate the powers of arrest, detention and search Pg 336
P2 describe the rights of a detained person Pg 327		
P3 outline the powers the police have to search people and premises Pg 336	**M2** explain the powers the police have to search people and premises Pg 336	

To achieve a **pass** grade the evidence must show that the learner is able to:	To achieve a **merit** grade the evidence must show that, in addition to the pass criteria, the learner is able to:	To achieve a **distinction** grade the evidence must show that, in addition to the pass and merit criteria, the learner is able to:
P4 describe the pre-trial procedure in criminal courts in a given situation Pg 343	**M3** compare the pre-trial and trial process in given situations in the Magistrates' and Crown Court, using one example of a summary and an indictable offence Pg 351	**D2** evaluate the criminal court process Pg 354
P5 describe how the criminal trial process works in both the Magistrates' and Crown Court, using one example each of a summary and an indictable offence Pg 351		
P6 describe the powers of the courts in sentencing offenders and the routes and grounds for appeal in criminal cases in a given situation, using one example of a summary and an indictable offence Pg 354	**M4** explain a selected criminal court's sentencing powers and the grounds for appeal in a given situation, using one example of a summary and an indictable offence Pg 354	

The requirements of a lawful arrest and the regulations regarding detention of suspected offenders

'**Arrest**' is the act of depriving someone of their freedom by taking them into custody. The word normally relates to the act when carried out by the police or some other 'lawful authority'.

Detention is the act of depriving someone of their freedom (i.e. keeping them in custody) over a period of time.

A lawful arrest is an arrest which is allowed under the law. The circumstances in which arrest (or detention) are lawful are listed in the Human Rights Act 1998.

Arrest with or without warrant

A **warrant** is a document issued by a magistrate, district judge or judge, permitting the police to do something. An arrest warrant permits the police (or some other arresting agency such as Customs or immigration officers) to arrest somebody.

See pages 317–319 below for more on when arrests can be carried out with or without warrants

case study 17.1 — Lawful arrest/detention

Everyone has the right to 'liberty and security of person' except in the following cases:

(a) the lawful detention of a person after conviction by a competent court;

(b) the lawful arrest or detention of a person for non-compliance with the lawful order of a court or in order to secure the fulfilment of any obligation prescribed by law;

(c) the lawful arrest or detention of a person effected for the purpose of bringing him before the competent legal authority on reasonable suspicion of having committed an offence or when it is reasonably considered necessary to prevent his committing an offence or fleeing after having done so;

(d) the detention of a minor by lawful order for the purpose of educational supervision or his lawful detention for the purpose of bringing him before the competent legal authority;

(e) the lawful detention of persons for the prevention of the spreading of infectious diseases, of persons of unsound mind, alcoholics or drug addicts or vagrants;

(f) the lawful arrest or detention of a person to prevent his effecting an unauthorised entry into the country or of a person against whom action is being taken with a view to deportation or extradition.

Source: Human Rights Act 1998, Article 5

activity
INDIVIDUAL WORK

1. How do the police, immigration officers and Customs officers know whether an arrest is lawful or not? State as many ways as you can by which officers can find out when or how arrests are lawful.

2. Search the internet and other media for examples of unlawful arrest. Explain why unlawful arrest is a serious problem.

Differences between arrest made by police officers and an arrest by a private citizen

Arrests are normally made by police officers (or people such as Customs officers who have similar roles and powers of arrest). When the police carry out an arrest they do so under powers given them by the Police and Criminal Evidence Act 1984. The police are recommended to make arrests only if it is necessary.

The police have clear guidelines to follow when arresting people.

case study 17.2 — Power to arrest

1.3 The use of the power must be fully justified and officers exercising the power should consider if the necessary objectives can be met by other, less intrusive means. Arrest must never be used simply because it can be used. Absence of justification for exercising the powers of arrest may lead to challenges should the case proceed to court. When the power of arrest is exercised it is essential that it is exercised in a nondiscriminatory and proportionate manner.

Source: Police and Criminal Evidence Act 1984, Code G, Code of Practice for the Statutory Power of Arrest by Police Officers

activity
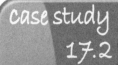
INDIVIDUAL WORK

1. What **justifications** are given when a police officer is carrying out an arrest?

2. Give as many reasons as you can why the police should try to use the power of arrest in a '**proportionate** manner'.

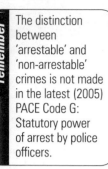

remember

The distinction between 'arrestable' and 'non-arrestable' crimes is not made in the latest (2005) PACE Code G: Statutory power of arrest by police officers.

remember

The present caution was introduced in the Criminal Justice and Public Order Act 1994.

Police officers must give a **caution** when making an arrest if they are going to ask questions about a crime. The caution here takes the form of a warning, using the following words: 'You do not have to say anything. But it may harm your defence if you do not mention when questioned something which you later rely on in court. Anything you do say may be given in evidence.' The caution has two purposes:

■ To encourage suspects to tell what they know.

■ To indicate what may happen if they do not speak, or do not tell the truth.

Police officers who make an arrest have to record the following details:

■ The nature and circumstances of the offence leading to the arrest.

■ The reason or reasons why arrest was necessary.

■ The giving of the caution.

■ Anything said by the person at the time of arrest.

Police arrests can be made with or without a warrant depending on the circumstances outlined as in case study 17.3 and on pages 317–319 below.

Arrests by a private citizen are allowed, but only in certain situations. These are explained in case study 17.4. The citizen's power of arrest was extended by the Serious Organised Crime and Police Act 2005 and came into effect on 1 January 2006.

www.askthe.police.uk/content/Q508.htm

case study 17.3

Guidelines for arrest

2.9 The criteria are that the arrest is necessary:

(a) to enable the name of the person in question to be ascertained (in the case where the constable does not know, and cannot readily ascertain, the person's name, or has reasonable grounds for doubting whether a name given by the person as his name is his real name)

(b) correspondingly as regards the person's address ...

(c) to prevent the person in question –
(i) causing physical injury to himself or any other person;
(ii) suffering physical injury;
(iii) causing loss or damage to property;
(iv) committing an offence against public decency (only applies where members of the public going about their normal business cannot reasonably be expected to avoid the person in question); or
(v) causing an unlawful obstruction of the highway;

(d) to protect a child or other **vulnerable person** from the person in question

(e) to allow the prompt and effective investigation of the offence or of the conduct of the person in question.

Source: Police and Criminal Evidence Act 1984, Code G, Code of Practice for the Statutory Power of Arrest by Police Officers

activity
GROUP WORK

1. Why is it necessary to itemise all of the circumstances in which a police officer may arrest someone in this way?

2. Explain the purpose of the parts in brackets in (a) and (c)(iv) above.

case study 17.4 — Citizen's arrest

24A Arrest without warrant: other persons

(1) A person other than a constable may arrest without a warrant–

    (a) anyone who is in the act of committing an indictable offence;

    (b) anyone whom he has reasonable grounds for suspecting to be committing an indictable offence.

(2) Where an indictable offence has been committed, a person other than a constable may arrest without a warrant–

    (a) anyone who is guilty of the offence;

    (b) anyone whom he has reasonable grounds for suspecting to be guilty of it.

(3) But the power of summary arrest conferred by subsection (1) or (2) is exercisable only if–

    (a) the person making the arrest has reasonable grounds for believing that for any of the reasons mentioned in subsection (4) it is necessary to arrest the person in question; and

    (b) it appears to the person making the arrest that it is not reasonably practicable for a constable to make it instead.

(4) The reasons are to prevent the person in question–

    (a) causing physical injury to himself or any other person;

    (b) suffering physical injury;

    (c) causing loss of or damage to property; or

    (d) making off before a constable can assume responsibility for him.

Source: Serious Organised Crime and Police Act (SOCPA) 2005, Section 110

In this case study an 'indictable' offence is a serious crime, of the kind that could be tried at the Crown Court. A summary arrest is an arrest without a warrant. 'Exercisable' means allowed by law.

activity — GROUP WORK

1. If you saw somebody committing a serious offence, in what circumstances would you consider arresting them yourself? Discuss this with a friend.

2. What are the advantages and disadvantages of having a citizens' power of arrest?

Table 17.1 Summary of differences between arrest by a police officer and a citizen's arrest

Aspect	Police arrest	Citizen's arrest
Warrant	Can be done with or without a warrant	An arrest warrant would not be given to a citizen
Obligation	The police have to carry out an arrest if the criteria for an arrest are met (i.e. it is a duty that comes with the job)	A citizen has no legal duty to arrest a criminal, only a civic obligation (i.e. as a 'good citizen'). A citizen can just walk away
Procedure	The police have to follow procedures outlined above	A citizen only has to make it clear to the person that they are under arrest, and prevent them from running off
Afterwards	The arrested person is taken into custody by the police	The arrested person is handed over to the police at the earliest possible opportunity

case study 17.5 — Constable's powers of arrest

A constable may arrest without warrant in relation to any offence ... A constable may arrest anyone:

- who is about to commit an offence or is in the act of committing an offence
- whom the officer has reasonable grounds for suspecting is about to commit an offence or to be committing an offence
- whom the officer has reasonable grounds to suspect of being guilty of an offence which he or she has reasonable grounds for suspecting has been committed
- anyone who is guilty of an offence which has been committed or anyone whom the officer has reasonable grounds for suspecting to be guilty of that offence.

Source: PACE Code G: Statutory power of arrest by police officers

activity
INDIVIDUAL WORK

1. What is the difference between this statement of a constable's powers and the statement in case study 17.4?

2. What is the relationship between the authorisation given in this extract and the 'necessity **criteria**' listed in case study 17.3 above?

Reasonable grounds for suspecting

PACE Code G, the code of practice for the statutory power of arrest by police officers, identifies two elements of a lawful arrest. These are:

1. 'A person's involvement or suspected involvement or attempted involvement in the commission of a criminal offence'.

2. 'Reasonable grounds for believing that the person's arrest is necessary'.

'Reasonable grounds' for an arrest includes both of these. It would not be reasonable (i.e. sensible) to arrest someone if there was nothing whatsoever to suggest that they had anything to do with a crime. Equally it would not be reasonable (or necessary) to arrest somebody if there was no possibility of their harming other people, or themselves, or running off to escape justice.

In practice it is often reasonable to arrest someone thought to be involved in a crime, because the fact of being involved in a crime could well make them likely to harm others or to run off.

When a person is arrested there is rarely enough evidence to prove on the spot that they have committed the crime. They are therefore arrested 'on suspicion', i.e. there are circumstances which would make a reasonably intelligent person think that they might well be involved in a crime of a certain level of seriousness.

activity
INDIVIDUAL WORK 17.1

P1

M1

You are training police cadets. Produce a handout in two parts. The first part should state the differences between an arrest with a warrant and an arrest without a warrant, listing the main circumstances in which each of the two kinds of arrest can be used.

The second part should explain when arrest and detention are lawful, and the rules the police must follow when they are arresting or detaining people.

Arrest with a warrant

An arrest warrant is a piece of paper from a magistrate or judge giving permission to the police to arrest a named person for a specific reason.

Arrest warrants are issued by the courts when people fail at attend at court to answer their **bail** or when people do not pay their fines. Normally the Crown Prosecution Service asks the court for a warrant when someone does not appear at the fines office or when fines are not paid.

Arrest warrants can also be used when people suspected of a serious crime have to be found. With the introduction of the European arrest warrants, these can be used to arrest a person suspected of cross-border crime in the EU.

Arrest without a warrant

The circumstances in which a police constable (i.e. any police officer) can arrest someone without a warrant are listed in case study 17.5 above.

In addition officers can arrest anybody without a warrant in situations which meet the arrest criteria given in case study 17.3 above.

Other statutory rights of arrest

Statutory rights of arrest are situations in which it is lawful to arrest somebody.

Arrest as a preventative measure

It is lawful for the police and other 'arresting authorities' to arrest people if they have reasonable grounds for believing that the person is likely to do harm to themselves or others.

See parts (c) and (d) in case study 17.3 above for a list of situations in which the police can arrest someone in order to prevent harm

Breach of the peace

A breach of the peace is a situation where an individual or group of people threatens to act in an aggressive or dangerous manner. It can happen either in public or private places and can relate to any behaviour which is either violent or likely to cause violence in the very near future. 'Breach' means a break in something protective (e.g. a dam). 'The peace' here refers to the normal state of society when people can live their lives without having to worry much about their own safety or that of other people. Both the police and ordinary citizens have a legal right to arrest people whom they reasonably believe to be committing a breach of the peace.

Public order offences

> **remember**
>
> SOCPA is the Serious Organised Crime and Police Act 2005.

These are all offences involving violence between individuals and groups. Most are covered by the Public Order Act 1986. Drunk and disorderly behaviour is covered by the Criminal Justice Act 1967. All of these offences are arrestable offences if the criteria in section 24A PACE 1984 (as amended by section 110 SOCPA 2005) are satisfied.

Time limits

After a person has been arrested, there are limits to the length of time they can be held in police detention before being charged.

Young people or people who are 'mentally vulnerable' are less likely to be detained for a long time before being charged, and 24 hours' detention is normally considered the maximum for such people.

Table 17.2 Public order offences

Name of offence	Section in Part 1 of the Public Order Act 1986	Key features
Riot	1	Twelve or more persons present together used or threatened unlawful violence for a common purpose; and that the conduct of them (taken together) was such as to cause a person of reasonable firmness present at the scene to fear for his personal safety
Violent disorder	2	Three or more persons present together used or threatened unlawful violence so that the conduct of them (taken together) would cause a person of reasonable firmness present at the scene to fear for his or her personal safety
Affray	3	A person has used or threatened unlawful violence towards another and his conduct is such as would cause a person of reasonable firmness present at the scene to fear for his personal safety
Using threatening, abusive or insulting words or behaviour causing fear of or provoking violence	4	These similar public order offences are all arrestable if the arrest criteria listed in case study 17.3 above are met
Using threatening, abusive or insulting words or behaviour, or disorderly behaviour intending to and causing harassment, alarm or distress	4A	As above
Using threatening, abusive or insulting words or behaviour, or disorderly behaviour likely to cause harassment, alarm or distress	5	As above
Drunk and disorderly behaviour	Section 91 Criminal Justice Act 1967	A person is in a public place, drunk and guilty of disorderly behaviour.

Beyond this, the rules are different for criminal suspects and terrorist suspects. Rules for criminal suspects are outlined in Section 43 of the Police and Criminal Evidence Act 1984. Rules for terrorist suspects are based on the Terrorism Act 2000 and the Terrorism Act 2006.

Table 17.3 Length of time in custody – criminal offences

Length of time in police detention	Responsible for extension
24 hours	No extension needed
+12	Officer of rank of superintendent or above
+36	Magistrate
+36	Magistrate

The total detention period for a criminal suspect without charge is 96 hours. If after 96 hours the suspect has still not been charged, he or she must be released.

Table 17.4 Length of time in custody – terrorist suspects

Length of time in police detention	Responsible for extension
48 hours	No extension needed
+7 days	District judge, following application by an officer of rank of superintendent or above, or by a crown prosecutor
+7 days	Either: (for a short extension which will not take the period of detention beyond 14 days) District judge, following application by an officer of rank of superintendent or above, or by a crown prosecutor Or: (if detention will go on beyond 14 days after arrest) a High Court judge
+7 days	High Court judge, after application as above

In 2007 the total time that a terrorist suspect could be kept in custody without being charged was 28 days.

Rights of a detained person

People in police detention have a variety of rights which the police must respect unless there are pressing reasons why they should not.

These rights were established in the Police and Criminal Evidence Act 1984 (see page 326 below).

Responsibility for providing these rights rests with the custody officer. The **custody officer** is a person (usually a police sergeant) whose job it is to ensure that the detainee's needs are met and their human rights are respected. The custody officer has no connection with the case, and must make sure that the arrangements for detainees comply with the PACE codes of practice.

Figure 17.1 Main rights of detainees in police custody

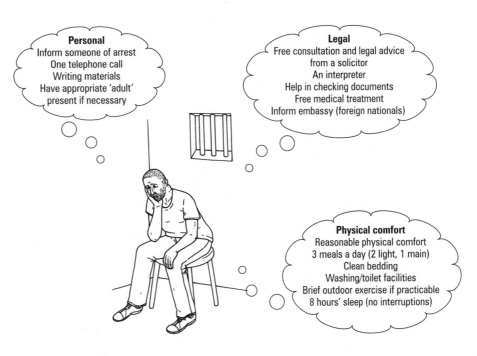

Right to have someone informed

The detained person has a right under PACE Code C 'not to be held **incommunicado**'. In other words, a friend, relative or guardian has to be informed that the person is in police detention if the detained person requests it. Unless there are operational or other important reasons that dictate otherwise, the detainee should be allowed to make one phone call of a 'reasonable length' to a friend or relative.

Right to legal advice

Detainees can have free legal advice either from a solicitor of their choice, or a 'duty solicitor' who is usually part of a rota of local solicitors who give independent and confidential advice and representation to arrested people. If a solicitor chosen by the detainee refuses to give advice or representation, another solicitor must be found if the detainee wants one. The detainee and the solicitor must be able to talk in private, and their communications are '**privileged**', i.e. they do not have to be revealed to the police or the courts.

If detainees do not want a solicitor, they are not compelled to have one.

Right to silence

The right to silence which is a traditional feature of English law was changed by the Criminal Justice and Public Order Act 1994. Accused people can of course still refuse to answer questions put to them by the police, but when they are brought to trial, this silence can now be seen as evidence of guilt. If a person is silent about something during police questioning, but answers the same question in court, juries and magistrates are allowed to draw unfavourable conclusions (e.g. that the defendant has made up an excuse since being arrested). This situation is summed up in the caution given to suspects when they are arrested and before they are interviewed:

> You do not have to say anything. But it may harm your defence if you do not mention when questioned something which you later rely on in court. Anything you do say may be given in evidence.

DNA and other samples

Individuals in police custody are sometimes required to give **DNA** and other samples for identification purposes. The rules for taking and preserving such samples are given in PACE Code D: Code of practice for the identification of persons by police officers.

DNA (deoxyribonucleic acid) is a very complex protein whose molecules contain genetic 'tags' or instructions which determine many of our characteristics. Samples of DNA can be processed in a forensic laboratory to give a profile, which looks a bit like a bar-code, which is different for each individual. The chances of any two people having the same genetic profile (other than identical twins) are extremely remote. DNA identification is therefore a powerful tool for linking suspects to a scene of crime, since the profile of

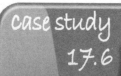

case study 17.6   **Old caution (before 1994)**

The caution before 1994 was: 'You do not have to say anything, but anything you do say may be taken down and used against you in evidence.

activity GROUP WORK

What are the differences between the old caution and the present one? Which do you prefer and why?

the suspect can be checked against that found in traces of body fluids or other matter found at the crime scene. In addition the police keep a database of genetic profiles which enables a 'speculative search' to be made, the purpose of which is to match a genetic profile found at a crime scene with any other genetic profile on the database. Since many developed countries now keep **DNA profile** databases of people accused of crimes, this speculative search can be an international one. Given the ease of modern transport and the increased importance of cross-border crime, people-trafficking and international terrorism, these speculative searches can help to solve serious crimes. But they are also an infringement of people's individual privacy and help to encourage fears of a worldwide police state.

Samples, which include fingerprints and footprints as well as DNA, can be:

- Obtained by consent.
- Obtained by the use of 'reasonable force' from suspects who do not consent.

Consent for a speculative search must be given in writing.

Issues to do with keeping or destroying DNA samples and profiles, or fingerprints, or footwear impressions, etc. are covered in Annex F of PACE Code D. Samples taken from non-suspects should normally be destroyed. However, they may be kept if the person gives their written consent. Samples from suspects or people convicted may be kept.

Police interviews

The rules governing police interviews are complex, and there is not enough space to go into them in detail in this book. Basic principles are set out in PACE Code C: Detention, treatment and questioning. The technicalities are given in Code E: Audio recording of interviews with suspects and Code F: Visual recording of interviews. In addition to any taped interview a written record must also be made, which should either be the exact words or an accurate summary of them, and signed by the suspect (if the suspect agrees).

Figure 17.2 DNA profiles: our individual bar-codes

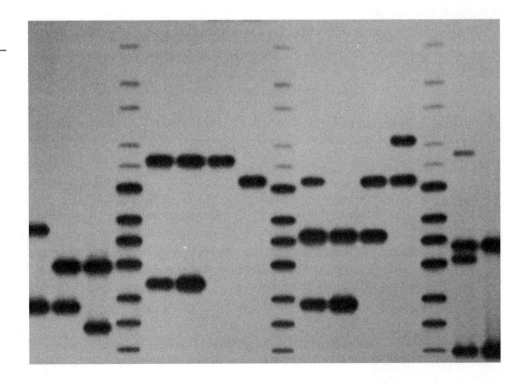

case study 17.7

Samples and DNA

Fingerprints, footwear impressions or samples, and the information derived from samples, taken in connection with the investigation of an offence which are not required to be destroyed, may be retained after they have fulfilled the purposes for which they were taken but may be used only for purposes related to the prevention or detection of crime, the investigation of an offence or the conduct of a **prosecution** in, as well as outside, the UK and may also be subject to a speculative search. This includes checking them against other fingerprints, footwear impressions and DNA records held by, or on behalf of, the police and other law enforcement authorities in, as well as outside, the UK.

Source: PACE Code D; Annex F; Section 4

activity
GROUP WORK

1. Are you in favour of DNA records being retained and used in this way? Give your reasons.

2. It is said that the DNA records of many young people are being kept (illegally) by the police after they should have been destroyed. What is your attitude to this?

3. What are the arguments for and against having everybody's DNA profile on a national police database?

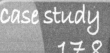

case study 17.8

Police interview procedures

4.4 The interviewer should tell the suspect about the recording process. The interviewer shall:

   (a) say the interview is being audibly recorded

   (b) subject to paragraph 2.3,[*] give their name and rank and that of any other interviewer present

   (c) ask the suspect and any other party present, e.g. a solicitor, to identify themselves

   (d) state the date, time of commencement and place of the interview

   (e) state the suspect will be given a notice about what will happen to the copies of the recording.

4.5 The interviewer shall:

- caution the suspect, see Code C, section 10

- remind the suspect of their entitlement to free legal advice, see Code C, paragraph 11.2.

*Officers do not have to identify themselves if it could lead to a risk of violence against them by associates of the accused, e.g. in cases of serious organised crime or suspected terrorism.

Source: PACE Code E

activity
INDIVIDUAL WORK

1. Look up the articles (rights) in the Human Rights Act 1998.

2. Explain how these regulations for police interviews uphold the human rights of the accused person.

Tape recording

This can be either an audio or video recording. It is recommended but not compulsory, and in any case a written **transcript** has to be made. If suspects insist on having only a written record, this is allowable. Every effort has to be made to protect and secure the master copy of the recording, which will be used by the Crown Prosecution Service and, possibly, in the trial itself. A second copy is made which is used by the police and other investigators.

Rights of interviewee

Interviewees have the right to:

- Eight hours' uninterrupted rest/sleep in any period of 24 hours while being questioned
- Adequate heat, light and ventilation in the interview room.
- Breaks at meal times and at two-hour intervals during questioning.
- An interpreter if requested.
- Remain silent without any 'adverse inferences being drawn' (i.e. without the silence being taken as a sign of guilt) and only if they wish to have a solicitor and have not (yet) been provided with one.
- A solicitor present during the interview if they wish.
- An 'appropriate adult' (for juveniles or people who are 'mentally vulnerable').

An appropriate adult can be a parent, friend, social worker, etc., preferably of the accused's own choice. Appropriate adults can take an active role, explaining questions or objecting to them, but they are not normally allowed to prevent questioning taking place.

Additional rights include:

- Every person present must be identified to the interviewee.
- Any complaints by the interviewee must be recorded.

Right to silence

See page 322 above and 'Rights of interviewee' above.

 www.homeoffice.gov.uk. **(All PACE codes of practice can be downloaded from this site)**

Searches

Searches outside police stations are covered by PACE Code A: Stop and search and recording of public encounters and PACE Code B: Searching of premises and seizure of property.

Searches of detained persons inside police stations are covered by PACE Code C, Annex A. This annex (section) deals with strip searches (taking off all clothes and searching the clothes and outer skin of the suspect) and intimate searches (searching body orifices other than the mouth). Except in urgent cases an intimate search can only be carried out by a doctor or nurse.

Fingerprints and body samples

The correct taking of fingerprints, body samples (including DNA), impressions of footwear and other impressions is covered by PACE Code D. The aim of taking such samples is to compare them with samples taken at the scene of the crime or from a victim. The Code is intended to ensure, among other things, that such evidence is only taken, used and stored 'when justified and necessary for preventing, detecting or investigating crime'. The taking of samples in connection with driving offences, immigration control and some terrorism suspects is not covered by Code D. Fingerprints and other samples can be taken either with a person's consent or using reasonable force if consent is not given and if the person is suspected of a 'recordable offence' (an offence which carries a prison sentence). Under PACE, fingerprints cannot be taken from someone under the age of 10.

Body samples can be either intimate or non-intimate. 'Intimate' means 'a dental impression or sample of blood, semen or any other tissue fluid, urine, or pubic hair, or a swab taken from any part of a person's genitals or from a person's body orifice other than the mouth' (Code D 6.1). 'Non-intimate' includes: hair (not pubic), nail scrapings, saliva, some swabs and skin impressions of parts of people's bodies other than fingerprints. Written consent is always needed before intimate samples are given (if consent is refused, it may be taken as evidence of guilt), and intimate samples can only be taken with the authorisation of an officer of inspector rank or above. Written consent is needed for a non-intimate sample except in a few circumstances involving imprisonable offences mentioned in Code D, 6.6.

Codes of practice

These are the Police and Criminal Evidence Act 1984 Codes of Practice – a series of books totalling over 70,000 words outlining the powers and duties which the police have when investigating crimes. The aims of these codes of practice are to:

■ Protect the police from accusations of wrongdoing.

■ Protect the human rights of offenders.

■ Ensure fairness and consistency in police behaviour.

■ Ensure that evidence has been correctly obtained so that it will stand up in court.

PACE Codes of practice are regulations which the police have to follow. Breaking the rules will not in itself cause an officer to appear in court, but in an extreme case it could mean that a person dies in police custody. This could lead to private prosecutions and disastrous publicity which would at the least ruin the careers of officers involved and might bring the police as a whole into disrepute. Breaking PACE codes can also lead to cases being thrown out in court because the evidence is not considered valid – a serious matter for the police and for the victims of that particular crime (and excellent news for the criminals concerned).

Legislation

The law governing police treatment of suspects both before and after arrest is the Police and Criminal Evidence Act 1984. This was brought in after the 1981 Brixton Riots and the publication of the Scarman Report on the police response to those riots.

The codes of practice made under Section 66

The codes of practice were set up in Sections 60, 66 and 67 of the PACE Act 1984. These codes are not laws in the sense that the PACE Act 1984 is a law; they are drawn up by the Home Office in consultation with the Home Affairs Select Committee (a group of MPs who discuss and investigate police work and similar matters), laid before Parliament (so they can be considered by MPs but not debated) and are passed by the Home Secretary. As stated above, PACE codes of practice give detailed direction to the police about how they should deal with suspects and collect evidence.

The Serious Organised Crime and Police Act 2005 (SOCPA)

This important Act, passed to deal with the increasing amount of this kind of crime, has strengthened police powers of arrest by, in effect, abolishing the old distinction between arrestable and non-arrestable offences. Constables now have wide powers to arrest without a warrant provided that certain criteria are met. These criteria are laid out in SOCPA, section 110, and have been incorporated into PACE Code of Practice G: Power of arrest.

As a result of SOCPA police and magistrates have less paperwork to deal with arrests, and decisions to arrest people can be made more quickly.

activity
GROUP WORK
17.2

P2

Each choose a different offence for which a young person might be detained in a police station. Then carry out a role-play in which a custody officer states and, where appropriate, explains the rights of a detainee in police custody. Take turns in playing the roles of a detainee and a custody officer. Afterwards, carry out a peer assessment of each custody officer's description of the rights of the detained person.

The regulations regarding the search of people and premises

Stop and search

Police powers to stop and search people are covered by PACE Code A: Exercise by police officers of statutory powers of stop and search.

The right to stop and search people and vehicles in a public place

There are many laws which give police powers to search people and vehicles in public places. Four main ones are shown in Table 17.5.

Table 17.5 Powers to search people and vehicles in public places

Act	What the police have power to search for
Misuse of Drugs Act 1971	Drugs
Criminal Justice Act 1988	Offensive weapons – especially knives and pointed objects
Criminal Justice and Public Order Act 1994	Offensive weapons
Terrorism Act 2000	Anything that might be used for a terrorist act

The powers given by these Acts are included in the PACE codes of practice which are updated from time to time to take account of new laws. This means that the police have up-to-date guidance, all in one place, on what they can or cannot do when gathering evidence of crimes they are investigating.

Reasonable grounds

Grounds are reasons, facts or observations which support an action.

These are explained in the Acts which give the police power to search. For example, in the Terrorist Act 2000 there must be reasons for suspecting that a person might be carrying something that could be used for a terrorist act. In a recent case the sight of gas canisters in a car parked near a London nightclub constituted reasonable grounds for carrying out a search under this Act. The grounds were reasonable because gas canisters are explosive and are not usually found in cars parked near nightclubs. If a pub had a reputation for allowing drugs to be bought and sold on the premises, and the clientele seemed different from what might normally be expected at a pub, this too might be reasonable grounds for stopping and searching.

Occasionally, for example outside football stadiums, the police can carry out searches of everybody. Here the reasonable grounds are not suspicion of particular individuals, but the need to reassure the public and to limit risks of hooliganism and other violence within the stadium.

Reasonable grounds or 'reasonable suspicion' cannot be based on stereotypes, e.g. stopping and searching people because they are black, have scruffy clothes or are under 25. Normally reasonable suspicion is based on intelligence (e.g. tip-offs) or the sight of something suspicious and out of the ordinary (e.g. someone stuffing a large object under their jacket).

Prohibited articles

Prohibited articles are things which people should not be carrying in public, or which they should not have in their possession. Some articles, such as class A drugs or unlicensed guns, are prohibited anyway. Others, such as kitchen knives, are OK in the kitchen but not, say, at a football match. Table 17.5 indicates that different articles are covered by different Acts. The main classes of prohibited articles are drugs, weapons and stolen goods. Others include crossbows, intoxicating liquor (at football matches) and poaching equipment. The Terrorism Acts 2000 and 2006 prohibit anything which could be used to promote terrorism, ranging from chemicals and electronic equipment through to things like propaganda leaflets and suspicious photographs and maps.

See Pace Code A, Annex A for a summary of prohibited articles. Further details can be found in the Acts referred to

Procedures to be followed

PACE Code A gives detailed instructions on search procedures. The main points are:

- Searches must be fair, responsible, respectful and brief, without unlawful discrimination.
- There must be reasonable grounds for suspicion.
- The purpose of the search must be explained to the person (or owner of vehicle or premises) being searched.
- Officers must try to get people to consent and may only use force as a last resort.
- Searches should last no longer than necessary.
- In a public place, people can only be asked to remove their outer coat or jacket and gloves. Further searches must be out of public view.
- People can be required to remove disguises and face coverings.
- A proper search record must be kept (see below) except in the case of mass searches (e.g. outside football grounds).

A record is required for each person and each vehicle searched (see case study 17.10). Searches are normally carried out by police officers, but the power can be delegated to other trained people. Community support officers, for example, have some powers to stop and search.

Searching an arrested person

Procedures for searching arrested people are outlined in PACE Code C.

Rights of police to search a person when arrested

The police have wide rights to search a person when arrested. Preliminary searches of outer garments including, say, the removal of a T-shirt, can be done in a police vehicle or other place out of public view. But it must be done by an officer of the same sex as the arrested person, and out of sight of anyone of the opposite sex 'unless the person being searched specifically requests it' (see Code A 3.6). More thorough searches are normally carried out at a police station.

case study 17.9 — Searches

3.8 Before any search of a detained person or attended vehicle takes place the officer must take reasonable steps to give the person to be searched or in charge of the vehicle the following information:

(a) that they are being detained for the purposes of a search;

(b) the officer's name (except in the case of enquiries linked to the investigation of terrorism, or otherwise where the officer reasonably believes that giving his or her name might put him or her in danger, in which case a warrant or other identification number shall be given) and the name of the police station to which the officer is attached;

(c) the legal search power which is being exercised; and

(d) a clear explanation of:

   (i) the purpose of the search in terms of the article or articles for which there is a power to search; and

   (ii) in the case of powers requiring reasonable suspicion (see paragraph 2.1(a)), the grounds for that suspicion; or

   (iii) in the case of powers which do not require reasonable suspicion (see paragraph 2.1(b), and (c)), the nature of the power and of any necessary authorisation and the fact that it has been given

Source: PACE Code A

activity — INDIVIDUAL WORK

Explain how each of the activities listed in the case study can:

1. Ensure as far as possible that the search is successful.
2. Help maintain good relations between the police and the public.

Searches at a police station should be done as soon as possible. The custody officer can carry out or authorise a search as long as it only involves the removal of outer clothing. Searches are likely if a detainee is expected to be in custody for some time, or if they behave in a way which suggests they should be searched (e.g. appearing to be violent or under the influence of drugs). The custody officer keeps an inventory of all objects found.

Intimate searches

These are dealt with in PACE Code C, Annex A. They can only be authorised by an officer of inspector or higher rank, and must normally be done by a registered doctor or nurse. The purpose is to find offensive weapons or class A drugs concealed in body orifices other than the mouth.

There are special arrangements for intimate searches of juveniles and vulnerable adults. In urgent cases where the safety of the detainee or others is at stake and a doctor or nurse cannot be brought in quickly enough, a police officer can carry out the search.

Besides the detainee, two people must be present during the search, and must be of the same sex as the person being searched.

The search record must show:

■ Who authorised the search.

■ The grounds for the search.

- Why the search was necessary.
- Which parts of the detainee's body were searched.
- Who did the search.
- Who was present.
- The result of the search.

Strip searches

These involve the removal of more than outer clothing. They must be done 'only if it is considered necessary to remove an article which a detainee would not be allowed to keep, and the officer reasonably considers the detainee might have concealed such an article'. The police officer doing the search must be of the same sex as the detainee. Detainees should not normally have to take off all their clothes at once. They may be asked to show their genital or anal regions, but without any physical contact. If such contact is needed it becomes an intimate search (see above).

There are special arrangements for young people and vulnerable adults and an **appropriate adult** can be present if the detainee agrees.

---

case study 17.10   Search record

4.3 **The following information must always be included in the record of a search even if the person does not wish to provide any personal details:**

  (i)   the name of the person searched, or (if it is withheld) a description;
  (ii) a note of the person's self-defined ethnic background; ...
  (iii) when a vehicle is searched, its registration number; ...
  (iv) the date, time, and place that the person or vehicle was first detained;
  (v)   the date, time and place the person or vehicle was searched (if different from (iv));
  (vi) the purpose of the search;
  (vii) the grounds for making it, ... the nature of the power and of any necessary authorisation and the fact that it has been given; ...
  (viii) its outcome (e.g. arrest or no further action);
  (ix) a note of any injury or damage to property resulting from it;
  (x)   subject to paragraph 3.8(b)*, the identity of the officer making the search. ...

*(except in the case of enquiries linked to the investigation of terrorism, or otherwise where the officer reasonably believes that giving his or her name might put him or her in danger, in which case a warrant or other identification number shall be given)

NB: The omitted sections (indicated by ellipses (...)) are cross-references to other paragraphs.

Source: PACE Code A

activity
GROUP WORK

1. What are the arguments for and against recording searches in this way?
2. Why do the police have to record the ethnic backgrounds of people searched?

Time limits

There are no exact time limits, but intimate and strip searches should be carried out as soon as reasonably possible after arrest – especially if the detainee or other people might be put at risk by whatever is concealed.

Searching premises

The regulations for searching premises are set out in *PACE Code B: Code of practice for searches of premises by police officers and the seizure of property found by police officers on persons or premises.*

The manner in which these searches are carried out is given in PACE Code B, but the power for the search comes from the relevant Act of Parliament. Table 17.6 outlines some of these.

Table 17.6 Acts that convey power for a search

Act	Object of search
Theft Act 1968, section 26	Stolen goods
Misuse of Drugs Act 1971, section 23	Controlled drugs
Terrorism Act 2000, Schedule 5, para. 1	Anything potentially linked to terrorism
Criminal Justice Act 1988, section 139B	Knives, offensive weapons, etc. in schools
Explosives Act 1875, section 73(b)	Explosives

Search warrants

> *remember*
>
> For the information on search warrants (and many other things) talk to police officers or people who work in the courts.

These are papers issued to constables by district judges or judges giving the police legal authority (under named laws) to carry out searches for specified items.

Requirements of a warrant

The procedure for applying for a search warrant is normally as follows:

1. Officers check the accuracy of their information about the need for a search and a search warrant.
2. They ascertain what is being looked for and where it might be.
3. They collect information on the premises and their occupier.
4. They check if any previous searches have been done there.
5. They make an application to a judge of the High Court, a circuit judge, a recorder or a district judge for a search warrant under PACE Schedule 1. (Schedules are instructions which normally appear near the end of an Act of Parliament.)
6. The application is made with written authority from an officer of the rank of inspector or above.
7. The application has to go to a circuit judge if the search is under the powers given in Schedule 5 of the Terrorism Act 2000.
8. Officers consult the local police/community liaison officer (especially if the search is likely to upset people in the community, or cause other problems).
9. The application is made in writing specifying:

    (a) the relevant Act;
    (b) whether the warrant is for one or more premises;
    (c) the premises to be searched;
    (d) the object of the search;
    (e) the grounds for the application;
    (f) how evidence being searched for relates to the investigation.

Figure 17.3 Searching premises

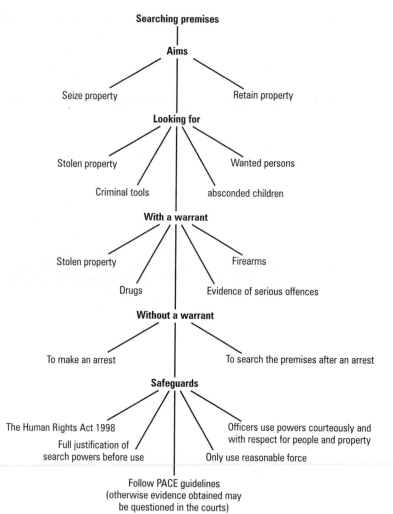

Figure 17.4 outlines the issues involved in seeking consent (agreement) from an occupier before searching premises. Consent does not always have to be obtained, for example where it would frustrate the object of the search by giving the occupiers an opportunity to hide evidence of an offence.

A search should be carried out only when it is needed to find the kind of things being looked for. For example, there is no need to look in a person's dressing table for a stolen television. Searches should stop once the items being looked for are found.

Powers to enter premises without a warrant

Officers who have arrested someone for an **indictable offence** can search the premises where the arrest takes place, or they can search promises where the arrested person was shortly before the arrest took place, without having a warrant.

Immigration officers have the power under the Immigration Act 1971 to enter and search premises without a warrant.

Seizing of goods

In this context 'seizing goods' means that the police remove things which they have found during a search and keep them as possible evidence of an offence.

Officers can seize anything:

- Covered by a warrant.

- Which appears to be evidence of an offence and which needs to be seized so it does not 'disappear'.

- Which needs to be 'sifted' (examined) elsewhere (e.g. documents or computers).

> **remember**
>
> An indictable offence is a serious offence which must be tried in the Crown Court, and which can carry a sentence of more than six months' imprisonment or a £5,000 fine.

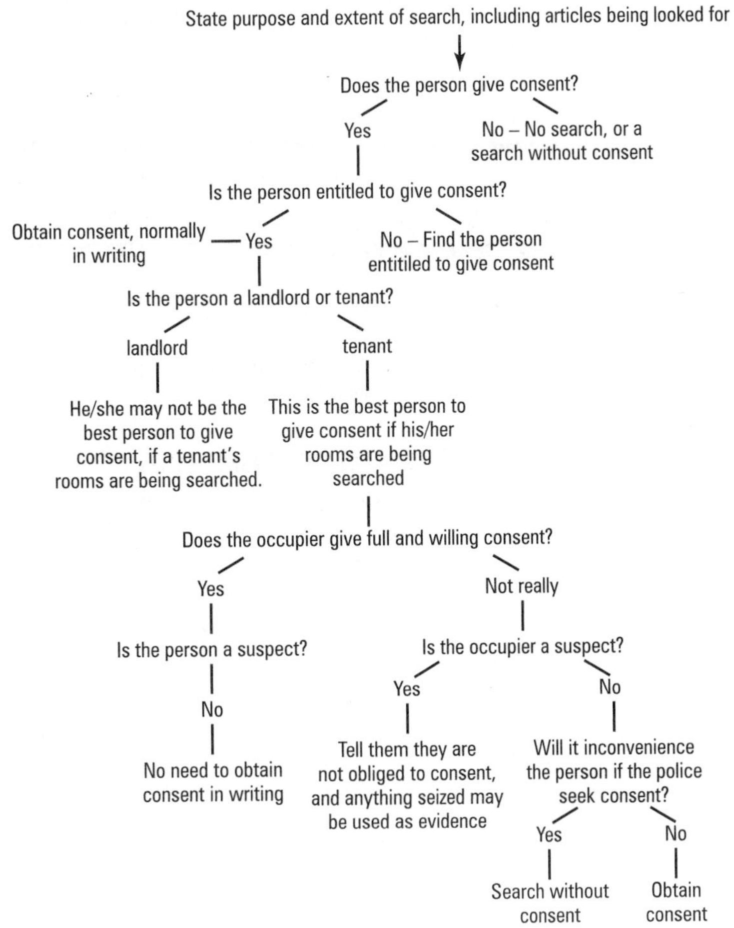

Figure 17.4 Searches of premises with consent

State purpose and extent of search, including articles being looked for

↓

Does the person give consent?

Yes — No – No search, or a search without consent

Is the person entitled to give consent?

Obtain consent, normally in writing — Yes — No – Find the person entitled to give consent

Is the person a landlord or tenant?

landlord — tenant

He/she may not be the best person to give consent, if a tenant's rooms are being searched. — This is the best person to give consent if his/her rooms are being searched

Does the occupier give full and willing consent?

Yes — Not really

Is the person a suspect? — Is the occupier a suspect?

No — Yes — No

No need to obtain consent in writing — Tell them they are not obliged to consent, and anything seized may be used as evidence — Will it inconvenience the person if the police seek consent?

Yes — No

Search without consent — Obtain consent

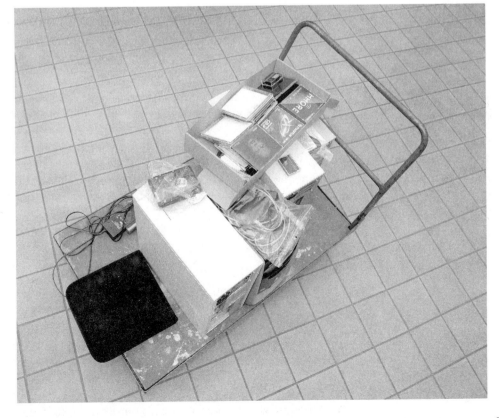

Figure 17.5 Property seized by the police may have to be sifted later

The police cannot seize things which are subject to legal privilege (e.g. letters between a lawyer and client).

Officers can photograph or copy items which may be evidence but which do not need to be seized, and warn the suspect (or the owner) that they will be breaking the law if they get rid of the items. People from whom property has been seized for further examination have a right to be present during that further examination.

Things seized can be retained for use at a trial or for further forensic examination. Property that is retained must be kept securely.

Seized property can be returned to the person it was seized from once it is not needed for evidence purposes unless someone else has more right to it. People claiming property which has been seized by the police should apply for it through a magistrates' court under the Police (Property) Act 1897.

Unlawful entry and searches

A lawful search is a search which is carried out for a purpose and in a manner which is laid down by law. Though the Police and Criminal Evidence Act Code B gives guidance on how searches should be carried out, other Acts also give guidance. This makes the lawfulness of searches quite complicated. For example, part of the Criminal Justice and Police Act 2001 deals with searches where it is expected to find a mixture of material which is and is not **admissible** in court (e.g. in major fraud cases where there are vast amounts of documentation some of which may be correspondence between lawyers and the defendants). Material found in searches done under this Act must by law be kept separate from material found in searches based on other Acts and special procedures must be followed for sifting the material. The complexity of regulations dealing with searches makes it more likely that some aspect of the search is unlawful. Furthermore, phrases such as 'only use reasonable force when this is considered necessary and proportionate to the circumstances' leave plenty of room for legal argument as to whether force used in any given search really was 'necessary and proportionate to the circumstances'. Another aspect of unlawful searching is the excessive targeting of young people and people from ethnic minorities.

Remedies for those affected by unlawful entry and searches

If the police carry out an unlawful search of a person, vehicle or premises there are various things people can do to get a remedy – which in this case can be an apology, disciplinary action taken against police officers concerned, repair of damage caused or compensation through the courts.

One option for people affected by an unlawful entry and/or search is to complain to the police. Such complaints can be dealt with in the ways described in case study 17.11.

Not all complaints are followed up. Besides the two options in case study 17.11, complaints can be dealt with by dispensation (agreement by the IPCC that the complaint need not be followed up), withdrawal (the complainant decides not to continue with the complaint) and discontinuation (stopping the complaints procedure for other reasons).

Table 17.7 on page 336 shows the number of complaints received by the Independent Police Complaints Commission relating to searches in 2005/06.

Case study 17.12 gives an account of a case where complaints against the police were upheld.

Most serious complaints (as Table 17.7 shows) do not succeed. Nevertheless, some do, and if the police are taken to court they may have to pay out large sums in compensation.

The figures in case study 17.13 relate to all cases of police misconduct by the Metropolitan Police, not simply cases involving searches, which are probably a fairly small percentage.

case study 17.11

Dealing with complaints

Local resolution: for less serious complaints, such as rudeness or incivility, a complainant may agree to local resolution. Usually this involves a local police supervisor handling the complaint and agreeing with the complainant [on] a way of dealing with it. This might be: an explanation or information to clear up a misunderstanding; an apology on behalf of the force; and/or an outline of what actions are to be taken to prevent similar complaints occurring in the future.

Investigation: in other circumstances (or if the complainant declines local resolution) it may be decided that a complaint requires a thorough examination of the incident. This involves the appointment of an Investigating Officer who will look into a complaint and produce a report which will state whether or not each allegation is substantiated.

Source: Gleeson, E. and Dady, H. Police Complaints: Statistics for England and Wales 2005/2006. *IPCC Research and Statistics Series* Paper 5, p. 37

activity
GROUP WORK

Explain the advantages and disadvantage of these two types of remedy.

case study 17.12

Complaint upheld

'Police Stop and Search Was Unlawful' – says IPCC Commissioner

West Midlands Police unlawfully stopped and searched a Wolverhampton man and his son and thus unlawfully detained them, according to the Independent Police Complaints Commission (IPCC).

Police officers had stopped and searched Mr Ranjit Singh Sahota and his son, Mr Amarjit Singh Sahota, aged 21 at the time of the incident, in Woden Road, Heathtown, Wolverhampton on Saturday 11th October 2003 at around 7.00pm, the day an England v Turkey football match was being broadcast on satellite TV. Police had argued they were using an order they had issued under Section 60 of the Criminal Justice and Public Order Act 1994 covering the whole of the local command unit, an area covering approximately half of Wolverhampton, because of concern that there might be violence associated with venues broadcasting the match. Neither Mr Sahota nor his son was at or near such a venue when they were stopped. Neither was arrested as a result of the stop and search.

Mr Sahota complained to West Midlands Police about being stopped and searched when he and his son were going about their lawful business, and twice declined to have the matter settled informally. Officers from the Professional Standards Department of West Midlands Police then investigated the complaint but found it unsubstantiated. The outcome was reported to the IPCC. The Commissioner handling the case, John Crawley, required further investigations and discovered that the basis upon which an Inspector had authorised the Section 60 order was fundamentally flawed.

Source: IPCC

activity
GROUP WORK

Explain in as much detail as you can the effects that decisions like this might have on the police and their work.

case study
17.13

The cost of civil litigation

The MPA is naturally concerned with the increasing costs of **civil litigation**. Civil court proceedings of alleged police misconduct are increasingly being pursued. For example in 1979 only 7 cases against the police in London were heard, resulting in damages of £1,991 being paid. In 1986, 126 cases were heard; in 1994/95 it was 731, and 1000 in 1996/7. Damage payments tripled from £1.3 million in 1994/5 to £3.9 million in 1999/2000.

Source: Equal Opportunity and Diversity Board (EODB) of the MPA, Report of the MPA Scrutiny on MPS Stop and Search Practice 2004

activity
GROUP WORK

Do you think increased litigation against the police improves the service they give? Discuss, and give your views.

Table 17.7 Complaints about searches received by the IPCC in 2005/06

Complaints of unlawful searches – category	Number	Percentage of total complaints received by IPCC	Unsuccessful complaints after IPCC investigation (%)
Breach of PACE Code A on stop and search	336	0.9	91
Breach of PACE Code B on searching of premises and seizure of property	868	2.1	88

activity
GROUP WORK
17.3

P3

You are police officers searching a person and premises for prohibited items. Devise and, if possible, video a role-play in which you outline the police's search powers to an unwilling individual whose person and premises are then searched. The person must only be searched as they would be in a public place. (If you are being assessed, provide individual evidence to your tutor that you have researched the police powers for searching people and premises.)

activity
INDIVIDUAL WORK
17.4

M2

Produce a leaflet suitable for a citizens' advice organisation summarising police powers for searching people and premises, indicating how they protect the rights of individuals and how they help to ensure that evidence obtained can be used in court.

activity
INDIVIDUAL WORK
17.5

D1

Write an article suitable for a human rights magazine assessing the police powers of arrest, detention and search in relation to their:
1. Human rights implications.
2. Effectiveness in obtaining admissible evidence.
3. Workability from a police point of view.

Pre-trial procedure in criminal courts

The criminal courts are the magistrates' courts and the Crown Court. Pre-trial procedure includes all of the things that have to be done after a person has been charged with an offence and before their case is heard in court.

Categories of criminal offences

From the point of view of the courts there are three categories of criminal offence:

- **Summary offences**. These are relatively minor cases which are tried at a magistrates' court. They include things like minor assault and driving offences.

- Either-way offences. These are cases of medium seriousness which can be tried at the Crown Court or at a **magistrates' court**. The defendant (usually following a solicitor's advice) can choose.

- Indictable-only offences. These are the most serious cases, such as murder, manslaughter, rape and robbery. They are always heard at the Crown Court.

Bail

Bail is an arrangement to ensure that a person who has been charged with an offence does not have to be kept in custody but will turn up at court on the day of their trial.

There are two kinds of bail:

- Conditional bail. This is where the person charged with the offence is released, but only on condition that they do (or do not do) certain things between the time of their release on bail and their appearance in court. Examples of such **conditions** are observing a curfew between certain hours each day, reporting regularly to a police station, having a sum of money paid to the court which will be forfeited if the defendant does not turn up, or keeping away from another person linked to the case. Conditional bail is imposed when:

    - there appears to be some risk of another offence between the date of release from police custody and the planned date of appearance in court; or

    - there is a risk that the accused person will not turn up in court on the day.

- Unconditional bail. The person charged is released and no conditions are imposed between the time of release and the planned appearance in court. Unconditional bail is granted when the police or the courts are fairly sure that the person charged will not re-offend before the date of the trial, and will turn up at the trial as planned.

Police powers to grant bail

These are outlined in PACE Code C. There is some difference between the power of the police to grant bail and the power of the courts.

The Bail Act 1976

The Bail Act 1976 is the main law setting out how and when bail should be granted either by the police or by the courts.

The Act states that after people have been charged they have a general right to bail unless there is some good reason why they should not be granted it.

Offenders need not be granted bail if the court believes:

1. That the defendant will:

    (a) abscond (disappear);

    (b) commit an offence while on bail;

    (c) influence or intimidate witnesses or 'obstruct the course of justice'.

2. That the defendant should be kept in custody for their own protection or well-being.

3. That the defendant is already in custody.

4. More time is needed to allow a decision on whether to grant bail or not.

5. The defendant has been arrested for absconding or for breaking bail conditions.

6. The offence was a serious one and committed while the defendant was already on bail for another offence.

Breach of bail means that the offender can be arrested by a police officer without a warrant.

The police can grant bail, under the Act, but police bail is less of an entitlement than court bail. The police can attach conditions to ensure that the defendant:

- Surrenders to custody (i.e. turns up at court on the arranged day).

- Does not commit an offence while on bail.

- Does not interfere with witnesses or obstruct the course of justice.

Other provisions include the following:

- A person on bail has a duty to surrender to custody and to make him/herself available for reports (e.g. pre-sentence reports).

- Bail should normally be refused for suspects of murder and other very serious crimes.

- Conditions include tagging and a requirement to live in a bail hostel (however, this can only be authorised by the courts, not the police).

- Offenders can apply to a court for variation of their bail if they think the conditions are too strict.

- Offenders have a right to a copy of all bail decisions by the court.

- The prosecution can demand to know from a court why bail is being allowed if they have already argued against it. In indictable or triable either-way offences this can lead to the imposing of more conditions or withholding bail altogether.

- Absconding from bail is an offence. Courts may issue a warrant for arrest.

 www.justice.gov.uk. The UK Statute Law Database (a useful site – but it takes time to learn how to use it!)

Table 17.8 Bail

Police bail	Court bail
People who have been arrested and charged do not have an automatic right to police bail. The police can release people on bail but do not have the same powers as the courts to impose conditions. However, they can impose some conditions, such as reporting at regular times to a police station. When the police grant bail it is either to return at a later date to the police station, or to appear at a court on a given date at a given time. The police can only grant bail before the first court hearing; if bail is granted after that it is the responsibility of the court. Police are able to grant 'street bail' for minor offenders. This power, which started in 2006, enables officers to require a minor offender to meet them at a later time or date, or to report to the police station – perhaps to be charged and then released again on normal police bail	Magistrates' courts can grant bail when hearings are adjourned (e.g. for further reports) or when the offender will be committed (sent) to the Crown Court. Courts can impose a wide range of conditions (see page 337 above) and can also permit exceptions (e.g. X cannot visit Y except to see the children, under supervision, at a fixed time). Courts are allowed to vary the conditions imposed in police bail if the person bailed applies to them for a variation and the application seems justified. The Criminal Justice and Police Act 2001 allows the courts to electronically tag children and young people who persistently offend while on bail. The courts can impose curfews and instruct young people to appear at the door when a police officer comes to check that the offender is at home

Restrictions on bail

Restrictions on bail take two forms:

- Conditions, which are outlined on page 337 above.
- Prohibitions, when people are not eligible for bail.

The main prohibitions are for offenders in indictable (serious) crimes such as homicide and rape. Such offenders are kept on **remand**, in custody (prison) until the trial date in order to ensure their attendance at trial and to protect the public.

There have been complaints that some people accused of less serious crimes have been denied the right to bail because they have no fixed address or for similar reasons – and this has led to accusations of discrimination in the bail/remand system. There are also restrictions on bail for immigration detainees, who have a legal right to apply for bail but who, according to the National Coalition of Anti-Deportation Campaigns, have obstacles, some of them unauthorised, put in the way of their applications.

www.ncadc.org.uk/about/index.htm

Access to legal advice and representation

Most people charged with crime are on less than average incomes and cannot afford to pay a lawyer themselves. However, it is a fundamental human right that all people should be equal under the law. Article 6 part 3(c) of the Human Rights Act 1998 states:

> Everyone charged with a criminal offence has the following [right ...]
>
> (c) to defend himself in person or through legal assistance of his own choosing or, if he has not sufficient means to pay for legal assistance, to be given it free when the interests of justice so require;

Duty solicitors

The purpose of **duty solicitors** is to give free legal advice and help to people who are either accused or witnesses at police stations and magistrates' courts who feel that they need legal help. They attend police stations and courts to give this help and advice on a rota basis.

Duty solicitors have two main jobs:

1. To go to police stations to advise and help people who otherwise have no legal representation.
2. To help and defend people at magistrates' courts when they need legal representation and do not have it.

Besides their legal qualification, duty solicitors need to hold a qualification called the Criminal Litigation Accreditation Scheme Police Station Qualification. (This is based mainly on a portfolio of relevant experience plus an 'examination' consisting of relevant role-plays.)

Duty solicitors should be distinguished from solicitors chosen by people who are being held at police stations. Solicitors representing their detained clients are doing what is called 'own-client' work. This may well be publicly funded (as duty solicitors are), but it does not fit into the rotas provided and is not part of the duty solicitor scheme.

Funding and representation for litigation

This is a complex issue and the law has changed recently, making applications for financial help in legal actions more difficult for people.

remember

You should try to talk to people such as duty solicitors to get a fuller understanding of this part of the unit.

Legal aid in criminal cases is arranged by the Criminal Defence Service. It takes the following forms:

- Free legal advice at a police station. This can come either from the duty solicitor or from the client's own solicitor if he or she is attached to the Criminal Defence Service.

- The right to consult a solicitor at any time when in police detention (except for some serious cases where this right can be put off until a later time).

- Advice and assistance about a criminal case even for a person who has not been charged with a criminal offence. There is a means test for this kind of help, and people can only get it free if they are on low incomes or on income support or jobseeker's allowance.

Full legal representation for a criminal defence can be obtained if someone has a Representation Order. This is awarded by the court following a means test and an 'interests of justice' test. In 2007 anybody with an annual income of more than £21,487 was not eligible for legal aid in a *magistrates' court* (except in rare cases where they were allowed legal aid despite having a higher income than this following a 'hardship review'). The interests of justice test is linked to the possibility of a person losing their job or having to go to prison if they are found guilty. People facing this risk qualify on 'interests of justice' grounds for legal representation. For the Crown Court, because the cases and the sentences are much more serious, all defendants are entitled to free and full legal representation.

The paragraphs above refer to legal aid or help well in advance of the hearing. People who have had no such help beforehand will get some free legal advice and representation when their case is heard in a magistrates' court whatever their financial position.

Prosecutors

Prosecutors are lawyers who use evidence collected by the police or some other prosecuting body such as the Health and Safety Executive to make a case in a criminal court against a defendant. In the English legal system most prosecution is carried out by the Crown Prosecution Service.

Role of the Crown Prosecution Service

Until the mid 1980s the police prepared their own prosecutions, collecting evidence and arguments to convict the people they caught and charged with offences. However, it became clear that this system increasingly overloaded the police with work and led to badly prepared cases which then failed in court, wasting police time and public money. The Prosecution of Offences Act 1985 changed the system by creating the Crown Prosecution Service, a body composed mainly of lawyers whose job is to:

- Collect evidence and information from the police through a process called disclosure.
- Decide whether the evidence is sufficient in quantity and quality to proceed with the case.
- Prepare the case in a way that will stand up in court.
- Present and argue the case in front of magistrates or a judge.

The Crown Prosecution Service started work in 1986.

Code for crown prosecutors

The code for crown prosecutors is a 24-page booklet showing the main principles that crown prosecutors should follow in their work. The essential points of the code are that prosecutions must be carried out which:

1. Are in the public interest.

2. Have a realistic chance of success.

3. Reflect the wishes and needs of the victims of crime.

Figure 17.6 The role of the Crown Prosecution Service

Role	Purpose	Responsibilities
Getting information about offences from the police	Provide an independent prosecution service	Uphold justice by supporting the police
Advising the police before they charge offenders		Uphold the rights of victims by helping to ensure that criminals are punished
Building the prosecution case by organising evidence and arguments within the framework of the law		Accurately assess the needs of victims and the evidence of witnesses
Presenting the case fairly in court		Inspire the confidence of the public
		Provide value for taxpayers' money

The code is easy to read and understand. It is intended for the public to read it and not just lawyers. Here is a brief and very simple outline of what it says:

1. Introduction – why a code is needed.

2. General principles – fairness:

   (a) Cases must be heard in the interests of justice and not simply to obtain a conviction.

   (b) There is a duty to give guidance to investigators.

   (c) The Human Rights Act 1998 must be followed.

3. The decision to prosecute – introduces the idea of the Full Code Test and the Threshold Test (see point 5).

4. Cases are reviewed as they are prepared, to ensure that prosecution should go ahead. The CPS is finally responsible for deciding if a case goes ahead.

5. The Full Code Test. This has two stages:

   (a) Evidential stage. Will the evidence provide 'a realistic prospect of conviction'? Will it be accepted by a judge, jury or magistrate? Is it admissible (usable) in court? Is it reliable? Are there any problems over the identity of the defendant or the credibility of witnesses?

   (b) Public interest stage. If the following are true, the prosecution is more likely to be in the public interest:

   (i)   the offence carries a heavy sentence;

   (ii)   property will be recovered if the prosecution succeeds;

   (iii)   a weapon was used;

   (iv)   the victim was a public servant, e.g. a police officer or nurse;

   (v)   the defendant was in a position of trust;

   (vi)   the defendant was a ringleader;

   (vii) the offence was planned beforehand;

   (viii) it was a group offence;

   (ix)   the victim has suffered;

   (x)   a child was harmed;

   (xi)   discrimination, e.g. racism, sexism, was involved;

   (xii) people have been corrupted;

   (xiii) there are relevant previous convictions;

   (xiv) the offence happened while under a court order, e.g. bail;

   (xv)   the offence is likely to be repeated;

(xvi) the offence is a common problem in the area;

(xvii) ordinary people would want the prosecution to go ahead.

Prosecution is less in the public interest if:

(i)   the penalty is small;

(ii)   the defendant is already under sentence;

(iii) the offence was a genuine error;

(iv)   the effects were minor;

(v)   the offence happened a long time ago;

(vi)   prosecution may harm the victim's state of mind;

(vii) the defendant is old or ill;

(viii) the defendant has paid compensation or tried to right the wrong;

(ix)   'details may be made public that could harm sources of information, international relations or national security'.

Victims should be kept informed of decisions which affect them, but the CPS is acting for the state (the people as a whole) not the victim personally.

6. The Threshold Test. This is a preliminary test to decide if there is a reasonable chance that the suspect has committed an offence, and that it is in the public interest to charge the suspect. It is applied mostly in serious cases where the suspect is in custody, and there is a lack of evidence for a proper Full Code Test.

7. Selection of charges. Charges chosen by the CPS should reflect the seriousness of the crime yet carry a reasonable chance of success.

8. Diversion. Sometimes measures other than prosecution should be considered, such as cautions for adults, and reprimands and final warnings for young people.

9. Mode of trial. The CPS should decide whether a case goes to the magistrates' or Crown Court.

10. The CPS does not have to accept guilty pleas, and should not do so if it will result in an unfairly lenient sentence for a serious crime.

11. Prosecutors should give background information to the courts and challenge untrue statements made by defence lawyers.

12. The CPS has a right to restart a prosecution if new evidence appears.

Other prosecutors

Although the Crown Prosecution Service is responsible for the great bulk of prosecutions in England and Wales, there are other 'prosecuting authorities' – bodies which can prosecute people, firms, etc. The CPS has a convention of understanding with the following 16. This means that they follow broadly similar principles when preparing prosecutions, and will cooperate wherever possible:

■ Department for Business, Enterprise and Regulatory Reform.

■ Serious Fraud Office (SFO).

■ HM Customs and Excise.

■ Health and Safety Executive (HSE).

■ Department for Work and Pensions (DWP).

■ Inland Revenue.

■ Environment Agency.

■ Department for Environment Food and Rural Affairs (Defra).

■ Intervention Board.

■ Bank of England.

- Army Prosecuting Authority.
- Royal Air Force Prosecuting Authority.
- Royal Navy Prosecuting Authority.
- Maritime and Coastguard Agency.
- Occupational Regulatory Authority.
- Civil Aviation Authority.

Other bodies, such as local authorities, can also act as prosecuting authorities. Though there is no formal convention between them and the CPS there is an understanding that each will be prepared to cooperate with the other. This understanding is based on the Prosecution of Offences Act 1985 section 6(2) which gives the CPS a right to take over the prosecutions of other prosecution authorities if necessary.

www.cps.gov.uk

See Unit 15, pages 248–250 for details of prosecutions by the Health and Safety Executive

Private prosecutions

A private prosecution is a criminal court action by an individual or a private organisation against someone or some organisation which they believe has done them wrong, and broken the law in doing so. The aim may be to gain compensation, to get a public admission of guilt or indeed to publicise a wrongdoing and encourage a change in the law. The right to bring a private prosecution is given in the Prosecution of Offences Act 1985. However, the Crown Prosecution Service also has the right to take over the prosecution (in the public interest) and either continue it, stop it or allow it to continue as a private prosecution.

Private prosecutions are not the same as civil actions where a person seeks compensation for a wrong through the *civil* courts. Civil actions are much more likely to succeed than private prosecutions. People can bring civil proceedings against public authorities such as the police under, say, the Human Rights Act 1998 and will, if they are eligible, receive financial help through legal aid.

Plea bargaining

Accused persons are expected to plead guilty or not guilty to the offence with which they are charged. **Plea bargaining** is the process of giving the defendant a more lenient sentence if they plead guilty in advance of a case. It has traditionally been illegal in Britain (but is widely practised in the US). There have been suggestions that it should be introduced in England and Wales for fraud cases (which are difficult and expensive to try) and terrorist offences (in order to get more information without having to make it public in court).

activity
GROUP WORK
17.6

P4

Design and produce a flow chart showing clearly the procedures that have to be gone through before a trial in a particular kind of criminal court, in relation to a named offence. (If you are being assessed, provide evidence of your own research and input into the project.)

How the criminal trial process works in both Magistrates' and Crown Courts

Magistrates' court

Ninety-seven per cent of criminal cases are tried in a magistrates' court.

Summary trial process

In a summary trial (the kind of trial which takes place at a magistrates' court), the charge is read out to the defendant who is asked whether they are pleading guilty or not guilty to the charge. If they plead guilty the magistrates make a decision on the sentence, and there is no need for lawyers to argue the case. If the defendant pleads not guilty the prosecuting solicitor outlines the case and, perhaps with witnesses, shows that the evidence proves that the defendant is guilty of the charge beyond reasonable doubt. The defence solicitor then argues either that the defendant is not guilty of any crime, not guilty of the crime they have been charged with, or (even if he or she is guilty) that there are reasons why the person should only receive a lenient sentence. After hearing the arguments and listening to the witnesses (if any) the three magistrates usually go into a back room and decide whether the defendant is guilty and, if so, what the sentence should be. They then come out and the chief magistrate, often a district judge, gives the verdict and the sentence. Sometimes there are social workers' and other reports linked to the case. These are called 'pre-sentence reports'. If the magistrates have not had time to look at them (e.g. because they were submitted late) the case may have to be adjourned until a later date before a decision is reached.

Guilty pleas; not guilty pleas

Everybody who is being tried at a criminal court has to say before the trial whether they are (or believe they are) guilty of the offence they have been charged with. This is called a plea. If a person pleads guilty the argument in the case can be left out, and the person is sentenced. If someone pleads not guilty then the trial, with the prosecution and defence arguments and witnesses, goes ahead.

Triable either way offences

A range of offences of medium seriousness are called **triable either way** offences because they can be tried either in a magistrates' court or in the Crown Court. Offences

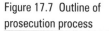
You will be able to get useful and interesting information by visiting your local courts and talking to the people who work there.

Figure 17.7 Outline of prosecution process

Source: Adapted from 'A guide to the criminal justice system in England and Wales, RDS communication and Development Unit', Home Office, 2000

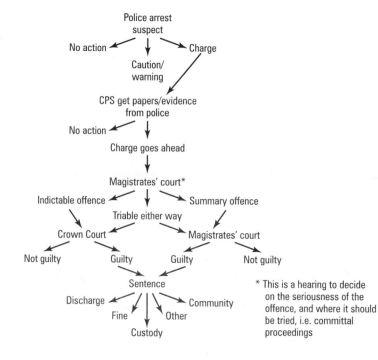

of this type include assaults causing injury, theft and burglary. The defendant (together with a solicitor) can choose which court to be tried in (though this right may be abolished before long). Equally the magistrates' court – which considers the situation at the person's first attendance – may decide where such a case should be tried.

Plea before venue

This is the process of making a plea in a magistrates' court, described in the previous paragraph. Statistically, defendants who have a choice between a magistrates' and Crown Court hearing get a better deal (on average) in the Crown Court, because juries tend to be more lenient than magistrates. However, the choice is a gamble because the Crown Court can give much heavier sentences, and the defendant may (if he or she is paying a lawyer) end up paying much higher costs.

Mode of trial

This refers to whether the trial takes place in the Crown Court or a magistrates' court.

Defendant's election

This is the choice by the defendant in an either-way case to have the case heard in front of a jury (i.e. in the Crown Court) rather than by magistrates. 'Election' here simply means 'choice'.

Committal proceedings

This is the proper name for the first attendance of a defendant at a magistrates' court. All defendants, however serious their crime, have to attend a magistrates' court first so that a decision can be made as to which kind of court they should be tried in. Normally these proceedings are secret in the sense that they cannot be reported in the media unless the defendant wishes to have them reported (which rarely happens).

Role of the legal adviser (clerk)

The legal adviser, formerly known as the 'clerk of the court', is a legally qualified person, usually a solicitor, who advises the magistrates about the law. The role is needed because most magistrates do not have formal legal training: their training is in how to be a magistrate, not in the law as such.

Youth courts

These are branches of magistrates' courts and deal with all except the most serious cases involving offences by young people. The magistrates are given special training and the hearings are in private.

remember

Youth courts deal with people aged 10–17.

Role of lay magistrates

Lay magistrates are magistrates with no formal legal training. Their role is to listen to cases and help decide whether defendants are guilty and what sentence (if any) is suitable for the defendant. Lay magistrates work part time, for a minimum of 26 half-day sittings each year (i.e. about once a fortnight). On a typical magistrates' 'bench' (three seats at the front of the court) there are two lay magistrates and one legally qualified district judge. Magistrates ideally come from a range of social, economic, cultural and ethnic backgrounds so that they can have a balanced view of crime. In practice, a disproportionate number of lay magistrates in most places are white, middle class and middle aged. The fact that they are lay people is important: their job is to see offenders and offences as normal well-meaning and law-abiding members of the public would do, and so give sentences which are within the limits laid down by law and are what most people would think was reasonable or just in the circumstances.

Role of district judge

The **district judge** is a legally trained magistrate. Before 2000, district judges were called stipendiary magistrates. They are full time, unlike lay magistrates, and receive a full salary. The district judge's role is often to 'take the chair', i.e. to act as chief magistrate. District judges can also listen to cases alone, and make their decisions about them without the assistance of the other two magistrates. District judges often work in the bigger cities or specialise in longer and more complex cases.

The role of a district judge in a magistrates' court should not be confused with that of the district judges who sit in county courts and who deal with civil law.

Crown Court

> **remember**
>
> 'Crown Court' is always singular, and always has capital Cs.

There are 78 branches of the Crown Court in England and Wales. The cases they deal with are serious ones, which are sent to them after a committal hearing in a magistrates' court. They deal with any offence for which the sentence can be more than six months' imprisonment or a £5000 fine.

Trial by jury

A jury is a group of 12 people chosen at random, using the **electoral roll**, who are then called to a court to decide the outcome of a case. Juries are used mainly in the Crown Court but can occasionally be used in a civil court to help decide a complex case such as a libel case, and they can also be used in the coroner's court. The role of the jury is to listen to a trial in an unbiased way and, using the evidence and any points made during the summing up by the prosecution, the defence and the judge, decide whether the defendant is guilty or not guilty of the offence with which they have been charged. The conclusion is reached after the trial when the jury go into a room to discuss what they have heard. They aim to reach a unanimous verdict, i.e. one on which they all agree. However, for some cases the jury may be able to decide a case by reaching a majority verdict of, say, 10 to two if the judge agrees. If the jury cannot reach even a majority verdict it is said to be split (or 'hung'). When this happens the jury is dismissed and the judge may order a retrial.

Implications of trial by jury

The implications of trial by jury are:

- That it is morally right for people to be able to judge the guilt of their peers (equals).
- That it is an acceptable duty of a citizen to carry out jury service.
- That ordinary people have enough understanding, common sense and goodwill to make a fair judgment on criminal cases.
- That the majority are usually right.

In the English system of justice there is a long tradition of using juries, and a general belief (despite some serious miscarriages of justice) that juries are usually correct in their decisions.

Composition of the jury

A jury is composed of 12 people aged between 18 and 70 who have lived in Britain for at least five years since the age of 13 and are registered as voters on the electoral roll. They must not be mentally disordered or disqualified from jury service because of criminal convictions.

People can be excused or have their jury service deferred for a number of reasons, e.g. for being police or prison officers or being in the armed forces.

See Book 1, Unit 22, pages 388–390

Juries are vetted using police checks to ensure that nobody sitting on them is a convicted criminal. Barristers for the prosecution or defence can challenge a juror if they appear to be biased, or there is a clear reason why they might be biased, in a particular case.

Juries Act 1974

This is the law which governs how juries are run in England and Wales at the present time.

The issues that the Act covers are:

- Qualification for jury service.
- **Summoning**. The electoral register is the basis for jury selection.
- Withdrawal or alteration of jury summonses.
- Jury panels (lists of people summoned).
- Summoning in exceptional circumstances.
- Attendance and service.
- Excusal for previous jury service.
- Excusal for certain persons and discretionary excusal.
- Discharge of people incapable of acting as jurors.
- The ballot and swearing of jurors.
- Challenge.
- Separation (of juries).
- Views (e.g. crime scenes).
- Refreshment.
- Continuation of criminal trial on death or discharge of juror.
- Majority verdicts.
- Judgments: stay or reversal.
- Payment for jury service.
- Offences (things jurors should not do).

At the end there are lists, called schedules, which give further details of:

- Persons ineligible (by profession).
- Persons disqualified (by criminal record).
- People 'excusable as of right' (e.g. MPs and doctors).

The full Act can be found at www.justice.gov.uk

Criminal Justice Act 2003

case study 17.14

Reasons for not having a trial by jury

The condition is that the complexity of the trial or the length of the trial (or both) is likely to make the trial so burdensome to the members of a jury hearing the trial that the interests of justice require that serious consideration should be given to the question of whether the trial should be conducted without a jury.

Source: Criminal Justice Act 2003, Section 43

activity
GROUP WORK

Do you think this is a sufficient reason to deny defendants the right of trial by jury? Explain your viewpoint.

The Criminal Justice Act 2003 made the following changes to the provisions of the Jury Act 1974:

1. Certain complex fraud cases can be conducted without a jury.

2. Serious crime trials can be conducted without a jury if the judge thinks there is a risk of jury tampering (e.g. jury members being bribed or intimidated by people linked to the accused).

3. A judge who believes a jury has been tampered with can discharge the jury and either continue the case without a jury or terminate the case.

Advantages and disadvantages of the jury system

These are largely a matter of personal or public opinion. It is not possible to compare the effectiveness of different trial procedures in the way that scientists might compare the effectiveness of different washing powders. The following are suggestions.

Advantages:

- The jury system is largely popular with the public.

- The system is believed to act as a safeguard for the defendant's human rights.

- The system involves the community in its own justice.

Disadvantages:

- Juries chosen from the electoral role are predominantly white, middle class and not young, and therefore they fail to represent some communities.

- Juries can make wrong decisions due to having naïve attitudes and a lack of specialised knowledge, especially when dealing with fraud and other unfamiliar types of crime.

- The system disrupts the lives and work of the jurors.

- Dominant personalities in a jury may force members to agree to verdicts they do not really accept.

- Juries can be tampered with or 'nobbled' in various ways.

- The majority may not always be right.

- The system is fairly costly to run.

Sentencing powers

A sentence is a punishment which is given by a court to an offender. Sentences vary in type and seriousness according to the type and seriousness of the offence, the type of

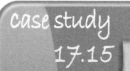

A jury's understanding

case study 17.15

Gentlemen of the jury, the facts of this distressing and important case have already been put before you some four or five times, twice by prosecuting counsel, twice by counsel for the defence, and once at least by each of the various witnesses who have been heard; but so low is my opinion of your understanding that I think it necessary, in the simplest language, to tell you the facts again.

Source: Herbert, A.P. (2001) Uncommon Law. House of Stratus, UK
(first published 1935)

activity
GROUP WORK

What are the implied criticisms of the jury system in this extract, and how valid do you think they are?

court at which the defendant appears and the circumstances of the defendant. There are very many different kinds of sentence (see below). Many of them involve restrictions of freedom.

The courts also have the power to impose fines on certain types of offender. If these are not paid, then the offender is likely to be imprisoned.

Adult Court Bench Book (2006) Judicial Studies Board (www.jsboard.co.uk/ magistrates/adult_court/index.htm)

Magistrates' court sentencing powers and limitations

The maximum custodial sentence that a magistrates' court can impose is six months' imprisonment. The maximum fine is £5000 for an adult offender, £1000 for a person under 18 and £250 for a person under 14.

Crown Court sentencing and restrictions

The Crown Court can impose sentences of up to and including life imprisonment, and for major crimes it can also impose an unlimited fine. However, fines cannot be imposed for the crimes of murder and treason.

Murder carries a 'mandatory life sentence' – in other words, the sentence has to be life imprisonment. There is at present a good deal of uncertainty, though, on what life imprisonment actually means, since in England and Wales it rarely means a whole lifetime. In practice it usually means a minimum of 15 years spent behind bars, followed by a release on licence. If the murder is especially shocking the judge can recommend a 'whole life order' under Section 269 of the Criminal Justice Act 2003.

> **remember**
>
> The case of Ian Huntley and the Soham murders has led to much discussion about 'whole life' sentences. Whole life can mean 40 or more years in prison.

Range of sentences available

The courts have a vast range of sentences, or even combinations of sentences (such as imprisonment and a fine together), at their disposal.

A government body, the Sentencing Guidelines Council, was formed in 2004. It brings out online booklets called Guidelines which give detailed information on sentences or '**tariffs**' and the ways in which these sentences can be varied according to the circumstances of the case.

Many offences carry maximum sentences. For example, under the Misuse of Drugs Act 1971, Section 5(2): 'It is an offence for a person to have a controlled drug in his possession'. This is an either-way offence. The maximum sentence for this offence at a magistrates' court is either six months' imprisonment or £5000 fine. But at the Crown

---

case study 17.16 | Purposes of a sentence

The purposes of a sentence are:

- Punishment
- Reduction of crime
- Reform and rehabilitation
- Protection of the public
- Reparation.

Source: Judicial Studies Board

activity
INDIVIDUAL WORK

Explain what each of these purposes means and how it might work.

Court the maximum sentence for the same offence is either seven years' imprisonment or a £5000 fine.

For any given offence magistrates or judges have considerable freedom to vary the sentence as long as it does not exceed the maximum sentence allowed under the law. Within these statutory limits the seriousness of an offence is measured by:

- Culpability – how much is the offender to blame?
- Harm – how much was the victim harmed by the offence?

The Sentencing Guidelines Council publishes lists of 'aggravating' and 'mitigating' factors which judges and magistrates should consider once they have a general idea of the offender's culpability and the harm done by the offence. **Aggravating** factors, e.g. 'use of a weapon to frighten or injure a victim', are circumstances which make the offence more serious than it would normally be. **Mitigating** factors, e.g. 'the fact that the offender played only a minor role in the offence', reduce the seriousness of the offence and may lead to a more lenient sentence.

Sentences can be reduced if defendants plead guilty at an early opportunity. This is, in effect, a reward for showing that they realise they have done wrong. Credit is also sometimes given for willing cooperation with the police or other authorities.

There are also sentencing 'thresholds'. These are levels of seriousness above which a custodial sentence, for example, is appropriate. The rule is:

> 'Having assessed the seriousness of an individual offence, sentencers must consult the sentencing guidelines for an offence of that type for guidance on the factors that are likely to indicate whether a custodial sentence or other disposal is most likely to be appropriate.'

Types of sentence include the following:

- Deferred sentence.
- Conditional/absolute discharge.
- Community sentences.
- Imprisonment.
- Suspended prison sentence.
- Fine.
- Compensation order.
- Deprivation or forfeiture order.
- Disqualification (driving).
- **Restitution**.
- Binding over to be of good behaviour.

www.jsboard.co.uk/downloads/acbb_complete_07.pdf **Magistrates' Bench Book**
www.sentencing-guidelines.gov.uk/docs/Guilty_plea_guideline.pdf
www.lawteacher.net/lawcases.html

Appeals from criminal courts

The law is not perfect, and the courts can make mistakes, for example by passing a guilty verdict when a person is innocent or by giving too harsh or too lenient a sentence. The process of **appeal** is used when there is reason to believe that a court has made a mistake and that there has been 'a miscarriage of justice'.

See page 353 below for more on 'grounds of appeal'

Figure 17.8 Prison: the harshest sentence given by the British courts

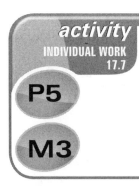

activity

INDIVIDUAL WORK 17.7

P5

M3

Visit the magistrates' and Crown Court and take notes of one or more trials in each. Then write a report of a trial in a magistrates' court and a trial in the Crown Court, describing what happens in all of the different stages. In the report's conclusion you should give a detailed comparison of the two processes. Your report should be suitable for informing volunteers who work in a legal advice centre for young people.

Figure 17.9 has the highest courts at the top. Arrows show which higher court hears appeals from which lower court. The Divisional Court is a section of the High Court. The Court of Appeal has a Civil and a Criminal division.

Appeals from magistrates' court to the Crown Court

An appeal against a decision of a magistrates' court has to reach the Crown Court in writing not later than 21 days after the decision. Grounds of appeal must be given. The magistrates' court officer sends the appeal to the Crown Court. The magistrates have to send relevant court records. The Crown Court fixes a hearing and informs the appellant, the magistrates' court officer and any other interested person. There is no jury in an appeal of this kind – the case is heard by a Crown Court judge and two magistrates.

www.ccrc.gov.uk/

Figure 17.9 The criminal courts structure, showing routes of appeal

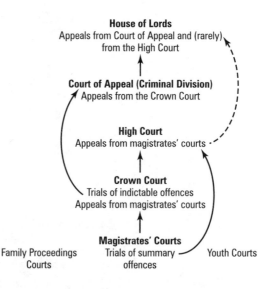

Appeals to the Queen's Bench Divisional Court by way of case stated

Divisional courts and administrative courts are parts of the High Court. Both are able to deal with appeals from magistrates' courts. The difference between the two types of court is that administrative courts have only one judge, while divisional courts usually have two. Appeals from magistrates' courts, sometimes called judicial reviews, are usually heard by a divisional court.

The High Court will hear appeals from magistrates' courts if they are based on a possible misinterpretation by a magistrates' court of a point of law. The appeal is done 'by way of case stated'. A stated case is an outline of a case in which the main points agreed on by both the prosecution and the defence can be included. A case stated by the magistrates' court for an appeal to the High Court has to state the facts found by the court and the question or questions of law or jurisdiction on which the opinion of the High Court is sought. Unfortunately for the appellant, an appeal of this sort disqualifies the person from appealing to the Appeal Court (Criminal Division) (see below).

Further appeals to the House of Lords

The House of Lords will probably be replaced by a Supreme Court in 2009, which will take over the House of Lords' traditional role as the 'highest court in the land'. At present (2007) the House of Lords hears appeals on major cases which are of public importance or interest, especially if it is likely that some binding ruling (decision that other courts must follow) is needed on a difficult legal point. Appeals to the House of Lords usually come from the Court of Appeal but can, in exceptional cases, come from the High Court.

Appeals from the Crown Court by the defendant

Appeals against apparently wrong decisions by the Crown Court can go to the Court of Appeal. The system is shown in Figure 17.10.

The first part of the process is application for leave (permission) to appeal. This is considered by a single judge. If leave is refused the application can be resubmitted and reconsidered, this time by a panel of three judges.

If leave to appeal is approved either by the single judge or the panel of three, there is an appeal hearing before a full court in the Court of Appeal. If leave to appeal is not approved, the case is referred to the Criminal Cases Review Commission, who investigate cases where they may have been a miscarriage of justice. They act as a safety net and can refer an appeal back to the Court of Appeal (Criminal Division) even after the court itself has refused leave to appeal. At the end of the process the appeal

Figure 17.10 Appeals from
the Crown court

Source: Criminal Cases Review
Committee

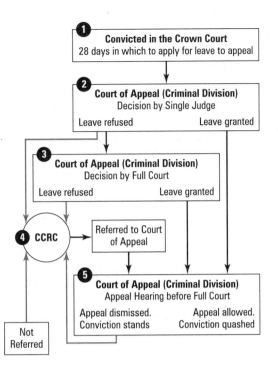

can either fail, and the Crown Court conviction stands, or it can succeed, in which case
the original conviction is **quashed** (deleted).

Appeals can also be made to the High Court from the Crown Court. As with similar
appeals from a magistrates' court the appeal has to be based on a point of law (not on
anything else, such as new evidence coming to light). The appeals application is sent
to the judge who tried the case, and the judge can then send the case stated to the
High Court. The judge has the right to refuse to state the case if he or she thinks the
application is 'frivolous' (e.g. pointless or based on a simple misunderstanding). The
judge then has to send a certificate stating reasons for refusal to the applicant. If the
High Court does not accept the refusal a 'mandatory order' can be sent, compelling the
judge to state the case.

Leave to appeal

Whether leave to appeal is granted by any higher court will depend very much on the
grounds for appeal. The grounds for appeal are the reasons why an appeal is thought to
be necessary. There are many possible grounds for appeal; below is a list of some of the
more common ones:

> *remember*
>
> It will be useful to
> invite a lawyer as
> a visiting speaker
> to discuss some of
> these grounds in
> more detail.

- Insufficient evidence.

- Refusal of no case to answer submission.

- Perverse verdict.

- Wrongful admission of evidence.

- Misdirection on evidence.

- The appearance of new evidence after the case.

- Wrong interpretation of law during trial.

Court of Appeal's powers

The Court of Appeal (Criminal Division) has the power to overturn decisions of lower
courts if an appeal by a defendant is successful. It also has the power to support appeals
which go from it to the House of Lords. In addition it can hear appeals from prosecuting
authorities against court judgments which they feel have been too lenient.

Appeals by the prosecution

Judges and even juries have a good deal of freedom and independence under the English justice system. This means that not everybody agrees with every court decision. While defendants and some human rights activists may often feel that the courts are too strict, there are others who feel that they are too lenient.

From time to time prosecuting authorities such as the Crown Prosecution Service appeal to the Court of Appeal (Criminal Division) against a court decision which they feel has been too lenient. To do this they have to write to the Attorney General (the chief legal adviser to the government) stating details of the case and reasons why they are not happy with the court's decision. There is a concern among politicians and the Attorney General that the courts sometimes let off offenders too lightly (especially in high-profile murder and sexual offence cases). This leads to criticism of the government from the media and the public, and goes against the government's intentions to make justice more victim friendly.

Appeals to the House of Lords

If they feel a case is deserving, even though an appeal has failed in the Court of Appeal (Criminal Division), the Court of Appeal will make an application to the House of Lords to hear the appeal themselves and come to a final decision. The procedure is either that the Court of Appeal makes an oral application to the House of Lords, or the House of Lords will itself send out an instruction called a 'practice direction' to the Registrar of the Court of Appeal, stating that they wish to hear an appeal in a particular case. This is where the case is one which has public importance, or where an important legal principle is at stake.

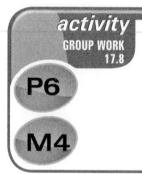

activity

GROUP WORK
17.8

P6

M4

Do a presentation suitable for police cadets or trainee community support officers summarising the sentencing powers of the criminal courts and the ways in which defence and prosecution can appeal against the outcome. Then give a more detailed explanation of a criminal court's sentencing powers and the possible grounds for appeal in particular cases, using one example from a magistrates' court and one from the Crown Court.

activity

INDIVIDUAL WORK
17.9

D2

Write a full report on the procedures used in the criminal courts before, during and after trials, assessing how effective all of these procedures are in ensuring justice both for the community and for the defendant. Your report should be suitable as an information resource for use by volunteers in a citizens' advice bureau.

Progress Check

1. State the six circumstances in which an arrest is lawful.
2. State the main differences between police powers of arrest and a citizen's power of arrest.
3. When are arrests carried out:
   (a) With a warrant?
   (b) Without a warrant?
4. Outline the rules about how long a suspect can be kept in custody before being charged.
5. Give five rights of an arrested person.
6. State the rights of suspects during police questioning.
7. Give eight rules that the police should follow when stopping and searching someone.
8. What are the main requirements of a search warrant?
9. What can a member of the public do if their house is unlawfully searched by the police?
10. What is conditional bail? State five possible conditions.
11. Explain, with examples, the differences between exclusion, exemption and deferral in relation to jury service.
12. What is the role of a duty solicitor?
13. Explain the Full Code Test and the Threshold Test, as carried out by Crown prosecutors.
14. Outline the differences between summary, either-way and indictable offences.
15. State the five purposes of a sentence.
16. Name 10 kinds of sentence.

UNIT 18

Understanding Behaviour in Public Sector Employment

This unit covers:

- Different approaches to psychology and their benefits to public services
- Different types of communication behaviour
- Possible areas of conflict between individual and group behaviour
- The different ways of overcoming possible conflicts between groups and individuals through the use of effective conflict management techniques

This unit is about understanding how people behave, and using that understanding in public service work.

It begins with an introduction to psychology and the different theories psychologists have put forward to try to explain human behaviour.

The unit then goes on to explore the different ways in which we can deal with other people. In particular it shows how we can get our point of view across in an effective and acceptable manner.

The third part of the unit analyses conflict – arguments, disagreements and protests – investigating how and why conflict happens.

The final part outlines methods of reducing or resolving conflict which are used in the public services.

To achieve a **pass** grade the evidence must show that the learner is able to:	To achieve a **merit** grade the evidence must show that, in addition to the pass criteria, the learner is able to:	To achieve a **distinction** grade the evidence must show that, in addition to the pass and merit criteria, the learner is able to:
P3 describe the benefits of understanding approaches to psychology within the public services Pg 369	**M3** compare the effectiveness of two different methods of overcoming conflict between individuals working in any area of public service employment Pg 396	
P4 describe the types of, and reasons for, conflict in the public services Pg 390		
P5 describe ways of overcoming conflict between groups and individuals Pg 390		

Different approaches to psychology and their benefits to public services

The public sector includes all government-run public services and any other agencies or activities paid for by the taxpayer or government.

Psychology is a word which is often used and easily misunderstood. It comes from ancient Greek words which mean 'study of the mind'. For many people, though, it has come to mean the study of human behaviour.

The main reason for this split in meaning is that some people believe that the mind, including ideas and consciousness, can be studied, while other people believe that the mind is a set of experiences which is different for each one of us, and is therefore too personal or subjective to be studied.

Approaches

Approaches are theories or ways of thinking about a subject.

The different approaches to psychology can be separated into two main types:

- Those which claim it is possible to study the mind directly by focusing on what people think and believe.

- Those which claim that the mind cannot be studied: all we can study is what people do, and how they behave, and in particular how they respond to stimuli.

These types are subdivided into named 'theories' or 'schools of psychology'. Because their ideas are not fixed, and because psychology is about people and can never be a science in the sense that, say, chemistry is, these different theories are often called 'approaches'.

Humanistic

Humanistic psychology is a set of beliefs that affirm (uphold) the value of the individual and the ability of individuals to understand and solve their own problems.

The *Collins English Dictionary* defines humanistic psychology as 'psychology that emphasises feelings and emotions and the better understanding of the self in terms of observation of oneself and one's relations with others'.

Humanistic psychology includes the following ideas:

■ The individual's own perceptions, experiences, thoughts, inner feelings and self-image are the key to understanding that individual.

■ People are inherently good, and are capable of development and self-improvement.

■ People have inbuilt intentions: consciousness is directed by something within the self.

■ Everybody seeks meaning, value and creativity.

■ People are not machines or animals; each of us is a conscious, unique individual.

■ People have choices and responsibilities and are aware of them.

■ People are best understood through 'qualitative research' based on their perceived experiences (not 'quantitative research' such as surveys or experiments).

■ What we think about ourselves and about the world is more important than the theories or beliefs that other people might try to impose on us.

■ It is healthy for people to believe in their own value and potential goodness.

Criticisms of humanistic psychology are as follows:

■ It takes people's feelings, ideas and beliefs at face value.

■ It makes statements which are unscientific because they cannot be shown to be false.

■ It contains ideas such as 'self-actualisation' which have never been clearly defined.

■ It can suggest that people are not mentally ill when they are.

■ It appears to support the status quo (it makes no attempt to change, question or improve society).

The most famous humanist psychologists are Abraham Maslow and Carl Rogers.

Abraham Maslow, 1908–70

Maslow is famous for his theory of human needs, which he expresses as a hierarchy or pyramid. At the bottom he has 'deficit needs', which are needs based on a lack of life's essentials. In his view thirst is a classic deficit need; it expresses itself as a need for something (water) which is lacking. As a need it is even lower in the pyramid than hunger because (he argues) a person who is both hungry and thirsty will drink first. This is because people can live for months without food, but can only live a day or two without water.

According to Maslow the basic needs are physiological (bodily) needs, and these have to be satisfied first before other needs which come higher in the pyramid can be satisfied. But once a person's needs for food, water, shelter and rest have been fulfilled, Maslow argued that a condition of 'homeostasis' (balance) has been reached in these needs, and a human being then starts reaching up the pyramid to satisfy more complex needs. Thus a person who has food, drink and shelter starts thinking about safety (e.g. living not in a tent but in a house with a lockable door). When this need is satisfied, the person has belonging needs – the need to belong to a community. At this stage, people are keen to conform and fit in, rather as new recruits to the army might actively want to have their hair cut so it is the same length as everybody else's. Belonging needs may also include needs to have a family or some close companionship. When these needs too have been satisfied a person looks for esteem, that is, respect or admiration from others. This is like the reasonably well-off married person who starts looking for promotion and advancement at work – all of the needs lower down the pyramid having been satisfied. The same needs might be satisfied by becoming captain of a sports team or chairperson of a committee. When all of these needs have been satisfied Maslow argued that some people (about 2% in his view) wish to achieve some higher aim, some form of intellectual and emotional fulfilment which he calls 'self-actualisation'. He considered that people such as great artists, scientists and humanitarian figures come into this category.

This theory, especially the part about self-actualisation, sounds elitist to many people nowadays, and suggests that the people Maslow most admired were people like himself. (He was a respected university professor in the US.) But nevertheless in the 1950s, '60s and '70s his theory was highly influential in changing the ways businesses and other organisations (such as public services) were run. Out went the old authoritarian systems where people were motivated by being threatened with the sack if they did not toe the line. In came new systems of management where people were given responsibility and the chance to earn the esteem which was (Maslow had suggested) a far better motivator at this level than fear. The productivity figures in industries and other workplaces where Maslow's ideas were applied went up and that suggested there was a good deal of truth in Maslow's theory.

(See more on page 369 below.)

Figure 18.1 Maslow's pyramid of human needs

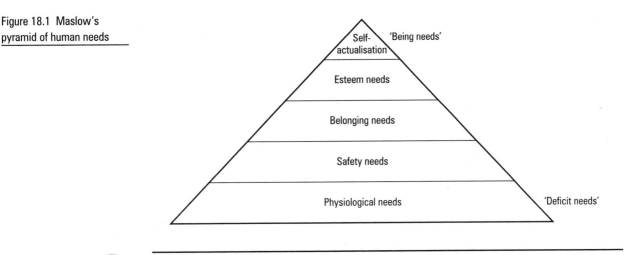

 http://webspace.ship.edu/cgboer/maslow.html

Carl Rogers, 1902–87

Carl Rogers was an American psychiatrist, attempting to heal people's mental illnesses by **counselling** and **psychotherapy**. His work was influenced by, but at the same time reacted against, the work of Sigmund Freud (see below).

Unlike Freud, who believed there were violent destructive forces hidden in the human mind, Rogers believed people are basically good and healthy and that they are inclined to have a correct view of themselves. He therefore saw the negative features of people's lives, such as mental illness and criminality, as abnormal and against the natural constructive tendency that most people have. He believed that people are motivated towards good actions and towards bettering themselves by a built-in life force which we all have and which he called 'the actualising tendency'. He believed that human history, with its progress towards 'civilisation', development and a more caring attitude towards other people, was evidence of that tendency.

Rogers based both his own thinking and the therapy he gave his patients on three principles:

1. Congruence – genuineness, honesty with the client.

2. Empathy – the ability to feel what the client feels.

3. Respect – acceptance, unconditional positive regard towards the client.

'Unconditional positive regard' means that the therapist should treat the client or patient in an uncritical way, showing goodwill at all times. The therapist should never impose conditions such as saying, 'If you do that, I will be very unhappy'. Such a statement,

Rogers believes, has a negative effect because it widens the gap between the patient's 'real' and 'ideal' selves. The real self is what the patient thinks he or she is really like; the ideal self is what the patient wants to be like. The '**incongruence**' caused by the difference between real and ideal selves is what causes neurosis (mild mental illness). If the difference is very great it causes psychosis (serious mental illness of the type that used to be called 'madness').

Rogers called his therapy 'non-directive' or 'client-centred'. He would not contradict or advise his clients. His technique was one of reflection – saying something which was more or less what the patient said, but using slightly different words, intended to encourage the patient to go on speaking. The long-term aim was to get patients to cure themselves by drawing out their 'goodness' and 'self-knowledge' so that, in effect, they cured themselves.

Rogers' work has been very influential in psychotherapy and counselling. To some extent 'Rogerian counsellors' mimic the behaviour of true friends, by avoiding critical and destructive comments. The aim is to build confidence, improve people's self esteem, and so make them feel better about themselves. When they feel good about themselves, patients or clients will be able to resolve their own problems.

The advantages of Rogerian counselling are:

- It is less difficult to carry out than most other types of counselling, psychotherapy or psychiatry.
- Even if it does not work it is unlikely to do serious harm.
- It can be useful in easing depression.
- It works relatively well with children and young people.

The disadvantages are:

- It will not help people who are mentally ill because of some physical or chemical (i.e. medical) problem.
- It is not effective in dealing with **phobias** and other relatively serious disorders.
- It is essentially unscientific and depends very much on the communicative skills and human sympathy of the counsellor.

John B Watson, 1878–1958

Watson was a US university professor who later went into the advertising industry. He had the idea that psychology should be studied not through people's thoughts and consciousness, but through the way they behaved.

He was influenced by experiments involving teaching rats to run through mazes and thought that human beings should be studied in similar ways. This was because **behaviour** could be observed, measured and objectively recorded but human thoughts and consciousness could not. He believed that 'psychology' which discussed thoughts and consciousness could never be a science because thoughts and consciousness could neither be predicted nor observed.

Watson established 'behaviourism' as an approach to psychology. Behaviourism is the study of animal or human behaviour in relation to its causes. To use more scientific language, it is the study of responses to stimuli. Watson was particularly interested in '**conditioning**', the idea (developed by Pavlov and Lorenz) that repeated exposure to a stimulus would create, even in people, an 'automatic' response which would become built into the person's behaviour patterns. Watson carried out a famous experiment on an orphan boy he called 'little Albert', where a supposedly unemotional and unimaginative child was conditioned to be terrified of rats. Before the experiment the child was shown not to be afraid of rats. The basis of the experiment was that every time the child saw the rat Watson caused a loud unpleasant noise to be made behind the child by clanging a metal bar. Terrified by the noise, the child cried every time he saw the rat, and before long would cry on seeing the rat even if the bar was not clanged.

remember

'Behaviourism' is spelt 'behaviorism' in US English. Most internet sites dealing with behaviourism spell it the US way.

case study 18.1 **Behaviourism**

Psychology as the behaviorist views it is a purely objective experimental branch of natural science. Its theoretical goal is the prediction and control of behavior. Introspection forms no essential part of its methods, nor is the scientific value of its data dependent upon the readiness with which they lend themselves to interpretation in terms of consciousness. The behaviorist, in his efforts to get a unitary scheme of animal response, recognizes no dividing line between man and brute ...

In a system of psychology completely worked out, given the response the stimuli can be predicted; given the stimuli the response can be predicted.

Source: Watson, John B. (1913) *Psychology as the Behaviorist Views it*. First published in Psychological Review, 20, 158–77.

 http://psychclassics.yorku.ca/index.htm

activity
GROUP WORK

What do you think are the advantages and disadvantages of trying to make psychology an 'exact science'?

The child also became terrified of anything furry. Watson believed that people could be educated and controlled using similar patterns of conditioning through stimulus and response.

Watson's aim was to make psychology a science which could be studied through hypothesis, experiment and observation like physics and chemistry and which could discover predictable rules about human behaviour. He was against the idea of making a connection between people's behaviour and their thoughts; behaviour should be studied for its own sake. Thoughts, whatever they may be, were not suitable subjects for scientific study.

Behaviourism is not humanism, and it is not interested in how people view themselves or whether they have reached a self-actualising stage, etc. Its application is in controlling behaviour and it can be linked to education, advertising and some public service work. A recent interesting example is the use of CCTV and loudspeaker announcements to stop litter dropping and minor antisocial behaviour in Middlesbrough. Opponents of behaviourism argue that it claims we have no free will and reduces us from humans to animals. They also feel that the techniques of behaviourism can be abused and used to **brainwash** people, and if applied in experiments like the 'little Albert' one, or in 'curing' mental illness, they infringe human rights.

Fritz Perls, 1893–1970
Fritz Perls, sometimes called Frederick Perls, was born in Germany but fled to South Africa, then to the US, to escape the Nazis. He is famous for pioneering work in Gestalt therapy, a form of psychotherapy which was popular from the 1950s to the 1980s and has had lasting effects not only in the treatment of mental illness but also in education and the way we see ourselves.

The origins of Gestalt therapy were in **Gestalt psychology**, a form of humanistic psychology. Gestalt psychology is humanistic because it is interested in what people think, feel and imagine.

Gestalt psychology originated in the nineteenth century and studied the way in which we process the raw material of what we see (shapes, colours and lines) together into experiences which are 'more than the sum of their parts'. Gestalt itself is a German word meaning 'a unified whole'. Gestalt psychology produced 'laws' about the ways we see our surroundings and give meanings to the things we see. Gestalt laws can be defined as principles for organising sensations. They include:

- Pragnanz – the urge to organise out perceptions into the best possible Gestalt.

- Law of closure – we will fill gaps. It looks like a rectangle even though there's a gap in it (see Figure 18.2a).

- Law of similarity – we group similar items together. We notice the line of 'o's in Figure 18.2b because they are similar:

- Law of proximity – what is close together belongs together. The dots look like a fish because they are close together (see Figure 18.2c).

- Law of symmetry – the symmetrical shapes of the paired brackets are noticed before the proximity of the back-to-back brackets (in Figure 18.2d).

- Law of continuity. We see Figure 18.2e as two continuous lines which cross, not as four lines which meet or four touching angles.

- Figure-ground. For most people the faces are noticed before the vase in Figure 18.2f. Where a more meaningful image is next to a less meaningful one, we notice the meaningful one first and imagine it is closer to us.

Gestalt therapy, as developed by Fritz Perls, his wife Laura Perls and their associates in the 1950s, stressed the importance of how we perceive and experience things rather than what we know or have been taught they are. The aim is to develop self-awareness. Gestalt therapists interact with patients and try to share their experiences. The object is to achieve 'insight', a sudden understanding of the interacting sensations and emotions which go to make up a person's life (or their perception of their life). This type of therapy was often used to give deeper meaning to the lives of clients who were not mentally ill, rather than to treat patients who had been diagnosed as mentally ill.

Gestalt therapy was popular in the 'swinging sixties'. Because it broke down barriers between therapist and client it has been criticised for encouraging unethical or unprofessional behaviour when carried out by the wrong kinds of people. However, its

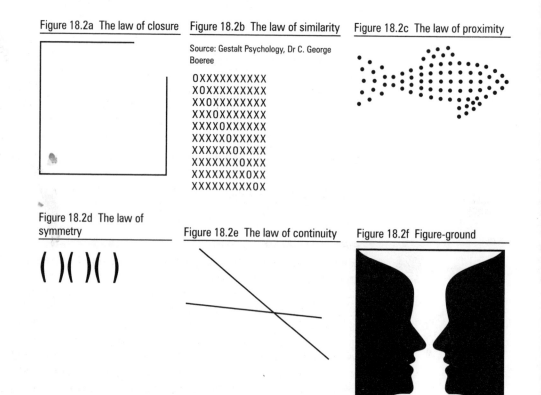

Figure 18.2a The law of closure

Figure 18.2b The law of similarity

Source: Gestalt Psychology, Dr C. George Boeree

```
OXXXXXXXXXX
XOXXXXXXXXX
XXOXXXXXXXX
XXXOXXXXXXX
XXXXOXXXXXX
XXXXXOXXXXX
XXXXXXOXXXX
XXXXXXXOXXX
XXXXXXXXOXX
XXXXXXXXXOX
```

Figure 18.2c The law of proximity

Figure 18.2d The law of symmetry

( )( )( )

Figure 18.2e The law of continuity

Figure 18.2f Figure-ground

emphasis on interaction and active involvement gives it some value in education since the theory of it is related to active learning and also to 'conductive education' and other methods used to help children with severe learning difficulties.

Cognitive

The word '**cognitive**' means learning. Cognitive psychology is therefore psychology which relates to learning and understanding. Many psychologists have been interested in the process of learning; perhaps the most famous is Jean Piaget (1896–1980) who studied the mental development of children and broke it down into a number of stages. More modern cognitive psychology is about things like problem solving, and the thought-related aspects of the kind of **stimulus**-response actions that were studied by the behaviourists. Cognitive psychology has been of great interest to educationalists and theorists as it has shown how different people learn in different ways, and how learning is a cyclical process. This has affected the way syllabuses (including your BTEC specifications) have been designed.

Cognitive psychology is concerned with making valid rules and generalisations about learning processes. This may sound limiting, but in fact it is arguable that nearly all kinds of human behaviour are learned in some way or other. Cognitive psychology has also given rise to an important type of psychotherapy (a way of treating mental conditions through talking with patients). This is called cognitive behavioural therapy. Cognitive behavioural therapy has a wide range of practical applications and is now the most popular form of psychotherapy in Britain.

Like most forms of psychotherapy, cognitive behavioural therapy originated in the US. The two main inventors of the technique were Aaron Beck and Albert Ellis.

Beck, born 1921

Aaron T. Beck made a name for himself as a psychiatrist and a professor of psychiatry in the US. He has used cognitive therapy to treat a wide range of problems including **depression**, suicide, anxiety disorders, panic disorders, alcoholism, drug abuse and personality disorders. Others have used similar methods to treat eating disorders, phobias and **post-traumatic stress disorder**. The therapy can be used by itself or in conjunction with programmes of medication to treat serious psychiatric disorders such as bipolar disorder (formerly known as manic depression) and schizophrenia.

The aim of cognitive therapy is to treat sufferers of conditions such as anxiety and depression by showing them how to increase objectivity and get rid of destructive thinking. Put simply, it teaches them how to think more realistically and positively about their situation, to identify the things that can be changed and the things that cannot be changed, and to teach them strategies for putting this new knowledge into practice. This element of teaching distinguishes cognitive therapy from other kinds of psychotherapy, which work by revealing inner mental truths and enabling patients to cure themselves.

Another of Beck's contributions was to create lists of identifying characteristics of people with certain kinds of mental problem. These he called 'inventories' and they include his Depression Inventory, Anxiety Inventory, Hopelessness Scale and Suicide Intent Scale. These inventories enabled at-risk people to be identified and treated at an early stage of their mental illness.

Ellis, 1913–2007

Albert Ellis is the originator of Rational Emotive Behavior Therapy. This helps clients to learn about the attitudes, expectations and personal rules which are causing them distress. The aim of Ellis's form of cognitive behavioural therapy is to develop in patients a philosophy and approach to life that will help them with work, living with others, parenting, education, etc. The therapist, through examining the patient's past and present difficulties, tries to stop them from taking things too personally. Patients are given methods and ideas to help them think more realistically and calmly. The approach is cognitive in that it develops the patient's understanding, and behavioural in that it teaches ways of using that new understanding to solve the patient's problems. Activities such as homework and skills training are included in Ellis's cognitive behavioural therapy. Skills taught and practised include communication skills and assertiveness. Patients are given individual plans to tackle their particular difficulties.

An interesting feature of Ellis's methods is the use of ideas from ancient philosophers such as Marcus Aurelius and Epictetus to help give patients a calmer and more balanced approach to their own problems.

Cognitive behavioural therapy is more practical and down-to-earth than most other kinds of therapy. It addresses specific problems and proposes definite solutions. It moves from examining the patient's thoughts to setting tasks for the patient such as keeping a diary and practising new and less self-destructive thinking and behaviour. In this way it plans for the future after therapy, so that the gains made are not lost later. Unlike most humanist therapies which deal with thinking and self-image, cognitive behavioural therapy blends thought and action. The clear focus of cognitive behavioural therapy, and the emphasis on practical outcomes, which are observable and measurable, have made it the most widely used form of psychotherapy.

Psychoanalytic (e.g. Freud)

Freud, 1856–1939

Sigmund Freud lived most of his life in Vienna, Austria and died in England. He was a pioneer of psychiatry, and by studying his patients he developed many theories about the development of workings of the human mind. He wrote a number of highly influential books whose effects spread well beyond the fields of psychology and psychotherapy.

Below is a list of some of Freud's main ideas:

1. Topography of the mind (i.e. a surface view):

    (a) The conscious mind. This includes everything we know here and now.

    (b) The preconscious mind. This is knowledge and memory which is easily accessible even though we are not thinking about it at the moment.

    (c) The unconscious mind. Experiences, ideas and emotions which we have forgotten (or think we have forgotten). The unconscious mind is 'bigger' than the conscious and preconscious mind, and though we may not be directly aware of it, it deeply influences our emotions and our desires.

2. Structure of the mind. Freud divides the world of the mind into three parts: the ego, the super-ego and the id.

    (a) The id ('it' in Latin) is there at birth; the other parts develop later. The id follows the pleasure principle, is a mass of unfulfilled desires, and has no morality.

    (b) The ego ('I' in Latin). This is the conscious and rational part of our minds. It follows the reality principle and examines reality in order to ensure survival.

    (c) Super-ego – this is the conscience (based on punishment) and also the 'perfect self' (based on rewards). This is the moral part of the mind.

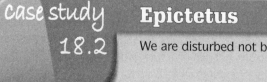

case study 18.2   **Epictetus**

We are disturbed not by events, but by the views which we take of them.

Source: Epictetus, AD 100

activity
GROUP WORK   With a friend, discuss a situation which has happened to you and where this statement of Epictetus could have applied.

Figure 18.3 Topography and structure of the mind – Freud's ideas: the 'iceberg' model

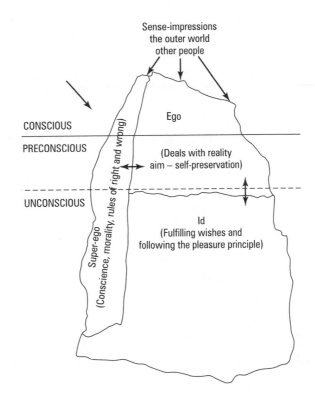

Sense-impressions
the outer world
other people

CONSCIOUS

Ego

PRECONSCIOUS

(Deals with reality
aim – self-preservation)

UNCONSCIOUS

Super-ego
(Conscience, morality, rules of right and wrong)

Id
(Fulfilling wishes and
following the pleasure principle)

According to Freud, mental illness is caused by the id and the super-ego disturbing the ego. Many of these disturbances can be traced back to traumatic or painful events in early life (which have often been forgotten by the conscious mind, but which lurk in the unconscious mind). Freud identifies mental development stages that have to be passed through successfully if a person is to become a fully functioning adult. These stages are all based on 'sexual' pleasure and are shown in Table 18.1.

Table 18.1 Mental development stages identified by Freud

Stage	Age (approx.)	Explanation
Oral	0–1½	The baby gets sexual pleasure from sucking and chewing
Anal	1½–4	Sexual pleasure linked to bowel movements
Phallic	4–8	Awareness of penis in boys, lack of penis in girls
Latency	8–12	A period of relatively low sexual awareness
Genital	12–adulthood	Sexual awareness becomes firmly linked to the genital regions

Freud had a name for sexual desire: 'libido'. He also believed that people have a life-wish, which he called 'Eros' and a death-wish called 'Thanatos', and that these affect the behaviour of the libido.

Psychoanalysis

Freud developed a famous technique for treating the illnesses of his patients, which he called **psychoanalysis**. The patient lies in comfort on a couch and the psychoanalyst tries, by talking with the patient, to bring out the disturbances in the unconscious mind which are causing the mental illness. One of the most well-known methods is 'free association', where a word is spoken and the patient then responds with the first word that comes to mind. From the associated words the psychoanalyst is able to build up a picture of what is wrong with the patient. Freudian psychoanalysis also examines and interprets the patient's dreams. The overall aim is to break through the defence

One of the key problems with psychology is that we have the human mind studying itself. This makes it different from all other kinds of study.

mechanisms of the patient, achieve a realisation of what the problem is (often with an outburst of relieving emotion called 'catharsis') and so cure the condition.

Freud believed that even when patients were telling lies, they were revealing truths. If they made mistakes ('Freudian slips') they too were revealing. His methods were not scientific in the behaviourist sense, for they could not make universal predictions or produce measurable results. His ideas were not the kind of ideas that could be 'falsified' (disproved) using scientific method. Some of his opponents felt, and still do, that he made psychology into a kind of bogus religion and said all sorts of unprovable things about the human mind.

On the other hand, most modern psychologists think Freud's ideas have at least some truth in them. He mapped the mind and gave us words to describe it. His methods had a vast influence on humanistic, gestalt and even cognitive behaviourist psychotherapy. Freud argued in his books that people were not rational, that they were obsessed with sex, and they could not be easily predicted or understood. His ideas caused uproar among some religious groups and have deeply influenced generations of writers, film-makers and artists. His methods are not now the most widely used, but his ideas changed western culture and the way people think more than those of any other psychologist.

activity
INDIVIDUAL WORK 18.1

P2

Produce a leaflet suitable for trainee counsellors outlining the main types of psychology and summarising the work of one major psychologist for each approach.

Nature versus nurture

This is an ongoing argument about whether our minds, thoughts, emotions and behaviour (especially the last of these) are more influenced by **heredity** (nature) or environment (nurture).

Heredity is the process of passing down characteristics (in all living creatures) from parents to offspring through DNA, the chemical that 'encodes' many of our physical characteristics. The active parts of DNA which contain these inherited 'instructions' or 'blueprints' are called 'genes'. However, this process is more complex than it sounds because there are different types of genes (e.g. dominant and recessive), and many genetically determined characteristics such as hair colour are the product of a number of genes.

Nurture is also a complex process involving all the so-called '**agencies of social control**'. The main ones are the family, the peer group, education, the media, religion and the law.

Some characteristics such as eye colour are known to be entirely the result of heredity (nature). Nobody can bring up a child to have blue eyes! Other characteristics such as the language we speak are entirely the result of the environment we are brought up in.

Table 18.2 Nature or nurture

Nature	Both	Nurture
Eye colour	Height	Language
Sex (male or female)	Weight	Religion
	IQ scores	
	Ability at sport	

But many of our characteristics, including most of the important ones, have both genetic and environmental roots. Though it is rare for identical twins (who are genetically the same) to be split up and reared separately from birth, it has happened and the impact of the adoptive family is surprisingly strong. If one twin was well fed and the other malnourished, the well-fed one would grow significantly taller and stronger than the malnourished one. The IQ scores of adopted children on average resemble more closely the IQ scores of their adoptive parents than their biological parents (though this effect is thought to diminish when the children reach adulthood).

In these characteristics where both nature and nurture have an effect, it is very hard to distinguish which of the two is more important.

The main importance of the argument is probably a political one. Belief that nature is more important than nurture is associated in the public mind with the attempts of the German Nazis in the 1930s and 1940s to selectively breed children who would be fair-haired, blue-eyed and belong to a kind of super-race. The Nazis also exterminated six million Jews. In Britain, the 'nature' side of the belief is associated with politically right-wing thinking, while the 'nurture' side is associated with left-wing thinking. Left-wing politicians have traditionally argued that poverty and a poor environment disadvantage people, and therefore nurture matters.

> *remember*
>
> Teachers tend to stress the importance of nurture because they like to feel that they can make a difference to the children they teach.

Free will versus determinism

This argument is rather similar to the previous one, only it is about morality rather than human characteristics and abilities.

Free will is the belief that we can, and do, choose between different actions as we live our lives. **Determinism** is the belief that our actions are caused by our environment, and that we have no real control over what we do.

The two ideas both have relevance for public service work.

People who say that crime is caused by social deprivation, bad upbringing, poor education or drug habits are taking a determinist view by implying that criminals are made to commit crimes by factors that are outside their control. Modern criminology also takes a determinist view by saying that opportunity is the key factor in determining whether a crime takes place: the burglary is caused by the open window, not by the burglar freely deciding to do a wrongful act.

By contrast, nearly all religion and morality is based on the idea that people have free will, and that we can choose to do the right and wrong thing. In our everyday lives we tend to believe that we and others have choices. The law, too, takes a free-will view: the offender has a choice whether to commit crime or not, has chosen to do so, and should therefore be punished.

> *remember*
>
> From a psychological viewpoint determinism is similar to behaviourism. It says we respond to stimuli and have no choice as to how we respond.

Which is right – social science or the law? Philosophers have been worrying about free will and determinism for hundreds of years – and they still cannot agree. The common-sense position is probably that we have free will in some situations but not others. And since we have a moral sense we may well have both a right and a duty to use our free will when we can.

Benefits

The different approaches to psychology have influenced the way society operates and the way we live and work together – and this is particularly true of the public services.

For individuals

For ordinary people the effects of psychology have been mainly beneficial. Reasons include:

■ A chance to get treated effectively for various mental conditions and illnesses which appeared untreatable (e.g. post traumatic stress disorder (PTSD). In World War I (1914–18) PTSD, then called 'shell shock', led to 306 British soldiers being shot for cowardice.

Figure 18.4 Did they choose to offend, or couldn't they help it?

- An increased awareness of and sympathy for the suffering of mentally ill people among the general public.

Staff

- Staff of large organisations now have counselling and **occupational health** services which help to solve psychological problems – such as stress – which affect them either as individuals or in their work.

- Psychologists investigating **work study** (efficiency; time and motion study) and **ergonomics** (physical and mental comfort and well-being in the workplace) have made workplaces safer and less stressful.

- Psychology has led to an improved understanding of behaviour such as harassment and bullying, and ways to tackle such behaviour – both by changing the attitudes of bullies and by improving the self-esteem of people who are bullied.

- Education, training, briefing and similar activities have been made more effective as a result of research by cognitive psychologists which shows how people learn, and the range of methods that suit learners best.

- There is better treatment available for drug and addiction problems (including alcohol and smoking) as a result of psychological research.

- Psychology has wide application in policing, e.g. through crime pattern analysis, offender profiling, effective interviewing techniques and the proposed identification of people with dangerous personality disorders.

- Twenty per cent of prisoners are said to suffer from psychological disorders: an understanding of these is of clear benefit to prison officers and other workers.

Customers

Psychology is not always beneficial to customers in shops and supermarkets. This is because Freudian and other types of psychology are used in advertising, which is sometimes seen as exploiting customers by encouraging them to spend more than they can afford. Put in Freudian terms, the aim of advertising is to get under the guard of the ego, bypass the 'conscience' of the super-ego and appeal to the pleasure principle in the id, thus giving the customer a strong, partly unconscious desire to buy the product.

However, dealing effectively with the public often demands skills like those used in humanistic counselling – listening skills and the use of '**reflection**' to gain the person's goodwill. This is especially true in professions such as nursing, social work or teaching. But such skills are also used by peacekeeping forces, community support officers and anybody else who works closely with the public and hopes to get their cooperation.

For teams and organisations (e.g. motivated workforces)

The contribution of psychology to teams and organisations is mainly in the area of how people are motivated. The breakthrough was made by Abraham Maslow, who saw that people who are reasonably well paid and have friends and family are most likely to be motivated by esteem needs and self-actualisation. Esteem needs in this context are the good opinions of the rest of the team and promotion in the organisation. People's need for self-actualisation (self-fulfilment) can be satisfied by giving them more responsibility, and the power to express their creativity and individuality by making plans and decisions.

Maslow's ideas were developed and popularised by the US management expert Douglas McGregor in *The Human Side of Enterprise*.

McGregor, D. (1960) The Human Side of Enterprise, McGraw-Hill, New York (republished in 2006)

www.accel-team.com/

www.businessballs.com/

Partly thanks to humanistic psychology modern leadership is less authoritarian and more democratic or participative. This improves job satisfaction.

Team development is a learning curve which is now better practised and understood thanks to the insights of cognitive psychology. Cognitive psychology teaches that different people learn in different ways, and that active learning ('learning by doing') is often more effective than traditional methods of 'chalk and talk'.

Financial

Money as a reward for effort is a motivating factor. Rewards and their effects were closely studied by behaviourist psychologists such as J.B. Watson and B.F. Skinner. They saw behaviour as being dictated by positive and negative stimuli which operated as rewards and punishments. It was possible, for example, to teach pigeons to feed themselves by pecking a lever in their cage which released a seed (a process called operant conditioning).

In humanist psychology too money is a motivating factor, though it comes fairly low down on Maslow's hierarchy. It is therefore (according to Maslow) a more powerful motivator for people who are underpaid!

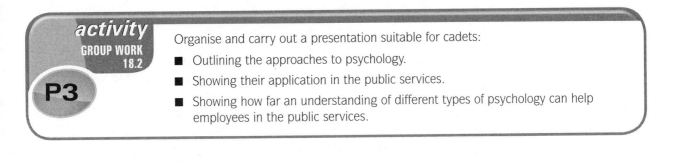

activity
GROUP WORK 18.2

P3

Organise and carry out a presentation suitable for cadets:

■ Outlining the approaches to psychology.

■ Showing their application in the public services.

■ Showing how far an understanding of different types of psychology can help employees in the public services.

Carry out research for a careers adviser on how far the different approaches to psychology, and a knowledge of those types of psychology, can affect people working in a particular public service. Your research should be presented in the form of a report.

Different types of communication behaviour

Aggressive

Aggressive behaviour is behaviour which attacks and seeks to hurt another person, either mentally or physically.

Key features

Most of us learn to recognise aggressive behaviour from our earliest years, and most of us are sometimes aggressive ourselves. Aggression – the desire to fight or to impose our will on others – is present in nearly everybody. It is an emotion which appears to be necessary for survival, and we can see aggressive behaviour not only in humans but in many animals.

There are times when aggression can be used constructively or to a good purpose. Usually this is when it is channelled into a socially acceptable activity such as sport. Aggression is also a necessary element in the work of the armed forces, though it must be strictly controlled and directed towards the enemy, following the rules of engagement.

Aggression is often paired with avoidance, as a 'fight or flight' reaction (the choice is to stand up and fight or to run away). Aggression can also be a 'displaced' emotion (for example an attempt to hide fear or feelings of inadequacy). Wrongly used aggression causes pain to others, is linked to bullying and harassment, and can result in unacceptable behaviour of many kinds.

Physical and/or verbal aggression of anger or dominance
Aggression can be either physical or verbal.

Physical aggression means hitting, shoving, thumping, biting, kicking, stabbing or shooting people, etc., but in a wider sense it can also include threatening or offensive body language such as insulting gestures, standing too close to somebody, staring, refusing to make eye contact, pulling faces, dressing in a manner intended to hurt other people's feelings or showing a lack of respect through posture or stance. Some antisocial behaviour such as urinating in the street, graffiti, dropping litter, playing loud music and even vomiting in public may be regarded as aspects of physical aggression.

Verbal aggression is the use of language to hurt people's feelings, belittle them, humiliate them, ridicule them or weaken their position with other people. It can be used directly against the intended victim or (in a more **passive-aggressive** manner) by criticising them when speaking to other people, 'backbiting', spreading rumours etc. Verbal aggression is normally done through speech, but it can be done through writing – by abusive graffiti, writing hostile letters or newspaper articles or even posting hurtful messages on the internet. Again it can be directed at the victim or it can take the more indirect form of influencing other people against the victim.

The causes of physical and verbal aggression are many. Aggression may result from:

■ Anger.

■ Psychological causes or mental unbalance/illness on the part of the aggressor.

■ Revenge for a perceived wrong done by the victim of the aggression.

■ Sexual jealousy.

- Loss of status, loss of power, helplessness or frustration (or the fear or threat of these).
- The desire to move higher in an informal chain of command or 'pecking order' and achieve dominance in a group.
- The sexual or other pleasure that aggressors sometimes get from bullying and harassment, e.g. a sense of power, sadism.
- Disagreements or differences in culture, ideology, religion or other beliefs.
- An upbringing or environment that rewards aggressive behaviour (e.g. abusive parents, violent gang membership).
- A response to the aggression of others.
- Media influence (e.g. violent videos; songs with violent lyrics).
- Drugs or alcohol.

Dominance

What these causes have in common is that they are all related to the desire for power or the fear of losing power. Dominance is power, relative to the people around us. Many groups of people, e.g. street gangs, develop informal hierarchies, with the leader being someone who is tougher, more aggressive, more ruthless or more resourceful than the rest. Dominance is not always achieved through aggressive behaviour, but usually there is an element of aggression in dominant people, as we can see, for example, in the behaviour, body-language and speeches of politicians.

Unexpected sudden aggressive reactions

Aggressive behaviour is often shown by sudden movements or threatening gestures, mood swings, or the use of unexpectedly harsh or abusive language. Sometimes these unexpected reactions are warnings. The aggressive person may do them deliberately, or they might just 'come out' – but aggression is aggression whether it is conscious or not.

Poor listening skills

Some aggression results from misunderstanding. This can mean various kinds of poor communication skills: saying something rude when it was not intended; hearing a statement as rude when it was not meant to be rude. In such situations it is not always clear whether the speaker or the listener is at fault. These misunderstandings can occur

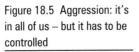

remember

Achieving dominance is a useful skill in the public services, but it must be done by acceptable methods.

Figure 18.5 Aggression: it's in all of us – but it has to be controlled

more easily in a diverse society where the use of English varies. A word such as 'stupid' for example, is likely to appear even more insulting to a person for whom English is not the first language. It will also be more insulting to a younger person than an older person. People who work in the public services and are likely to deal with aggression should develop their own listening and speaking skills, and try to be sensitive to language which could cause offence or be misunderstood.

Lack of self-esteem or inability to control a situation other than with anger

Research seems to indicate that aggression in young people is linked to low self-esteem.

Placing the rights of the aggressor above the rights of the other party

In simple terms, this means that aggressive people usually think that they are right and the other person is wrong. Being aware of things like this is important for public service workers – especially the police, teachers, NHS workers or social workers who from time to time are likely to come across aggression from members of the public. When reporting or dealing with incidents it is useful to be able to distinguish aggression – and this 'I'm right and you're wrong' attitude is characteristic of aggressive behaviour.

Avoiding responsibility

Another characteristic of aggressive behaviour (similar to the above) is that the aggressor feels – or claims – that they are not to blame. This makes it difficult to reason with them, which perhaps suits them because they feel more comfortable with behaving aggressively (since they are used to it) than with trying to behave in any other way. The avoidance of responsibility may also suggest that the person had an upbringing where they were routinely punished – and saying they were not to blame was a way of avoiding that punishment.

Avoidance

Avoidance is a series of techniques used by people to limit or cut off interaction between themselves and others. It is a type of communication behaviour because even though it is non-communicative it sends out signals to others.

Key features

The aims of avoidance, for the person who practises it, can be:

- To reduce the risk of **confrontation**.
- To escape aggression.
- To show non-involvement and detachment.
- To show lack of interest or commitment.
- To show dislike or disagreement in a passive way.

Avoidance behaviour can be seen by others as cowardly, uncooperative, evasive, snobbish or passive-aggressive. It is not a problem to others in the same way that aggressive behaviour is, because it does not directly threaten other people and is always non-violent. But avoidance can be a serious long-term problem for the person practising avoidance, for example:

- When avoiding or refusing school, education, work, medical treatment, etc.
- When failing to carry out necessary work duties.
- In the forming or maintaining of relationships with others.

Avoidance behaviour in children is sometimes linked to separation anxiety disorder, and comes from fear of leaving home and going to school. In adults it can be linked to social phobia (fear of people or company), agoraphobia (fear of open spaces) and other anxiety disorders (feelings of intense fear without good reason). In many cases, though, avoidance is not so much a sign of mental illness as a personality trait which can harm the 'avoider', undermine personal relationships and have a negative effect at work.

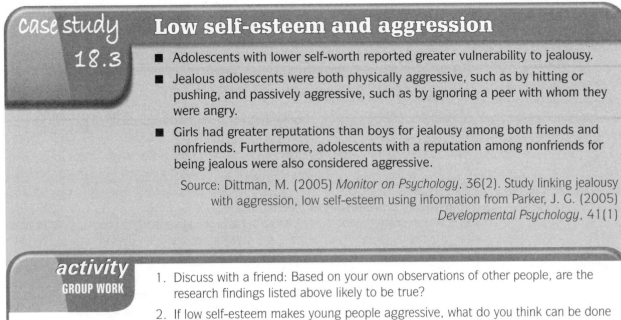

case study 18.3

Low self-esteem and aggression

- Adolescents with lower self-worth reported greater vulnerability to jealousy.
- Jealous adolescents were both physically aggressive, such as by hitting or pushing, and passively aggressive, such as by ignoring a peer with whom they were angry.
- Girls had greater reputations than boys for jealousy among both friends and nonfriends. Furthermore, adolescents with a reputation among nonfriends for being jealous were also considered aggressive.

Source: Dittman, M. (2005) *Monitor on Psychology*, 36(2). Study linking jealousy with aggression, low self-esteem using information from Parker, J. G. (2005) *Developmental Psychology*, 41(1)

activity
GROUP WORK

1. Discuss with a friend: Based on your own observations of other people, are the research findings listed above likely to be true?
2. If low self-esteem makes young people aggressive, what do you think can be done to raise their self-esteem?

Used to evade confrontation

Avoidance is a strategy to prevent confrontation (e.g. disagreements or arguments). It can take the form of physically missing appointments (e.g. tutorials, counselling sessions or meetings where the 'avoider' expects to be criticised for something). Or it can take the form of evasiveness in conversation, e.g. not expressing opinions even when other people are saying what they think, or agreeing with people simply to avoid an argument.

In public service work avoidance is generally not a good idea as the purpose of most public service work is to seek out problems, confront them and solve them. However, when dealing with difficult or argumentative people (e.g. people who are drunk), or people for whom one has a deep-seated dislike or disagreement, some avoidance is needed. For example, if police officers arrest a paedophile, they may have to practise avoidance in order not to show an unprofessional anger at the nature of the crime.

Apparent desire not to be bothered with consequences

Avoidance can be a form of detachment: 'Not my problem, mate!'. Avoidance may sound like laziness, but it is not always a bad thing. People working in the public services have many demands made on them – they cannot satisfy all of them. Prioritising some commitments may mean avoiding or neglecting others. This is why public service workers need to have a sense of responsibility – so that they do what they must do and can avoid doing what is not their responsibility.

Refusal to recognise a problem

> **remember**
> Avoidance can lead to moral cowardice, e.g. knowing that someone is doing something wrong, yet doing nothing about it.

Freud identified the mental state of 'denial' – the refusal to recognise a problem. People practising avoidance as a type of communication behaviour will say, 'Oh – it'll be fine!', when it is clear to everybody else that 'it' will not be. Obviously people are not always going to agree on whether something is a problem or not, but a systematic tendency to underestimate or deny problems is a sign of avoidance behaviour. This, of course, can be dangerous (for example if someone persistently underestimates risks) and it can lead to a failure to act in emergency situations.

Deliberately side-stepping confrontational situations

As with other aspects of avoidance behaviour, there are times when this may be justified. Not all confrontations are worth bothering with. But to side-step a situation simply because it is confrontational is harmful to the avoider (dodging the issue can become a habit) and may harm the other person as well, for the confrontation may be for their own good. In the interests of efficiency, public service workers may side-step some unnecessary confrontations, but as a rule they should be willing and able to confront problems (and 'problem people') when necessary.

Not answering the telephone

This is typical avoidance behaviour, especially if done out of fear, laziness or a desire to be uncooperative. (The same is true of failing to deal with messages on an answering machine.)

On the other hand, if a person is talking to a client on a serious matter, it is bad practice to interrupt the conversation and answer the phone.

Not attending a pre-arranged meeting

This is unacceptable avoidance behaviour (unless of course there is good reason for not attending the meeting – in which case the meeting, or the other person, should be told in advance). If the meeting is not wanted it should never be arranged in the first place.

From the point of view of people working in public services, it is always a good thing to attend meetings. You get to know more, you can influence decisions, and it is more difficult for people to talk about you behind your back because you are there!

Development of elaborate plans to avoid a situation

This avoidance technique is widely used by politicians and others when they wish to achieve a difficult aim without using, or threatening, force. How well such methods work depends on the type of situation to be avoided. Years of elaborate planning to avoid conflict in Northern Ireland appear to be paying off – and though there may be avoidance involved, avoidance which saves lives has a good deal to be said for it. At a more personal level though, it is often better to tackle a situation head-on rather than waste time and energy planning to avoid it. In public service work, which should be transparent and accountable, and where there is always more to be done than there is time to do it, it is normally best to deal with everyday situations in straightforward and direct ways.

Submissive or accommodating behaviour

Submissive behaviour involves fitting in, obeying or conforming to the will of others. It means setting aside your own feelings, wishes or ideas of what is right or wrong, and accepting other people's wishes, plans, intentions or actions. The basic attitude is: 'I'll do it, if you want it.'

Accommodating behaviour is also submissive or obliging behaviour – but it is not necessarily a bad thing. Of course other people's wishes should be taken into consideration when making a decision, but they should not normally be the overriding factor.

Key features

Key features of submissive behaviour include:

- Agreeing with other people all the time, even when you do not really agree.
- Being too obedient and compliant.
- Not sticking up for yourself or your point of view in an argument.
- Keeping quiet and being inconspicuous in a group.
- Excessive conformity.
- Allowing yourself to be teased, bullied or harassed and doing nothing about it.
- Not complaining when you have good reason to complain.
- Doing jobs for other people which they should be doing themselves.

- Lending/giving people money or things in order to 'buy' friendship.
- Being unnecessarily helpful or generous; allowing yourself to be exploited.

Allowing personal views or thoughts to be misconstrued

One of the bad things about submissive behaviour is that it undermines our individuality and makes us into the servants of other people, following their wishes, voicing their opinions and copying their actions. Submissive people give away their rights to their own views and their unique qualities, and seem happy to be misunderstood or not understood at all. This is harmful to the submissive person because they cannot take full responsibility for their actions, nor can they develop their character and abilities to the full. Submission harms people's ability to make meaningful adult relationships, it limits their experience of life, can imprison people in a kind of extended childhood and may make them dependent rather than independent.

The fact that they do not even feel free to express their views openly means that they have allowed other people (or the fear of other people) to impose censorship on them.

It can be instilled by parents or other early influences

Submission is often (deliberately or not) instilled by parents and schooling. The subtext (i.e. the underlying message) of much parenting and schooling is: 'You will obey!'

With young children this is necessary for their own safety, but as children grow older they should, by stages, be allowed to have more autonomy (i.e. independence). At adolescence there is normally a phase of 'rebellion' against parental or school wishes. This may not be particularly violent or extreme, but the end result is usually that young people achieve their independence through a struggle for freedom, and can see themselves as the equal of others, with full rights and responsibilities. With submissive people either the parents or schooling have been too authoritarian, the peer group has been ineffective or unsupportive, or the person him or herself has not been able to rebel successfully during the adolescent phase of self-assertion.

This is not to suggest that submissive behaviour is 'incurable'. Nor are submissive people any less able than others. It simply means that to fulfil themselves (achieving Maslow's 'self-actualisation') they have to change their behaviour so that they can, when necessary, be **assertive**.

The individual can experience immediate pleasure from pleasing others

Traditional religion places value on being submissive and putting the needs of others before our own needs. Other people can encourage submissive behaviour by thanking us and complimenting us on our helpfulness. This satisfies 'esteem needs' and being submissive can have a lot to do with wanting to be liked, wanted and needed. There is also a sexist dimension to submissive behaviour, for in many traditional cultures women are expected to be submissive (while men are expected to be dominant).

Need to keep all situations calm

Submissive people dislike conflict, shouting, threats of violence and actual violence. They have a tendency to believe in 'peace at any price'. They are more concerned with avoiding conflict than with solving the cause of the conflict. This could be a problem in police or other uniformed service work, where situations are not always calm and sometimes have to be confronted head on.

Whatever the faults of submissive behaviour, though, it is less damaging than aggressive behaviour. A degree of submissive behaviour can be useful in some situations. As a short-term, one-off tactic it may be effective in dealing with aggressive people. (For example, police advice is to give your bag to a mugger if they try to snatch it.) But otherwise, submissive behaviour should always be part of a wider range of possible responses.

Not wanting to say 'no' to unreasonable requests

Anybody has a right to say 'no' to an unreasonable request. One of the main weaknesses of submissive behaviour is that it leaves a person open to manipulation or exploitation – when saying 'no' clearly would put an end to the problem.

> **remember**
>
> No communication behaviour is always good or always bad. But in most cases assertiveness is best.

Not wanting to draw personal attention

Fear of being 'shown up' is sometimes a motive for submissive behaviour. And there are times when most people would rather not attract personal attention. Nevertheless, there are other times (especially in public service work) when it is necessary to attract attention and be noticed. Shyness – often a sign of sensitivity – can be overcome by people who want to overcome it, and then they can use their sensitivity to help others.

Lack of self-esteem

Self-esteem is self-respect, a person's sense of their own value. People brought up in poverty or by parents who are too authoritarian, or people who do badly at school or who get picked on for some reason, may have low self-esteem as a result. Some studies (see page 372 above) suggest that low self-esteem can cause people to use inappropriate communication behaviour, e.g. being too aggressive or too submissive.

Submissive behaviour leading to aggressive outbursts

A final reason for not always behaving submissively is that very few people genuinely feel submissive all the time. People take advantage of submissive behaviour and may become bullying, abusive or over-familiar because of it. In such circumstances a person who is being too submissive may think, 'Enough is enough!' and become suddenly aggressive.

Assertive

This is the kind of communication behaviour which is easiest and most effective in the long term. It enables a person to act honestly, professionally, directly and effectively – and minimises stress both for themselves and the people around them.

Key features

The key features of assertive communication behaviour are as follows:

- It is clear, honest and direct.
- It expresses goodwill.
- It says what you want.
- It says why you want it.
- It says what you want the other person to do.

It is not aggressive, avoiding or submissive. The aim is to get the outcome that you want.

Pleading, threatening, shouting, sarcasm, play-acting, wheedling, seeking pity, teasing and disrespect are all non-assertive and should be avoided in situations where you are making requests.

Mistaken association with aggression

Assertion is not aggression. It is not the same as bullying, threatening or imposing your will on someone. Assertion demands respect, but it also shows respect.

Issues related to sexual stereotyping of women

It is sometimes believed that women cannot – or should not – be assertive. This view comes either from a misunderstanding of assertion, or a misunderstanding of women and their role in modern society. The fact that women have so often been exploited and abused in the past highlights the need for women to be assertive in the present.

There is still a problem in British society, and in some workplaces, as far as the treatment of women by men is concerned. One of the biggest arguments in favour of assertive behaviour is that it demands that people are treated with respect, as equals, without harassment, discrimination, sexism or any other sort of unfair pressure.

Protecting own space and rights without isolating space and rights of others

Space is both physical and psychological. Assertive communication respects the physical space of others (e.g. by not standing over them, pawing them or shoving your face in theirs). It also respects their psychological space (and human rights) by avoiding

remember

Assertive communication is not just for the day job. It works in private life as well.

unwanted personal remarks, needling about politics and religion, or any other kind of unwelcome and unprofessional behaviour.

Identification of own needs

Assertive communication is often about getting what you want – but not at the other person's expense. It involves using the word 'I'. The following shows the three-part structure of an assertive communication:

A: Hi Ben – how you doing?

B: I'd be doing a bit better if Mr Bean hadn't lost my assignment

A: He's just lost mine as well, the *******. Hey – I know what I was going to say to you –

B: What's that?

A: This rucksack of yours that you've been keeping in my locker for the past week …

B: Yes? What about it?

A: I'd like you to take it out, and put it in your own locker now you've got one.

B: What – now? I've got a bus to catch.

A: Yes – but I've got to put this tent away, so I'd rather you took it now.

This conversation splits into three parts:

- Up to 'Hey' – an introduction which establishes goodwill.
- Up to 'week' – a statement of the problem.
- To the end – a statement of the solution to the problem and a reason.

Both parties benefit from increased effectiveness

Assertive communications work because they are worded in such a way as to show that both parties benefit if the request is complied with. In the above example the benefit to A is that he can put his tent in his locker, and get rid of B's rucksack. The benefit to B

---

case study 18.4 — Assertiveness

Assertiveness involves the following:

- being clear about what you feel, what you need and how it can be achieved
- being able to communicate calmly without attacking another person
- saying 'yes' when you want to, and saying 'no' when you mean 'no' (rather than agreeing to do something just to please someone else)
- deciding on, and sticking to, clear boundaries – being happy to defend your position, even if it provokes conflict
- being confident about handling conflict if it occurs
- understanding how to negotiate if two people want different outcomes
- being able to talk openly about yourself and being able to listen to others
- having confident, open body language
- being able to give and receive positive and negative feedback
- having a positive, optimistic outlook.

Source: BUPA

---

activity GROUP WORK

Using the guidelines above, discuss situations from your own experience where assertiveness worked, or where you (or someone else) should have been assertive but were not.

is that he remains on good terms with A. They can then join forces and tackle Mr Bean (assertively, of course) about their missing assignments.

Finding a workable compromise

If a compromise is required it is much easier if the people disagreeing approach the problem in an assertive way. This is because, through assertive communication, they can each say what they really think, and people do not have to guess what is in the other's mind (which can easily be the case with avoidance or **submissive** behaviour). Respect is generated, plus a serious desire to sort out the problem in a way which satisfies both parties.

Acknowledging another's point of view, involves clear direct communication, exploring ways to resolve problems

These aspects of assertive communication are interrelated. They all help people who disagree to reach agreement or a compromise which is workable and well understood by both sides.

In public service work this approach is essential most of the time because it:

- Generates confidence between the worker and the client or member of the public.
- Recognises that policing and other activities are done 'by consent' – in other words, effective policing would not be possible without the broad cooperation of the public.
- Is open and above-board, and so helps to give the public service a good image.
- Reduces stress, and limits the risk of aggression.
- Communicates efficiently and therefore saves time and effort, and minimises misunderstanding and wrong decisions.
- Shows respect by treating other people as adults and as equals.
- Is non-sexist, non-racist and not culturally biased: assertive communication is understood and appreciated by people of all backgrounds.

Benefits of understanding behaviour

Understanding behaviour can take two forms:

- Passive – being able to 'read' and interpret the behaviour of others (including underlying aspects which may not be immediately obvious).
- Active – being able to adjust and adapt your behaviour to the needs of the situation and the people you are dealing with.

For individuals (e.g. staff, customers)

As Figure 18.6 shows, there are plenty of benefits in understanding behaviour. These benefits are both personal (in our daily lives) and professional (in our dealings with people and organisations at work). The benefits are especially great in public service work, because so much of it is to do with communication.

Benefits for staff (i.e. public service staff) are shown in Figure 18.6. The biggest benefit of all, from a professional point of view, is that of being able to maximise control over other people – either for their own good or for the good of society. The second-biggest benefit is that of being able to understand other people and their needs.

Benefits for customers are that they are more likely to take advice or control from people who express themselves clearly and who inspire respect.

For teams

For teams and their leaders it is important to be able to understand the behaviour of team members in order to work effectively and efficiently together and to develop team spirit. It is also important for teams to understand the behaviour of other individuals and teams they come in contact with (they may be superior officers, partner teams, members of other agencies, etc.). In **inter-agency working**, which is increasingly used,

Figure 18.6 The benefits of understanding behaviour

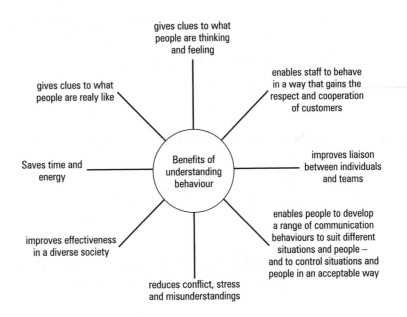

understanding behaviour improves team relationships and helps the different teams in the partnership to work efficiently and harmoniously together. Teams therefore give a better service, and people gain more job satisfaction from their work.

For organisations (e.g. motivated workforces)

We have already seen (page 369 above) that a knowledge of psychological theory can help managers to improve the motivation and performance of their workforce. This is as true in the public sector as it is in the private sector.

An understanding of communication behaviour will help to increase productivity and motivate a workforce:

■ By reducing the time spent on communication, for if training in assertive behaviour is given both misunderstandings and negative communication behaviour such as **avoidance** should go down.

■ By increasing the accuracy and effectiveness of communication – again by reducing the risk of misunderstandings.

■ By decreasing conflict and **stress** – again caused by inappropriate use of avoidance or submissive behaviour.

■ By increasing job satisfaction: good communication empowers people because they understand what is going on and feel that they are participating more effectively.

The benefits of understanding communication behaviour will be equally marked in the relationship between the organisation and the public. If the fire and rescue service were to practice avoidance and not answer the phone in an emergency, fire and accident casualties would go up – and the public would not be impressed. Without a good understanding of communication behaviour in the public services there would be increased problems of lack of feedback and the non-completion of tasks, and both quantity and quality of service would go down.

Financial

Good communication within an organisation, and between an organisation and its clients, stakeholders and the public are good for the finance of an organisation. For a commercial organisation good communication raises profits. For a public service it increases the amount of work done for the public and therefore saves – or makes better use of – taxpayers' money.

remember
All behaviour is a form of communication because people observe and interpret it.

remember
Modern public service work requires the fast and accurate communication of huge amounts of information.

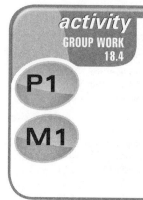

You are giving a presentation to school pupils. Prepare and perform a short drama or role-play illustrating the main types of communication behaviour. Then give a short presentation:

- Describing how these communication behaviours are used in the public services.
- Explaining how using and understanding different communication behaviours helps people working in public services to do their job better.
- Examining the effects of different types of communication behaviour on public service workers and the public they deal with.

Keep all of your written notes and other materials.

Possible areas of conflict between individual and group behaviour

Uniformed public service workers such as the police, prison officers and soldiers on peacekeeping duties may find themselves having to deal with potential conflict between themselves and members of the public, prisoners or conflicting groups within an occupied country (such as Iraq, Kosovo, the Democratic Republic of Congo or Afghanistan).

In dealing with such potential conflict the following may well be needed:

- Some understanding of crowd psychology.
- An understanding of individual psychology (especially aggression and its causes and risks).
- Knowledge of the reasons underlying the potential conflict (e.g. unruly gathering of young people, football supporters, new road-building protest, political demonstration).
- Strategic aims (why action has to be taken).
- Knowledge of own powers and their limits, e.g. public order laws, rules of engagement.
- Knowledge of materials, equipment, back-up.
- Knowledge of the physical setting of the conflict.
- Knowledge of the possible effect of any action on the community.
- A risk assessment of the situation.

Types of conflict

Conflicts can be classified into different types (Table 18.3). As the table shows, there are many possible ways of resolving, stopping or reducing conflict – but not all are equally effective or acceptable.

> **remember**
>
> If you want to work in a uniformed public service, you should make a point of studying conflict and how it can be resolved.

Table 18.3 Types of conflict

Type	Characteristics	Ways of dealing with it
Between individuals	Can be physical or verbal	Physical: threats, fighting; other people breaking up the fight; prosecution may result, depending on seriousness of incident. Verbal: reconciliation, mediation or separation
Individual v. group	Mainly verbal. Often semi-official, e.g. police officer v. youths; teacher v. class; complainant v. public service	If assertive behaviour does not work, either avoidance or back-up is needed by the individual. Making plans to avoid such conflict in advance (see page 374) may be the best tactic if the conflict is foreseen. Submissive behaviour may help if the individual is being beaten up. Shouting for help and (rarely) aggression may protect the individual
Group v. group	Verbal or physical. This is common in our society. Can be legal (e.g. political conflict, business competition) or illegal (e.g. gang warfare, **sectarian** violence)	Peaceful resolution: negotiation, compromise, debate, mediation by a third party or by chosen or elected representatives; civil courts, public inquiries, a public vote to settle the issue, changes in the law. In international disputes the United Nations or leaders of other countries may try to settle the dispute peacefully. Non-peaceful resolution: Fighting until victory is achieved; peacekeeping forces set up; feuding with violence (as in the Mafia); also threats and sanctions
Caused by conflict of interests	This is a conflict caused by one person or group having what another person or group wants, or threatening what another person or group has. Power, money or sex are usually at the root of such conflicts	These range from disputes between individuals ('He pinched my girlfriend – I'll get him for that!') through disputes about property to political and military conflicts about land and resources. They may be mixed up with ideological conflicts (see below). They may involve public order, e.g. police v. looters or football hooligans. They are resolved by (a) deterrence – show of force; (b) fighting – actual force; (c) policing, legal, economic or political action; or (d) negotiation; or a combination of these
Ideological conflicts	These are based on culture, beliefs, political ideas or religion. They are usually mixed up with conflicts of interest (e.g. religious discrimination mixed up with economic or political discrimination)	These can be dealt with (a) by avoidance, i.e. refusing to quarrel about such matters, agreeing to differ; (b) by mediation and negotiation between different communities where there is tension. The mediation can be done by chosen community leaders or a mediating body such as the Commission for Racial Equality; (c) by police action, possibly linked to mediation; (d) through the courts; (e) by political action which outlaws discrimination; (f) by giving economic help to disadvantaged communities; (g) by violence or fighting and, in international disputes, by warfare

Between two individuals

Conflicts between individuals do not usually involve official bodies in the first place. If neighbours argue about loud music, barking dogs or cypress hedges the dispute is at first between the neighbours themselves. If the neighbours use assertive methods to communicate, acting as reasonable beings and saying what they really think, the problem will almost certainly get solved in a quick, straightforward manner with no great expense. If aggression is used to tackle the problem, eventually the police or council will be called, and criminal proceedings – not for the cause of the conflict so much as the conflict itself – will follow. Avoidance by one party may lead to the other party getting aggressive, so that too may result in court action. (Avoidance in the sense of moving house would solve the problem – but at a cost.) Submission by one individual to the other may 'buy' peace for a time, but is unlikely to be an effective solution in the long run. It could lead to an aggressive outburst by the submissive person, or to depression or ill-health in a person suffering from the antisocial behaviour of a neighbour.

A challenge from a member of the public against a council official

In this example the conflict is between an individual and an elected body. If the individual chooses to deal with the conflict through submission (accepting the will of the council) the conflict will not develop, though the individual may well be left feeling badly treated. If the individual chooses the avoidance route, the outcome will depend on the reason for the conflict in the first place. If the conflict is because the individual has not paid council tax, or is breaking the law (e.g. by using domestic premises for an industrial purpose), avoidance of the issue will lead to the individual being taken to court. If the individual responds to the conflict aggressively (e.g. by threatening to break the legs of a council official) court action will result. But if the individual responds assertively, complaining clearly through the available official channels, the outcome could be something like that in case study 18.5 below.

www.lgo.org.uk/index.php (Local Government Ombudsman)

Between an individual and a group

The form this type of conflict takes depends very much on the reason for the conflict, who is involved, whether either the individual or the group has any kind of official status, and whether there is a risk of violence. The essential point in physical conflict is that (except in kung fu movies) an unarmed individual will not win a physical fight against a group.

A police officer and a protesting group

A number of points should be considered:

■ Conflict does not automatically spring up between a police officer and a protesting group unless the group are doing something unlawful or are protesting against the police. In other situations, protesters (e.g. peace protesters, or a silent vigil) may see the police as their protectors against, say, right-wing extremists.

■ Crowd psychology is not as well understood, nor as easy to study, as the psychology of the individual. Indeed, it is sometimes seen as sociology, since it involves the behaviour of groups. Max Weber, a sociologist who was broadly in sympathy with humanism, argued that crowds were normally rational and reflected the norms and values of the people making them up. He also believed that crowds, though

---

case study 18.5 — Complaint about antisocial behaviour

'Mr Hurst' (not his real name) experienced regular problems from antisocial behaviour (ASB) by a gang of youths who gathered in a park close to his home. He complained that the Council did not properly investigate the disturbances he reported and that it did not take prompt action to resolve the problems he was caused.

The Ombudsman found that a number of Council departments involved had failed to follow the Council's procedures for dealing with complaints about antisocial behaviour and, as a result, Mr Hurst's complaints were not properly investigated. This led to delays in taking action, and so Mr Hurst and his family suffered a prolonged period of uncertainty, anxiety and distress.

The Ombudsman found maladministration causing injustice and the Council agreed to pay Mr Hurst compensation of £2000.

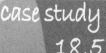

activity
GROUP WORK

What could have happened if Mr Hurst had decided to take a passive, avoidance or aggressive approach to the problem?

case study 18.6

Father attacked by gang

A father of two young children was stabbed to death by a gang of youths after he asked them to stop making a noise outside his home.

Steven Nyembo-Ya-Muteba, 40, told about a dozen teenagers to move away from the stairwell of a block of flats because they were keeping him awake. The youths left the low-rise flats in Hackney, east London, shortly after 10pm on Sunday night, but at least one returned and stabbed Mr Nyembo-Ya-Muteba.

The victim, a university maths student, was taken to a nearby hospital but died from his wounds. He leaves two daughters, aged five and six, and his wife, also a student, who was described as 'devastated' by the killing.

Source: 'Father of two murdered after confronting youths', *The Independent*, 3 October 2006, by Jason Bennetto, crime correspondent

activity
GROUP WORK

When should citizens 'have a go'? What are the arguments for and against this?

---

essentially passive, could be manipulated by charismatic leaders. Freud believed that the collective emotion of the crowd overcame the individual emotions of the people in it. Gustave Le Bon believed crowds became depersonalised and '**deindividuated**', and could then be whipped up to an animal-like frenzy by a certain type of leader. Durkheim said crowds did not reflect the feelings or interests of the individuals who made them up, but he did believe that they could become highly excitable and experience collective emotion – whose main value was to remind people that they were essentially social beings. Convergence theory states that crowds develop their identity and group purpose from the people who make them up. Emergent-norm theory sees crowds as fluid and unpredictable, making up their emotions and reactions as they go along.

What these brief (and oversimplified) summaries show is that crowds can vary enormously and our understanding of them is incomplete. Theoretical psychology is of limited usefulness in crowd policing if the crowd appears unexpectedly, though it may be more useful if the crowd is known about in advance (e.g. with a pre-planned demonstration) and the police have been able to make proper preparations for controlling it.

If there is conflict between a police officer and a protesting group, the officer must take 'proportionate action', as case study 18.7 below shows. (The case study is about how the police should treat people caught in possession of cannabis.)

Public demonstrations (e.g. anti-war rallies)
Conflict at demonstrations can be:

- Between the demonstrators and the authorities (e.g. the police or, in some countries, the army).
- Between different groups of demonstrators (e.g. militant left- and right-wing groups).

If the demonstration is a march, there is a legal duty under the Public Order Act 1986 to inform the police in advance. This enables the police to prepare. Techniques for dealing with demonstrators face to face will be assertive: making clear announcements (if necessary) stating what the demonstrators should do. However, preparation is often based on avoidance – for example, directing the route of the march away from potential trouble spots and keeping opposed groups of demonstrators away from each other.

case study 18.7 — Proportionate action

Police sometimes have to make quick decisions based on what is presented to them. Providing you made your decision on an honestly held belief that you were taking action that was both proportionate and necessary in light of what you knew at the time then your action should be justified even if additional evidence later comes to light.

Source: Cannabis; Guidance on Policing – Use of Cannabis Warnings

activity — GROUP WORK

What are the strengths and weaknesses of giving this kind of advice to police officers?

If there is a conflict between the police and demonstrators the police will give an order to disperse. This must comply with the Human Rights Act 1998 (since the right to demonstrate is a legal human right).

case study 18.8 — Police powers to disperse groups

Once an authorisation has been granted for a relevant locality, the Act permits a constable in uniform or a designated PCSO to give one or more of the following directions which:

■ Require the persons in the group to disperse either immediately or within a given time and manner specified by the officer giving the direction;

■ Require those persons who do not live within the relevant locality to leave the relevant locality or any part of it either immediately, or within a given time and manner, specified by the officer giving the direction;

■ Prohibit the return of those persons who do not live within the relevant locality from returning to that locality or any part of it for a period as stated in the direction, but in any case not exceeding 24 hours.

A direction may be given:

■ Orally;

　• To any person individually or to two or more persons together.

This direction may be withdrawn or varied by the person who gave it.

This does not prevent police officers in plain clothes from carrying out observations or gathering evidence.

Source: Practice advice on part 4 of the Anti-Social Behaviour Act 2003 (Police Powers to Disperse Groups), 2005. Produced on behalf of the Association of Chief Police Officers by the National Centre for Policing Excellence

activity — GROUP WORK

■ How effective do you think these measures would be in preventing violent conflict?

■ What purposes can you think of for plain-clothes officers carrying out observations or gathering evidence?

Interdepartmental conflict

This kind of conflict can occur in public services or between public services and other agencies when they are working in partnership. For example, it might happen in a Crime and Disorder Reduction Partnership if one of the lead agencies thought another agency was not pulling its weight or was carrying out actions which had not been agreed on.

Public services such as the police or the fire and rescue service, who might get involved in this kind of dispute, would obviously prefer to settle it privately in a professional manner before evidence of the conflict reached the public or the media. An officer of some seniority, probably in the police, would arrange steps to resolve the conflict. This would probably happen by **mediation** – possibly talking separately to team leaders who were at loggerheads and then organising a **reconciliation**. The purpose of these arrangements would be to 'draw a line under' the conflict and make a new start, using agreed action plans which would allow both sides to begin a new phase of their work without being humiliated.

Where ambitious or committed people work together, this kind of conflict is not unusual. If the friction can be dealt with assertively, and parties do not resort to aggression, avoidance or submission, it is usually possible to resolve the conflict to everyone's satisfaction. Occasionally it may be necessary to go further, for example to use the organisation's grievance system, transfer people to different teams or take disciplinary action.

Reasons for conflict

Possible reasons for conflict are shown in Table 18.4.

Table 18.4 Possible reasons for conflict

Between individuals	Between groups
Incompatibility which neither individual fully understands (sometimes explained vaguely as 'chemistry not right')	Xenophobia – a dislike of outsiders which may include racism and other forms of stereotyping or prejudice
Differences of education, class or culture (these need not and should not lead to conflict, but they can do if the individuals concerned allow them to)	Cultural, racial or religious differences
	Political or ideological differences
	Social and economic inequality
Harassment, bullying (aggressive behaviour towards a non-aggressive person)	Excessive loyalty to own group
	Competition for jobs, land, housing, etc.
Insecurity or low self-esteem (leads individuals to be defensive, aggressive, feel threatened, etc.)	A real or imagined grudge
	Rapid social and economic change
Competition at work (e.g. for promotion, approval of boss, etc.)	The capitalist system
	Negative propaganda and rabble-rousing
Manipulative, troublemaking behaviour by third parties	A history of enmity or conflict
Disagreements about how a job should be done	The feeling that there is something to be gained by getting into a conflict
Ideological, political or religious differences	
Racism or sexism	The feeling that nobody has the power or authority to stop the conflict
Confusion of professional and personal roles (e.g. sexual or personal involvement with or rejection by a workmate)	An enjoyment of fighting (e.g. between rival football supporters)
Effects of alcohol, stress, mental illness, family problems, etc.	Causes such as animal rights which bring people into conflict with each other
An abusive or aggressive upbringing	Education or traditions which reward conflict
Inner conflicts within self	The availability of weapons
	Gang culture
	Media such as films and music which appear to glorify violence and conflict
	The belief that a particular conflict is morally justified

Though conflict may not always be a bad thing, it should be minimised. The causes should be tackled, and lessons learned.

Most management/ staff conflicts are about pay, conditions of service, or threatened redundancies.

Management and staff conflicts can also result from disciplinary or grievance-related issues, such as indiscipline or harassment.

It ought to be added that, as human beings, our history is a history of struggle and conflict. Our attitude to conflict is ambivalent (two-sided). TV, films, newspapers and other media are full of stories of conflict. Our sports use the rules of conflict and turn it into recreation and entertainment. Conflict causes much anxiety and suffering, and yet we admire people who 'take a stand'.

Non-assimilation and isolation of individuals at work

This can be a reason for, and a result of, conflict. It has the effect of undermining teamwork and reducing job satisfaction for the person(s) isolated.

Management and staff conflicts

According to the social, political and economic thinker Karl Marx (1818–83), conflicts between management and staff are inevitable wherever there is a system of 'bosses and workers' (i.e. a capitalist system). The reason he puts forward (with great force and many arguments which there is no room to explain here) is that what is good for the management is bad for the staff and vice versa. The management want workers to do as much work as possible for as little pay as possible; the workers want to do as little work as possible for as much pay as possible. According to Marx workers are exploited and will be until the economic system is changed, probably (he says) by violent revolution. In Britain the violent revolution has not come, but the conflict is there in the form of strikes and other industrial action.

However, some uniformed services, such as the armed forces, the police and the prison service, are not allowed to take industrial action. Armed forces pay is regularly reviewed by the Ministry of Defence and the Armed Forces Pay Review Body – a committee set up for the purpose.

The police also have special arrangements.

The fire and rescue service has a trade union, the Fire Brigades Union, who negotiate with the employers for increased pay or better conditions. When these negotiations break down the fire and rescue service sometimes goes on strike – but they will still usually respond to emergencies.

Public disquiet relating to a local government or central government issue

'Disquiet' – a feeling of unhappiness or anxiety – will only turn into 'conflict' if:

- People feel strongly enough about the issue and
- Enough people get involved.

Local government issues that cause disquiet are council decisions about things such as:

- New roads and industrial or housing developments.
- Planning decisions which might result in noise, litter or other kinds of public nuisance.
- New developments that threaten woodlands or sites of special scientific interest.
- Other developments affecting the scenery or landscape – especially wind turbines ('wind farms').
- Arrangements for asylum seekers.
- Closure of hospitals or schools.

Conflict arising from local government issues is:

- In the local community, between those who are for and against the council decision.
- Between those who are against the council decision and the council itself.

Forms that the conflict can take include:

- The setting up of local organisations and pressure groups to fight the council decision.

case study 18.9

Police pay

Police pay is negotiated by the **Police Federation** and is reviewed on an annual basis with changes coming into effect every September.

i www.policeuk.com/

activity
GROUP WORK

1. What are the arguments for and against having the above system for fixing police salaries?
2. How effective do you think the police system will be for resolving pay disputes between them and their employers?
3. Do you think the fire and rescue service (see below) should have a similar system?

Figure 18.7 Most uniformed public services are not allowed to strike

- Enlisting the help of national organisations such as Greenpeace.
- Writing letters to the council, to local MPs and to central government.
- Fierce debates within the council chamber.
- Local press coverage, including hostile letters and biased articles.
- Leaflet, poster and sticker campaigns.
- Marches and demonstrations.
- Delays in planning applications and the planning process.
- In large protests: sit-ins, encampments, **vigils** and more permanent though usually peaceful demonstrations.
- Attempts to evict protesters.
- The arrival of large groups of sympathisers from other parts of the country, if the case is well publicised.
- Court hearings and public inquiries.
- People standing as independent MPs in general elections to publicise the local conflict.

The different ways of overcoming possible conflicts between groups and individuals through the use of effective conflict management techniques

Winston Churchill (1875–1965), the British prime minister in World War II, famously said 'jaw jaw is better than war war' meaning that conflicts are best solved by getting round a table and talking, rather than by fighting. At any level, talking is a better conflict management technique than fighting. It is cheaper, easier, more humane, more controllable and (if it succeeds) more permanent.

Conflict management techniques

These are methods or actions which can reduce, prevent or solve conflict.

Prevention of conflict

Prevention of conflict means stopping potential conflict from even starting.

However, conflict is not always a bad thing. It is natural for humans to disagree, and often it is better if the disagreements are out in the open. For conflicts to be sorted out they first have to be understood, and sometimes they cannot be fully understood until they have started.

Prevention of conflict can be achieved by brutality. When Saddam Hussein was dictator of Iraq there were few terrorist attacks and, it is said, the residents of Baghdad did not need to lock their doors. Sectarian conflict (e.g. between Sunnis and Shiites) was suppressed by the police, the secret police and other security organisations that existed in Baghdad in those days.

The methods of conflict prevention used by Saddam Hussein only work as long as there is a ruthless dictatorial government. They do not tackle the causes of conflict, so they cannot provide a lasting solution. In any case, they are not acceptable in a modern western democracy. In Britain there is an open society, and generally conflict cannot be prevented by violence or by secret methods.

In any case, the vast majority of conflicts are peaceful, relatively minor (except perhaps to those involved at the time) and can be solved by peaceful means using discussion, mediation, negotiation, administrative changes and similar techniques.

Team building with colleagues

Team building is an enjoyable and sociable activity which enables the members of a new team to get to know and understand each other in a stress-free setting away from the pressures of work. This is likely to prevent or reduce future conflict by:

- Allowing differences to be identified and sorted out early in the relationship.
- Giving team members an understanding of each other so that they know what to expect of others.
- Identifying people's preferred team roles.
- Enabling friendships to start and develop.
- Reducing the tension caused by working with, and being judged by, people who are not well known.
- Allowing the team to share achievements and develop team spirit and respect for each other.

Link — Team roles – see Book 1, Unit 4, pages 154–156

remember

Monitoring of community relations by police and peacekeepers, using consultation and intelligence gathering, is used to forestall conflicts between gangs, factions, ethnic communities, etc.

remember

In community conflicts the public services can play a role in mediation, negotiation, and other procedures which reduce escalation.

Early identification of situations

Team leaders should monitor their teams and carry out reasonably frequent appraisals to make sure that everybody is happy with the way things are going. Monitoring does not mean prying and spying – it can be done in a friendly and non-judgemental way. If problems are arising between team members which could develop into conflicts, minimal action – such as a few private words, or a slight rearrangement of people's roles – may be enough to prevent a possible conflict.

Reducing escalation

The **escalation** of a conflict, sometimes called 'ratcheting up' or 'raising the stakes', is the period when a conflict is getting more serious. The aim for a team leader is to prevent this happening, for it is during the escalation period that attitudes harden and the conflict becomes more bitter or deep-rooted.

People involved in a conflict also have a duty to stop it escalating. Conflict may not be bad in itself, because it may be a sign that actions must be taken (e.g. by management) which will benefit everybody, but the more personal or vindictive conflicts get, the more harmful they become – especially to the participants. Participants in a conflict can stop it if they can talk to each other assertively, and with a genuine desire to resolve the conflict.

If they cannot do this themselves, they should talk to line managers or other appropriate people and get them to sort it out through mediation and negotiation. If those do not work, the process should move on through the appropriate grievance procedure and administrative or disciplinary action.

Attitude/behaviour cycle

Attitude is defined as 'a general evaluation, or assessment, of the people, objects and ideas that surround us'. It is divided into three parts: affect (our feelings), cognition (what we know) and behaviour (the way the attitude is expressed in action). Attitude and behaviour are therefore aspects of the same thing.

In Figure 18.8 attitudes (feelings and opinions) harden as the conflict escalates. At the same time the actions taken by the opposing groups in the conflict become more extreme. The media and outsiders get drawn into the conflict as it develops. The cycle will eventually be brought to an end either by a legal victory for one side or the other, or a **public inquiry** which will enable people to argue their points in an assertive manner. If the wind farm is built the protesters will have to take avoidance action, putting up

Figure 18.8 Attitude/ behaviour cycle – conflict arising from proposed wind farm development

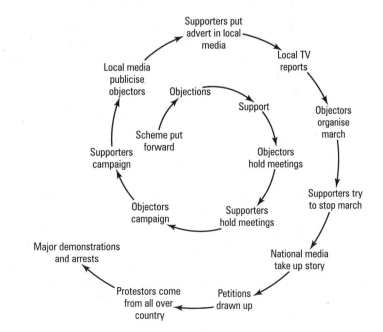

with it or moving away. If the protesters win, the developers will move somewhere else (avoidance). Divided opinion in the local community will heal very slowly.

Aronson, E., Wilson, T. D. and Akert, R. (2006) *Social Psychology*, 6th edn, Prentice Hall, Englewood Cliffs (NJ)

Using assertive behaviour
Using assertive behaviour is the easiest single way of overcoming conflict. For people in leadership positions assertive behaviour is an essential skill although, as we have seen, it sometimes needs to be used in conjunction with other forms of communication behaviour such as avoidance.

Link

Pages 376–378 above explain assertive behaviour and its advantages

activity
INDIVIDUAL WORK
18.5

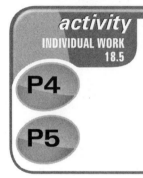

Produce a fact-sheet for a citizens' advice centre outlining the kinds of conflict which can take place in the public services. Suggest reasons for each kind, and set out the ways in which conflict – whether between individuals, groups or a combination of the two – can be prevented or resolved.

Style of management

Public sector management involves the organisation and motivation of workers, and ensuring that the best use is made of resources (e.g. that time and money are not wasted).

Management, like any other communication-based activity, can be assertive, aggressive, avoiding or submissive. The styles used depend on:

■ The personality or mood of the manager.

■ The characters and expectations of the people being managed.

■ The traditions of the institution.

■ The work/activity being managed.

■ Outside pressures on the team.

Assertiveness

As we have seen, assertiveness is saying what you want in a clear, open, direct yet non-confrontational way. It involves saying 'I' as in 'I would like …' rather than 'You' as in 'You must …'. An assertive communication typically consists of a three-part statement. The first part shows that you are not hostile. The second part says what you want. The third part, which is optional, says why you want it. Example: 'Hi Jane. I'd like you to take my place at the meeting this afternoon.'

Ways of speaking and behaving

Since human beings are not telepathic, the way that managers speak and behave is a major source of information about their characters, abilities and attitudes. What the manager says is important, but the way the manager says it, and then behaves, is very important too.

Aggressive

In the example about Jane above, an aggressive manager might say: 'I notice you've been sitting around chatting and painting your nails all afternoon, Jane, so it's about time you did some work. Now get off your backside and go to that meeting I was going to go to – and I'll check that you've gone, so don't try and skive off.' This is aggressive because it contains unnecessary personal comment, sarcasm and a threat. If it is said in a jokey way, then it is too familiar as well, and familiarity is linked to aggression because it risks invading a person's private space – either physical or psychological.

Submissive

A submissive manager might say: 'I'm sorry to be a nuisance yet again and ask you to fill in for me, but would it be too much to just sort of ask you to drop in on that meeting I was supposed to go to? It'll be pretty boring … and I don't expect you to stay the whole time. I'd go myself but I'm afraid I have to go to the dentist to get my impacted wisdom tooth seen to … though I suppose I could change the appointment. What do you think?' The submissive manager wastes a good deal of time being apologetic or unclear, and if Jane wanted to take advantage of the situation by saying she was too busy to go to the meeting, she would probably get away with it.

Assertive

This has already been shown above.

The importance of finding a style of management which relates well to the needs of employees is shown in case study 18.10.

Giving feedback

Feedback is comments on work that someone has done. The aim of feedback is to give information which is useful to the person who has done the work. Useful feedback should include praise – if it is deserved.

There is not much point in praising work that is no good, though submissive managers might do it. But deserved praise motivates the subordinate, who is probably working to satisfy esteem needs and who probably knows the work is good. If work that deserves praise is not praised, there is a risk that the subordinate might feel that the manager is grumpy, unappreciative or simply does not like them.

Constructive criticism

If it is done properly, criticism can be a good learning experience. It might not motivate as well as praise, but it gives more helpful information to someone who wants to improve in their job. Constructive criticism is analytical in that it picks out the main

---

case study 18.10 **Management style**

There are loads (of disputes), constantly. I could go on forever. The place is just a bit nuts. They don't work to a normal structure like any other organisation I have ever worked for. And because of the way it works, people have a lot of issues and because they don't have a clear structure, they don't have clear policies, everybody does their own thing and you've got people who are not qualified to do jobs, it's just so vague really.

Source: Supervisor in a dispute, quoted in ACAS Research Paper: *The Acas small firms' mediation pilot: Research to explore parties' experiences and views on the value of mediation* (2005)

activity
INDIVIDUAL WORK

Examine your workplace or college. What management structures and policies are there to prevent conflict between individuals or employees?

points for action or improvement. It should give some indication (but not too much) as to how improvements might be made. The person being criticised should be left feeling that they have learned something worthwhile.

Destructive criticism

This is criticism which aims to humiliate the person who did the work. It is counterproductive because it fails to motivate the person, gives no useful learning points, generates conflict and is, in fact, an easy way to make an enemy.

Formal actions

Formal actions – rules, dress codes, respect for rank and disciplinary procedures – play a significant role in reducing the risk of conflict between employees in the uniformed public services.

Codes of behaviour (e.g. formal)

These exist in most uniformed public services and may be very detailed and elaborate, as they are in the armed forces. The greater the risk of internal conflict, the more formal and prescriptive (demanding) the code of behaviour. Behaviour codes in the armed forces reflect the fact that the services are mainly composed of large numbers of young, energetic and sometimes testosterone-driven males who are trained for conflict and could do plenty of damage if they wanted to.

 Link

Book 1, Unit 5, pages 189–193

www.ipcc.gov.uk/ (Police Code of Conduct)
www.army.mod.uk (Queen's Regulations)

Internal sanctions

These are discipline procedures, and include the kind of summary justice which is given out by a commanding officer and used for relatively minor administrative offences in the armed forces. They also include the systems of verbal and written warnings and reprimands used in civilian public services.

www.acas.org.uk (ACAS Code of Practice 1: Disciplinary and grievance procedures)

Retraining of employees

In cases of serious internal conflict which does not, however, warrant dismissal, employees can be retrained or transferred to other departments. If the conflict takes the form of bullying, it is normally better to move the bully not the victim.

Use of internal mediators or advisers

ACAS is a publicly-funded body which carries out resolution of workplace disputes in both the public and private sector. It carries out mediation for large-scale disputes involving pay, conditions and large numbers of workers, and small-scale disputes such as quarrels between individuals and departments, as well as mediating conflict over grievance and disciplinary issues. It can enlist the help of other more specialised organisations such as the Equal Opportunities Commission or the Commission for Racial Equality.

remember
Your college or workplace may have a code of conduct. Check it out. How effective do you think it is?

www.acas.org.uk/index.aspx?articleid=301
www.eoc.org.uk/
www.cre.gov.uk/

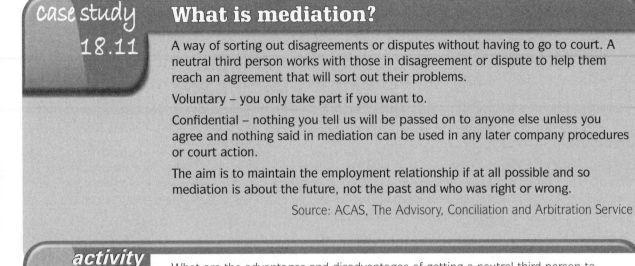

case study 18.11 — What is mediation?

A way of sorting out disagreements or disputes without having to go to court. A neutral third person works with those in disagreement or dispute to help them reach an agreement that will sort out their problems.

Voluntary – you only take part if you want to.

Confidential – nothing you tell us will be passed on to anyone else unless you agree and nothing said in mediation can be used in any later company procedures or court action.

The aim is to maintain the employment relationship if at all possible and so mediation is about the future, not the past and who was right or wrong.

Source: ACAS, The Advisory, Conciliation and Arbitration Service

activity — GROUP WORK

What are the advantages and disadvantages of getting a neutral third person to settle disputes?

Case study 18.12 relates to research by ACAS on the success of mediation in the public and private sector, and in charities.

Mediation can be done both internally (i.e. by a manager in the same organisation as the parties who are in conflict) or externally (by a mediator brought in from an outside organisation such as ACAS, or a private mediation company). Internal mediation

case study 18.12 — Mediation

For most parties the mediation went according to their expectations and the experience was positive. The key positive feature of mediation was identified by parties as the external mediator, whose role in enabling parties to set out their case to each other and to find a way to reach agreement was seen as **invaluable**. Other features of mediation identified as contributing to the value of the process, included being obliged to spend time with the other party, listening, explaining, **negotiating** and also the iterative [step-by-step] process of composing the agreement. In constructing an agreement point by point, parties were enabled to find solutions in small steps rather than all at once.

Negative experiences were about the length and stress of the meetings, the problems of confronting the other party and the persistent problem of the mediation format not being the investigative form desired. Some parties felt that they were not as skilled as the other party at setting out their case and acting in their own interests.

Source: The Acas small firms mediation pilot, research to explore parties' experiences and views on the value of mediation, Ref: 04/05 2005. Prepared by: John Seargeant on behalf of Acas Research and Evaluation

activity — INDIVIDUAL WORK

1. What are the differences between a 'mediation format' and an 'investigative form'?

2. Why would some people in a dispute or conflict feel strongly that the investigative form was better than the mediation format?

works well if the mediator is a patient, fair-minded, sympathetic and understanding person, and if the people in dispute are basically keen to get the dispute over and done with. External mediation is better in a major conflict where internal managers are not impartial, or where special skills and understanding are needed to resolve the conflict.

Facilitative mediation allows the people in conflict to talk to the mediator and develop their own preferred solutions to the conflict, which the mediator then communicates to the other parties. Directive mediation is slightly more formal, in that the mediator uses his or her expertise and lays out formal options, giving advice where needed. It is therefore more like adjudication (judgment) in the eyes of the people who are in conflict.

Mediation typically takes from half a day to a day to accomplish. The basic format is that the mediator meets with each side in the conflict; then, having done the groundwork and being fairly sure that an agreement or compromise is possible, a meeting between the two sides is arranged. Normally – though not always – the meeting is followed by agreement and the conflict is resolved.

Record-keeping relating to individuals

Record keeping refers mainly to the written records of disciplinary or grievance-based disputes, or to records taken at regular staff appraisals by team leaders or other appraisers of employees.

Records kept are used to keep track of any disciplinary or grievance action so it does not get forgotten or overlooked. They will also back up any legal or tribunal action that results from a conflict. In addition they may affect the kind of reference that workers get from their employers if they apply for another job, or for promotion or a more specialised role in the same organisation.

Informal actions

Mentoring (e.g. buddy systems, role models)

Mentoring is an informal or formal arrangement where a senior employee helps new employees to settle into their job. The idea is that the **mentor** gives advice and

---

case study 18.13

Acas advice

It is important, and in the interests of both employers and employees, to keep written records during the disciplinary process. Records should include:

- The complaint against the employee;
- The employee's defence.
- Findings made and actions taken.
- The reason for actions taken.
- Whether an appeal was lodged.
- The outcome of the appeal.
- Any grievances raised during the disciplinary procedure.
- Subsequent developments.

---

activity
INDIVIDUAL WORK

1. Research information about the methods of resolving disputes or conflict used in your college or workplace.
2. Collect examples of the documentation used in your college or workplace.

guidance at the 'point of need', i.e. when the new employee needs to know. It is a partial alternative to formal training.

Though mentors might not often have to resolve disputes, they certainly have a role in preventing them from happening in the first place by ensuring that new employees and probationers (in the police) know what is expected of them.

The **buddy system** is an arrangement where two people work together or keep in close contact so that they can give support and back-up at work. The system can operate in dangerous workplaces, e.g. firefighters on operations, but can also be a form of mentoring where each buddy gives advice and feedback to the other. It is used in the police where pairs of officers work together, e.g. on patrols. Like mentoring, the buddy system reduces the likelihood of workplace conflict arising in the first place. And if there is a conflict, the fact of having a supportive buddy at work can make the experience less stressful.

Role models are people we see as setting a good example, and whom we wish to imitate in some way. Whether they are helpful in reducing or dealing with conflict is hard to say; it depends on the role model!

Sharing best practice

It can help to reduce conflict within teams if the leader sets up a system of standardisation of work practices or ways of agreeing on how particular jobs should be done. Besides improving the quality of work done, this reduces the risk of disagreements arising out of people doing the same jobs in different ways.

Increased socialisation between employees

Socialisation between employees is often a good thing as it develops friendships and increases job satisfaction. However, there can be problems. If people are excluded from social activities, or feel forced to take part in social activities when they do not want to, the effects may be counterproductive. Furthermore, underlying conflicts may surface in a social setting and become worse as a result – especially if the socialisation involves drinking and 'letting your hair down', as is the case with some office Christmas parties.

Use of humour to diffuse situations

Skilful managers can use humour to put people in a good mood and to relieve tension by putting a different slant on a situation. A cheerful and humorous workplace atmosphere will normally increase job satisfaction and decrease tendencies towards conflict. However, not all humour is good natured or well meant. Sarcastic hurtful humour can be an aspect of aggressive behaviour, and taunts, practical jokes and teasing can anger people and increase conflict.

Demonstrating acts of gratitude and politeness

Gratitude normally means thanking people and showing appreciation of what they have done. In a workplace this should be done verbally. If you are writing a note or email to someone who has helped you in some way, you should normally include an expression of thanks. Politeness means showing consideration for other people in ways which are acceptable in that workplace.

remember
If newcomers are seen as 'too polite' it is generally regarded as a less serious fault than being 'not polite enough'.

Excessive politeness may sometimes be seen as submissive behaviour, while the absence of politeness can be seen as aggressive. Apologising for mistakes is sometimes necessary, but then again apology is submissive behaviour: it should not be done too often or it loses its meaning. Some people apologise and explain at the same time. This may be counterproductive since the explanation (or excuse) devalues the apology, and the apology may make the explanation unnecessary.

activity
INDIVIDUAL WORK
18.6

M3

D1

Write an article for an in-house public service newspaper or magazine examining two different ways of sorting out workplace disputes between individuals. Your article should:

- Give a reasoned comparison of their effectiveness.
- Assess their usefulness by working out their cost-effectiveness and any moral and human rights implications.

Progress Check

1. What are the main points of humanistic, behaviourist, cognitive, Gestalt and psychoanalytic psychology?
2. Nature or nurture – which matters more to public service workers? Give your reasons.
3. List as many ways as you can in which public services use the findings or theories of psychology.
4. State the key features of aggressive and submissive communication behaviour.
5. Outline what is meant by assertive communication behaviour.
6. In what ways does assertive behaviour help to uphold the rights of women?
7. How can people working in a given uniformed public service benefit by understanding behaviour?
8. What are the main causes of conflicts between individuals in the workplace?
9. Why, and how, can conflict happen between individuals and local or national government?
10. State five ways of preventing conflict in the workplace.
11. What is mediation and how is it done?

Glossary

Abseiling
a method of going down cliffs using ropes, a harness and steel clips (also called rappelling).

Accelerant
fuel used by an arsonist to make a fire burn hotter or faster.

Accession countries
countries that have recently joined the EU.

Accountable
(a) open to inspection, not secret; (b) responsible.

Achievable
a goal or aim is said to be 'achievable' when the team or person attempting it has the ability, knowledge, strength or other qualities needed to reach it successfully.

Act
a (large, complex) law.

Activity centre
a place which provides outdoor activities such as climbing, canoeing, etc.

Administration
(a) 'paperwork' (often done with computers now), to make an organisation run smoothly; (b) organisation and delivery (e.g. of justice through the courts).

Administrative action (in the armed forces)
minor punishments and warnings for minor offences in the armed forces, carried out by a commanding officer.

Admissible (evidence)
evidence which can be used in court.

Adventure Activities Licensing Authority
government-backed organisation licensing activity centres and promoting outdoor safety.

Adventurous
involving challenging and exciting activities.

Adversarial
of a court system, based on a contest between opponents (e.g. prosecution and defence). The British court system is mainly adversarial, but public inquiries are inquisitorial (see 'inquisitorial').

Aerobic capacity
a measure of the amount of oxygen used by a person during exercise.

Affirmation
a legally binding promise (not an oath) used by some people before giving evidence in court.

Agencies of social control
the family, peer group, school, religion, the media or anything else which influences our beliefs and behaviour as we grow up.

Agency
any organisation acting for someone else (especially for the public or the government). Loosely, any civilian public service, volunteer organisation or government-backed body.

Agenda
(a) a series of plans; (b) a list of topics to be discussed at a meeting.

Aggravated (of offences)
made more serious than normal (e.g. by racism or a high level of violence).

Aggravating
circumstances or actions that make anything unpleasant (e.g. a crime) more serious.

Aid agencies
international organisations such as the UN, Oxfam, Save the Children which help relieve famine and do other humanitarian work in poor countries.

Aim
(a) an intention; (b) a general statement of what you (or an organisation) plan to do (e.g. 'to reduce car crime').

Aiming off
in navigation, choosing a course which is not the shortest route to your destination, in order to meet a road, track or other feature which you can then follow to your destination.

'Airwave'
a kind of digital radio technology used by the emergency services to help them work together at major incidents.

Amendments
changes (in the law).

Analytical (of thinking)
picking out the main points from a mass of information, and understanding their importance.

Antisocial behaviour
low-level crime, e.g. vandalism, noise, heavy drinking in public, etc.

Appeal
a request to a higher court for a retrial.

Appraisal
a procedure where an employee speaks to their line manager about their ambitions, performance and training requirements, etc. in the job. It is partly assessment, partly self-assessment, and partly a chance for the employee to talk about their medium- and long-term career aims.

Appropriate adult
a person (e.g. social worker or guardian) allowed to be present at police questioning of a young person or vulnerable adult.

Aptitude
ability.

Armed Forces Pay Review Body
the people who decide what people working in the armed forces should be paid.

Arrest
depriving a crime suspect of their freedom.

Arresting agency
the police, HM Revenue and Customs, and any other organisation which is allowed by law to arrest people.

Assassination
killing a prominent politician or other individual for a political or religious reason.

Assertive
being direct, confident and honest without being aggressive.

Asylum
a place of safety from persecution (e.g. in another country).

At-risk register
an official list of children thought to be at risk of abuse.

Attack point
a landmark from which you can take bearings and navigate.

Attitude/behaviour cycle
a sequence of events where attitudes (opinions) become more extreme and behaviour (e.g. protests) also gets more extreme, for example in a campaign or dispute.

Audacity
having daring ideas and the courage to carry them out.

Audit
an inspection of how money is spent and whether an organisation is getting value for money.

Audit Commission
a government body which inspects public service spending.

Authorisation
official permission.

Authority
(a) the power or right to enforce obedience; (b) a government-backed body with a controlling function, e.g. a police authority.

Autonomy
independence (of countries, or regions of bigger countries).

Avian
to do with birds.

Avoidance
the techniques of avoiding disagreements and confrontations in the workplace.

Bail
an arrangement to ensure that a person who is charged with an offence and released will turn up in court when needed.

Basic Command Unit (BCU)
a neighbourhood policing group.

Battalion
group of around 650 soldiers.

Battlegroup
any large group (500+) of soldiers.

Bearings
directions expressed in degrees using three figures, e.g. 045 is north-east.

Beat
a police officer's area of responsibility, e.g. in a town centre.

Beat manager
a police officer who organises the policing of a given area, often with the help of community support officers.

Behaviour
actions (usually of people or animals) which can be observed, recorded and scientifically studied.

Behaviourism (US spelling 'behaviorism')
the study of human or animal behaviour in relation to its causes.

Behaviourist
to do with how we react to stimuli or events.

Belay
a method of safeguarding a climber by tying on to the rock-face or some other support.

Best value
a government measure of the effectiveness of a public service.

Bilateral (of agreements)
involving two agencies or countries.

Biometric
based on digitally recorded exact measurements of people's faces, etc.

Biometric passports
a kind of passport (not yet fully developed) containing exact information about certain body measurements which, in theory, would be useless if stolen and impossible to forge.

BNP (British National Party)
a racist political party.

Body composition
amount of body fat.

Body mass index (BMI)
a measure of a person's weight in relation to their height.

Boom
inflatable dam or barrier for channelling water, etc.

Bovine TB
a cattle disease caused by a bacterium which may be transmitted by badgers and other wildlife. It is no longer dangerous to humans, but it threatens the livelihoods of cattle farmers.

Brainwash
a term loosely used to mean forcing people to change their beliefs by repeated bullying, propaganda, preaching, etc.

Breach of bail
disobeying the conditions of bail.

Briefing
(a) giving instructions before a task starts; (b) holding a meeting to inform and review while a task is ongoing.

Brigade
group of 5000 soldiers.

Glossary

British Crime Survey
a yearly government survey of victims of crime, which is thought to give a reliable indication of whether crime levels are going up or down.

Bronze command
the operational (on-site) level of emergency management.

Buddy system
two people working together closely as 'partners' in a public service.

Business continuity management (BCM)
methods of ensuring that businesses survive disasters, emergencies and other severe disruption; emergency planning and tabletop exercises.

Bureaucratic
involving a lot of office work and paperwork.

Call centres
another name for emergency service control rooms.

Camming
a method of jamming something in a crack to help a rock-climber.

Capitalist
(a) (of a political or economic system) based on free trade, competition between private companies and relative freedom from government interference; (b) (of a person) someone who believes in the capitalist system; (c) someone who runs a private company or business in competition with other companies or businesses.

Carbon footprints
the carbon dioxide pollution caused by an activity, e.g. driving to work produces a carbon footprint; walking to work doesn't.

Carbon trading
the buying and selling of certificates which are issued by governments and which give firms a right to pollute the environment with carbon dioxide up to an agreed limit. A firm which is going to pollute beyond its agreed limit can buy a certificate from a firm which is going to pollute less than its agreed limit. The system is intended to provide encouragement to firms to pollute less, without setting quotas (limits) which might damage the country's economic performance.

Cardiovascular fitness
condition of heart and blood vessels.

Career development
(a) promotion; (b) specialisation in a particular kind of work.

Casualty
(a) a person who is killed in an emergency; (b) a person who is injured in an emergency.

Casualty bureau
a temporary office which deals with information about the dead and injured in a major incident.

Catching feature
something that tells you that you have gone too far (when navigating).

Category 1 responders
local authorities and the emergency services, who have a special responsibility under the Civil Contingencies Act 2004 to work together, plan for and respond to major incidents.

Category 2 responders
other organisations such as electricity, gas and water companies which also have a role to play in dealing with major incidents under the Civil Contingencies Act 2004.

Caution
a warning given to arrested people by the police that they must tell the truth: 'You do not have to say anything. But it may harm your defence if you do not mention when questioned something which you later rely on in Court. Anything you do say may be given in evidence.'

CCTV
closed circuit television.

Centralised (of command, etc.)
coming from a few major control rooms rather than lots of little ones.

Chain of command
rank structure.

Charter
a list of rights, freedoms or duties.

Chatter
words relating to terrorism or organised crime which can be monitored in emails and on mobile phone networks, etc.

Cholera
a serious bacterial disease caused by poor sanitation or floods in tropical countries and producing large amounts of watery diarrhoea.

Circuit judge
a judge in the Crown Court.

Citizen-focused
doing what the public really want.

Civil community
ordinary people.

Civil contingencies
major emergencies.

Civil justice
the court system for seeking compensation and for settling disputes between people, firms and other organisations.

Civil power
the police or the government (or both).

Civilian (staff)
non-uniformed people who work for a uniformed public service.

Climatic
to do with long-term weather trends, or the 'average' weather over many years.

Coalition
a group of countries or organisations acting together without a formal treaty or agreement.

COBRA
the government's top disaster management committee.

Codes of practice
official instructions on the correct way to do a job.

Cognitive
to do with learning and understanding.

Cognitive-behavioural therapy
a way of 'teaching' people to overcome mental problems such as anxieties and phobias.

Cohesion (community)
everybody supporting everybody else (i.e. with less poverty, crime and antisocial behaviour).

Cohesive (of communities)
where people are able to get on with each other and lead an active, enjoyable social life. The word is used by the government to describe a thriving community.

Cold War (1945–89)
a period of bad relations between the West and Soviet (communist) Russia. It happened because their political and economic systems (capitalism and communism) were incompatible. Each side tried to increase its power and influence, and weaken the other, using propaganda, political manoeuvring, economic pressure, threats of war and by arming 'liberation movements' in poorer countries.

Collation (of information)
collecting, filing and storing (either on paper or in computer databases).

Collecting features
landmarks you can pass and identify while navigating.

Command
the art of setting tasks for other people to do.

Command task
any action which requires a team and a commander for it to be carried out (it can be either a real or simulated task).

Commissioned
refers to officers of the rank of 2nd Lieutenant or above who have completed their training.

Common
(a) shared; (b) often seen.

Communist
describes a country following an extreme form of socialism in which the government runs everything and private industry is not allowed to develop.

Communities
groups of people who have geographical, social, economic or cultural characteristics, e.g. local communities, farming communities, the gay community.

Community sentence
a serious non-prison sentence with strict conditions and supervision, used for persistent offenders.

Company
group of around 100 soldiers.

Competence
ability to do a task to a good standard.

Competences
skills.

Competencies
abilities or skills.

Complainant
the person or organisation suing another person or organisation in a civil court.

Components of fighting power
weapons, people, plans; everything that is needed in a war effort.

Computer modelling
predicting future trends using computer programs and information processing techniques.

Conditioning
(a) the automatic association of one event with another, based on frequent experience (e.g. salivating when a dinner bell rings); (b) a learned response which happens so often that it becomes automatic.

Conditions
requirements or restrictions imposed by the courts against people who are out on bail, or who are serving sentences in the community (e.g. not going to football matches if the offence involves football violence).

Conditions of service
pay, holidays, pensions, medical care and other rights of workers.

Conflict of interest
a situation where the correct course of action will not necessarily have the best outcome for some parties.

Confrontation
an open disagreement or quarrel.

Constitution
a big list of laws, treaties, rights and responsibilities agreed on by a country or a group of countries.

Consulate
an office run by British diplomats in a foreign country.

Contentious (of statements)
provocative or likely to cause trouble.

Contingencies
emergencies or major incidents.

Control
(a) checking or monitoring the progress of a task; (b) feeding information or instructions to people on a continuous basis.

Control centre
the place where the emergency services get incoming emergency calls, and decide what to do about them (especially the first response).

Control points
markers used in orienteering.

Convention
an international agreement (often human rights, setting standards for treatment of prisoners of war, etc.).

Coordination
working closely together on a big project.

Cordon
a barrier or line of tape around an area of temporarily restricted access (e.g. an accident scene). The aim is to keep the public out.

Core duties
main or basic roles and responsibilities.

Coroner
a kind of judge who investigates the causes of violent or unexplained deaths, using evidence collected by the police, pathologists, etc.

Correctional
to do with stopping offenders from re-offending.

Corrupted
bribed, influenced or threatened to do something which is against the law.

Cost/benefit analysis
an examination of the benefits gained in an operation against the costs (i.e. was it worth it?).

Council of the European Union
a meeting of government ministers from each EU member country .

Counselling
sorting out people's mental problems by listening to them (and, sometimes, setting tasks to help them overcome those problems).

Counterfeiting
forgery.

Coup
the violent overthrow of one government by another (usually done by an army general).

Court martial
a British military court (hears cases where the accused is a military person who commits an offence linked to military work).

Creative (of thinking)
imaginative and original.

Crime trend
an increase or decrease in the amount of crime (or of a given type of crime) over a period of time.

Criminal Cases Review Commission
a body which examines cases which might be sent to a higher court on appeal.

Criminal Injuries Compensation Authority
a government body which pays compensation to some victims of violent crime.

Criminal justice
the court system for dealing with offenders who have been charged by the police.

Criminal justice system
police, criminal courts, probation, prison, etc.

Criminal liability
the possibility of being tried for a criminal offence.

Criminalise
to make an action, e.g. money-laundering, illegal.

Criminology
the study of crime, crime trends, crime patterns and ways of reducing crime.

Criteria (arrest)
the factors which make an arrest lawful, e.g. 'to prevent a person suffering physical injury'.

Crown Court
the court which tries the 3% of offences which are really serious.

Crown Prosecution Service
the body which prepares police prosecutions and argues the police case in court.

Cultural
to do with language, lifestyle, religion and customs.

Custodial (of sentences)
in prison, a young offender's institution, or some other secure place.

Custody officer
the person (often a sergeant) at a police station who looks after detained people.

Debriefing
a structured assessment of how well a task went, after it has finished. The aim is to learn how to do better next time.

Decentralised
local commanders have the power to make decisions.

Decontamination
cleaning (e.g. of toxic dust from clothing).

Defendant
the person in a court who is accused of a crime.

Defibrillating
controlling the heartbeat during a heart attack.

Deindividuated (of crowds)
taken over by group or collective emotion.

Delegation
giving tasks and responsibilities to subordinates (people lower down the chain of command).

Demand management
satisfying people's needs effectively and efficiently.

Democracy
a type of government with free and secret elections, a Parliament, and laws which support individual freedom and human rights.

Democratically elected
chosen by the people in a general election.

Deport
officially remove a person to another country.

Depression
a mental illness whose symptoms are feelings of sadness and despair.

Designated
labelled or classified.

Design out crime
build houses, flats, estates, etc. in a way which does not give encouragement or cover to muggers, burglars, etc.

Designated
chosen.

Destabilising
likely to cause anger and fighting.

Detailed control
a type of control where subordinates have to be monitored very closely. Rarely used these days.

Determinism
the idea that the environment determines what we do and we have no real choice.

Deterrent
anything which puts people off committing crimes or attacking a country.

Development plan
a written plan with targets, outlining how a person will improve certain skills over a period of time.

Deviant behaviour
behaviour which is regarded as strange or unacceptable by most people. (It may or may not be criminal.)

Dictatorship
a country ruled by a person or group of people who have not been democratically elected.

Diction
speech (pronunciation).

Diplomatic
to do with representatives of one country talking to and negotiating with representatives of another. In Britain diplomacy is mainly organised by the Foreign Office and done through ambassadors.

Direct report
an immediate subordinate.

Direction
giving instructions or advice on how something should be done.

Disclosing
(of information) revealing or sharing information which has been secret.

Discrimination
treating people unfairly for reasons of sex, race, age, disability, etc.

Disorder
(a) rioting, unruly behaviour, behaviour that 'disturbs the peace';
(b) illness or condition (often a mental illness).

Disseminate
the act of sharing information with those who need it.

Dissemination (of information)
communicating information widely to the people or services that need it.

Distal
long-term, distant.

District judge
a paid, legally qualified magistrate.

Diversion
of measures designed to keep people away from crime, or from prosecution (e.g. final warning).

Diversity
(a) differences between people; (b) people from different ethnic and cultural backgrounds living and working together happily and on equal terms, respecting each others' differences .

Division
group of 20,000 soldiers.

DNA
deoxyribonucleic acid (a chemical in the body which carries genetic information and can be used to identify offenders).

DNA profile
the lines resulting from DNA analysis which are different for each individual.

Doctrine
theory (of policing, warfare, etc.).

Dossier
a file of information.

Downstream oil
oil spills in rivers and water supplies. The oil flows with the water and causes problems a long way from where the pollution started. (Downstream = in the direction of the flow of the water course or river.)

Duty solicitor
a solicitor who advises (free of charge) accused people who do not have a solicitor of their own.

Dysentery
a water-borne disease carried by protozoa or bacteria which causes inflammation and ulcers in the intestine, leading to fever and severe diarrhoea.

E-coli
a kind of deadly food poisoning caused by bacteria and linked with poor hygiene in food preparation areas in places such as butchers' shops or in hospitals and nursing homes.

Economic
to do with industry, trade, wealth, taxes, money, etc.

Economy (the)
trade, commerce and industry in the country as a whole.

Effective (of work, systems, etc.)
good; achieves what it sets out to do.

Efficient
achieving a good result with a minimum of cost, effort, etc.

Either way
see 'Triable either way'.

Electoral roll
a list of all the people living in an area who are eligible to vote at elections.

El Nino
the name of a current in the Pacific Ocean that appears in certain years and is thought to upset the world's weather systems, causing disastrous floods and droughts in other parts of the world.

Embezzlement
stealing money from an employer over a period of time.

Emergency
(a) a situation that needs quick action by the emergency services;
(b) a major incident, a disaster, or the immediate threat of a disaster.

Emergency Planning Unit
an organisation set up by a local authority to produce emergency plans, in consultation with the emergency and other relevant services.

Empathy
the ability to understand another person's feelings or point of view without necessarily agreeing with them.

Environment Agency
a government-run organisation which deals with flooding, pollution, etc.

Epidemic
an outbreak of a (usually infectious) disease affecting many people.

Equal opportunities
fair, decent and equal treatment for all workers whatever their sex, background, religion, etc.

Ergonomics
the study of how to fit the workplace to the human body and human actions.

Escalation
the progressive worsening of a conflict or other problem.

Esteem
being valued or respected.

Ethics
moral principles (knowing the difference between right and wrong).

Ethnic
of people with roots in the traditions and culture of a specific geographical area. (NB: the word is an adjective, not a noun.)

Ethnic cleansing
the killing or displacement of one ethnic group by another.

Ethnicity
aspects of behaviour, lifestyle, language, culture or belief linked to the geographical origins of an individual or a group of people.

Ethos
the character, spirit and attitudes of an organisation.

European Commission
the unelected ruling body of the EU.

European Parliament
the elected law-making body of the European Union.

Evacuation
removing large numbers of people from a disaster area to a place of safety.

Evaluating
judging the success of a piece of work by measuring its good effects against what it has cost.

Executive
the part of government which puts laws into practice (government departments).

Explosive device
(sometimes called an 'improvised explosive device' (IED)) home-made bomb.

Explosive ordnance disposal (EOD)
bomb disposal.

Extended policing family
the police and anybody who works with or for them.

Extinguishing media
substances such as water and foam which will put out fires.

Extradition
the deportation of a person to another country (at the other country's request) in order to stand trial there.

Extrajudicial
without justice or court action, based only on 'intelligence received' (of killings of suspected terrorists).

Financial accountability
responsible for money and explaining how it has been spent.

Firebreaks
places where trees or bushes have been cut so that forest fires cannot spread.

Fluency
skill and speed.

Forensic
to do with solving crimes through the careful analysis of evidence.

Formative (of reviews, assessment, etc.)
done while a project is going on.

Free enterprise
the right of people to start their own companies, compete with others and get rich.

Free market
a system encouraging private industry and free private enterprise, e.g. by getting rid of customs duties and by minimising government control.

Free will
the idea that we can choose what to do.

Functional command
the command of a number of services which are cooperating on a shared task. Related to 'joint command' and uses techniques similar to 'mission command'.

Funding
money given to a public service or similar organisation (usually from the government).

Gauge
an instrument or device for measuring or controlling fluids, gases, etc.

GDP (Gross Domestic Product)
a measure of the total wealth of a country.

Generic
general; relating to many aspects of a particular job, e.g. map-reading is a generic skill for soldiers.

Genocide
the organised large-scale killing of a particular ethnic group, with the aim of wiping out that group.

Geology
the study of rock types.

Gestalt psychology
a kind of psychology which studies the way we perceive things, emotions and ideas.

Globalisation
increased links, communication, trade and transport with all parts of the world.

Glorifies
praises or supports.

Gold
the strategic (top) level of command in a major incident.

Gold command
see 'Gold'.

Governing body
an organisation which sets out rules, procedures, safety measures and standards for a sporting activity.

Grand strategic
command of the armed forces by the government, in line with Britain's long-term strategic plans.

Grievance
a complaint within an organisation (e.g. about working conditions or harassment).

Grounds
a reason for doing an action (e.g. grounds for searching a building).

Handlines
ropes fixed to cave walls to help people move safely.

Handrail
something like a wall or a stream which you can follow when navigating.

Harness
a safety device to stop climbers, etc. from falling.

Hazard
something that might cause harm.

Hazchem
a system of codes used for identifying the contents of road and rail tankers, etc.

Health and Safety Commission (HSC)
the body in charge of safety in British workplaces.

Health and Safety Executive (HSE)
a body of inspectors run by the HSC.

Health and safety policy statement
a notice which an employer has to put up by law explaining to workers the safety arrangements in that workplace.

Heredity
the passing down of genes and associated characteristics (e.g. eye colour) from parents to children.

Heyphone
a kind of telephone which works in caves.

Hierarchy
a rank order, from the lowest to the highest, or from the highest to the lowest.

Holocaust
the genocide (mass murder) of 6 million Jews in Germany during World War II.

Homophobic
to do with a hatred (or extreme fear) of homosexuality .

Humanistic
refers to psychology (and other beliefs) which emphasise the value and importance of individual feelings and thoughts.

Humanitarian (of work)
work to relieve suffering, famine, etc.

Hurricane
a circular storm about 500 miles across, with wind speeds up to about 200 mph. Sometimes called a typhoon or a cyclone. (It is not the same as a tornado or 'twister', which is a spiralling cloud with high wind speeds and ferocious weather inside it that can kill people and demolish buildings over a narrow track about 50 yards wide.)

Hydraulic
operated by fluid (e.g. water) under pressure.

Hyperthermia
heat-stroke; overheating of the body.

Hypothermia
when the body becomes dangerously cold.

Idealised
too good to be true.

Ideological (of conflicts)
conflicts to do with widely differing or extreme political beliefs.

Ideology
a set of (usually extreme) political beliefs.

Illicit
illegal (especially in the sense of avoiding paying tax), e.g. illicit whisky distillation.

Implement
put into practice; do.

Incident
any unexpected or dangerous event which requires the call-out of the emergency services.

Incident Commander
the person in charge of an emergency response in the fire and rescue service.

Incident grading
a way of assessing how serious an emergency incident is.

Incident manager
the person in overall control of the emergency response to a serious incident.

Incommunicado
unable (or not allowed) to speak to anyone.

Incongruence
a psychological term meaning that there is a big difference between what someone thinks they are and what they would like to be.

Independent Police Complaints Commission
a body of experts not connected with the police who investigate serious complaints against the police and any deaths which happen as a result of police action.

Index line
a line under the housing of a compass, in line with the 'direction of travel arrow', used for reading bearings.

Indictable offence
a serious offence which must be tried at the Crown Court.

Infrastructure
roads, railways, electricity, water and gas supplies, telephones and other services needed by the community and industry.

Initial (of training)
first or basic training, after a person has joined a uniformed service.

Initiative
(a) a project or new idea; (b) originality in thinking or planning.

Inner city
areas of low income and old housing, often with social problems, around the middle of many of Britain's large towns and cities.

Inquisitorial
of an inquiry, by a judge which aims to get at the truth. (Compare with 'adversarial'.)

Inshore
near the coast (of coastal waters).

Instigating
setting up.

Institutions
branches of huge international organisations such as the EU, the UN or NATO.

Institutions
organisations which are often part of a bigger organisation (e.g. UNESCO is an institution within the UN).

Insurgents
armed rebels using terrorist tactics.

Intelligence
information, in the police (crime related) or the armed forces (to do with enemy strength, plans, movements, etc.).

Intelligence-led (of policing)
police actions based on information received about expected criminal activity, rather than simply responding to a crime after it has been reported.

Intensive supervision and surveillance programmes (ISSP)
community-based sentences for young offenders.

Inter-agency
involving a number of public services and other groups (e.g. the local authority) working together.

Interagency cooperation
how the police, fire and rescue and other services work together on an emergency incident.

Inter-agency working
partnerships; different bodies (e.g. police and social services) working together .

Interests (British)
companies, energy supplies, etc. outside Britain which are linked to Britain and Britain's economic, political or military well-being.

Interoperability
the ability of teams from different services to work well together on the same task.

Introspection
looking into one's own thoughts.

Invaluable
extremely useful.

Islamist
name given to an anti-Western political belief, which claims to come from the teachings of the Qur'an, and can be linked to terrorism.

Jargon
specialised technical language .

Job description
a statement of what a particular job involves list of duties, etc.

Joined up
used of partnerships between agencies such as police and social services to tackle crime, so that the public services do not work against each other and so that all problems are dealt with.

Joined-up government
a system of partnership and liaison between different public services, to ensure that there are no gaps in provision for, say, young offenders.

Judiciary
the people who apply and interpret laws (judges and courts).

Justification
full explanation showing why an action has been done.

Karabiner
a large metal clip.

Labelling
classifying or stereotyping people in a way which can have harmful effects on them.

Leadership
'the art of motivating people towards a common objective'.

Left-wing
linked to communism or socialism – supports workers against bosses, state control, high taxes, large public services and high wages for ordinary workers.

Legal accountability
can be taken to court.

Legionnaires' disease
a sometimes deadly flu-like disease caused by a bacterium which can be spread through hot-water systems, steam-based central heating, etc.

Legislation
laws.

Legislative
law-making.

Legislature
the part of a government which makes laws.

Levees
a kind of river embankment built to prevent flooding on very flat, low-lying land.

Liaise
work together, share information or cooperate with another organisation, public service, etc.

Lichen
a mossy fungus that grows on rocks and can make them slippery.

Life opportunities
chances to succeed in life.

Lifted (of fingerprints)
removed using plastic film so that they can be preserved and studied in the laboratory.

Litigation
taking someone to (normally a civil) court; suing someone.

Live exercise
a practice emergency response using real people, vehicles and equipment to deal with a mock emergency.

Live links
a video link so that a child, vulnerable victim or vulnerable witness does not have to come to court in person to answer questions.

Local Resilience Forum
a non-statutory body set up in each police area to coordinate the emergency planning of local authorities and emergency services within that area.

Local resolution
dealing with a complaint against the police at the police station (i.e. not taking it further).

Log
a diary or written day-by-day record of things done (e.g. on an expedition).

Logarithmic
a mathematical system based on the squares, cubes, etc. ('powers') of numbers such as 10 or two. It is used in the Richter scale of earthquake intensity. The relationship between 5 and 7 on the Richter scale is the same as the relationship between 10 to the power 5 and 10 to the power 7 (i.e. $10 \times 10 \times 10 \times 10 \times 10 = 100,000$ to $10 \times 10 \times 10 \times 10 \times 10 \times 10 \times 10 = 10,000,000$). Thus an earthquake measuring 7 on the Richter scale is 100 times more powerful than one measuring 5.

Logistics
the transport of people and weapons by the armed forces.

Loyalty
steady unselfish support for a leader, team, organisation, etc.

Magistrates' court
the type of court which tries less-serious offences (97% of all offences that come to court).

Major incident
a disaster or a large-scale emergency with the loss or possible loss of lives and property.

Malicious ignitions
starting a fire with criminal intent – arson.

Management
the art of organising and motivating people so that they work effectively and efficiently.

Managerial
to do with motivating people and organising their workloads.

Manoeuvres
moves.

Manoeuvrist
a system of command and control which maximises the mobility and speed of response of military units.

Mapping progress
recording, checking or planning progress.

Marshalling area
a place near a disaster scene where vehicles can be parked, people can rest, and briefing or debriefing can take place.

Measures
actions (often to do with safety).

Mediation
a technique for solving disputes by getting a third person to act as a go-between.

Mentor
an older employee who is given the role of helping a younger employee to settle into a workplace. The system is used with police probationers.

MI5
Government agency working for security within the UK ('spying').

MI6
Government agency working for British security but outside the UK ('spying').

Milestone
an intermediate target.

Militants
civilians who are prepared to break the law (and sometimes to fight or kill) to support an ideology.

Military strategic
the major war or defence planning by the Ministry of Defence and the Joint Chiefs of Staff (the heads of each of the armed forces).

Ministry of Justice
the government department in charge of the courts and the prison and probation services.

Mission
a style of command used in the armed forces which gives freedom to subordinates to decide how a task will be carried out.

Mission statement
(a) a statement outlining the purpose or aims of a public service; (b) (in command and control) – an instruction giving a task and a purpose (but not saying how the task should be done).

Mitigating
circumstances or actions that make something (e.g. a crime) less serious.

MO
the recognisable working methods or 'trademarks'; of individual criminals.

Money laundering
making money which comes from crime appear legal (e.g. by investing it in legal businesses).

Monitoring
frequent checking.

Monopoly
a situation where the government or one company is the only producer of certain goods or services.

Moral courage
saying or doing the right thing even when it is unpopular.

Morality
the study, or knowledge, of right and wrong.

Mountaineering
climbing steep, high, rocky or snowy mountains.

Multi-agency
used to describe a partnership between (usually) several public services, local government and other organisations.

Multi-agency debrief
a collective review of the performance of emergency workers from a range of organisations (e.g. police, fire and rescue, ambulance, local authority, etc.) after a major incident.

Multilateral
(of agreements) involving a number of agencies or countries.

Multinational force
a large number of soldiers, etc. from a range of allied countries fighting or working in a given country such as Afghanistan.

Mutate (of viruses or other living organisms)
to undergo genetic changes which result in changes of behaviour or appearance.

National Crime Recording Standard
a system of recording crimes which the police have to follow so that their crime figures are more reliable, and can be compared from one area to another.

National Intelligence Model
a system for sharing police information in order to discover patterns of crime.

National occupational standards
a list of definitions of all the main tasks which are carried out by people in civilian public services.

National Offender Management Service
The organisation which both the prison service and probation service belong to, and which is overseen by the Ministry of Justice.

National Policing Improvement Agency
a body that produces plans, manuals and policies to make the police more effective. (Has replaced 'Centrex'.)

Nationalisation
the taking over of private companies or services by the government.

Nationalism
strong support for one's own country, sometimes linked with contempt or dislike for other countries.

Navigation
finding your way in open country or at sea.

Negotiating
sorting out problems through discussion and give and take.

Non-commissioned
of soldiers, etc. who have never taken the full officers' training; 'other ranks' (NATO Code 'OR').

Norm
(a) a socially accepted pattern of behaviour; (b) a statistical average.

Nurture
a word sometimes used to describe the effect of the family environment on a growing child.

Oath
swearing by a god, or on a holy book, that a person will tell the truth in court.

Objective
(a) (training) a clear statement of a learning outcome, e.g. 'A body belay is demonstrated' saying what must be done and how it must be done in order to show that the skill has been learned; (b) a limited aim or target of a public service or a project; (c) without bias, prejudice or personal opinions.

Obliterated
hidden, rubbed out, made invisible.

Occupational health
health care in the workplace (common in the uniformed public services).

Officiousness
bossiness, nosiness .

Off-piste
off the main ski run.

Old Bailey
the Central Criminal Court in London (EC4) where major criminal trials are heard.

Ombudsman
an office which deals independently with complaints against some public services (e.g. Prisons Ombudsman). Some services, such as the police in England and Wales, do not have an ombudsman.

OODA Loop
the decision and execution cycle: (Observe, Orient, Decide, Act).

Operational (of emergency services)
to do with the practical achievement of a task (i.e. work done by firefighters or police constables 'on the ground').

Operational command (of armed forces)
the planning of major military actions (NB: this is very different from the way the emergency services use the word 'operational').

Operational debrief
a team review of how well an emergency response (or any other job or activity) has gone.

Opportunity theories
explanations of crime which say that it is the chance of doing a crime (and getting away with it) which causes the crime, not the mentality of the criminal.

Oppressed
treated cruelly or harshly over a long time .

Order
(a) a court order, a condition or requirement added to a sentence (e.g. curfew); (b) an instruction or a command; (c) a state of peacefulness and normality in society – as in 'law and order'.

OSPRE
(Objective Structured Performance-Related Examination) – an examination taken by police constables who wish to become sergeants, and sergeants who wish to become inspectors.

Overheads
costs, such as administration and support services, which are not directly connected with the main work of a company or public service.

Over-represented
more of them than expected.

Pandemic
a worldwide or very large-scale epidemic.

Paramedic
(a) to do with emergency medical care outside, or before reaching, hospital; (b) a qualified person who gives emergency medical care.

Parole Board
a body which supervises the possible early release of long-term prisoners.

Partnership
a group made up of members of different services and organisations, working together on a project.

Passive aggressive
showing aggression in devious or roundabout ways (e.g. talking about somebody in a negative way behind their back, while pretending to be friendly to their face).

Pathogens
any germs (viruses, bacteria, etc.) which cause disease.

Pathologist
a doctor who can carry out post-mortem examinations to determine cause of death.

Patient transport service
routinely taking out-patients, non-urgent cases, etc. to and from hospital.

Performance indicator
a defined measure of how well a public service is doing a particular job.

Personality cult
excessive admiration of a person, and the slavish following of their ideas.

Phab
a charity for integrating disabled people into the community.

Phobia
a powerful fear or hatred which is not based on reason.

Pitches
vertical sections of a rock climb.

Plant
flammable material heaped up by an arsonist.

Platoon
group of around 30 soldiers.

Plea bargaining
getting a lesser sentence by pleading guilty when (or soon after being) charged.

Police authority
a body of local councillors who set a budget and decide priorities for the local police.

Police Federation (the)
the professional organisation which represents police officers and negotiates their pay rises with the government.

Police state
a country where the police are all-powerful, and can arrest people for no good reason.

Policy
(a) strategy, long-term plan; (b) a planned approach which can be altered if necessary. (The word is used in politics and in emergency planning.)

Policy framework
a set of basic plans and rules.

Political accountability
either able to be voted out if something goes wrong (e.g. of an MP or government minister) or with a duty to justify to politicians (e.g. in a Parliamentary committee) actions taken (by a public service)

Political climate
what the public or politicians think is a good idea at any given time.

Post
a job title, e.g. 'warfare officer', 'watch assistant'.

Post-traumatic stress disorder (PTSD)
an illness involving anxiety, nightmares, flashbacks, etc. which affects some people after exposure to horrific events.

Potential
the ability to do well (in a career, etc.).

Powers
the things that the police and the courts are allowed to do when dealing with offenders or witnesses (more generally, what people are allowed to do by law).

PPE
personal protective equipment (safety clothing, etc.).

Practical (of thinking)
based on what is possible and sensible.

Precedence
seniority, higher rank.

Press briefing
an organised event where the public services talk about a specific problem (emergency, crime, etc.) to journalists or television people. Sometimes called a 'press conference', especially if questions can be asked freely.

Pressure group
an organisation which campaigns on a single issue such as human rights or the environment.

Primary care
first medical attention after an accident, or on arriving at hospital.

Primary Care Trust
the organisation in charge of local health care – pharmacists, dentists, opticians, especially GPs, health visiting and district nursing (but not hospitals).

Primary legislation
Acts of Parliament (major laws), e.g. Crime and Disorder Act 1998.

Prior
previous.

Prioritise
to decide which case or action is most urgent, and to do it first.

Private-sector support
(financial) help from organisations which are not run by the government.

Privatisation
the taking over of government services by private companies. The aim is to lower taxes and increase competition.

Privileged
used of any material (e.g. letters between a lawyer and client) which is always confidential and therefore cannot be used as evidence in a criminal court.

Proactive
trying to stop crime, attacks, etc. before they happen.

Probation (in the police, etc.)
a period (usually two years) between being accepted and being finally confirmed as a police constable. This is a learning period when the recruit is 'on approval' and is easier to sack if he or she is unsuitable.

Pro Bono
Latin phrase that translates as 'for the good [of the public']. It means free of charge.

Procedures
systems for ensuring that a task is done successfully, safely, correctly or legally.

Productivity
the amount of useful work done in a given time, for a given cost.

Professional accountability
responsible for doing a job well.

Prohibition notice
a written order from the Health and Safety Executive inspectors preventing unsafe machinery, buildings, etc. from being used, or preventing any form of unsafe behaviour by workers.

Promulgate
to announce, explain or put into effect.

Propaganda
writing, films, TV programmes, etc. which push a political view in a biased manner .

Proportionate
with reasonable force; with moderation.

Proscribed
banned by the government (used of terrorist groups).

Prosecuting authority
any body such as the Crown Prosecution Service or the Health and Safety Executive that has a legal right or duty to prepare a case against a person or organisation accused of breaking the law.

Prosecution
(a) Civil – taking someone to court; (b) Criminal – the process of preparing and pleading the case against someone charged with a criminal offence.

Provider
a person, organisation, club, company or public service which arranges (adventurous) activities for the public or for young people.

Prusik
a knot which enables someone to climb a long rope.

Psychoanalysis
a form of psychotherapy used to discover hidden memories which may be causing disturbance or mental ilness.

Psychoanalytic
a method of finding causes of mental illness or states of mind through word-association.

Psychological
to do with the way people think or behave, either individually or in groups.

Psychology
(a) the study of the mind; (b) the systematic study of human behaviour.

Psychometric (tests)
tests for measuring thinking abilities.

Psychopathy
(a) mental illness; (b) a condition where serious criminals feel no sense of guilt.

Psychotherapy
the professional treatment of mental illness by a range of counselling and other methods.

Public inquiry
a government-backed investigation (of a disaster or other major issue), usually chaired by a judge, and open to the public.

Quality
(a) an aspect of personality, e.g. patience; (b) the standard of work, as assessed through targets, feedback, surveys and statistics.

Quashed
deleted, cancelled (of a conviction).

Rabies
a fatal disease of animals and humans, which can be passed on by the bites of infected dogs, etc. Extinct in Britain, but present still in Africa and some other parts of the world.

Radicalism
the belief that a society or government should be completely changed.

Ramifications
(a) branches, links or connections between one organisation and another; (b) different aspects of a complex problem.

Rank
the level of power, responsibility or seniority in a public service, e.g. constable, sergeant, inspector.

Reactive
dealing with a problem after it has happened.

Realistic
an aim is 'realistic' if a team or person has the time or money needed to achieve it.

Reckonable service
work which counts towards a pension.

Reconciliation
the peaceful ending of a disagreement.

Red Crescent
the name given to the Red Cross in Muslim countries.

Referendum
a nationwide vote on a single issue or question (e.g. should Britain change to the euro?).

Reflection (in counselling)
deliberately echoing what a person says (or even imitating their posture) in order to express sympathy and understanding.

Reflectorised (road signs and markings)
coated with tiny glass beads which reflect headlamps.

Regime change
the replacement of one government, or style of government, with another.

Regiment
group of around 650 soldiers.

Regional Resilience Teams
nine disaster management and advice teams based in each of the nine English regional government offices.

Regulation
a law passed by the government which is narrow and specific in its powers. Sometimes called a 'statutory instrument'.

Regulatory
checking up on industries, governments, etc.

Rehydration
supplying water or fluid to people who badly need it.

Reinforcement
encouragement due to the expectation or memory of a reward.

Reinforcement schemes
agreements between fire and rescue services to back each other up in a major emergency, as required by the Fire and Rescue Services Act 2004.

Remand
custody (imprisonment) before trial.

Remit
duty; job description.

Rendezvous point
a place within the cordons of an emergency incident scene where different agencies working on the site can meet in order to plan or make operational decisions.

Reparation
an action carried out by a person found guilty of a crime, in order to compensate either the victim in particular or society in general.

Repeat victimisation
the tendency of some people or companies to be frequent victims of crime (often by the same person).

Repressive
(of laws) unfair, discriminatory, likely to cause suffering.

Reprimand
tell off; 'a reprimand' is a telling-off.

Resilience
(a) government measures to combat major threats such as terrorism or natural disasters; (b) (of a country) the ability to withstand emergencies; (c) toughness and flexibility.

Resilience
a word used by the government to describe effective disaster response.

Resolution
a statement by the UN Security Council demanding action by a country which the Council accuses of breaking international law.

Response vehicles
any public service vehicle which rushes to the scene of an emergency.

Restitution
the replacement of property which has been stolen or damaged.

Restorative justice
a system of discouraging offenders from reoffending by arranging for them to meet their victims (with the victim's consent) and compensate them in some way.

Resuscitation
reviving unconscious people.

Retaliation
quick revenge or military action against an attacker.

Review
assess strengths and weaknesses of a project, activity, etc.

Risk
the chance of someone being harmed by a given hazard.

Risk assessment
a systematic, written examination of the possible dangers of an activity or environment, together with ideas for reducing those risks and a record of whether those risks have actually been reduced.

Risk rating
a figure to show how dangerous an activity is.

Role
any kind of work carried out by a public service, e.g. fighting fires.

Role model
a person with (usually good) qualities which other people want to imitate.

Role structure
modern name for a rank structure. The focus is on the work done rather than the job title.

Route card
a written plan of a walk showing estimated times of arrival, etc.

Rules of engagement
the (usually secret) rules that the armed forces have to follow in a particular operation, e.g. when and why they are allowed to shoot.

Salvage
saving property or removing accident wreckage for recycling.

Samaritans
an organisation which counsels victims of crime and others who feel depressed or suicidal.

Sanctions
(a) a ban on trade (or trade in certain goods, such as armaments) with another country; (b) punishments, e.g. for minor offences in the army.

Scenario
the setting for a mock disaster or emergency, which can be used as a basis for emergency planning exercises.

Secessionist (of a political group)
wanting to form an independent country out of a section of a larger country. Similar to 'separatist'.

Secondary legislation
Statutory Instruments; Regulations (minor laws), e.g. The Reporting of Injuries, Diseases and Dangerous Occurrences Regulations 1995 (RIDDOR).

Sectarian (conflict)
conflict between religious or ethnic groups within a larger community.

Section
small group of 6–10 soldiers.

Self-esteem
whether a person feels good about themselves or not. A person who feels insecure or worthless is said to have 'low self-esteem'.

Self-worth
see 'Self-esteem'.

Senior investigating officer (SIO)
the person in charge of the scene of an serious incident (usually a policeman).

Senior Investigating Officer
the person in overall charge of the investigation of the causes of a major incident.

Sentence
a punishment by a court.

Separatist
fighting for independence from another country.

Shia Muslims (sometimes called 'Shiites')
Muslims who believe that the leadership of Islam should have passed to a direct descendant of the Prophet Mohammed.

Shift
a single period of work at a workplace, e.g. 9–5.

Silver command
the tactical (middle) level of command in a major incident.

Simulation
a form of training or assessment where people 'act out' a realistic situation.

Skill
a learnable ability.

Smearing
a friction grip for the feet in rock climbing, where as much of the sole as possible is pressed flat against the rock.

Snatch rescue
saving someone quickly, e.g. from a burning building.

Social exclusion
the loss of normal freedoms, rights and pleasures for reasons of poverty, disability, age or discrimination.

Socialists
people whose political beliefs include giving more benefits to the poor, greater rights and better pay for low-paid workers, and higher taxes especially for the rich.

Socio-economic
to do with people's occupations (jobs) and wealth ('social class').

Sociological
to do with the way society is organised, or with social and economic factors, e.g. culture, lifestyle, poverty .

Solidarity Fund
a sum of money kept by the European Union which is used to help EU countries in the event of a disaster.

Specific (e.g. of a task)
clearly defined and with strict limits.

Sponsoring
giving money and other support (e.g. to terrorism).

Squadron
group of 100 soldiers.

Stabilisation
paramedic action to stop a seriously ill person from dying before getting to hospital.

Stakeholders
people who carry out, or are involved in the success of, a project, initiative or activity (e.g. a Crime and Disorder Reduction Partnership).

Standard scale
a list of the fines normally given in a magistrates' court.

Standardised
following a normal pattern.

State of emergency
a situation in which the government gives itself, the police and the army extra powers to control people and their activities during a major national emergency (e.g. a natural disaster or serious political unrest).

Statistics
figures collected through surveys or by other methods which have been processed or sorted in order to reveal some underlying truth (e.g. crime statistics).

Statutory
set up by law (i.e. by the government).

Statutory Performance Indicators
targets for defined public service activities which are laid down by law.

Stereotyping
taking a highly oversimplified and/or wrong view of a particular group of people, e.g. 'women are bad drivers'.

Stewardship
care.

Stimulus
an action which produces a reaction (response) in a living creature (e.g. a loud noise that makes someone jump).

Strategy
(a) a large-scale, long-term plan; (b) a method, as in 'motivational strategy'.

Stress
Feelings of tension, anger and anxiety caused by the pressure of work, by poor workplace relationships or by personal/family problems. In severe cases it can lead to mental and physical illness.

Submissive
of behaviour, where a person is always trying to please other people or failing to stick up for themselves when there is a disagreement.

Subordinates
people of lower rank; people under an officer's command.

Subsidiary
less important.

Summary justice
quick disciplinary action on a subordinate by a commanding officer (for a minor or 'administrative' breaking of the rules).

Summary offence
a minor offence which can be tried in a magistrates' court or dealt with by a fixed penalty, etc.

Summative (of reviews, assessment, etc.)
done when a project is finished.

Summit
a meeting of top world leaders.

Summoning
calling someone for jury service.

Sunni Muslims
Muslims who accept that the leadership of Islam passed to Abu Bakr on the Prophet's death.

Superpower
a country like the US which is richer and more powerful than any other country.

Super-state
a name given to a group of countries joined together, in which each country loses some of its independence.

Supervisors
managers who keep an eye on the workforce or the team(s) they lead.

Surveillance
watching (often from a distance).

Sustainable
can survive or keep going without outside help (can describe communities or the environment).

Syndicate
share or distribute news stories.

Tabletop scenario
an outline of a possible disaster giving all the information (e.g. facts and figures) needed to carry out emergency response planning exercises.

Tactics
short- or medium-term plans.

Taliban
Islamist (anti-western) fighters in Afghanistan.

Target
a measurable improvement of performance in a named activity to be achieved by a definite date.

Tariff
a range of sentences linked to the seriousness of different crimes.

Tasking
briefing (instructions) which tells a team what to do but not how to do it.

Technical competence
skill at an action or process (e.g. at skiing).

Technical skills
(a) skill with technology, e.g. computers; (b) specialist skills, used in a particular kind of work, e.g. 'control and restraint' in the prison service.

Technician
a highly qualified mechanic, working on the maintenance of hi-tech equipment.

Tectonic
to do with movements or deformities of the Earth's crust.

Telemark
a skiing technique where the heel is not fixed to the ski, allowing greater freedom of movement and tighter turns.

Tempo (of warfare)
the speed or rapidity with which events happen or decisions are taken.

Tender
a specialised fire engine.

Terrain
land or environment for adventurous activities; the surface of the ground, e.g. rocky terrain.

Terrorism
violent attacks designed to frighten and shock civilians and to grab media attention.

Theoretical (of thinking)
based on principles, possibilities, hypotheses and underlying rules.

Trade barriers
taxes, duties or prohibition on the trading of goods between one country and another.

Trailer
a method used by arsonists to help a fire spread quickly.

Transcript
the written version of words which have been recorded on tape (e.g. in police interviews).

Transformational (of leadership)
changes people and the way they look at life and work.

Treaty
a binding agreement between two or more countries, usually for economic benefits or military cooperation.

Trend
a change, e.g. in crime figures – over a period of time.

Triable either way
fairly serious offences where defendants can choose to be tried either in the Crown Court or in a magistrates' court.

Triage
sorting casualties to identify the most urgent cases at the scene of a major incident.

Troop
group of around 16 soldiers.

Tsunami
a wave (that is sometimes huge), caused by an earthquake under the sea.

Unstaffed
'unmanned' (of level crossings).

Utility
to do with gas, water, electricity and telephone networks.

Variable message signs (matrix signals)
large motorway signs which can give a range of different messages using a grid of small lights.

Vetting
checking.

Vicarious
refers to emotions which we get from watching or hearing about other people's experiences. For example, people get vicarious pleasure by watching films in which they imagine themselves to be the hero or heroine.

Vigil
a peaceful or silent demonstration, often about a human rights issue.

Violation
serious breaking of human rights laws.

Volume crime
crime carried out by people who commit a lot of crime in a short time.

Volume offenders
criminals who are very active and commit a huge number of burglaries, etc.

Vulnerable person
people who can easily be hurt; the very young, very old, mentally ill, etc. who may need help if they are charged with a crime or acting as witnesses.

War criminals
people who deliberately kill, rape, persecute, etc. civilians during wartime.

Warrant
a piece of paper issued by a magistrate allowing the police to search a place or arrest a person.

Wastage
people leaving a job (after they have been trained).

Weapons of mass destruction (WMD)
chemical, biological, radiological or nuclear weapons intended to kill large numbers of ordinary people.

Welfare (of teams)
well-being, happiness, health and safety.

Witness Care Unit
an organisation which protects witnesses and looks after them when they go to court .

Work study
the study of how to do a job in the most efficient possible way.

Workstream
an area of government planning, activity and spending.

Youth Justice Board
a central government committee which supervises youth justice in England and Wales.

Youth Offending Teams (YOTs)
local authority teams which coordinate the sentencing and other treatment of young offenders.

Index